Fourteenth Century
VERSE & PROSE

D0817024

Fourteenth Century

VERSE & PROSE

edited by

KENNETH SISAM

OXFORD

AT THE CLARENDON PRESS

Oxford University Press, Walton Street, Oxford OX2 6DP

Oxford New York Toronto
Delhi Bombay Calcutta Madras Karachi
Petaling Jaya Singapore Hong Kong Tokyo
Nairobi Dar es Salaam Cape Town
Melbourne Auckland

and associated companies in
Berlin Ibadan

Oxford is a trade mark of Oxford University Press

Published in the United States
by Oxford University Press, New York

First Published 1921
Twenty-second impression 1992

ISBN 0 19 811391 9
ISBN 0 19 871093 3 (paperback)

Printed and bound in
Great Britain by Biddles Ltd
Guildford and King's Lynn

CONTENTS

INTRODUCTION

I

Two periods of our early history promise most for the future of English literature—the end of the seventh with the eighth century; the end of the twelfth century with the thirteenth.

In the first a flourishing vernacular poetry is secondary in importance to the intellectual accomplishment of men like Bede and Alcuin (to name only the greatest and the last of a line of scholars and teachers) who, drawing their inspiration from Ireland and still more from Italy direct, made all the knowledge of the time their own, and learned to move easily in the disciplined forms of Latin prose.

During the second the impulse again came from without. In twelfth-century France the creative imagination was set free. In England, which from the beginning of the tenth century had depended more and more on France for guidance, the nobles, clergy, and entertainers, in whose hands lay the fortunes of literature, had a community of interest with their French compeers that has never since been approached. So England shared early in the break with tradition; and during the thirteenth century the native stock is almost hidden by the brilliant growth of a new graft.

Every activity of the mind was quickened. A luxuriant invention of forms distinguished the Gothic style in architecture. All the decorative arts showed a parallel enrichment. Oxford (at least to insular eyes) was beginning to rival Paris in learning, and to contribute to the over-production of clerks which at first extended the province of the Church, and finally, by breaking the bounds set between ecclesiastics and laymen, played an important part in the secularization of letters. The friars, whose foundation was the last great reform of the mediaeval Church, were at the height of their good fame; and one of them, the Franciscan Roger Bacon, by his work in philosophy, criticism, and physical science, raised the name of English thinkers to an eminence unattained since Bede. If among the older monastic orders feverish and sometimes extravagant reforms are symptoms of decline, the richness of Latin chronicles like those of Matthew Paris of St. Albans is evidence that in some of the great abbeys the monks were still learned and eloquent. Nor was Latin the only medium in which educated Englishmen were at home. They wrote French familiarly, and to some extent repaid their debt to France by transcribing and preserving Continental compositions that would else have perished.

Apart from all these activities, the manifestations of a new spirit in English vernacular works are so important, and the break with the past is so sharp, that the late twelfth century and the thirteenth would be chosen with more justice than Chaucer's time as the starting-point for a study of modern literature.

Then romance was established in English, whether we use the word to mean the imaginative searching of dark places, or in the more general sense of story-telling unhampered by a too strict regard for facts. Nothing is more remarkable in pre-Conquest works than the Anglo-Saxon's dislike of exaggeration and his devotion to plain matter of fact. Here is the account of the whales in the far North that King Alfred received from Ohthere (a Norseman, of course, but it is indifferent):—' they are eight and forty ells long, and the biggest fifty ells long '. Compare with this parsimony the full-blooded description of the griffins in *Mandeville*:—' But o griffoun hath the body more gret, and is more strong, þanne eight lyouns, of suche lyouns as ben o this half; and more gret and strongere þan an hundred egles suche as we han amonges vs, &c. ', and you have a rough measure of the progress of fiction.

To take pleasure in stories is not a privilege reserved for favoured generations : but special conditions had transformed this pleasure into a passion. When Edward I became King in 1272, Western Europe had enjoyed a long period of internal peace, during which national hatreds burnt low. The breaking down of barriers between Bretons and French, Welsh and English, brought into the main stream of European literature the Celtic vein of idealism and delicate fancy. At the universities, in the Crusades, in the pilgrimages to Rome or Compostella, the nations mingled, each bringing from home some contribution to the common stock of stories ; each gaining new experiences of the outside world, fusing them, and repeating them with embellishments. To those who stayed at home came the minstrels in the heyday of their craft—they were freemen of every Christian land who reported whatever was marvellous or amusing—and at second hand the colours of the rediscovered world seemed no less brave. It was an age greedy for entertainment that fed a rich sense of comedy on the jostling life around it; and to serve its ideals called up the great men of the past—Orpheus opening the way to fairyland, the heroes of the Trojan war, Alexander ; Arthur and the Knights of the Round Table and Merlin the enchanter ; Charlemagne with his peers—or won back from the shadows not Eurydice alone, but Helen and Criseyde, Guinevere and Ysolde, Rymenhild and Blaunche-flour.

While she still claimed to direct public taste, the Church could not be indifferent to the spread of romance. A policy of uniform repression was no longer possible. Her real

power to suppress books was ineffective to bind busy tongues
and minds; popular movements were assured of a measure
of practical tolerance when order competed with order and
church with church for the goodwill of the people; and even
if the problem had been well defined, a disciplined attitude
unvarying throughout all the divisions of the Church was not
to be expected when her mantle covered clerks ranging in
character from the strictest ascetic to that older Falstaff who
passed under the name of Golias and found his own Muse in
the tavern,—

> *Tales versus facio quale vinum bibo;*
> *Nihil possum scribere nisi sumpto cibo;*
> *Nihil valet penitus quod ieiunus scribo,—*
> *Nasonem post calices carmine praeibo!*

So it came about that while some of the clergy denounced all
minstrels as 'ministers of Satan', others made a truce with
the more honest among them, and helped them to add to
their repertories the lives of saints. Officially 'trifles and
trotevales' were still censured: but it seemed good to mould
the *chansons de geste* to pious uses,[1] and to purify the court
of King Arthur, which popularity had led into dissolute ways,
by introducing the quest of the Graal. And if Rolle preached
sound doctrine when he ranked among the Sins of the
Mouth 'to syng seculere sanges and lufe þam', their style
and music were not despised as baits to catch the ears of the
frivolous: when a singer began

> Ase y me rod þis ender dai
> By grene wode to seche play,
> Mid herte y þohte al on a may,
> Suetest of alle þinge,—

[1] For illustrations from Old French, see *Les Légendes Épiques* by
Professor Joseph Bédier, 4 vols., Paris 1907-, a book that maintains the
easy pre-eminence of the French school in the appreciation of mediaeval
literature.

the lover of secular songs would be tempted to listen ; but he would stay to hear a song of the Joys of the Virgin, to whose cult the period owes its best devotional poetry.

The power of the Church to mould the early growth of vernacular literature is so often manifested that there is a risk of underestimating the compromises and surrenders which are the signs of its wane. The figures of romance invaded the churches themselves, creeping into the carvings of the portals, along the choir-stalls, and into the historiated margins of the service books. Ecclesiastics collected and multiplied stories to adorn their sermons or illustrate their manuals of vices and virtues. In the lives of saints marvels accumulated until the word 'legend' became a synonym for an untrue tale. Though there are moments in the fourteenth century when the preponderance of the clerical over the secular element in literature seems as great as ever, by the end of the Middle Ages the trend of the conflict is plain. It is the Church that draws back to attend to her own defences, which the domestic growth of pious fictions has made everywhere vulnerable. But imaginative literature, growing always stronger and more confident, wins full secular liberty.

Emancipation from the bondage of fact, and to some extent from ecclesiastical censorship, coincided with the acquisition of a new freedom in the form of English poetry. Old English had a single metre—the long alliterative line without rime. It was best suited to narrative; it was un-musical in the sense that it could not be sung ; it had marked proclivities towards rant and noise ; and like blank verse it degenerated easily into mongrel prose.

Degeneration was far advanced in the eleventh century ; and about the end of the twelfth some large-scale experiments show that writers were no longer content with the old medium. In *Layamon*, the last great poem in this metre before the fourteenth century, internal rime and assonance are common. Orm adopted the unrimed *septenarius* from Latin, but counted his syllables so faithfully as to produce an intolerable monotony. Then French influence turned the scale swiftly and decisively in favour of rime, so that in the extant poetry of the thirteenth century alliteration is a secondary principle or a casual ornament, but never takes the place of rime.

The sudden and complete eclipse of a measure so firmly rooted in tradition is surprising enough; but the wealth and elaborateness of the new forms that replaced it are still more matter for wonder. It is natural to think of the poets before Chaucer as children learning their art slowly and painfully, and often stumbling on the way. Yet in this one point of metrical technique they seem to reach mastery at a bound.

That the development of verse forms took place outside of English is part of the explanation. Rimed verse had its origin in Church Latin. In the monastic schools the theory of classical and post-classical metres was a principal study; and the practical art of chant was indispensable for the proper conduct of the services. Under these favourable conditions technical development was rapid, so that in such an early example of the rimed stanza as the following, taken from a poem that Godescalc wrote in exile about the year 845,—

> *Magis mihi, miserule,*
> *Flere libet, puerule,*
> *Plus plorare quam cantare*
> *Carmen tale iubes quale,*
> *Amor care.*
> *O, cur iubes canere?*[1]—

the arrangement of longer and shorter lines, the management of rime or assonance, and the studied grouping of consonant sounds, give rather the impression of too much than too little artifice.

[1] *Poetae Latini Aevi Carolini*, vol. iii (ed. L. Traube), p. 731.

From Church Latin rime passed into French, and with the twelfth century entered on a new course of development at the hands of the *trouvères* and the minstrels. The *trouvères*, or 'makers', studied versification and music as a profession, and competed in the weaving of ingenious patterns. Since their living depended on pleasing their audience, those minstrels who were not themselves composers spared no pains to sing or recite well the compositions of others; and good execution encouraged poets to try more difficult forms.

The varied results obtained in two such excellent schools of experience were offered to the English poets of the thirteenth century in exchange for the monotony of the long line; and their choice was unhesitating. In an age of lyrical poetry they learned to sing where before they could only declaim: and because the great age of craftsmanship had begun, the most intricate patterns pleased them best. Chaucer was perhaps not yet born when the over-elaboration of riming metres in English drew a protest from Robert Mannyng:[1] and when, after a period of hesitancy, rimed verse regained its prestige in Chaucer's prime, nameless writers again chose or invented complex stanza forms and sustained them throughout long poems. If *The Pearl* stood alone it might be accounted a literary *tour de force*: the York and Towneley plays compel the conclusion that a high standard of metrical workmanship was appreciated by the common people.

Thus far, by way of generalization and without the *caveats* proper to a literary history, I have indicated some aspects of the preceding period that are important for an understanding

> If it were made in *ryme couwee*,
> Or in strangere, or *enterlacé*,
> Þat rede Inglis it ere inowe
> Þat couthe not haf coppled a kowe,
> Þat outhere in *couwee* or in *baston*
> Som suld haf ben fordon. (*Chronicle*, Prologue, ll. 85 ff.)

of the fourteenth century. But it would be misleading to pass on without a word of reservation. There is reason to suppose that the extant texts from the thirteenth century give a truer reflection of the tastes of the upper classes, who were in closest contact with the French, than of the tastes of the people. But however this may be, they do not authorize us to speak for every part of the country. All the significant texts come from the East or the South—especially the western districts of the South, where an exceptional activity is perhaps to be connected with the old preference of the court for Winchester. In the North and the North-West a silence of five centuries is hardly broken.

II

Judged by what survives, the literary output of the first half of the fourteenth century was small in quantity ; though it must be remembered that, unlike the thirteenth and six-teenth centuries which made a fresh start and depended almost entirely on their own production, the fourteenth inherited and enjoyed a good stock of verse, to which the new compositions are a supplement.

Our first impression of this new material is negative and disappointing. The production of rimed romances falls off: their plots become increasingly absurd and mechanical; the action, so swift in the early forms, moves sluggishly through a maze of decorative descriptions ; and their style at its best has the pretty inanity of *Sir Thopas*. The succession of merry tales—such as *Dame Siriz*, or *The Fox and the Wolf* [1] where Reynard, Isengrim, and Chauntecleer make their first bow in English—is broken until the appearance of the *Canterbury Tales* themselves. To find secular lyrics we

[1] Both are in Bodleian MS. Digby 86 (about 1280), and are accessible in G. H. McKnight's *Middle English Humorous Tales*, Boston 1913.

must turn to the very beginning or the very end of the century, and Chaucer himself does not recover the fresh gaiety of the earlier time.

The decline of these characteristic thirteenth-century types becomes less surprising when we notice that literature has changed camps. The South, more especially the South-West, is now almost silent: the North and the North-West reach their literary period. Minot and Rolle are Northerners, Wiclif is a Yorkshireman by birth, the York and Towneley Miracle cycles are both from the North, and with Barbour the literature of the Scots dialect begins; Robert Mannyng belongs to the North-East Midlands; while *Sir Gawayne*, *The Pearl*, and *The Destruction of Troy* represent the North-West. This predominance in the present volume rests on no mere chance of selection, since the Northern (Egerton) version of *Mandeville* might have been preferred to the Cotton; and if the number of extracts were to be increased, the texts that first come to mind—*Cursor Mundi* (about 1300),[1] *Prick of Conscience* (about 1340), *Morte Arthure* (about 1360), the Chester Plays—are Northern and North-Western.

It is impossible to give more than a partial explanation of the change in the area of production. But as the kinds of poetry that declined early in the fourteenth century are those that owed most to French influence, it is reasonable to assume that in the South the impulse that produced them had spent its force. The same pause is observable at the same time in France, where it coincides with the transition from oral poetry to more reflective compositions written for the eye of a reader. It is the pause between the passing of the minstrels and the coming of men of letters.

[1] Early English Text Society, ed. R. Morris. Unless other editions are mentioned, the longer works which are not represented by specimens may be read among the Early English Texts.

Such changes were felt first in the centres of government, learning, and commerce, whence ideas and fashions spread very slowly to the country districts. At this time the North, and above all the North-West, was the backward quarter of England, thinly populated and in great part uncultivated. An industrial age had not yet dotted it with inland cities ; and while America was still unknown the western havens were neglected.[1] In these old-fashioned parts the age of minstrel poetry was prolonged, and the wave of inspiration from France, though it came late, stirred the North and North-West after the South had relapsed into mediocrity or silence.

So, about the middle of the century, imaginative poetry found a new home in the West-Midlands. As before, poets turned to French for their subjects, and often contented themselves with free adaptation of French romances. They accepted such literary conventions as the Vision, which was borrowed from the *Roman de la Rose* to be the frame of *Wynnere and Wastoure* (1352)[2] and *The Parlement of the Thre Ages*,[3] before it was used in *Piers Plowman* and *The Pearl* and by Chaucer. But time and distance had weakened the French influence, and the new school of poets did not catch, as the Southern poets did, the form and spirit of their models.

They preferred the unrimed alliterative verse, which from pre-Conquest days must have lived on in the remote Western counties without a written record ; and for a generation rime is overshadowed. The suddenness and importance of this revival in a time otherwise barren of poetry will appear from a list of the principal alliterative poems that are commonly assigned to the third quarter of the century :— *Wynnere and*

[1] See p. 150.
[2] Ed. Sir Israel Gollancz, Oxford 1920.
[3] Ed. Gollancz, Oxford 1915.

Wastoure, The Parlement of the Thre Ages, Joseph of Arimathie (the first English Graal romance), *William of Palerne, Piers Plowman* (A-text), *Patience, Sir Gawayne and the Green Knight, The Destruction of Troy, Morte Arthure.*

At the time alliterative verse was fitted to become the medium of popular literature. Prose would not serve, because its literary life depends on books and readers. Up to the end of the century (if we exclude sermons and religious or technical treatises, where practical considerations reinforced a Latin tradition) the function of prose in English literature is to translate Latin or French prose;[1] and even this narrow province is sometimes invaded by verse. Yet it was not easy to write verse that depended on number of syllables, quantity, or rime. The fall of inflexions brought confusion on syllabic metres; there were great changes in the quantity and quality of vowels; and these disturbances affected the dialects unevenly.[2] It must have been hard enough for a poet to make rules for himself: but popularity involved the recital of his work by all kinds of men in all kinds of English, when the rimes would be broken and the rhythm lost. It is perhaps unfair to call Michael of Northgate's doggerel (p. 33) to witness the misfortunes of rimed metres. But the text of *Sir Orfeo* from the Auchinleck manuscript shows how often Englishmen who were nearly contemporary with the composer had lost the tune of his verses. The more fortunate makers of alliterative poems, whose work depended on the stable yet elastic frame of stress and initial consonants, possessed a master-key to the dialects.

Adaptability made easier the diffusion of alliterative verse: but its revival was not due to a deliberate choice on practical grounds. It was a phase of a larger movement, which may

[1] Chaucer's prose rendering of the *Metra* of Boethius is an apparent exception, but Jean de Meung's French prose version lay before him.
[2] See the Appendix.

be described as a weakening of foreign and learned influences, and a recovery of the native stock. And the metrical form is only the most obvious of the old-fashioned elements that reappeared. In spirit, too, the authors of the alliterative school have many points of kinship with the Old English poets. They are more moderate than enthusiastic. Left to themselves, their imaginations move most easily among sombre shapes and in sombre tones. They have not the intellectual brilliance and the wit of the French poets; and when they laugh—which is not often—the lightness of the thirteenth century is rarer than the rough note of the comic scenes in the Towneley plays. It is hard to say how much the associations and aptitudes of the verse react on its content: but *Sumer is icumen in*, which is the essence of thirteenth-century poetry, is barely conceivable in Old English, where even the cuckoo's note sounded melancholy; and it would come oddly from the poets of the middle fourteenth century, who have learned from the French *trouvères* the convention of spring, with sunshine, flowers, and singing birds, but seem unable to put away completely the memory of winter and rough weather.

In the last quarter of the century the tide of foreign influence runs strong again; and the work of Gower and Chaucer discloses radical changes in the conditions of literature which are the more important because they are permanent. The literary centre swings back to the capital—London now instead of Winchester—which henceforth provides the models for authors of any pretensions throughout England and across the Scottish border. In Chaucer we have for the first time a layman, writing in English for secular purposes, who from the range and quality of his work may fairly claim to be ranked among men of letters. The strictly clerical writers had been content to follow the Scriptures, the Fathers and commentators, the service books and legendaries; and Chaucer

does not neglect their tradition.[1]   The minstrels had exploited
a popular taste for merry tales 'that sownen into synne';
and he borrowed so gladly from them that many have doubted
his repentance.[2] But his models are men of letters:—the
Latin poets headed by Ovid, who was Gower's favourite too ;
French writers, from the satirical Jean de Meung to makers
of studied 'balades, roundels, virelayes' like Machaut and
Deschamps ; and the greater Italian group—Boccaccio,
Petrarch, and Dante. Keeping such company, he was bound
to reject the rusticity of the alliterative school, and the middle
way followed by those who added a tag of rime at the end of
a rimeless series (as in *Sir Gawayne*), or invented stanzas in
which alliteration remains, but is subservient to rime (as in
The Pearl and the York plays). After his day, even for
Northerners who wish to write well, there will be no more
'*rum-ram-ruf* by lettre '.[3]

III

In outlining the main movements of the century, I have
mentioned incidentally the fortunes of certain kinds of composition,—the restriction of the lyrical form to devotional
uses ; the long dearth in the records of humorous tales ; the
decadence of romances in rime, and the flourishing of alliterative romances. The popular taste for stories was still unsatisfied, and guided authors, from Robert Mannyng to Chaucer,

[1]   And for to speke of other holynesse,
        He hath in prose translated Boece,
        And of the Wrechede Engendrynge of Mankynde
        As man may in pope Innocent ifynde,
        And made the Lyfe also of Seynt Cecile ;
        He made also, gon ys a grete while,
        Origenes upon the Maudeleyne.
                    (*Legend of Good Women*, Prologue A, ll. 424 ff.)
[2] *Parson's Tale*, at the end.
[3] *Prologue to Parson's Tale*, l. 43.

in their choice of subjects or method of treatment. Translators were busier than ever in making Latin and French works available to a growing public who understood no language but English ; and of necessity the greater number of our specimens are translations, ranging from the crude literalness of Michael of Northgate to the artistic adaptation seen in Gower's tales. But the chief new contribution of the century is the vernacular Miracle Play, with which the history of the English drama begins.

Miracle plays grew out of the services for the church festivals of Easter and Christmas. Towards the end of the tenth century a representation of the Three Maries at the Sepulchre is provided for in the English Easter service. Later, the Shepherds seeking the Manger and the Adoration of the Magi are represented in the services for the Christmas season. In their early form these dramatic ceremonies consist of a few sentences of Latin which were sung by the clergy with a minimum of dignified action.

From the eleventh to the thirteenth century the primitive form underwent a parallel development in all parts of Europe. Records of Miracles in England are at this time scanty and casual :—Matthew Paris notes one at Dunstable because precious copes were borrowed for it from St. Albans, and were accidentally burnt ; another, given in the churchyard at Beverley, is mentioned because a boy who had climbed to a post of vantage in the church, and thence higher to escape the sextons, fell and yet took no harm. But the scantiness of references before 1200 is in itself evidence of growth without active enemies, and the few indications agree with the general trend observable on the Continent. The range of subjects was extended to include the acts of saints, and the principal scenes of sacred history from the Fall of Lucifer to the Last Judgement. Single scenes were elaborated to something like the scale familiar in Middle English. By the end of the twelfth century French begins to appear beside or in place of Latin; the French verses were spoken, not sung; the plays were often acted outside the church; and it may be assumed that laymen were admitted as performers alongside the minor clergy, who seem to have been the staunchest supporters of the plays.

The Miracle had become popular, and there is soon evidence of its perversion by the grotesque imaginings of the people. In 1207 masking and buffoonery in the churches at Christmas came under the ban of Pope Innocent III, and his prohibition was made permanent in the Decretals. Henceforth we must look for new developments to the Miracles played outside the church. To these freedom from the restraints of the sacred building did not bring a better reputation. Before 1250 the most influential churchman of the time, Bishop Grosseteste of Lincoln, who was far from being a kill-joy, urged his clergy to stamp out Miracles; and later William of Wadington, and Robert Mannyng his translator, while allowing plays on the Resurrection and the Nativity if decently presented in the church, condemn the Miracles played in open places, and blame those of the clergy who encouraged them by lending vestments to the performers.[1]

From the first three-quarters of the fourteenth century, which include the critical period for the English Miracles, hardly a record survives. The memoranda on which the history of the English plays is based begin toward the end of the century, and the texts are drawn from fifteenth- and sixteenth-century manuscripts. Hence it will be simplest to set out the changes that were complete by 1400 without attempting to establish their true sequence; and to disregard the existence, side by side with the fully developed types, of all the gradations between them and the primitive form that might result from stunted growth or degeneration.

[1] *Handlyng Synne*, ll. 4640 ff.

The early references point to the representation of single plays or small groups of connected scenes; and such isolated pieces survive as long as there are Miracles : Hull, for instance, specialized on a play of Noah's Ship. But now we have to record the appearance of series or cycles of plays, covering in chronological order the whole span of sacred history. Complete cycles were framed on the Continent as early as the end of the thirteenth century. In England they are represented by the York, Towneley (Wakefield), and Chester plays, and the so-called *Ludus Coventriae*.[1] There are also records or fragments of cycles from Beverley, Coventry, Newcastle-upon-Tyne, and Norwich. The presentation of the cycle sometimes occupied a day (York), sometimes two or three successive days (Chester), and sometimes a part was carried over to the next year's festival (*Ludus Coventriae*).

The production of a long series of scenes in the open requires fine weather, and once the close connexion with the church services had been broken, there was a tendency to throw forward the presentation into May or June. The Chester plays were given in Whitsun-week—at least in later times. But normally the day chosen in fourteenth-century England was the Feast of Corpus Christi (the first Thursday after Trinity Sunday), which was made universal throughout the Church in 1311. So the Miracles get the generic name of 'Corpus Christi Plays'.

The feature of the Corpus Christi festival was its procession. As a result either of inclusion in this procession or of imitation, the cycles came to be played processionally: each play had its stage on wheels which halted at fixed

---

[1] These are not the Coventry plays, of which only two survive, but a cycle of plays torn from their local connexions (ed. J. O. Halliwell, Shakespeare Society, 1841). The title is due to a seventeenth-century librarian, who possibly had heard of no Miracle cycle but the famous one at Coventry.

stations in the streets, and at each station the play was re-enacted. This was the usage at York, Wakefield, Chester, Coventry, and Beverley. The older practice of presentation on fixed stages was followed in the *Ludus Coventriae.*

Our last records from the end of the thirteenth century indicated that the open-air Miracle had been disowned by the Church from which it sprang. Yet a century later proces-sional performances appear on a scale that postulates strong and competent management. In the interim the control of the great cycles had passed from the clergy to the munici-palities, who laid upon each guild of craftsmen within their jurisdiction the duty of presenting a play. Ecclesiastics still wrote Miracles, and occasionally performed them ; but when Canterbury, London, Salisbury, Winchester, Oxford, which have no extant texts and few records of popular performances, are named against York, Wakefield, Chester, Coventry, Beverley, it is obvious that official Church influences were no longer the chief factor in the development of Miracles. For their growth and survival in England the cycles depended on the interest of powerful corporations, willing to undertake the financial responsibility of their production, and able to main-tain them against the attacks of the Lollards, or change of policy in the orthodox Church, or the fickleness of fashion in entertainment.

The steps by which the English guilds assumed the guardianship of the plays cannot now be retraced. We must be content to note that the undertaking called for just that combination of religious duty, civic patriotism, and pride of craft that inspired the work of the guilds in their best days. And the clergy had every reason to welcome the disciplining by secular authority of a wayward offspring that had grown beyond their own control The York texts, which bring us nearest to the time when the corporations and guilds first took charge of the Miracles, are very creditable to the taste of the city, and must represent a reform on the irresponsible productions that scandalized the thirteenth century. The vein of coarseness in some of the comic scenes of the Towneley group seems to be due to a later recrudescence of incongruous elements.

The last great change to be noted was inevitable when the plays became popular: they were spoken in English and in rimed verse, with only an occasional tag or stage direction or hymn in Latin to show their origin. The variety of the texts, and of the modes and purposes of their representation, make it impossible to assign a date to the transition that would be generally applicable; and its course was not always the same. There is an example of direct translation from Latin in the Shrewsbury fragments,[1] which contain one actor's cues and parts in three plays : first the Latin foundation is given in verse or prose, and then its expansion in English alternate rime. That translations were sometimes made from the French is proved by the oldest known manuscript of a Miracle in English—an early fourteenth-century fragment of a Nativity play, consisting of a speech in French followed by its rendering in the same stanza form.[2] But there is no reason to doubt that as English gained ground and secularization became more complete, original composition appeared side by side with translation.[3]

[1] Shrewsbury School MS. Mus. iii. 42 (early fifteenth century), ed. Skeat, *Academy*, January 4 and January 11, 1890. The fragments are (i) the part of the Third Shepherd in a Nativity play ; (ii) the part of the third Mary in a Resurrection play; (iii) the part of Cleophas in *Pilgrims to Emmaus*. Manly, who reprints the fragments in *Specimens of the Pre-Shaksperean Drama*, vol. i (1900), pp. xxvi ff., notes that these plays seem to have been church productions rather than secular.

[2] See *The Times Literary Supplement* of May 26 and June 2, 1921. The fragment comes from Bury St. Edmunds. The dialect is E. Midland.

[3] On the production of Miracle plays see L. Toulmin Smith, Introduction to *York Plays*, Oxford 1885 ; and A. F. Leach in *An English Miscellany presented to Dr. Furnivall*, pp. 205 ff.

For one other kind of writing the fourteenth century is notable—its longer commentaries on contemporary life and the art of living. In the twelfth century England had an important group of satirical poets who wrote in Latin; and in the thirteenth there are many French and a few English satires. Their usual topic was the corruption of the religious orders, varied by an occasional attack on some detail of private folly, such as extravagance in dress or the pride of serving-men. These pieces are mostly in the early French manner, where so much wit tempers the indignation that one doubts whether the satirist would be really happy if he succeeded in destroying the butts of his ridicule.

This is not the spirit of the fourteenth century, when a darker side of life is turned up and reported by men whose eyes are not quick to catch brightness. The number of short occasional satires in English increases, but they are seldom gay. The greater writers—Rolle, Wiclif, Langland, Gower—were obsessed by the troubles of their time, and are less satirists than moralists. Certainly the events of the century gave little cause for optimism. The wane of enthusiasm throughout Europe and the revival of national jealousies are evident very early in the failure of all attempts to organize an effective Crusade after 1291, when the Turks conquered the last Christian outposts in Palestine. There was no peace, for the harassing wars with Scotland were followed by the long series of campaigns against France that sapped the strength of both countries for generations. The social and economic organization was shaken by the severest famines (1315–21) and the greatest pestilence (1349) in English history, and both famine and plague came back more than once before the century was done. The conflict of popes and anti-popes divided the Western Church, while England faced the domestic problem of Lollardry. There was civil revolt in 1381; and the century closed with the deposition of

Richard II. A modern historian balances the account with the growth of parliamentary institutions, the improving status of the labouring classes, and the progress of trade : but in so far as these developments were observable at all by contemporary writers, they were probably interpreted as signs of general decay.

In such an atmosphere the serene temper with which Robert Mannyng handles the sins and follies of his generation did not last long. Rolle tried to associate with men in order to improve their way of life : but his intensely personal attitude towards every problem, and the low value he set on the quality of reasonableness, made success impossible ; and after a few querulous outbursts against his surroundings, he found his genius by withdrawing into pure idealism.

Wiclif was the one writer who was also a practical reformer. Having made up his mind that social evils could be remedied only through the Church, and that the first step was a thorough reform of the government, doctrine, and ministers of the Church, he acted with characteristic logic. The vices and follies of the people he regarded as secondary, and refused to dissipate his controversial energies upon them. His strength was reserved for a grim, ordered battle against ecclesiastical abuses ; and while he pulled down, he did not neglect to lay foundations that outlasted his own defeat.

Piers Plowman gives a full picture of the times and their bewildering effect on the mind of a sincere and moderate man. Its author belonged to the loosely organized secular clergy who, by reason of their middle position, served as a kind of cement in a ramshackle society. He has no new system and no practical schemes of reform to expound—only perplexing dreams of a simple Christian who, with Conscience and Reason as his guides, faces in turn the changing shapes of evil. He attacks them bravely enough, and still they seem to evade him ; because he shrinks from destroying their roots when he finds them too closely entwined with things to which his habits or affections cling. In the end he cannot find a sure temporal foothold: yet he has no vision of a Utopia to come in which society will be reorganized by men's efforts. That idea brought no comfort to his generation who, standing on the threshold of a new order, looked longingly backward.

Passing over Gower, whose direct studies of contemporary conditions were written in Latin and French, we come round again to Chaucer. He has not Rolle's idealism, or Wiclif's fighting spirit, or Langland's earnestness—in fact, he has no great share of moral enthusiasm. A man of the world with keen eyes and the breadth of outlook and sympathy that Gower lacked, he is at home in a topsy-turvy medley of things half-dead with things half-grown, and the thousand disguises of convention and propriety through which the new life peeped to mock at its puzzled and despairing repressors were to him a never-ending entertainment. *Ubique iam abundat turpitudo terrena*, says Rolle in an alliterative flight, *vilissima voluptas in viris vacillat; . . . bellant ut bestiae; brevviantur beati; nullus est nimirum qui nemini non nocet.* That was one side, but it was not the side that interested Chaucer. He had the spirit of the thirteenth-century poets grown up, with more experience, more reflection, and a mellower humour, but not less good temper and capacity for enjoyment. He no longer laughs on the slightest occasion for sheer joy of living: but he would look elvishly at Richard Rolle—a hermit who made it a personal grievance that people left him solitary, a fugitive from his fellows who unconsciously satisfied a very human and pleasing love for companionship and admiration by becoming the centre of a coterie of women recluses. A world that afforded such infinite amusement to a quiet observer was after all not a bad place to live in.

IV

Chaucer, who suffers when read in extracts, is not represented in this book, although without him fourteenth-century literature is a body without a head. But in the choice of literary forms and subjects, I have aimed at illustrating the variety of interest that is to be found in the writings of lesser men.

It may be asked whether the choice of specimens gives a true idea of the taste and accomplishment of the age. This issue is raised by Professor Carleton Brown's Afterword in the second volume of his *Register of Middle English Religious and Didactic Verse*, a book that will be to generations of investigators a model of unselfish research. There he emphasizes the popularity of long poems, and especially of long didactic poems, as evidenced by the relatively great number of manuscript copies that survive. *The Prick of Conscience* leads with ninety-nine manuscripts, against sixty-nine of *The Canterbury Tales*, and forty-seven of *Piers Plowman*. What is to be said of a book that, impoverished by the exclusion of Chaucer, passes by also the most popular poem of his century?

I would rest an apology on the conditions under which manuscript copies came into being and survived; and begin with Michael of Northgate as he brings his *Ayenbyte* to an end in the October of 1340, before the short days and the numbing cold should come to make writing a pain. The book has no elegance that would commend it to special care, for Dan Michael is a dry practical man, as indifferent to the graces of style as to the luxury of silky vellum and miniatures stiff with gold and colour. But from his cell it goes into the library of his monastery—a library well ordered and well catalogued, and (as if to guarantee security) boasting the continuous possession of books that Gregory the Great gave to the first missionaries. We know its place exactly—the fourth shelf of press XVI. And there it remained safe until the days of intelligent private collectors, passing finally with the Arundel library to the British Museum. The course was not often so smooth, for of two dozen manuscripts left by Michael to St. Augustine's, Dr. James, in the year 1903, could identify only four survivors in as many different libraries. But the example is enough to illustrate a proposition that will not easily be refuted:—the chances of an English mediaeval manuscript surviving greatly depend on its eligibility for a place in the library of a religious house, since these are the chief sources of the manuscripts that have come down to us.

The attitude of the Church towards the vernacular literature of the later Middle Ages did not differ materially from her attitude towards the classics in earlier times, though the classics had always the greater dignity. Literary composition as a pure art was not encouraged. Entertainment for its own sake was discountenanced. The religious houses were to be centres of piety and learning; and if English were admitted at all in the strongholds of Latin and French, a work of unadorned edification like *The Prick of Conscience* would make very suitable reading for those who craved relaxation from severer studies. There were, of course, individuals among the professed religious who indulged a taste for more worldly literature; but the surviving catalogues of libraries that were formed under the eye of authority show a marked discrimination in favour of didactic works.

In England the private libraries of fourteenth-century laymen were relatively insignificant. But Guy, Earl of Warwick, in 1315 left an exceptionally rich collection to the Abbey of Bordesley, which failed to conserve the legacy. The list was first printed in Todd's *Illustrations of Gower and Chaucer* (1810),[1] and (among devotional works and lives of saints that

[1] p. 161.

merge into religious romances like *Joseph of Arimathea and the Graal, Titus and Vespasian,* and *Constantine*) it includes most of the famous names of popular history:—Lancelot, Arthur and Modred; Charlemagne, Doon of Mayence, Aimery of Narbonne, Girard de Vienne, William of Orange, Thibaut of Arraby, Doon of Nanteuil, Guy of Nanteuil, William Longespée, Fierebras; with two Alexander romances, a *Troy Book,* a *Brut;* the love story of *Amadas e Idoine;* the romance *de Guy e de la Reygne 'tut enterement';* a book of physic and surgery; and a miscellany—*un petit rouge livere en lequel sount contenuz mous diverses choses.* Yet even a patron so well disposed to secular poems did little to perpetuate the manuscripts of English verse. His education enabled him to draw from the fountain head, and most of his books were French.

Neither in the libraries of the monasteries, nor in the libraries of the great nobles, should we expect to find a true mirror of popular taste. The majority of the people knew no language but English; and the relative scarcity of books of every kind, which even among the educated classes made the hearers far outnumber the readers, was at once a cause and a symptom of illiteracy: the majority of the people could not read. This leads to a generalization that is cardinal for every branch of criticism:—up to Chaucer's day, the greater the popularity of an English poem, the less important becomes the manuscript as a means of early transmission. The text, which would have been comparatively safe in the keeping of scribe, book, and reader, passes to the uncertain guardianship of memorizer, reciter, and listener; so that sometimes it is wholly lost, and sometimes it suffers as much change in a generation as would a classical text in a thousand years. Already Robert Mannyng laments the mutilation of *Sir Tristrem* by the 'sayers' (who could hardly be expected to avoid faults of improvisation and omission in the recitation of so long a poem from memory);[1] and his regret would have been keener if he could have looked ahead another hundred years to see how the texts of the verse romances paid the price of popularity by the loss of crisp phrases and fresh images, and the intrusion of every mode of triteness.

Of course manuscripts of the longer secular poems were made and used,—mean, stunted copies from which the travelling entertainer could refresh his memory or add to his stock of tales; fair closet copies that would enable well-to-do admirers to renew their pleasure when no skilled minstrel was by; and, occasionally, compact libraries of romance, like the Auchinleck manuscript, which must have been the treasure of some great household that enjoyed 'romanz-reding *on þe bok*'—the pastime that encouraged the rise of prose romances in the late Middle Ages. But as a means of circulation for popular verse, distinguished from learned verse and from prose, the book was of secondary importance in its own time, and was always subject to exceptional risks. The fates of three stories in different kinds, all demonstrably favourites in the fourteenth century, will be sufficient illustration: of *Floris and Blaunche-flour*, one of the best of the early romances in the courtly style,

[1]
> I see in song, in sedgeyng tale
> Of Erceldoun and of Kendale,
> Non þam says as þai þam wroght,
> And in þer sayng it semes noght.
> Þat may þou here in *Sir Tristrem*—
> Ouer gestes it has þe steem,
> Ouer alle þat is or was,
> If men it sayd as made Thomas:
> But I here it no man so say,
> Þat of som copple som is away.
>
> (*Chronicle*, Prologue, ll. 93 ff.)

Robert blames the vanity of the reciters more than their memories, on the excellence of which Petrarch remarks in his account of the minstrels: *Sunt homines non magni ingenii, magnae vero memoriae, magnaeque diligentiae* (to Boccaccio, *Rerum Senilium*, Bk. v, ep. ii).

several manuscripts survive, but when all are assembled the beginning of the story is still wanting; of *Havelok*, typical of the homely style, one imperfect copy and a few charred fragments of another are extant; of the *Tale of Wade*, that was dear to ' olde wydwes ',[1] and yet considered worthy to entertain the noble Criseyde,[2] no text has come down. Evidently, to determine the relative popularity of the longer tales in verse we need not so much a catalogue of extant manuscripts, as a census, that cannot now be taken, of the repertories of the entertainers.

If the manuscript life of the longer secular poems was precarious, the chances of the short pieces—songs, ballads, jests, comic dialogues, lampoons—were still worse. Since they were composed for the day without thought of the future, and were no great charge on the ordinary memory, the chief motives for writing them down were absent; and no doubt the professional minstrel found that to secure his proprietary rights against competitors, he must be chary of giving copies of his best things. Many would never be put into writing; some were jotted down on perishable wax; but parchment, always too expensive for ephemeral verse, was reserved for special occasions. In France, in the thirteenth century, Henri d'Andeli adds a touch of dignity to his poem celebrating the memory of a distinguished patron by inscribing it on parchment instead of the wax tablets he used for lighter verses.[3]

---

[1] Chaucer, *Merchant's Tale*, ll. 211 ff.

[2] Chaucer, *Troilus and Criseyde*, Bk. iii, l. 614.

[3] *Et icil clers qui ce trova . . .*
   Por ce qu'il est de verite,
   Ne l'apele mie flablel,
   Ne l'a pas escrit en tablel,
   Ainz l'a escrit en parchamin:
   Par bois, per plains et par chamins,
   Par bors, par chateals, par citez
   Vorra qu'il soit bien recitez.

   (*Œuvres*, ed. A. Héron, Paris 1881, p. 40.)

In England in 1305, a West-Country swashbuckler, whom
fear of the statute against *Trailebastouns* kept in the green-
wood, relieves his offended dignity by composing a poem
half apologetic, half minatory, and chooses as the safest way
of publication to write it on parchment and throw it in the
high road :—

> *Cest rym fust fet al bois desouz vn lorer,*
> *La chaunte merle, russinole, e crye l'esperuer.*
> *Escrit estoit en parchemyn pur mout remenbrer,*
> *Et gitté en haut chemyn, qe vm le dust trouer.*[1]

These loose sheets or tiny rolls[2] rarely survive, and the preservation of their contents, as of pieces launched still more
carelessly on the world, depends on the happy chance of
inclusion in a miscellany; quotation in a larger work; or
entry on a fly-leaf, margin, or similar space left blank in a book
already written.

Most productive, though not very common in the fourteenth
century, are the miscellanies of short pieces—volumes like
Earl Guy's 'little red book containing many divers things'—
in which early collectors noted down the scraps that interested

---

[1] 'This rime was made in the wood beneath a bay-tree, where black-
bird and nightingale sing and the sparrow-hawk cries. It was written
on parchment for a record, and flung in the high road so that folk
should find it.' *The Political Songs of England*, ed. T. Wright
(London 1839), p. 236.

[2] A rare example of a roll made small for convenience of carrying is
the British Museum Additional MS. 23986. It is about three inches
wide and, in its imperfect state, twenty-two inches long, so that when
rolled up it is not much bigger than one's finger. On the inside it
contains a thirteenth-century *Song of the Barons* in French (T. Wright,
Political Songs, 1839, pp. 59 ff.); on the outside, two scenes from
a Middle English farce called *Interludium de Clerico et Puella* (Chambers,
Mediaeval Stage, vol. ii, pp. 324 ff.) which, like so many happy experiments of the earlier time, appears to have no successor in the fourteenth
century.

them. A codex of West-Country origin, MS. Harley 2253 in the British Museum, preserves among French poems such as the complaint of the *Trailebastoun*, a group of English songs that includes *Lenten is Come* and *Alysoun*. Most of its numbers are unique, and the loss of this one volume would have swept away the best part of our knowledge of the early Middle English secular lyrics.

Of survival by quotation there is an example in the history of the Letter of Theodric, which lies behind Mannyng's tale of the Dancers of Colbek; and the circumstances are worth lingering over both for the number of by-paths they open to speculation, and for the glimpse they give of Wilton in a century from which there are few records of the nunnery outside the grim, tax-gatherer's entries of Domesday.

A few years before the Conquest, Theodric the foreigner, still racked by the curse that was laid on Bovo's company, made his way from the court of Edward the Confessor to the shrine of St. Edith. As he walked through the quiet valley to Wilton in the spring of the year, we may be sure the thought came to him that here at last was the spot where a man wearied with wandering from land to land, from shrine to shrine, might hope to be cured and to set up his rest. From the moment he reaches the abbey it is impossible not to admire his feeling for dramatic effect. By a paroxysm of quaking he terrifies the peasants; but to the weeping nuns he tells his story discreetly; and, lest a doubt should remain, produces from his scrip a letter in which St. Bruno, the great Pope Leo IX, vouches for all. It is notable that at this stage the convent appear to have taken no steps to record a story so marvellous and so well authenticated; and had Theodric continued his restless wandering we should know of him as little as is known of three others from the band of carollers, who had preceded him at Wilton with a similar story. But when he obtains leave to sleep beside

the shrine of St. Edith, and in the morning of the great feast
of Lady Day wakes up healed, exalting the fame of their
patron saint who had lifted the curse where all the saints of
Europe had failed, then, and then only, the convent order that
an official record should be made, and the letter copied : *Hec
in presencia Brichtive ipsius loci abbatisse declarata et patriis
litteris*[1] *sunt mandata.*   Henceforth it exists only as a chapter
in the Acts of St. Edith, and as such it lay before Robert of
Brunne. Of the other communities or private persons visited
by Theodric (who, whether saint or *faitour*, certainly did
not produce his letter for the first and last time at Wilton)
none have preserved his memory. It would be hard to find
a better example of the power of the clergy in early times to
control the keys to posterity, or of the practical considerations
which, quite apart from merit or curiosity, governed the
preservation of legends.

But it is the verses casually jotted down in unrelated books
that bring home most vividly the slenderness of the thread of
transmission. A student has committed *Now Springs the
Spray* to solitary imprisonment between the joyless leaves of
an old law book. The song of the Irish Dancer and *The
Maid of the Moor* were scribbled, with some others from
a minstrel's stock, on the fly-leaf of a manuscript now in the
Bodleian. On a blank page of another a prudent man (who
used vile ink, long since faded) has written the verses that
banish rats, much as a modern householder might treasure

---

[1] *Patriis litteris* according to Schröder and Gaston Paris means
'English language', but if it is not a mere flourish, it means rather
the 'English script' in which the Latin letter was copied, as distinct
from the foreign hand of Theodric's original letter. What 'English
script' meant at Wilton in 1065 is a question of some delicacy. The
spelling *Folcpoldus* for *Folcwoldus* in some later copies of the Wilton
text must be due to confusion of *þ* and Anglo-Saxon p = *w*. This would
be decisive for 'Anglo-Saxon script' if it occurred anywhere but in
a proper name.

up some annihilating prescription.   To these waifs the chance
of survival did not come twice, and to a number incalculable
it never came.

It has been the purpose of this digression to bring the
extant literature into perspective : not to raise useless regrets
for what is lost, since we can learn only from what remains ;
nor to contest the value of statistics of surviving copies as
a proof of circulation, provided the works compared are
similar in length and kind, and are represented in enough
manuscripts to make figures significant ; nor yet to deny that
didactic verse bulks large in the output of the fourteenth
century : it could not be otherwise in an anxious age, when
the scarcity of remains gives everything written in English
a place in literary history, and when for almost everything
verse was preferred to prose.   And it seemed better to redress
the balance of chance by stealing from the end of the
thirteenth century a few fragments that following generations
would not forget, than to lend colour to the suggestion that
ninety-nine of the men of Chaucer's century enjoyed *The
Prick of Conscience* for every one that caught up the refrain
of *Now Springs the Spray*, or danced through *The Maid of
the Moor*, or sang the praises of Alison.

V

However much a maker of excerpts may stretch his com-
mission to give variety, it is in vain if the reader will not do
his part ; for it lies with him to find interest.   Really no
effective attack can be made on a crust of such diversified
hardness until the reader looks at his text as a means of
winning back something of the life of the past, and feels
a pleasure in the battle against vagueness.

The first step is to find out the verbal meaning.   Strange
words, that force themselves on the attention and are easily

found in dictionaries and glossaries, try a careful reader less than groups of common words—such lines as

> *Þe fairest leuedi, for þe nones,*
> *Þat miȝt gon on bodi and bones* II 53–4

which, if literally transposed into modern English, are nonsense. Those who think it is beneath the dignity of an intelligent reader to weigh such gossamer should turn to Zupitza's commentary on the Fifteenth Century Version of *Guy of Warwick*,[1] and see how a master among editors of Middle English relishes every phrase, missing nothing, and yet avoiding the opposite fault of pressing anything too hard. For these tags, more or less emptied of meaning through common use, and ridiculous by modern standards, have their importance in the economy of spoken verse, where a good voice carried them off. They helped out the composer in need of a rime; the reciter on his feet, compelled to improvise; and the audience who, lacking the reader's privilege to linger over close-packed lines, welcomed familiar turns that by diluting the sense made it easier to receive.

Repeated reading will bring out clearly the formal elements of style—the management of rime and alliteration in verse, the grouping and linking of clauses in prose, the cadences in both verse and prose: and before the value of a word or phrase can be settled it is often necessary to inquire how far its use was dictated by technical conditions, compliance with which is sometimes ingenuous to the point of crudity. Where a prose writer would be content with *Mathew sayth*, an alliterative poet elaborates (VIII *a* 234) into:

> *Mathew with mannes face mouthed þise wordis*

and in such a context *mouthed* cannot be pressed. The frequent oaths in the speeches in *Piers Plowman* are no more than counters in the alliteration: being meaningless they are

---

[1] Early English Text Society, extra series, 1875–6.

selected to prop up the verse, just as the barrenest phrases in the poem *On the Death of Edward III* owe their inclusion to the requirements of rime. Again, it will be easier to acquiesce in a forced sense of *bende* in

On bent much baret bende v 47

when it is observed that rime and alliteration so limit the poet's choice that no apter word could be used. Conversely, in the absence of disturbing technical conditions, a reader who finds nonsense should suspect his understanding of the text, or the soundness of the text, before blaming the author.

When the sense expressed and the methods of expression have been studied, it remains to examine the implications of the words—an endless task and perhaps the most entertaining of all. Take as a routine example the place where the Green Knight, preparing a third time to deliver his blow, says to Gawayne—

Halde þe now þe hyʒe hode þat Arþur þe raʒt,
And kepe þy kanel at þis kest, ʒif hit keuer may

v 229 f.

A recent translator renders very freely :

'but yet thy hood up-pick,
Haply 'twill cover thy neck when I the buffet strike'— though the etiquette of decapitation, and the delicacy of the stroke that the Green Knight has in mind, require just the opposite interpretation :—Gawayne's hood has become disarranged since he bared his neck (v 188), and the Green Knight wants a clear view to make sure of his aim. An observation of Gaston Paris on the Latin story of the Dancers of Colbek will show how much an alert mind enriches the reading of a text with precise detail. From the incident of Ave's arm he concludes that the dancers did not form a closed ring, but a line with Bovo leading (1 55) and Ave, as the last comer (1 43–54), at its end, so that she had one arm free which her brother seized in his attempt to drag her away (1 111 ff).

Intensive reading should be combined with discursive. Intensive reading cultivates the habit of noticing detail ; and it is a sound rule of textual criticism to interpret a composition first in the light of the evidence contained within itself. For instance, the slight flicker in the verse

> *Sche most wiþ him no lenger abide* ii 330

should recall as surely as a cross-reference the earlier line

> *No durst wiþ hir no leng abide* ii 84

and raise the question whether in both places in the original work the comparative had not the older form *leng*. Discursive reading is a safeguard against the dangers of a narrow experience, and especially against the assumption that details of phrase, style, or thought are peculiar to an author or composition, when in fact they are common to a period or a kind. A course of both will enable the reader to cope with a school of critics who rely on superficial resemblances to strip the mask from anonymous authors and attach their works to some favoured name. Whether *Sir Gawayne* and *The Destruction of Troy* are from the same hand is still seriously debated. Both are alliterative poems ; but it is impossible to read ten lines from each aloud without realizing the wide gap that divides their rhythms. The differences of spirit are more radical still. The facility of the author of *The Destruction* is attained at the cost of surrender to the metre. Given pens, ink, vellum, and a good original, he could go on turning out respectable verses while human strength endured. And because his meaning is all on the surface, the work does not improve on better acquaintance. The author of *Sir Gawayne* is an artist who never ceases to struggle with a harsh medium. He has the rare gift of visualizing every scene in his story : image succeeds image, each so sharply drawn as to suggest that he had his training in one of the schools of miniature-painting for which early England was famous. It is this gift of the painter that, more than likeness of dialect or juxtaposition in the manuscript, links *Sir Gawayne* with *The Pearl*.

It cannot be too strongly urged that the purpose of a worker in Middle English should be nothing less than to read sensitively, with the fullest possible understanding. Of such a purpose many *curricula* give no hint. Nor could it be deduced readily from the latest activities of research, where the tendency is more and more to leave the main road (which should be crowded if the study is to thrive) for side-tracks and by-paths of side-tracks in which the sense of direction and proportion is easily lost.

That much may be accomplished by specialists following a single line of approach has been demonstrated by the philologists, who have burrowed tirelessly to present new materials to a world which seldom rewards their happiest elucidations with so much as a ' Well said, old mole !' The student of literature (in the narrower modern sense of the word) brings a new range of interests. He will be disappointed if he expects to find a finished art, poised and sustained, in an age singularly afflicted with growing pains ; but there are compensations for any one who is content to catch glimpses of promise, and—looking back and forward, and aside to France—to take pleasure in tracing the rise and development of literary forms and subjects. It is still not enough. The specialist in language as a science, or in literature as an art, may find the Sixth Passus of *Piers Plowman* (VIII *a*) or the Wiclifite sermon (XI *b*) of secondary interest. Yet both are primary documents, the one for the history of society, the other for the history of religion.

There is no escape from a counsel of perfection :—whoever enters on a course of mediaeval studies must reckon as a defect his lack of interest in any side of the life of the Middle Ages ; and must be deaf to those who, like the fox in Aesop that had lost its tail, proclaim the benefits of truncation. The range of knowledge and experience was then more than in later times within the compass of a single mind and life. And so much that is necessary to a full understanding has been lost that no possible source of information should be shut out willingly. It is an exercise in humility to call up in all its details some scene of early English life (better a domestic scene than one of pageantry) and note how much is blurred.

Every blur is a challenge. There are few familiar subjects in which a beginner can sooner reach the limits of recorded knowledge. The great scholars have found time to chart only a fraction of their discoveries; and the greatest could not hope or wish for a day when the number of quests worth the making would be appreciably less.

This book had its origin in a very different project. Professor Napier had asked me to join him in producing for the use of language students a volume of specimens from the Middle English dialects, with an apparatus strictly linguistic. The work had not advanced beyond the choice of texts when his death and my transfer to duties in which learning had no part brought it to an end. When later the call came for a book that would introduce newcomers to the fourteenth century, I was able to bring into the changed plan his favourite passage from *Sir Gawayne*, and to draw upon the notes of his lectures for its interpretation. It is a small part of my debt to the generous and modest scholar whose mastery of exact methods was an inspiration to his pupils.

I am obliged to the Early English Text Society and to the Clarendon Press for permission to use extracts from certain of their publications; to the librarians who have made their manuscripts available, or have helped me to obtain facsimiles; to Mr. J. R. R. Tolkien who has undertaken the preparation of the Glossary, the most exacting part of the apparatus; and to Mr Nichol Smith who has watched over the book from its beginnings.

THE TEXTS

A SINGLE manuscript is chosen as the basis of each text, and neither its readings nor its spellings are altered if they can reasonably be defended. Where correction involves substitution, the substituted letters are printed in italics, and the actual reading of the manuscript will be found in the Foot-notes (or occasionally in the Notes). Words or letters added to complete the manuscript are enclosed in caret brackets ⟨ ⟩. Corrupt readings retained in the text are indicated by daggers † †. Paragraphing, punctuation, capitals, and the details of word division are modern, and contractions are expanded without notice, so that the reader shall not be distracted by difficulties that are purely palaeographical. A final *e* derived from OFr. *é(e)* or *ie*, OE. *-ig*, is printed *é*, to distinguish it from unaccented final *e* which is regularly lost in Modern English.

The extracts have been collated with the manuscripts, or with complete photographs, except Nos. IV (Thornton MS.), VIII *b*, XI *a*, and XVII, the manuscripts of which I have not been able to consult. The foot-notes as a rule take no account of conjectural emendations, variants from other manuscripts, or minutiae like erasures and corrections contemporary with the copy.

SELECT BIBLIOGRAPHY[1]

DICTIONARIES.

*A New English Dictionary on Historical Principles, ed. Sir J. A. H. Murray, H. Bradley, W. A. Craigie, C. T. Onions, Oxford 1888–1928 [quoted as *N.E.D.*].

*Stratmann, F. A. A Middle English Dictionary, new edn. by H. Bradley, Oxford 1891.

BIBLIOGRAPHICAL.

*Brown, Carleton, and Robbins, Rossell H. The Index of Middle English Verse, New York 1943 (The Index Society).

*Hammond, Miss E. P. Chaucer: A Bibliographical Manual, New York 1908.

Kennedy, G. K. A Bibliography of Writings on the English Language, Cambridge and New Haven 1927.

*Wells, J. E. A Manual of Writings in Middle English, 1050–1400, New Haven 1916; Supplements, 1919, 1923, 1926, etc.

LITERATURE AND LEARNING.

Chambers, E. K. The Mediaeval Stage, 2 vols., Oxford 1903.

Clark, J. W. The Care of Books, Cambridge (new edn.) 1909.

Ker, W. P. English Literature, Mediaeval, London 1912.

Legouis, E. Chaucer (transl. L. Lailavoix), London 1913.

Lowes, J. L. Geoffrey Chaucer, London 1934.

Rashdall, H. The Universities of Europe in the Middle Ages, 2nd edition by F. M. Powicke and A. B. Emden, 3 vols., Oxford 1936.

CHURCH HISTORY.

*Dugdale, Sir William, Monasticon Anglicanum, new edn. by Caley, Ellis and Bandinel, 6 vols., London 1846. [Gives detailed histories of the English religious houses.]

Knowles, D., The Religious Orders in England, Cambridge 1950–5.

Pantin, W. A., The English Church in the Fourteenth Century, Cambridge 1955.

---

[1] Books primarily of reference are distinguished by an asterisk. Details relating to texts, manuscript sources, editions, monographs, and articles that have appeared in periodicals, will be found in the bibliographical manuals cited.

GENERAL HISTORY.

Ashley, W. J. *An Introduction to English Economic History and Theory*, 2 vols., London 1888-93.

Bateson, Mary. *Mediaeval England (1066-1350)*, London 1903. [A brief and exact social history.]

Crump, C. G. and Jacob, E. F. (editors). *The Legacy of the Middle Ages*, Oxford 1927.

Gasquet, Cardinal F. A. *The Black Death of 1348 and 1349*, London, 2nd edn. 1908.

Jusserand, J. J. *English Wayfaring Life in the Middle Ages* (transl. L. Toulmin Smith), London 1889, &c.; revised 1921. [Invaluable.]

McKisack, M. *The Fourteenth Century (1307-1399)*, Oxford 1959.

Oman, Sir Charles Wm. C. *The Great Revolt of 1381*, Oxford 1906.

Poole, A. L. (editor). *Medieval England*, Oxford 1958.

Reville, A., et Petit-Dutaillis, Ch. *Le Soulèvement des Travailleurs d'Angleterre en 1381*, Paris 1898.

Riley, H. T. *Memorials of London and London Life (1270-1419)*, London 1868.

Salzman, L. F. *English Industries of the Middle Ages*, Oxford 1924. *English Trade in the Middle Ages*, Oxford 1931.

Smith, S. Armitage. *John of Gaunt*, London 1904.

Stenton, Lady D. M. *English Society in the Early Middle Ages*, London 1951. [Excellent.]

Trevelyan, G. M. *England in the Age of Wycliffe*, London 1899; new edn., 1909. [A brilliant study.]

Workman, H. B. *John Wyclif*, 2 vols., Oxford 1927.

WORKS RELATING CHIEFLY TO FRANCE.

Enlart, C. *Le Costume* (vol. iii of his *Manuel d'Archéologie Française*), Paris 1916.

Evans, Joan. *Life in Medieval France*, Oxford 1925.

Faral, E. *Les Jongleurs en France au Moyen Âge*, Paris 1910.

Paris, G. *La Littérature Française au Moyen Âge*, Paris, 5th edn. 1909. [A model handbook.]

I

ROBERT MANNYNG OF BRUNNE'S
HANDLYNG SYNNE

Begun 1303

What is known of Robert Mannyng of Brunne is derived from
his own works. In the Prologue to *Handlyng Synne* he writes:

> To alle Crystyn men vndir sunne,
> And to gode men of Brunne,
> And speciali, alle be name,
> Þe felaushepe of Symprynghame,
> Roberd of Brunne greteþ ʒow
> In al godenesse þat may to prow,
> Of Brunne Wake yn Kesteuene,
> Syxe myle besyde Sympryngham euene;
> Y dwelled yn þe pryorye
> Fyftene ʒere yn cumpanye. . . .

And in the Introduction to his *Chronicle*:

> Of Brunne I am; if any me blame,
> Robert Mannyng is my name;
> Blissed be he of God of heuene
> Þat me Robert with gude wille neuene!
> In þe third Edwardes tyme was I,
> When I wrote alle þis story,
> In þe hous of Sixille I was a throwe;
> Danʒ Robert of Malton, þat ʒe know,
> Did it wryte for felawes sake
> When þai wild solace make.

From these passages it appears that he was born in Brunne,
the modern Bourne, in Lincolnshire, called *Brunne Wake* because
it was a possession of the Wake family; and that he belonged to
the Gilbertine Order. Sempringham was the head-quarters of
the Order, and the dependent priory of Sixhill in N. Lincolnshire
was near by. It has been suggested, without much evidence, that
he was a lay brother, and not a full canon.

His *Chronicle of England* was completed in 1338. It falls into two parts, distinguished by a change of metre and source. The first, edited by Furnivall in the Rolls Series (2 vols. 1887), extends from the Flood to A.D. 689, and is based on Wace's *Brut*, the French source of Layamon's *Brut*. The second part, edited by Hearne, 2 vols., Oxford 1725, extends from A.D. 689 to the death of Edward I, and is based on the French *Chronicle* of a contemporary, who is sometimes called Pierre de Langtoft, sometimes Piers of Bridlington, because he was a native of Langtoft in Yorkshire, and a canon of the Austin priory at Bridlington in the same county. Mannyng's *Chronicle* has no great historical value, and its chief literary interest lies in the references to current traditions and popular stories.

Handlyng Synne is a much more valuable work. It was begun in 1303 :

> Dane Felyp was mayster þat tyme
> Þat y began þys Englyssh ryme ;
> Þe ȝeres of grace fyl þan to be
> A þousynd and þre hundred and þre.
> In þat tyme turnede y þys
> On Englyssh tunge out of Frankys
> Of a boke as y fonde ynne,
> Men clepyn þe boke ' Handlyng Synne '.

The source was again French—the *Manual de Pechiez* attributed to a contemporary Northerner William of Wadington. The popularity of such treatises on the Sins may be judged from the number of works modelled upon them : e.g. the *Ayenbyte of Inwyt*, Gower's *Confessio Amantis*, and Chaucer's *Parson's Tale*. Their purpose was, as Robert explains, to enable a reader to examine his conscience systematically and constantly, and so to guard himself against vice.

Two complete MSS. of *Handlyng Synne* are known : British Museum MS. Harley 1701 (about 1350–75), and MS. Bodley 415, of a slightly later date. An important fragment is in the library of Dulwich College. The whole text, with the French source, has been edited by Furnivall for the Roxburghe Club, and later for the Early English Text Society. It treats, with the usual wealth of classification, of the Commandments, the Sins, the Sacraments, the Requisites and Graces of Shrift. But such a bald summary gives no idea of the richness and variety of its content. For Mannyng, anticipating Gower, saw the opportunities that the illustrative stories offered to his special gifts, and spared no pains in their telling. A few examples are added from his own knowledge. More often he expands Wadington's outlines, as in the tale of the Dancers of Colbek. Here the French source is brief and colourless. But the English translator had found a fuller Latin version—clearly the same as that printed from Bodleian MS. Rawlinson C 938 in the preface to Furnivall's Roxburghe Club edition—and from it he produced the well-rounded and lively rendering given below.

Robert knew that a work designed to turn 'lewde men' from the ale-house to the contemplation of their sins must grip their attention; and in the art of linking good teaching with entertainment he is a master. He has the gift of conveying to his audience his own enjoyment of a good story. His loose-knit conversational style would stand the test of reading aloud to simple folk, and he allows no literary affectations, no forced metres or verbiage, to darken his meaning :

> Haf I alle in myn Inglis layd
> In symple speche as I couthe,
> Þat is lightest in mannes mouthe.
> I mad noght for no disours,
> Ne for no seggers, no harpours,
> But for þe luf of symple men
> Þat strange Inglis can not ken;
> For many it ere þat strange Inglis
> In ryme wate neuer what it is,
> And bot þai wist what it mente,
> Ellis me thoght it were alle schente.
>
> (*Chronicle*, ll. 72 ff.)

The simple form reflects the writer's frankness and directness. He points a moral fearlessly, but without harshness or self-righteousness. And the range of his sympathies and interests makes *Handlyng Synne* the best picture of English life before Langland and Chaucer.

I. ROBERT MANNYNG OF BRUNNE

THE DANCERS OF COLBEK

MS. Harley 1701 (about A.D. 1375); ed. Furnivall, ll. 8987 ff.

KAROLLES, wrastlynges, or somour games,   1
Whoso euer haunteþ any swyche shames
Yn cherche, oþer yn chercheȝerd,
Of sacrylage he may be aferd;
Or entyrludes, or syngynge,   5
Or tabure bete, or oþer pypynge—
Alle swyche þyng forbodyn es
Whyle þe prest stondeþ at messe.
Alle swyche to euery gode preste ys lothe,
And sunner wyl he make hym wroth   10
Þan he wyl, þat haþ no wyt,
Ne vndyrstondeþ nat Holy Wryt.
And specyaly at hygh tymes
Karolles to synge and rede rymys
Noght yn none holy stedes,   15
Þat myȝt dysturble þe prestes bedes,
Or ȝyf he were yn orysun
Or any ouþer deuocyun:
Sacrylage ys alle hyt tolde,
Þys and many oþer folde.   20
But for to leue yn cherche for to daunce,
Y shal ȝow telle a ful grete chaunce,
And y trow þe most þat fel
Ys soþe as y ȝow telle;
And fyl þys chaunce yn þys londe,   25
Yn Ingland, as y vndyrstonde,
Yn a kynges tyme þat hyght Edward
Fyl þys chau⟨n⟩ce þat was so hard.

21 for (2nd) *om. MS. Bodley 415.*   24 Ys as soþ as þe gospel *MS. Bodley.*

Hyt was vppon a Crystemesse nyȝt
Þat twelue folys a karolle dyȝt,   30
Yn wodehed, as hyt were yn cuntek,
Þey come to a tounne men calle Colbek.
Þe cherche of þe tounne þat þey to come
Ys of Seynt Magne, þat suffred martyrdome ;
Of Seynt Bukcestre hyt ys also,   35
Seynt Magnes suster, þat þey come to.
Here names of alle þus fonde y wryte,
And as y wote now shul ȝe wyte :
Here lodesman, þat made hem glew,
Þus ys wryte, he hyȝte Gerlew.   40
Twey maydens were yn here coueyne,
Mayden Merswynde and Wybessyne.
Alle þese come þedyr for þat enchesone
Of þe prestes doghtyr of þe tounne.

Þe prest hyȝt Robert, as y kan ame ;   45
Aȝone hyght hys sone by name ;
Hys doghter, þat þese men wulde haue,
Þus ys wryte, þat she hyȝt Aue.
Echoune consented to o wyl
Who shuld go Aue oute to tyl,   50
Þey graunted echone out to sende
Boþe Wybessyne and Merswynde.

Þese wommen ȝede and tolled here oute
Wyþ hem to karolle þe cherche aboute.
Beu⟨u⟩ne ordeyned here karollyng ;   55
Gerlew endyted what þey shuld syng.
Þys ys þe karolle þat þey sunge,
As telleþ þe Latyn tunge :
   ' *Equitabat Beuo per siluam frondosam,*
Ducebat secum Merswyndam formosam.   60
Quid stamus ? cur non imus ?'
   ' By þe leued wode rode Beuolyne,

Wyþ hym he ledde feyre Merswyne.
Why stonde we? why go we noght?'
Þys ys þe karolle þat Grysly wroght;   65
Þys songe sunge þey yn þe chercheȝerd—
Of foly were þey no þyng aferd—
Vnto þe matynes were alle done,
And þe messe shuld bygynne sone.

Þe preste hym reuest to begynne messe,   70
And þey ne left þerfore neuer þe lesse,
But daunsed furþe as þey bygan,
For alle þe messe þey ne blan.

Þe preste, þat stode at þe autere,
And herd here noyse and here bere,   75
Fro þe auter down he nam,
And to þe cherche porche he cam,
And seyd 'On Goddes behalue, y ȝow forbede
Þat ȝe no lenger do swych dede,
But comeþ yn on feyre manere   80
Goddes seruyse for to here,
And doþ at Crystyn mennys lawe;
Karolleþ no more, for Crystys awe!
Wurschyppeþ Hym with alle ȝoure myȝt
Þat of þe Vyrgyne was bore þys nyȝt.'   85
For alle hys byddyng lefte þey noȝt,
But daunsed furþ, as þey þoȝt.
Þe preste þarefor was sore agreued;
He preyd God þ<del>a</del>t he on beleuyd,
And for Seynt Magne, þat he wulde so werche—   90
Yn whos wurschyp sette was þe cherche—
Þat swych a veniaunce were on hem sent,
Are þey oute of þat stede were went,
Þat ⟨þey⟩ myȝt euer ryȝt so wende

78 behalue] halfe *MS. Bodley.*   94 þey] *so MS. Bodley* : *om.*
MS. Harley.

Vnto þat tyme tweluemonth ende; 95
(Yn þe Latyne þat y fonde þore
He seyþ nat 'tweluemonth' but 'euermore';)
He cursed hem þere alsaume
As þey karoled on here gaume.

    As sone as þe preste hadde so spoke 100
Euery hand yn ouþer so fast was loke
Þat no man myȝt with no wundyr
Þat tweluemo(n)þe parte hem asundyr.

    Þe preste ȝede yn, whan þys was done,
And commaunded hys sone Aȝone 105
Þat ⟨he⟩ shulde go swyþe aftyr Aue,
Oute of þat karolle algate to haue.
But al to late þat wurde was seyd,
For on hem alle was þe veniaunce leyd.

    Aȝone wende weyl for to spede; 110
Vnto þe karolle as swyþe he ȝede,
Hys systyr by þe arme he hente,
And þe arme fro þe body wente.

Men wundred alle þat þere wore,
And merueyle mowe ȝe here more, 115
For, seþen he had þe arme yn hand,
Þe body ȝede furþ karoland,
And noþer ⟨þe⟩ body ne þe arme
Bledde neuer blode, colde ne warme,
But was as drye, with al þe haunche, 120
As of a stok were ryue a braunche.

    Aȝone to hys fadyr went,
And broght hym a sory present:
'Loke, fadyr,' he seyd, 'and haue hyt here,
Þe arme of þy doghtyr dere, 125
Þat was myn owne syster Aue,
Þat y wende y myȝt a saue.

106 he] *so MS. Bodley.*   118 þe] *so MS. Bodley.*

Þy cursyng now sene hyt ys
Wyth veniaunce on þy owne flessh.
Fellyche þou cursedest, and ouer sone;   130
Þou askedest veniaunce,—þou hast þy bone.'
    Ʒow þar nat aske ʒyf þere was wo
Wyth þe preste, and wyth many mo.
Þe prest, þat cursed for þat daunce,
On some of hys fyl harde chaunce.   135
He toke hys doghtyr arme forlorn
And byryed hyt on þe morn;
Þe nexte day þe arme of Aue
He fonde hyt lyggyng aboue þe graue.
He byryed ⟨hyt⟩ on anouþer day,   140
And eft aboue þe graue hyt lay.
Þe þrydde tyme he byryed hyt,
And eft was hyt kast oute of þe pyt.
Þe prest wulde byrye hyt no more,
He dredde þe veniaunce ferly sore;   145
Ynto þe cherche he bare þe arme,
For drede and doute of more harme,
He ordeyned hyt for to be
Þat euery man myʒt wyth ye hyt se.

    Þese men þat ʒede so karolland,   150
Alle þat ʒere, hand yn hand,
Þey neuer oute of þat stede ʒede,
Ne none myʒt hem þenne lede.
Þere þe cursyng fyrst bygan,
Yn þat place aboute þey ran,   155
Þat neuer ne felte þey no werynes
As many †bodyes for goyng dost†,
Ne mete ete, ne drank drynke,
Ne slepte onely alepy wynke.

136-7 forlorn̄ . . . morn̄ *MS.*   140 hyt] *so MS. Bodley : om. MS
Harley.*

Ny3t ne day þey wyst of none,　　　　　　160
Whan hyt was come, whan hyt was gone;
Frost ne snogh, hayle ne reyne,
Of colde ne hete, felte þey no peyne;
Heere ne nayles neuer grewe,
Ne solowed cloþes, ne turned hewe;　　　165
Þundyr ne ly3tnyng dyd hem no dere,
Goddys mercy ded hyt fro hem were;—
But sungge þat songge þat þe wo wro3t:
'Why stonde we? why go we no3t?'

What man shuld þyr be yn þys lyue　　　170
Þat ne wulde hyt see and þedyr dryue?
Þe Emperoure Henry come fro Rome
For to see þys hard dome.
Whan he hem say, he wepte sore
For þe myschefe þat he sagh þore.　　　175
He ded come wry3tes for to make
Coueryng ouer hem, for tempest sake.
But þat þey wroght hyt was yn veyn,
For hyt come to no certeyn,
For þat þey sette on oo day　　　　　　180
On þe touþer downe hyt lay.
Ones, twyys, þryys, þus þey wro3t,
And alle here makyng was for no3t.
Myght no coueryng hyle hem fro colde
Tyl tyme of mercy þat Cryst hyt wolde.　　185

Tyme of grace fyl þurgh Hys my3t
At þe tweluemonth ende, on þe 3ole ny3t.
Þe same oure þat þe prest hem banned,
Þe same oure atwynne þey †woned†;
Þat houre þat he cursed hem ynne,　　　190
Þe same oure þey 3ede atwynne,
And as yn twynkelyng of an ye

171 Þat] Þat hyt *MS. Harley.*

Ynto þe cherche gun þey flye,
And on þe pauement þey fyl alle downe
As þey had be dede, or fal yn a swone.   195
    Þre days styl þey lay echone,
Þat none steryd oþer flesshe or bone,
And at þe þre days ende
To lyfe God graunted hem to wende.
Þey sette hem vpp and spak apert   200
To þe parysshe prest, syre Robert:
' Þou art ensample and enchesun
Of oure long confusyun;
Þou maker art of oure trauayle,
Þat ys to many grete meruayle,   205
And þy traueyle shalt þou sone ende,
For to þy long home sone shalt þou wende.'
    Alle þey ryse þat yche tyde
But Aue,—she lay dede besyde.
Grete sorowe had here fadyr, here broþer;   210
Merueyle and drede had alle ouþer;
Y trow no drede of soule dede,
But with pyne was broght þe body dede.
Þe fyrst man was þe fadyr, þe prest,
Þat deyd aftyr þe doȝtyr nest.   215
Þys yche arme þat was of Aue,
Þat none myȝt leye yn graue,
Þe Emperoure dyd a vessel werche
To do hyt yn, and hange yn þe cherche,
Þat alle men myȝt se hyt and knawe,   220
And þenk on þe chaunce when men hyt sawe.
    Þese men þat hadde go þus karolland
Alle þe ȝere, fast hand yn hand,
Þogh þat þey were þan asunder
Ȝyt alle þe worlde spake of hem wunder.   225

221 men] þey *MS. Bodley.*

Þat same hoppyng þat þey fyrst ȝede,
Þat daunce ȝede þey þurgh land and lede,
And, as þey ne myȝt fyrst be vnbounde,
So efte togedyr myȝt þey neuer be founde,
Ne myȝt þey neuer come aȝeyn   230
Togedyr to oo stede certeyn.

Foure ȝede to þe courte of Rome,
And euer hoppyng aboute þey nome,
†Wyth sundyr lepyst† come þey þedyr,
But þey come neuer efte togedyr.   235
Here cloþes ne roted, ne nayles grewe,
Ne heere ne wax, ne solowed hewe,
Ne neuer hadde þey amendement,
Þat we herde, at any corseynt,
But at þe vyrgyne Seynt Edyght,   240
Þere was he botened, Seynt Teodryght,
On oure Lady day, yn lenten tyde,
As he slepte here toumbe besyde.
Þere he had hys medycyne
At Seynt Edyght, þe holy vyrgyne.   245

Brunyng þe bysshope of seynt Tolous
Wrote þys tale so merueylous;
Seþþe was hys name of more renoun,
Men called hym þe pope Leoun.
Þys at þe court of Rome þey wyte,   250
And yn þe kronykeles hyt ys wryte
Yn many stedys beȝounde þe see,
More þan ys yn þys cuntré.
Þarfor men seye, an weyl ys trowed,
'Þe nere þe cherche, þe fyrþer fro God'.   255

So fare men here by þys tale,
Some holde hyt but a troteuale,

Yn oþer stedys hyt ys ful dere
And for grete merueyle þey wyl hyt here.
A tale hyt ys of feyre shewyng,   260
Ensample and drede aȝens cursyng.
Þys tale y tolde ȝow to ⟨make⟩ ȝow aferde
Yn cherche to karolle, or yn chercheȝerde,
Namely aȝens þe prestys wylle:
Leueþ whan he byddeþ ȝow be stylle.   265

II

SIR ORFEO

Sir Orfeo is found in three MSS.: (1) the Auchinleck MS. (1325–1350), a famous Middle English miscellany now in the Advocates' Library, Edinburgh; (2) British Museum MS. Harley 3810 (fifteenth century); (3) Bodleian MS. Ashmole 61 (fifteenth century). Our text follows the Auchinleck MS., with ll. 1–24 and ll. 33–46 supplied from the Harleian MS. A. J. Bliss, *Sir Orfeo*, Oxford 1954, prints all the texts.

The story appears to have been translated from a French source into South-Western English at the beginning of the fourteenth century. It belongs to a group of 'lays' which claim to derive from Brittany, e.g. *Lai le Freine*, which has the same opening lines (1–22); *Emaré*; and Chaucer's *Franklin's Tale*.

The story of Orpheus and Eurydice was known to the Middle Ages chiefly from Ovid (*Metamorphoses* x) and from Virgil (*Georgics* iv). King Alfred's rendering of it in his *Boethius* is one of his best prose passages, despite the crude moralizing which makes Orpheus's backward glance at Eurydice before she is safe from Hades a symbol of the backslider's longing for his old sins. The Middle English poet has a lighter and daintier touch. The Greek myth is almost lost in a tale of fairyland, the earliest English romance of the kind; and to provide the appropriate happy ending, Sir Orfeo is made successful in his attempt to rescue Heurodis. The adaptation of the classical subject to a mediaeval setting is thorough. An amusing instance is the attempt in the Auchinleck MS. to give the poem an English interest by the unconvincing assurance that *Traciens* (which from 'Thracian' had come to mean 'Thrace') was the old name of Winchester (ll. 49–50). Probably we have in this MS. a copy of the rendering given by some minstrel at Winchester.

⟨Wᴇ redyn ofte and fynde ywryte,
As clerkes don us to wyte,
The layes that ben of harpyng
Ben yfounde of frely thing.
Sum ben of wele, and sum of wo,   5
And sum of ioy and merthe also ;
Sum of trechery, and sum of gyle,
And sum of happes þat fallen by whyle;
Sum of bourdys, and sum of rybaudry,
And sum þer ben of the feyré.   10
Of alle þing þat men may se,
Moost o loᴜe forsoþe þey be.
In Brytayn þis layes arne ywryte,
Furst yfounde and forþe ygete,
Of aventures þat fillen by dayes,   15
Wherof Brytouns made her layes.
When þey myght owher heryn
Of aventures þat þer weryn,
Þey toke her harpys wiþ game,
Maden layes and ȝaf it name.   20

Of aventures þat han befalle
Y can sum telle, but nouȝt all.
Herken, lordyngys þat ben trewe,
And y wol ȝou telle of Sir Orphewe.⟩
Orfeo was a king,   25
In Inglond an heiȝe lording,
A stalworþ man and hardi bo,
Large and curteys he was also.
His fader was comen of King Pluto,
And his moder of King Iuno,   30
Þat sum time were as godes yhold,
For auentours þat þai dede and told.

---

ll. 1–24 *from Harl.* 3810 : *em. MS.*   ll. 7–8 *follow* ll. 9–10 *in Harl.*   12 o loue] to lowe *Harl.*   26 In Inglond] And in his tyme *Harl.*

⟨Orpheo most of ony þing
Louede þe gle of harpyng;
Syker was euery gode harpoure   35
Of hym to haue moche honoure.
Hymself loued for to harpe,
And layde þeron his wittes scharpe.
He lernyd so, þer noþing was
A better harper in no plas;   40
In þe world was neuer man born
Þat ones Orpheo sat byforn,
And he myȝt of his harpyng here,
He schulde þinke þat he were
In one of þe ioys of Paradys,   45
Suche ioy and melody in his harpyng is.⟩
    Þis king soiournd in Traciens,
Þat was a cité of noble defens;
For Winchester was cleped þo
Traciens wiþouten no.   50
Þe king hadde a quen of priis,
Þat was ycleped Dame Herodis,
Þe fairest leuedi, for þe nones,
Þat miȝt gon on bodi and bones,
Ful of loue and of godenisse;   55
Ac no man may telle hir fairnise.
    Bifel so in þe comessing of May,
When miri and hot is þe day,
And oway beþ winter-schours,
And eueri feld is ful of flours,   60
And blosme breme on eueri bouȝ
Oueral wexeþ miri anouȝ,
Þis ich quen, Dame Heurodis,
Tok to maidens of priis,

33–46 *from Harl. 3810*: *om. MS.*   49–50 *om. Harl., Ashm.*
    51 Þe king] He *Harl.* : And *Ashm.*

And went in an vndrentide   65
To play bi an orchard side,
To se þe floures sprede and spring.
And to here þe foules sing.

    Þai sett hem doun al þre
Vnder a fair ympe-tre,   70
And wel sone þis fair quene
Fel on slepe opon þe grene.
Þe maidens durst hir nouȝt awake,
Bot lete hir ligge and rest take.
So sche slepe til afternone,   75
Þat vndertide was al ydone.

Ac as sone as sche gan awake,
Sche crid and loþli bere gan make,
Sche froted hir honden and hir fet,
And crached hir visage, it bled wete ;   80
Hir riche robe hye al torett,
And was reuey⟨se⟩d out of hir witt.

Þe tvo maidens hir biside
No durst wiþ hir no leng abide,
Bot ourn to þe palays ful riȝt,   85
And told boþe squier and kniȝt
Þat her quen awede wold,
And bad hem go and hir athold.

Kniȝtes vrn, and leuedis also,
Damisels sexti and mo,   90
In þe orchard to þe quen hye come,
And her vp in her armes nome,
And brouȝt hir to bed atte last,
And held hir þere fine fast ;
Ac euer sche held in o cri,   95
And wold vp and owy.

    When Orfeo herd þat tiding,

---

82 reueysed] rauysed *Ashm.*: reueyd *MS.*: wode out *Harl.*

Neuer him nas wers for no þing.
He come wiþ kniȝtes tene
To chaumber riȝt bifor þe quene,   100
And biheld, and seyd wiþ grete pité:
'O lef liif, what is te,
Þat euer ȝete hast ben so stille,
And now gredest wonder schille?
Þi bodi, þat was so white ycore,   105
Wiþ þine nailes is al totore.
Allas! þi rode, þat was so red,
Is al wan as þou were ded;
And also þine fingres smale
Beþ al blodi and al pale.   110
Allas! þi louesom eyȝen to
Lokeþ so man doþ on his fo.
A! dame, ich biseche merci.
Lete ben al þis reweful cri,
And tel me what þe is, and hou,   115
And what þing may þe help now.'
    Þo lay sche stille atte last,
And gan to wepe swiþe fast,
And seyd þus þe king to:
'Allas! mi lord, Sir Orfeo,   120
Seþþen we first togider were,
Ones wroþ neuer we nere,
Bot euer ich haue yloued þe
As mi liif, and so þou me.
Ac now we mot delen ato;   125
Do þi best, for y mot go.'
    'Allas!' quaþ he, 'forlorn icham.
Whider wiltow go, and to wham?
Whider þou gost, ichil wiþ þe,
And whider y go, þou schalt wiþ me.'   130
'Nay, nay, sir, þat nouȝt nis;

Ichil þe telle al hou it is:
As ich lay þis vndertide,
And slepe vnder our orchard-side,
Þer come to me to fair kniȝtes   135
Wele y-armed al to riȝtes,
And bad me comen an heiȝing,
And speke wiþ her lord þe king.
And ich answerd at wordes bold,
Y n⟨o⟩ durst nouȝt, no y nold.   140
Þai priked oȝain as þai miȝt driue;
Þo com her king also bliue,
Wiþ an hundred kniȝtes and mo,
And damisels an hundred also,
Al on snowe-white stedes;   145
As white as milke were her wedes:
Y no seiȝe neuer ȝete bifore
So fair creatours ycore.
Þe king hadde a croun on hed,
It nas of siluer, no of gold red,   150
Ac it was of a precious ston,
As briȝt as þe sonne it schon.
And as son as he to me cam,
Wold ich, nold ich, he me nam,
And made me wiþ him ride   155
Opon a palfray, bi his side,
And brouȝt me to his palays,
Wele atird in ich ways,
And schewed me castels and tours,
Riuers, forestes, friþ wiþ flours,   160
And his riche stedes ichon;
And seþþen me brouȝt oȝain hom
Into our owhen orchard,
And said to me þus afterward:
"Loke, dame, to-morwe þatow be   165

Riȝt here vnder þis ympe-tre,
And þan þou schalt wiþ ous go,
And liue wiþ ous euermo ;
And ȝif þou makest ous ylet,
Whar þou be, þou worst yfet,   170
And totore þine limes al,
Þat noþing help þe no schal;
And þei þou best so totorn,
ȝete þou worst wiþ ous yborn." '

   When King Orfeo herd þis cas,   175
'O we !' quaþ he, 'allas, allas !
Leuer me were to lete mi liif,
Þan þus to lese þe quen mi wiif l'
He asked conseyl at ich man,
Ac no man him help no can.   180

   Amorwe þe vndertide is come,
And Orfeo haþ his armes ynome,
And wele ten hundred kniȝtes wiþ him
Ich y-armed stout and grim ;
And wiþ þe quen wenten he   185
Riȝt vnto þat ympe-tre.
Þai made scheltrom in ich a side,
And sayd þai wold þere abide,
And dye þer euerichon,
Er þe quen schuld fram hem gon.   190
Ac ȝete amiddes hem ful riȝt
Þe quen was oway ytuiȝt,
Wiþ fairi forþ ynome ;
Men wist neuer wher sche was bicome.

   Þo was þer criing, wepe and wo.   195
Þe king into his chaumber is go,
And oft swoned opon þe ston,
And made swiche diol and swiche mon
Þat neiȝe his liif was yspent:

Þer was non amendement.   200

   He cleped togider his barouns,
Erls, lordes of renouns;
And when þai al ycomen were,
'Lordinges,' he said, 'bifor ʒou here
Ich ordainy min heiʒe steward   205
To wite mi kingdom afterward;
In mi stede ben he schal,
To kepe mi londes ouer al.
For, now ichaue mi quen ylore,
Þe fairest leuedi þat euer was bore,   210
Neuer eft y nil no woman se.
Into wildernes ichil te,
And liue þer euermore
Wiþ wilde bestes in holtes hore.
And when ʒe vnderstond þat y be spent,   215
Make ʒou þan a parlement,
And chese ʒou a newe king.
Now doþ ʒour best wiþ al mi þing.'

   Þo was þer wepeing in þe halle,
And grete cri among hem alle;   220
Vnneþe miʒt old or ʒong
For wepeing speke a word wiþ tong.
Þai kneled adoun al yfere,
And praid him, ʒif his wille were,
Þat he no schuld nouʒt fram hem go.   225
'Do way!' quaþ he, 'it schal be so.'

   Al his kingdom he forsoke;
Bot a sclauin on him he toke;
He no hadde kirtel no hode,
Schert, ⟨no⟩ no noþer gode.   230
Bot his harp he tok algate,
And dede him barfot out atte ʒate;

No man most wiþ him go.

O way! what þer was wepe and wo,
When he, þat hadde ben king wiþ croun,   235
Went so pouerlich out of toun!
Þurch wode and ouer heþ
Into þe wildernes he geþ.
Noþing he fint þat him is ays,
Bot euer he liueþ in gret malais.   240
He þat hadde ywerd þe fowe and griis,
And on bed þe purper biis,
Now on hard heþe he liþ,
Wiþ leues and gresse he him wriþ.
He þat hadde had castels and tours,   245
Riuer, forest, friþ wiþ flours,
Now, þei it comenci to snewe and frese,
Þis king mot make his bed in mese.
He þat had yhad kniȝtes of priis
Bifor him kneland, and leuedis,   250
Now seþ he noþing þat him likeþ,
Bot wilde wormes bi him strikeþ.
He þat had yhad plenté
Of mete and drink, of ich deynté,
Now may he al day digge and wrote   255
Er he finde his fille of rote.
In somer he liueþ bi wild frut
And berien bot gode lite;
In winter may he noþing finde
Bot rote, grases, and þe rinde.   260
Al his bodi was oway duine
For missays, and al tochine.
Lord! who may telle þe sore
Þis king sufferd ten ȝere and more?
His here of his berd, blac and rowe,   265
To his girdelstede was growe.

His harp, whereon was al his gle,
He hidde in an holwe tre;
And, when þe weder was clere and briȝt,
He toke his harp to him wel riȝt,   270
And harped at his owhen wille.
Into alle þe wode þe soun gan schille,
Þat alle þe wilde bestes þat þer beþ
For ioie abouten him þai teþ;
And alle þe foules þat þer were   275
Come and sete on ich a brere,
To here his harping afine,
So miche melody was þerin;
And when he his harping lete wold,
No best bi him abide nold.   280
    He miȝt se him bisides
Oft in hot vndertides
Þe king o fairy wiþ his rout
Com to hunt him al about,
Wiþ dim cri and bloweing;   285
And houndes also wiþ him berking;
Ac no best þai no nome,
No neuer he nist whider þai bicome.
And oþer while he miȝt him se
As a gret ost bi him te   290
Wele atourned ten hundred kniȝtes,
Ich y-armed to his riȝtes,
Of cuntenaunce stout and fers,
Wiþ mani desplaid baners,
And ich his swerd ydrawe hold,   295
Ac neuer he nist whider þai wold.
And oþer while he seiȝe oþer þing:
Kniȝtes and leuedis com daunceing
In queynt atire, gisely,
Queynt pas and softly;   300

Tabours and trunpes ȝede hem bi,
And al maner menstraci.
   And on a day he seiȝe him biside
Sexti leuedis on hors ride,
Gentil and iolif as brid on ris,—   305
Nouȝt o man amonges hem þer nis.
And ich a faucoun on hond bere,
And riden on haukin bi o riuere.
Of game þai founde wel gode haunt,
Maulardes, hayroun, and cormeraunt;   310
Þe foules of þe water ariseþ,
Þe faucouns hem wele deuiseþ;
Ich faucoun his pray slouȝ.
Þat seiȝe Orfeo, and louȝ:
'Parfay!' quaþ he, 'þer is fair game,   315
Þider ichil, bi Godes name!
Ich was ywon swiche werk to se.'
He aros, and þider gan te.
To a leuedi he was ycome,
Biheld, and haþ wele vndernome,   320
And seþ bi al þing þat it is
His owhen quen, Dam Heurodis.
ȝern he biheld hir, and sche him eke,
Ac noiþer to oþer a word no speke.
For messais þat sche on him seiȝe,   325
Þat had ben so riche and so heiȝe,
Þe teres fel out of her eiȝe.
Þe oþer leuedis þis yseiȝe,
And maked hir oway to ride,
Sche most wiþ him no lenger abide.   330
   'Allas!' quaþ he, 'now me is wo.
Whi nil deþ now me slo?
Allas! wreche, þat y no miȝt

333 wreche] wroche MS.

Dye now after þis siȝt !
Allas ! to long last mi liif,   335
When y no dar nouȝt wiþ mi wiif,
No hye to me, o word speke.
Allas ! whi nil min hert breke ?
Parfay ! ' quaþ he, ' tide wat bitide,
Whider so þis leuedis ride,   340
Þe selue way ichil streche ;
Of liif no deþ me no reche.'

His sclauain he dede on also spac,
And henge his harp opon his bac,
And had wel gode wil to gon,—   345
He no spard noiþer stub no ston.
In at a roche þe leuedis rideþ,
And he after, and nouȝt abideþ.

When he was in þe roche ygo
Wele þre mile oþer mo,   350
He com into a fair cuntray,
As briȝt so sonne on somers day,
Smoþe and plain and al grene,
Hille no dale nas þer non ysene.

Amidde þe lond a castel he siȝe,   355
Riche and real, and wonder heiȝe.
Al þe vtmast wal
Was clere and schine as cristal ;
An hundred tours þer were about,
Degiselich, and bataild stout ;   360
Þe butras com out of þe diche,
Of rede gold y-arched riche ;
Þe vousour was anow⟨rn⟩ed al
Of ich maner diuers aumal.
Wiþin þer wer wide wones   365
Al of precious stones.
Þe werst piler on to biholde

Was al of burnist gold.
Al þat lond was euer liȝt,
For when it schuld be þerk and niȝt,   370
Þe riche stones liȝt gonne,
As briȝt as doþ at none þe sonne.
No man may telle, no þenche in þouȝt
Þe riche werk þat þer was wrouȝt;
Bi al þing him þink þat it is   375
Þe proude court of Paradis.

In þis castel þe leuedis aliȝt;
He wold in after, ȝif he miȝt.
Orfeo knokkeþ atte gate,
Þe porter was redi þerate,   380
And asked what he wold haue ydo.
'Parfay!' quaþ he, 'icham a minstrel, lo!
To solas þi lord wiþ mi gle,
ȝif his swete wille be.'
Þe porter vndede þe ȝate anon,   385
And lete him into þe castel gon.

Þan he gan bihold about al,
And seiȝe †ful† liggeand wiþin þe wal
Of folk þat were þider ybrouȝt,
And þouȝt dede, and nare nouȝt.   390
Sum stode wiþouten hade,
And sum non armes nade,
And sum þurch þe bodi hadde wounde,
And sum lay wode, ybounde,
And sum armed on hors sete,   395
And sum astrangled as þai ete,
And sum were in water adreynt,
And sum wiþ fire al forschreynt;
Wiues þer lay on childbedde,
Sum ded, and sum awedde;   400
And wonder fele þer lay bisides

Riȝt as þai slepe her vndertides.
Eche was þus in þis warld ynome,
Wiþ fairi þider ycome.
Þer he seiȝe his owhen wiif,   405
Dame Heurodis, his lef liif,
Slepe vnder an ympe-tre :
Bi her cloþes he knewe þat it was he.

And when he hadde bihold þis meruails alle,
He went into þe kinges halle.   410
Þan seiȝe he þer a semly siȝt,
A tabernacle blisseful and briȝt,
Þerin her maister king sete,
And her quen fair and swete.
Her crounes, her cloþes, schine so briȝt,   415
Þat vnneþe bihold he hem miȝt.

When he hadde biholden al þat þing,
He kneled adoun bifor þe king.
'O lord,' he seyd, 'ȝif it þi wille were,
Mi menstraci þou schust yhere.'   420
Þe king answerd : 'What man artow,
Þat art hider ycomen now ?
Ich, no non þat is wiþ me,
No sent neuer after þe ;
Seþþen þat ich here regni gan,   425
Y no fond neuer so folehardi man
Þat hider to ous durst wende,
Bot þat ichim wald ofsende.'
'Lord,' quaþ he, 'trowe ful wel,
Y nam bot a pouer menstrel ;   430
And, sir, it is þe maner of ous
To seche mani a lordes hous ;
Þei we nouȝt welcom no be,
ȝete we mot proferi forþ our gle.'

Bifor þe king he sat adoun,   435
And tok his harp so miri of soun,
And tempreþ his harp, as he wele can,
And blisseful notes he þer gan,
Þat al þat in þe palays were
Com to him for to here,   440
And liggeþ adoun to his fete,
Hem þenkeþ his melody so swete.
Þe king herkneþ and sitt ful stille,
To here his gle he haþ gode wille;
Gode bourde he hadde of his gle,   445
Þe riche quen also hadde he.

When he hadde stint his harping,
Þan seyd to him þe king:
'Menstrel, me likeþ wele þi gle.
Now aske of me what it be,   450
Largelich ichil þe pay.
Now speke, and tow miȝt asay.'
'Sir,' he seyd, 'ich biseche þe
Þatow woldest ȝiue me
Þat ich leuedi, briȝt on ble,   455
Þat slepeþ vnder þe ympe-tre.'
'Nay,' quaþ þe king, 'þat nouȝt nere!
A sori couple of ȝou it were,
For þou art lene, rowe, and blac,
And sche is louesum, wiþouten lac;   460
A loþlich þing it were forþi
To sen hir in þi compayni.'

'O sir,' he seyd, 'gentil king,
ȝete were it a wele fouler þing
To here a lesing of þi mouþe,   465
So, sir, as ȝe seyd nouþe,
What ich wold aski, haue y schold,
And nedes þou most þi word hold'

Þe king seyd : 'Seþþen it is so,
Take hir bi þe hond, and go ;   470
Of hir ichil þatow be bliþe.'

He kneled adoun, and þonked him swiþe ;
His wiif he tok bi þe hond,
And dede him swiþe out of þat lond,
And went him out of þat þede,—   475
Riȝt as he come þe way he ȝede.

So long he haþ þe way ynome,
To Winchester he is ycome,
Þat was his owhen cité ;
Ac no man knewe þat it was he.   480
No forþer þan þe tounes ende
For knoweleche ⟨he⟩ no durst wende,
Bot wiþ a begger y⟨n⟩ bilt ful narwe,
Þer he tok his herbarwe,
To him and to his owhen wiif,   485
As a minstrel of pouer liif,
And asked tidinges of þat lond,
And who þe kingdom held in hond.
Þe pouer begger in his cote
Told him euerich a grot :   490
Hou her quen was stole owy
Ten ȝer gon wiþ fairy ;
And hou her king en exile ȝede,
Bot no man nist in wiche þede ;
And hou þe steward þe lond gan hold :   495
And oþer mani þinges him told.

Amorwe, oȝain nonetide,
He maked his wiif þer abide ;
Þe beggers cloþes he borwed anon,
And heng his harp his rigge opon,   500
And went him into þat cité,

478 Winchester] Traciens *Ashm.*: Crassens *Harl.*

Þat men miȝt him bihold and se.
Erls and barouns bold,
Buriays and leuedis him gun bihold.
'Lo,' þai seyd, 'swiche a man!   505
Hou long þe here hongeþ him opan!
Lo, hou his berd hongeþ to his kne!
He is yclongen also a tre!'

'And as he ȝede in þe strete,
Wiþ his steward he gan mete,   510
And loude he sett on him a crie:
'Sir steward,' he seyd, 'merci!
Icham an harpour of heþenisse;
Help me now in þis destresse!'
Þe steward seyd: 'Com wiþ me, come;   515
Of þat ichaue þou schalt haue some.
Euerich gode harpour is welcom me to,
For mi lordes loue Sir Orfeo.'

In þe castel þe steward sat atte mete,
And mani lording was bi him sete.   520
Þer were trompour⟨s⟩ and tabourers,
Harpours fele, and crouders.
Miche melody þai maked alle,
And Orfeo sat stille in þe halle,
And herkneþ.   When þai ben al stille,   525
He toke his harp and tempred schille,
Þe bli⟨sse⟩fulest notes he harped þere
Þat euer ani man yherd wiþ ere;
Ich man liked wele his gle.

Þe steward biheld and gan yse,   530
And knewe þe harp als bliue.
'Menstrel,' he seyd, 'so mot þou þriue,
Where hadestow þis harp, and hou?
Y pray þat þou me telle now.'
'Lord,' quaþ he, 'in vncouþe þede,   535

Þurch a wildernes as y ȝede,
Þer y founde in a dale
Wiþ lyouns a man totorn smale,
And wolues him frete wiþ teþ so scharp.
Bi him y fond þis ich harp;   540
Wele ten ȝere it is ygo.'
'O,' quaþ þe steward, 'now me is wo!
Þat was mi lord Sir Orfeo.
Allas! wreche, what schal y do,
Þat haue swiche a lord ylore?   545
A way! þat ich was ybore!
Þat him was so hard grace yȝarked,
And so vile deþ ymarked!'
Adoun he fel aswon to grounde.
His barouns him tok vp in þat stounde,   550
And telleþ him hou it geþ—
It nis no bot of manes deþ.

    King Orfeo knewe wele bi þan
His steward was a trewe man
And loued him as he auȝt to do,   555
And stont vp and seyt þus: 'Lo,
Steward, herkne now þis þing:
ȝif ich were Orfeo þe king,
And hadde ysuffred ful ȝore
In wildernisse miche sore,   560
And hadde ywon mi quen owy
Out of þe lond of fairy,
And hadde ybrouȝt þe leuedi hende
Riȝt here to þe tounes ende,
And wiþ a begger her in ynome,   565
And were miself hider ycome
Pouerlich to þe, þus stille,
For to asay þi gode wille,
And ich founde þe þus trewe,
Þou no schust it neuer rewe: 570

Sikerlich, for loue or ay,
Þou schust be king after mi day.
And ȝif þou of mi deþ hadest ben bliþe,
Þou schust haue voided also swiþe.'

Þo al þo þat þerin sete   575
Þat it was King Orfeo vnderȝete,
And þe steward him wele knewe;
Ouer and ouer þe bord he þrewe,
And fel adoun to his fet;
So dede euerich lord þat þer sete,   580
And al þai seyd at o criing:
'ȝe beþ our lord, sir, and our king!'
Glad þai were of his liue.
To chaumber þai ladde him als biliue,
And baþed him, and schaued his berd,   585
And tired him as a king apert.
And seþþen wiþ gret processioun
Þai brouȝt þe quen into þe toun,
Wiþ al maner menstraci.
Lord! þer was grete melody!   590
For ioie þai wepe wiþ her eiȝe
Þat hem so sounde ycomen seiȝe.

Now King Orfeo newe coround is,
And his quen Dame Heurodis,
And liued long afterward;   595
And seþþen was king þe steward.

Harpours in Bretaine after þan
Herd hou þis meruaile bigan,
And made herof a lay of gode likeing,
And nempned it after þe king;   600
Þat lay 'Orfeo' is yhote,
Gode is þe lay, swete is þe note.
Þus com Sir Orfeo out of his care.
God graunt ous alle wele to fare.

III

MICHAEL OF NORTHGATE'S AYENBYTE OF INWYT

A.D. 1340.

Michael of Northgate was a monk of St. Augustine's, Canterbury. From a library catalogue of the monastery it appears that he was a lover of books, for he is named as the donor of twenty-five MSS., a considerable collection for those days. Their titles show a taste not merely for religious works, but for science—mathematics, chemistry, medicine, as they were known at the time. Four of these MSS. have been traced, and one of them, British Museum MS. Arundel 57, is Michael's autograph copy of the *Ayenbyte*. On folio 2 of the MS. are the words: *Þis boc is Dan Michelis of Northgate, ywrite an Englis of his oȝene hand, þet hatte 'Ayenbyte of Inwyt'; and is of the boc-house of Saynt Austines of Canterberi, mid þe lettres .CC.* 'CC.' is the press-mark given in the catalogue. A note at the end of the text shows that it was finished on October 27, 1340:

Ymende þet þis boc is uolueld ine þe eue of þe holy apostles Symon an Iudas [i.e. Oct. 27] *of ane broþer of the cloystre of Sauynt Austin of Canterberi, in the yeare of oure Lhordes beringe 1340.*

The *Ayenbyte* has been edited for the Early English Text Society by R. Morris. The title means literally 'Remorse of Conscience', but from the contents of the work it would appear that the writer meant rather 'Stimulus to the Conscience', or 'Prick of Conscience'. It is in fact a translation from the French *Somme des Vices et des Vertues*, compiled by Friar Lorens in 1279 for King Philip le Hardi, and long held to be the main source of Chaucer's *Parson's Tale*. Caxton rendered the *Somme* into English prose as *The Royal Book*. It treats of the Commandments, the Creed, the Seven Deadly Sins, the Seven Petitions of the Paternoster, and the Seven Gifts of the Holy Spirit.

Dan Michael's purpose is stated in some doggerel lines at the end:

> Nou ich wille þet ye ywyte
> Hou hit is ywent
> Þet þis boc is ywrite
> Mid Engliss of Kent.
> Þis boc is ymad uor lewede men,
> Vor uader, and uor moder, and uor oþer ken,
> Ham uor to berȝe uram alle manyere zen,
> Þet ine hare inwytte ne bleue no uoul wen.

His translation is inaccurate, and sometimes unintelligible, and the treatment is so barren of interest that the work seems to have fallen flat even in its own day, when the popular appetite for edification was keen and unspoiled. But if its literary merit is slight, linguistically it is one of the most important works in Middle English. It provides a long prose text, exactly dated and exactly localized ; we have the author's autograph copy to work from ; and the dialect is well distinguished. These circumstances, unique in Middle English, make it possible to study the Kentish dialect of the mid-fourteenth century under ideal conditions.

HOW MERCY INCREASES TEMPORAL GOODS.

Hou Merci multiplieþ þe timliche guodes, hyerof we habbeþ uele uayre uorbisnen, huerof ich wille hier zome telle. Me ret of Saint Germain of Aucerre þet, þo he com uram Rome, ate outguoinge of Melane, he acsede at onen of his diaknen yef he hedde eny zeluer, and he ansuerede þet he ne hedde bote þri pans, uor Say⟨n⟩t Germayn hit hedde al yeue to pouren. Þanne he him het þet he his ssolde yeue to þe poure, uor God hedde ynoȝ of guode, huerof he hise uedde uor þane day. Þe dyacne mid greate pine and mid greate grochinge yeaf þe tuaye pans, and ofhild þane þridde. Þe sergont of ane riche kniȝte him broȝte ane his lhordes haf tuo hondred pans. Þo clepede he his dyacne, and him zede þet he hedde benome þe poure ane peny, and yef he hedde yeue þane þridde peny to þe poure, þe kniȝt him hedde yzent þri hondred pans.

15

Efterward me ret ine þe lyue of Ion þe Amoner, þet wes
zuo ycleped uor þe greate elmesses þet he dede: A riche
ientilman wes yrobbed of þieues, zuo þet him naȝt ne blefte.
He him com to playni to þe uorzede manne, and he him
20 zede his cas.   He hedde greate reuþe þerof, and het his
desspendoure þet he him yeaue uyftene pond of gold.   Þe
spendere, be his couaytise, ne yeaf bote vyf.   An haste a
gentil wymman wodewe zente to þe uore-yzede Ion uif
hondred pond of gold.   Þo he clepede his spendere, and him
25 acsede hou moche he hedde yyeue to þe kniȝte.   He ansuerede
'vyftene pond.'   Þe holy man ansuerede þet 'nay, he ne
hedde bote vyf'; and huanne he hit wiste þe ilke zelue þet
his hedde onderuonge, zuo zayde to his spendere þet yef he
hedde yyeue þe viftene pond þet he hedde yhote, oure Lhord
30 him hede yzent be þe guode wyfman a þouzond and vyf
hondred pond.   And huanne he acsede ate guode wyfman,
þo he hedde hise ycleped, hou moche hi hedde him ylete, hi
andzuerede þet uerst hi hedde ywrite ine hare testament þet
hi him let a þousend and vyf hondred pond.   Ac hi lokede
35 efterward ine hare testament, and hi yzeȝ þe þousend pond
defaced of hire write, and zuo ylefde þe guode wyfman þet
God wolde þet hi ne zente bote vif hondred.

Efterward Saint Gregori telþ þet Saint Boniface uram þet
he wes child he wes zuo piteuous þet he yaf ofte his kertel
40 and his sserte to þe poure uor God, þaȝ his moder him byete
ofte þeruore.   Þanne bevil þet þet child yzeȝ manie poure þet
hedden mezeyse.   He aspide þet his moder nes naȝt þer.
An haste he yarn to þe gerniere, and al þet his moder hedde
ygadered uor to pasi þet yer he hit yaf þe poure.   And þo
45 his moder com, and wyste þe ilke dede, hy wes al out of hare
wytte.   Þet child bed oure Lhorde, and þet gernier wes an
haste al uol.

Efterward þer wes a poure man, ase me zayþ, þet hedde
ane cou ; and yhyerde zigge of his preste ine his prechinge

þet God zede ine his spelle þet God wolde yelde an hondred- 5o
uald al þet me yeaue uor him. Þe guode man, mid þe rede
of his wyue, yeaf his cou to his preste, þet wes riche. Þe
prest his nom bleþeliche, and hise zente to þe oþren þet he
hedde. Þo hit com to euen, þe guode mannes cou com hom
to his house ase hi wes ywoned, and ledde mid hare alle þe 55
prestes ken, al to an hondred. Þo þe guode man yzeʒ þet,
he þoʒte þet þet wes þet word of þe Godspelle þet he hedde
yyolde; and him hi weren yloked beuore his bissoppe aye
þane prest. Þise uorbisne sseweþ wel þet merci is guod
chapuare, uor hi deþ wexe þe timliche guodes.   6c

IV

RICHARD ROLLE OF HAMPOLE

D. 1349.

Richard Rolle was born at Thornton-le-Dale, near Pickering, in Yorkshire. He was sent to Oxford, already a formidable rival to the University of Paris ; but the severer studies were evidently uncongenial to his impulsive temperament. He returned home without taking orders, improvised for himself a hermit's dress, and fled into solitude. His piety attracted the favour of Sir John and Lady Dalton, who gave him a cell on their estate. Here, in meditation, he developed his mystical religion. He did not immure himself, or cut himself off from human companionship. For a time he lived near Anderby, where was the cell of the recluse Margaret Kirkby, to whom he addressed his *Form of Perfect Living*. Another important work, *Ego Dormio et Cor Meum Vigilat*, was written for a nun of Yedingham (Yorks.). Towards the end of his life he lived in close friendship with the nuns of Hampole, and for one of them he wrote his *Commandment of Love to God*. At Hampole he died in 1349, the year of the Black Death. By the devout he was regarded as a saint, and had his commemoration day, his office, and his miracles ; but he was never canonized.

He wrote both in Latin and in English, and it is not always easy to distinguish his work from that of his many followers and imitators. The writings attributed to him are edited by C. Horstmann, *Yorkshire Writers*, 2 vols., London 1895-6. Besides the prose works noted above, he wrote, at the request of Margaret Kirkby, a *Commentary on the Psalms* (ed. Bramley, Oxford 1884), based on the Latin of Peter Lombard. A long didactic poem in Northern English, the *Prick of Conscience*, has been attributed to him from Lydgate's time onwards; but his authorship has recently been questioned, chiefly on the ground that the poem is without a spark of inspiration. It is not certain that he wrote *Love is Life*, which is included here because it expresses in characteristic language his central belief in the personal bond, the burning love, between God and man. The piece is an early linking together of two poems originally separate, the second beginning with line 69. See S. Wilson, *Review of English Studies*, N.S. x (1959), pp. 337 ff., who notes several better readings from MS. Longleat 29, e.g. 3 *þe* trauel; 20 *with* wyn; 55 *lyuyng* (Lat. *vita*) for lykyng.

With Rolle began a movement of devotional piety, which, as might be expected from its strong appeal to the emotions, was taken up first among religious women; and signs of a striving for effect in his style suggest that the hermit was not indifferent to the admiration of his followers. He brings to his teaching more heart than mind. He escapes the problems of the world, which seemed so insistent to his contemporaries, by denying the world's claims. His ideas and temperament are diametrically opposed to those of the other great figure in the religious life of fourteenth-century England—Wiclif, the schoolman, politician, reformer, controversialist. Yet they have in common a sincerity and directness of belief that brushes aside conventions, and an enthusiasm that made them leaders in an age when the Church as a whole suffered from apathy.

A. LOVE IS LIFE.

Cambridge University Library MS. DD. 5. 64, III (about 1400) f. 38 a.

⟨L⟩uf es lyf þat lastes ay, þar it in Criste es feste,
For wele ne wa it chaunge may, als wryten has men wyseste.
Þe nyght it tournes intil þe day, þi trauel intyll reste;
If þou wil luf þus as I say, þou may be wyth þe beste.

Lufe es thoght wyth grete desyre of a fayre louyng;   5
Lufe I lyken til a fyre þat sloken may na thyng;
Lufe vs clenses of oure syn; luf vs bote sall bryng;
Lufe þe Keynges hert may wyn; lufe of ioy may syng.

Þe settel of lufe es lyſt hee, for intil heuen it ranne;
Me thynk in erth it es sle, þat makes men pale and wanne; 10
Þe bede of blysse it gase ful nee, I tel þe as I kanne:
Þof vs thynk þe way be dregh, luf copuls God and manne.

Lufe es hatter þen þe cole; lufe may nane beswyke.
Þe flawme of lufe wha myght it thole, if it war ay ilyke? 14
Luf vs comfortes, and mase in qwart, and lyftes tyl heuenryke;
Luf rauysches Cryste intyl owr hert; I wate na lust it lyke.

Lere to luf, if þou wyl lyfe when þou sall hethen fare;
All þi thoght til Hym þou gyf þat may þe kepe fra kare:
Loke þi hert fra Hym noght twyn, if þou in wandreth ware;
Sa þou may Hym welde and wyn, and luf Hym euermare. 20

Iesu, þat me lyfe hase lent, intil Þi lufe me bryng!
Take til Þe al myne entent, þat Þow be my ȝhernyng.
Wa fra me away war went, and comne war my couaytyng,
If þat my sawle had herd and hent þe sang of Þi louyng.

Þi lufe es ay lastand, fra þat we may it fele; 25
Þarein make me byrnand, þat na thyng gar it kele.
My thoght take into Þi hand, and stabyl it ylk a dele,
Þat I be noght heldand to luf þis worldes wele.

If I lufe any erthly thyng þat payes to my wyll,
And settes my ioy and my lykyng when it may comm me tyll,
I mai drede of partyng, þat wyll be hate and yll: 31
For al my welth es bot wepyng when pyne mi saule sal spyll.

Þe ioy þat men hase sene es lyckend tyl þe haye,
Þat now es fayre and grene, and now wytes awaye.
Swylk es þis worlde, I wene, and bees till Domesdaye, 35
All in trauel and tene, fle þat na man it maye.

If þou luf in all þi thoght, and hate þe fylth of syn,
And gyf Hym þi sawle þat it boght, þat He þe dwell within,
Als Crist þi sawle hase soght, and þerof walde noght blyn,
Sa þou sal to blys be broght, and heuen won within. 40

Þe kynd of luf es þis, þar it es trayst and trew,
To stand styll in stabylnes, and chaunge it for na new.
Þe lyfe þat lufe myght fynd, or euer in hert it knew,
Fra kare it tornes þat kyend, and lendes in myrth and glew.

For now, lufe þow, I rede, Cryste, as I þe tell,   45
And with aungels take þi stede: þat ioy loke þou noght sell!
In erth þow hate, I rede, all þat þi lufe may fell,
For luf es stalworth as þe dede, luf es hard as hell.

Luf es a lyght byrthen; lufe gladdes ȝong and alde;
Lufe es withowten pyne, as lofers hase me talde;   50
Lufe es a gastly wyne, þat makes men bygge and balde;
Of lufe sal he na thyng tyne þat hit in hert will halde.

Lufe es þe swettest thyng þat man in erth hase tane;
Lufe es Goddes derlyng; lufe byndes blode and bane.
In lufe be owre lykyng, I ne wate na better wane,   55
For me and my lufyng lufe makes bath be ane.

Bot fleschly lufe sal fare as dose þe flowre in May,
And lastand be na mare þan ane houre of a day,
And sythen syghe ful sare þar lust, þar pryde, þar play,
When þai er casten in kare til pyne þat lastes ay.   60

When þair bodys lyse in syn, þair sawls mai qwake and drede,
For vp sal ryse al men, and answer for þair dede.
If þai be fonden in syn, als now þair lyfe þai lede,
Þai sal sytt hel within, and myrknes hafe to mede.

Riche men þair hend sal wryng, and wicked werkes sal by   65
In flawme of fyre, bath knyght and keyng, with sorow schamfully.
If þou wil lufe, þan may þou syng til Cryst in melody;
Þe lufe of Hym ouercoms al thyng, þarto þou traiste trewly.

45 For now] Forþi *MS. Lambeth 853.*   51 wyne] = wynne *MS.*
65 hend] handes *MS., apparently altered from* hend.

⟨I⟩ sygh and sob, bath day and nyght, for ane sa fayre of hew!
Þar es na thyng my hert mai light, bot lufe þat es ay new. 70
Wha sa had Hym in his syght, or in his hert Hym knew,
His mournyng turned til ioy ful bryght, his lang(yng) intil
    glew.

In myrth he lyfes, nyght and day, þat lufes þat swete chylde;
It es Iesu, forsoth I say, of al mekest and mylde.
Wreth fra hym walde al away, þof he wer neuer sa wylde, 75
He þat in hert lufed Hym þat day fra euel He wil hym schylde.

Of Iesu mast lyst me speke, þat al my bale may bete;
Me thynk my hert may al tobreke when I thynk on þat swete;
In lufe lacyd He hase my thoght, þat I sal neuer forgete. 79
Ful dere me thynk He hase me boght with blodi hende and fete.

For luf my hert es bowne to brest, when I þat faire behalde;
Lufe es fair þare it es fest, þat neuer will be calde;
Lufe vs reues þe nyght-rest, in grace it makes vs balde;
Of al warkes luf es þe best, als haly men me talde.

Na wonder gyf I syghand be, and sithen in sorow be sette: 85
Iesu was nayled apon þe tre, and al blody forbette.
To thynk on Hym es grete pyté—how tenderly He grette—
Þis hase He sufferde, man, for þe, if þat þou syn wyll lette.

Þare es na tonge in erth may tell of lufe þe swetnesse.
Þat stedfastly in lufe kan dwell, his ioy es endlesse. 90
God schylde þat he sulde til hell, þat lufes and langand es,
Or euer his enmys sulde hym qwell, or make his luf be lesse.

Iesu es lufe þat lastes ay, til Hym es owre langyng;
Iesu þe nyght turnes to þe day, þe dawyng intil spryng.
Iesu, thynk on vs now and ay, for þe we halde oure keyng; 95
Iesu, gyf vs grace, as þou wel may, to luf þe withowten endyng.

69 I] so MS. Lambeth 853.   72 langyng] so MS. Longleat 29:
sang MS.

B. THE NATURE OF THE BEE.

(The Thornton MS. (before 1450); ed. Horstmann, vol. i, p. 193.)

Moralia Ricardi Heremite de Natura Apis.

THE bee has thre kyndis. Ane es þat scho es neuer ydill, and scho es noghte with thaym þat will noghte wyrke, bot castys thaym owte, and puttes thaym awaye. Anothire es þat when scho flyes scho takes erthe in hyr fette, þat scho be noghte lyghtly ouerheghede in the ayere of wynde. The 5 thyrde es þat scho kepes clene and bryghte hire wyngez.

Thus ryghtwyse men þat lufes God are neuer in ydyllnes. For owthyre þay ere in trauayle, prayand, or thynkande, or redande, or othere gude doande; or withtakand ydill mene, and schewand thaym worthy to be put fra þe ryste of heuene, 10 for þay will noghte trauayle here.

Þay take erthe, þat es, þay halde þamselfe vile and erthely, that thay be noghte blawene with þe wynde of vanyté and of pryde. Thay kepe thaire wynges clene, that es, þe twa commandementes of charyté þay fulfill in gud concyens, and 15 thay hafe othyre vertus, vnblendyde with þe fylthe of syne and vnclene luste.

Arestotill sais þat þe bees are feghtande agaynes hym þat will drawe þaire hony fra thayme. Swa sulde we do agaynes deuells, þat afforces thame to reue fra vs þe hony of poure 20 lyfe and of grace. For many are, þat neuer kane halde þe ordyre of lufe ynence þaire frendys, sybbe or fremmede. Bot outhire þay lufe þaym ouer mekill, settand thaire thoghte vnryghtwysely on thaym, or þay luf thayme ouer lyttill, yf þay doo noghte all as þey wolde till þame. Swylke kane 25 noghte fyghte for thaire hony, forthy þe deuelle turnes it to wormes, and makes þeire saules oftesythes full bitter in

22 ynence] ynesche MS.   23 mekill] MS. follows with: or that
lufe þame ouer lyttill, caught up from below.

angwys, and tene, and besynes of vayne thoghtes, and oþer
wrechidnes.   For thay are so heuy in erthely frenchype þat
30 þay may noghte flee intill þe lufe of Iesu Criste, in þe wylke
þay moghte wele forgaa þe lufe of all creaturs lyfande in
erthe.

Wharefore, accordandly, Arystotill sais þat some fowheles
are of gude flygliyng, þat passes fra a lande to anothire.
35 Some are of ill flyghynge, for heuynes of body, and for⟨þi⟩
þaire neste es noghte ferre fra þe erthe.   Thus es it of
thayme þat turnes þame to Godes seruys.   Some are of gude
flyeghynge, for thay flye fra erthe to heuene, and rystes
thayme thare in thoghte, and are fedde in delite of Goddes
40 lufe, and has thoghte of na lufe of þe worlde.   Some are þat
kan noghte flyghe fra þis lande, bot in þe waye late theyre herte
ryste, and delyttes þaym in sere lufes of mene and womene,
als þay come and gaa, nowe ane and nowe anothire.   And in
Iesu Criste þay kan fynde na swettnes ; or if þay any tyme
45 fele oghte, it es swa lyttill and swa schorte, for othire thoghtes
þat are in thayme, þat it brynges thaym till na stabylnes.

⟨F⟩or þay are lyke till a fowle þat es callede strucyo or storke,
þat has wenges, and it may noghte flye for charge of body.
Swa þay hafe vndirstandynge, and fastes, and wakes, and
50 semes haly to mens syghte ; bot thay may noghte flye to lufe
and contemplacyone of God, þay are so chargede wyth othyre
affeccyons and othire vanytés.

THE SEVEN GIFTS OF THE HOLY GHOST.

(Chap. xi of *The Form of Perfect Living* ; ed. Horstmann, vol. I,
p. 196.)

Þe seuene gyftes of þe Haly Gaste, þat ere gyfene to men
and wymmene þat er ordaynede to þe ioye of heuene, and
55 ledys theire lyfe in this worlde reghtwysely.   Thire are thay :—
Wysdome, Undyrstandynge, Counsayle, Strenghe, Connynge,

Peté, the Drede of God. Begynne we at Consaile, for þareof
es myster at the begynnynge of oure werkes, þat vs myslyke
noghte aftyrwarde. With thire seuene gyftes þe Haly Gaste
teches sere mene serely.   60

Consaile es doynge awaye of worldes reches, and of all
delytes of all thyngez þat mane may be tagyld with, in thoghte
or dede, and þarwith drawynge intill contemplacyone of
Gode.

Undyrstandynge es to knawe whate es to doo, and whate 65
es to lefe, and þat that sall be gyffene, to gyffe it to thaym
þat has nede, noghte till oþer þat has na myster.

Wysedome es forgetynge of erthely thynges and thynkynge
of heuen, with discrecyone of all mens dedys. In þis gyfte
schynes contemplacyone, þat es, Saynt Austyne says, a gastely 70
dede of fleschely affeccyones, thurghe þe ioye of a raysede
thoghte.

Strenghe es lastynge to fullfill gude purpose, þat it be
noghte lefte, for wele ne for waa.

Peté es þat a man be mylde, and gaynesay noghte Haly 75
Writte whene it smyttes his synnys, whethire he vndyrstand
it or noghte ; bot in all his myghte purge he þe vilté of syne
in hyme and oþer.

Connynge es þat makes a man of gude ⟨hope⟩, noghte
ruysand hyme of his reghtewysnes, bot sorowand of his 80
synnys, and þat man gedyrs erthely gude anely to the
honour of God, and prow to oþer mene þane hymselfe.

The Drede of God es þat we turne noghte agayne till oure
syne thurghe any ill eggyng. And þan es drede perfite in vs
and gastely, when we drede to wrethe God in þe leste syne 85
þat we kane knawe, and flese it als venyme.

60 teches] towches *Cambridge MS. DD. s. 64.*   63 þar] þat *MS.
Thornton.*   69 mens] *so Cambridge MS. DD. s. 64* = mene *MS.
Thornton.*   79 hope] *from Cambridge MS. DD. s. 64 : om. MS.
Thornton.*   84 þan] *Cambridge MS. DD. s. 64* : þen *MS. Arundel so71*
þat *MS. Thornton.*

V

SIR GAWAYNE AND THE GRENE KNIGHT

About 1350–75.

Sir Gawayne has been admirably edited by Sir F. Madden for the Bannatyne Club, 1839; by R. Morris for the Early English Text Society; and in a useful students' edition by E. V. Gordon and J. R. R. Tolkien, Oxford 1925. It is found in British Museum MS. Nero A X, together with three other alliterative poems, named from their first words *Pearl*, *Patience*, and *Cleanness*. *Pearl* supplies the next specimen; *Patience* exemplifies the virtue by the trials of Jonah; *Cleanness* teaches purity of life from Scriptural stories. All these poems are in the same handwriting; all are in a West-Midland dialect; all appear to be of the same age; and none is without literary merit. For these reasons, which are good but not conclusive, they are assumed to be by the same author. Attempts to identify this author have been unsuccessful.

The story runs as follows :

King Arthur is making his Christmas feast with his court at Camelot. On New Year's Day he declares that he will not eat until he has seen or heard some marvel. The first course of the feast is barely served when a tall knight, clad all in green, with green hair, and a green horse to match, rides into the hall. He carries a holly bough and a huge axe, and tauntingly invites any knight to strike him a blow with the axe, on condition that he will stand a return blow on the same day a year hence. Gawayne accepts the challenge and strikes off the Green Knight's head. The Green Knight gathers up his head, gives Gawayne an appointment for next New Year's Day at the Green Chapel, and rides off.

The year passes, and Gawayne, despite the fears of the court, sets out in quest of the Green Chapel. On Christmas Eve he arrives at a splendid castle, and finding that the Green Chapel is close at hand, accepts an invitation to stay and rest until New Year's Day. On each of three days the knight of the castle goes hunting, and persuades Gawayne to rest at home. They make an agreement that each shall give the other whatever he gets. The lady of the castle makes love to Gawayne, and kisses him once on the first day, twice on the second day, thrice on the third day; and on the third day she gives him her girdle, which he accepts because it has the magic power of preserving the wearer from wounds. Each evening he duly gives the kisses to the knight, and receives in return the spoils of the hunting of deer and boar and fox. But he conceals the girdle.

The extract begins with Gawayne preparing on New Year's morning to stand the return blow at the Green Chapel.

The poem ends by the Green Knight revealing that he is himself the lord of the castle; that he went to Arthur's court at the suggestion of Morgan la Fay; that he had urged his wife to make love to Gawayne and try his virtue; and that he would not have harmed him at all, if he had not committed the slight fault of concealing the girdle. Gawayne returns to the court, bearing the girdle as a sign of his shame, and tells his story. The knights of the court agree in future to wear a bright green belt for Gawayne's sake.

Sir Gawayne is admittedly the best of the alliterative romances. It must have come down to us practically as it was written by the poet, for it is free from the flatness and conventional phrasing which is characteristic of romances that have passed through many popular recensions. The descriptions of nature, of armour and dresses, the hunting scenes, and the love making, are all excellently done; and the poet shows the same richness of imagination and skill in producing pictorial effects that are so noticeable in *Pearl*. He has too a quiet humour that recalls Chaucer in some of his moods.

THE TESTING OF SIR GAWAYNE.

British Museum MS. Nero A X (about 1400); ed. R. Morris, ll. 2069 ff.
Facsimile of MS. ed. Sir Israel Gollancz, E. E. T. S. 1924.

THE brygge watȝ brayde doun, and þe brode ȝateȝ
Vnbarred and born open vpon boþe halue.
Þe burne blessed hym bilyue, and þe bredeȝ passed;
Prayses þe porter bifore þe prynce kneled,
Gef hym God and goud day, þat Gawayn He saue,   5
And went on his way with his wyȝe one,
Þat schulde teche hym to tourne to þat tene place
Þer þe ruful race he schulde resayue.
Þay boȝen bi bonkkeȝ þer boȝeȝ ar bare;
Þay clomben bi clyffeȝ þer clengeȝ þe colde.   10
Þe heuen watȝ vp halt, bot vgly þer vnder,—
Mist muged on þe mor, malt on þe mounteȝ,
Vch hille hade a hatte, a myst-hakel huge.
Brokeȝ byled and breke bi bonkkeȝ aboute,
Schyre schaterande on schoreȝ, þer þay doun schowued.   15
Wela wylle watȝ þe way þer þay bi wod schulden,
Til hit watȝ sone sesoun þat þe sunne ryses
     þat tyde.
     Þay were on a hille ful hyȝe,
     Þe quyte snaw lay bisyde;   20
     Þe burne þat rod hym by
     Bede his mayster abide.
'For I haf wonnen yow hider, wyȝe, at þis tyme,
And now nar ȝe not fer fro þat note place
Þat ȝe han spied and spuryed so specially after.   25
Bot I schal say yow for soþe, syþen I yow knowe,
And ȝe ar a lede vpon lyue þat I wel louy,
Wolde ȝe worch bi my wytte, ȝe worþed þe better.
Þe place þat ȝe prece to ful perelous is halden.
Þer woneȝ a wyȝe in þat waste, þe worst vpon erþe,   30

For he is stiffe and sturne, and to strike louies,
And more he is þen any mon vpon myddelerde,
And his body bigger þen þe best fowre
Þat ar in Arþureȝ hous, Hestor, oþer oþer.
He cheueȝ þat chaunce at þe chapel grene,   35
Þer passes non bi þat place so proude in his armes
Þat he ne dyngeȝ hym to deþe with dynt of his honde;
For he is a mon methles, and mercy non vses,
For be hit chorle oþer chaplayn þat bi þe chapel rydes,
Monk oþer masse-prest, oþer any mon elles,   40
Hym þynk as queme hym to quelle as quyk go hymseluen.
Forþy I say þe, as soþe as ȝe in sadel sitte,
Com ȝe þere, ȝe be kylled, may þe, knyȝt, rede—
Trawe ȝe me þat trwely—þaȝ ȝe had twenty lyues
  to spende.   45
  He hatȝ wonyd here ful ȝore,
  On bent much baret bende,
  Aȝayn his dynteȝ sore
  ȝe may not yow defende.
'Forþy, goude Sir Gawayn, let þe gome one,   50
And gotȝ away sum oþer gate, vpon Goddeȝ halue!
Cayreȝ bi sum oþer kyth, þer Kryst mot yow spede,
And I schal hyȝ me hom aȝayn, and hete yow fyrre
Þat I schal swere bi God and alle His gode halȝeȝ,
As help me God and þe halydam, and oþeȝ innoghe,   55
Þat I schal lelly yow layne, and lance neuer tale
Þat euer ȝe fondet to fle for freke þat I wyst.'
'Grant merci,' quod Gawayn, and gruchyng he sayde :
'Wel worth þe, wyȝe, þat woldeȝ my gode,
And þat lelly me layne I leue wel þou woldeȝ.   60
Bot helde þou hit neuer so holde, and I here passed,
Founded for ferde for to fle, in fourme þat þou telleȝ,
I were a knyȝt kowarde, I myȝt not be excused.

  37 dyngeȝ] dynneȝ *MS.* 63 not] mot *MS.*

Bot I wyl to þe chapel, for chaunce þat may falle,
And talk wyth þat ilk tulk þe tale þat me lyste,   65
Worþe hit wele oþer wo, as þe wyrde lykeȝ
      hit hafe.
    Þaȝe he be a sturn knape
    To stiȝtel, and stad with staue,
    Ful wel con Dryȝtyn schape   70
    His seruaunteȝ for to saue.'
'Mary!' quod þat oþer mon, 'now þou so much spelleȝ
Þat þou wylt þyn awen nye nyme to þyseluen,
And þe lyst lese þy lyf, þe lette I ne kepe.
Haf here þi helme on þy hede, þi spere in þi honde,   75
And ryde me doun þis ilk rake bi ȝon rokke syde
Til þou be broȝt to þe boþem of þe brem valay.
Þenne loke a littel on þe launde, on þi lyfte honde,
And þou schal se in þat slade þe self chapel,
And þe borelych burne on bent þat hit kepeȝ.   80
Now fareȝ wel, on Godeȝ half! Gawayn þe noble;
For alle þe golde vpon grounde I nolde go wyth þe,
Ne bere þe felaȝschip þurȝ þis fryth on fote fyrre.'
Bi þat þe wyȝe in þe wod wendeȝ his brydel,
Hit þe hors with þe heleȝ as harde as he myȝt,   85
Lepeȝ hym ouer þe launde, and leueȝ þe knyȝt þere
      al one.
    'Bi Goddeȝ self!' quod Gawayn,
    'I wyl nauþer grete ne grone;
    To Goddeȝ wylle I am ful bayn,   90
    And to Hym I haf me tone.'
Thenne gyrdeȝ he to Gryngolet, and gedereȝ þe rake,
Schowueȝ in bi a schore at a schaȝe syde,
Rideȝ þurȝ þe roȝe bonk ryȝt to þe dale;
And þenne he wayted hym aboute, and wylde hit hym þoȝt,
And seȝe no syngne of resette bisydeȝ nowhere,   96

       69 and] & & *MS.*

Bot hyȝe bonkkeȝ and brent vpon boþe halue,
And ruȝe knokled knarreȝ with knorned stoneȝ;
Þe skweȝ of þe scowtes skayned hym þoȝt.
Þenne he houed, and wythhylde his hors at þat tyde,   100
And ofte chaunged his cher þe chapel to seche:
He seȝ non suche in no syde, and selly hym þoȝt
Sone, a lyttel on a launde, a lawe as hit we⟨re⟩,
A balȝ berȝ bi a bonke, þe brymme bysyde,
Bi a forȝ of a flode þat ferked þare;   105
Þe borne blubred þerinne as hit boyled hade.
Þe knyȝt kacheȝ his caple, and com to þe lawe,
Liȝteȝ doun luflyly, and at a lynde tacheȝ
Þe rayne and his riche with a roȝe braunche.
Þenne he boȝeȝ to þe berȝe, aboute hit he walkeȝ,   110
Debatande with hymself quat hit be myȝt.
Hit hade a hole on þe ende and on ayþer syde,
And ouergrowen with gresse in glodes aywhere,
And al watȝ holȝ inwith, nobot an olde caue,
Or a creuisse of an olde cragge, he couþe hit noȝt deme   115
        with spelle.
       'Wel Lorde,' quod þe gentyle knyȝt,
       'Wheþer þis be þe grene chapelle?
       He⟨re⟩ myȝt aboute mydnyȝt
       Þe dele his matynnes telle!   120
'Now iwysse,' quod Wowayn, 'wysty is here;
Þis oritore is vgly, with erbeȝ ouergrowen;
Wel bisemeȝ þe wyȝe wruxled in grene
Dele here his deuocioun on þe deueleȝ wyse.
Now I fele hit is þe fende, in my fyue wytteȝ,   125
Þat hatȝ stoken me þis steuen to strye me here.
Þis is a chapel of meschaunce, þat chekke hit bytyde!
Hit is þe corsedest kyrk þat euer I com inne!'
With heȝe helme on his hede, his launce in his honde,
He romeȝ vp to þe rokke of þo roȝ woneȝ.   130

Þene herde he, of þat hyȝe hil, in a harde roche,
Biȝonde þe broke, in a bonk, a wonder breme noyse.
Quat ! hit clatered in þe clyff, as hit cleue schulde,
As one vpon a gryndelston hade grounden a syþe ;
What ! hit wharred and whette, as water at a mulne ; 135
What ! hit rusched and ronge, rawþe to here.
Þenne 'Bi Godde !' quod Gawayn, 'þat gere as I trowe
Is ryched at þe reuerence me, renk, to mete
  bi rote.
  Let God worche, we loo !   140
  Hit helppeȝ me not a mote.
  My lif þaȝ I forgoo,
  Drede dotȝ me no lote.'
Thenne þe knyȝt con calle ful hyȝe :
'Who stiȝtleȝ in þis sted, me steuen to holde ? 145
For now is gode Gawayn goande ryȝt here.
If any wyȝe oȝt wyl, wynne hider fast,
Oþer now oþer neuer, his nedeȝ to spede.'
'Abyde,' quod on on þe bonke abouen ouer his hede,
'And þou schal haf al in hast þat I þe hyȝt ones.' 150
ȝet he rusched on þat rurde rapely a þrowe,
And wyth quettyng awharf, er he wolde lyȝt ;
And syþen he keuereȝ bi a cragge, and comeȝ of a hole,
Whyrlande out of a wro wyth a felle weppen,
A Deneȝ ax nwe dyȝt, þe dynt with ⟨t⟩o ȝelde, 155
With a borelych bytte bende by þe halme,
Fyled in a fylor, fowre fote large,—
Hit watȝ no lasse bi þat lace þat lemed ful bryȝt,—
And þe gome in þe grene gered as fyrst,
Boþe þe lyre and þe leggeȝ, lokkeȝ and berde, 160
Saue þat fayre on his fote he foundeȝ on þe erþe,
Sette þe stele to þe stone, and stalked bysyde.
Whan he wan to þe watter, þer he wade nolde,

He hypped ouer on hys ax, and orpedly strydeȝ,
Bremly broþe on a bent þat brode watȝ aboute,   165
    on snawe.
      Sir Gawayn þe knyȝt con mete,
      He ne lutte hym no þyng lowe;
      Þat oþer sayde 'Now, sir swete,
      Of steuen mon may þe trowe.   170

'Gawayn,' quod þat grene gome, 'God þe mot loke!
Iwysse þou art welcom, wyȝe, to my place,
And þou hatȝ tymed þi trauayl as truee mon schulde,
And þou knoweȝ þe couenaunteȝ kest vus bytwene:
At þis tyme twelmonyth þou toke þat þe falled,   175
And I schulde at þis nwe ȝere ȝeply þe quyte.
And we ar in þis valay verayly oure one;
Here ar no renkes vs to rydde, rele as vus likeȝ.
Haf þy helme of þy hede, and haf here þy pay.
Busk no more debate þen I þe bede þenne   180
When þou wypped of my hede at a wap one.'
'Nay, bi God' quod Gawayn, 'þat me gost lante l
I schal gruch þe no grwe for grem þat falleȝ.
Bot styȝtel þe vpon on strok, and I schal stonde stylle
And warp þe no wernyng to worch as þe lykeȝ,   185
    nowhare.'
      He lened with þe nek, and lutte,
      And schewed þat schyre al bare,
      And lette as he noȝt dutte;
      For drede he wolde not dare.   190

Then þe gome in þe grene grayþed hym swyþe,
Gedereȝ vp hys grymme tole Gawayn to smyte;
With alle þe bur in his body he ber hit on lofte,
Munt as maȝtyly as marre hym he wolde:
Hade hit dryuen adoun as dreȝ as he atled,   195
Þer hade ben ded of his dynt þat doȝty watȝ euer.

    172 welcom] welcon *MS.*   179 þy (1st)] þy þy *MS.*

Bot Gawayn on þat giserne glyfte hym bysyde,
As hit com glydande adoun on glode hym to schende,
And schranke a lytel with þe schulderes for þe scharp yrne.
Þat oþer schalk wyth a schunt þe schene wythhaldeȝ,   200
And þenne repreued he þe prynce with mony prowde wordeȝ :
'Þou art not Gawayn,' quod þe gome, 'þat is so goud
          halden,
Þat neuer arȝed for no here, by hylle ne be vale,
And now þou fles for ferde er þou fele harmeȝ !
Such cowardise of þat knyȝt cowþe I neuer here.   205
Nawþer fyked I ne flaȝe, freke, quen þou myntest,
Ne kest no kauelacion, in kyngeȝ hous Arthor.
My hede flaȝ to my fote, and ȝet flaȝ I neuer ;
And þou, er any harme hent, arȝeȝ in hert ;
Wherfore þe better burne me burde be called   210
          þerfore.'
          Quod Gawayn ' I schunt oneȝ,
          And so wyl I no more ;
          Bot þaȝ my hede falle on þe stoneȝ,
          I con not hit restore.   215
Bot busk, burne, bi þi fayth ! and bryng me to þe poynt.
Dele to me my destiné, and do hit out of honde,
For I schal stonde þe a strok, and start no more
Til þyn ax haue me hitte : haf here my trawþe.'
' Haf at þe þenne ! ' quod þat oþer, and heueȝ hit alofte,   220
And wayteȝ as wroþely as he wode were.
He mynteȝ at hym maȝtyly, bot not þe mon ryueȝ,
Withhelde heterly h⟨i⟩s honde, er hit hurt myȝt.
Gawayn grayþely hit bydeȝ, and glent with no membre,
Bot stode stylle as þe ston, oþer a stubbe auþer   225
Þat raþeled is in roché grounde with roteȝ a hundreth.
Þen muryly efte con he mele, þe mon in þe grene :
' So now þou hatȝ þi hert holle, hitte me bihou⟨e⟩s.
Halde þe now þe hyȝe hode þat Arþur þe raȝt,

And kepe þy kanel at þis kest, ȝif hit keuer may.'   230
Gawayn ful gryndelly with greme þenne sayde :
'Wy ! þresch on, þou þro mon, þou preteȝ to longe.
I hope þat þi hert arȝe wyth þyn awen seluen.'
'For soþe,' quod þat oþer freke, 'so felly þou spekeȝ,
I wyl no lenger on lyte lette þin ernde   235
      riȝt nowe.'
    Þenne tas he hym stryþe to stryke,
    And frounses boþe lyppe and browe.
    No meruayle þaȝ hym myslyke
    Þat hoped of no rescowe.   240
He lyftes lyȝtly his lome, and let hit doun fayre,
With þe barbe of þe bitte bi þe bare nek,
Þaȝ he homered heterly, hurt hym no more,
Bot snyrt hym on þat on syde, þat seuered þe hyde ;
Þe scharp schrank to þe flesche þurȝ þe schyre grece   245
Þat þe schene blod ouer his schulderes schot to þe erþe,
And quen þe burne seȝ þe blode blenk on þe snawe,
He sprit forth spenne fote more þen a spere lenþe,
Hent heterly his helme, and on his hed cast,
Schot with his schuldereȝ his fayre schelde vnder,   250
Braydeȝ out a bryȝt sworde, and bremely he spekeȝ ;—
Neuer syn þat he watȝ burne borne of his moder
Watȝ he neuer in þis worlde wyȝe half so blyþe—
'Blynne, burne, of þy bur, bede me no mo !
I haf a stroke in þis stede withoute stryf hent,   255
And if þow recheȝ me any mo, I redyly schal quyte,
And ȝelde ȝederly aȝayn—and þerto ȝe tryst—
      and foo.
    Bot on stroke here me falleȝ—
    Þe couenaunt schop ryȝt so   260
    ⟨Schapen⟩ in Arþureȝ halleȝ—
    And þerfore, hende, now hoo !'

       237 he] he he *MS.*

The haþel heldet hym fro, and on his ax rested,
Sette þe schaft vpon schore, and to þe scharp lened,
And loked to þe leude þat on þe launde ȝede, 265
How þat doȝty, dredles, deruely þer stondeȝ
Armed, ful aȝleȝ : in hert hit hym lykeȝ.
Þenn he meleȝ muryly wyth a much steuen,
And wyth a ry⟨n⟩kande rurde he to þe renk sayde :
' Bolde burne, on þis bent be not so gryndel. 270
No mon here vnmanerly þe mysboden habbe⟨ȝ⟩
Ne kyd, bot as couenaunde at kyngeȝ kort schaped.
I hyȝt þe a strok and þou hit hatȝ ; halde þe wel payed.
I relece þe of þe remnaunt of ryȝtes alle oþer.
Iif I deliuer had bene, a boffet paraunter 275
I couþe wroþeloker haf waret,—to þe haf wroȝt anger.
Fyrst I mansed þe muryly with a mynt one,
And roue þe wyth no rof sore, with ryȝt I þe profered
For þe forwarde þat we fest in þe fyrst nyȝt,
And þou trystyly þe trawþe and trwly me haldeȝ, 280
Al þe gayne þow me gef, as god mon schulde.
Þat oþer munt for þe morne, mon, I þe profered,
Þou kyssedes my clere wyf, þe cosseȝ me raȝteȝ.
For boþe two here I þe bede bot two bare myntes
boute scaþe. 285
    Trwe mon trwe restore,
    Þenne þar mon drede no waþe.
    At þe þrid þou fayled þore,
    And þerfor þat tappe ta þe.
For hit is my wede þat þou wereȝ, þat ilke wouen girdel, 290
Myn owen wyf hit þe weued, I wot wel forsoþe.
Now know I wel þy cosses, and þy costes als,
And þe wowyng of my wyf : I wroȝt hit myseluen.
I sende hir to asay þe, and sothly me þynkkeȝ
On þe fautlest freke þat euer on fote ȝede. 295
As perle bi þe quite pese is of prys more,

So is Gawayn, in god fayth, bi oþer gay knyȝteȝ.
Bot here yow lakked a lyttel, sir, and lewté yow wonted ;
Bot þat watȝ for no wylyde werke, ne wowyng nauþer,
Bot for ȝe lufed your lyf; þe lasse I yow blame.' 300
Þat oþer stif mon in study stod a gret whyle,
So agreued for greme he gryed withinne ;
Alle þe blode of his brest blende in his face,
Þat al he schrank for schome þat þe schalk talked.
Þe forme worde vpon folde þat þe freke meled : 305
' Corsed worth cowarddyse and couetyse boþe !
In yow is vylany and vyse þat vertue disstryeȝ.'
Þenne he kaȝt to þe knot, and þe kest lawseȝ,
Brayde broþely þe belt to þe burne seluen :
' Lo ! þer þe falssyng ! foule mot hit falle ! 310
For care of þy knokke cowardyse me taȝt
To acorde me with couetyse, my kynde to forsake,
Þat is larges and lewté þat longeȝ to knyȝteȝ.
Now am I fawty and falce, and ferde haf ben euer
Of trecherye and vntrawþe : boþe bityde sorȝe 315
          and care !
       I biknowe yow, knyȝt, here stylle,
         Al fawty is my fare ;
       Leteȝ me ouertake your wylle
       And efte I schal be ware.' 320
Thenn loȝe þat oþer leude, and luflyly sayde :
' I halde hit hardily hole, þe harme þat I hade.
Þou art confessed so clene, beknowen of þy mysses,
And hatȝ þe penaunce apert of þe poynt of myn egge,
I halde þe polysed of þat plyȝt, and pured as clene 325
As þou hadeȝ neuer forfeted syþen þou watȝ fyrst borne ;
And I gif þe, sir, þe gurdel þat is golde-hemmed,
For hit is grene as my goune. Sir Gawayne, ȝe maye
Þenk vpon þis ilke þrepe, þer þou forth þryngeȝ

322 haidily] hardilyly *MS.*

Among prynces of prys; and þis a pure token　　　　330
Of þe chaunce *at* þe grene chapel *of* cheualrous knyʒteʒ.
And ʒe schal in þis nwe ʒer aʒayn to my woneʒ,
And we schyn reuel þe remnaunt of þis ryche fest
　　　　ful bene.'
　　　　　　Þer laþed hym fast þe lord,　　　　335
　　　　　　And sayde ' With my wyf, I wene,
　　　　　　We schal yow wel acorde,
　　　　　　Þat watʒ your enmy kene.'
' Nay, for soþe,' quod þe segge, and sesed hys helme,
And hatʒ hit of hendely, and þe haþel þonkkeʒ,　　　　340
' I haf soiorned sadly ; sele yow bytyde !
And He ʒelde hit yow ʒare þat ʒarkkeʒ al menskes !
And comaundeʒ me to þat cortays, your comlych fere,
Boþe þat on and þat oþer myn honoured ladyeʒ,
Þat þus hor knyʒt wyth hor kest han koyntly bigyled.　　　　345
Bot hit is no ferly þaʒ a fole madde,
And þurʒ wyles of wymmen be wonen to sorʒe,
For so watʒ Adam in erde with one bygyled,
And Salamon with fele sere, and Samson eftsoneʒ
Dalyda dalt hym hys wyrde, and Dauyth þerafter　　　　350
Watʒ blended with Barsabe, þat much bale þoled.
Now þese were wrathed wyth her wyles, hit were a wynne
　　　　huge
To luf hom wel, and leue hem not, a leude þat couþe.
For þes wer forne þe freest, þat folʒed alle þe sele
Exellently of alle þyse oþer vnder heuenryche　　　　355
　　　　　　þat mused ;
　　　　　　And alle þay were biwyled
　　　　　　With wymmen þat þay vsed.
　　　　　　Þaʒ I be now bigyled,
　　　　　　Me þink me burde be excused.'　　　　360

VI

THE PEARL

ABOUT 1375.

The facts leading to the presumption that *Pearl* and *Sir Gawayne* are by the same author have been mentioned in the prefatory note to *Sir Gawayne*. But the poems are markedly different in subject and tone. *Pearl*, like Chaucer's *Death of Blanche the Duchess*, is an elegy cast in the vision form made popular by the *Roman de la Rose*. The subject is a little girl, who died before she was two years old, and the treatment is deeply religious. Her death is symbolized as the loss of a pearl without spot, that slipped from its owner's hand through the grass into the earth.

On a festival day in August, the poet, while mourning his loss, falls asleep on his child's grave. His spirit passes to a land of flowers and rich fruits, where birds of flaming hues sing incomparably, where the cliffs are of crystal and beryl, and a river runs in a bed of gleaming jewels. On the other side of the river, which is lovelier still, sits a maiden dressed all in white, with coronet and ornaments of pearl. The poet recognizes his lost child, but cannot call to her for wonder and dread, until she rises and salutes him. He complains that since her loss he has been a joyless jeweller. She rebukes him gently; she is not lost, but made safe and beautiful for ever. Overjoyed, he says he will cross the river and live with her in this paradise; but she warns him against such presumption, for since Adam's fall the river may be crossed only by the way of death. He is in despair to think that now that his Pearl is found, he must still live joyless, apart from her; but he is bidden to resign himself to God's will and mercy, because rebellion will avail him nothing.

At this point begins the argument on salvation by grace or salvation by works which is here reprinted.

The maiden then continues the discussion, explaining that 'the innocent are ay safe by right', and that only those who come as little children can win the bliss sought by the man who sold his all for a matchless pearl.

Next the poet asks whence her beauty comes, and what her office is. She replies that she is one of the brides of Christ, whom St. John in the Apocalypse saw arrayed for the bridal in the New Jerusalem. He asks to see their mansions, and by special grace is allowed to view the holy city from without. He sees it as St. John saw it, gleaming with gold, with its pillars of precious stone, its gates of pearl; its streets lighted by a divine radiance, so that there is no need of moon or sun. There is no church or chapel or temple there : God himself is the minister, and Christ is the sacrifice. Mortal eye could not bear the splendour, and he stood 'as stylle as dased quayle'. At evening came the procession of the virgin brides of Christ, each bearing on her breast the pearl of perfect happiness. The Lamb leads them, in pearl-white robes, his side bleeding, his face rapt; while elders make obeisance, and angels sing songs of joy as He nears the throne of God.

Suddenly the poet sees his Pearl among her companions. Overcome with longing and delight, he tries to cross the river, only to wake in the garden where he fell asleep. Henceforth he is resigned to the pleasure of the Prince of Heaven.

The reader will be able to judge the author's poetical gift from the selection, which has been chosen as one of the less ornate passages. Even here the form distracts attention from the matter by its elaborateness. A difficult rime scheme is superimposed on the alliterative line; stanza is interlinked with stanza; each group of five stanzas is distinguished by a similar refrain, and bound to the preceding and following groups by repetition in the first and last lines. So too the close of the poem echoes the beginning. With such intricacy of plan, it is not surprising that the rime is sometimes forced, and the sense strained or obscure. It is rather a matter for wonder that, in so long a work, the author was able to maintain his marvellous technique without completely sacrificing poetry to metrical gymnastics.

The highly wrought, almost overwrought, effect is heightened when the poem is read as a whole. If *Piers Plowman* gives a realistic picture of the drabness of mediaeval life, *Pearl*, more especially in the early stanzas, shows a richness of imagery and a luxuriance in light and colour that seem scarcely English. Yet they have their parallels in the decorative art of the time—the elaborate carving in wood and stone; the rich colouring of tapestries, of illuminated books and painted glass; the designs of the jewellers, goldsmiths, and silversmiths, which even the notaries who made the old inventories cannot pass without a word of admiration. The *Pearl* reminds us of the tribute due to the artists and craftsmen of the fourteenth century.

The edition by E. V. Gordon, Oxford 1953, is handy. The minor edition by Sir I. Gollancz, 1921, includes a translation.

THE PEARL, ll. 361–612.

(MS. Cotton Nero A X (about 1400).)

THENNE demed I to þat damyselle :
  ' Ne worþe no wrathþe vnto my Lorde,
If rapely ⟨I⟩ raue, spornande in spelle ;
My herte watȝ al wyth mysse remorde,
As wallande water gotȝ out of welle.   5
I do me ay in Hys myserecorde ;
Rebuke me neuer wyth wordeȝ felle,
Þaȝ I forloyne, my dere endorde,
Bot *k*yþeȝ me kyndely your coumforde,
Pytosly þenkande vpon þysse :   10
Of care and me ȝe made acorde,
Þat er watȝ grounde of alle my blysse.

  ' My blysse, my bale, ȝe han ben boþe,
Bot much þe bygger ȝet watȝ my mon ;
Fro þou watȝ wroken fro vch a woþe,   15
I wyste neuer quere my perle watȝ gon.

9 kyþeȝ] lyþeȝ *MS*

Now I hit se, now leþeʒ my loþe;
And, quen we departed, we wern at on;
God forbede we be now wroþe,
We meten so selden by stok oþer ston.   20
Þaʒ cortaysly ʒe carp con,
I am bot mol and manereʒ mysse;
Bot Crystes mersy, and Mary, and Ion,
Þise arn þe grounde of alle my blysse.

'In blysse I se þe blyþely blent,   25
And I a man al mornyf mate;
ʒe take þeron ful lyttel tente,
Þaʒ I hente ofte harmeʒ hate.
Bot now I am here in your presente,
I wolde bysech, wythouten debate,   30
ʒe wolde me say in sobre asente
What lyf ʒe lede erly and late.
For I am ful fayn þat your astate
Is worþen to worschyp and wele, iwysse;
Of alle my ioy þe hyʒe gate   35
Hit is, *and* grounde of alle my blysse.'

'Now blysse, burne, mot þe bytyde,'
Þen sayde þat lufsoum of lyth and lere,
'And welcum here to walk and byde,
For now þy speche is to me dere.   40
Maysterful mod and hyʒe pryde,
I hete þe, arn heterly hated here.
My Lorde ne loueʒ not for to chyde,
For meke arn alle þat woneʒ Hym nere;
And when in Hys place þou schal apere,   45
Be dep deuote in hol mekenesse;
My Lorde þe Lamb loueʒ ay such chere,
Þat is þe grounde of alle my blysse.

22 manereʒ] marereʒ *MS.*   36 and] in *MS.*

'A blysful lyf þou says I lede;
Þou woldeȝ knaw þerof þe stage.   50
Þow wost wel when þy perle con schede
I watȝ ful ȝong and tender of age;
Bot my Lorde þe Lombe, þurȝ Hys Godhede,
He toke myself to Hys maryage,
Corounde me quene in blysse to brede   55
In lenghe of dayeȝ þat euer schal wage;
And sesed in alle Hys herytage
Hys lef is, I am holy Hysse;
Hys prese, Hys prys, and Hys parage
Is rote and grounde of alle my blysse.'   60

'Blysful,' quod I, 'may þys be trwe?—
Dyspleseȝ not if I speke errour—
Art þou þe quene of heueneȝ blwe,
Þat al þys worlde schal do honour?
We leuen on Marye þat grace of grewe,   65
Þat ber a barne of vyrgynflour;
Þe croune fro hyr quo moȝt remwe
Bot ho hir passed in sum fauour?
Now, for synglerty o hyr dousour,
We calle hyr Fenyx of Arraby,   70
Þat freles fleȝe of hyr fasor,
Lyk to þe quen of cortaysye.'

'Cortayse Quen,' þenne s⟨a⟩yde þat gaye,
Knelande to grounde, folde vp hyr face,
'Makeleȝ Moder and myryest May,   75
Blessed Bygynner of vch a grace!'
Þenne ros ho vp and con restay,
And speke me towarde in þat space:
'Sir, fele here porchaseȝ and fongeȝ pray,
Bot supplantoreȝ none wythinne þys place.   80
Þat emperise al heueneȝ hatȝ,

And vrþe and helle in her bayly;
Of erytage ȝet non wyl ho chace,
For ho is quen of cortaysye.

'The court of þe kyndom of God alyue   85
Hatȝ a property in hytself beyng:
Alle þat may þerinne aryue
Of alle þe reme is quen oþer kyng,
And neuer oþer ȝet schal depryue,
Bot vchon fayn of oþereȝ hafyng,   90
And wolde her corouneȝ wern worþe þo fyue
If possyble were her mendyng.
Bot my Lady, of quom Iesu con spryng,
Ho haldeȝ þe empyre ouer vus ful hyȝe;
And þat dyspleseȝ non of oure gyng,   95
For ho is quene of cortaysye.

'Of courtaysye, as saytȝ Saynt Poule,
Al arn we membreȝ of Iesu Kryst;
As heued and arme and legg and naule
Temen to hys body ful trwe and t⟨r⟩yste,   100
Ryȝt so is vch a Krysten sawle
A longande lym to þe Mayster of myste.
Þenne loke what hate oþer any gawle
Is tached oþer tyȝed þy lymmeȝ bytwyste:
Þy heued hatȝ nauþer greme ne gryste   105
On arme oþer fynger þaȝ þou ber byȝe:
So fare we alle wyth luf and lyste
To kyng and quene by cortaysye.'

'Cortaysé,' quod I, 'I leue,
And charyté grete, be yow among,   110
Bot my speche þat yow ne greue,

.   .   .   .   .   .

Þyself in heuen ouer hyȝ þou heue,

112 *a line omitted in MS.*

To make þe quen þat watȝ so ȝonge.
What more honour moȝte he acheue   115
Þat hade endured in worlde stronge,
And lyued in penaunce hys lyueȝ longe,
Wyth bodyly bale hym blysse to byye?
What more worschyp moȝt he fonge,
Þen corounde be kyng by cortaysé?   120

'That cortaysé is to fre of dede,
ȝyf hyt be soth þat þou coneȝ saye;
Þou lyfed not two ȝer in oure þede;
Þou cowþeȝ neuer God nauþer plese ne pray,
Ne neuer nawþer Pater ne Crede;   125
And quen mad on þe fyrst day!
I may not traw, so God me spede,
Þat God wolde wryþe so wrange away;
Of countes, damysel, par ma fay!
Wer fayr in heuen to halde asstate,   130
Oþer elleȝ a lady of lasse aray;
Bot a quene!—hit is to dere a date.'

'Þer is no date of Hys godnesse,'
Þen sayde to me þat worþy wyȝte,
'For al is trawþe þat He con dresse,   135
And He may do no þynk bot ryȝt,
As Mathew meleȝ in your messe,
In sothful Gospel of God Almyȝt,
In sample he can ful grayþely gesse,
And lykneȝ hit to heuen lyȝte: 140
   "My regne," He saytȝ, "is lyk on hyȝt
To a lorde þat hade a uyne, I wate.
Of tyme of ȝere þe terme watȝ tyȝt,
To labor vyne watȝ dere þe date.

119 he] ho *M.S.*

'" Þat date of ȝere wel knawe þys hyne.
Þe lorde ful erly vp he ros,
To hyre werkmen to hys vyne,
And fyndeȝ þer summe to hys porpos.
Into acorde þay con declyne
For a pené on a day, and forth þay gotȝ,   150
Wryþen and worchen and don gret pyne,
Keruen and caggen and man hit clos.
Aboute vnder, þe lorde to marked totȝ,
And ydel men stande he fyndeȝ þerate.
'Why stande ȝe ydel?' he sayde to þos;   155
'Ne knawe ȝe of þis day no date?'

'" 'Er date of daye hider arn we wonne;'
So watȝ al samen her answar soȝt;
'We haf standen her syn ros þe sunne,
And no mon byddeȝ vus do ryȝt noȝt.'   16c
'Gos into my vyne, dotȝ þat ȝe conne,'
So sayde þe lorde, and made hit toȝt;
'What resonabele hyre be naȝt be runne
I yow pay in dede and þoȝte.'
Þay wente into þe vyne and wroȝte,   16
And al day þe lorde þus ȝede his gate,
And nw men to hys vyne he broȝte,
Welneȝ wyl day watȝ passed date.

'" At þe date of day of euensonge,
On oure byfore þe sonne go doun,   17
He seȝ þer ydel men ful stronge,
And sa⟨y⟩de to hem wyth sobre soun:
'Wy stonde ȝe ydel þise dayeȝ longe?'
Þay sayden her hyre watȝ nawhere boun.
'Gotȝ to my vyne, ȝemen ȝonge,   175
And wyrkeȝ and dotȝ þat at ȝe moun.'

164 pay] pray *MS*.   169 date of day] day of date *MS*.
172 hem] hen *MS*.

Sone þe worlde bycom wel broun,
Þe sunne watȝ doun, and hit wex late;
To take her hyre Ŀe mad sumoun;
Þe day watȝ al apassed date.   180

'" The date of þe daye þe lorde con knaw,
Called to þe reue: 'Lede, pay þe meyny;
Gyf hem þe hyre þat I hem owe;
And fyrre, þat non me may reprené,
Set hem alle vpon a rawe,   185
And gyf vchon ilyche a peny;
Bygyn at þe laste þat standeȝ lowe,
Tyl to þe fyrste þat þou atteny.'
And þenne þe fyrst bygonne to pleny,
And sayden þat þay hade trauayled sore: 190
' Þese bot on oure hem con streny;
Vus þynk vus oȝe to take more.

'"'More haf we serued, vus þynk so,
Þat suffred han þe dayeȝ hete,
Þenn þyse þat wroȝt not houreȝ two,   195
And þou dotȝ hem vus to counterfete.'
Þenne sayde þe lorde to on of þo:
' Frende no waning I wyl þe ȝete;
Take þat is þyn owne and go.
And I hyred þe for a peny agrete,   200
Quy bygynneȝ þou now to þrete?
Watȝ not a pené þy couenaunt þore?
Fyrre þen couenaunde is noȝt to plete.
Wy schalte þou þenne ask more?

'"'More weþer †louyly† is me my gyfte   205
To do wyth myn quat so me lykeȝ?
Oþer elleȝ þyn yȝe to lyþer is lyfte
For I am goude and non byswykeȝ?''

178 and] & & MS.   186 ilyche] ilyche MS.

'Þus schal I,' quod Kryste, ' hit skyft.
Þe laste schal be þe fyrst þat stryke3,   210
And þe fyrst be laste, be he neuer so swyft;
For mony ben calle⟨d⟩, þa3 fewe be myke3.' "
Þus pore men her part ay pyke3,
Þa3 þay com late and lyttel wore ;
And þa3 her sweng wyth lyttel atslyke3,   215
Þe merci of God is much þe more.

' More haf I of ioye and blysse hereinne,
Of ladyschyp gret and lyue3 blom,
Þen alle þe wy3e3 in þe worlde my3t wynne
By þe way of ry3t to aske dome.   220
Wheþer welnygh now I con bygynne—
In euentyde into þe vyne I come—
Fyrst of my hyre my Lorde con mynne,
I wat3 payed anon of al and sum.
3et oþer þer werne þat toke more tom,   225
Þat swange and swat for long 3ore,
Þat 3et of hyre no þynk þay nom,
Paraunter no3t schal to3ere more.'

Then more I meled and sayde apert :
' Me þynk þy tale vnresounable ;   230
Godde3 ry3t is redy and euermore rert,
Oþer Holy Wryt is bot a fable ;
In Sauter is sayd a verce ouerte
Þat speke3 a poynt determynable :
" Þou quyte3 vchon as hys desserte,   235
Þou hy3e Kyng ay pretermynable."
Now he þat stod þe long day stable,
And þou to payment com hym byfore,
Þenne þe lasse in werke to take more able,
And euer þe lenger þe lasse þe more.'   240

'Of more and lasse in Godeȝ ryche,'
Þat gentyl sayde, 'lys no ioparde,
For þer is vch mon payed ilyche,
Wheþer lyttel oþer much be hys rewarde,
For þe gentyl Cheuentayn is no chyche;   245
Queþersoeuer He dele nesch oþer harde,
He laueȝ Hys gyfteȝ as water of dyche,
Oþer goteȝ of golf þat neuer charde.
Hys fraunchyse is large þat euer dard
To Hym þat matȝ in synne rescoghe;   250
No blysse betȝ fro hem reparde,
For þe grace of God is gret inoghe.

243 ilyche] inlyche *MS.*

VII

THE GEST HYSTORIALE OF THE
DESTRUCTION OF TROY

About 1375.

The Fall of Troy was one of the most popular subjects of mediaeval story. Lydgate wrote a *Troy Book* about 1420; fragments of another are attributed to 'Barbour', whose identity with the author of *The Bruce* has been questioned; a third version, anonymous, is known as the *Laud Troy Book*; and Caxton chose as the first work to be printed in English the *Recuyell of the Historyes of Troye* (about 1474). More famous than any of these full histories are two single stories detached from the cycle: Jason's Quest of the Golden Fleece, which is admirably told by Gower in the fifth book of his *Confessio Amantis*; and the Love of Troilus and Cressida, which gave a theme both to Chaucer and to Shakespeare.

The *Gest Hystoriale of the Destruction of Troy*, from which our extracts are taken, is a free rendering of the prose *Historia Troiana* finished in 1287 by Guido de Columna (most probably the modern Terranova in Sicily). The translation, which appears to have been made in the North or North-West Midlands in the second half of the fourteenth century, is preserved only in an imperfect fifteenth-century MS. at the Hunterian Museum, Glasgow. In the Early English Text Society's print, edited by Panton and Donaldson, the text extends to over 14,000 lines.

The table of contents prefixed to the MS. promises ' *the nome of the knight þat causet it* [sc. *the story*] *to be made, and the nome of hym that translatid it out of Latyn into Englysshe* '; but the extant MS. does not fulfil the promise. The execution suggests a set task and a journeyman poet. Phrases are repeated carelessly; there is a great deal of padding; the versification is monotonous; and the writer is too often at the mercy of the alliteration to maintain a serious level. Yet he is not a slavish or a dull translator. The more romantic elements of the story, such as the matter of the *Odyssey*, had already been whittled away in his original, and he shows little desire or capacity to restore them. But he knew as well as the Old English poets the forcefulness of alliterative verse in scenes of violence, and describes with unflagging zest and vigour the interminable battles of the siege, and storms such as that which wrecked the fleet of Ajax.

The Prologue is a curious example of the pseudo-critical attitude of the Middle Ages. Homer is despised as a teller of impossible tales, and a partisan of the Greeks,—for Hector is the popular hero of the mediaeval versions. The narratives of Dares Phrygius and Dictys Cretensis, products of the taste for fictitious history that spread westward from Greek-speaking lands in the fourth and following centuries, are accepted as reliable documents ; and Guido de Columna as their authoritative literary interpreter. No mention is made of Benoît de Sainte-Maure, whose *Roman de Troie*, written in French about 1184, served as source to Guido, and, directly or indirectly, as inspiration to the whole body of Western writers who dealt with the ' Matter of Troy '. For these lapses the English translator need not be held responsible. On the merits of Homer, Dares, Dictys, and Guido de Columna, he probably accepted without question the word of his master Guido.

PROLOGUE.

Maistur in magesté, Maker of alle,
Endles and on, euer to last !
Now, God, of þi grace, graunt me þi helpe,
And wysshe me with wyt þis werke for to ende
Of aunters ben olde of aunsetris nobill,   5
And slydyn vppon shlepe by slomeryng of age ;

Of stithe men in stoure, strongest in armes,
And wisest in wer, to wale in hor tyme,
Þat ben drepit with deth, and þere day paste,
And most out of mynd for þere mecull age.   10
Sothe stories ben stoken vp, and straught out of mynde,
And swolowet into swym by swiftenes of yeres,
For new þat ben now next at our hond,
Breuyt into bokes for boldyng of hertes,
On lusti to loke with lightnes of wille,   15
Cheuyt throughe chaunce and chaungyng of peopull;
Sum tru for to traist, triet in þe ende,
Sum feynit o fere and ay false vnder.

Yche wegh as he will warys his tyme,
And has lykyng to lerne þat hym list after.   20
But olde stories of stithe þat astate helde
May be solas to sum þat it segh neuer,
Be writyng of wees þat wist it in dede,
With sight for to serche of hom þat suet after,
To ken all the crafte how þe case felle   25
By lokyng of letturs þat lefte were of olde.

Now of Troy for to telle is myn entent euyn,
Of the stoure and þe stryffe when it distroyet was.
Þof fele yeres bene faren syn þe fight endid,
And it meuyt out of mynd, myn hit I thinke,   30
Alss wise men haue writen the wordes before,
Left it in Latyn for lernyng of vs.

But sum poyetis full prist þat put hom þerto
With fablis and falshed fayned þere speche,
And made more of þat mater þan hom maister were.   35
Sum lokyt ouer litle, and lympit of the sothe.
Amonges þat menye, to myn hym be nome,
Homer was holden haithill of dedis
Qwiles his dayes enduret, derrist of other,

Þat with the Grekys was gret, and of Grice comyn.　40
He feynet myche fals was neuer before wroght,
And turnet þe truth, trust ye non other.
Of his trifuls to telle I haue no tome nowe,
Ne of his feynit fare þat he fore with:
How goddes foght in the filde, folke as þai were!　45
And other errours vnable, þat after were knowen,
That poyetis of prise have preuyt vntrew:
Ouyde and othir þat onest were ay,
Virgille þe virtuus, verrit for nobill,
Thes dampnet his dedys, and for dull holdyn.　50

　　But þe truth for to telle, and þe text euyn,
Of þat fight, how it felle in a few yeres,
Þat was clanly compilet with a clerke wise,
On Gydo, a gome þat graidly hade soght,
And wist all þe werkes by weghes he hade,　55
That bothe were in batell while the batell last,
And euþer sawte and assembly see with þere een.
Thai wrote all þe werkes wroght at þat tyme
In letturs of þere langage, as þai lernede hade:
Dares and Dytes were duly þere namys.　60
Dites full dere was dew to the Grekys,
A lede of þat lond, and logede hom with.
The tother was a tulke out of Troy selfe,
Dares, þat duly the dedys behelde.
Aither breuyt in a boke on þere best wise,　65
That sithen at a sité somyn were founden,
After, at Atthenes, as aunter befell.
The whiche bokes barely, bothe as þai were,
A Romayn ouerraght, and right hom hymseluyn,
That Cornelius was cald to his kynde name.　70
He translated it into Latyn for likyng to here,
But he shope it so short þat no shalke might
Haue knowlage by course how þe case felle;

For he brought it so breff, and so bare leuyt,
Þat no lede might have likyng to loke þerappon ;   75
Till þis Gydo it gate, as hym gráce felle,
And declaret it more clere, and on clene wise.

In this shall faithfully be founden, to the fer ende,
All þe dedis bydene as þai done were:
How þe groundes first grew, and þe grete hate,   80
Bothe of torfer and tene þat hom tide aftur.
And here fynde shall ye faire of þe felle peopull :
What kynges þere come of costes aboute ;
Of dukes full doughty, and of derffe erles,
That assemblid to þe citie þat sawte to defend ;   85
Of þe Grekys þat were gedret how gret was þe nowmber,
How mony knightes þere come, and kynges enarmede,
And what dukes thedur droghe for dedis of were ;
What shippes þere were shene, and shalkes within,
Bothe of barges and buernes þat broght were fro Grese ; 90
And all the batels on bent þe buernes betwene ;
What duke þat was dede throughe dyntes of hond,
Who fallen was in fylde, and how it fore after.
Bothe of truse and of trayne þe truthe shalt þu here,
And all the ferlies þat fell, vnto the ferre ende.   95

Fro this prologe I passe, and part me þerwith.
Frayne will I fer, and fraist of þere werkes,
Meue to my mater, and make here an ende.

EXPLICIT PROLOGUE.

THE XXXI BOKE: OF THE PASSAGE OF THE
GREKYS FRO TROY (ll. 12463-12547).

Hyt fell thus, by fortune, þe fairest of þe yere
Was past to the point of the pale wintur.   100
Heruest, with the heite and the high sun,
Was comyn into colde, with a course low.

Trees, thurgh tempestes, tynde hade þere leues,
And briddes abatid of hor brem songe ;
The wynde of the west wackenet aboue,   105
Blowyng full bremly o the brode ythes ;
The clere aire ouercast with cloudys full thicke,
With mystes full merke mynget with showres.
Flodes were felle thurgh fallyng of rayne,
And wintur vp wacknet with his wete aire.   110
    The gret nauy of the Grekes and the gay kynges
Were put in a purpos to pas fro the toune.
Sore longit þo lordis hor londys to se,
And dissiret full depely, doutyng no wedur.
Þai counted no course of the cold stormys,   115
Ne the perellis to passe of the pale windes.
Hit happit hom full hard in a hondqwile,
And mony of þo mighty to misse of hor purpos.
    Thus tho lordes in hor longyng laghton þe watur,
Shotton into ship mony shene knightes,   120
With the tresowre of þe toune þai token before,
Relikes full rife, and miche ranke godes.
Clere was the course of the cold flodis,
And the firmament faire, as fell for the wintur.
Thai past on the pale se, puld vp hor sailes,   125
Hadyn bir at þere backe, and the bonke leuyt.
Foure dayes bydene, and hor du nyghtis,
Ful soundly þai sailed with seasonable windes.
    The fyft day fuersly fell at the none,
Sodonly the softe winde vnsoberly blew ;   130
A myste and a merkenes myngit togedur ;
A thonder and a thicke rayne þrublet in the skewes,
With an ugsom noise, noy for to here ;
All flasshet in a fire the firmament ouer ;
Was no light but a laite þat launchit aboue :   135
Hit skirmyt in the skewes with a skyre low,

Thurgh the claterand clowdes clos to the heuyn,
As the welkyn shuld walt for wodenes of hete;
With blastes full bigge of the breme wyndes,
Walt vp the waghes vpon wan hilles.　　　　140
Stith was the storme, stird all the shippes,
Hoppit on hegh with heste of the flodes.
The sea was vnsober, sondrit the nauy,
Walt ouer waghes, and no way held,
Depertid the pepull, pyne to behold,　　　　145
In costes vnkowthe; cut down þere sailes,
Ropis al torochit, rent vp the hacches,
Topcastell ouerturnyt, takelles were lost.
The night come onone, noye was the more!

All the company cleane of the kyng Telamon,　　150
With þere shippes full shene, and þe shire godis,
Were brent in the bre with the breme lowe
Of the leymonde laite þat launchit fro heuyn,
And euyn drownet in the depe, dukes and other!

Oelius Aiax, as aunter befelle,　　　　155
Was stad in the storme with the stith windes,
With his shippes full shene and the shire godes.
Thrifty and þriuaund, thretty and two
There were brent on the buerne with the breme low,
And all the freikes in the flode floterand aboue.　　160

Hymseluyn in the sea sonkyn belyue,
Swalprit and swam with swyngyng of armys.
ȝet he launchet to lond, and his lyf hade,
Bare of his body, bretfull of water,
In the slober and the slicche slongyn to londe;　　165
There he lay, if hym list, the long night ouer,
Till the derke was done, and the day sprang;
Þare sum of his sort, þat soght were to lond
And than wonen of waghes, with wo as þai might,

166-7 and also 168-9 *transposed in MS.*

Laited þere lord on the laund-syde, 170
If hit fell hym by fortune the flodes to passe.
   Þan found þai the freike in the fome lye,
And comford hym kyndly, as þere kyd lord ;
With worship and wordes wan hym to fote.
Bothe failet hym the fode and the fyne clothes. 175
   Thus þere goddes with gremþ with þe Grekes fore,
Mighty Myner⟨u⟩a, of malis full grete,
For Telamon, in tene, tid for to pull
Cassandra the cleane out of hir cloise temple.
Thus hit fell hom by fortune of a foule ende, 180
For greuyng þere goddes in hor gret yre.
Oftsythes men sayn, and sene is of olde,
Þat all a company is cumbrit for a cursed shrewe.

171 hym] hom *MS.*

VIII

PIERS PLOWMAN

(1362–1400)

By WILLIAM LANGLAND

Recent criticism of *Piers Plowman* has done more to weaken
the hold of opinions once generally accepted than to replace them
by others better founded. It is still most probable that 'Long
Will', who is more than once mentioned in the text as the poet,
was William Langland. The earliest external evidence of his
home and parentage is given in a fifteenth-century note in MS.
Dublin D 4. 1, of which both the matter and the vile Latinity
bear the stamp of genuineness: 'Memorandum quod Stacy de
Rokayle, pater Willielmi de Langlond, qui Stacius fuit generosus,
et morabatur in Schiptone under Whicwode, tenens domini le
Spenser in comitatu Oxon., qui praedictus Willielmus fecit librum
qui vocatur Perys Ploughman.' Shipton-under-Wychwood is near
Burford in Oxfordshire. The poem shows familiarity with the
Malvern Hills and the streets of London; but it is hard to say
how much is fact and how much is fiction in the references to
Long Will in the text itself, more especially the description of
his London life added as the Sixth Passus in Version C, and
reproduced here as the second extract.

Since Skeat's edition for the Early English Text Society, the
many manuscripts have been grouped into three main types. The
shortest, or A-text, appears from internal evidence to have been
written about 1362. The B-text (about 1377) has the most compact manuscript tradition. It is distinguished by considerable
additions throughout, and by the reconstruction and expansion of
the visions of Dowel, Dobet, Dobest, which make up the second
half of the poem. The C-text, the latest and fullest form, appears

to have been completed in the last decade of the fourteenth century.

Until recently it has been assumed that these three versions represent progressive revisions by the author. But Professor Manly has found considerable support for his view that more than one writer—perhaps as many as five—had a share in the work. For the present, judgement on this question, and on the intricate problem of the relations of the different versions, is suspended until the results of a complete re-examination of all the MSS. are available. It would not be surprising to find that even when this necessary work is done differences of opinion on the larger questions remain as acute as ever.

It is impossible in short space to give an outline of the whole work, which describes no less than eleven visions. The structure is loose, and allegory is developed or dropped with disconcerting abruptness, for the writer does not curb his vigorous imagination in the interests of formal correctness.

The first part is the best known. On a May morning the poet falls asleep on the Malvern Hills and sees a ' Field full of Folk ', where all classes of men are busy about their occupations, more particularly the nefarious occupations that engage the attention of the moralist. Holy Church explains that a high tower in the Field is the home of Truth; and that a ' deep dale ' is the Castle of Care, where Wrong dwells with the wicked. She points out Falseness, who is about to marry Lady Meed (i.e. Reward, whether deserved reward or bribe). Lady Meed and her company are haled before the King, who, with Reason and Conscience as his guides, decides her case, and upholds the plea of Peace against Wrong.

The second vision is prefaced (in the C-text only) by the passage printed as the second selection. The poet falls asleep again, and sees Conscience preaching to the people in the Field. Representatives of the Seven Deadly Sins are vividly described. They are brought to penitence, and all set out in search of Truth. But no one knows the way. A palmer who wears the trophies of many pilgrimages to distant saints is puzzled by their inquiries, for he has never heard of pilgrims seeking Truth. Then Peter the Plowman comes forward and explains the way in allegorical terms. Here the first extract begins. The second vision closes with a general pardon given by Truth to Piers Plowman in this simple form:

> Do wel, and haue wel, and God shal haue þi sowle;
> And do yuel, and haue yuel, hope þow non other
> But after þi ded-day þe Deuel shal haue þi sowle.

The several visions of the second part make up the lives of Dowel, Dobet, and Dobest. Piers Plowman is there identified with Christ, and the poem ends with Conscience, almost overcome by sin, setting out resolutely in search of Piers.

First impressions of mediaeval life are usually coloured by the courtly romances of Malory and his later refiners. Chaucer brings us down to reality, but his people belong to a prosperous middle-class world, on holiday and in holiday mood. *Piers Plowman* stands alone as a revelation of the ignorance and misery of the lower classes, whose multiplied grievances came to a head in the Peasants' Revolt of 1381. It must not be supposed that Langland idealized the labourers. Their indolence and improvidence are exposed as unsparingly as the vices of the rich; and Piers himself is not so much a representative of the English workman in the fourteenth century as a character drawn straight from the Gospels. Still, such an eager plea for humbleness, simplicity, and honest labour, could not fail to encourage the political hopes of the poor, and we see in John Ball's letter (p. 160) that 'Piers Plowman' had become a catchword among them. The poet himself rather deprecates political action. His satire is directed against the general slackening of the bonds of duty that marked the last years of an outworn system of society. For the remedy of abuses he appeals not to one class but to all: king, nobles, clergy, and workers must model their lives on the pattern of the Gospels.

A. FROM THE B-TEXT, PASSUS VI.

Bodleian MS. Laud 581 (about 1400).

'This were a wikked way, but whoso hadde a gyde
That wolde folwen vs eche a fote:' þus þis folke hem
    mened.

Quatȝ Perkyn þe plouman: 'Bi Seynt Peter of Rome!

I haue an half-acre to erye bi þe heigh way.
Hadde I eried þis half-acre, and sowen it after,   5
I *wolde* wende with ȝow, and þe way teche.'
    ' Þis were a longe lettynge,' quod a lady in a sklayre;
' What sholde we wommen worche þerewhiles?'
    ' Somme shal sowe ⟨þe⟩ sakke,' quod Piers, ' for shedyng
        of þe whete;
And ȝe, louely ladyes, with ȝoure longe fyngres,   10
Þat ȝe han silke and sendal to sowe, whan tyme is,
Chesibles for chapclleynes, cherches to honoure;
Wyues and wydwes wolle and flex spynneth,
Maketh cloth, I conseille ȝow, and kenneth so ȝowre
        douȝtres;
Þe nedy and þe naked, nymmeth hede how hii liggeth,   15
And casteth hem clothes, for so comaundeth Treuthe.
For I shal lene hem lyflode, but ȝif þe londe faille,
Flesshe and bred, bothe to riche and to pore,
As longe as I lyue, for þe Lordes loue of heuene.
And alle manere of men þat þorw mete and drynke lyb-
        beth,   20
Helpith hym to worche wiȝtliche þat wynneth ȝowre fode.'
    ' Bi Crist !' quod a knyȝte þo, ' he kenneth vs þe best;
Ac on þe teme trewly tauȝte was I neuere.
Ac kenne me,' quod þe knyȝte, ' and, bi Cryst ! I wil assaye.'
    ' Bi seynt Poule !' quod Perkyn, ' ȝe profre ȝow so faire,   25
Þat I shal swynke, and swete, and sowe for vs bothe,
And oþer laboures do for þi loue al my lyf tyme,
In couenaunt þat þow kepe Holi Kirke and myselue
Fro wastoures and fro wykked men þat þis worlde struyeth;
And go hunte hardiliche to hares and to foxes,   30
To bores and to brockes þat breketh adown myne hegges,
And go affaite þe faucones wilde foules to kille,
For suche cometh to my croft, and croppeth mȝ whete.'

6 wolde] wil *MS*.

Curteislich þe knyȝte þanne comsed þise wordes :
'By my power, Pieres,' quod he, 'I pliȝte þe my treuthe   35
To fulfille þis forward, þowȝ I fiȝte sholde ;
Als longe as I lyue, I shal þe mayntene.'

'ȝe, and ȝit a poynt,' quod Pieres, 'I preye ȝow of more ;
Loke ȝe tene no tenaunt, but Treuthe wil assent.
And þowgh ȝe mowe amercy hem, late Mercy be taxoure,
And Mekenesse þi mayster, maugré Medes chekes ;   41
And þowgh pore men profre ȝow presentis and ȝiftis,
Nym it nauȝte, an auenture ȝe mowe it nauȝte deserue ;
For þow shalt ȝelde it aȝein at one ȝeres ende
In a ful perillous place, Purgatorie it hatte.   45
And mysbede nouȝte þi bondemen, þe better may þow
    spede ;
Þowgh he be þyn vnderlynge here, wel may happe in
    heuene
Þat he worth worthier sette and with more blisse :
      Amice, ascende superius.
For in charnel atte chirche cherles ben yuel to knowe,   50
Or a kniȝte fram a knaue þere,—knowe þis in þin herte.
And þat þow be trewe of þi tonge, and tales þat þow
    hatie,
But if þei ben of wisdome or of witte, þi werkmen to
    chaste.
Holde with none harlotes, ne here nouȝte her tales,
And nameliche atte mete suche men eschue,   55
For it ben þe deueles disoures, I do þe to vnderstande.'

'I assente, bi Seynt Iame !' seyde þe kniȝte þanne,
'Forto worche bi þi wordes þe while my lyf dureth.'

'And I shal apparaille me,' quod Perkyn, 'in pilgrimes
    wise,
And wende with ȝow I wil til we fynde Treuthe,   60
And cast on me my clothes, yclouted and hole,
My cokeres and my coffes, for colde of my nailles,

And hange myn hoper at myn hals, in stede of a scrippe,
A busshel of bredcorne brynge me þerinne,
For I wil sowe it myself; and sitthenes wil I wende 65
To pylgrymage, as palmers don, pardoun forto haue.
Ac whoso helpeth me to erie or sowen here, ar I wende,
Shal haue leue, bi owre Lorde, to lese here in heruest,
And make hem mery þeremydde, maugré whoso bigruc-
    cheth it.
And alkyn crafty men, þat konne lyuen in treuthe, 70
I shal fynden hem fode, þat feithfulliche libbeth.' ..
   (Dame 'Worche-whan-tyme-is' Pieres wyf hiȝte ;
His douȝter hiȝte ' Do-riȝte-so- or-þi-dame-shal-þe-bete ';
His sone hiȝte ' Suffre-þi-souereynes- to-hauen-her-wille-,
Deme-hem-nouȝte-, for-, if-þow-doste-, þow-shalt-it-dere-
    abugge.') 75
  ' Late God yworth with al, for so His worde techeth ;
For now I am olde and hore, and haue of myn owen,
To penaunce and to pilgrimage I wil passe with þise
    other.
Forþi I wil, or I wende, do wryte my biqueste.
  In Dei nomine, amen, I make it myseluen. 80
He shal haue my soule þat best hath yserued it,
And fro þe fende it defende, for so I bileue,
Til I come to His acountes, as my *Credo* me telleth,
To haue a relees and a remissioun on þat rental I leue.
Þe kirke shal haue my caroigne and kepe my bones, 85
For of my corne and catel he craued þe tythe ;
I payed it hym prestly, for peril of my soule,
Forthy is he holden, I hope, to haue me in his masse,
And mengen in his memorye amonge alle Crystene.
  My wyf shal haue of þat I wan with treuthe, and nomore,
And dele amonge my douȝtres and my dere children ; 91
For þowgh I deye todaye, my dettes ar quitte ;
I bare home þat I borwed, ar I to bedde ȝede.

And with þe residue and þe remenaunte, bi þe rode of
    Lukes !
I wil worschip þerwith Treuthe bi my lyue,   95
And ben his pilgryme atte plow, for pore mennes sake.
My plow-fote shal be my pyk-staf, and picche atwo þe
    rotes,
And helpe my culter to kerue, and clense þe forwes.'
    Now is Perkyn and his pilgrymes to þe plowe faren ;
To erie þis halue-acre holpyn hym manye.   100
Dikeres and delueres digged vp þe balkes ;
Þerewith was Perkyn apayed, and preysed hem faste.
Other werkemen þere were þat wrouȝten ful ȝerne ;
Eche man in his manere made hymself to done,
And some, to plese Perkyn, piked vp þe wedes.   105
    At heighe pryme Peres lete þe plowe stonde,
To ouersen hem hymself, and whoso best wrouȝte
He shulde be huyred þerafter whan heruest-tyme come.
    And þanne seten somme and songen atte nale,
And hulpen erie his half-acre with ' how ! trollilolli ! '   110
    ' Now, bi þe peril of my soule ! ' quod Pieres, al in pure
        tene,
' But ȝe arise þe rather, and rape ȝow to worche,
Shal no greyne þat groweth glade ȝow at nede ;
And þough ȝe deye for dole, þe deuel haue þat reccheth ! '
    Tho were faitoures aferde, and feyned hem blynde ;   115
Somme leyde here legges aliri, as suche loseles conneth,
And made her mone to Pieres, and preyde hym of grace :
' For we haue no lymes to laboure with, lorde, ygraced be ȝe !
Ac we preye for ȝow, Pieres, and for ȝowre plow bothe,
Þat God of His grace ȝowre grayne multiplye,   120
And ȝelde ȝow of ȝowre almesse þat ȝe ȝiue vs here ;
For we may nouȝte swynke ne swete, suche sikenesse vs
    eyleth.'
    ' If it be soth,' quod Pieres, ' þat ȝe seyne, I shal it sone
        asspye.

ȝe ben wastoures, I wote wel, and Treuthe wote þe sothe,
And I am his olde hyne, and hiȝte hym to warne   125
Which þei were in þis worlde his werkemen appeyred.
ȝe wasten þat men wynnen with trauaille and with tene,
Ac Treuthe shal teche ȝow his teme to dryue,
Or ȝe shal ete barly bred and of þe broke drynke.
But if he be blynde, *or* broke-legged, or bolted with yrnes,
He shal ete whete bred and drynke with myselue,   131
Tyl God of his goodnesse amendement hym sende.
Ac ȝe myȝte trauaille as Treuthe wolde, and take mete and
      huyre
To kepe kyne in þe felde, þe corne fro þe bestes,
Diken, or deluen, or dyngen vppon sheues,   135
Or helpe make morter, or bere mukke afelde.
In lecherye an in losengerye ȝe lyuen, and in sleuthe,
And al is þorw suffrance þat veniaunce ȝow ne taketh.

   Ac ancres and heremytes, þat eten but at nones,
And namore er morwe, myne almesse shul þei haue,   140
And of my catel to cope hem with þat han cloistres and
      cherches.
Ac Robert Renne-aboute shal nouȝte haue of myne,
Ne posteles, but þey preche conne, and haue powere of
      þe bisschop;
They shal haue payne and potage, and make hemself at ese,
For it is an vnresonable religioun þat hath riȝte nouȝte of
      certeyne.'   145
And þanne gan a Wastoure to wrath hym, and wolde haue
      yfouȝte,
And to Pieres þe plowman he profered his gloue;
A Brytonere, a braggere, abosted Pieres als :—
' Wiltow or neltow, we wil haue owre wille
Of þi flowre and of þi flessche, fecche whan vs liketh,   150
And make vs myrie þermyde, maugré þi chekes!'

      130 or] and *MS.*

Thanne Pieres þe plowman pleyned hym to þe knyȝte,
To kepe hym, as couenaunte was, fram cursed shrewes,
And fro þis wastoures wolues-kynnes, þat maketh þe worlde
    dere :
' For þo waste, and wynnen nouȝte, and þat ilke while   155
Worth neuere plenté amonge þe poeple þerwhile my plow
    liggeth.'
    Curteisly þe knyȝte þanne, as his kynde wolde,
Warned Wastoure, and wissed hym bettere,
' Or þow shalt abugge by þe lawe, by þe ordre þat I bere !'
    ' I was nouȝt wont to worche,' quod Wastour, ' and now
        wil I nouȝt bigynne ',   160
And lete liȝte of þe lawe, and lasse of þe knyȝte,
And sette Pieres at a pees, and his plow bothe,
And manaced Pieres and his men ȝif þei mette eftsone.
    · Now, by þe peril of my soule !' quod Pieres, ' I shal
        apeyre ȝow alle !'
And houped after Hunger, þat herd hym atte firste :   165
' Awreke me of þise wastoures,' quod he ' þat þis worlde
    schendeth !'
    Hunger in haste þo hent Wastour bi þe mawe,
And wronge hym so bi þe wombe þat bothe his eyen
    wattered.
He buffeted þe Britoner aboute þe chekes,
Þat he loked like a lanterne al his lyf after.   170
He bette hem so bothe, he barste nere here guttes ;
Ne hadde Pieres with a pese-lof preyed Hunger to cesse,
They hadde ben doluen bothe, ne deme þow non other.
' Suffre hem lyue,' he seyde ' and lete hem ete with hogges,
Or elles benes and bren ybaken togideres,   175
Or elles melke and mene ale ; ' þus preyed Pieres for hem.
    Faitoures for fere herof flowen into bernes,
And flapten on with flayles fram morwe til euen,
That Hunger was nouȝt so hardy on hem for to loke,

For a potful of peses þat Peres hadde ymaked.   180
An heep of heremites henten hem spades,
And ketten here copes, and courtpies hem made,
And wenten as werkemen with spades and with schoueles,
And doluen and dykeden to dryue aweye Hunger.

Blynde and bedreden were botened a þousande,   185
Þat seten to begge syluer ; sone were þei heled.
For þat was bake for Bayarde was bote for many hungry,
And many a beggere for benes buxome was to swynke,
And eche a pore man wel apayed to haue pesen for his
    huyre,
And what Pieres preyed hem to do as prest as a sperhauke.
And þereof was Peres proude, and put hem to werke,   191
And ȝaf hem mete as he myȝte aforth, and mesurable huyre.

Þanne hadde Peres pité, and preyed Hunger to wende
Home into his owne erde, and holden hym þere :
' For I am wel awroke now of wastoures, þorw þi myȝte.   195
Ac I preye þe, ar þow passe,' quod Pieres to Hunger,
' Of beggeres and of bidderes what best be ⟨to⟩ done ?
For I wote wel, be þow went, þei wil worche ful ille ;
For myschief it maketh þei beth so meke nouthe,
And for defaute of her fode þis folke is at my wille.   200
Þey are my blody bretheren,' quod Pieres, ' for God bouȝte
    vs alle ;
Treuthe tauȝte me ones to louye hem vchone,
And to helpen hem of alle þinge ay as hem nedeth.
And now wolde I witen of þe what were þe best,   204
An how I myȝte amaistrien hem, and make hem to worche.'

' Here now,' quod Hunger ' and holde it for a wisdome :
Bolde beggeres and bigge, þat mowe her bred biswynke,
With houndes bred and hors bred holde vp her hertis,
Abate hem with benes for bollyng of her wombe ;
And ȝif þe gomes grucche, bidde hem go swynke,   210
And he shal soupe swettere whan he it hath deseruid.

And if þow fynde any freke, þat fortune hath appeyred
Or any maner fals men, fonde þow suche to cnowe;
Conforte hym with þi catel, for Crystes loue of heuene;
Loue hem and lene hem, so lawe of God techeth:—   215
    Alter alterius onera portate.
And alle maner of men þat þow myȝte asspye
That nedy ben and nauȝty, helpe hem with þi godis;
Loue hem, and lakke hem nouȝte; late God take þe
    veniaunce;
Theigh þei done yuel, late þow God aworthe:—   220
    Michi vindictam, et ego retribuam.
And if þow wil be graciouse to God, do as þe Gospel
    techeth,
And bilow þe amonges low men; so shaltow lacche grace:—
    Facite vobis amicos de mamona iniquitatis.'
'I wolde nouȝt greue God,' quod Piers, 'for al þe good
    on grounde;   225
Miȝte I synnelees do as þow seist?' seyde Pieres þanne.
'ȝe, I bihote þe,' quod Hunger, 'or ellis þe Bible lieth;
Go to Genesis þe gyaunt, þe engendroure of vs alle:—
"*In sudore* and swynke þow shalt þi mete tilye,
And laboure for þi lyflode," and so owre Lorde hyȝte.   230
And Sapience seyth þe same, I seigh it in þe Bible:—
"*Piger pro frigore* no felde nolde tilye,
And þerfore he shal begge and bidde, and no man bete his
    hunger."
Mathew with mannes face mouthed þise wordis:—
þat *seruus nequam* had a nam, and for he wolde nouȝte
    chaffare,   235
He had maugré of his maistre for euermore after,
And binam ⟨hym⟩ his mnam, for he ne wolde worche,
And ȝaf þat mnam to hym þat ten mnames hadde;
And with þat he seyde, þat Holi Cherche it herde,
"He þat hath shal haue, and helpe þere it nedeth,   240

And he þat nouȝt hath shal nouȝt haue, and no man hym
    helpe ;
And þat he weneth wel to haue, I wil it hym bireue."

    Kynde Witt wolde þat eche a wyght wrouȝte,
Or in dykynge, or in deluynge, or trauaillynge in preyeres,
Contemplatyf lyf or actyf lyf, Cryst wolde men wrouȝte.   245
Þe Sauter seyth in þe psalme of *Beati omnes*,
Þe freke þat fedeth hymself with his feythful laboure,
He is blessed by þe boke, in body and in soule :—

        Labores manuum tuarum, etc.'

    'ȝet I prey ȝow,' quod Pieres, '*par charité !* and ȝe kunne
Eny leef of lechecraft, lere it me, my dere.   251
For somme of my seruauntȝ, and myself bothe,
Of al a wyke worche nouȝt, so owre wombe aketh.'

    'I wote wel,' quod Hunger, 'what sykenesse ȝow eyleth ;
ȝe han maunged ouermoche, and þat maketh ȝow grone.   255
Ac I hote þe,' quod Hunger, 'as þow þyne hele wilnest,
That þow drynke no day ar þow dyne somwhat.
Ete nouȝte, I hote þe, ar hunger þe take,
And sende þe of his sauce to sauoure with þi lippes ;
And kepe some tyl sopertyme, and sitte nouȝt to longe ;   260
Arise vp ar appetit haue eten his fulle.
Lat nouȝt Sire Surfait sitten at þi borde. . . .
And ȝif þow diete þe þus, I dar legge myne eres
Þat Phisik shal his furred hodes for his fode selle,
And his cloke of Calabre, with alle þe knappes of golde,   265
And be fayne, bi my feith, his phisik to lete,
And lerne to laboure with londe, for lyflode is swete ;
For morthereres aren mony leches, Lorde hem amende !
Þei do men deye þorw here drynkes, ar Destiné it wolde.'

    'By Seynt Poule !' quod Pieres, 'þise aren profitable
    wordis.   270
Wende now, Hunger, whan þow wolt, þat wel be þow
    euere,

For this is a louely lessoun; Lorde it þe forȝelde!'

'Byhote God,' quod Hunger, 'hennes ne wil I wende,
Til I haue dyned bi þis day, and ydronke bothe.'

'I haue no peny,' quod Peres 'poletes forto bigge,   275
Ne neyther gees ne grys, but two grene cheses,
A fewe cruddes and creem, and an hauer-cake,
And two loues of benes and bran ybake for my fauntis;
And ȝet I sey, by my soule, I haue no salt bacoun
Ne no kokeney, bi Cryst, coloppes forto maken.   280
Ac I haue percil, and porettes, and many koleplantes,
And eke a cow and a kalf, and a cart-mare
To drawe afelde my donge þe while þe drought lasteth.
And bi þis lyflode we mot lyue til Lammasse tyme;
And bi þat I hope to haue heruest in my croft,   285
And þanne may I diȝte þi dyner as me dere liketh.'

Alle þe pore peple þo pesecoddes fetten,
Benes and baken apples þei brouȝte in her lappes,
Chibolles and cheruelles and ripe chiries manye,
And profred Peres þis present to plese with Hunger.   290
Al Hunger eet in hast, and axed after more.
Þanne pore folke for fere fedde Hunger ȝerne
With grene poret and pesen—to poysoun Hunger þei þouȝte.
By þat it neighed nere heruest, newe corne cam to chepynge;
Þanne was folke fayne, and fedde Hunger with þe
          best,   295
With good ale, as Glotoun tauȝte, and gerte Hunger go
          slepe.

And þo wolde Wastour nouȝt werche, but wandren aboute
Ne no begger ete bred that benes inne were,
But of coket, or clerematyn, or elles of clene whete
Ne none halpeny ale in none wise drynke,   300
But of þe best and of þe brounest þat in borgh is to selle.

Laboreres þat haue no lande to lyue on but her handes,
Deyned nouȝt to dyne aday nyȝt-olde wortes;

May no peny-ale hem paye, ne no pece of bakoun,
But if it be fresch flesch, other fische, fryed other bake,   305
And that *chaude* or *plus chaud*, for chillyng of here mawe.
And but if he be heighlich huyred, ellis wil he chyde,
And þat he was werkman wrouȝt waille þe tyme;
Aȝeines Catones conseille comseth he to iangle :—

> *Paupertatis onus pacienter ferre memento.*   310

He greueth hym aȝeines God, and gruccheth aȝeines resoun,
And þanne curseth he þe kynge, and al his conseille after,
Suche lawes to loke, laboreres to greue.
Ac whiles Hunger was her maister, þere wolde none of hem
       chyde,
Ne stryue aȝeines his statut, so sterneliche he loked.   315
   Ac I warne ȝow, werkemen, wynneth while ȝe mowe,
For Hunger hide⟨r⟩ward hasteth hym faste,
He shal awake with water wastoures to chaste.
Ar fyue ⟨ȝere⟩ be fulfilled suche famyn shal aryse,
Thorwgh flodes and þourgh foule wederes frutes shul faille;
And so sayde Saturne, and sent ȝow to warne :   321
Whan ȝe se þe sonne amys, and two monkes hedes,
And a mayde haue þe maistrie, and multiplied bi eight,
Þanne shal Deth withdrawe, and Derthe be Iustice,
And Dawe þe Dyker deye for hunger,   325
But if God of his goodnesse graunt vs a trewe.

B.   FROM THE C-TEXT, PASSUS VI, ll. 1–104.

MS. Phillips 8231 (about 1400).

THUS ich awaked, wot God, wanne ich wonede on Cornehulle,
Kytte and ich in a cote, cloþed as a lollere,
And lytel *ylete* by, leyue me for soþe,
Among lollares of London and lewede heremytes;
For ich made of þo men as Reson me tauhte.   5

3 And a lytel ich let by *MS.*

For as ich cam by Conscience, wit Reson ich mette,
In an hote heruest, wenne ich hadde myn hele,
And lymes to labore with, and louede wel fare,
And no dede to do bote drynke and to slepe :
In hele and in vnité on me aposede,   10
Romynge in remembraunce, thus Reson me aratede :—
'Canstow seruen,' he seide, 'oþer syngen in a churche,
Oþer coke for my cokers, oþer to þe cart picche,
Mowe, oþer mowen, oþer make bond to sheues,
Repe, oþer be a repereyue, and aryse erliche,   15
Oþer haue an horne and be haywarde, and liggen oute
        a nyghtes,
And kepe my corn in my croft fro pykers and þeeues ?
Oþer shappe shon oþer cloþes, oþer shep oþer kyn kepe,
⟨H⟩eggen oþer harwen, oþer swyn oþer gees dryue,
Oþer eny kyns craft þat to þe comune nudeþ,   20
Hem þat bedreden be bylyue to fynde ? '
'Certes,' ich seyde, 'and so me God helpe,
Ich am to waik to worche with sykel oþer with sythe,
And to long, leyf me, lowe for to stoupe,
To worchen as a workeman eny wyle to dure.'   25
'Thenne hauest þow londes to lyue by,' quath Reson, 'oþer
        lynage riche
That fynden þe þy fode ? For an hydel man þow semest,
A spendour þat spende mot, oþer a spille-tyme,
Oþer beggest þy bylyue aboute ate menne hacches,
Oþer faitest vpon Frydays oþer feste-dayes in churches,   30
The wiche is lollarene lyf, þat lytel ys preysed
Þer Ryghtfulnesse rewardeþ ryght as men deserueþ :—
        Reddit unicuique iuxta opera sua.
Oþer þow ert broke, so may be, in body oþer in membre,
Oþer ymaymed þorw som myshap werby þow myȝt be ex-
        cused ? '   35

'Wanne ich ȝong was,' quath ich, ' meny ȝer hennes,
My fader and my frendes founden me to scole,
Tyl ich wiste wyterliche wat Holy Wryt menede,
And wat is best for þe body, as þe Bok telleþ,
And sykerest for þe soule, by so ich wolle continue.   40
And ȝut fond ich neuere, in faith, sytthen my frendes deyden,
Lyf þat me lyked, bote in þes longe clothes.
Hyf ich by laboure sholde lyue and lyflode deseruen,
That labour þat ich lerned best *perwith* lyue ich sholde :—

    In eadem uocatione qua uocati estis.   45

And ich lyue in Londene and on Londen bothe ;
The lomes þat ich laboure with and lyflode deserue
Ys *Paternoster*, and my Prymer, *Placebo* and *Dirige*,
And my Sauter som tyme, and my Seuene Psalmes.
Thus ich synge for hure soules of suche as me helpen,   50
And þo þat fynden me my fode vochen saf, ich trowe,
To be wolcome wanne ich come oþerwyle in a monthe,
Now with hym and now with hure ; and þusgate ich begge
Withoute bagge oþer botel bote my wombe one.
And also, moreouer, me þynkeþ, syre Reson,   55
Men sholde constreyne no clerke to knauene werkes ;
For by lawe of *Leuitici,* þat oure Lord ordeynede,
Clerkes þat aren crouned, of kynde vnderstondyng,
Sholde noþer swynke, ne swete, ne swere at enquestes,
Ne fyghte in no vauntwarde, ne hus fo greue :—   60

    Non reddas malum pro malo.

For it ben aires of heuene alle þat ben crounede,
And in queer in churches Cristes owene mynestres :—

    Dominus pars hereditatis mee ; & alibi : *Clementia non*
      constringit.

Hit bycomeþ for clerkus Crist for to seruen,   65
And knaues vncrouned to cart and to worche.

<hr>

44 þerwith] þerhwit *MS.*   62 alle] and alle *MS.*   63 in churches]
and in kirkes *Ilchester MS.*

For shold no clerk be crouned bote yf he ycome were
Of franklens and free men, and of folke yweddede.
Bondmen and bastardes and beggers children,
Thuse bylongeþ to labour, and lordes children sholde seruen,
Bothe God and good men, as here degree askeþ;   71
Some to synge masses, oþer sitten and wryte,
Rede and receyue þat Reson ouhte spende;
And sith bondemenne barnes han be mad bisshopes,
And barnes bastardes han ben archidekenes,   75
And sopers and here sones for seluer han be knyghtes,
And lordene sones here laborers, and leid here rentes to
      wedde,
For þe ryght of þes reame ryden aȝens oure enemys,
In confort of þe comune and þe kynges worshep,
And monkes and moniales, þat mendinauns sholden fynde, 80
Han mad here kyn knyghtes, and knyghtfees purchase⟨d⟩,
Popes and patrones poure gentil blod refuseþ,
And taken Symondes sone seyntewarie to kepe.
Lyf-holynesse and loue han ben longe hennes,
And wole, til hit be wered out, or oþerwise ychaunged.   85
      Forþy rebuke me ryght nouht, Reson, ich ȝow praye;
For in my conscience ich knowe what Crist wolde þat ich
      wrouhte.
Preyers of ⟨a⟩ parfyt man and penaunce discret
Ys þe leueste labour þat oure Lord pleseþ.
Non de solo,' ich seide, 'for soþe *uiuit homo,*   90
Nec in pane et pabulo, þe *Paternoster* witnesseþ:
Fiat uoluntas tua fynt ous alle þynges.'
Quath Conscience, 'By Crist! ich can nat see this lyeþ;
Ac it semeth nouht parfytnesse in cytees for to begge,
Bote he be obediencer to pryour oþer to mynstre.'   95
'That ys soth,' ich seide 'and so ich byknowe
That ich haue tynt tyme, and tyme mysspended;

92 tua] tuas MS.

And ʒut, ich hope, as he þat ofte haueþ chaffared,
Þat ay hath lost and lost, and at þe laste hym happed
He bouhte suche a bargayn 'ie was þe bet euere,   100
And sette hus lost at a lef at þe laste ende,
Suche a wynnynge hym warth þorw wyrdes of hus grace :—
            Simile est regnum celorum thesauro abscondito in agro,
                et cetera ;
            Mulier que inuenit dragmam, et cetera ;
So hope ich to haue of Hym þat his almyghty   105
A gobet of Hus grace, and bygynne a tyme
Þat alle tymes of my tyme to profit shal turne.'
    'Ich rede þe,' quath Reson þo 'rape þe to bygynne
Þe lyf þat ys lowable and leel to þe soule '—
'ʒe, and continue,' quath Conscience ; and to þe churche ich
        wente.   110

            99 laste] latiste *MS.*

IX

MANDEVILLE'S TRAVELS

Mandeville's Travels were originally written in French, perhaps in 1356 or 1357. Their popularity was immediate, and Latin and English translations soon appeared. The English texts published show three forms. The first, imperfect, is the text of the early prints. The second, from Cotton MS. Titus C xvi (about 1400–25), was first printed in 1725, and is followed in the editions by Halliwell, 1839 and 1866, and by Hamelius, 1919. The third, from Egerton MS. 1982 (about 1400–25), has been edited for the Roxburghe Club by G. F. Warner, with the French text, and an excellent apparatus. Our selections follow the Cotton MS.

The *Travels* fall into two parts : (i) a description of the routes to the Holy Land, and an account of the Holy Places; (ii) a narrative of travel in the more distant parts of Asia. Throughout the author poses as an eyewitness. But in fact the book is a compilation, made without much regard to time or place. For the first part William de Boldensele, who wrote in 1336 an account of a visit to the Holy Land, is the main source. The second part follows the description of an Eastern voyage written by Friar Odoric of Pordenone in 1330. Other materials from the mediaeval encyclopaedists are woven in, and there is so little trace of original observation that it is doubtful whether the author travelled far beyond his library.

In the preface he claims to be Sir John Mandeville, an Englishman born at St. Albans. The people of St. Albans were driven to desperate shifts to explain the absence of his tomb from their abbey; but until 1798 it was actually to be seen at the church of the Guillemins, Liège, with this inscription :

' Hic iacet vir nobilis Dom Ioannes de Mandeville, alias dictus ad Barbam, Miles, Dominus de Campdi, natus de Anglia, medicinae professor, devotissimus orator, et bonorum suorum largissimus pauperibus erogator, qui, toto quasi orbe lustrato, Leodii diem vitae suae clausit extremum A.D. MCCCLXXII, mensis Nov. die xvii.'

A Liège chronicler, Jean d'Outremeuse (d. 1399), who claims the invidious position of his confidant and literary executor, gives further details : Mandeville was 'chevalier de Montfort en Angleterre'; he was obliged to leave England because he had slain a nobleman ; he came to Liège in 1343 ; and was content to be known as ' Jean de Bourgogne dit à la Barbe '.

Now Jean de Bourgogne, with whom Sir John Mandeville is identified by d'Outremeuse, is known as the writer of a tract on the Plague, written at Liège in 1365. Further, the Latin text of the *Travels* mentions that the author met at Liège a certain ' Johannes ad Barbam ', recognized him as a former physician at the court of the Sultan of Egypt, and took his advice and help in the writing of the *Travels*.

Again, in 1322, the year in which Sir John Mandeville claims to have left England, a Johan de Burgoyne was given good reason to flee the country, because a pardon, granted to him the previous year for his actions against the Despensers, was then withdrawn. Curiously enough, a John Mandeville was also of the party opposed to the Despensers.

Nothing has come of the attempts to attach the clues—St. Albans, Montfort, Campdi, the arms on the tomb at Liège—to the English family of Mandeville. It seems likely that ' Sir John Mandeville' was an alias adopted by Jean de Bourgogne, unless both names cover Jean d'Outremeuse. The Epilogue to the Cotton version shows how early the plausible fictions of the text had infected the history of its composition.

It is clear that the English versions do not come from the hand of the writer of the *Travels*, who could not have been guilty of such absurdities as the translation of *montaignes* by ' þe hille of Aygnes' in the Cotton MS. But whoever the author was, he shows a courtesy and modesty worthy of a knight, begging those with more recent experience to correct the lapses of his memory, and remembering always the interests of later travellers, who might wish to glean some marvels still untold. He might well have pleaded in the fourteenth century that the time had not come when prose fiction could afford to throw off the disguise of truth.

[THE VOIAGE AND TRAVAILE OF SIR

IOHN MAUNDEVILE, KT.]

British Museum MS. Cotton Titus C xvi (about 1400–25).

From chap. xiv (xviii), f. 65 b.

ETHIOPE is departed in two princypall parties; and þat is in the Est partie, and in the Meridionall partie, the whiche partie meridionall is clept Moretane. And the folk of þat contree ben blake ynow, and more blake þan in the toþer 5 partie; and þei ben clept Mowres. In þat partie is a well, þat in the day it is so cold þat no man may drynke þereoffe; and in the nyght it is so hoot þat no man may suffre hys hond þerein. And beȝonde þat partie, toward the South, to passe by the See Occean, is a gret lond and a gret contrey. But 10 men may not duell þere, for the feruent brennynge of the sonne, so is it passynge hoot in þat contrey.

In Ethiope all the ryueres and all the watres ben trouble, and þei ben somdell salte, for the gret hete þat is þere. And the folk of þat contree ben lyghtly dronken, and han but litill 15 appetyt to mete . . .

In Ethiope ben many dyuerse folk, and Ethiope is clept 'Cusis.' In þat contree ben folk þat han but o foot; and þei gon so blyue þat it is meruaylle; and the foot is so large þat it schadeweth all the body aȝen the sonne, whanne þei wole lye 20 and reste hem.

In Ethiope, whan the children ben ȝonge and lytill, þei ben all ȝalowe; and whan þat þei wexen of age, þat ȝalownesse turneth to ben all blak. In Ethiope is the cytee of Saba.

and the lond of the whiche on of the þre Kynges, þat presented oure Lord in Bethleem, was kyng offe.   25

Fro Ethiope men gon into Ynde be manye dyuerse con-
treyes. And men clepen the high Ynde 'Emlak'. And Ynde is
devyded in þre princypall parties; þat is: the more, þat is
a full hoot contree; and Ynde the lesse, þat is a full atempree
contrey, þat streccheth to the lond of Medé; and the þridde 30
part, toward the Septentrion, is full cold, so þat for pure cold
and contynuell frost the water becometh cristall.

And vpon tho roches of cristall growen the gode dyamandes,
þat ben of trouble colour. ȝalow cristall draweth ⟨to⟩ colour
lyke oylle. And þei ben so harde þat no man may pollysch 35
hem; and men clepen hem 'dyamandes' in þat contree, and
'hamese' in anoþer contree. Othere dyamandes men fynden
in Arabye, þat ben not so gode; and þei ben more broun and
more tendre. And oþer dyamandes also men fynden in the
Ile of Cipre, þat ben ȝit more tendre; and hem men may wel 40
pollische. And in the lond of Macedoyne men fynden
dyamaundes also. But the beste and the moste precyiouse
ben in Ynde.

And men fynden many tyme harde dyamandes in a masse,
þat cometh out of gold, whan men puren it and fynen it out 45
of the myne, whan men breken þat masse in smale peces.
And sum tyme it happeneth þat men fynden summe as grete
as a pese, and summe lasse; and þei ben als harde as þo of
Ynde.

And all be it þat men fynden gode dyamandes in Ynde, 50
ȝit natheles men fynden hem more comounly vpon the roches
in the see, and vpon hilles where the myne of gold is. And þei
growen many togedre, on lytill, another gret. And þer ben
summe of the gretnesse of a bene, and summe als grete as an
hasell-note. And þei ben square and poynted of here owne 55
kynde, boþe abouen and benethen, withouten worchinge of
mannes hond.

And þei growen togedre, male and femele. And þei ben norysscht with the dew of heuene. And þei engendren
60 comounly, and bryngen forth smale children, þat multiplyen and growen all the ȝeer. I haue often tymes assayed þat ȝif a man kepe hem with a lityll of the roche, and wete hem with May dew oftesithes, þei schull growe eueryche ȝeer; and the smale wole wexen grete. For right as the fyn perl congeleth
65 and wexeth gret of the dew of heuene, right so doth the verray dyamand; and right as the perl, of his owne kynde, taketh roundnesse, right so the dyamand, be vertu of God, taketh squarenesse.

And men schall bere the dyamaund on his left syde; for
70 it is of grettere vertue þanne, þan on the right syde. For the strengthe of here growynge is toward the North, þat is the left syde of the world, and the left partie of man is, whan he turneth his face toward the Est.

And ȝif ȝou lyke to knowe the vertues of þe dyamand, as
75 men may fynden in þe Lapidarye, þat many men knowen noght, I schall telle ȝou, as þei beȝonde the see seyn and affermen, of whom all science and all philosophie cometh from.

He þat bereth the dyamand vpon him, it ȝeueth him hardy-
80 nesse and manhode, and it kepeth the lemes of his body hole. It ȝeueth him victorye of his enemyes, in plee and in werre, ȝif his cause be rightfull; and it kepeth him þat bereth it in gode wytt; and it kepeth him fro strif and ryot, fro euyll sweuenes, from sorwes, and from enchauntementes, and from fantasyes
85 and illusiouns of wykked spirites. And ȝif ony cursed wycche or enchauntour wolde bewycche him þat bereth the dyamand, all þat sorwe and myschance schall turne to himself, þorgh vertue of þat ston. And also no wylde best dar assaylle the man þat bereth it on him. Also the dyamand scholde ben
90 ȝouen frely, withouten coueytynge, and withouten byggynge; and þan it is of grettere vertue. And it maketh a man more

strong and more sad aȝenst his enemyes. And it heleth him þat is lunatyk, and hem þat the fend pursueth or trauayleth. And ȝif venym or poysoun be brought in presence of the dyamand, anon it begynneth to wexe moyst, and for to 95 swete.

Þere ben also dyamandes in Ynde þat ben clept 'violastres', —for here colour is liche vyolet, or more browne þan the violettes,—þat ben full harde and full precyous. But ȝit sum men loue not hem so wel as the oþere. But in soth to 100 me, I wolde louen hem als moche as þe oþere; for I haue seen hem assayed. Also þere is anoþer maner of dyamandes þat ben als white as cristall, but þei ben a lityll more trouble; and þei ben gode and of gret vertue, and all þei ben square and poynted of here owne kynde. And summe 105 ben six squared, summe four squared, and summe þre, as nature schapeth hem.

And þerfore whan grete lordes and knyghtes gon to seche worschipe in armes, þei beren gladly the dyamaund vpon hem. I schal speke a litill more of the dyamandes, allþough 110 I tarye my matere for a tyme, to þat ende þat þei þat knowen hem not be not disceyued be gabberes þat gon be the contree, þat sellen hem. For whoso wil bye the dyamand, it is nede-full to him þat he knowe hem, because þat men counterfeten hem often of cristall þat is ȝalow; and of saphires of cytryne 115 colour, þat is ȝalow also; and of the saphire loupe; and of many oþer stones. But, I tell ȝou, theise contrefetes ben not so harde; and also the poyntes wil breken lightly; and men may esily pollissche hem. But summe werkmen, for malice, wil not pollische hem, to þat entent to maken men beleue þat þei may 120 not ben pollisscht. But men may assaye hem in this manere: First schere with hem, or write with hem, in saphires, in cristall, or in oþer precious stones. After þat men taken the ademand, þat is the schipmannes ston, þat draweth the nedle to him, and men leyn the dyamand vpon the ademand, and leyn the nedle 125

before the ademand; and ȝif the dyamand be gode and vertuous, the ademand draweth not the nedle to him, whils the dyamand is þere present. And this is the preef þat þei beȝonde the see maken. Natheles it befalleth often tyme þat the gode dyamand
130 leseth his vertue, be synne and for incontynence of him þat bereth it. And þanne is it nedfull to make it to recoueren his vertue aȝen, or ell it is of litill value.

Chap. xxvi (xxx), f. 112 a.

Now schall I seye ȝou sewyngly of contrees and yles þat
135 ben beȝonde the contrees þat I haue spoken of. Wherfore I seye ȝou, in passynge be the lond of Cathaye toward the high Ynde, and toward Bacharye, men passen be a kyngdom þat men clepen 'Caldilhe', þat is a full fair contré. And bere groweth a maner of fruyt, as þough it weren gowrdes;
140 and whan þei ben rype, men kutten hem ato, and men fynden withinne a lytyll best, in flesch, in bon, and blode as þough it were a lytill lomb, withouten wolle. And men eten bothe the frut and the best: and þat is a gret merueylle. Of þat frute I haue eten, allþough it were wondirfull: but þat I knowe wel,
145 þat God is merueyllous in his werkes. And natheles I tolde hem of als gret a merueyle to hem, þat is amonges vs: and þat was of the Bernakes. For I tolde hem þat in oure contree weren trees þat baren a fruyt þat becomen briddes fleeynge; and þo þat fellen in the water lyuen; and þei þat fallen on the erthe
150 dyen anon; and þei ben right gode to mannes mete. And hereof had þei als gret meruaylle þat summe of hem trowed it were an inpossible thing to be. In þat contré ben longe apples of gode sauour, whereof ben mo þan an hundred in a clustre, and als manye in another: and þei han grete longe leves and
155 large, of two fote long or more. And in þat contree, and in oþer contrees þere abouten, growen many trees, þat beren clowe gylofres, and notemuges, and grete notes of Ynde, and of canell, and of many oþer spices. And þere ben vynes þat beren so grete grapes þat a strong man scholde haue

ynow to done for to bere o clustre with all the grapes. In 160
þat same regioun ben the mountaynes of Caspye þat men
clepen 'Vber' in the contree. Betwene þo mountaynes the
Iewes of ten lynages ben enclosed, þat men clepen Goth and
Magoth; and þei mowe not gon out on no syde. Þere weren
enclosed twenty two kynges with hire peple, þat dwelleden 165
betwene the mountaynes of Syŧhye. Þere Kyng Alisandre
chacede hem betwene þo mountaynes; and þere he thoughte
for to enclose hem þorgh werk of his men. But whan he
saugh þat he myghte not don it, ne bryng it to an ende, he
preyed to God of Nature þat He wolde parforme þat þat he 170
had begonne. And all were it so þat he was a payneme,
and not worthi to ben herd, ȝit God of His grace closed the
mountaynes togydre; so þat þei dwellen þere, all faste
ylokked and enclosed with high mountaynes alle aboute, saf
only on o syde; and on þat syde is the See of Caspye. Now 175
may sum men asken: sith þat the see is on þat o syde, wherfore
go þei not out on the see syde, for to go where þat hem lyketh?
But to this questioun I schal answere: þat See of Caspye goth
out be londe, vnder the mountaynes, and renneth be the desert
at o syde of the contree; and after it streccheth vnto the endes 180
of Persie. And allþough it be clept a see, it is no see, ne
it toucheth to non oþer see; but it is a lake, the grettest of the
world. And þough þei wolden putten hem into þat see, þei
ne wysten neuer where þat þei scholde arryuen. And also
þei conen no langage but only hire owne, þat no man 185
knoweth but þei: and þerfore mowe þei not gon out. And
also ȝee schull vnderstonde þat the Iewes han no propre
lond of hire owne, for to dwellen inne, in all the world, but
only þat lond betwene the mountaynes. And ȝit þei ȝelden
tribute for þat lond to the queen of Amazoine, the whiche þat 190
maketh hem to ben kept in cloos full diligently, þat þei schull
not gon out on no syde, but be the cost of hire lond. For
hire lond marcheth to þo mountaynes. And often it hath

befallen þat summe of þe Iewes han gon vp the mountaynes,
95 and avaled down to the valeyes : but gret nombre of folk ne
may not do so.   For the mountaynes ben so hye, and so
streght vp, þat þei moste abyde þere, maugree hire myght.
For þei mowe not gon out, but be a litill issue þat was
made be strengthe of men ; and it lasteth wel a four grete
200 myle.   And after is þere ȝit a lond all desert, where men
may fynde no water, ne for dyggynge, ne for non other þing :
wherfore men may not dwellen in þat place.   So is it full of
dragounes, of serpentes, and of oþer venymous bestes, þat no
man dar not passe, but ȝif it be be strong wynter.   And þat
205 streyt passage men clepen in þat contree 'Clyron'.   And þat
is the passage þat the Queen of Amazoine maketh to ben kept.
And þogh it happene sum of hem, be fortune, to gon out,
þei conen no maner of langage but Ebrew, so þat þei can
not speke to the peple.   And ȝit natheles, men seyn þei schull
210 gon out in the tyme of Antecrist, and þat þei schull maken
gret slaughter of Cristene men.   And þerfore all the Iewes
þat dwellen in all londes lernen allweys to speken Ebrew,
in hope þat whan the oþer Iewes schull gon out, þat þei may
vnderstonden hire speche, and to leden hem into Cristendom,
215 for to destroye the Cristene peple.   For the Iewes seyn þat
þei knowen wel be hire prophecyes þat þei of Caspye schull
gon out and spreden þorghout all the world ; and þat the
Cristene men schull ben vnder hire subieccioun als longe as
þei han ben in subieccioun of hem.   And ȝif þat ȝee wil wyte
220 how þat þei schull fynden hire weye, after þat I haue herd
seye, I schall tell ȝou.   In the tyme of Antecrist, a fox
schall make þere his †traynet†, and mynen an hole, where
Kyng Alisandre leet make the ȝates : and so longe he schall
mynen and percen the erthe, til þat he schall passe þorgh
225 towardes þat folk.   And whan þei seen the fox, they schull
haue gret merueylle of him, because þat þei saugh neuer
such a best.   For of all oþere bestes þei han enclosed

amonges hem, saf only the fox. And þanne þei schulle
chacen him and pursuen him so streyte, till þat he come to
the same place þat he cam fro.   And þanne þei schulle 230
dyggen and mynen so strongly, till þat þei fynden the ȝates
þat King Alisandre leet make of grete stones and passynge
huge, wel symented and made stronge for the maystrie. And
þo ȝates þei schull breken, and so gon out, be fyndynge of
þat issue.   235

Fro þat lond gon men toward the lond of Bacharie, where
ben full yuele folk and full cruell.   In þat lond ben trees þat
beren wolle, as þogh it were of scheep; whereof men maken
clothes, and all þing þat may ben made of wolle.   In þat
contree ben many ipotaynes, þat dwellen som tyme in the 240
water, and somtyme on the lond: and þei ben half man and
half hors, as I haue seyd before; and þei eten men, whan þei
may take hem.   And þere ben ryueres and watres þat ben
fulle byttere, þree sithes more þan is the water of the see.   In
þat contré ben many griffounes, more plentee þan in ony 245
other contree.   Sum men seyn þat þei han the body vpward
as an egle, and benethe as a lyoun: and treuly þei seyn soth
þat þei ben of þat schapp.   But o griffoun hath the body more
gret, and is more strong, þanne eight lyouns, of suche lyouns
as ben o this half; and more gret and strongere þan an 250
hundred egles, suche as we han amonges vs.   For o griffoun
þere wil bere fleynge to his nest a gret hors, ȝif he may fynde
him at the poynt, or two oxen ȝoked togidere, as þei gon at the
plowgh.   For he hath his talouns so longe and so large and grete
vpon his feet, as þough þei weren hornes of grete oxen, or of 255
bugles, or of kyȝn; so þat men maken cuppes of hem, to drynken
of.   And of hire ribbes, and of the pennes of hire wenges, men
maken bowes full stronge, to schote with arwes and quarell.

From þens gon men be many iourneyes þorgh the lond of
Prestre Iohn, the grete emperour of Ynde.   And men clepen 260
his roialme the Yle of Pentexoire.

EPILOGUE.

Þere ben manye oþer dyuerse contrees and manye oþer
merueyles beȝonde, þat I haue not seen: wherfore of hem
I can not speke propurly, to tell ȝou the manere of hem.
265 And also in the contrees where I haue ben, ben manye
mo dyuersitees of many wondirfull thinges þanne I make
mencioun of, for it were to longe thing to deuyse ȝou the
manere.   And þerfore þat þat I haue deuysed ȝou of certeyn
contrees, þat I haue spoken of before, I beseche ȝoure worthi
270 and excellent noblesse þat iſ suffise to ȝou at this tyme.   For
ȝif þat I deuysed ȝou all þat is beȝonde the see, another man
peraunter, þat wolde peynen him and trauaylle his body for
to go into þo marches for to encerche þo contrees, myghte
ben blamed be my wordes, in rehercynge manye straunge
275 thinges; for he myghte not seye no thing of newe, in the
whiche the hereres myghten hauen ouþer solace or desport or
lust or lykyng in the herynge.   For men seyn allweys þat
newe thinges and newe tydynges ben plesant to here.
Wherfore I wole holde me stille, withouten ony more rehercyng
280 of dyuersiteeȝ or of meruaylles þat ben beȝonde, to þat entent
and ende þat whoso wil gon into þo contrees, he schall
fynde ynowe to speke of, þat I haue not touched of in no
wyse.

And ȝee schull vndirstonde, ȝif it lyke ȝou, þat at myn
285 hom comynge I cam to Rome, and schewed my lif to oure
holy fadir the Pope, and was assoylled of all þat lay in my
conscience, of many a dyuerse greuous poynt, as men mosten
nedes þat ben in company, dwellyng amonges so many
a dyuerse folk of dyuerse secte and of beleeve, as I haue ben.
290 And amonges all, I schewed hym this tretys, þat I had made
after informacioun of men þat knewen of thinges þat I had
not seen myself; and also of merueyles and customes þat
I hadde seen myself, as fer as God wolde ȝeue me grace:

and besoughte his holy fadirhode þat my boke myghte ben examyned and corrected be avys of his wyse and discreet conseill. And oure holy fader, of his special grace, remytted my boke to ben examyned and preued be the avys of his seyd conseill. Be the whiche my boke was preeued for trewe; in so moche þat þei schewed me a boke, þat my boke was examynde by, þat comprehended full moche more be an hundred part; be the whiche the *Mappa Mundi* was made after. And so my boke (all be it þat many men ne list not to ȝeue credence to no þing, but to þat þat þei seen with hire eye, ne be the auctour ne the persone neuer so trewe) is affermed and preued be oure holy fader, in maner and forme as I haue seyd.

And I Iohn Maundevyll knyght aboueseyd, (allþough I be vnworthi) þat departed from oure contrees and passed the see the ȝeer of grace 1322, þat haue passed many londes and manye yles and contrees, and cerched manye full strange places, and haue ben in many a full gode honourable companye, and at many a faire dede of armes, all be it þat I dide none myself, for myn vnable insuffisance; and now I am comen hom, mawgree myself, to reste, for gowtes artetykes þat me distreynen, þat diffynen the ende of my labour, aȝenst my will, God knoweth. And þus takynge solace in my wrechched reste, recordynge the tyme passed, I haue fulfilled þeise thinges and putte hem wryten in this boke, as it wolde come into my mynde, the ȝeer of grace 1356 in the 34th ȝeer þat I departede from oure contrees. Wherfore I preye to all the rederes and hereres of this boke, ȝif it plese hem, þat þei wolde preyen to God for me, and I schall preye for hem. And alle þo þat seyn for me a *Paternoster*, with an *Aue Maria*, þat God forȝeue me my synnes, I make hem parteneres and graunte hem part of all the gode pilgrymages, and of all the gode dedes þat I haue don, ȝif ony ben to his plesance; and noght only of þo, but of all þat euere I schall

do vnto my lyfes ende. And I beseche Almyghty God,
fro whom all godenesse and grace cometh fro, þat He
330 vouchesaf of His excellent mercy and habundant grace to
fullfylle hire soules with inspiracioun of the Holy Gost, in
makynge defence of all hire gostly enemyes here in erthe,
to hire saluacioun, bothe of body and soule ; to worschipe and
thankynge of Him þat is þree and on, withouten begynnynge
335 and withouten endyng ; þat is withouten qualitee good,
withouten quantytee gret ; þat in alle places is present, and
all thinges conteynynge ; the whiche þat no goodnesse may
amende, ne non euell empeyre ; þat in perfyte Trynytee
lyueth and regneth God, be alle worldes and be all tymes.
340 Amen, Amen, Amen.

X

THE BRUCE

Written in 1375 by JOHN BARBOUR.

John Barbour was archdeacon of Aberdeen, an auditor of the Scottish exchequer, and a royal pensioner. Consequently a number of isolated records of his activities have been preserved. In 1364 he was granted a safe-conduct to travel with four students to Oxford. In 1365 and 1368 he had permission to travel through England so that he might study in France. The notices of his journeys, his offices, and his rewards point to a busy and successful life. He died in 1395.

According to Wyntoun, Barbour's works were (1) *The Bruce*; (2) *The Stewartis Oryginalle* (or *Pedigree of the Stewarts*), now lost; (3) a *Brut*, which some have identified with extant fragments of a Troy Book (see the prefatory note to No. VII), and others with (2) *The Stewartis Oryginalle*.

The Bruce is found in two late MSS., both copied by John Ramsay; the first, St. John's College, Cambridge, MS. G 23, in the year 1487; the second, now at the Advocates' Library, Edinburgh, in 1489. It has been edited by Skeat for the Early English Text Society, and for the Scottish Text Society. The poem is valuable for the history, more especially the traditional history, of the period 1304–33. Barbour speaks of it as a romance, and the freedom and vividness of the narrative, with its hero-worship of Robert Bruce and Douglas, place it well above the ordinary chronicle. But far from disclaiming historical accuracy, Barbour prides himself that truth well told should have a double claim to popularity:

> Storys to rede ar delitabill
> Suppos that thai be nocht bot fabill:
> Than suld storys that suthfast wer,
> And thai war said on gud maner,

> Hawe doubill plesance in heryng :
> The fyrst plesance is the carpyng,
> And the tothir the suthfastnes,
> That schawys the thing rycht as it wes.

He did not misjudge the taste of his country, and *The Bruce*, with which the Scottish contribution to English literature begins, long held its place as the national epic of Scotland.

The specimen describes an incident in the unsuccessful siege of Berwick, 1319, after five quiet days.

THE BRUCE, Bk. xvii, ll. 593 ff.

St. John's College (Cambridge) MS. G 23 (A. D. 1487).

> Thai ⟨that⟩ at the sege lay,
> Or it wes passit the fift day,
> Had maid thame syndry apparale
> To gang eftsonis till assale.
> Of gret gestis ane sow thai maid   5
> That stalward heling owth it had,
> With armyt men enew tharin,
> And instrumentis als for to myne.
> Syndry scaffatis thai maid vithall
> That war weill hyar than the wall,   10
> And ordanit als that by the se
> The toune suld weill assalȝeit be.
>
> And thai vithin that saw thame swa
> So gret apparale schap till ma,
> Throu Cra*bb*is consale, that ves sle,   15
> Ane cren thai haf gert dres vp hye,
> Rynand on quhelis, that thai mycht bring
> It quhar neid war of mast helping.
> And pik and ter als haf thai tane,
> And lynt ⟨and⟩ hardis, with brynstane,   20
> And dry treis that weill wald byrne,
> And mellit syne athir othir in ;

15 Crabbis] Craggis *MS.* : Crabys *MS. Edinburgh.*

And gret flaggatis tharof thai maid,
Gyrdit with irnebandis braid;
Of thai flaggatis mycht mesurit be   25
Till a gret twnnys quantité.
Thai flaggatis, byrnand in a baill,
With thair cren thoucht thai till availl,
And, gif the sow come to the wall,
Till lat thame byrnand on hir fall,   30
And with ane stark cheyne hald thame thar
Quhill all war brint ⟨vp⟩ that ves thar.

  Engynys alsua for till cast
Thai ordanit and maid redy fast,
And set ilk man syne till his ward;   35
And Schir Valter, the gude Steward,
With armyt men suld ryde about,
And se quhar at thar var mast dout,
And succur thar with his menʒhe.

  And quhen thai into sic degré   40
Had maid thame for thair assaling,
On the Rude-evyn in the dawing.
The Inglis host blew till assale.
Than mycht men with ser apparale
Se that gret host cum sturdely.   45
The toune enveremyt thai in hy,
And assalit with sa gud will, —
For all thair mycht thai set thartill,—
That thai thame pressit fast of the toune.
Bot thai that can thame abandoune   50
Till ded, or than till woundis sare,
So weill has thame defendit thare
That ledderis to the ground thai slang,
And vith stanys so fast thai dang
Thair fais, that feill thai left lyand,   55
Sum ded, sum hurt, and sum swavnand.

Bot thai that held on fut in hy
Drew thame avay deliuerly,
And skunnyrrit tharfor na kyn thing,
Bot went stoutly till assalyng ;   60
And thai abovin defendit ay,
And set thame till so harde assay,
Quhill that feill of thame voundit war,
And thai so gret defens maid thar,
That thai styntit thair fais mycht.   65
Apon sic maner can thai ficht
Quhill it wes neir noyne of the day.

   Than thai without, in gret aray,
Pressit thair sow toward the wall ;
And thai within weill soyne gert call   70
The engynour that takyne was,
And gret manans till him mais,
And swoir that he suld de, bot he
Provit on the sow sic sutelté
That he tofruschyt hir ilke deill.   75
And he, that has persauit weill
That the dede wes neir hym till,
Bot gif he mycht fulfill thar will,
Thoucht that he all his mycht vald do :
Bendit in gret hy than wes scho,   80
And till the sow wes soyn evin set.
In hye he gert draw the cleket,
And smertly swappit out the stane,
That evyn out our the sow is gane,
And behynd hir a litill we   85
It fell, and than thai cryit hye
That war in hir : 'Furth to the wall,
For dreid⟨les⟩ it is ouris all.'

63 Quhill] How *MS.*   64 And] þat *MS.*   75 tofruschyt]
till frusche *MS.*

The engynour than deliuerly
Gert bend the gyne in full gret hy,   90
And the stane smertly swappit out.
It flaw ⟨out⟩ quhedirand with a rout,
And fell richt evin befor the sow.
Thair hertis than begouth till grow,
Bot ȝeit than with thair mychtis all   95
Thai pressit the sow toward the wall,
And has hir set thar*to* iuntly.

The gynour than gert bend in hy
The gyne, and swappit out the stane,
That evin toward the lift is gane,   100
And with gret wecht syne duschit doune
Richt by the wall, in a randoune,
That hyt the sow in sic maner
That it that wes the mast summer,
And starkast for till stynt a strak,   105
In swndir with that dusche he brak.
The men ran out in full gret hy,
And on the wallis thai can cry
That 'thair sow ferryit wes thair !'

Iohne Crab, that had his geir all ȝar,   110
In his faggatis has set the fyre,
And our the wall syne can thame wyre,
And brynt the sow till brandis bair.

With all this fast assalȝeand war
The folk without, with felloune ficht ;   115
And thai within with mekill mycht
Defendit manfully thar stede
Intill gret auentur of dede.
The schipmen with gret apparale
Com with thair schippes till assale,   120
With top-castellis warnist weill,

97 tharto] þar in *MS.*

And wicht men armyt intill steill;
Thair batis vp apon thair mastis
Drawyn weill hye and festnyt fast is,
And pressit with that gret atour   125
Toward the wall.   Bot the gynour
Hit in ane hespyne with a stane,
And the men that war tharin gane
Sum dede, *sum* dosnyt, ⟨come doun⟩ vyndland.
Fra thine furth durst nane tak vpon hand   130
With schippes pres thame to the vall.

    But the laiff war assalȝeand all
On ilk a syde sa egyrly,
That certis it wes gret ferly
That thai folk sic defens has maid,   135
For the gret myscheif that thai had:
For thair wallis so law than weir
That a man richt weill with a sper
Micht strik ane othir vp in the face,
As eir befor tald till ȝow was;   140
And feill of thame war woundit sare,
And the layf so fast travaland war
That nane had tume rest for till ta,
Thair aduersouris assailȝeit swa.
Thai war within sa stratly stad   145
That thar wardane with *him* had
Ane hundreth men in cumpany
Armyt, that wicht war and hardy,
And raid about for till se quhar
That his folk hardest pressit war,   150
Till releif thame that had mister,
Com syndry tymes in placis ser
Quhar sum of the defensouris war
All dede, and othir woundit sare,

129 Sum dede dosnyt sum dede vyndland *MS.*   146 him] þame *MS.*

Swa that he of his cumpany   155
Behufit to leiff thair party;
Swa that, be he ane cours had maid
About, *of* all *the* men he had
Thair wes levit with him bot ane,
That he ne had thame left ilkane   160
To releve quhar he saw mister.
    And the folk that assalȝeand wer
At Mary-ȝet behevin had
The barras, and a fyre had maid
At the drawbrig, and brynt it doune.   165
And war thringand in gret foysoune
Richt in the ȝet, ane fire till ma.
And thai within gert smertly ga
Ane to the wardane, for till say
How thai war set in hard assay.   170
And quhen Schir Valter Steward herd
How men sa stratly with thame ferd,
He gert cum of the castell then
All that war thar of armyt men,—
For thar that day assalȝeit nane,—   175
And with that rout in hy is gane
Till Mary-ȝet, and till the wall
Is went, and saw the myscheif all,
And vmbethoucht hym suddandly,
Bot gif gret help war set in hy   180
Tharto, thai suld burne vp the ȝet
With the fire *he* fand tharat.
    Tharfor apon gret hardyment
He suddanly set his entent,
And gert all wyde set vp the ȝet,   185
And the fyre that he fand tharat

158 of] to *MS.*   the] to *MS.*   182 With] And *MS.*   he fand]
haffand *MS.*

With strinth of men he put avay.
He set hym in full hard assay,
For thai that war assalȝeand thar
Pressit on hym with vapnys bair,   190
And he defendit with all his mycht.

    Thar mycht men se a felloune fieht :
With staffing, stoking, and striking
Thar maid thai sturdy defending,
For with gret strynth of men the ȝet   195
Thai defendit, and stude tharat,
Magré thair fais, quhill the nycht
Gert thame on bath halfis leif the ficht.

XI

JOHN WICLIF

D. 1384.

Like Richard Rolle, Wiclif was a Yorkshireman by birth. Of
his career at Oxford little is known until 1360, when he is
described as 'master of Balliol'. From Balliol he was presented
to the living of Fillingham, and, after a series of preferments, he
accepted in 1374 the rectory of Lutterworth, which he held till
his death in 1384.

Wiclif's life was stormy. His acknowledged pre-eminence as
a theologian and doctor in the University did not satisfy his active
and combative mind. 'False peace', he said, 'is grounded in
rest with our enemies, when we assent to them without with-
standing; and sword against such peace came Christ to send.'
He lacked neither enemies nor the moral courage to withstand
them.

At first, under the powerful patronage of John of Gaunt, he
entered into controversies primarily political, opposing the right
of the Pope to make levies on England, which was already over-
burdened with war-taxation, and to appoint foreigners to English
benefices. On these questions popular opinion was on his side.

He proceeded to attack the whole system of Church government, urging disendowment; rejecting the papal authority, which
had been weakened in 1378 by the fierce rivalry of Urban VI
and Clement VII; attacking episcopal privileges, the established religious orders, and the abuse of indulgences, pardons,
and sanctuary. Still his opinions found a good deal of popular
and political support.

Then in 1380 he publicly announced his rejection of the doctrine of transubstantiation. From the results of such a heresy
his friends could no longer protect him. Moderate opinion
became alarmed and conservative after the Peasants' Revolt of
1381. Richard II was no friend of heretics. John of Gaunt,
himself unpopular by this time, commanded silence. And in 1382

the secular party in Oxford were compelled, after a struggle, to condemn and expel their favourite preacher and his followers. Wiclif retired to Lutterworth, and continued, until struck down by paralysis in the last days of 1384, to inspire his 'poor preachers'—the founders of the Lollard sect which lived on to join forces with Lutheranism in the sixteenth century—and to develop in a series of Latin and English works the doctrines that later came to be associated with Puritanism.

His authorship is often doubtful. In the interests of orthodoxy the early MSS. of his writings were ruthlessly destroyed, as in the famous bonfire of his works at Carfax, Oxford, in 1411. And his followers included not only the simple folk from whom later the 'poor priests' were recruited, but able University men, trained in his new doctrines, bred in the same traditions, and eager to emulate their master in controversy. So his share in the famous Wiclif Bible (ed. Forshall and Madden, Oxford 1850) is still uncertain. Part of the translation seems to have been made by Nicholas of Hereford, and a later recension is claimed for another Oxford disciple, John Purvey. But Wiclif probably inspired the undertaking, for to him, as to the later Puritans, the word of the Bible was the test by which all matters of belief, ritual, and Church government must be tried; and he was particularly anxious, in opposition to the established clergy and the friars, that laymen should read it in their own language. Contemporaries, friend and foe, ascribe the actual translation to him. John Huss, the Bohemian reformer, who was martyred in 1416 for teaching Wiclif's doctrines, states that Wiclif 'translated all the Bible into English'. Arundel, Archbishop of Canterbury, is equally positive when he writes to the Pope in 1412 that 'the son of the Old Serpent filled up the cup of his malice against Holy Church by the device of a new translation of the Scriptures into his native tongue'.

The first selection, chapter xv of the *De Officio Pastorali* (ed. Matthew, pp. 429 f.), states the case for translation : see Workman's *Wyclif*, ii. p. 329. In the second (ed. Matthew, pp. 188 ff.) some essential points of Wiclif's teaching are explained.

In abuse of his opponents he maintains the sturdy tradition of controversy that still survives in Milton's prose. The style

is rugged and vigorous; the thought logical and packed close.
And it is easy to see the source of his strength. In an age
whose evils were patent to all, many reproved this or that
particular abuse, but the system as a whole passed unchallenged.
Wiclif, almost alone in his generation, had the reasoning power
to go to the root of the matter, and the moral courage not only
to state fearlessly what, rightly or wrongly, he found to be the
source of evil, but to insist on basic reform. It is difficult
nowadays, when modern curiosity has made familiar the practice
of mining among the foundations of beliefs, society, and government, to realize the force of authority that was ranged against
unorthodox reformers in the fourteenth century. If the popular
support he received indicates that this force was already
weakening, Wiclif must still be reckoned among the greatest of
those who broke the way for the modern world.

A. THE TRANSLATION OF THE BIBLE.

De Officio Pastorali, chap. xv.

MS. Ashburnham XXVII (15th century).

ANT heere þe freris wiþ þer fautours seyn þat it is heresye
to write þus Goddis lawe in English, and make it knowun to
lewid men. And fourty signes þat þey bringen for to shewe an
heretik ben not worþy to reherse, for nouȝt groundiþ hem but
nygromansye.   5

It semyþ first þat þe wit of Goddis lawe shulde be tauȝt in
þat tunge þat is more knowun, for þis wit is Goddis word.
Whanne Crist seiþ in þe Gospel þat boþe heuene and erþe
shulen passe, but His wordis shulen not passe, He vndirstondith
bi His woordis His wit. And þus Goddis wit is Hooly Writ, 10
þat may on no maner be fals. Also þe Hooly Gost ȝaf to
apostlis wit at Wit Sunday for to knowe al maner langagis, to
teche þe puple Goddis lawe þerby ; and so God wolde þat þe
puple were tauȝt Goddis lawe in dyuerse tungis. But what
man, on Goddis half, shulde reuerse Goddis ordenaunse and 15
His wille ?

And for þis cause Seynt Ierom trauelide and translatide þe
Bible fro dyuerse tungis into Lateyn, þat it myȝte be aftir
translatid to oþere tungis. And þus Crist and His apostlis
20 tauȝten þe puple in þat tunge þat was moost knowun to þe
puple. Why shulden not men do nou so?

And herfore autours of þe newe law, þat weren apostlis of
Iesu Crist, writen þer Gospels in dyuerse tungis þat weren
more knowun to þe puple.

25 Also þe worþy reume of Fraunse, notwiþstondinge alle
lettingis, haþ translatid þe Bible and þe Gospels, wiþ oþere
trewe sentensis of doctours, out of Lateyn into Freynsch.
Why shulden not Engliȝschemen do so? As lordis of
Englond han þe Bible in Freynsch, so it were not aȝenus
30 resoun þat þey hadden þe same sentense in Engliȝsch; for
þus Goddis lawe wolde be betere knowun, and more trowid,
for onehed of wit, and more acord be bitwixe reumes.

And herfore freris han tauȝt in Englond þe Paternoster in
Engliȝsch tunge, as men seyen in þe pley of ȝork, and in
35 many oþere cuntreys. Siþen þe Paternoster is part of Matheus
Gospel, as clerkis knowen, why may not al be turnyd to
Engliȝsch trewely, as is þis part? Specialy siþen alle Cristen
men, lerid and lewid, þat shulen be sauyd, moten algatis sue
Crist, and knowe His lore and His lif. But þe comyns of
40 Engliȝschmen knowen it best in þer modir tunge; and þus it
were al oon to lette siche knowing of þe Gospel and to lette
Engliȝschmen to sue Crist and come to heuene.

Wel y woot defaute may be in vntrewe translating, as
myȝten haue be many defautis in turnyng fro Ebreu into
45 Greu, and fro Greu into Lateyn, and from o langage into
anoþer. But lyue men good lif, and studie many persones
Goddis lawe, and whanne chaungyng of wit is foundun,
amende þey it as resoun wole.

Sum men seyn þat freris trauelen, and þer fautours, in þis
50 cause for þre chesouns, þat y wole not aferme, but God woot

wher þey ben soþe. First þey wolden be seun so nedeful to
þe Engliȝschmen of oure reume þat singulerly in her wit layȝ
þe wit of Goddis lawe, to telle þe puple Goddis lawe on what
maner euere þey wolden. And þe secound cause herof is
seyd to stonde in þis sentense : freris wolden lede þe puple in 55
techinge hem Goddis lawe, and þus þei wolden teche sum,
and sum hide, and docke sum. For þanne defautis in þer lif
shulden be lesse knowun to þe puple, and Goddis lawe shulde
be vntreweliere knowun boþe bi clerkis and bi comyns. Þe
þridde cause þat men aspien stondiþ in þis, as þey seyn : alle 60
þes newe ordris dreden hem þat þer synne shulde be knowun,
and hou þei ben not groundid in God to come into þe chirche ;
and þus þey wolden not for drede þat Goddis lawe were
knowun in Engliȝsch ; but þey myȝten putte heresye on men
ȝif Engliȝsch toolde not what þey seyden.   65

God moue lordis and bischops to stonde for knowing of
His lawe !

B. OF FEIGNED CONTEMPLATIVE LIFE.

Corpus Christi College (Cambridge) MS. 296 (1375–1400), p. 165.

OF feyned contemplatif lif, of song, of þe Ordynal of
Salisbury, and of bodely almes and worldly bysynesse of
prestis ; hou bi þes foure þe fend lettiþ hem fro prechynge
of þe Gospel.—

First, whanne trewe men techen bi Goddis lawe wit and 5
reson, þat eche prest owiþ to do his myȝt, his wit, and his
wille to preche Cristis Gospel, þe fend blyndiþ ypocritis to
excuse hem by feyned contemplatif lif, and to seie þat, siþ it
is þe beste, and þei may not do boþe togidre, þei ben nedid
for charité of God to leue þe prechynge of þe Gospel, and 10
lyuen in contemplacion.

7 fend] fendis *MS*.

See nowe þe ypocrisie of þis false seiynge. Crist tauȝt and dide þe beste lif for prestis, as oure feiþ techiþ, siþ He was God and myȝte not erre. But Crist preched þe Gospel, and
15 charged alle His apostlis and disciplis to goo and preche þe Gospel to alle men. Þan it is þe beste lif for prestis in þis world to preche þe Gospel.

Also God in þe olde lawe techiþ þat þe office of a prophete is to schewe to þe peple here foule synnys. But eche prest
20 is a prophete bi his ordre, as Gregory seyþ vpon þe Gospellis. Þanne it is þe office of eche prest to preche and telle þe synnys of þe peple ; and in þis manere schal eche prest be an aungel of God, as Holy Writt seiþ.

Also Crist and Ion Baptist leften desert and precheden þe
25 Gospel to here deþ þerfore ; and þis was most charité ; for ellis þei weren out of charité, or peierid in charité, þat myȝte not be in hem boþe, siþ þe ton was God, and no man after Crist was holyere þan Baptist, and he synned not for þis prechynge.

Also þe holy prophete Ieromye, halwid in his moder
30 wombe, myȝtte not be excused fro prechynge bi his con-templacion, but chargid of God to preche þe synnes of þe peple, and suffre peyne þerfore, and so weren alle þe pro-phetis of God.

A Lord ! siþ Crist and Ion Baptist and alle þe prophetis of
35 God weren nedid bi charité to come out of desert to preche to þe peple, and leue here sol⟨it⟩arie preiere, hou dore we fonnyd heretikys seie þat it is betre to be stille, and preie oure owen fonnyd ordynaunce, þan to preche Cristis Gospel ?

Lord ! what cursed spirit of lesyngis stiriþ prestis to close
40 hem in stonys or wallis for al here lif, siþ Crist comaundiþ to alle His apostlis and prestis to goo into alle þe world and preche þe Gospel. Certis þei ben opyn foolis, and don pleynly aȝenst Cristis Gospel ; and, ȝif þei meyntenen þis errour, þei ben cursed of ⟨God⟩, and ben perilous ypocritis and
45 heretikis also. And siþ men ben holden heretikis þat done

aȝenst þe popis lawe, ⟨and þe beste part of þe popis lawe⟩ seiþ pleynly þat eche þat comeþ to presthod takiþ þe office of a bedele, or criere, to goo bifore Domesday to crie to þe peple here synnes and vengaunce of God, whi ben not þo prestis heretikis þat leuen to preche Cristis Gospel, and 50 compelle oþere treue men to leue prechynge of þe Gospel? Siþ þis lawe is Seynt Gregoryes lawe, groundid opynly in Goddis lawe and reson and charité; and oþere lawes of þe peple ben contrarie to Holy Writt and reson and charité, for to meyntene pride and coueitise of Anticristis worldly clerkis. 55

But ypocritis allegen þe Gospel,—þat Magdaleyne chees to hereself þe beste part whanne she saat bisiden Cristis feet and herde His word. Soþ it is þat þis meke sittynge and deuout herynge of Cristis wordis was best to Magdeleyne, for sche hadde not office of prechynge as prestis han, siþ sche was 60 a womman, þat hadde not auctorité of Goddis lawe to teche and preche opynly. But what is þis dede to prestis, þat han expresse þe comaundement of God and men to preche þe Gospel? Where þei wolen alle be wommen in ydelnesse, and suen not Iesu Crist in lif and prechynge þe Gospel, þat 65 He comandiþ Hymself boþe in þe olde lawe and newe?

Also þis pesible herynge of Cristis word and brennynge loue þat Magdeleyne hadde was þe beste part, for it schal be ende in heuene of good lif in þis world. But in þis *world* þe beste lif for prestis is holy lif in kepynge Goddis hestis, and 70 trewe prechynge of þe Gospel, as Crist dide, and chargid alle His prestis to do ⟨þe same⟩. And þes ypocritis wenen þat here dremys and fantasies of hemself ben contemplacion, and þat prechynge of þe Gospel be actif lif; and so þei menen þat Crist tok þe worse lif for þis world, and nedid alle His prestis 75 to leue þe betre and take þe worse lif; and þus þes fonnyd ypocritis putten errour in Iesu Crist. But who ben more heretikis?

66 þe] þo *MS.*   67 pesible] posible *MS.*   69 world] lii *MS.*

Also þes blynde ypocritis alleggen þat Crist biddiþ vs preie
80 euermore, and Poul biddiþ þat we preie wiþoute lettynge, and
þan we prestis may not preche, as þei feynen falsly. But
here þes ypocritis schullen wite þat Crist and Poul vnderstonden of preiere of holy lif, þat eche man doþ as longe as
he dwelliþ in charité; and not of babelynge of lippis, þat no
85 man may euere do wiþouten cessynge; for ellis no man in þis
world myȝte fulfille þe comaundement of Crist; and þis techiþ
Austyn and oþere seyntis.

And siþ men þat fulfillen not Goddis lawe, and ben out of
charité, ben not acceptid in here preiynge of lippis,—for here
90 preiere in lippis is abhomynable, as Holy Writt seiþ bi
Salomon,—þes prestis þat prechen not þe Gospel, as Crist
biddiþ, ben not able to prele ⟨God⟩ for mercy, but disceyuen
hemself and þe peple, and dispisen God, and stiren Hym to
wraþþe and vengaunce, as Austyn and Gregory and oþere
95 seyntis techen.

And principaly þes ypocritis þat han rentes, and worldly
lordischipes, and parische chirchis approprid to hem, aȝenst
Holy Writt boþe old and newe, by symonye and lesyngis *on*
Crist and His apostelis, for stynkynge gronyngys and abite of
100 holynesse, and *for* distroiynge of Goddis ordynaunce, and for
singuler profession maade to foolis and, in cas, to fendis of
helle,—þes foolis schullen lerne what is actif lif and contemplatif bi Goddis lawe, and þanne þei myȝtten wite þat þei
han neiþer þe ton ne þe toiþer, siþ þei chargen more veyn
105 statutis *of* synful men, and, in cas, ⟨of⟩ deuelys, þan þei
chargen þe heste of God, and werkis of mercy, and poyntis
of charité. And þe fende blyndiþ hem so moche, þat þei seyn
indede þat þei moten neuere preie to p*l*esynge of God, siþ þei
vnablen hemself to do þe office of prestis bi Goddis lawe, and
110 purposen to ende in here feyned deuocion, þat is blasphemye
to God.

98 on] & *MS.*   100 for (1st)] fro *MS.*   105 of (1st)] & *MS.*
108 plesynge] preisynge *MS. altered later.*

Also bi song þe fend lettiþ men to studie and preche þe
Gospel; for siþ mannys wittis ben of certeyn mesure and
myȝt, þe more þat þei ben occupied aboute siche mannus
song, þe lesse moten þei be sette aboute Goddis lawe. For 115
þis stiriþ men to pride, and iolité, and oþere synnys, and so
vnableþ hem many gatis to vnderstonde and kepe Holy
Writt, þat techeþ mekenesse, mornynge for oure synnys and
oþere mennus, and stable lif, and charité. And ȝit God in all
þe lawe of grace chargiþ not siche song, but deuocion in 120
herte, trewe techynge, and holy spekynge in tonge, and goode
werkis, and holy lastynge in charité and mekenesse. But
mannus foly and pride stieþ vp euere more and more in þis
veyn nouelrie.

First men ordeyned songe of mornynge whanne þei weren 125
in prison, for techynge of þe Gospel, as Ambrose, *as* men
seyn, to putte awey ydelnesse, and to be not vnoccupied in
goode manere for þe tyme. And þat songe and our⟨e⟩ acordiþ
not, for oure stiriþ to iolité and pride, and here stiriþ to
mornynge, and to dwelle lenger in wordis of Goddis lawe. 130
Þan were matynys, and masse, and euensong, *placebo* and
dirige, and comendacion, and matynes of Oure Lady, ordeyned
of synful men to be songen wiþ heiȝe criynge, to lette men
fro þe sentence and vnderstondynge of þat þat was þus
songen, and to maken men wery, and vndisposid to studie 135
Goddis lawe for akyng of hedis. And of schort tyme þanne
⟨weren⟩ more veyn iapis founden : deschaunt, countre note,
and orgon, and smale brekynge, þat stiriþ veyn men to
daunsynge more þan ⟨to⟩ mornynge ; and herefore ben many
proude lorelis founden and dowid wiþ temperal and worldly 140
lordischipis and gret cost. But þes foolis schulden drede þe
scharpe wordis of Austyn, þat seiþ: 'As oft as þe song likiþ
me more þan doþ þe sentence þat is songen, so oft I confesse
þat I synne greuously.'

126 as (2nd)] and *MS.*   128 oure] oþer *MS.*

145   And ȝif þes knackeris excusen hem bi song in þe olde lawe,
seie þat Crist, þat best kepte þe olde lawe as it schulde be
aftirward, tauȝt not ne chargid vs wiþ sich bodely song, ne ony
of His apostlis, but wiþ deuocion in herte, and holy lif, and
trewe prechynge, and þat is ynowþȝ and þe beste.   But who
150 schulde þanne charge vs wiþ more, oure þe fredom and
liȝtnesse of Cristis lawe?

And ȝif þei seyn þat angelis heryen God bi song in heuene,
seie þat we kunnen not þat song ; but þei ben in ful victorie
of here enemys, and we ben in perilous bataíle, and in þe
155 valeye of wepynge and mornynge ; and oure song lettiþ vs
fro betre occupacion, and stiriþ vs to many grete synnes, and
to forȝete vs self.

But oure flecshly peple haþ more lykynge in here bodely
eris in sich knackynge and taterynge, þan in herynge of
160 Goddis lawe, and spekynge of þe blisse of heuene; for þei
wolen hire proude prestis and oþere lorelis þus to knacke
notis for many markis and poundis.   But þei wolen not ȝeue
here almes to prestis and children to lerne and teche
Goddis lawe.   And þus, bi þis nouelrie of song, is Goddis
165 lawe vnstudied and not kepte, and pride and oþere grete
synnys meyntenyd.

And þes fonnyd lordis and peple gessen to haue more þank
of God, and ⟨to⟩ worschipe Hym more, in haldynge vp of
here owen nouelries wiþ grete cost, þan in lernynge, and
170 techynge, and meyntenynge of his lawe, and his seruauntis,
and his ordynaunce.   But where is more disceit in feiþ, hope
and charité?   For whanne þer ben fourty or fyfty in a queer,
þre or foure proude lorellis schullen knacke þe most deuout
seruyce þat no man schal here þe sentence, and alle oþere
175 schullen be doumbe, and loken on hem as foolis.   And þanne
strumpatis and þeuys preisen Sire Iacke, or Hobbe, and
Williem þe proude clerk, hou smale þei knacken here notis;

154 bataile] baitale *MS.*

and seyn þat þei seruen wel God and Holy Chirche, whanne
þei dispisen God in His face, and letten oþere Cristene men of
here deuocion and compunccion, and stiren hem to worldly 180
vanyté.   And þus trewe seruyce of God is lettid, and þis veyn
knackynge for oure iolité and pride is preised abouen þe mone.

Also þe Ordynalle of Salisbury lettiþ moche prechynge of
þe Gospel ; for folis chargen þat more þan þe maundementis
of God, and to studie and teche Cristis Gospel.   For ȝif 185
a man faile in his Ordynale, men holden þat grete synne, and
reprouen hym þerof faste ; but ȝif a preste breke þe hestis of
God, men chargen þat litel or nouȝt.   And so ȝif prestis seyn
here matynes, masse, and euensong aftir Salisbury vsse, þei
hemself and oþere men demen it is ynowȝ, þouþ þei neiþer 190
preche ne teche þe hestis of God and þe Gospel.   And þus
þei wenen þat it is ynowȝ to fulfille synful mennus ordynaunce,
and to leue þe riȝtfulleste ordynaunce of God, þat He chargid
prestis to performe.

But, Lord ! what was prestis office ordeyned bi God bifore 195
þat Salisbury vss was maad of proude prestis, coueitous
and dronkelewe ?   Where God, þat dampneþ alle ydelnesse,
chargid hem not at þe ful wiþ þe beste occupacion for hemself and oþere men ?   Hou doren synful folis chargen Cristis
prestis wiþ so moche nouelrie, and euermore cloute more to, 200
þat þei may not frely do Goddis ordynaunce ?   For þe Iewis
in þe olde lawe haden not so manye serymonyes of sacrifices
ordeyned bi God as prestis han now riȝttis and reulis maade
of synful men   And ȝit þe olde lawe in þes charious customes
mosten nedes cesse for fredom of Cristis Gospel.   But þis 205
fredom is more don awei bi þis nouelrie þan bi customes of
þe olde lawe.   And þus many grete axen where a prest may,
wiþouten dedly synne, seie his masse wiþouten matynys ; and
þei demen it dedly synne a prest to fulfille þe ordynaunce of
God in his fredom, wiþoute nouelrie of synful men, þat lettiþ 210

prestis fro þe betre occupacion ; as ʒif þei demen it dedly synne
to leue þe worse þing, and take þe betre, whanne þei may not
do boþe togidre.

And þus, Lord! Þin owen ordynaunce þat þou madist for
215 þi prestis is holden errour, and distroied for þe fonnyd nouelrie
of synful foolis, and, in cas, of fendis in helle.

But here men moste be war þat vnder colour of þis fredom
þei ben betre occupied in þe lawe of God to studie it and teche
it, and not slouʒ ne ydel in ouermoche sleep, and vanyté, and
220 oþer synnes, for þat is þe fendis panter.

See now þe blyndnesse of þes foolis. Þei seyn þat a prest
may be excused fro seiynge of masse, þat God comaundid
Himself to þe substance þerof, so þat he here on. But he
schal not be excused but ʒif he seie matynes and euensong
225 himself, þat synful men han ordeyned ; and þus þei chargen
more here owene fyndynge þan Cristis comaundement.

A Lord ! ʒif alle þe studie and traueile þat men han now
abowte Salisbury vss, wiþ multitude *of* newe costy portos,
antifeners, graielis, and alle oþere bokis, weren turned into
230 makynge of biblis, and in studiynge and techynge þerof, hou
moche schulde Goddis lawe be forþered, and knowen, and
kept, and now in so moche it is hyndrid, vnstudied, and
vnkept. Lord ! hou schulden riche men ben excused þat
costen so moche in grete schapellis, and costy bokis of mannus
235 ordynaunce, for fame and nobleie of þe world, and wolen not
spende so moche aboute bokis of Goddis lawe, and for to
studie hem and teche hem : siþ þis were wiþoute comparison
betre on alle siddis, and lyʒttere, and sykerere ?

But ʒit men þat knowen þe fredom of Goddis ordynaunce
240 for prestis to be þe beste, wiþ grete sorow of herte seyn here
matynes, masse, and euensong, whanne þei schulden ellis be
betre occupied, last þei sclaundren þe sike conscience of here
breþeren, þat ʒit knowen not Goddis lawe. God brynge þes

228 of] & *M.S.*

prestis to þe fredom to studie Holy Writt, and lyue þerafter,
and teche it oþer men frely, and to preie as long and as 245
moche as God meueþ hem þerto, and ellis turne to oþere
medeful werkis, as Crist and His apostlis diden; and þat þei
ben not constreyned to blabre alle day wiþ tonge and grete
criynge, as pies and iaies, þing þat þei knowen not, and to
peiere here owen soule for defaute of wis deuocion and charité! 250

Also bysynesse of worldly occupacion of prestis lettiþ
prechynge of þe Gospel, for þei ben so besy ⟨þer⟩aboute, and
namely in herte, þat þei þenken litel on Goddis lawe, and han
no sauour þerto. And seyn þat þei don þus for hospitalité,
and to releue pore men wiþ dedis of charité. But, hou euere 255
men speken, it his for here owen couetise, and lustful lif in
mete and drynk and precious cloþis, and for name of þe world
in fedynge of riche men; and litel or nouȝt comeþ frely to
pore men þat han most nede.

But þes prestis schulden sue Crist in manere of lif and 260
trewe techynge. But Crist lefte sich occupacion, and His
apostlis also, and weren betre occupied in holy preiere and
trewe techynge of þe Gospel. And þis determinacion and ful
sentence was ȝouen of alle þe apostlis togidre, whanne þei
hadden resceyued þe plenteuous ȝiftis of þe Holy Gost. Lord! 265
where þes worldly prestis ⟨ben⟩ wisere þan ben alle þe apostlis
of Crist? It semeth þat þei ben, or ellis ⟨þei ben⟩ fooles.

Also Crist wolde not take þe kyngdom whan þe puple
wolde haue maad Him kyng, as Iones Gospel telleþ. But if
it haade be a prestis office to dele aboute þus bodi⟨ly⟩ almes, 270
Crist, þat coude best haue do þis office, wolde haue take þes
temperal goodis to dele hem among poeuere men. But He
wolde not do þus, but fley, and took no man of þe aposteles
wiþ him, so faste He hiede. Lord! where worldly prestis
kunnen bettere don þis partinge of worldly goodis *þan* Iesu 275
Crist?

And ȝif þei seyn þat Crist fedde þe puple in desert with bodily almes, manye þousand, as þe Gospel saiþ : þat dide
180 Crist by miracle, to shewe His godhede, and to teche prestes houȝ þei schulden fede gostly Cristene men by Goddis word. For so dide Cristis aposteles, and hadde not whereof to do bodily almes, whan þei miȝten haue had tresour and iuelis ynowe of kynggis and lordis.

185 Also Peter saiþ in Dedis of Apostlis to a pore man þat to him neiþer was gold ne siluer ; and ȝit he performede wel þe office of a trewe prest.   But oure prestis ben so bysye aboute worldly occupacioun þat þei semen bettere bailyues or reues þan gostly prestis of Iesu Crist.   For what man is so bysy
190 aboute marchaundise, and oþere worldly doyngis, as ben preostes, þat shulden ben lyȝt of heuenly lif to alle men abouten hem ?

But certes þei shulde be as bysy aboute studyinge of Goddys lawe, and holy preyer, not of *Famulorum*, but of holy
195 desires, and clene meditacioun of God, and trewe techinge of þe Gospel, as ben laboreris aboute worldly labour for here sustenaunce.   And muche more bysie, ȝif þei miȝten, for þey ben more holden for to lyue wel, and ⟨ȝeue⟩ ensaumple of holi lif to þe puple, and trewe techinge of Holy Writ, þanne þe
300 people is holden to ȝyue hem dymes or offringis or ony bodily almes.   And þerfore prestis shulde not leue ensaumple of good lif, and studyinge of Holi Writ, and trewe techinge þerof, ne ⟨for⟩ bodily almes, ne for worldly goodis, ne for sauynge of here bodily lif.

305 And as Crist sauede þe world by writynge and techinge of foure Euaungelistis, so þe fend casteþ to dampne þe world and prestis for lettynge to preche þe Gospel by þes foure : by feyned contemplacioun, by song, by Salisbury vse. and by worldly bysynes of prestis.

310 God for His mercy styre þes prestis to preche þe Gospel in word, in lif ; and be war of Sathanas disceitis.   Amen.

XII

JOHN GOWER

D. 1408.

John Gower, a Londoner himself, came of a good Kentish family. Chaucer must have known him well, for he chose him as his attorney when leaving for the Continent in 1378, and, with the dedication of *Troilus and Criseyde*, labelled him for ever as 'moral Gower'. Gower's marriage with Agnes Groundolf, probably a second marriage, is recorded in 1398. Blindness came on him a few years later. His will, dated August 15, 1408, was proved on October 24, 1408, so that his death must fall between those two points. By his own wish he was buried in St. Saviour's, Southwark, the church of the canons of St. Mary Overy, to whom he was a liberal benefactor.

On his tomb in St. Saviour's Church, Gower is shown with his head resting on three great volumes, representing his principal works—the *Speculum Meditantis*, the *Vox Clamantis*, and the *Confessio Amantis*.

The *Speculum Meditantis*, or *Mirour de l'Omme*, is a handbook of sins and sinners, written in French.

The *Vox Clamantis*, written in Latin, covers similar ground. Opening with a vision of the Peasants' Revolt of 1381, the poet passes in review the faults of the different grades of society—clergy, nobles, labourers, traders, lawyers—and ends with an admonition to the young King Richard II.

In his English work, the *Confessio Amantis*, he expressly abandons the task of setting the world to rights, and promises to change his style henceforth. Now he will sing of Love. The machinery of the poem is suggested by the great source of mediaeval conventions, the *Roman de la Rose*. On a May morning the poet, a victim of love, wanders afield and meets the

Queen of Love (cp. the beginning of Chaucer's *Legend of Good Women*). She bids him confess to her priest Genius. Genius hears the confession, sustaining with some incongruity the triple rôle of high priest of Love, Christian moralist, and entertainer— for it is he who tells the stories which, woven about the frame- work of the Seven Deadly Sins, make the real matter of the poem.

The first form of the *Confessio* was completed in 1390. It con- tains a Prologue in which the suggestion for the poem is ascribed to Richard II, and an Epilogue in his praise. In this version the Queen of Love at parting gives Gower a message for Chaucer :

> And gret wel Chaucer whan ye mete,
> As mi disciple and mi poete :
> For in the floures of his youthe
> In sondri wise, as he wel couthe,
> Of ditees and of songes glade,
> The whiche he for mi sake made,
> The lond fulfild is overal.
> Wherof to him in special
> Above alle othre I am most holde.
> Forthi now, in hise daies olde,
> Thow schalt him telle this message,
> That he upon his latere age,
> To sette an ende of alle his werk,
> As he which is myn owne clerk,
> Do make his testament of love,
> As thou hast do thi schrifte above,
> So that mi Court it mai recorde.

In the final form, completed in 1392–3, Richard's name dis- appears from the Prologue; the dedication to his popular rival, Henry of Lancaster, is made prominent ; the eulogy in the Epilogue is dropped ; and with it the compliment to Chaucer. Whether this last omission is due to chance, or to some change in the relations between the two poets, is not clear.

In his own day Gower was ranked with Chaucer. His reputa- tion was still high among the Elizabethans ; and he has the dis- tinction of appearing as Chorus in a Shakespearian play—*Pericles* —of which his story of *Apollonius of Tyre*, in Bk. viii of the *Con- fessio*, was the immediate source.

A selection gives a very favourable impression of his work. He has a perfect command of the octosyllabic couplet ; an easy style, well suited to narrative ; and a classic simplicity of expression for which the work of his predecessors in Middle English leaves us unprepared. Throughout the whole of the *Confessio Amantis*, more than 30,000 lines, the level of workmanship is remarkable, and almost every page shows some graceful and poetical verses.

Yet the poem as a whole suffers from the fault that Gower tried to avoid:

> It dulleth ofte a mannes wit
> To him that schal it aldai rede.

One defect, obvious to a modern reader, would hardly be noticed by his contemporaries : he often incorporates in his poetry matter proper only to an encyclopaedia, such as the discourse on the religions of the world in Bk. v, or that on Philosophy in Bk. vii. Another is more radical: for all his wide reading, his leading ideas lack originality. It is hardly a travesty to say that the teaching of his works amounts to this : ' In the moral world, avoid the Seven Deadly Sins in the five sub-classifications of each ; in the political world keep your degree without presuming '. Such a negative and conventional message cannot sustain the fabric of three long poems. Their polished and facile moralizing becomes almost exasperating if it be remembered that the poet wrote when a whole system of society was falling, and falling noisily, about him. Modern taste rejects Gower the moralist and political writer, and his claim to present as apart from historical value rests on the delightful single stories which served as embroidery to his serious themes.

The extracts are taken from the admirable edition by G. C. Macaulay : ' The Works of John Gower ', 4 vols., Oxford 1899–1902.

A. CEIX AND ALCEONE.

From Bk. iv, ll. 2927 ff.

THIS finde I write in Poesie :
Ceïx the king of Trocinie
Hadde Alceone to his wif,
Which as hire oghne hertes lif

Him loveth; and he hadde also   5
A brother, which was cleped tho
Dedalion, and he per cas
Fro kinde of man forschape was
Into a goshauk of liknesse;
Wherof the king gret hevynesse   10
Hath take, and thoghte in his corage
To gon upon a pelrinage
Into a strange regioun,
Wher he hath his devocioun
To don his sacrifice and preie,   15
If that he mihte in eny weie
Toward the goddes finde grace
His brother hele to pourchace,
So that he mihte be reformed
Of that he hadde be transformed.   20

     To this pourpos and to this ende
This king is redy for to wende,
As he which wolde go be schipe;
And for to don him felaschipe
His wif unto the see him broghte,   25
With al hire herte and him besoghte
That he the time hire wolde sein
Whan that he thoghte come aȝein:
'Withinne,' he seith, ' tuo monthe day.
And thus in al the haste he may   30
He tok his leve, and forth he seileth,
Wepende and sche hirself beweileth,
And torneth hom, ther sche cam fro.

     Bot whan the monthes were ago,
The whiche he sette of his comynge,   35
And that sche herde no tydinge,
Ther was no care for to seche:
Wherof the goddes to beseche

Tho sche began in many wise,
And to Iuno hire sacrifise   40
Above alle othre most sche dede,
And for hir lord sche hath so bede
To wite and knowe hou that he ferde,
That Iuno the goddesse hire herde,
Anon and upon this matiere   45
Sche bad Yris hir messagere
To Slepes hous that ⟨sc⟩he schal wende,
And bidde him that he make an ende,
Be swevene and schewen al the cas
Unto this ladi, hou it was.   50

This Yris, fro the hihe stage
Which undertake hath the message,
Hire reyny cope dede upon,
The which was wonderli begon
With colours of diverse hewe,   55
An hundred mo than men it knewe;
The hevene lich unto a bowe
Sche bende, and so she cam doun lowe,
The god of Slep wher that sche fond;
And that was in a strange lond,   60
Which marcheth upon Chymerie:
For ther, as seith the Poesie,
The God of Slep hath mad his hous,
Which of entaille is merveilous.

Under an hell ther is a cave,   65
Which of the sonne mai noght have,
So that noman mai knowe ariht
The point betwen the dai and nyht:
Ther is no fyr, ther is no sparke,
Ther is no dore, which mai charke,   70
Wherof an yhe scholde unschette,
So that inward ther is no lette.

And for to speke of that withoute,
Ther stant no gret tree nyh aboute
Wher on ther myhte crowe or pie   75
Alihte, for to clepe or crie;
Ther is no cok to crowe day,
Ne beste non which noise may;
The hell bot al aboute round
Ther is growende upon the ground   80
Popi, which berth the sed of slep,
With othre herbes suche an hep.
A stille water for the nones
Rennende upon the smale stones,
Which hihte of Lethes the rivere,   85
Under that hell in such manere
Ther is, which ȝifth gret appetit
To slepe.   And thus full of delit
Slep hath his hous; and of his couche
Withinne his chambre if I schal touche,   90
Of hebenus that slepi tree
The bordes al aboute be,
And for he scholde slepe softe,
Upon a fethrebed alofte
He lith with many a pilwe of doun.   95
The chambre is strowed up and doun
With swevenes many thousendfold.
     Thus cam Yris into this hold,
And to the bedd, which is al blak,
Sche goth, and ther with Slep sche spak,   100
And in the wise as sche was bede
The message of Iuno sche dede.
Ful ofte hir wordes sche reherceth,
Er sche his slepi eres perceth;
With mochel wo bot ate laste   105
His slombrende yhen he upcaste

And seide hir that it schal be do.
   Wherof among a thousend tho
Withinne his hous that slepi were,
In special he ches out there   110
Thre, whiche scholden do this dede :
The ferste of hem, so as I rede,
Was Morpheüs, the whos nature
Is for to take the figure
Of what persone that him liketh,   115
Wherof that he ful ofte entriketh
The lif which slepe schal be nyhte ;
And Ithecus that other hihte,
Which hath the vois of every soun,
The chiere and the condicioun   120
Of every lif, what so it is :
The thridde suiende after this
Is Panthasas, which may transforme
Of every thing the rihte forme,
And change it in an other kinde.   125
Upon hem thre, so as I finde,
Of swevenes stant al thapparence,
Which other while is evidence,
And other while bot a iape.
   Bot natheles it is so schape,   130
That Morpheüs be nyht al one
Appiereth until Alceone
In liknesse of hir housebonde
Al naked ded upon the stronde,
And hou he dreynte in special   135
These othre tuo it schewen al :
The tempeste of the blake cloude,
The wode see, the wyndes loude,
Al this sche mette, and sih him dyen ;
Wherof that sche began to crien,   140

Slepende abedde ther sche lay,
And with that noise of hire affray
Hir wommen sterten up aboute,
Whiche of here ladi were in doute,
And axen hire hou that sche ferde;   145
And sche, riht as sche syh and herde,
Hir swevene hath told hem everydel:
And thei it halsen alle wel
And sein it is a tokne of goode.

Bot til sche wiste hou that it stode,   150
Sche hath no confort in hire herte,
Upon the morwe and up sche sterte,
And to the see, wher that sche mette
The bodi lay, withoute lette
Sche drowh, and whan that sche cam nyh,   155
Stark ded, hise armes sprad, sche syh
Hire lord flietende upon the wawe.
Wherof hire wittes ben withdrawe,
And sche, which tok of deth no kepe,
Anon forth lepte into the depe   160
And wolde have cawht him in hire arm.

This infortune of double harm
The goddes fro the hevene above
Behielde, and for the trowthe of love,
Which in this worthi ladi stod,   165
Thei have upon the salte flod
Hire dreinte lord and hire also
Fro deth to lyve torned so
That thei ben schapen into briddes
Swimmende upon the wawe amiddes.   170
And whan sche sih hire lord livende
In liknesse of a bridd swimmende,
And sche was of the same sort,
So as sche mihte do desport,

Upon the ioie which sche hadde 171
Hire wynges bothe abrod sche spradde,
And him, so as sche mai suffise,
Beclipte and keste in such a wise,
As sche was whilom wont to do :
Hire wynges for hire armes tuo 180
Sche tok, and for hire lippes softe
Hire harde bile, and so ful ofte
Sche fondeth in hire briddes forme,
If that sche mihte hirself conforme
To do the plesance of a wif, 185
As sche dede in that other lif :
For thogh sche hadde hir pouer lore,
Hir will stod as it was tofore,
And serveth him so as sche mai.

Wherof into this ilke day 190
Togedre upon the see thei wone,
Wher many a dowhter and a sone
Thei bringen forth of briddes kinde ;
And for men scholden take in mynde
This Alceoun the trewe queene, 195
Hire briddes ʒit, as it is seene,
Of Alceoun the name bere.

B. ADRIAN AND BARDUS.

From Bk. v, ll. 4937 ff.

To speke of an unkinde man,
I finde hou whilom Adrian,
Of Rome which a gret lord was,
Upon a day as he per cas
To wode in his huntinge wente, 5
It hapneth at a soudein wente,

After his chace as he poursuieth,
Thurgh happ, the which noman eschuieth,
He fell unwar into a pet,
Wher that it mihte noght be let.   10
The pet was dep and he fell lowe,
That of his men non myhte knowe
Wher he becam, for non was nyh
Which of his fall the meschief syh.

   And thus al one ther he lay   · 15
Clepende and criende al the day
 For socour and deliverance,
Til a3ein eve it fell per chance,
A while er it began to nyhte,
A povere man, which Bardus hihte,   20
Cam forth walkende with his asse,
And hadde gadred him a tasse
Of grene stickes and of dreie
To selle, who that wolde hem beie,
As he which hadde no liflode,   25
Bot whanne he myhte such a lode
To toune with his asse carie.
And as it fell him for to tarie
That ilke time nyh the pet,
And hath the trusse faste knet,   30
He herde a vois, which cride dimme,
And he his ere to the brimme
Hath leid, and herde it was a man,
Which seide, ‘ Ha, help hier Adrian,
And I wol 3iven half mi good.’   35

   The povere man this understod,
As he that wolde gladly winne,
And to this lord which was withinne
He spak and seide, ‘ If I thee save,
What sikernesse schal I have   40

Of covenant, that afterward
Thou wolt me ȝive such reward
As thou behihtest nou tofore ? '

That other hath his othes swore
Be hevene and be the goddes alle, 45
If that it myhte so befalle
That he out of the pet him broghte,
Of all the goodes whiche he oghte
He schal have evene halvendel.

This Bardus seide he wolde wel; 50
And with this word his asse anon
He let untrusse, and therupon
Doun goth the corde into the pet,
To which he hath at the ende knet
A staf, wherby, he seide, he wolde 55
That Adrian him scholde holde.
Bot it was tho per chance falle,
Into that pet was also falle
An ape, which at thilke throwe,
Whan that the corde cam doun lowe, 60
Al sodeinli therto he skipte
And it in bothe hise armes clipte.
And Bardus with his asse anon
Him hath updrawe, and he is gon.
But whan he sih it was an ape, 65
He wende al hadde ben a iape
Of faierie, and sore him dradde :
And Adrian eftsone gradde
For help, and cride and preide faste,
And he eftsone his corde caste ; 70
Bot whan it cam unto the grounde,
A gret serpent it hath bewounde,
The which Bardus anon up drouh.
And thanne him thoghte wel ynouh

It was fantosme, bot yit he herde   75
The vois, and he therto ansuerde,
'What wiht art thou in Goddes name?
   'I am,' quod Adrian, 'the same,
Whos good thou schalt have evene half.'
Quod Bardus, 'Thanne a Goddes half   80
The thridde time assaie I schal':
And caste his corde forth withal
Into the pet, and whan it cam
To him, this lord of Rome it nam,
And therupon him hath adresced,   85
And with his hand ful ofte blessed,
And thanne he bad to Bardus hale.
And he, which understod his tale,
Betwen him and his asse, al softe,
Hath drawe and set him up alofte   90
Withouten harm, al esely.
   He seith noght ones 'grant merci,'
Bot strauhte him forth to the cité,
And let this povere Bardus be.
And natheles this simple man   95
His covenant, so as he can,
Hath axed; and that other seide,
If so be that he him umbreide
Of oght that hath be speke or do,
It schal ben venged on him so,   100
That him were betre to be ded.
   And he can tho non other red,
But on his asse aȝein he caste
His trusse, and hieth homward faste:
And whan that he cam hom to bedde,   105
He tolde his wif hou that he spedde.
Bot finaly to speke oght more
Unto this lord he dradde him sore.

So that a word ne dorste he sein.

    And thus upon the morwe aȝein, 110
In the manere as I recorde,
Forth with his asse and with his corde
To gadre wode, as he dede er,
He goth ; and whan that he cam ner
Unto the place where he wolde, 115
He hath his ape anon beholde,
Which hadde gadred al aboute
Of stickes hiere and there a route,
And leide hem redy to his hond,
Wherof he made his trosse and bond. 120
Fro dai to dai and in this wise
This ape profreth his servise,
So that he hadde of wode ynouh.

    Upon a time and as he drouh
Toward the wode, he sih besyde 125
The grete gastli serpent glyde,
Til that sche cam in his presence,
And in hir kinde a reverence
Sche hath him do, and forth withal
A ston mor briht than a cristall 130
Out of hir mouth tofore his weie
Sche let doun falle, and wente aweie
For that he schal noght ben adrad.
Tho was this povere Bardus glad,
Thonkende God and to the ston 135
He goth and takth it up anon,
And hath gret wonder in his wit
Hou that the beste him hath aquit,
Wher that the mannes sone hath failed,
For whom he hadde most travailed. 140

    Bot al he putte in Goddes hond,
And torneth hom, and what he fond

Unto his wif he hath it schewed;
And thei, that weren bothe lewed,
Acorden that he scholde it selle.   145
And he no lengere wolde duelle,
Bot forth anon upon the tale
The ston he profreth to the sale;
And riht as he himself it sette,
The iueler anon forth fette   150
The gold and made his paiement ;
Therof was no delaiement.

   Thus whan this ston was boght and sold,
Homward with ioie manyfold
This Bardus goth; and whan he cam   155
Hom to his hous and that he nam
His gold out of his purs, withinne
He fond his ston also therinne,
Wherof for ioie his herte pleide,
Unto his wif and thus he seide,   160
'Lo, hier my gold, lo, hier mi ston!'
His wif hath wonder therupon,
And axeth him hou that mai be.
'Nou, be mi trouthe! I not,' quod he,
'Bot I dar swere upon a bok   165
That to my marchant I it tok,
And he it hadde whan I wente:
So knowe I noght to what entente
It is nou hier, bot it be grace.
Forthi tomorwe in other place   170
I wole it fonde for to selle,
And if it wol noght with him duelle,
Bot crepe into mi purs aȝein,
Than dar I saufly swere and sein
It is the vertu of the ston.'   175

   The morwe cam, and he is gon

To seche aboute in other stede
His ston to selle, and he so dede,
And lefte it with his chapman there.
Bot whan that he cam elleswhere 180
In presence of his wif at hom,
Out of his purs and that he nom
His gold, he fond his ston withal.
And thus it fell him overal,
Where he it solde in sondri place, 185
Such was the fortune and the grace.

Bot so wel may nothing ben hidd,
That it nys ate laste kidd:
This fame goth aboute Rome
So ferforth that the wordes come 190
To themperour Iustinian;
And he let sende for the man,
And axede him hou that it was.
And Bardus tolde him al the cas,
Hou that the worm and ek the beste, 195
Althogh thei maden no beheste,
His travail hadden wel aquit;
Bot he which hadde a mannes wit,
And made his covenant be mouthe,
And swor therto al that he couthe, 200
To parte and ʒiven half his good,
Hath nou forʒete hou that it stod,
As he which wol no trouthe holde.

This Emperour al that he tolde
Hath herd, and thilke unkindenesse 205
He seide he wolde himself redresse.
And thus in court of iuggement
This Adrian was thanne assent,
And the querele in audience
Declared was in the presence 210

Of themperour and many mo;
Wherof was mochel speche tho
And gret wondringe among the press.
    Bot ate laste natheles
For the partie which hath pleigned   215
The lawe hath diemed and ordeigned
Be hem that were avised wel,
That he schal have the halvendel
Thurghout of Adrianes good.

    And thus of thilke unkinde blod   220
Stant the memoire into this day,
Wherof that every wys man may
Ensamplen him, and take in mynde
What schame it is to ben unkinde;
Aȝein the which reson debateth,   225
And every creature it hateth.

XIII

JOHN OF TREVISA'S TRANSLATION OF
HIGDEN'S POLYCHRONICON

1387.

Ranulph Higden (d. 1364) was a monk of St. Werburgh's at
Chester, and has been doubtfully identified with the 'Randal
Higden' who is said to have travelled to Rome to get the Pope's
consent to the acting of the Chester miracle plays in English.

His *Polychronicon*, so called because it is the chronicle of many
ages, is a compilation covering the period from the Creation to
1352. In the fourteenth and fifteenth centuries it was the
favourite universal history ; and the First Book, which deals with
general geography, has still a special interest for the light it
throws on the state of knowledge in Chaucer's day.

Two English prose translations are known : Trevisa's, completed in 1387, and modernized and printed by Caxton in 1482 ;
and an anonymous rendering made in the second quarter of the
fifteenth century. Both are printed, with Higden's Latin, in the
edition by Babington and Lumby, Rolls Series, 9 vols., 1865–86.

John of Trevisa was a Cornishman. He was a fellow of Exeter
College, Oxford, from 1362 to 1365 ; and was one of those expelled
from Queen's College for 'unworthiness' in 1379. He became
vicar of Berkeley, and at the request of Sir Thomas Berkeley
undertook the translation of the *Polychronicon*. In 1398 he
brought to an end another long work, the translation of *Bartholomaeus de Proprietatibus Rerum*, the great encyclopaedia of natural
science at this time. He died at Berkeley in 1402.

Trevisa was a diligent but not an accurate or graceful trans-

lator. He rarely adds anything from his own knowledge, though
we have an example in the account of the reform of teaching at
Oxford while he was there. The interest of his work depends
chiefly on the curiosity of some passages in his originals.

A. THE MARVELS OF BRITAIN.

Chap. xlii.

MS. Tiberius D. vii (about 1400), f. 39 a.

In Brytayn buþ hoot welles wel arayed and yhyȝt to þe vse
of mankunde. Mayster of þulke welles ys þe gret spyryt of
Minerua. Yn hys hous fuyr duyreþ alwey, þat neuer
chaungeþ into askes, bote þar þe fuyr slakeþ, hyt changeþ
5 ynto stony clottes.

Yn Brytayn buþ meny wondres. Noþeles foure buþ most
wonderfol. Þe furste ys at Pectoun. Þar bloweþ so strong
a wynd out of þe chenes of þe eorþe þat hyt casteþ vp aȝe
cloþes þat me casteþ yn. Þe secunde ys at Stonhenge
10 bysydes Salesbury. Þar gret stones and wondur huge buþ
arered an hyȝ, as hyt were ȝates, so þat þar semeþ ȝates
yset apon oþer ȝates. Noþeles hyt ys noȝt clerlych yknowe
noþer parceyuet houȝ and wharfore a buþ so arered and
so wonderlych yhonged. Þe þridde ys at Cherdhol. Þer
15 ys gret holwenes vndur eorþe. Ofte meny men habbeþ
ybe þerynne, and ywalked aboute wiþynne, and yseye ryuers
and streemes, bote nowhar conneþ hy fynde non ende. Þe
feurþe ys þat reyn ys yseye arered vp of þe hulles, and anon
yspronge aboute yn þe feeldes. Also þer ys a gret pond þat
20 conteyneþ þre score ylondes couenable for men to dwelle
ynne. Þat pound ys byclypped aboute wiþ six score rooches.
Apon euerych rooch ys an egle hys nest; and þre score
ryuers eorneþ into þat pound, and non of ham alle eorneþ
into þe se, bot on. Þar ys a pound yclosed aboute wiþ a wal
25 of tyyl and of ston. Yn þat pound men wascheþ and baþeþ

wel ofte, and euerych man feeleþ þe water hoot oþer cold
ryȝt as a wol hymsylf. Þar buþ also salt welles fer fram þe
se, and buþ salt al þe woke long forto Saturday noon, and
fersch fram Saturday noon forto Moneday. Þe water of þis
welles, whanne hyt ys ysode, turneþ into smal salt, fayr and 30
whyyt. Also þar ys a pond þe water þerof haþ wondur
worchyng, for þey al an ost stood by þe pond, and turnede
þe face þyderward, þe water wolde drawe ⟨hem⟩ vyolentlych
toward þe pond, and weete al here cloþes. So scholde hors
be drawe yn þe same wyse. Bote ȝef þe face ys aweyward 35
fram þe water, þe water noyeþ noȝt. Þer ys a welle ⟨þat⟩ non
streem eorneþ þarfram noþer þerto, and ȝet four maner fysch
buþ ytake þarynne. Þat welle ys bote twenty foot long, and
twenty foot brood, and noȝt deop bote to þe kneo, and
ys yclosed wiþ hyȝ bankkes in euerych syde. 40

Yn þe contray aboute Wynchestre ys a den. Out of þat
den alwey bloweþ a strong wynd, so þat no man may endure
for to stonde tofor þat den. Þar ys also a pond þat turneþ
tre into yre and hyt be þerynne al a ȝer, and so tren buþ
yschape into whestones. Also þer ys yn þe cop of an hul 45
a buryel. Euerych man þat comeþ and meteþ þat buriel
a schal fynde hyt euene ryȝt of hys oune meete; and ȝef a
pylgrym oþer eny wery man kneoleþ þerto, anon a schal be
al fersch, and of werynes schal he feele non nuy.

Fast by þe Ministre of Wynburney, þat ys noȝt fer fram 50
Bathe, ys a wode þat bereþ moche fruyt. ȝef þe tren of þat
wode falle into a water oþer grounde ⟨þat⟩ þar ys nyȝ, and
lygge þar al a ȝer, þe tren teorneþ ynto stoones.

Vndur þe cité of Chestre eorneþ þe ryuer Dee, þat now
todeleþ Engelond and Wales. Þat ryuer euerych monthe 55
chaungeþ hys fordes, as men of þe contray telleþ, and leueþ
ofte þe chanel. Bote wheþer þe water drawe more toward
Engelond oþer toward Wales, to what syde þat hyt be, þat ȝer
men of þat syde schal habbe þe wors ende and be ouerset, and

60 þe men of þe oþer syde schal habbe þe betre ende and be
at here aboue. Whanne þe water chaungeþ so hys cours, hyt
bodeþ such happes. Þis ryuer Dee eorneþ and comeþ out of
a lake þat hatte Pimbilmere. Yn þe ryuer ys gret plenté
of samon. Noþeles in þe lake ys neuer samon yfounde.

B. THE LANGUAGES OF BRITAIN.

Chap. lix.

As hyt ys yknowe houȝ meny maner people buþ in þis
ylond, þer buþ also of so meny people longages and tonges.
Noþeles Walschmen and Scottes, þat buþ noȝt ymelled wiþ
oþer nacions, holdeþ wel nyȝ here furste longage and speche,
5 bote ȝef Scottes, þat were som tyme confederat and wonede
wiþ þe Pictes, drawe somwhat after here speche. Bote þe
Fiemmynges þat woneþ in þe west syde of Wales habbeþ
yleft here strange speche, and spekeþ Saxonlych ynow. Also
Englyschmen, þeyȝ hy hadde fram þe bygynnyng þre maner
10 speche, Souþeron, Norþeron, and Myddel speche in þe
myddel of þe lond, as hy come of þre maner people of
Germania, noþeles by commyxstion and mellyng, furst wiþ
Danes and afterward wiþ Normans, in menye þe contray
longage ys apeyred, and som vseþ strange wlaffyng, chyteryng,
15 harryng, and garryng grisbittyng. Þis apeyryng of þe
burþtonge ys bycause of twey þinges. On ys for chyldern in
scole, aȝenes þe vsage and manere of al oþer nacions, buþ
compelled for to leue here oune longage, and for to construe
here lessons and here þinges a Freynsch, and habbeþ suþthe
20 þe Normans come furst into Engelond. Also gentil men
children buþ ytauȝt for to speke Freynsch fram tyme þat
a buþ yrokked in here cradel, and conneþ speke and playe
wiþ a child hys brouch; and oplondysch men wol lykne

hamsylf to gentil men, and fondeþ wiþ gret bysynes for to
speke Freynsch, for to be more ytold of.   25

[Þys manere was moche y-vsed tofore þe furste moreyn, and
ys seþthe somdel ychaunged. For Iohan Cornwal, a mayster
of gramere, chayngede þe lore in gramerscole and construccion
of Freynsch into Englysch; and Richard Pencrych lurnede
þat manere techyng of hym, and oþer men of Pencrych, so þat 30
now, þe 3er of oure Lord a þousond þre hondred foure score
and fyue, of þe secunde kyng Richard after þe Conquest
nyne, in al þe gramerscoles of Engelond childern leueþ
Frensch, and construeþ and lurneþ an Englysch, and habbeþ
þerby avauntage in on syde, and desavauntage yn anoþer. 35
Here avauntage ys þat a lurneþ here gramer yn lasse tyme
þan childern wer ywoned to do. Disavauntage ys þat now
childern of gramerscole conneþ no more Frensch þan can
here lift heele, and þat ys harm for ham and a scholle passe
þe se and trauayle in strange londes, and in meny caas also.40
Also gentil men habbeþ now moche yleft for to teche here
childern Frensch.] Hyt semeþ a gret wondur hou3 Englysch,
þat ys þe burþ-tonge of Englyschmen, and here oune longage
and tonge, ys so dyuers of soon in þis ylond ; and þe longage
of Normandy ys comlyng of anoþer lond, and haþ on maner 45
soon among al men þat spekeþ hyt ary3t in Engelond.
[Noþeles þer ys as meny dyuers maner Frensch yn þe rem of
Fraunce as ys dyuers manere Englysch in þe rem of Engelond.]

Also of þe forseyde Saxon tonge, þat ys deled a þre, and
ys abyde scarslych wiþ feaw vplondysch men, and ys gret 50
wondur, for men of þe est wiþ men of þe west, as hyt were
vnder þe same party of heuene, acordeþ more in sounyng
of speche þan men of þe norþ wiþ men of þe souþ. Þerfore
hyt ys þat Mercii, þat buþ men of myddel Engelond, as hyt
were parteners of þe endes, vndurstondeþ betre þe syde 55
longages, Norþeron and Souþeron, þan Norþeron and Souþeron
vndurstondeþ eyþer oþer.

Al þe longage of þe Norþhumbres, and specialych at ȝork, ys so scharp, slyttyng, and frotyng, and vnschape, þat we 60 Souþeron men may þat longage vnneþe vndurstonde. Y trowe þat þat ys bycause þat a buþ nyȝ to strange men and aliens, þat spekeþ strangelych, and also bycause þat þe kynges of Engelond woneþ alwey fer fram þat contray ; for a buþ more yturnd to þe souþ contray, and ȝef a goþ to þe norþ contray, 65 a goþ wiþ gret help and strengthe.

Þe cause why a buþ more in þe souþ contray þan in þe norþ may be betre cornlond, more people, more noble cytés, and more profytable hauenes.

XIV

POLITICAL PIECES

In the thirteenth century political poems were written chiefly in Latin or French. In the fourteenth century a steadily growing tendency to use English witnesses the increased interest of the people in politics and social questions. The fullest collections are those edited by T. Wright, *Political Songs of England* (John to Edward II), Camden Society, 1839; and *Political Poems and Songs* (Edward III to Richard III), Rolls Series, 2 vols., 1859–61.

The selections A and B are from the poems of Laurence Minot, of which the best edition is the third by J. Hall, Oxford 1914. Minot was a better patriot than a poet, and his boisterous contempt for the Scots and French reflects the spirit of England in the early days of Edward III's greatness.

The empty phrases in which the anonymous piece C abounds do not disguise a note of despair. The long war with France was becoming more and more hopeless. The plague that added to its miseries had carried off Henry, first Duke of Lancaster, in 1361. The Black Prince, to whom the nation looked for guidance, had died in 1376. The inglorious old age of Edward III ended in the following year. But there remained the hope, soon to be falsified, that the boy king Richard II would steer the ship of state to safety.

D is the earliest text of the letter which John Ball addressed to the Essex members of the Great Society of Peasants on the eve of the revolt of 1381. It shows how deep an impression the characters and allegorical form of *Piers Plowman* had made on the oppressed serfs and labourers, and it gives some idea of the vague and incoherent thinking that brought ruin on their enterprise. Ball, who had defied established authority all his life, was freed from prison by the rebels, became a ringleader, and preached to their assembly on Blackheath a famous sermon with the text :

> When Adam dalf, and Eve span,
> Who was then the gentleman ?

A few weeks later he was executed by sentence of Lord Chief Justice Tressilian, who had been charged by the King to take vengeance on the rebels.

The distich E sums up briefly the history of a year which turned moderate men against Richard II.   A fuller contemporary picture of the events that led to his deposition is found in the alliterative poem *Richard the Redeles* (called *Mum and the Sothsegger* since the discovery of a new fragment) which Skeat attributed, probably wrongly, to the author of *Piers Plowman*.

A. ON THE SCOTS (ABOUT 1333).

By LAURENCE MINOT.

MS. Cotton Galba E. ix (about 1425), f. 52 a.

Now for to tell ʒou will I turn
Of batayl of Banocburn

SKOTTES out of Berwik and of Abirdene
At þe Bannokburn war ʒe to kene ;
Þare slogh ʒe many sakles, als it was sene,
And now has King Edward wroken it, I wene.
   It es wrokin, I wene, wele wurth þe while !   5
   War ʒit with þe Skottes for þai er ful of gile !

Whare er ʒe Skottes of Saint Iohnes toune ?
Þe boste of ʒowre baner es betin all doune.
When ʒe bosting will bede, Sir Edward es boune
For to kindel ʒow care, and crak ʒowre crowne.   10
   He has crakked ʒowre croune, wele worth þe while
   Schame bityde þe Skottes, for þai er full of gile !

Skottes of Striflin war steren and stout,
Of God ne of gude men had þai no dout.
Now haue þai, þe pelers, priked obout,   15
Bot at þe last Sir Edward rifild þaire rout.
   He has rifild þaire rout, wele wurth þe while!
   Bot euer er þai vnder bot gaudes and gile.

Rughfute riueling, now kindels þi care;
Berebag with þi boste, þi biging es bare;   20
Fals wretche and forsworn, whider wiltou fare?
Busk þe vnto Brig, and abide þare.
   Þare, wretche, saltou won, and wery þe while;
   Þi dwelling in Dondé es done for þi gile.

Þe Skottes gase in Burghes and betes þe stretes;   25
Al þise Inglis men harmes he hetes;
Fast makes he his mone to men þat he metes,
Bot fone frendes he findes þat his bale betes.
   Fune betes his bale, wele wurth þe while!
   He vses al threting with gaudes and gile.   30

Bot many man thretes and spekes ful ill
Þat sum tyme war better to be stane-still.
Þe Skot in his wordes has wind for to spill,
For at þe last Edward sall haue al his will.
   He had his will at Berwik, wele wurth þe while!   35
   Skottes broght him þe kayes,—bot get for þaire gile.

B. THE TAKING OF CALAIS (1347).

By Laurence Minot.

MS. Cotton Galba E. ix (about 1425), f. 55 b.

How Edward als þe romance sais
Held his sege bifor Calais.

Calays men, now mai 3e care,
And murni⟨n⟩g mun 3e haue to mede;

Mirth on mold get ȝe no mare,
Sir Edward sall ken ȝow ȝowre crede.
Whilum war ȝe wight in wede   5
To robbing rathly for to ren ;
Mend ȝow sone of ȝowre misdede :
ȝowre care es cumen, will ȝe it ken.

Kend it es how ȝe war kene
Al Inglis men with dole to dere.   10
Þaire gudes toke ȝe al bidene,
No man born wald ȝe forbere.
ȝe spared noght with swerd ne spere
To stik þam, and þaire gudes to stele.
With wapin and with ded of were   15
Þus haue ȝe wonnen werldes wele.

Weleful men war ȝe iwis,
Bot fer on fold sall ȝe noght fare :
A bare sal now abate ȝowre blis
And wirk ȝow bale on bankes bare.   20
He sall ȝow hunt, als hund dose hare,
Þat in no hole sall ȝe ȝow hide ;
For all ȝowre speche will he noght spare,
Bot bigges him right by ȝowre side.

Biside ȝow here þe bare bigins   25
To big his boure in winter-tyde,
And all bityme takes he his ines
With semly se⟨r⟩gantes him biside.
Þe word of him walkes ful wide—
Iesu saue him fro mischance !   30
In bataill dar he wele habide
Sir Philip and Sir Iohn of France.

Þe Franche men er fers and fell,
And mase grete dray when þai er dight;
Of þam men herd slike tales tell,   35
With Edward think þai for to fight,
Him for to hald out of his right,
And do him treson with þaire tales:
Þat was þaire purpos, day and night,
Bi counsail of þe Cardinales.   40

Cardinales with hattes rede
War fro Calays wele thre myle;
Þai toke þaire counsail in þat stede
How þai might Sir Edward bigile.
Þai lended þare bot litill while   45
Till Franche men to grante þaire grace:
Sir Philip was funden a file,
He fled and faght noght in þat place.

In þat place þe bare was blith,
For all was funden þat he had soght.   50
Philip þe Valas fled ful swith
With þe batail þat he had broght.
For to haue Calays had he thoght
All at his ledeing, loud or still;
Bot all þaire wiles war for noght: 55
Edward wan it at his will.

Lystens now, and ȝe may lere,
Als men þe suth may vnderstand,
Þe knightes þat in Calais were
Come to Sir Edward sare wepeand.   60
In kirtell one, and swerd in hand,
And cried, 'Sir Edward, þine ⟨we⟩ are.
Do now, lord, bi law of land
Þi will with vs for euermare'.

Þe nobill burgase and þe best   65
Come vnto him to haue þaire hire.
Þe comun puple war ful prest
Rapes to bring obout þaire swire.
Þai said all : ' Sir Philip, oure syre,
And his sun, Sir Iohn of France,   70
Has left vs ligand in þe mire,
And broght vs till þis doleful dance.

Our horses þat war faire and fat
Er etin vp ilkone bidene ;
Haue we nowþer conig ne cat   75
Þat þai ne er etin, and hundes kene
Al er etin vp ful clene—
Es nowther leuid biche ne whelp—
Þat es wele on oure sembland sene,
And þai er fled þat suld vs help.'   80

A knight þat was of grete renowne—
Sir Iohn de Viene was his name—
He was wardaine of þe toune
And had done Ingland mekill schame.
For all þaire boste þai er to blame,   85
Ful stalworthly þare haue þai streuyr.
A bare es cumen to mak þam tame,
Kayes of þe toun to him er gifen.

Þe kaies er ʒolden him of þe ʒate,—
Lat him now kepe þam if he kun.   90
To Calais cum þai all to late,
Sir Philip, and Sir Iohn his sun.
Al war ful ferd þat þare ware fun,
Þaire leders may þai barely ban.
All on þis wise was Calais won :   95
God saue þam þat it sogat wan !

C. ON THE DEATH OF EDWARD III, A.D. 1377.

Bodleian MS. Vernon (about 1400), f. 410ᵇ.

A! DERE God, what mai þis be,
Þat alle þing weres and wasteþ awai?
Frendschip is but a vanyté,
Vnneþe hit dures al a day.
Þei beo so sliper at assai,   5
So leof to han, and loþ to lete,
And so fikel in heore fai,
Þat selden iseiȝe is sone forȝete.

I sei hit not wiþouten a cause,
And þerfore takes riht good hede,   10
For ȝif ȝe construwe wel þis clause,
I puit ȝou holly out of drede
Þat for puire schame ȝor hertes wol blede
And ȝe þis matere wysli trete:
He þat was vr moste spede   15
Is selden iseye and sone forȝete.

Sum tyme an Englisch schip we had,
Nobel hit was and heih of tour,
Þorw al Cristendam hit was drad,
And stif wolde stande in vch a stour,   20
And best dorst byde a scharp schour,
And oþer stormes, smale and grete.
Now is þat schip, þat bar þe flour,
Selden seȝe and sone forȝete.

Into þat schip þer longed a rooþur   25
Þat steered þe schip and gouerned hit;
In al þis world nis such anoþur,
As me þinkeþ in my wit.

Whyl schip and roþur togeder was knit,
Þei dredde nouþer tempest, druyȝe nor wete;   30
Nou be þei boþe in synder flit,
Þat selden seyȝe is sone forȝete.

Scharpe wawes þat schip has sayled,
And sayed alle sees at auentur.
For wynt ne wederes neuer hit fayled   35
Whil þe roþur mihte enduir.
Þouȝ þe see were rouh or elles dimuir,
Gode hauenes þat schip wolde gete.
Nou is þat schip, I am wel suir,
Selde iseye and sone forȝete.   40

Þis goode schip I may remene
To þe chiualrye of þis londe;
Sum tyme þei counted nouȝt a bene
Beo al Fraunce, ich vnderstonde.
Þei tok and slouȝ hem with heore honde,   45
Þe power of Fraunce, boþ smal and grete,
And brouȝt þe king hider to byde her bonde:
And nou riht sone hit is forȝete.

Þat schip hadde a ful siker mast,
And a sayl strong and large,   50
Þat made þe gode schip neuer agast
To vndertake a þing of charge;
And to þat schip þer longed a barge
Of al Fraunce ȝaf nouȝt a clete;
To vs hit was a siker targe,   55
And now riht clene hit is forȝete.

Þe roþur was nouþer ok ne elm,—
Hit was Edward þe Þridde, þe noble kniht.
Þe Prince his sone bar vp his helm,
Þat neuer scoumfited was in fiht.   60

42 chilualrye *MS.*

The Kyng him rod and rouwed ariht;
Þe Prince dredde nouþur stok nor strete.
Nou of hem we lete ful liht:
Þat selde is seȝe is sone forȝete.

Þe swifte barge was Duk Henri,   65
Þat noble kniht and wel assayed,
And in his leggaunce worþili
He abod mony a bitter brayd.
Ȝif þat his enemys ouȝt outrayed,
To chastis hem wolde he not lete.   70
Nou is þat lord ful lowe ileyd:
Þat selde is seȝe is sone forȝete.

Þis gode Comunes, bi þe rode!
I likne hem to the schipes mast,
Þat with heore catel and heore goode   75
Mayntened þe werre boþ furst and last.
Þe wynd þat bleuȝ þe schip wiþ blast
Hit was gode preȝers, I sei hit atrete.
Nou is deuoutnes out icast,
And mony gode dedes ben clen forȝete.   80

Þus ben þis lordes ileid ful lowe:
Þe stok is of þe same rote;
An ympe biginnes for to growe
And ȝit I hope schal ben vr bote,
To holde his fomen vnder fote,   85
And as a lord be set in sete.
Crist leue þat he so mote,
Þat selden iseȝe be not forȝete!

Weor þat impe fully growe,
Þat he had sarri sap and piþ,   90
I hope he schulde be kud and knowe
For conquerour of moni a kiþ.

He is ful lyflich in lyme and liþ
In armes to trauayle and to swete.
Crist leeue we so fare him wiþ   95
Þat selden seȝe be neuer forȝete !

And þerfore holliche I ou rede,
Til þat þis ympe beo fully growe,
Þat vch a mon vp wiþ þe hede
And mayntene him, boþe heiȝe and lowe.   100
Þe Frensche men cunne boþe boste and blowe,
And wiþ heore scornes vs toþrete,
And we beoþ boþe vnkuynde and slowe,
Þat selden seȝe is sone forȝete.

And þerfore, gode sires, takeþ reward   105
Of ȝor douhti kyng þat dyȝede in age,
And to his sone, Prince Edward,
Þat welle was of alle corage.
Suche two lordes of heiȝ parage
I not in eorþe whon we schal gete ;   110
And nou heore los biginneþ to swage,
Þat selde iseȝe is sone forȝete.

D. JOHN BALL'S LETTER TO THE PEASANTS
OF ESSEX, 1381.

St. Albans MS. British Museum Royal 13. E. ix (about 1400), f. 287 a.

Iohon Schep, som tyme Seynte Marie prest of ȝork, and now ot Colchestre, greteth wel Iohan Nameles, and Iohan þe Mullere, and Iohon Cartere, and biddeþ hem þat þei bee war of gyle in borugh, and stondeth togidre in Godes name, 5 and biddeþ Peres Plouȝman go to his werk, and chastise

110 I] In *MS*.   4 togidre] togidedre *MS*.

wel Hobbe þe Robbere, and takeþ wiþ ȝow Iohan Trewman,
and alle hiis felawes, and no mo, and loke schappe ȝou to
on heued, and no mo.

    Iohan þe Mullere haþ ygrounde smal, smal, smal ;
    Þe Kynges sone of heuene schal paye for al.   10
    Be war or ye be wo ;
    Knoweþ ȝour freend fro ȝour foo ;
    Haueth ynow, and seith ' Hoo ' ;
    And do wel and bettre, and fleth synne,
    And sekeþ pees, and hold ȝou þerinne ;   15
and so biddeþ Iohan Trewman and alle his felawes.

E.   ON THE YEAR 1390–1.

St. John's College (Oxford) MS. 209, f. 57 a.

THE ax was sharpe, the stokke was harde,
In the xiiii yere of Kyng Richarde.

11 ye ǀ þe MS.

XV

MISCELLANEOUS PIECES IN VERSE

Under this head are grouped a number of short poems, representing forms of composition that survive only by fortunate chance.

A is a curious little song, which has been printed from Hale MS. 135 in *Modern Language Review*, vol. iv, p. 236, and reconstructed by Skeat at vol. v, p. 105. For a related French poem see H. E. Sandison, *The Chanson d'Aventure in M.E.*, 1913, p. 47.

B and C are the best-known lyrics of the important collection edited by Böddeker, *Altenglische Dichtungen des MS. Harley 2253*. Berlin 1878. They are literary and rather artificial in form.

D and E are minstrels' songs found, among other popular snatches, on a fly-leaf of Bodleian MS. Rawlinson D. 913, and edited by Heuser in *Anglia*, vol. xxx, p. 173. In E ll. 14–16 and ll. 17–19 are to be expanded on the model of ll. 7–13. For a Latin Nativity poem to this tune see R. L. Greene, *Speculum*, xxvii (1952), pp. 504 ff.

All these songs are early, and have a lightness and gaiety that become rare as the fourteenth century advances.

F is one of several English scraps (ed. Furnivall in *Political, Religious, and Love Poems*, E.E.T.S., pp. 249 ff.) that are found scattered through the Latin text of MS. Harley 7322. Most of the English pieces are without poetical merit, but in this one poem the writer has attained a perfect simplicity.

G, printed in Wright and Halliwell's *Reliquiae Antiquae*, 1845, vol. i, p. 144, has been recognized as the first of the English ballads. It is the only example before 1400 of the swift and dramatic movement, the sudden transitions, and the restrained expression, characteristic of the ballad style.

H, first printed in *Reliquiae Antiquae*, vol. i, p. 240, is the latest of the short pieces. With onomatopoeic effects it gives a vivid if unfriendly picture of a blacksmith's forge on a busy night.

I is a charm edited by Furnivall at p. 43 of the E.E.T.S. volume in which F appears.

A. NOW SPRINGS THE SPRAY.

Lincoln's Inn MS. Hale 135 (about 1300).

Nou sprinkes þe sprai,
Al for loue icche am so seek
Þat slepen I ne mai.

Als I me rode þis endre dai
O mi playinge,   5
Seih I hwar a litel mai
Bigan to singge :
' Þe clot him clingge !
Wai es him i louue-longinge
Sal libben ai !'   10
   Nou sprinkes, &c.

Son icche herde þat mirie note,
Þider I drogh ;
I fonde hire in an herber swot
Vnder a bogh,
With ioie inogh.   15
Son I asked : ' Þou mirie mai,
Hwi sinkestou ai ?'
   Nou sprinkes, &c.

Þan answerde þat maiden swote
Midde wordes fewe :
' Mi lemman me haues bihot   20
Of louue trewe :
He chaunges anewe.
Yiif I mai, it shal him rewe
Bi þis dai.'
   Nou sprinkes, &c.

---

4 þis endre dai als I me rode *MS.*; *corr. Skeat.*   5 playinge]
indistinct.   8 clingge] clingges *MS.*

B. SPRING.

MS. Harley 2253 (about 1325), f. 71 b.

LENTEN ys come wiþ loue to toune,
Wiþ blosmen and wiþ briddes roune,
   Þat al þis blisse bryngeþ.
Dayeseȝes in þis dales,
Notes suete of nyhtegales,   5
   Vch foul song singeþ.
Þe þrestelcoc him þreteþ oo,
Away is huere wynter wo,
   When woderoue springeþ.
Þis foules singeþ ferly fele,   10
Ant wlyteþ on huere †twynter† wele,
   Þat al þe wode ryngeþ.

Þe rose rayleþ hire rode,
Þe leues on þe lyhte wode
   Waxen al wiþ wille.   15
Þe mone mandeþ hire bleo,
Þe lilie is lossom to seo,
   Þe fenyl and þe fille.
Wowes þis wilde drakes;
†Milest† murgeþ huere makes,   20
   Ase strem þat strikeþ stille.
Mody meneþ, so doþ mo—
Ichot ycham on of þo,
   For loue þat likes ille.

Þe mone mandeþ hire lyht;   25
So doþ þe semly sonne bryht,
   When briddes singeþ breme.
Deawes donkeþ þe dounes;
Deores wiþ huere derne rounes,
   Domes for te deme;   30
      22 doþ] doh *MS.*

Wormes woweþ vnder cloude ;
Wymmen waxeþ wounder proude,
   So wel hit wol hem seme.
ȝef me shal wonte wille of on,
Þis wunne weole y wole forgon,   35
   Ant wyht in wode be fleme.

C. ALYSOUN.

MS. Harley 2253, f. 63 b.

BYTUENE Mersh and Aueril,
  When spray biginneþ to springe,
Þe lutel foul haþ hire wyl
  On hyre lud to synge.
Ich libbe in loue-longinge   5
  For semlokest of alle þynge ;
He may me blisse bringe—
  Icham in hire baundoun.
     An hendy hap ichabbe yhent ;
     Ichot from heuene it is me sent ;   10
     From alle wymmen mi loue is lent.
     And lyht on Alysoun.

On heu hire her is fayr ynoh,
  Hire browe broune, hire eȝe blake ;
Wiþ lossum chere he on me loh,   15
  Wiþ middel smal and wel ymake.
Bote he me wolle to hire take,
For te buen hire owen make,
Longe to lyuen ichulle forsake,
  And feye fallen adoun.   20
     An hendy hap, &c.

Nihtes when y wende and wake,
Forþi myn wonges waxeþ won,
Leuedi, al for þine sake
  Longinge is ylent me on.
  In world nis non so wyter mon   25
  Þat al hire bounté telle con;
  Hire swyre is whittore þen þe swon,
    And feyrest may in toune.
      An hend⟨y hap⟩, &c.

Icham for wowyng al forwake,
  Wery so water in wore,   30
Lest eny reue me my make,
  Ychabbe yȝyrned ȝore.
  Betere is þolien whyle sore
  Þen mournen euermore.
  Geynest vnder gore,   35
    Herkne to my roun.
      An hendi ⟨hap ichabbe yhent;
      Ichot from heuene it is me sent;
      From alle wymmen mi loue is lent,
        And lyht on Alysoun⟩.   40

D. THE IRISH DANCER.

Bodleian MS. Rawlinson D. 913.

Icham of Irlaunde,
  Ant of the holy londe
    Of Irlande.
Gode sire, pray ich þe,
  For of saynte charité,   5
  Come ant daunce wyt me
    In Irlaunde.
      4 þel ȝe *MS.*

E. THE MAID OF THE MOOR.

Bodleian MS. Rawlinson D. 913.

MAIDEN in the mor lay,
 In the mor lay,
Seuenyst fulle, seuenist fulle,
Maiden in the mor lay,
 In the mor lay,   5
Seuenistes fulle ant a day.

Welle was hire mete;
 Wat was hire mete?
 Þe primerole ant the,—
 Þe primerole ant the,—   10
Welle was hire mete;
Wat was hire mete?—
 The primerole ant the violet.

Welle ⟨was hire dryng⟩;
 Wat was hire dryng?   15
Þe chelde water of ⟨þe⟩ welle-spring.

Welle was hire bour;
 Wat was hire bour?
Þe rede rose an te lilie flour.

F. THE VIRGIN'S SONG.

British Museum MS. Harley 7322 (about 1375), f. 135 b.

IESU, swete sone dere!
 On porful bed list þou here,
And þat me greueþ sore;
For þi cradel is ase a bere,
Oxe and asse beþ þi fere: 5
 Weepe ich mai þarfore.

   7 was] wat *MS*

Iesu, swete, beo noth wroþ,
Þou ich nabbe clout ne cloþ
   Þe on for to folde,
   Þe on to folde ne to wrappe,   10
For ich nabbe clout ne lappe;
Bote ley þou þi fet to my pappe,
   And wite þe from þe colde.

G. JUDAS.

Trinity College (Cambridge) MS. B. 14. 39 (about 1300), f. 34 a.

HIT wes upon a Scere Þorsday þat vre Louerd aros;
Ful milde were þe wordes He spec to Iudas:

Iudas, þou most to Iurselem, oure mete for to bugge;
Þritti platen of seluer þou bere upo þi rugge.

Þou comest fer i þe brode stret, fer i þe brode strete;   5
Summe of þine cunesmen þer þou meist imete.

Imette wid is soster, þe swikele wimon:
'Iudas, þou were wrþe me stende þe wid ston, (*bis*)
For þe false prophete þat tou bileuest upon.'

'Be stille, leue soster, þin herte þe tobreke!   10
Wiste min Louerd Crist, ful wel He wolde be wreke.'

'Iudas, go þou on þe roc, heie upon þe ston,
Lei þin heued i my barm, slep þou þe anon.'

Sone so Iudas of slepe was awake,
Þritti platen of seluer from hym weren itake.   15

He drou hymselve bi þe top, þat al it lauede a blode;
Þe Iewes out of Iurselem awenden he were wode.

Foret hym com þe riche Ieu þat heiste Pilatus:
'Wolte sulle þi Louerd, þat hette Iesus?'

'I nul sulle my Louerd for nones cunnes eiste,   20
Bote hit be for þe þritti platen þat He me bitaiste.'

'Wolte sulle þi Lord Crist for enes cunnes golde ? '
'Nay, bote hit be for þe platen þat He habben wolde.'

In him com ur Lord gon, as is postles seten at mete :
'Wou sitte ye, postles, ant wi nule ye ete ? (*bis*)   25
Ic am iboust ant isold today for oure mete.'

Up stod him Iudas : 'Lord, am I þat ?
I nas neuer o þe stude þer me þe euel spec.'

Up him stod Peter, ant spec wid al is miste :
'Þau Pilatus him come wid ten hundred cnistes, (*bis*)   30
Yet ic wolde, Louerd, for þi loue fiste.'

'Stille þou be, Peter ! Wel I þe icnowe ;
Þou wolt fursake me þrien ar þe coc him crowe.'

H. THE BLACKSMITHS.

British Museum MS. Arundel 292 (about 1425–50), f. 71 b.

SWARTE smekyd smeþes smateryd wyth smoke
Dryue me to deth wyth den of here dyntes.
Swech noys on nyghtes ne herd men neuer :
What knauene cry and clateryng of knockes !
Þe cammede kongons cryen after 'col, col !'   5
And blowen here bellewys, þat al here brayn brestes :
'Huf, puf !' seith þat on ; 'haf, paf !' þat oþer.
Þei spyttyn and spraulyn and spellyn many spelles ;
Þei gnauen and gnacchen, þei gronys togydere,
And holdyn hem hote wyth here hard hamers.   10
Of a bole-hyde ben here barm-fellys ;
Here schankes ben schakeled for the fere-flunderys ;
Heuy hamerys þei han, þat hard ben handled,

Stark strokes þei stryken on a stelyd stokke :
Lus, bus ! las, das ! rowtyn be rowe.   15
Swech dolful a dreme þe deuyl it todryue !
Þe mayster longith a lityl, and lascheth a lesse,
Twyneth hem tweyn, and towchith a treble :
Tik, tak ! hic, hac ! tiket, taket ! tyk, tak !
Lus, bus ! lus, das ! swych lyf thei ledyn   20
Alle cloþemerys : Cryst hem gyue sorwe !
May no man for brenwaterys on nyght han hys rest !

I. RATS AWAY.

Bodleian MS. Rawlinson C. 288, f. 113 (15th-century writing, blurred).

I comawnde alle þe ratones þat are here abowte,
Þat non dwelle in þis place, withinne ne withowte,
Thorgh þe vertu of Iesu Crist, þat Mary bare abowte,
Þat alle creatures owyn for to lowte,
And thorgh þe vertu of Mark, Mathew, Luke, an Ion,—   5
Alle foure Awangelys corden into on,—
Thorgh þe vertu of Sent Geretrude, þat mayde clene,
    God graunte þat grace
    Þat ⟨non⟩ raton dwelle in þe place
Þat here namis were nemeled in ;   10
And thorgh þe vertu of Sent Kasi.
Þat holy man, þat prayed to God Almyty
    For skathes þat þei deden
    Hys medyn
Be dayes and be nyȝt,   15
God bad hem flen and gon out of euery manesse syȝt.
Dominus Deus Sabaot ! Emanuel, þe gret Godes name !
I betweche þes place from ratones and from alle oþer schame.
God saue þis place fro alle oþer wykked wytes,
Boþe be dayes and be nytes ! *et in nomine Patris et Filii,* &c.   20

13 skathes] t *altered from* f (?) *MS.*

XVI

THE YORK PLAY 'HARROWING OF HELL'

British Museum MS. Addit. 35290 (about 1430–40), f. 193 b.

The miracle play *Harrowing of Hell* is assigned to the craft of Saddlers in the York cycle, edited by Miss L. Toulmin-Smith, Oxford 1885, pp. 372 ff. This is the text reproduced below. It is also found, though in a less perfect form, among the *Towneley Plays*, ed. England and Pollard, E.E.T.S., 1897, pp. 293 ff.

All the mediaeval stories of Christ's Descent into Hell are based on the gospel of Nicodemus, which seems to date from the fourth century, though the legend is referred to nearly two centuries earlier. This apocryphal narrative was popular throughout the Middle Ages. There is a prose translation in late Anglo-Saxon, and a Middle English verse rendering supplies some of the phrases in the play.

Two points deserve notice for their bearing on the development of miracles. A trace of their origin in the services of the Church is seen in the use made of the Scriptural passage 'Attollite portas, principes, vestras, et elevamini portae aeternales, et introibit rex gloriae', the dramatic possibilities of which were recognized in ritual from an early date. And the growing taste for comic scenes is met, without prejudice to the serious characters, by the rudimentary buffoonery of the Devil and his companions.

DRAMATIS PERSONAE.

ADAME	IOHANNES BAPTISTA	BELLIALL
EUA	MOYSES	MICHILL (Archangel)
ISAIAH	BELSABUB	PRIMUS DIABOLUS
SYMEON	SATTAN	SECUNDUS DIABOLUS
IESUS	DAUID	

[SCENE I, *outside the gates of Hell.*]

1. ⟨*Iesus.* M⟩anne on molde, be meke to me,
   And haue thy Maker in þi mynde,
   And thynke howe I haue tholid for þe
   With pereles paynes for to be pyned.

The forward of my Fadir free   5
Haue I fulfillid, as folke may fynde,
Þerfore aboute nowe woll I bee
Þat I haue bought for to vnbynde.
Þe feende þame wanne with trayne,
Thurgh frewte of erthely foode;   10
I haue þame getyn agayne
Thurgh bying with my bloode.

2. And so I schall þat steede restore
   Fro whilke þe feende fell for synne;
   Þare schalle mankynde wonne euermore   15
   In blisse þat schall neuere blynne.
   All þat in werke my werkemen were,
   Owte of thare woo I wol þame wynne,
   And some signe schall I sende before
   Of grace, to garre þer gamys begynne.   20
   A light I woll þei haue
   To schewe þame I schall come sone;
   My bodie bidis in graue
   Tille alle thes dedis be done.

3. My Fadir ordand on þis wise   25
   Aftir His will þat I schulde wende,
   For to fulfille þe prophicye⟨s⟩,
   And als I spake my solace to spende.
   My frendis, þat in me faith affies,
   Nowe fro ther fois I schall þame fende,   30
   And on the thirde day ryght vprise,
   And so tille heuen I schall assende.
   Sithen schall I come agayne
   To deme bothe goode and ill
   Tille endles ioie or peyne;   35
   Þus is my Fadris will.

14 Fro] For *MS.*

[SCENE II, *Hell; at one side Limbo, enclosing the patriarchs and prophets; a light shines across.*]

4. *Adame.*   Mi bretheren, harkens to me here,
Swilke hope of heele neuere are we hadde.
Foure thowsande and sex hundereth ʒere
Haue we bene heere in †þis stedde†.   40
Nowe see I signe of solace seere,
A glorious gleme to make vs gladde,
Wherfore I hope oure helpe is nere,
And sone schall sesse oure sorowes sadde.
Eua.   Adame, my husband hende,   45
Þis menys solas certayne;
Suoh light gune on vs lende
In Paradise full playne.

5. *Isaiah.*   Adame, we schall wele vndirstande;
I, Ysaias, as God me kende,   50
I prechid in Neptalym þat lande,
And ʒabulon, even vntill ende.
I spake of folke in mirke walkand,
And saide a light schulde on þame lende;
This lered I whils I was leuand,   55
Nowe se I God þis same hath sende.
Þis light comes all of Criste,
Þat seede, to saue vs nowe,
Þus is my poynte puplisshid.
But Symeon, what sais þou?   60

6. *Symeon.*   Þhis, my tale of farleis feele,
For in þis temple His frendis me fande;
I hadde delite with Hym to dele,
And halsed homely with my hande.
I saide, 'Lorde, late thy seruaunt lele   65
Passe nowe in pesse to liffe lastand,

40 in þis stedde] in darknes stad *Towneley*.   49 Isaiah] Isaac *MS.*

For nowe myselfe has sene Thy hele,
Me liste no lengar to liffe in lande.'
Þis light Þou hast purueyed
To folkes Þat liffis in leede,   70
Þe same Þat I Þame saide,
I see fulfillid in dede.

7. *Iohan. Baptista.*   Als voyce criand to folke I kende
Þe weyes of Criste, als I wele kanne;
I baptiste Hym with bothe my hande   75
Euen in Þe floode of flume Iordanne.
Þe Holy Goste fro heuene discende
Als a white dowue doune on Hym Þanne;
The Fadir voice, my mirthe to mende,
Was made to me euen als manne,   80
'This is my Sone,' he saide,
'In whome me paies full wele.'
His light is on vs laide,
He comes oure cares to kele.

8. *Moyses.*   Of Þat same light lernyng haue I,   85
To me Moyses He mustered his myght,
And also vnto anodir, Hely,
Wher we were on an hille on hight.
Whyte as snowe was His body,
And His face like to Þe sonne to sight: 90
No man on molde was so myghty
Grathely to loke agaynste Þat light;
Þat same light se I nowe
Shynyng on vs sarteyne,
Wherfore trewly I trowe   95
We schalle sone passe fro payne.

9. *i Diabolus.*   Helpe! Belsabub! to bynde Þer boyes,
Such harrowe was neuer are herde in helle.

ii Diab.   Why rooris þou soo, Rebalde? þou royis ;
What is betidde, canne þou ought telle?   100
i Diab.   What I heris þou noȝt þis vggely noyse?
Þes lurdans þat in Lymbo dwelle,
Þei make menyng of many ioies,
And musteres grete mirthe þame emell.
ii Diab.   Mirthe? nay, nay, þat poynte is paste,   105
More hele schall þei neuer haue.
i Diab.   Þei crie on Criste full faste,
And sais he schal þame saue.

10. *Belsabub.*   ȝa, if he saue þame noght, we schall,
For they are sperde in speciall space ;   110
Whils I am prince and principall
Schall þei neuer passe oute of þis place.
Calle vppe Astrotte and Anaball
To giffe þer counsaille in þis case,
Bele-Berit and Belial,   115
To marre þame þat swilke maistries mase.
Say to Satan oure sire,
And bidde þame bringe also
Lucifer louely of lyre.
i Diab.   Al redy, lorde, I goo.   120

11. *Iesus* [*Without*].   *Attollite portas, principes,*
Oppen vppe, ȝe princes of paynes sere,
Et eleuamini eternales,
Youre yendles ȝatis þat ȝe haue here.
Sattan.   What page is þere þat makes prees,   125
And callis hym kyng of vs in fere?
Dauid [*in Limbo*].   I lered leuand, withouten lees,
He is a kyng of vertues clere.
A ! Lorde, mekill of myght,
And stronge in ilke a stoure,   130
In batailes ferse to fight,
And worthy to wynne honnoure.

12. *Sattan.*   Honnoure! in þe deuel way, for what dede?
All erthely men to me are thrall;
þe lady þat calles hym lorde in leede   135
Hadde neuer ȝitt herberowe, house, ne halle.
   i Diab.   Harke, Belsabub! I haue grete drede,
For hydously I herde hym calle.
   Belliall.   We! spere oure ȝates, all ill mot þou spede!
And sette furthe watches on þe wall.   140
And if he calle or crie
To make vs more debate,
Lay on hym þan hardely,
And garre hym gang his gate.

13. *Sattan.*   Telle me what boyes dare be so bolde   145
For drede to make so mekill draye.
   i Diab.   Itt is þe Iewe þat Iudas solde
For to be dede, þis othir daye.
   Sattan.   O we! þis tale in tyme is tolde,
þis traytoure traues⟨es⟩ vs alway;   150
He schall be here full harde in holde,
Loke þat he passe noght, I þe praye.
   ii Diab.   Nay, nay, he will noȝt wende
Away or I be ware,
He shappis hym for to schende   155
Alle helle, or he go ferre.

14. *Sattan.*   Nay, faitour, þerof schall he faile,
For alle his fare I hym deffie;
I knowe his trantis fro toppe to taile,
He leuys with gaudis and with gilery.   160
þerby he brought oute of oure bale,
Nowe late, Laȝar of Betannye,
þerfore I gaffe to þe Iewes counsaille
þat þei schulde alway garre hym dye.

I entered in Iudas   165
Þat forwarde to fulfille,
Þerfore his hire he has,
Allway to wonne here stille.

15. *Belsabub.*   Sir Sattanne, sen we here þe saie
Þat þou and þe Iewes wer same assente,   170
And wotte he wanne Laȝar awaye,
Þat tille vs was tane for to tente,
Trowe þou þat þou marre hym maye
To mustir myghtis, what he has mente?
If he nowe depriue vs of oure praye,   175
We will ȝe witte whanne þei are wente.
Sattan.   I bidde ȝou be noȝt abasshed,
But boldely make youe boune
With toles þat ȝe on traste,
And dynge þat dastard doune.   180

16. *Iesus* [*Without*].   *Principes, portas tollite,*
Vndo youre ȝatis, ȝe princis of pryde,
Et introibit rex glorie,
Þe kyng of blisse comes in þis tyde.
                    [*Enters the gates of Hell.*
Sattan.   Owte! harrowe ⟨what harlot⟩ is hee   185
Þat sais his kyngdome schall be cryed?
Dauid [*in Limbo*].   Þat may þou in my Sawter see
For þat poynte *I* prophicie⟨d⟩.
I saide þat he schuld breke
Youre barres and bandis by name,   190
And on youre werkis take wreke;
Nowe schalle ȝe see þe same.

17. *Iesus.*   Þis steede schall stonde no lenger stoken;
Opynne vppe, and latte my pepul passe!

170 þe] ȝe *MS.*   185 what harlot] *from Towneley MS.*: *om
MS.*   188 I] *of MS.*

Diabolus. Owte! beholdes, oure baill is brokynne,   195
And brosten are alle oure bandis of bras.
Telle Lucifer alle is vnlokynne.
Belsabub.   What þanne, is Lymbus lorne? allas!
Garre Satan helpe þat we wer wroken;
Þis werke is werse þanne euere it was.   200
Sattan.   I badde ȝe schulde be boune
If he made maistries more;
Do dynge þat dastard doune,
And sette hym sadde and sore.

18. *Belsabub.*   ȝa, sette hym sore, þat is sone saide,   205
But come þiselffe and serue hym soo;
We may not bide his bittir braide,
He wille vs marre and we wer moo.
Sattan.   What! faitours, wherfore are ȝe ferde?
Haue ȝe no force to flitte hym froo?   210
Belyue loke þat my gere be grathed,
Miselffe schall to þat gedlyng goo.
[*To Iesus.*]   Howe! belamy, abide,
With al thy booste and bere,
And telle to me þis tyde,   215
What maistries makes þou here?

19. *Iesus.*   I make no maistries but for myne,
Þame wolle I saue, I telle þe nowe;
Þou hadde no poure þame to pyne,
But as my prisoune for þer prowe   220
Here haue þei soiorned, noght as thyne,
But in thy warde, þou wote wele howe.
Sattan.   And what deuel haste þou done ay syne,
Þat neuer wolde negh þame nere, or nowe?
Iesus.   Nowe is þe tyme certayne   225
Mi Fadir ordand before

Þat they schulde passe fro payne,
And wonne in mirthe euer more.

20. *Sattan.*   Thy fadir knewe I wele be sight,
He was a write his mette to wynne,   230
And Marie me menys þi modir hight,
Þe vttiremeste ende of all þi kynne.
Who made þe be so mekill of myght?
Iesus.   Þou wikid feende, latte be thy dynne !
Mi Fadir wonnys in heuen on hight,   235
With blisse þat schall neuere blynne.
I am His awne sone,
His forward to fulfille ;
And same ay schall we wonne,
And sundir whan we wolle.   240

21. *Sattan.*   God⟨ys⟩ sonne ! þanne schulde þou be ful
    gladde,
Aftir no catel neyd thowe craue !
But þou has leued ay like a ladde,
And in sorowe, as a symple knaue.
Iesus.   Þat was for hartely loue I hadde   245
Vnto mannis soule, it for to saue ;
And for to make þe mased and madde,
And by þat resoune þus dewly to haue
Mi godhede here, I hidde
In Marie modir myne,   250
For it schulde noȝt be kidde
To þe, nor to none of thyne.

22. *Sattan.*   A ! þis wolde I were tolde in ilke a toune.
So, sen þou sais God is thy sire,
I schall þe proue, be right resoune,   255
Þou motes His men into þe myre.

242 neyd thowe craue] þus þe I telle *first hand.*   244 as] *added*
later MS.   knaue] braide *first hand.*

To breke His bidding were þei boune,
And, for they did at my desire,
Fro Paradise He putte þame doune
In helle here to haue þer hyre.　　260
And thyselfe, day and nyght,
Has taught al men emang
To do resoune and right,
And here werkis þou all wrang.

23. *Iesus.*　I wirke noght wrang, þat schal þow witte,　265
If I my men fro woo will wynne;
Mi prophetis playnly prechid it,
All þis note þat nowe begynne.
Þai saide þat I schulde be obitte,
To hell þat I schulde entre in,　　270
And saue my seruauntis fro þat pitte,
Wher dampned saulis schall sitte for synne.
And ilke trewe prophettis tale
Muste be fulfillid in mee;
I haue þame boughte with bale,　　275
And in blisse schal þei be.

24. *Sattan.*　Nowe sen þe liste allegge þe lawes,
Þou schalte be atteynted, or we twynne,
For þo þat þou to wittenesse drawes
Full even agaynste þe will begynne.　　280
Salamon saide in his sawes
Þat whoso enteres helle withynne
Shall neuer come oute, þus clerkis knawes,
And þerfore, felowe, leue þi dynne.
Iob, þi seruaunte, also　　285
Þus in his tyme gune telle,
Þat nowthir frende nor foo
Shulde fynde reles in helle,

25. *Iesus.*   He saide full soth, þat schall þou see,
       Þat in helle may be no reles,   290
       But of þat place þan preched he
       Where synffull care schall euere encrees.
       And in þat bale ay schall þou be,
       Whare sorowes sere schall neuer sesse,
       And for my folke þerfro wer free,   295
       Nowe schall þei passe to þe place of pees.
       Þai were here with my wille,
       And so schall þei fourthe wende,
       And þiselue schall fulfille
       Þer wooe withouten ende.   300

26. *Sattan.*   O wel þanne se I howe þou menys emang
       Some mesure with malice to melle,
       Sen þou sais all schall noȝt gang,
       But some schalle alway with vs dwelle.
       Iesus.   ȝaa, witte þou wele, ellis were it wrang,   305
       Als cursed Cayme þat slewe Abell,
       And all þat hastis hemselue to hange,
       Als Iudas and Archedefell,
       Datan and Abiron,
       And alle of þare assente ;   310
       Als tyrantis euerilkone
       Þat me and myne turmente.

27. And all þat liste noght to lere my lawe,
       Þat I haue lefte in lande nowe newe,
       Þat is my comyng for to knawe,   315
       And to my sacramente pursewe,
       Mi dede, my rysing, rede be rawe,
       Who will noght trowe, þei are noght trewe,
       Vnto my dome I schall þame drawe,
       And luge þame worse þanne any Iewe.   320

And all þat likis to leere
My lawe, and leue þerbye,
Shall neuere haue harmes heere,
But welthe, as is worthy.

28. *Sattan.*   Nowe here my hande, I halde me paied;   325
Þis poynte is playnly for oure prowe;
If þis be soth þat þou hast saide,
We schall haue moo þanne we haue nowe.
Þis lawe þat þou nowe late has laide
I schall lere men noȝt to allowe,   330
Iff þei it take, þei be betraied,
For I schall turne þame tyte, I trowe.
I schall walke este and weste,
And garre þame werke wele werre.
Iesus.   Naye, feende, þou schall be feste,   335
Þat þou schalte flitte not ferre.

29. *Sattan.*   Feste l þat were a foule reasoune,
Nay, bellamy, þou bus be smytte.
Iesus.   Mighill l myne aungell, make þe boune,
And feste yone fende, þat he noght flitte.   340
And Deuyll, I comaunde þe go doune
Into thy selle where þou schalte sitte.   [*Satan sinks.*
Sattan.   Owt, ay l herrowe l helpe Mahounde l
Nowe wex I woode oute of my witte.
Belsabub.   Sattan, þis saide we are,   345
Nowe schall þou fele þi fitte.
Sattan.   Allas l for dole and care,
I synke into helle pitte.   [*Falls into the pit.*

30. *Adame.*   A l Iesu Lorde, mekill is þi myght,
That mekis þiselffe in þis manere,   350
Vs for to helpe, as þou has hight,
Whanne both forfette, I and my feere.

347 dole] dolee *MS.*

Here haue we leuyd withouten light
Foure thousand and six hundred ȝere;
Now se I be þis solempne sight   355
Howe Thy mercy hath made vs clere.
Eue. A! Lorde, we were worthy
Mo turmentis for to taste,
But mende vs with mercye,
Als þou of myght is moste.   360

31. *Baptista.*   A! Lorde, I loue þe inwardly,
That me wolde make þi messengere
Thy comyng in erth for to crye,
And teche þi faith to folke in feere;
And sithen before þe for to dye,   365
And bringe boodworde to þame here,
How þai schulde haue Thyne helpe in hye :
Nowe se I all þi poyntis appere.
Als Dauid prophete trewe
Ofte tymes tolde vntill vs,   370
Of þis comyng he knewe,
And saide it schulde be þus.

32. *Dauid.*   Als I haue saide, ȝitt saie I soo,
Ne derelinquas, Domine,
Animam meam ⟨in⟩ inferno,   375
Leffe noght my saule, Lorde, aftir þe,
In depe helle where dampned schall goo,
Ne suffre neuere †saules fro þe be†
The sorowe of þame þat wonnes in woo
Ay full of filthe, †þat may repleye†.   380
Adame.   We thanke His grete goodnesse
He fette vs fro þis place,
Makes ioie nowe more and lesse ;
Omnis.   We laude God of His grace.

356 clere] clene *MS.*

33. *Iesus.* Adame and my frendis in feere,   385
Fro all youre fooes come fourth with me,
ʒe schalle be sette in solas seere,
Wher ʒe schall neuere of sorowes see.
And Mighill, myn aungell clere,
Ressayue þes saules all vnto þe,   390
And lede þame als I schall þe lere
To Paradise with playe and plenté.

[They come out of Limbo.

Mi graue I woll go till,
Redy to rise vpperight,
And so I schall fulfille   395
That I before haue highte.

34. *Michill.* Lorde, wende we schall aftir þi sawe,
To solace sere þai schall be sende,
But þat þer deuelis no draught vs drawe,
Lorde, blisse vs with þi holy hende.   400
Iesus. Mi blissing haue ʒe all on rawe,
I schall be with youe, wher ʒe wende,
And all þat lelly luffes my lawe,
þai schall be blissid withowten ende.
Adame. To þe, Lorde, be louyng,   405
þat vs has wonne fro waa,
For solas will we syng,
Laus Tibi cum gloria.   *[Exeunt.*

XVII

THE TOWNELEY PLAY OF NOAH

Towneley MS. (about 1475), ff. 76 ff.

The Towneley Miracles, so called because the manuscript belonged in recent times to the library of Towneley Hall in Lancashire, are edited by England and Pollard, E.E.T.S., 1897. The cycle is a composite one—for instance it includes a later form of the York play *Harrowing of Hell* (No. XVI, above)—but it is distinguished by a group of plays and interpolated scenes which seem to have been specially composed for representation at Wakefield. Formally this group is marked by the use of a peculiar nine-lined stanza, riming a a a a b c c c b, with central rimes in the first four lines. The rough vigour of the comic scenes is still more distinctive, and there can be little doubt that all are the work of one man. The specimen of his style most often reprinted is *The Second Shepherd's Play*, which has an original and purely secular comic plot. The *Play of Noah* is more typical of the English Miracle in its later development. This subject was always popular with early playwrights, for the Ark made a spectacle, and the traditional quarrels of Noah and his wife gave scope for contests in fisticuffs and rough raillery—the stuff of primitive comedy.

DRAMATIS PERSONAE.

Noe	Primus Filius	Prima Mulier
Deus	Secundus Filius	Secunda Mulier
Vxor Noe	Tercius Filius	Tercia Mulier

1. *Noe.* Myghtfull God veray, Maker of all that is,
   Thre persons withoutten nay, oone God in endles blis,
   Thou maide both nyght and day, beest, fowle, and fysh,
   All creatures that lif may wroght Thou at Thi wish,

   As Thou wel myght;   5
   The son, the moyne, verament,
   Thou maide, the firmament,
   The sternes also full feruent
   To shyne Thou maide ful bright.

2. Angels Thou maide ful euen, all orders that is,   10
   To haue the blis in heuen; this did Thou, more and les,
   Full mervelus to neuen; yit was ther vnkyndnes
   More bi foldis seuen then I can well expres;
        For whi?
   Of all angels in brightnes   15
   God gaf Lucifer most lightnes,
   Yit prowdly he flyt his des,
        And set hym euen Hym by.

3. He thoght hymself as worthi as Hym that hym made,
   In brightnes, in bewty, therfor He hym degrade,   20
   Put hym in a low degré soyn after, in a brade,
   Hym and all his menye, wher he may be vnglad
        For euer.
   Shall thay neuer wyn away
   Hence vnto Domysday,   25
   Bot burne in bayle for ay;
        Shall thay neuer dysseuer.

4. Soyne after, that gracyous Lord to his liknes maide man,
   That place to be restord euen as He began,
   Of the Trinité bi accord, Adam and Eue that woman,   30
   To multiplie without discord, in Paradise put He thaym,
        And sithen to both
   Gaf in commaundement
   On the Tre of Life to lay no hend.
   Bot yit the fals feynd   35
        Made Hym with man wroth,

5. Entysyd man to glotony, styrd him to syn in pride;
   Bot in Paradise, securly, myght no syn abide,
   And therfor man full hastely was put out in that tyde,
   In wo and wandreth for to be, in paynes full vnrid   40
        To knowe,

Fyrst in erth, *and* sythen in hell
With feyndis for to dwell,
Bot He his mercy mell
    To those that will Hym trawe. 45

6. Oyle of mercy He hus hight, as I haue hard red,
To euery lifyng wight that wold luf Hym and dred;
Bot now before His sight euery liffyng leyde,
Most party day and nyght, syn in word and dede
    Full bold; 50
Som in pride, ire, and enuy,
Som in couete*i*s and glotyny,
Som in sloth and lechery,
    And other wise many fold.

7. Therfor I drede lest God on vs will take veniance, 55
For syn is now alod, without any repentance.
Sex hundreth yeris and od haue I, without distance,
In erth, as any sod, liffyd with grete grevance
    Allway;
And now I wax old, 60
Seke, sory, and cold,
As muk apon mold
    I widder away.

8. Bot yit will I cry for mercy and call:
Noe, Thi seruant, am I, Lord ouer all! 65
Therfor me, and my fry shal with me fall,
Saue from velany, and bryng to Thi hall
    In heuen;
And kepe me from syn
This warld within; 70
Comly Kyng of mankyn,
    I pray The, here my stevyn!
      [God appears above.]

9.   *Deus.*   Syn I haue maide all thyng that is liffand,
Duke, emperour, and kyng, with Myne awne hand,
For to haue thare likyng, bi see and bi sand,   75
Euery man to My bydyng shuld be bowand
      Full feruent,
That maide man sich a creatoure,
Farest of favoure;
Man must luf Me paramoure   80
      By reson, and repent.

10.   Me thoght I shewed man luf when I made hym to be
All angels abuf, like to the Trynyté;
And now in grete reprufe full low ligis he,
In erth hymself to stuf with syn that displeases Me   85
      Most of all.
Veniance will I take
In erth for syn sake;
My grame thus will I wake
      Both of grete and small.   90

11.   I repente full sore that euer maide I man;
Bi me he settis no store, and I am his soferan;
I will distroy therfor both beest, man and woman,
All shall perish, les and more; that bargan may thay ban
      That ill has done.   95
In erth I se right noght
Bot syn that is vnsoght;
Of those that well has wroght
      Fynd I bot a fone.

12.   Therfor shall I fordo all this medill-erd   100
With floodis that shall flo and ryn with hidous rerd;
I haue good cause therto; for Me no man is ferd.
As I say shal I do—of veniance draw My swerd,
      And make end

Of all that beris life,   105
Sayf Noe and his wife,
For thay wold neuer stryfe
    With Me, then Me offend.

13. Hym to mekill wyn, hastly will I go
    To Noe my seruand, or I blyn, to warn hym of his wo.
    In erth I se bot syn reynand to and fro,   111
    Emang both more and myn, ichon other fo
        With all thare entent.
    All shall I fordo
    With floodis that shall floo;   115
    Wirk shall I thaym wo
        That will not repent.

        [God descends and addresses Noah.]

14. Noe, My freend, I thee commaund, from cares the to keyle,
    A ship that thou ordand of nayle and bord ful wele.
    Thou was alway well-wirkand, to Me trew as stele,   120
    To My bydyng obediand: frendship shal thou fele
        To mede.
    Of lennthe thi ship be
    Thre hundreth cubettis, warn I the,
    Of heght euen thirté,   125
        Of fyfty als in brede.

15. Anoynt thi ship with pik and tar, without and als within,
    The water out to spar—this is a noble gyn;
    Look no man the mar, thre chese chambres begyn;
    Thou must spend many a spar this wark or thou wyn   130
        To end fully.
    Make in thi ship also
    Parloures oone or two,
    And houses of offyce mo
        For beestis that ther must be.   135

        129 chese] chefe *MS.*

16. Oone cubite on hight a wyndo shal thou make;
    On the syde a doore, with slyght, beneyth shal thou take;
    With the shal no man fyght, nor do the no kyn wrake.
    When all is doyne thus right, thi wife, that is thi make,
        Take in to the;   140
    Thi sonnes of good fame,
    Sem, Iaphet, and Came,
    Take in also ⟨t⟩hame,
        Thare wifis also thre.

17. For all shal be fordone that lif in land, bot ye,   145
    With floodis that from abone shal fall, and that plenté;
    It shall begyn full sone to rayn vncessantlé,
    After dayes seuen be done, and induyr dayes fourty,
        Withoutten fayll.
    Take to thi ship also   150
    Of ich kynd beestis two,
    Mayll and femayll, bot no mo,
        Or thou pull vp thi sayll,

18. For thay may the avayll when al this thyng is wroght.
    Stuf thi ship with vitayll, for hungre that ye perish noght.
    Of beestis, foull, and catayll, for thaym haue thou in
        thoght,   156
    For thaym is My counsayll that som socour be soght
        In hast.
    Thay must haue corn and hay,
    And oder mete alway.   160
    Do now as I the say,
        In the name of the Holy Gast.

19. *Noe.* A! *benedicite*! what art thou that thus
    Tellys afore that shall be? Thou art full mervelus!
    Tell me, for charité, thi name so gracius.   165
        Deus. My name is of dignyté, and also full glorius
        To knowe.

l am God most myghty,
Oone God in Trynyty,
Made the and ich man to be;   170
    To luf Me well thou awe.

20.   *Noe.* I thank The, Lord so dere, that wold vowchsayf
Thus low to appere to a symple knafe.
Blis vs, Lord, here, for charité I hit crafe,
The better may we stere the ship that we shall hafe, 175
    Certayn.
    Deus. Noe, to the and to thi fry
My blyssyng graunt I;
Ye shall wax and multiply
    And fill the erth agane,   180

21. When all thise floodis ar past, and fully gone away.
    Noe. Lord, homward will I hast as fast as that I may;
My ⟨wife⟩ will I frast what she will say,   [*Exit* Deus.]
And I am agast that we get som fray
    Betwixt vs both;   185
For she is full tethee,
For litill oft angré;
If any thyng wrang be,
    Soyne is she wroth.
        Tunc perget ad vxorem.

22. God spede, dere wife, how fayre ye?   190
    Vxor. Now, as euer myght I thryfe, the wars
    I thee see.
Do tell me belife where has thou thus long be?
To dede may we dryfe, or lif, for the,
    For want.
When we swete or swynk,   195
Thou dos what thou thynk,
Yit of mete and of drynk
    Haue we veray skant.

23.   *Noe.*   Wife, we ar hard sted with tythyngis new.

  Vxor.   Bot thou were worthi be cled in Stafford blew;

For thou art alway adred, be it fals or trew,   201

Bot God knowes I am led, and that may I rew,

  Full ill;

For I dar be thi borow,

From euen vnto morow   205

Thou spekis euer of sorow;

  God send the onys thi fill !

24.   We women may wary all ill husbandis;

I haue oone, bi Mary that lowsyd me of my bandis !

If he teyn, I must tary, how so euer it standis,   210

With seymland full sory, wryngand both my handis

  For drede.

  Bot yit other while,

What with gam and with gyle,

I shall smyte and smyle,   215

  And qwite hym his mede.

25.   *Noe.*   We ! hold thi tong, ram-skyt, or I shall the still.

  Vxor.   By my thryft, if thou smyte, I shal turne the

    vntill.

  Noe.   We shall assay as tyte.   Haue at the, Gill !

Apon the bone shal it byte.

  Vxor.   A, so, Mary ! thou smytis ill !   220

  Bot I suppose

I shal not in thi det

Flyt of this flett !

Take the ther a langett

  To tye vp thi hose !   225

26.   *Noe.*   A ! wilt thou so? Mary ! that is myne.

  Vxor.   Thou shal thre for two, I swere bi Godis pyne !

  Noe.   And I shall qwyte the tho, in fayth, or syne.

  Vxor.   Out apon the, ho !

Noe.   Thou can both byte and whyne
    With a rerd;   230
For all if she stryke,
Yit fast will she skryke ;
In fayth, I hold none slyke
    In all medill-erd.

27. Bot I will kepe charyté, for I haue at do.   235
    Vxor. Here shal no man tary the, I pray the go to ı
Full well may we mys the, as euer haue I ro ;
To spyn will I dres me.
    Noe.   Wel fare well, lo ;
    Bot wife,
Pray for me beselé   240
To eft I com vnto the.
    Vxor. Euen as thou prays for me,
    As euer myght I thrife.   [*Exit* Vxor.]

28.   *Noe.* I tary full lang fro my warke, I traw ;
Now my gere will I fang, and thederward draw ;   245
I may full ill gang, the soth for to knaw,
Bot if God help amang, I may sit downe daw
    To ken ;
Now assay will I
How I can of wrightry,   250
In nomine patris, et filii,
    Et spiritus sancti. Amen.

29. To begyn of this tree my bonys will I bend,
I traw from the Trynyté socoure will be send ;
It fayres full fayre, thynk me, this wark to my hend ; 255
Now blissid be He that this can amend.
    Lo, here the lenght,
Thre nundreth cubettis euenly;
Of breed, lo, is it fyfty ;
The heght is euen thyrty   260
    Cubettis full strenght.

30. Now my gowne will I cast and wyrk in my cote,
    Make will I the mast or I flyt oone foote;
    A! my bak, I traw, will brast! This is a sory note!
    Hit is wonder that I last, sich an old dote,   265
        All dold,
    To begyn sich a wark!
    My bonys ar so stark,
    No wonder if thay wark,
        For I am full old.   270

31. The top and the sayll both will I make,
    The helme and the castell also will I take,
    To drife ich a nayll will I not forsake,
    This gere may neuer fayll, that dar I vndertake
        Onone.   275
    This is a nobull gyn,
    Thise nayles so thay ryn
    Thoro more and myn
        Thise bordis ichon.

32. Wyndow and doore, euen as He saide,   280
    Thre ches chambre, thay ar well maide,
    Pyk and tar full sure therapon laide;
    This will euer endure, therof am I paide;
        For why?
    It is better wroght   185
    Then I coude haif thoght.
    Hym that maide all of noght
        I thank oonly.

33. Now will I hy me, and no thyng be leder,
    My wife and my meneye to bryng euen heder.   290
    Tent hedir tydely, wife, and consider,
    Hens must vs fle, all sam togeder,
        In hast.

Vxor. Whi, syr, what alis you?
Who is that asalis you? 295
To fle it avalis you
    And ye be agast.

34.   *Noe.* Ther is garn on the reyll other, my dame.
    Vxor. Tell me that ich a deyll, els get ye blame.
    Noe. He that cares may keill—blissid be His name!—
He has ⟨het⟩ for oure seyll to sheld vs fro shame, 301
    And sayd
All this warld aboute
With floodis so stoute,
That shall ryn on a route, 304
    Shall be ouerlaide.

35. He saide all shall be slayn, bot oonely we,
Oure barnes that ar bayn, and thare wifis thre.
A ship He bad me ordayn, to safe vs and oure fee;
Therfor with all oure mayn thank we that fre, 310
    Beytter of bayll.
Hy vs fast, go we thedir.
    Vxor. I wote neuer whedir,
I dase and I dedir
    For ferd of that tayll. 315

36.   *Noe.* Be not aferd, haue done, trus sam oure gere,
That we be ther or none, without more dere.
    Primus filius. It shall be done full sone. Brether,
        help to bere.
    Secundus filius. Full long shall I not hoyne to do my
        devere,
Brether sam. 320
    Tercius filius. Without any yelp,
At my myght shall I help.
    Vxor. Yit, for drede of a skelp,
    Help well thi dam.

37.   *Noe.*   Now ar we there as we shuld be ;   325
Do get in oure gere, oure catall and fe,
Into this vessell here, my chylder fre.
  Vxor.   I was neuer bard ere, as euer myght I the,
    In sich an oostré as this.
In fath, I can not fynd   330
Which is before, which is behynd.
Bot shall we here be pynd,
    Noe, as haue thou blis ?

38.   *Noe.*   Dame, as it is skill, here must vs abide grace ;
Therfor, wife, with good will, com into this place.   335
  Vxor.   Sir, for Iak nor for Gill will I turne my face,
Till I haue on this hill spon a space
    On my rok.
Well were he myght get me !
Now will I downe set me ;   340
Yit reede I no man let me,
    For drede of a knok.

39.   *Noe.*   Behold to the heuen the cateractes all,
Thai are open full euen, grete and small,
And the planettis seuen left has thare stall.   345
Thise thoners and levyn downe gar fall
    Full stout
Both halles and bowers,
Castels and towres.
Full sharp ar thise showers   350
    That renys aboute.

40.   Therfor, wife, haue done, com into ship fast.
  Vxor.   Yei, Noe, go cloute thi shone, the better will
    thai last.
  Prima mulier.   Good moder, com in sone, for all is
    ouercast
Both the son and the mone.

 Secunda mulier.   And many wynd blast   355
  Full sharp.
Thise floodis so thay ryn,
Therfor, moder, come in.
  Vxor.   In fayth, yit will I spyn ;
  All in vayn ye carp.   360

41. *Tercia mulier.*   If ye like ye may spyn, moder, in the
   ship.
  Noe. Now is this twyys com in, dame, on my frenship.
  Vxor. Wheder I lose or I wyn, in fayth, thi felowship
Set I not at a pyn.   This spyndill will I slip
  Apon this hill,   365
Or I styr oone fote.
  Noe.   Peter ! I traw we dote.
Without any more note
  Come in if ye will.

42. *Vxor.* Yei, water nyghys so nere that I sit not dry,   370
Into ship with a byr therfor will I hy
For drede that I drone here.
  Noe.   Dame, securly,
It bees boght ful dere ye abode so long by
  Out of ship.
  Vxor.   I will not, for thi bydyng,   375
Go from doore to mydyng.
  Noe.   In fayth, and for youre long taryyng
  Ye shal lik on the whyp.

43. *Vxor.* Spare me not, I pray the, bot euen as thou
   thynk,
Thise grete wordis shall not flay me.
  Noe.   Abide, dame, and drynk,   380
For betyn shall thou be with this staf to thou stynk ;
Ar strokis good ? say me.

Vxor.   What say ye, Wat Wynk?

Noe.   Speke!

Cry me mercy, I say!

    Vxor.   Therto say I nay.   385

    Noe.   Bot thou do, bi this day!

         Thi hede shall I breke.

44.   *Vxor.*   Lord, I were at ese, and hertely full hoylle,

Might I onys haue a measse of wedows coyll;

For thi saull, without lese, shuld I dele penny doyll,   390

So wold mo, no frese, that I se on this sole

     Of wifis that ar here,

For the life that thay leyd,

Wold thare husbandis were dede,

For, as euer ete I brede,   395

     So wold I oure syre were.

45.   *Noe.*   Yee men that has wifis, whyls they ar yong,

If ye luf youre lifis, chastice thare tong:

Me thynk my hert ryfis, both levyr and long,

To se sich stryfis wedmen emong.   400

     Bot I,

As haue I blys,

Shall chastyse this.

    Vxor.   Yit may ye mys,

     Nicholl Nedy!   405

46.   *Noe.*   I shall make þe still as stone, begynnar of blunder!

I shall bete the bak and bone, and breke all in sonder.

                           [*They fight.*]

    Vxor.   Out, alas, I am gone! Oute apon the, mans wonder!

    Noe.   Se how she can grone, and I lig vnder;

     Bot, wife,   410

In this hast let vs ho,
For my bak is nere in two.

   Vxor.   And I am bet so blo
    That I may not thryfe.

          [They enter the Ark.]

47.   *Primus filius.*   A! whi fare ye thus, fader and moder
      both?   415

   Secundus filius.   Ye shuld not be so spitus, standyng
    in sich a woth

   Tercius filius.   Thise ⟨floodis⟩ ar so hidus, with
    many a cold coth.

   Noe.   We will do as ye bid vs, we will no more be
    wroth,

    Dere barnes!

Now to the helme will I hent,   420
And to my ship tent.

   Vxor.   I se on the firmament,
    Me thynk, the seven starnes.

48.   *Noe.*   This is a grete flood, wife, take hede.

   Vxor.   So me thoght, as I stode; we ar in grete
    drede;   425

Thise wawghes ar so wode.

   Noe.   Help, God, in this nede!

As Thou art stereman good, and best, as I rede,
    Of all;

Thou rewle vs in this rase,
As Thou me behete hase.   430

   Vxor.   This is a perlous case.
    Help, God, when we call!

49.   *Noe.*   Wife, tent the stere-tre, and I shall asay
The depnes of the see that we bere, if I may.

   Vxor.   That shall I do ful wysely. Now go thi way, 435

For apon this flood haue we flett many day
　　With pyne.
　　Noe. Now the water will I sownd :
A ! it is far to the grownd ;
This trauell I expownd　　　　　　　　　　　440
　　Had I to tyne.

50. Aboue all hillys bedeyn the water is rysen late
Cubettis fyfteyn, bot in a higher state
It may not be, I weyn, for this well I wate :
This forty dayes has rayn beyn ; it will therfor abate　445
　　Full lele.
This water in hast
Eft will I tast.
Now am I agast,
　　It is wanyd a grete dele.　　　　　　　　　　450

51. Now are the weders cest, and cateractes knyt,
Both the most and the leest.
　　Vxor.　　　　　　　　Me thynk, bi my wit,
The son shynes in the eest. Lo, is not yond it ?
We shuld haue a good feest, were thise floodis flyt
　　So spytus.　　　　　　　　　　　　　　455
　　Noe. We haue been here, all we,
Thre hundreth dayes and fyfty.
　　Vxor. Yei, now wanys the see ;
　　Lord, well is vs !

52. *Noe.* The thryd tyme will I prufe what depnes we
　　bere.　　　　　　　　　　　　　　460
　　Vxor. *H*ow long shall thou hufe ? Lay in thy lyne
　　there.
　　Noe. I may towch with my lufe the grownd evyn
　　here.

Vxor. Then begynnys to grufe to vs mery chere;
  Bot, husband,
What grownd may this be?   465
  Noe. The hyllys of Armonye.
  Vxor. Now blissid be He
    That thus for vs can ordand!

53.   *Noe.* I see toppys of hyllys he, many at a syght,
No thyng to let me, the wedir is so bright.   470
  Vxor. Thise ar of mercy tokyns full right.
  Noe. Dame, th*ou* counsell me, what fowll best myght,
    And cowth,
With flight of wyng
Bryng, without taryying,   475
Of mercy som tokynyng,
    Ayther bi north or southe?

54. For this is the fyrst day of the tent moyne.
    Vxor. The ravyn, durst I lay, will com agane sone;
As fast as thou may, cast hym furth, haue done;   480
He may happyn today com agane or none
    With grath.
  Noe. I will cast out also
Dowfys oone or two.
Go youre way, go,   485
    God send you som wathe!

55. Now ar thise fowles flone into seyr countré;
Pray we fast ichon, kneland on our kne,
To Hym that is alone worthiest of degré,
That He wold send anone oure fowles som fee   490
    To glad vs.
  Vxor. Thai may not fayll of land,
The water is so wanand.
  Noe. Thank we God Allweldand,
    That Lord that made vs!   495

56. It is a wonder thyng, me thynk, sothlé,
Thai ar so long taryyng, the fowles that we
Cast out in the mornyng.
   Vxor.   Syr, it may be
Thai tary to thay bryng.
   Noe.   The ravyn is a-hungrye
    Allway;   500
He is without any reson;
And he fynd any caryon,
As peraventure may be fon,
    He will not away.

57. The dowfe is more gentill, her trust I vntew,   505
Like vnto the turtill, for she is ay trew.
   Vxor.   Hence bot a litill she commys, lew, lew!
She bryngys in her bill som novels new;
    Behald!
It is of an olif tre   510
A branch, thynkys me.
   Noe.   It is soth, perdé,
    Right so is it cald.

58. Doufe, byrd full blist, fayre myght the befall!
Thou art trew for to trist, as ston in the wall;   515
Full well I it wist thou wold com to thi hall.
   Vxor.   A trew tokyn ist we shall be sauyd all:
    For whi?
The water, syn she com,
Of depnes plom   520
Is fallen a fathom
    And more, hardely.

59.   *Primus filius.*   Thise floodis ar gone, fader, behold.
   Secundus filius.   Ther is left right none, and that be
    ye bold.
   Tercius filius.   As still as a stone oure ship is stold.   525

Noe.   Apon land here anone that we were, fayn I wold,
   My childer dere,
Sem, Iaphet and Cam,
With gle and with gam,
Com go we all sam,   530
   We will no longer abide here.

60.   *Vxor.*   Here haue we beyn, Noy, long enogh
With tray and with teyn, and dreed mekill wogh.
   Noe.   Behald on this greyn nowder cart ne plogh
Is left, as I weyn, nowder tre then bogh,   535
   Ne other thyng;
Bot all is away;
Many castels, I say,
Grete townes of aray,
   Flitt has this flowyng.   540

61.   *Vxor.*   Thise floodis not afright all this warld so wide
Has mevid with myght on se and bi side.
   Noe.   To dede ar thai dyght, prowdist of pryde,
Euerich a wyght that euer was spyde
   With syn,   545
All ar thai slayn,
And put vnto payn.
   Vxor.   From thens agayn
   May thai neuer wyn?

62.   *Noe.*   Wyn? No, iwis, bot He that myght hase   550
Wold myn of thare mys, and admytte thaym to grace;
As He in bayll is blis, I pray Hym in this space,
In heuen hye with His to purvaye vs a place,
   That we,
With His santis in sight,   555
And His angels bright,
May com to His light:
   Amen, for charité.
              Explicit processus Noe.

NOTES

I

Dialect: North-East Midland of Lincolnshire.

Inflexions:—

VERB : pres. ind. 2 sg. *hast* 131.
          3 sg. *stondeþ* 8.
          3 pl. *calle* 32, *seye* 254 ; beside
                  dos 157 (see note).
     imper. pl. *comeþ* 80, *doþ* 82.
     pres. p. *karoland* (in rime) 117, 150, 222.
     strong pp. *wryte* 37, *fal* 195, *gone* 161.

PRONOUN 3 PERS. : fem. nom. *she* 48 ; pl. nom. *þey* 32 ; poss. *here* 37 ; obj. *hem* 39.

The inflexions are very much simplified as compared with those of the Kentish *Ayenbyte* (III), but the verse shows that final unaccented -*e* was better preserved in the original than in our late MS., e. g.

    And specyaly at hygh⟨è⟩ tymès 13.
    For to see þys hard⟨è⟩ dome 173.
    And at þe þre⟨è⟩ day⟨è⟩s endè 198.
    þat nonè myȝt⟨è⟩ leye yn grauè 217.

Sounds: $\bar{\varrho}$ is regular for OE. *ā* : *lothe* 9, *wroth* 10, &c. ; but the only decisive rime is *also* (OE. *alswā*) : *to* (OE. *tō*) 35–6, where $\bar{\varrho}$ after (*s*)*w* has become close $\bar{\varrho}$; see Appendix § 8. ii, note.

Syntax: the loose constructions, e. g. ll. 15 ff. (note), 134–5, 138–9, 216–19, are characteristic of the period.

The history of this legend is traced by E. Schröder, *Zeitschrift für Kirchengeschichte*, vol. xvii, 1896, pp. 94 ff., and, more summarily, by Gaston Paris, *Les Danseurs maudits*, Paris 1900. The circumstances from which it sprang appear to belong to the year 1021. Kölbigk, in Anhalt, Saxony, was the scene of the dance. In 1074 it is referred to as 'famous' by a German chronicler, who records the healing of one of the dancers in 1038 through the miraculous powers of St. Wigbert.

Mendicants who suffered from or could simulate nervous diseases like St. Vitus's dance, were quick to realize their opportunity, and two letters telling the story were circulated as credentials by pretended survivors of the band. Both are influenced in form by a sermon of St. Augustine of Hippo which embodies a similar story (Migne, *Patrologia*, vol. xxxviii, col. 1443). The first (Letter of Otbert), which claims to be issued by Peregrinus bishop of Cologne, spread rapidly through Western Europe. This was the version that Mannyng found in *Manual de Pechiez*. The second (Letter of Theodric) makes Bruno bishop of Toul, afterwards Pope Leo IX, vouch for the facts. In its extant form it derives from the Latin 'Legend of St. Edith of Wilton' by the monk Goscelin, who wrote about the year 1080 (see A. Wilmart, *Analecta Bollandiana* lvi, fasc. iii and iv, 1938). This was the text that Mannyng used. A later English version is found in the dreary fifteenth-century *Life of St. Editha* (ed. Horstmann, ll. 4063 ff.).

1 ff. *games*: Dances and shows in the churchyard were constantly condemned by the Church in the thirteenth and fourteenth centuries. In 1287 a synod at Exeter rules *ne quisquam luctas, choreas, vel alios ludos inhonestos in coemeteriis exercere praesumat, praecipue in vigiliis et festis sanctorum.* See Chambers, *The Mediaeval Stage*, vol. i, pp. 90 ff.

6. *or tabure bete*: Note the use of *bete* infin. as a verbal noun = *betyng*; cp. XI *b* 184–5.

10–12. 'And he (*sc.* a good priest) will become angered sooner than one who has no learning, and who does not understand Holy Writ.'

15 ff. *noght ... none*: An accumulation of negatives in ME. makes the negation more emphatic. Here the writer wavers between two forms of expression: (1) 'do not sing carols in holy places', and (2) 'to sing carols in holy places is sacrilege'.

25–8. *yn þys londe*, &c. The cure of Theodric, not the dance, took place in England. Brightgiva is said to have been abbess of Wilton at the time, and 'King Edward' is Edward the Confessor (1042–66).

34–5. The church of Kölbigk is dedicated to St. Magnus, of whom nothing certain is known. The memory of St. Bukcestre, if ever there was such a saint, appears to be preserved only in this story.

36. *þat þey come to*: Construe with *hyt* in l. 35.

37 ff. *Here names of alle*: The twelve followers of Gerlew are named in the Latin text, but Mannyng gives only the principal actors. The inconsistency is still more marked in the Bodleian MS., which after l. 40 adds:—

þe ouþer twelue here names alle
þus were þey wrete, as y can kalle.

Otherwise the Bodleian MS. is very closely related to the Harleian sharing most of its errors and peculiarities.

44. *þe prestes doghtyr of þe tounne*, 'the priest of the town's daughter'. In early ME. the genitive inflexion is not, as in Modern English, added to the last of a group of words: cp. XIV *d* 10 *Þe Kynges sone of heuene* 'the King of Heaven's son'. The same construction occurs in VIII *a* 19 *for þe Lordes loue of heuene* = 'for the love of the Lord of Heaven', and in VIII *a* 214; but in these passages the genitive is objective, and Modern English does not use the inflexion at all (note to I 83). The ME. and modern expressions have their point of agreement in the position of the genitive inflexion, which always precedes immediately the noun on which the genitive depends. Cp. notes to II 518, VI 23, and XIV *d* 1.

46. *Aȝone*: *ȝ* = *z* here. The name is *Azo* in the Latin.

55. *Beu⟨u⟩ne*: (derived from the accusative *Beuonem*)=*Beuo* of l. 59 and *Beuolyne* of l. 62. The form is properly *Bovo* not *Bevo*. Considerable liberties were taken with proper names to adapt them to metre or rime: e. g. l. 52 *Merswynde*; l. 63 *Merswyne*; cp. note to l. 246. This habit, and frequent miscopying, make it difficult to rely on names in mediaeval stories.

61. *Quid stamus? Cur non imus [hinc]?*: Terence, *Eunuchus*, l. 465.

65. *Grysly*: An error for *Gerlew*, Latin *Gerleuus*, from Low German *Gērlēf* = OE. *Gārlāf*.

83. *for Crystys awe*: In Modern English a phrase like *Christ's awe* could mean only 'the awe felt by Christ'. But in OE. *Cristes ege*, or *ege Cristes*, meant also 'the awe of Christ (which men feel)', the genitive being objective. In ME. the word order *eie Cristes* is dropped, but *Cristes eie* (or *awe*, the Norse form) is still regular for '(men's) fear of Christ'. Hence formal ambiguities like *þe Lordes loue of heuene* VIII *a* 19, which actually means '(men's) love of the Lord of Heaven', but grammatically might mean 'the Lord of Heaven's love (for men)'—see note to l. 44 above.

96-7. The Latin Letter of Theodric in fact has *ab isto officio ex Dei nutu amodo* (henceforth) *non cessetis*.

127. *a saue*: lit. 'have safe', i.e. 'rescue'. *Saue* is here adj.

128-9. *ys : flessh*: The rime requires the alternative forms *es* (as in l. 7) and *fles(s)*. Cp. note to VII 4.

132. *ȝow þar nat aske*: 'There is no need for you to ask'; *ȝow* is dative after the impersonal *þar*.

156-7. *werynes : dos*. The rime is false. Perhaps Mannyng wrote: *As many body for goyng es* [sc. *wery*], and a copyist misplaced *es*, writing: *As many body es for goyng*. If *body es* were read as *bodyes*, a new verb would then be added.

169. Note the irony of the refrain. The Letter of Otbert adds the picturesque detail that they gradually sank up to their waists in the ground through dancing on the same spot.

172. *Þe Emperoure Henry* : Probably Henry II of Germany, Emperor from 1014 to 1024. A certain vagueness in points of time and place would save the bearers of the letter from awkward questions.

188-9. *banned* : *woned.* The rime (OE. *bannan* and *wunian*) is false, and the use of *woned* 'remained' is suspicious. Mannyng perhaps wrote *bende* 'put in bonds': *wende* (= *ȝede* l. 191) 'went'; or (if the form *band* for *banned(e)* could be evidenced so early) *band* 'cursed' : *wand*, pret. of *winden*, 'went'.

195. *fal yn a swone* : So MS., showing that by the second half of the fourteenth century the pp. adj. *aswon* had been wrongly analysed into the indef. article *a* and a noun *swon.* Mannyng may have written *fallen aswone.* See Glossary, *s.v. aswone.*

234. *Wyth sundyr lepys* : 'with separate leaps'; but *Wyth* was probably added by a scribe who found in his original *sundyrlepys*, adv., meaning 'separately',—

> Kar suvent par les mains
> Des malvais escrivains
> Sunt livre corrumput.

240. *Seynt Edyght.* St. Edith (d. 984) was daughter of King Edgar, and a nun of Wilton. The rime is properly *Edit : Teodric*, for *t* and *k* are sufficiently like in sound to rime together in the best ME. verse ; cp. note to XV *g* 27.

246. *Brunyng . . . seynt Tolous* : Latin *Bruno Tullanus.* Robert probably did not hesitate to provide a rime by turning Toul into Toulouse. Bruno afterwards became Pope Leo IX (1049-54).

254-5. *trowed* : *God.* Read *trŏd*, a shortened form, revealed by rimes in North Midland texts. The identical rime occurs three times in Mannyng's *Chronicle* (ed. Hearne, p. 339; ed. Furnivall, ll. 7357-8, 8111-12); and, again with substitution of *troud* for *trod*, in *Havelok*, ll. 2338-9.

II

Dialect : South-Western, with some admixture of Northern forms due to a copyist.

Inflexions :—

VERB: pres. ind. 1 sg. *ichaue*, &c. (see note to l. 129).

> 2 sg. *makest* 169, *worst* 170.
>
> 3 sg. *geþ* (in rime) 238; contracted *fint* 239, *last* 335, *sitt* 443, *stont* 556.
>
> 2 pl. *ȝe beþ* 582.
>
> 3 pl. *strikeþ* 252 (proved by rime with 3 sg. *likeþ*).

imper. pl. *make* 216, *chese* 217 ; beside *doþ* 218.

pres. p. *berking* 286 (in rime with verbal sb.);
daunceing (in rime) 298. The forms *kneland*
250, *liggeand* 388, are due to a Northern
copyist.

strong pp. (various forms): *go* (: *wo*) 196, *ygo* (: *mo*)
349, *ydone* (: -*none*) 76, *comen* 29, *come* 181,
ycomen 203, *yborn* 174, *bore* 210.

infin. Note *aski* (OE. *acsian*) 467 (App. § 13 vii).

PRONOUN 3 PERS.: fem. nom. *he* 408, 446, *hye* 337, beside
sche 75, 77, &c.

pl. nom. *he* (in rime) 185, *hye* 91,
beside *þai* 32, 69, &c.; poss. *her*
'their' 87, 413, 415; obj. *hem*
69, &c.

NOUN: Note the plurals *honden* 79, *berien* 258.

The original text preserved final -*e* better than the extant
MSS., e. g.

And seyd⟨e⟩ þus þe king⟨e⟩ to 119.
Þat noþing help⟨e⟩ þe no schal 172.
Al þe vt⟨e⟩mast⟨e⟩ wal 357.
So, sir, as ꝛe seyd⟨e⟩ nouþè 466.

Sounds: *ǭ* for OE. *ā* is proved in rime: *biholde* (OE.
behǻldan): *gold* (OE. *gǿld*) 367–8 (cp. 467–8); and *yhote*
(OE. *gehāten*): *note* (OFr. *note*) 601–2.

The rime *frut* : *lite* 257–8 points to original *frut* : *lut* (OE. *lȳt*),
with Western *ü*, from OE. *ȳ*, riming with OFr. *ü*.

1–22. These lines, found also in *Lai le Freine*, would serve
as preface to any of the Breton lays, with the couplet ll. 23–4
as the special connecting link. In the Auchinleck MS., *Orfeo*
begins on a fresh leaf at l. 25, without heading or capitals to
indicate that it is a new poem. The leaf preceding has been
lost. There is good reason to suppose that it contained the
lines supplied in the text from the Harleian MS.

4. *frely*, 'goodly': *Lai le Freine* has *ferly* 'wondrous'.

12. MS. *moost to lowe*: means 'most (worthy) to be praised',
and there are two or three recorded examples of *to lowe* = *to
alowe* in this sense. But MS. Ashmole and the corresponding
lines in *Lai le Freine* point to *most o loue* 'mostly of love' as
the common reading. The typical 'lay' is a poem of moderate
length, telling a story of love, usually with some supernatural
element, in a refined and courtly style.

13. *Brytayn*, 'Brittany': so *Brytouns* 16 = 'Bretons'. Cp.
Chaucer, *Franklin's Tale, Prologue*, beginning

Thise olde gentil Britons in hir dayes
Of diverse aventures maden layes
Rymeyed in hir firste Briton tonge,
Whiche layes with hir instrumentz they songe, &c

20. The curious use of *it* after the plural *layes* is perhaps not original. *Lai le Freine* has : *And maked a lay and yaf it name.*

26. *In Inglond* : an alteration of the original text to give local colour. Cp. ll. 49–50 and l. 478.

29–30. *Pluto* : the King of Hades came to be regarded as the King of Fairyland ; cp. Chaucer, *Merchant's Tale*, l. 983 *Pluto that is the kyng of fairye.* The blunder by which Juno is made a king is apparently peculiar to the Auchinleck copy.

33–46. These lines are not in the Auchinleck MS., but are probably authentic. Otherwise little prominence would be given to Orfeo's skill as a harper.

41 ff. A confused construction : *In þe world was neuer man born* should be followed by ⟨*þat*⟩ *he* ⟨*ne*⟩ *schulde þinke*; but the writer goes on as if he had begun with ' every man in the world '. *And* = ' if '.

46. *ioy and* overload the verse, and are probably an unskilful addition to the text.

49–50. These lines are peculiar to the Auchinleck MS., and are clearly interpolated ; cp. l. 26 and l. 478. Winchester was the old capital of England, and therefore the conventional seat of an English king.

57. *comessing* : The metre points to a disyllabic form *comsing* here, and to *comsi* in l. 247.

80. *it bled wete* : In early English the clause which is logically subordinate is sometimes made formally co-ordinate. More normal would be *þat* (*it*) *bled wete* ' until (*or* so that) it bled wet '; i. e. until it was wet with blood.

82. *reuey*⟨*se*⟩*d* or some such form of *ravished* is probably right. *reneyd* ' apostate ' is a possible reading of the MS., but does not fit the sense. *N. E. D.* suggests *remeued*.

102. *what is te ?* : ' What ails you ? '; cp. l. 115. *Te* for *þe* after *s* of *is*. Such modifications are due either to dissimilation of like sounds, as *þ : s* which are difficult in juxtaposition ; or to assimilation of unlike sounds, as *þatow* 165, for *þat þow*.

115. ' What ails you, and how it came about ? '; cp. l. 102.

129. *ichil* = *ich wille* ; and so *ichaue* 209, *icham* 382, *ichot* XV *b* 23. These forms, reduced to *chill*, *cham*, &c., were still characteristic of the Southern dialect in Shakespeare's time : cp. *King Lear*, IV. vi. 239 *Chill not let go, Zir.*

131. *þat nouȝt nis* : ' That cannot be '; cp. l. 457 *þat nouȝt nere.*

157–8. *palays : ways.* The original rime was perhaps *palys : wys* ' wise '.

170. ' Wherever you may be, you shall be fetched.'

201–2. *barouns : renouns.* Forms like *renouns* in rime are usually taken over from a French original.

215. The overloaded metre points to a shorter word like *wite* for *vnderstond*.

216. *Make ȝou þan a parlement*: *ȝou* is not nom., but dat. 'for yourselves'. Observe that Orfeo acts like a constitutional English king.

241. *þe fowe and griis*: A half translation of OFr. *vair et gris*. *Vair* (Lat. *varius*) was fur made of alternate pieces of the grey back and white belly of the squirrel. Hence it is rendered by *fowe*, OE. *fāg* 'varicolor'. *Griis* is the grey back alone, and the French word is retained for the rime with *biis*, which was probably in the OFr. original.

258. *berien*: The MS. may be read *berren*, but it is better to assume that the *i* has been carelessly shaped by the scribe.

289. *him se*, 'see (for himself)', and similarly *slep þou þe* XV *g* 13. This reflexive use of the dative pronoun, which cannot be reproduced in a modern rendering, is common in OE. and ME., especially with verbs of motion; cp. note to XV *g* 24. But distinguish *went him* 475, 501, where *him* is accusative, not dative (OE. *wente hine*), because the original sense of *went* is 'turned', which takes a reflexive object.

342. *me no reche = I me no reche*. The alternative would be the impersonal *me no recheþ*.

343. *also spac = also bliue* 142 = *also swiþe* 574: 'straightway', &c.

363. MS. *auowed* (or *anowed*) is meaningless here. *Anow⟨rn⟩ed*, or the doubtful by-form *anow⟨r⟩ed* 'adorned', is probably the true reading.

364. *aumal*, 'enamel'. Holthausen's correction for *animal* (*Anglia*, vol. xlii, p. 427) is confirmed by the MS.

382. The line is too long—a fault not uncommon where direct speech is introduced, e. g. l. 419 and I 78. Usually a correct line can be obtained by dropping words like *quath he*, which are not as necessary in spoken verse as they are where writing alone conveys the sense. But sometimes the flaw may lie in the forms of address: l. 382 would be normal without *Parfay*; l. 419 may once have been:

> *And seyd 'Lord, ȝif þi wille were'*.

There is no task more slippery than the metrical reconstruction of ME. poems, particularly those of which the extant text derives from the original not simply through a line of copyists, but through a line of minstrels who passed on the verses from memory and by word of mouth.

388. The line seems to be corrupt, and, as usual, the Harleian and Ashmole MSS. give little help. *Ful* can hardly be a sb. meaning 'multitude' from the adj. *full*. Some form of *fele* (OE. *fela*) 'a great number' would give possible grammar and sense (cp. l. 401), but bad metre. Perhaps *ful* should be deleted

as a scribe's anticipation of *folk* in the next line ; for the construction *seiȝe . . . of folk* cp. XVI 388 ; and *Hous of Fame*, Bk. iii,
ll. 147 ff.

433. *Þei we nouȝt welcom no be* : Almost contemporary with
Sir Orfeo is the complaint of an English writer that the halls of
the nobles stood open to a lawyer, but not to a poet :

> *Exclusus ad ianuam poteris sedere*
> *Ipse licet venias, Musis comitatus, Homere !*

'Though thou came thyself, Homer, with all the Muses,
thou mightst sit at the door, shut out ! ', T. Wright, *Political
Songs* (1839), p. 209.

446. *hadde he*, 'had she'. For *he* (OE. *hēo*) = 'she' cp.
l. 408.

450. 'Now ask of me whatsoever it may be'. The plots of
mediaeval romances often depend on the unlimited promises of
an unwary king, whose honour compels him to keep his word.
So in the story of Tristram, an Irish noble disguised as a
minstrel wins Ysolde from King Mark by this same device, but
is himself cheated of his prize by Tristram's skill in music.

458. 'An ill-matched pair you two would be ! '

479. The halting verse may be completed by adding *sum
tyme* before *his*, with the Harley and Ashmole MSS.

483. *ybilt* of the MS. and editors cannot well be a pp. meaning
'housed'. I prefer to take *bilt* as sb. = *bild, build* 'a building';
and to suppose that *y* has been miswritten for *ȳ*, the contraction
for *yn*.

495. *gan hold*, 'held' ; a good example of the ME. use of
gan + infinitive with the sense of the simple preterite.

515. An unhappy suggestion *home* for the second *come* has
sometimes been accepted. But a careful Southern poet could
not rime *home* (OE. *hām*) and *some* (OE. *sŭm*). See note to
VI 224.

518. *For mi lordes loue Sir Orfeo*, 'for my lord Sir Orfeo's
love'. Logically the genitive inflexion should be added to both
of two substantives in apposition, as in OE. *on Herodes dagum
cyninges* 'in the days of King Herod'. But in ME. the first
substantive usually has the inflexion, and the second is uninflected ; cp. V 207 *kyngeȝ hous Arthor* 'the house of King
Arthur' ; and notes to I 44, VI 23.

544. *Allas ! wreche : wreche* refers to the speaker, as in l. 333.

551. *hou it geþ* — : The sense is hard to convey without some
cumbrous paraphrase like 'the inexorable law of this world — '.

552. *It nis no bot of manes deþ* : 'There is no remedy for
man's death', i. e. violent grief will do no good. Note *it nis*
'there is (not)'. In ME. the anticipated subject is commonly
it where we use *there*.

565. *in ynome*: '(had) taken up my abode'; *in* 'dwelling' = NE. 'inn'. But *her* may be for 'her' rather than 'here'; and Ashmole MS. points to *oure*. See ll. 484 f.

599. *herof* overloads the line and is omitted in the Ashmole MS.

III

Dialect: Pure Kentish of Canterbury.

Inflexions are well preserved, and are similar to those found in contemporary South-Western texts.

> VERB: pres. ind. 3 sg. *multiplieþ* 1; contracted *ret* 3, 16. 1 pl. *habbeþ* 2.
>
> strong pp. *yyeue* 25, *yhote* 29.
>
> PRONOUN 3 PERS.: the new forms *she, they, their, them* are not used. 3 sg. fem. nom. *hi* 32, *hy* 45; poss. *hare* 33, beside *hire* 36; pl. nom. *hi* 58. Note the objective form *his(e)* = 'her' 32, 53 (twice); and = 'them' 7, 8, 28.
>
> NOUN: plurals in *-en* occur: *uorbisnen* 2, *ken* 56. In *diaknen* 5, *-en* represents the dat. pl. inflexion.
>
> ADJECTIVE: *onen* dat. sg. 4, *oþren* dat. pl. 53, *þane* acc. sg. masc. 59, *þet (word)* nom. sg. neut. 57, show survivals rare even in the South at this date.

Sounds: Characteristic of the South-East is *ē* for OE. (West-Saxon) *ȳ*: *kertel* (OE. *cyrtel*) 39, *ken* (OE. *cȳ*) 56.

Old diphthongs are preserved in *greate* (OE. *grēat*) 9, *yeaf* 22. In *hyerof* 1, *yhyerde* 49, *hier* 2, *þieues* 18, *ye, ie* represent diphthongs developed in Kentish rather than simple close *ē*.

Initial *z* = *s* in *zome* 'some' 2, *zede* 'said' 12, *zuo* 'so' 17; and initial *u* = *f* in *uele* 2, *uayre* 2, *uram* 4, *bevil* 41, evidence dialectical changes which occurred also in the South-West.

Syntax: The constructions are distorted by slavish following of the French original; and see note to ll. 48–60.

3. Saint Germain of Auxerre (MS. *Aucerne*) is famous for his missions to Britain in the first half of the fifth century. This particular story is found in the *Acta Sanctorum* for July 31, p. 229.

16. St. John the Almoner (d. 616) was bishop of Alexandria. For the story see *Acta Sanctorum* for January 23, p. 115.

27-8. *and huanne he hit wiste þe ilke zelue þet his hedde onderuonge*: an obscure sentence. Perhaps: 'and when he, the same who had received them (i. e. John, who had received the five hundred pounds), knew it' (sc. the truth).

38. This tale of Boniface, bishop of Ferentia in Etruria, is told in the *Dialogues* of Gregory the Great, Bk. i, chap. 9. Its first appearance in English is in the translation of the *Dialogues*

made by Bishop Wærferth for King Alfred (ed. Hans Hecht, Leipzig 1900, pp. 67 ff.).

48–60. The French original of the passage, taken from an elegant fourteenth-century MS., Cotton Cleopatra A.V., fol. 144a, will show how slavishly Dan Michael followed his source :—

Apres il fu un poure home, sicom on dit, qui auoit une vache; e oi dire a son prestre en sarmon que Dieu disoit en leuangile que Dieu rendoit a cent doubles quanque on donast por lui. Le prodomme du conseil sa femme dona sa uache a son prestre, qui estoit riches. Le prestre la prist uolentiers, e lenuoia pestre auoec les autres quil auoit. Kant uint au soir, la uache au poure home sen uint a son hostel chies le poure homme, com ele auoit acoustume, e amena auoeques soi toutes les uaches au prestre, iukes a cent. Quant le bon home uit ce, si pensa que ce estoit le mot de leuangile que li auoit rendu; e li furent aiugiees deuant son euesque contre le prestre. Cest ensample moustre bien que misericorde est bone marchande, car ele multiplie les biens temporels.

58–9. 'And they were adjudged to him before his bishop against the priest', i. e. the bishop ruled that the poor man should have all the cows.

The French *fabliau* '*Brunain*' takes up the comic rather than the moral aspect of the story. A peasant, hearing the priest say that gifts to God are doubly repaid, thought it was a favourable opportunity to give his cow Blérain—a poor milker —to the priest. The priest ties her with his own cow Brunain. To the peasant's great joy, the unprofitable Blérain returns home, leading with her the priest's good cow.

IV

Dialect : Northern of Yorkshire.

Inflexions : are reduced almost as in Modern English.

VERB : pres. ind. 1 sg. *settes a* 30 ; beside uninflected *sygh a* 69, *sob a* 69.

    3 sg. *lastes a* 1.

    1 pl. *flese b* 86 : beside *we drede b* 85.

    3 pl. *lyse a* 61, *lufes b* 7, &c. ; beside *þay take*, *þay halde b* 12, &c., which agree with the Midland forms.

  pres. p. *lastand a* 25, *byrnand a* 26, riming with *hand*.

  strong pp. *wryten a* 2.

      Note the Northern and North Midland short forms *mase* 'makes' *a* 15, *tane* 'taken' *a* 53 (in rime).

PRONOUN 3 PERS.: sg. fem. *scho* *b* 1; pl. nom. *þai a* 60; poss. *þar a* 59 or *þair a* 65; obj. *thaym* *b* 2. The demonstrative *thire* 'these' at *b* 55, *b* 59 is specifically Northern.

Sounds: OE. *ā* is regularly represented by *ā*, not by *ǭ* of the South and most of the Midlands: *wa a* 2, *euermare a* 20, *balde* 'bold' *a* 51; *bane* (in rime) *a* 54.

ǭ becomes *ū* (*ū̃*?) in *gud*(*e*) *b* 9, *b* 15; and its length is sometimes indicated by adding *y*, as in *ruysand* 'vaunting' *b* 80.

---

a. This poem is largely a translation of sentences excerpted from Rolle's *Incendium Amoris*, cc. xl–xli (Miss Allen in *Mod. Lang. Review* for 1919, p. 320). Useful commentaries are his prose *Form of Perfect Living* (ed. Horstmann, vol. i, pp. 3 ff.), and *Commandment of Love to God* (ibid. pp. 61 ff.), which supply many parallels in thought and phrasing; see, for example, the note to l. 48 below.

a 1. *feste.* Not the adj. 'fast', but pp. 'fastened', and so in l. 82.

a 5. *louyng*, 'beloved one', here and in l. 56. This exceptional use of the verbal noun occurs again in *my ȝhernyng* 'what I yearn for', *a* 22; *my couaytyng* 'what I covet', *a* 23.

a 9–12. The meaning seems to be: 'The throne of love is raised high, for it (i. e. love) ascended into heaven. It seems to me that on earth love is crafty, for it makes men pale and wan. It goes very near to the bed of bliss (i. e. the bridal bed of Christ and the soul) I assure you. Though the way may seem long to us, yet love unites God and man.'

a 24. *louyng*, 'praise' here and in XVI 405, from OE. *lof* 'praise'; quite distinct from *louyng*, *lufyng*, in ll. 5 and 56.

a 36. *fle þat na man it maye*, 'which no man can escape'. See Appendix § 12, Relative.

a 42. *styll*, 'always' rather than 'motionless'.

a 43–4. Apparently 'the nature of love (*þat kyend*) turns from care the man (*þe lyfe*) who succeeds in finding love, or who ever knew it in his heart; and brings him to joy and delight.'

a 48. Cp. *Form of Perfect Living*, ed. Horstmann, vol. i, pp. 39–40: *For luf es stalworth als þe dede, þat slaes al lyuand thyng in erth; and hard als hell, þat spares noght till þam þat er dede.* In *The Commandment of Love* Rolle explains: *For als dede slas al lyuand thyng in bis worlde, sa perfite lufe slas in a mans sawle all fleschly desyres and erthly couaytise. And als hell spares noght til dede men, bot tormentes al þat commes bartill, alswa a man þat es in þis* [sc. the third, called 'Singular'] *degré of lufe noght anly he forsakes þe wretched solace of þis lyf, bot alswa he couaytes to sofer pynes for Goddes lufe.* (Ibid. p. 63.)

b 4. *scho takes erthe* : From the *Historia Animalium* attributed to Aristotle, Bk. ix, c. 21. This is the authority referred to at l. 18, and at l. 33 (Bk. ix, c. 9) ; but the citations seem to be second hand, as they do not agree closely with the text of the *Historia Animalium*.

b 21-2. 'For there are many who never can keep the rule of love towards their friends, whether kinsmen or not.' MS. *ynesche* has been variously interpreted ; but it must be corrected to *ynence*.

b 47. *strucyo or storke* : the ostrich, not the stork, is meant. Latin *struthio* has both meanings. On the whole, fourteenth-century translators show a fair knowledge of Latin, but the average of scholarship, even among the clergy, was never high in the Middle Ages. In the magnificent Eadwine Psalter, written at Canterbury Cathedral in the twelfth century, Ps. ci. 7 *similis factus sum pellicano* is rendered by ' I am become like to the skin of a dog ' (= *pelli canis*), though an ecclesiastic would recite this psalm in Latin at least once every week. The records of some thirteenth-century examinations of English clergy may be found in G. G. Coulton, *A Medieval Garner* (London 1910), pp. 270 ff. They include the classic answer of Simon, the curate of Sonning, who, being examined on the Canon of the Mass, and pressed to say what governed *Te* in *Te igitur, clementissime Pater, . . . supplices rogamus*, replied ' *Pater*, for He governeth all things '. As for French, Michael of Northgate, a shaky translator, is fortunate in escaping gross blunders in the specimen chosen (III) ; but the English rendering of Mandeville's *Travels* is full of errors ; see the notes to IX.

b 60. *teches* : better *toches*, according to the foot-note.

V

Alliterative Verse. The long lines in *Gawayne*, with *The Destruction of Troy*, *Piers Plowman*, and *The Blacksmiths* (XV *h*), are specimens of alliterative verse unmixed with rime, a form strictly comparable with Old English verse, from which it must derive through an unbroken oral tradition. While the detailed analysis of the Middle English alliterative line is complex and controversial, its general framework is describable in simple terms. It will be convenient to take examples from *Gawayne*, which shows most of the developments characteristic of Middle English.

1. The long line is divided by a caesura into two half lines, of which the second is the more strictly built so that the rhythm may be well marked. Each half line normally contains two principal stresses, e. g.

And wént on his wáy ‖ with his wýȝe óne 6.
Þat schulde téche hym to tóurne ‖ to þat téne pláce 7.
But three stresses are not uncommonly found in the first half
line :
Brókeȝ býled and bréke ‖ bi bónkkeȝ abóute 14 ;
and, even for the simpler forms in Old and Middle English, the
two-stress analysis has its opponents.

2. The two half lines are bound together by alliteration. In
alliteration *ch, st, s(c)h, sk,* and usually *sp,* are treated as single
consonants (see lines 64, 31, 15, 99, 25) ; any vowel may alliterate
with any other vowel, e. g.
Þis óritore is úgly ‖ with érbeȝ ouergrówen 122 ;
and, contrary to the practice of correct OE. verse, *h* may alliterate with vowels in *Gawayne* :
Hálde þe now þe hýȝe hóde ‖ þat Árþur þe ráȝt 229.
The háþel héldet hym fró ‖ and on his áx résted 263.

3. In correct OE. verse the alliteration falls on one or both of
the two principal stresses of the first half line, and invariably on
the first stress only of the second half line. This is the ordinary
ME. type :
Þat schulde téche hym to tóurne ‖ to þat téne pláce 7 ;
though verses with only one alliterating syllable in the first half
line, e. g.
Bot Í wyl to þe chápel ‖ for cháunce þat may fálle 64,
are less common in ME. than in OE. But in ME. the fourth
stress sometimes takes the alliteration also :
Þay clómben bi clýffeȝ ‖ þer cléngeȝ þe cólde 10.
And when there is a third stress in the first half line, five
syllables may alliterate :
Míst múged on þe mór ‖ mált on þe móunteȝ 12.
In sum, Middle English verse is richer than Old English in
alliteration.

4. In all these verses the alliteration of the first stress in the
second half line, which is essential in Old English, is maintained ;
but it is sometimes neglected, especially when the alliteration is
otherwise well marked :
With héȝe hélme on his héde ‖ his láunce in his hónde (129; cp. 75),
where the natural stress cannot fall on *his.*

5. So far attention has been confined to the stressed syllables,
around which the unstressed syllables are grouped. Clearly the
richer the alliteration, the more freedom will be possible in the
treatment of the unstressed syllables without undue weakening
of the verse form. In the first two lines of *Beowulf*—
Hwæt we Gárdéna ‖ in géardágum
Þéodcýninga ‖ þrým gefrúnon—
three of the half lines have the minimum number of syllables—
four—and the other has only five. In Middle English, with

more elaborate alliteration, the number of unstressed syllables
is increased, so that the minimum half line of four syllables is
rare, and often contains some word which may have had an
additional flexional syllable in the poet's own manuscript, e. g.

‖ *þe sélf⟨e⟩ chápel*   79.
‖ *árȝeȝ in hért⟨e⟩*   209.

The less regular first half line is found with as many as eleven
syllables; e.g.

And syþen he kéuereȝ bi a crágge ‖   153.

6. The grouping of stressed and unstressed syllables determines the rhythm. In Old English the falling rhythm predomi-
nates, as in ‖ *Gáwayn þe nóble* 81 ; and historically it is no
doubt correct to trace the development of the ME. line from
a predominantly falling rhythm. But in fact, owing to the
frequent use of unstressed syllables before the first stress (even
in the second half line where they are avoided in the OE. falling
rhythm) the commonest type is:

‖ *and þe bróde ȝáteȝ* 1,
(×   ×   ⊥ ×   ⊥ ×)

which from a strictly Middle English standpoint may be
analysed as a falling rhythm with introductory syllables
(× × | ⊥ × ⊥ ×), or as a rising rhythm with a weak ending
(× × ⊥ × ⊥ | ×). A careful reader, accustomed to the usage of
English verse, will have no difficulty in following the movement,
without entering into nice technicalities of historical analysis.

7. *The Destruction of Troy* is more regular than *Gawayne* in
its versification, and better preserves the Old English tradition.
Piers Plowman is looser and nearer to prose, so that the
alliteration sometimes fails altogether, e.g. Extract *a* 95, 138.
Such differences in technique may depend on date, on locality,
or on the taste, training, or skill of the author.

Dialect : West Midland of Lancashire or Cheshire. (There
is evidence of local knowledge in the account of Gawayne's ride
in search of the Green Chapel, ll. 691 ff. of the complete text.)

Vocabulary. *Sir Gawayne* shows the characteristic vocabulary of alliterative verse.

It is rich in number and variety of words—Norse, French,
and native. Besides common words like *race* 8, *wylle* 16, *kyrk*
128, *aȝ-* 267 (which displace native English forms *rēs*, *wylde*,
chyrche, *eie*), Norse gives *mug*(*g*)*ed* 12, *cayreȝ* 52, *scowtes* 99,
skayned 99, *wro* 154, *broþe* 165, *fyked* 206, *snyrt* 244, &c.
French are *baret* 47, *oritore* 122, *fylor* 157, *giserne* 197,
kauelacion 207, *frounses* 238, &c. *Myst-hakel* 13, *orpedly* 164
are native words ; while the rare *strype* 237 and *rapeled* 226 are
of doubtful origin.

Unless the alliteration is to be monotonous, there must be

many synonyms for common words like *man, kni3t*: e.g. *burne* 3, *wy3e* 6, *lede* 27, *gome* 50, *freke* 57, *tulk* 65, *knape* 68, *renk* 138, most of which survive only by reason of their usefulness in alliterative formulae. Similarly, a number of verbs are used to express the common idea 'to move (rapidly)': *bo3en* 9, *schowued* 15, *wonnen* 23, *ferked* 105, *rome3* 130, *keuere3* 153, *whyrlande* 154, &c. Here the group of synonyms arises from weakening of the ordinary prose meanings; and this tendency to use words in colourless or forced senses is a general defect of alliterative verse. For instance, it is hard to attach a precise meaning to *note* 24, *gedere3* 92, *glodes* 113, *wruxled* 123, *kest* 308.

The *Gawayne* poet is usually artist enough to avoid the worst fault of alliterative verse—the use of words for mere sound without regard to sense, but there are signs of the danger in the empty, clattering line:

> *Bremly brope on a bent pat brode wat3 aboute* 165.

Inflexions: The rime *wape : ta pe* 287-9 shows that organic final *-e* was sometimes pronounced in the poet's dialect.

VERB: pres. ind. 1 sg. *haf* 23 ; *leue* 60.

          2 sg. *spelle3* 72.

          3 sg. *prayses* 4 ; *tas* 237.

          2 pl. *3e han* 25.

          3 pl. *han* 345.

    imper. pl. *got3* (= *gǭs*) 51, *cayre3* 52.

    pres. p. normally *-ande*, e.g. *schaterande* 15 ; but very rarely *-yng*: *gruchyng* 58.

    strong pp. *born* 2, *wonnen* 23 ; *tone* (= *taken*) 91.

    The weak pa. t. and pp. show occasional *-(e)t* for *-(e)d*: *halt* 11, *fondet* 57, &c.

Note that present forms in *-ie(n)* are preserved, and the *t* extended to the past tense: *louy* (OE. *lufian*) 27, *louies* 31 ; *spuryed* 25.

PRONOUN 3 PERS.: pl. nom. *pay* 9 ; poss. *hor* 345, beside *her* 352 ; obj. *hom*, beside *hem* 353.

Sounds: *ǭ* for older *ā* is common, and is proved for the original by rimes like *more : restore* (OFr. *restorer*) 213-15, *pore : restore* 286-8. But *a* is often written in the MS.: *snaw* 20, 166 (note rimes), *halden* 29, &c.

u for OE. *y*, characteristic of Western dialects, is found especially in the neighbourhood of labial consonants: *spuryed* (OE. *spyrian*) 25 ; *muryly* 268, 277 ; *munt* vb. 194 and sb. 282 ; beside *myntes* 284, *lyfte* 78, *hille* 13.

u for OE. *eo* (normal ME. *e*) is another Western feature: *burne* 3, 21, &c., *rurde* 151.

aw for OE. *ēow* (normal ME. *ew, ow*) as in *trawe* 44, *trawpe* 219, *rawpe* 136, is still found in some Northern dialects.

Spelling: *3* (= *z*) is commonly written for final *s*: *brede3* 3,

&c.; even when the final *s* is certainly voiceless as in *forȝ*, 'force', 'torrent' 105, (*aȝ*-)*leȝ* 'fear-less' 267. *tȝ* is written for *s* in monosyllabic verbal forms, where it indicates the maintenance of voiceless final *s* under the stress (see rimes to *hatȝ* ' has ', VI 81): *watȝ* 'was' I, *gotȝ* 'goes' 51, &c. In early Norman French *s* had the sound *ts*, and so could be written *tz*, as in *Fitz-Gerald* ' son (Mod. Fr. *fils*) of Gerald'. But later, French (*t*)*s* fell together with *s* in pronunciation, so that the spelling *tz* was transferred to original *s*, both in fourteenth-century Anglo-French and in English.

qu- occurs for strongly aspirated *hw*- in *quyte* 'white' 20, *quat* 'what' 111; but the alliteration is with *w*, not with *k(w)*, e.g.
 And wyth quettyng *awharf, er he wolde lyȝt* 152.
The spelling *goud* 5, 50, &c., for *gōd* 'good' may indicate a sound change.

Notable is the carefully distinguished use of *ȝ* in *ȝe*, but *y* in *vow*, e.g. at ll. 23–6.

---

3. *blessed hym*, 'crossed himself'; cp. XII *b* 86.

4–6. 'He gives a word of praise to the porter,—⟨who⟩ kneeled before the prince (i.e. Gawayn) ⟨and who⟩ greeted him with "God and good day", and "May He save Gawayn!"—and went on his way, attended only by his man, who, &c.' Clumsiness in turning direct speech into reported speech is a constant source of difficulty in Middle English. For the suppressed relative cp. note to XIII *a* 36.

11. 'The clouds were high, but it was threatening below them.' *Halt* for *halet* pp. 'drawn up'.

16. 'The way by which they had to go through the wood was very wild.' Note the regular omission of a verb of motion after *shall, will*, &c. Cp. l. 64 *I wyl to þe chapel*; l. 332 *ȝe schal . . . to my woneȝ*, &c.

28. 'If you would act according to my wit (i.e. by my advice) you would fare the better.'

34. *Hestor, oþer oþer*, 'Hector, or any other'. Hector is quoted as the great hero of the Troy story, from which, and from the legends of Arthur, the Middle Ages drew their models of valour. The form *Hestor* occurs in Old French.

35. 'He brings it about at the green chapel ⟨that⟩', &c.

37. *dyngeȝ*: for MS. *dynneȝ*; Napier's suggestion.

41. 'He would as soon (lit. it seems to him as pleasant to) kill him, as be alive himself.'

43. 'If you reach that place you will be killed, I may warn you, knight.' Possibly *I, y*, has fallen out of the text after *y* of *may* (cp. VI 3), though there are clear instances in Old and Middle English where the pronominal subject must be understood from the context, e.g. I 168, VIII *a* 237, 273. Note the

transitions from plural *ȝe* to singular *þe* in ll. 42–3 ; and the evidence at l. 72 f. that *þou* could still be used in addressing a superior.

44. *Trawe ȝe me þat*: *trow* has here a double construction with both *me* and *þat* as direct objects.

56. 'That I shall loyally screen you, and never give out the tale that you fled for fear of any man that I knew.'

64. *for chaunce þat may falle*, 'in spite of anything that may happen'.

68–9. 'Though he be a stern lord (lit. a stern man to rule), and armed with a stave'. The short lines are built more with a view to rime than to sense.

72–4. 'Marry!' said the other, 'now you say so decidedly that you will take your own harm upon yourself, and it pleases you to lose your life, I have no wish to hinder you.'

76. *ryde me*: an instance of the rare ethic dative, which expresses some interest in the action of the verb on the part of one who is neither the doer of the action nor its object. Distinguish the uses referred to in the notes to II 289, XV *g* 24.

86. *Lepeȝ hym*, 'gallops'. For *hym*, which refers to the rider, not the horse, cp. note to XV *g* 24.

92. *Gryngolet*: the name of Gawayn's horse. *gedereȝ þe rake* seems to mean 'takes the path'. No similar transitive use of 'gather' is known.

95. *he wayted hym aboute*, 'he looked around him'. Cp. l. 221 *wayteȝ*, and note to l. 121.

99. 'The clouds seemed to him grazed by the crags'; i. e. the crags were so high that they seemed to him to scrape the clouds. I owe to Professor Craigie the suggestion that *skayned* is ON. *skeina* 'to graze', 'scratch'.

102–4. 'And soon, a little way off on an open space, a mound (as it appeared) seemed to him remarkable.'

107. *kacheȝ his caple*, 'takes control of his horse', i. e. takes up the reins again to start the horse after the halt mentioned at l. 100.

109. *his riche*: possibly 'his good steed'. The substantival use of an adjective is common in alliterative verse, e. g. l. 188 *þat schyre* (neck); 200 *þe schene* (axe); 245 *þe scharp* (axe); 343 *þat cortays* (lady). But it has been suggested that *brydel* has fallen out of the text after *riche*.

114. 'And it was all hollow within, nothing but an old cave.'

115 f. *he couþe hit noȝt deme with spelle*, 'he could not say ⟨which it was⟩'. For *deme* 'to speak', &c., cp. VI 1, XV *b* 29–30.

118. *Wheþer* commonly introduces a direct question and should not be separately translated. Cp. VI 205 and note to XI *a* 51.

121. *wysty is here*, 'it is desolate here'.   Note *Wowayn* =
Wauwayn, an alternative form of *Gawayn* used for the alliteration.   The alternation is parallel to that in *guardian : warden* ;
regard : reward XIV *c* 105 ; *guarantee : warranty* ; (*bi*)*gyled*
359 : (*bi*)*wyled* 357 ; *werre* 'war' beside French *guerre* ; *wait*
'watch' (as at l. 95) beside French *guetter* ; and is due to dialectal differences in Old French.   The Anglo-Norman dialect
usually preserved *w* in words borrowed from Germanic or Celtic,
while others replaced it by *gw, gu*, which later became simple *g*
in pronunciation.

125. *in my fyue wytteʒ* : construe with *fele*.

127. *þat chekke hit bytyde*, 'which destruction befall !' *þat ...*
hit = 'which'.   *chekke* refers to the checkmate at chess.

135. Had we not Chaucer's Miller and *The Reeves Tale*, the
vividness and intimacy of the casual allusions would show the
place of the flour-mill in mediaeval life.   Havelok drives out his
foes

> *So dogges ut of milne-hous* ;

and the Nightingale suggests as fit food for the Owl

> *one frogge*
> *Þat sit at mulne vnder cogge.*

These are records of hours spent by the village boys amid the
noise of grinding and rush of water, in times when there was no
rival mechanism to share the fascination of the water-driven
mill.

137–43. 'This contrivance, as I believe, is prepared, sir
knight, for the honour of meeting me by the way. Let God
work His will, Lo ! It helps me not a bit. Though I lose my
life, no noise causes me to fear.'   It has been suggested that *wel*
o⟨r w⟩oo 'weal or woe' should be read instead of the interjection
we loo !   But Gawayn's despair (l. 141) is not in keeping with
ll. 70 f., 90 f., or with the rest of his speech.   The looseness of
the short lines makes emendation dangerous.   Otherwise we
might read *Hit helppeʒ þe not a mote*, i. e. whatever happens,
mere noise will not help the Green Knight by making Gawayn
afraid ; or, alternatively, *hermeʒ* 'harms' for *helppeʒ*.

151. 'Yet he went on with the noise with all speed for a while,
and turned away ⟨to proceed⟩ with his grinding, before he would
come down.'   The nonchalance of the Green Knight is marked
throughout the poem.

155. *A Deneʒ ax* : the ordinary long-bladed battle-axe was
called a 'Danish' axe, in French *hache danoise*, because the
Scandinavians in their raids on England and France first proved
its efficiency in battle.

158. *bi þat lace*, '⟨measured⟩ by the lace'.   In *Gawayne*
(ll. 217 ff. of the full text) the axe used at the first encounter is
described.   It had :

> *A lace lapped aboute, þat louked at þe hede,*
> *And so after þe halme halched ful ofte,*
> *Wyth tryed tasseleȝ þerto tacched innoghe, &c.*

'A lace wrapped about ⟨the handle⟩, which was fastened at the ⟨axe's⟩ head, and was wound about the handle again and again, with many choice tassels fastened to it ', &c.

159. *as fyrst*, 'as at the first encounter ', i. e. when he rode into Arthur's hall. His outfit of green is minutely described at ll. 151 ff. of the full text.

162. *Sette þe stele to þe stone*: i. e. he used the handle of the axe as a support when crossing rough ground. *stele* = 'handle ', not ' steel '.

164. *hypped . . . strydeȝ*: note the frequent alternation of past tense and historic present. So ll. 3–4 *passed . . . prayses*; 107–8 *kacheȝ . . . com . . . liȝteȝ*; 280–1 *haldeȝ . . . gef*, &c.

169 f. ' Now, sweet sir, one can trust you to keep an appointment.'

175. *þat þe falled*, ' what fell to your lot ', i. e. the right to deal the first blow.

177. *oure one*, 'by ourselves '. To *one* 'alone' in early ME. the dative pronoun was added for emphasis, *him one, us one*, &c. Later and more rarely the possessive pronoun is found, as here. *Al(l)* was also used to strengthen *one*; so that there are six possible ME. types: (1) *one*, e. g. ll. 6, 50; (2) *him one*; (3) *his one*; (4) *al one = alone* l. 87; (5) *al him one*, or *him al one*; (6) *al his one*, or *his al one*.

181. *at a wap one*, ' at a single blow '.

183. ' I shall grudge you no good-will because of any harm that befalls me.'

189–90. ' And acted as if he feared nothing: he would not tremble (*dare*) with terror.'

196. He (Gawayn) who was ever valiant would have been dead from his blow there.'

200. It must not be supposed that the chief incidents of *Sir Gawayne* were invented by the English poet. The three strokes, for example, two of them mere feints and the third harmless, can be shown to derive from the lost French source, which has Irish analogues. See pp. 71–4 of *A Study of Gawain and the Green Knight* (London 1916), by Professor Kittredge, a safe guide in the difficult borderland of folklore and romance.

207. ' Nor did I raise any quibble in the house of King Arthur.' On *kyngeȝ hous Arthor* see note to ll 518.

222. *ryueȝ*: the likeness of *n* and *u* in MSS. of the time makes it impossible to say whether the verb is *riue* 'to cleave ', which is supported by l. 278, or *rine*, OE. *hrīnan*, ' to touch '.

230. ' And look out for your neck at this stroke, ⟨to see⟩ if it may survive.'

233. *I hope*: here, and often in ME., *hope* means 'believe', 'expect'.

250. Gawayn appears to have carried his shield on his back. By a movement of his shoulders he lets it fall in front of him, so that he can use it in defence.

258. *foo*, 'fiercely', adv. parallel with *ȝederly*.

269. *ry(n)kande*, 'ringing'; Napier's suggestion for MS. *rykande*.

271–2. 'Nobody here has ill-treated you in an unmannerly way, nor shown you ⟨discourtesy⟩': the object of *kyd* being understood from *vnmanerly mysboden. habbeȝ* for MS. *habbe* is Napier's reading.

278–9. 'And cleft you with no grievous wound, ⟨which⟩ I rightly ⟨merely⟩ proffered you, because of the compact we made fast', &c. It is better to assume a suppression of the relative, than to put a strong stop after *rof* and treat *sore* as sb. object of *profered*. This latter punctuation gives *sore* the chief stress in the line, and breaks the alliteration and rhythm, which is correct as long as *sore* is taken with *rof*, so that its stress is subordinated.

286–7. 'Let a true man truly repay—then one need dread no peril.'

291. *weued*: perhaps not a weak pa. t. of *weave-woven*, but rather means 'to give', from OE. *wǣfan*, 'to move'; *weue* in this sense occurs in *Gawayne* l. 1976.

294–5. 'And truly you seem to me the most faultless man that ever walked on foot.' The ME. construction, *on þe fautlest*, where *on* 'one' strengthens the superlative, is found in Chaucer, *Clerk's Tale* 212:

> *Thanne was she oon the faireste under sonne,*

and still survives in Shakespeare's time, e. g. *Henry VIII*, II. iv. 48 f. *one the wisest prince.* It has been compared with Latin *unus maximus*, &c. In modern English the apposition has been replaced, with weakening of the sense: *one* of *the* (*wisest*), &c.

298. *yow lakked . . . yow wonted*: impersonal, since *yow* is dative, 'there was lacking in you'.

319. 'Let me win your good-will', 'Pardon me'.

331. I have transposed MS. of *þe grene chapel* at *cheualrous knyȝteȝ*, because such a use of *at* is hardly conceivable. A copyist might easily make the slip. Cp. l. 35.

344. *Boþe þat on and þat oþer*: Besides the Green Knight's young wife, there was a much older lady in the castle, 'yellow', with 'rugh, ronkled chekeȝ', and so wrapped up

> *Þat noȝt watȝ bare of þat burde bot þe blake broȝes,*
> *Þe tweyne yȝen, and þe nase, þe naked lyppeȝ,*
> *And þose were soure to se, and sellyly blered.*
>
> *Gawayne* ll. 961–3.

350–1. 'And David afterwards, who suffered much evil, was ⟨morally⟩ blinded by Bathsheba.

352–6. 'Since these were injured with their wiles, it would be a great gain to love them well, and not believe them—for a man who could do it [cp. note to XI *b* 209]. For these (Adam, Solomon, &c.) were of old the noblest, whom all happiness followed, surpassingly, above all the others that lived beneath the heavens.' *mused* 'thought' is used for the rime, and means no more than 'lived'. ll. 354-6 amount to 'above all other men'.

VI

Dialect: West Midland, like *Gawayne*.

The metre occasionally gives clear evidence that final flexional *-e* of the original has not always been preserved in the extant MS., e. g.

> *Þaȝ cortaysly ȝe carp⟨è⟩ con*   21.

The most noteworthy verbal forms are:

pres. ind. 1 sg. *byswykeȝ* 208 (once only, in rime);

       2 sg. *þou quyteȝ* 235;

       3 sg. *leþeȝ* 17; *totȝ* (= *tǭs* = *tās* = *takes*) 153 (note).

       1 pl. *we leuen* 65; *we calle* 70;

       3 pl. *temen* 100 (and cp. ll. 151–2); *knawe* 145; but *þay gotȝ* 150, *pykeȝ* 213 (both in rime).

imperative pl. *dyspleseȝ* 62; *gos, dotȝ* 161.

pres. p. *spornande* 5.

pp. *runne* (in rime) 163, beside *wroken* 15, &c.

Characteristic Western forms are *burne* 37 (OE. *beorn*); *vrþe* 82 (OE. *eorþe*).

---

5. 'Like bubbling water that flows from a spring', i. e. his wild words rise from a heart that can no longer contain its affliction.

11-12. 'You, who were once the source of all my joy, made sorrow my companion.'

15. 'From the time when you were removed from every peril'. The child died before she was two years old (l. 123).

22. 'I am but dust, and lack manners.' The MS. has *marereȝ mysse*, which has been rendered 'botcher's waste'; but the poet is contrasting his own ill-mannered speech with the Pearl's courtesy.

23. 'But the mercy of Christ and of Mary and of John'. The genitive inflexion is confined to the noun immediately preceding *mersy*, while the two following nouns, which are logically

genitives with exactly the same construction as *Crystes*, remain uninflected. For analogies see note to II 518.

36. *and*: MS. *in*. The sign for *and* is easily mistaken for *ꝛ = in*. Cp. note to XVII 42.

48. *þat*, ' who '.

65. *þat . . . of*, 'from whom'; the later relative form *of quom* occurs at l. 93.

70. *Fenyx of Arraby*: the symbol of peerless perfection. Cp. Chaucer, *Death of Blanche the Duchess*, ll. 980–3

> Trewly she was to myn ye
> The soleyn Fenix of Arabye,
> For ther lyveth never but oon,
> Ne swich as she ne knew I noon.

71. 'which was faultless in form'; *fleȝe* 'flew' is used with weakened sense because a bird is normally thought of as on the wing.

74. *folde vp hyr face*, '⟨with⟩ her face upturned'; *folde* is pp.

91–2. 'And each would wish that the crowns of the others were five times as precious, if it were possible to better them.'

97. *Poule*: the common OFr. and ME. form, as at VIII *a* 25, 270, XI *b* 80. But the rime with *naule* 'nail' (ON. *nagl*) points to the form *Paule* for the original. The reference is to I Corinthians vi. 15 and xii. 12 ff.

100. *hys body*, 'its body', 'the body'. *t⟨r⟩yste*, Morris's emendation, is supported by the frequency of the phrase *trewe and tryste*. MS. *tyste* could only be explained as = *tyȝte* 'tight', with *st* for *ht*, like *myste* = *myȝte* at l. 102. See Appendix § 6 (end).

106. 'Because you wear a ring on arm or finger.'

109–11. 'I ⟨well⟩ believe that there is great courtesy and charity among you.' The construction of the next line (which conveys an apology, cp. l. 62) is not clear owing to the following gap in the MS.; nor is it easy to guess the missing rime word. *as emong* can rime with OE. *-ung-* (e.g. with *ȝonge*, ll. 114, 175), or with OE. *-ang-*; see the note to XVII 400.

116. *stronge* may be adj. 'violent' with *worlde*, but is more likely adv. 'severely'.

124–5. Note the cumulation of negatives. *cowþeȝ* has a double construction: 'You never knew how to please God nor pray to Him, nor ⟨did you know even⟩ the Paternoster and Creed.' The Lord's Prayer and the Apostles' Creed were prescribed by the Church as the elements of faith to be taught first to a child.

137. Matthew xx. 1–16.

139. 'He represented it very aptly in a parable.'

141. *My regne . . . on hyȝt*, 'My kingdom on high'.

145. *þys hyne*: the labourers. *This, these* are sometimes used in early English to refer to persons or things that have not been previously mentioned, but are prominent in the writer's mind.

Cp. xv *b* 4, 19; and the opening of Chaucer's *Prologue* to the *Franklin's Tale* quoted in the note to II 13.

150. *pené*: in ME. the final sound developed from OFr. -*é* (*e*) fell together with the sounds arising from OE. -*ig*, OFr. *ie*, &c. Hence *pené* or *peny* 186 (OE. *penig*); *reprené* 184 for *repreny*; *cortaysé* 120, 121, beside *cortaysye* 72, 84, 96. The acute accent is editorial.

153. 'At midmorning the master goes to the market.' *totʒ* (= *tp̄s*) = *tās*, contracted form of *takes* 'betakes himself'; cp. *tone* = *taken* V 91. The spelling and rimes with *o* (which cannot develop normally from *ă* lengthened in open syllables because this lengthening is everywhere later than the change *ā* > *p̄*) are usually explained as artificial. It is assumed that as Northern *bān* corresponded to Midland *bp̄n*, so from Northern *tá* 'take' an unhistorical Midland *tp̄* was deduced. But it is possible that the contraction of *tăke*(*n*), and consequent lengthening *tá*(*n*), is older than the ordinary lengthening *tăke* > *táke*, and also older than the development of *ā* to *p̄* in North Midland.

164. *I yow pay*: note the survival of the old use of the present to express future tense.

176. *þat at ʒe moun*, 'what you can'. *At* as a relative appears usually to be from Old Norse *at*, with the same sense, and it is not uncommon in Northern English. But *þat at* here is more likely the normal development of *bat bat* > *þat tat* (note to II 102) > *þat at*.

179. *sumoun* is infin. not sb.: 'he had ⟨them⟩ summoned'; cp. note to VIII *a* 79.

192. 'It seems to us we ought to receive more.' *Vus þynk* is a remnant of the old impersonal construction of *þynceþ* 'it seems'. In this phrase, probably owing to confusion with *we þynk*(*en*), the verb often has no flexional ending; cp. l. 192. *vus oʒe* is formed by analogy, the verb being properly personal; cp. *must vs* XVII 292, 334.

200. *And*, 'If'.

205–8. *More*, which is necessary for the metrical form, is best taken as conj. 'moreover', 'further'; *weþer* introduces a direct question (note to V 118). *louyly* is perhaps miswritten for *lauly* 'lawful', as the *Pearl-Gawayne* group often show the converse *au*, *aw* for normal *ou*, *ow*, e.g. *bawe* for *bowe*, *trawþe* for *trowþe*. 'Further, is my power to do what pleases me with my own lawful?' The meaning is fixed by Matthew xx. 15 'Is it not lawful for me to do what I will with mine own? Is thine eye evil because I am good?'

212. *mykeʒ*. In the few recorded examples *mik*, *myk* seems to mean 'an intimate friend'. Here it is used for the sake of rime in an extended sense 'chosen companion of the Lord'.

221 f. *Wheþer*, &c., 'Although I began ⟨only⟩ just now, coming into the vineyard in the eventide, ⟨yet⟩', &c.

224. Note the rime (OE. *sŭm*) with ON. *blóm(i)*, OE. *dóm, cóm.*
Such rimes occur occasionally in Northern texts of the fourteenth
century—never in the South.

233. Psalm lxii. 12 'Also unto Thee, O Lord, belongeth mercy;
for Thou renderest to every man according to his work.'

237-40. Loosely constructed. 'Now, if you came to payment
before him that stood firm through the long day, then he who
did less work would be more entitled to receive pay, and the
further ⟨it is carried⟩, the less ⟨work⟩, the more ⟨claim to be
paid⟩.'

249-51. On the meaning of these lines there is no agreement. Gollancz and Osgood interpret: 'That man's privilege
is great who ever stood in awe of Him (God) who rescues
sinners. From such men no happiness is withheld, for,' &c.
Yet it is difficult to believe that even a poet hard pressed would
use *dard to Hym* to mean ' feared Him '. One of several rival
interpretations will suffice to show the ambiguities of the text:
' His (God's) generosity, which is always inscrutable (lit. lay
hidden), is abundant to the man who recovers his soul from sin.
From such men no happiness is withheld ', &c. The sense and
construction of *dard* (for which the emendation *fard*, pret. of
fere 'to go', has been suggested, the rest of the interpretation
following Gollancz), and the obscurity of the argument, are the
chief obstacles to a satisfactory solution.

VII

Dialect: Irregular, but predominantly North-West Midland;
cp. V and VI.

Inflexions:—

VERB: pres. ind. 3 sg. *warys* 19, *has* 20.

        3 pl. *ben* 11, *sayn* 182, *haue* 31.

    pres. p. *claterand* 137, *priuaund* 158, *leymonde* 153;
beside *blowyng* 106, *doutyng* 114.

    strong pp. *slydyn* 6, *stoken* 11.

    The weak pp. and pa. t. have *-it*, *-(e)t* for *-(e)d*
drepit 9, *suet* 24.

PRONOUN 3 PERS.: pl. nom. *þai* 45; poss. *hor* 8, beside
þere 9, 10; obj. *hom* 24.

Sounds and Spelling: Northern and North Midland forms
are *qwiles* (= *whiles*) 39, *hondqwile* 117; and *wysshe* 4 (note).
West Midland indications are *buernes* 'men' 90, 91 = OE. *beorn*
(but *buerne* 'sea' 159 = OE. *burn-* is probably miswritten owing
to confusion with *buern* 'man'); and perhaps the spelling *u* in
unaccented syllables: *mecull* 10, *watur* 119, *wintur* 124.

4. *wysshe* = *wisse* 'guide'. In the North final *sh* was commonly pronounced *ss*; cp. note to 1 128–9, and the rimes in XVII 1–4. Conversely etymological *ss* was sometimes spelt *ssh*.

7–8. *strongest . . . and wisest . . . to wale*, 'the strongest . . . and wisest . . . that could be chosen' (lit. 'to choose').

15. *On lusti to loke*, 'pleasant to look upon'.

21 ff. A typical example of the vague and rambling constructions in which this writer indulges : apparently 'but old stories of the valiant ⟨men⟩ who ⟨once⟩ held high rank may give pleasure to some who never saw their deeds, through the writings of men who knew them at first hand (?) (*in dede*), ⟨which remained⟩ to be searched by those who followed after, in order to make known (*or* to know ?) all the manner in which the events happened, by looking upon letters (i. e. writings) that were left behind of old'.

45. Benoît de Sainte-Maure says the Athenians rejected Homer's story of gods fighting like mortals, but charitably explains that, as Homer lived a hundred years after the siege, it is no wonder if he made mistakes :

> *N'est merveille s'il i faillit,*
> *Quar onc n'i fu ne rien n'en vit.*
>
> *Prologue*, ll. 55–6.

53–4. 'That was elegantly compiled by a wise clerk—one Guido, a man who had searched carefully, and knew all the actions from authors whom he had by him.'   See Introductory note, pp. 68 f.

66–7. Cornelius Nepos was supposed to have found the Greek work of Dares at Athens when rummaging in an old cupboard (Benoît de Sainte-Maure, *Prologue*, ll. 77 ff.).

157. Note the slovenly repetition from l. 151. So l. 159 repeats l. 152.

168–9. I have transposed these lines, assuming that they were misplaced by a copyist. Guido's Latin favours the change, and the whole passage will illustrate the English translator's methods :

Oyleus uero Aiax qui cum 32 nauibus suis in predictam incidit tempestatem, omnibus nauibus suis exustis et submersis in mari, in suis uiribus brachiorum nando semiuiuus peruenit ad terram; et, inflatus pre nimio potu aque, uix se nudum recepit in littore, vbi usque ad superuenientis diei lucem quasi mortuus iacuit in arena, [et] de morte sua sperans potius quam de uita. Sed cum quidam ex suis nando similiter a maris ingluuie iam erepti nudi peruenissent ad littus, dominum eorum querunt in littore [et] si forsitan euasisset. Quem in arena iacentem inueniunt, dulcibus uerborum fouent affatibus, cum nec in uestibus ipsum nec in alio possunt subsidio refouere. (MS. Harley 4123, fol. 117 a—the bracketed words are superfluous.)

178. *Telamon* was not at the siege, and his name appears here and in l. 150 as the result of a tangle which begins in the confusion of Oyleus Ajax with Ajax the son of Telamon. In classical writers after Homer it is Oyleus Ajax who, at the sack of Troy, drags Cassandra from the temple of Minerva. This is the story in Dictys. Dares, like Homer, is silent. In Benoît de Sainte-Maure's poem (ll. 26211–16), the best MSS. name Oyleus Ajax as Cassandra's captor, but others have ' *Thelamon Aiax*', i. e. Ajax, the son of Telamon. Guido read Benoît in a MS. of the latter class, and accordingly makes *Telamonius Aiax* do the sacrilege. With the English translator this becomes *Telamon* simply (Bk. xxix, ll. 11993–7). So when later, in Bk. xxxi, he comes to describe the shipwreck, he replaces Guido's *Aiax* by *Telamon*, and spoils the story of Minerva's vengeance on the actual violator of her sanctuary.

VIII

Dialect: South Midland, with mixture of forms.

    a. VERB: pres. ind. 2 sg. *seist* 226, *wilnest* 256.

                        3 sg. *comaundeth* 16.

                        1 pl. *haue* 118, *preye* 119.

                        2 pl. *han* 11, *wasten* 127.

                        3 pl. *liggeth* 15, &c.; beside *ben* 50, *waste* 155.

        imper. pl. *spynneth* 13.

        pres. p. (none in *a*) ; *romynge b* 11.

        strong pp. *bake* 187, *ybake* 278, *ybaken* 175.

        Infinitives in -*ie* (OE. -*ian*) are retained: *erye* 4, *hatie* 52, *tilye* 229 (OE. *erian, hatian, tilian*).

    PRONOUN 3 PERS.: pl. nom. *þei* 126, &c., beside *hii* 15; poss. *her* 54 ; obj. *hem* 2.

    Sounds: OE. *y* often shows the Western development, as in *huyre(d)* 108, 133, &c.; *abugge* 75, 159; beside *bigge* 275. So *Cornehulle b* 1. But such forms were not uncommon in the London dialect of the time.

    b. The second extract has a more Southern dialectal colouring. Note especially the gen. pl. forms *lollarene* 31, *knauene* 56, *lordene* 77, continuing or extending the OE. weak gen. pl. in -*ena*; and *menne* 29, 74, retaining the ending of the OE. gen. pl. *manna.*

    The representation of unaccented vowels by *u* in *hure* (= 'their') 50, (= 'her') 53 ; (*h*)*us* 'his' 60, 101 ; *clerkus* 65, is commonest in Western districts. *h(w)* is no longer aspirated:

wanne I, *werby* 35, MS. *eggen* 19; and conversely *hyf* 'if' 43, *his* 'is' 105.

---

a 9. *for shedyng*, 'to prevent spilling'; and so *for colde* 62 'as a protection against cold'; *for bollyng* 209 'to prevent swelling'; *for chillyng* 306, &c.

a 11. *Þat ʒe han silke and sendal to sowe*: The construction changes as if Piers had begun: *Ich praye ʒow*, which is the reading in the C-text. The difficulty of excluding modern ideas from the interpretation of the Middle Ages is shown by the comment of a scholar so accomplished as M. Petit-Dutaillis: 'Il attaque les riches peu miséricordieux, les *dames charmantes aux doigts effilés*, qui ne s'occupent pas des pauvres' (*Soulève-ment*, p. lxii). But there is no hint of satire or reproach in the text. The poet, always conventional, assigns to high-born ladies the work which at the time was considered most fitting for them. So it is reported in praise of the sainted Isabella of France, sister of St. Louis: *Quand elle fust introduicte des lettres suffisamment, elle s'estudioit à apprendre à ouurer de soye, et faisoit estolles et autres paremens à saincte Eglise*—'When she was sufficiently introduced to letters, she set herself to learn how to work in silk, and made stoles and other vestments for Holy Church.' (Joinville, *Histoire d. S. Louys*, Paris 1668, pt. i, p. 169.)

a 19. *for þe Lordes loue of heuene*: cp. l. 214, and notes to I 44, I 83, II 518.

a 23. *on þe teme*, 'on this subject'; *teme* 'theme' is a correct form, because Latin *th* was pronounced *t*. The modern pronunciation is due to the influence of classical spelling.

a 32. *affaite þe*, 'tame for thyself'; cp. l. 64 (*I shal*) *brynge me* = 'bring (for myself)', and the note to II 289.

a 40–1. 'And though you should fine them, let Mercy be the assessor, and let Meekness rule over you, in spite of Gain.' This is a warning against abuse of the lord of the manor's power to impose fines in the manorial court with the object of raising revenue rather than of administering justice. Cp. Ashley, *Introduction to English Economic History*, vol. i (1894), pt. ii, p. 266. For *maugré Medes chekes* cp. l. 151.

a 49. Luke xiv. 10.

a 50. *yuel to knowe*, 'hard to distinguish'.

a 72–5. These clumsy lines, which are found in all versions, exemplify the chief faults in *Piers Plowman*: structural weakness and superfluous allegory.

a 79. *I wil . . . do wryte my biqueste*, 'I will have my will written'; *make*(*n*), *ger* (*gar*), and *lete*(*n*) are commonly used like *do*(*n*) with an active infinitive, which is most conveniently rendered by the passive; so *do wryte* 'cause to be written'; *dyd werche* 'caused to be made' I 218; *mad sumoun* 'caused to be summoned' VI 179; *gert dres vp* 'caused to be set up' X 16; *leet make* 'caused to be made' IX 223, &c.

a 80. *In Dei nomine, amen*: A regular opening phrase for wills.

a 84. ' I trust to have a release from and remission of my debts which are recorded in that book.' *Rental*, a book in which the sums due from a tenant were noted, here means 'record of sins '.

a 86. *he*: the parson, as representing the Church.

a 91. *douȝtres*. In l. 73 only one daughter is named. In the B-text, Passus xviii. 426, she is called *Kalote* (see note to *b* 2 below).

a 94. *bi þe rode of Lukes*: at Lucca (French *Lucques*) is a Crucifix and a famous representation of the face of Christ, reputed to be the work of the disciple Nicodemus. From Eadmer and William of Malmesbury we learn that William the Conqueror's favourite oath was ' By the Face of Lucca ! ', and it is worth noting that the frequent and varied adjurations in Middle English are copied from the French.

a 114. ' May the Devil take him who cares ! '

a 115 ff. *faitoures* (cp. ll. 185 ff.), who feigned some injury or disease to avoid work and win the pity of the charitable, multiplied in the disturbed years following the Black Death. Statutes were passed against them, and even against those who gave them alms (Jusserand, *English Wayfaring Life*, pp. 261 ff.). But the type was long lived. In the extract from *Handlyng Synne* (No. I), we have already a monument of their activities.

a 141. ' And those that have cloisters and churches (i. e. monks and priests) shall have some of my goods to provide themselves with copes.'

a 142. *Robert Renne-aboute*. The type of a wandering preacher; *posteles* are clearly preachers with no fixed sphere of authority, like the mendicant friars and Wiclif's ' poor priests '. Against both the regular clergy constantly complained that they preached without the authority of the bishop.

a 186. *Þat seten*: the MS. by confusion has *þat seten to seten to begge*, &c.

a 187. *þat was bake for Bayarde*: i. e. ' horse-bread' (l. 208), which used to be made from beans and peas only. *Bayard*, properly a ' bay horse', was, according to romance, the name of the horse given by Charlemagne to Rinaldo. Hence it became the conventional name for a horse, just as *Reynard* was appropriated to the fox. Chaucer speaks of *proude Bayard* (*Troilus*, Bk. i. 218) and, referring to an unknown story, *Bayard the blynde* (*Canon's Yeoman's Tale*, 860).

a 221. *Michi vindictam*: Romans xii. 19.

a 224. Luke xvi. 9.

a 229. **Genesis** iii. 19.

a 231. *Sapience*: the Book of Wisdom, but the quotation is actually from Proverbs xx. 4.

a 234. *Mathew with mannes face.* Each of the evangelists had his symbol: Matthew, a man; Mark, a lion; Luke, a bull; John, an eagle; and in early Gospel books their portraits are usually accompanied by the appropriate symbols.

a 235 ff. Matthew xxv. 14 ff.; Luke xix. 12 ff.

a 245. *Contemplatyf lyf or actyf lyf.* The merits of these two ways of life were endlessly disputed in the Middle Ages. In XI *b* Wiclif attacks the position of the monks and of Rolle's followers; and the author of *Pearl* (VI 61 ff.) takes up the related question of salvation by works or by grace.

a 246. Psalm cxxviii. 1.

a 264. Jusserand gives a brief account of the old-time physicians in *English Wayfaring Life*, pp. 177 ff. The best were somewhat haphazard in their methods, and the mountebanks brought discredit on the profession. Here are a few fourteenth-century prescriptions:

For hym that haves the squynansy [' *quinsy* '] :—

Tak a fatte katte, and fla hit wele and clene, and draw oute the guttes ; and tak the grees of an urcheon [' hedgehog '], and the fatte of a bare, and resynes, and feinygreke [' fenugreek '], and sauge [' sage '], and gumme of wodebynde, and virgyn wax: al this mye [' grate '] smal, and farse [' stuff '] the catte within als thu farses a gos : rost hit hale, and geder the grees, and enoynt hym tharwith. (*Reliquiae Antiquae*, ed. Wright and Halliwell (1841), vol. i, p. 51.)

3yf a woud hund hat ybite a man :—

Take tou(n)karsyn [' towncress '], and pulyole [' pennyroyal '], and seþ hit in water, and ȝef hym to drynke, and hit schal caste out þe venym: and ȝif þou miste [' might '] haue of þe hundys here, ley hit þerto, and hit schal hele hit. (*Medical Works of the Fourteenth Century*, ed. G. Henslow, London 1899, p. 19.)

A goud oynement for þe goute :—

Take þe grece of a bor, and þe grece of a ratoun, and cattys grece, and voxis grece, and hors grece, and þe grece of a brok [' badger ']; and take feþeruoye [' feverfew '] and eysyl [' vinegar '], and stampe hem togedre ; and take a litel lynnesed, and stampe hit wel, and do hit þerto ; and meng al togedre, and het hit in a scherd, and þerwith anoynte þe goute by the fuyre. Do so ofte and hit schal be hol. (Ibid., p. 20.)

a 284. *Lammasse tyme*: August 1, when the new corn (l. 294) would be in. On this day a loaf was offered as firstfruits: whence the name, OE. *hlāf-mæsse*.

a 307 ff. Owing to repeated famines, the wages of manual labour rose throughout the first half of the fourteenth century. A crisis was reached when the Black Death (1349) so reduced the number of workers that the survivors were able to demand wages on a scale which seemed unconscionable to their employers. By the Statute of Labourers (1350 and 1351) an attempt was made to force wages and prices back to the level of 1346. For a day's haymaking 1*d.* was to be the maximum wage ; for reaping 2*d.* or 3*d.* Throughout the second half of the fourteenth century vain attempts were made to enforce these maxima, and the penalties did much to fan the unrest that broke out in the Peasants' Revolt of 1381.

a 309–10. From Bk. i of the *Disticha* of Dionysius Cato, a collection of proverbs famous throughout the Middle Ages.

a 321. Saturn was a malevolent planet, as we see from his speech in Chaucer's *Knight's Tale,* 1595 ff.

a 324. *Deth* : the Plague.

b 1. *Cornehulle.* Cornhill was one of the liveliest quarters of fourteenth-century London, and a haunt of idlers, beggars, and doubtful characters. Its pillory and stocks were famous. Its market where, if *The London Lickpenny* is to be credited, dealing in stolen clothes was a speciality, was privileged above all others in the city. See the documents in Riley's *Memorials of London.*

b 2. *Kytte* : In the B-text, Passus xviii. 425–6, *Kytte* is mentioned again :

> and ri3t with þat I waked
> And called Kitte my wyf and Kalote my dou3ter.

b 4. *lollares of London* : The followers of Wiclif were called ' Lollards ' by their opponents ; but the word here seems to mean ' idlers ' as in l. 31. *lewede heremytes* : ' lay hermits ' : hermits were not necessarily in holy orders, and so far from seeking complete solitude, they often lived in the cities or near the great highways, where many passers would have opportunity to recognize their merit by giving alms. See Cutts, *Scenes and Characters of the Middle Ages,* pp. 93 ff.

b 5. ' For I judged those men as Reason taught me.' Skeat's interpretation—that *made of* means ' made verses about '—is forced. The sense is that the idlers and hermits thought little of the dreamer, and he was equally critical of them.

b 6. *as ich cam by Conscience* : ' as I passed by Conscience', referring to a vision described in the previous Passus, in which Conscience is the principal figure.

b 10 f. *In hele and in vnité,* ' in health and in my full senses ', and *Romynge in remembraunce* qualify *me.*

b 14. *Mowe oþer mowen,* ' mow or stack '. For these unrelated words see the Glossary.

b 16. *haywarde* : by derivation ' hedge-ward '. He watched over enclosures and prevented animals from straying among the crops. Observe that ME. nouns denoting occupation usually survive in surnames:—Baxter 'baker', Bow(y)er, Chapman, Dyer, Falconer, Fletcher 'arrow-maker', Fo(re)ster, Franklin, Hayward, Lister (= litster, 'dyer'), Palmer, Reeve(s), Spicer, Sumner, Tyler 'maker or layer of tiles', Warner 'keeper of warrens', Webb, Webster, Wright, Yeoman, &c.

b 20–1. 'Or craft of any kind that is necessary to the community, to provide food for them that are bedridden.'

b 24. *to long*, 'too tall': cp. B-text, Passus xv. 148 *my name is Longe Wille.* Consistency in such details in a poem full of inconsistencies makes it probable that the poet is describing himself, not an imagined dreamer.

b 33. Psalm lxii. 12.

b 45. 1 Corinthians vii. 20.

b 46 ff. Cp. the note to XI *b* 131 f. The dreamer appears to have made his living by saying prayers for the souls of the dead, a service which, from small beginnings in the early Middle Ages, had by this time withdrawn much of the energy of the clergy from their regular duties.   See note to XI *b* 140 f.

b 49. *my Seuene Psalmes*: the Penitential Psalms, normally **vi**, xxxii, xxxviii, li, cii, cxxx, cxliii, in the numbering of the Authorised Version. The *Prymer*, which contained the devotions supplementary to the regular Church service, included the Placebo, Dirige, and the Seven Psalms: see the edition by Littlehales for the Early English Text Society.

b 50. *for hure soules of suche as me helpen*: combines the constructions *for þe soules of suche as me helpen*, and *for hure soules þat me helpen.*

b 51. *vochen saf*: supply *me* as object, ' warrant me that I shall be welcome '.

b 61. 1 Thessalonians v. 15 ; Leviticus xix. 18.

b 63. *churches*: here and in l. 110 read the Norse form *kirkes* for the alliteration, as in *a* 28, 85.   But the English form also belongs to the original, for it alliterates with *ch* at *a* 12, 50.

b 64. *Dominus*, &c.: Psalm xvi. 5.

b 83. *Symondes sone*: a son of Simon Magus—one guilty of simony, or one who receives preferment merely because of his wealth.

b 90. Matthew iv. 4.

b 103-4. *Simile est*, &c.: Matthew xiii. 44.   *Mulier que*, &c.: Luke xv. 8 ff.

IX

Dialect: South-East Midland.

Vocabulary: A number of French words are taken over from the original, e.g. *plee* 81, *ryot* 83, *violastres* 97, *saphire loupe* 116, *gowrdes* 139, *clowe gylofres* 157, *canell* 158, *avaled*

195, *trayne* (for *taynere?*) 222, *bugles* 256, *gowtes artetykes* 314, *distreynen* 315.

Inflexions: Almost modern.

VERB: pres. ind. 3 sg. *schadeweth* 19, *turneth* 23.

3 pl. *ben* 4, *han* 14, *wexen* 22, *loue* 100.

pres. p. *fle(e)ynge* 148, 252; *recordynge* 317.

strong pp. *ȝouen* 90, *begonne* 171.

PRONOUN 3 PERS.: pl. *þei* 5; *here* 71; *hem* 20.

Sounds: OE. *ā* becomes *ǭ*: *hoot* 11, *cold* 31.

OE. *y* appears as *y* (= *i*): *byggynge* 90, *kyȝn* 'kine' 256; except regular *left* (hand) 69, 71, 72, where Modern English has also adopted the South-Eastern form of OE. *lyft*.

21–3. The French original says that the children have white *hair* when they are young, which becomes black as they grow up.

24–5. The belief that one of the Three Kings came from Ethiopia is based on Ps. lxviii. 31: 'Princes shall come out of Egypt, Ethiopia shall soon stretch out her hands unto God.' In mediaeval representations one of the three is usually a negro.

27. *Emlak*: miswritten for *Euilak*, a name for India taken from *Hævilah* of Genesis ii. 11.

28. *þat is : þe more*: *Ynde* has probably fallen out of the text after *is*.

34–5. *Ȝalow cristall draweth ⟨to⟩ colour lyke oylle*: the insertion of *to* is necessary to give sense, and is supported by the French: *cristal iaunastre trehant a colour doile.* (MS. Harley 4383, f. 34b.)

36–7. The translation is not accurate. The French has: *et appelle homme les dyamantz en ceo pais 'Hamese'.*

64 ff. It was supposed that the pearl-bearing shell-fish opened at low tide to receive the dew-drops from which the pearls grew.

74. *ȝif ȝou lyke*, 'if it please you', impersonal = French *si vous plest.*

75. *þe Lapidarye*, Latin *Lapidarium*, was a manual of precious stones, which contained a good deal of pseudo-scientific information about their natures and virtues, just as the *Bestiary* summed up popular knowledge of animals. A Latin poem by Marbod bishop of Rennes (d. 1123) is the chief source of the mediaeval lapidaries, and, curiously enough, there is a French prose text attributed by so intimate an authority as Jean d'Outremeuse to Mandeville himself. Several Old French texts have been edited by L. Pannier, *Les Lapidaires Français du Moyen Âge*, Paris 1882. Their high repute may be judged from the inclusion of no less than seven copies in the library of Charles V of France (d. 1380); and it is surprising that no complete ME. version is known. But much of the matter was absorbed into encyclopaedic

works like the *De Proprietatibus Rerum* of Bartholomaeus, which Trevisa translated.

97. Mistranslated.   The French has: *qi sont violastre, ou pluis broun qe violettes.*

100–1. *But in soth to me*: French: *Mes endroit de moy*, 'but for my part'; the English translator has rendered *en droit* separately.

108. *perfore*: the context requires the sense 'because', but the translator would hardly have used *perfore* had he realized that ll. 108–9 correspond to a subordinate clause in the French, and do not form a complete independent sentence.   He was misled by the bad punctuation of some French MSS., e.g. Royal 20 B. X and (with consequent corruption) Harley 4383.

136. *Cathaye*: China.   See the classic work of Colonel Yule, *Cathay and the Way Thither*, 2 vols., London 1866.   The modernization of the Catalan map of 1375 in vol. i gives a good idea of Mandeville's geography.

142. *withouten wolle*: the story of the vegetable lamb is taken from the Voyage of Friar Odoric, which is accessible in Hakluyt's *Voyages*.   Hakluyt's translation is reprinted, with the Eastern voyages of John de Plano Carpini (1246) and of William de Rubruquis (1253), in *The Travels of Sir John Mandeville*, ed. A. W. Pollard, London 1900.   The legend probably arose from vague descriptions of the cotton plant; and Mandeville makes it still more marvellous by describing as without wool the lamb which had been invented to explain the wool's existence.

143–4. *Of þat frute I haue eten*: This assertion seems to be due to the English translator.   The normal French text has simply: *et cest bien grant meruaille de ceo fruit, et si est grant oure* [= *œuvre*] *de nature* (MS. Royal 20 B. X, f. 70 b).

147. *the Bernakes*: The barnacle goose—introduced here on a hint from Odoric—is a species of wild goose that visits the Northern coasts in winter.   It was popularly supposed to grow from the shell-fish called 'barnacle', which attaches itself to floating timber by a stalk something like the neck and beak of a bird, and has feathery filaments not unlike plumage.   As the breeding place of the barnacle goose was unknown, and logs with the shell-fish attached were often found on the coasts, it was supposed that the shell-fish was the fruit of a tree, which developed in the water into a bird.   Giraldus Cambrensis, *Topographia Hibernica*, I. xv, reproves certain casuistical members of the Church who ate the barnacle goose on fast-days on the plea that it was not flesh; but himself vouches for the marvel.   The earliest reference in English is No. 11 of the Anglo-Saxon *Riddles*, of which the best solution is 'barnacle goose'.   For a full account see Max Müller's *Lectures on the Science of Language*, vol. ii, pp. 583–604.

157. *grete notes of Ynde,* 'coco-nuts'.

163-4. *Goth and Magoth*: see Ezekiel xxxviii and xxxix. The forms of the names are French.

170. *God of Nature*: Near the end of the *Travels* it is explained that all the Eastern peoples are Deists, though they have not the light of Christianity: *þei beleeven in God þat formede all thing and made the world, and clepen him 'God of Nature'.*

191-2. *þat þei schull not gon out on no syde, but be the cost of hire lond*: the general sense requires the omission of *but*, which has no equivalent in the original French text: *qils ne⟨nt⟩ issent fors deuers la coste de sa terre* (MS. Sloane 1464, f. 139 b). But some MSS. like Royal 20 B. x have *fors qe deuers*, a faulty reading that must have stood in the copy used by the Cotton translator. Cp. note to l. 108.

199-200. *a four grete myle*: renders the French *iiii grantz lieus*. There is no 'great mile' among English measures.

209 ff. In the Middle Ages references to the Jews are nearly always hostile. They were hated as enemies of the Church, and prejudice was hardened by stories, like that in the text, of their vengeance to come, or of ritual murder, like Chaucer's *Prioress's Tale*. England had its supposed boy martyrs, William of Norwich (d. 1144), and Hugh of Lincoln (d. 1255) whom the Prioress invokes:

> *O yonge Hugh of Lyncoln, slayn also*
> *With cursed Jewes, as it is notable,*
> *For it is but a litel while ago,*
> *Preye eek for us,* &c.

Religion was not the only cause of bitterness. The Jews, standing outside the Church and its laws against usury, at a time when financial needs had outgrown feudal revenues, became the money-lenders and bankers of Europe; and with a standard rate of interest fixed at over 40 per cent., debtors and creditors could hardly be friends. In England the Jews reached the height of their prosperity in the twelfth century, so that in 1188 nearly half the national contribution for a Crusade came from them. In the thirteenth century their privileges and operations were cut down, and they were finally expelled from the country in 1290 (see J. Jacobs, *The Jews of Angevin England*, 1893). The Lombards, whose consciences were not nice, took their place as financiers in fourteenth-century England.

222. *trayne*: read *taynere*, OFr. *taignere* 'a burrow'.

237-8. The cotton plant has already given us the vegetable lamb (l. 142). This more prosaic account is taken from the *Epistola Alexandri ad Aristotelem*: '*in Bactriacen ... penitus ad abditos Seres, quod genus hominum foliis arborum decerpendo lanuginem ex silvestri vellere vestes detexunt*' (Julius Valerius,

ed. B. Kübler, p. 194). From the same text come the hippo-
potami, the bitter waters (Kübler, p. 195), and the griffins (Kübler,
p. 217). The *Letter of Alexander* was translated into Anglo-
Saxon in the tenth century.

254 ff. *talouns* etc. : In the 1725 edition there is a reference to
'one 4 Foot long in the Cotton Library' with the inscription,
Griphi Unguis Divo Cuthberto Dunelmensi sacer, 'griffin's
talon, sacred to St. Cuthbert of Durham'. This specimen is now
in the Mediaeval Department of the British Museum, and is
really the slim, curved horn of an ibex. The inscription is late
(sixteenth century), but the talon was catalogued among the
treasures of Durham in the fourteenth century.

260. *Prestre Iohn*: Old French *Prestre Jean*, or 'John the
Priest', was reputed to be the Christian ruler of a great kingdom
in the East. A rather minatory letter professing to come from
him reached most of the princes of Europe, and was replied to
in all seriousness by Pope Alexander III. Its claims include
the lordship over the tribes of Gog and Magog whom Alexander
the Great walled within the mountains. Official missions were
sent to establish relations with him ; but neither in the Far East
nor in Northern Africa, where the best opinion in later times
located his empire, could the great king ever be found. The
history of the legend is set out by Yule in the article *Prester John*
in the *Encyclopaedia Britannica.*

261. *Yle of Pentexoire*: to Mandeville most Eastern countries
are 'isles'. *Pentexoire* in the French text of Odoric is a territory
about the Yellow River (Yule, *Cathay*, vol. i, p. 146).

262 ff. : For comparison the French text of the Epilogue is
given from MS. Royal 20 B. x, f. 83 a, the words in ⟨ ⟩ being
supplied from MS. Sloane 1464 :

'Il y a plusours autres diuers pais, et moutz dautres meruailles
par de la, qe ieo nay mie tout veu, si nen saueroye proprement
parler. Et meismement el pais en quel iay este, y a plusours
diuersetes dont ieo ne fais point el mencioun, qar trop serroit
long chose a tout deuiser. Et pur ceo qe ieo vous ay deuisez
dascuns pais, vous doit suffire quant a present. Qar, si ieo
deuisoie tout quantqez y est par de la, vn autre qi se peneroit
et trauailleroit le corps pur aler en celles marches, et pur sercher
la pais, serroit empeschez par mes ditz a recompter nuls choses
estranges, qar il ne purroit rien dire de nouelle, en quoy ly
oyantz y puissent prendre solaces. Et lem dit toutdis qe choses
nouelles pleisent. Si men taceray a tant, saunz plus recompter
nuls diuersetez qi soyent par de la, a la fin qe cis qi vourra aler
en celles parties y troeue assez a dire.

'Et ieo, Iohan Maundeuille dessudit, qi men party de nos pais
et passay le mer lan de grace mil cccxxii^de ; qi moint terre et
moint passage et moint pays ay puis cerchez ; et qy ay este en

moint bone compaignie et en molt beal fait, come bien qe ieo
(ne fuisse dignes, et) ne feisse vncqes ne beal fait ne beal
emprise ; et qi meintenant suy venuz a repos maugre mien, pur
goutes artetikes qi moy destreignont ; en preignan solacz en mon
cheitif repos, en recordant le temps passe, ay cestes choses
compilez et mises en escript, si come il me poet souuenir, lan de
grace mil ccc.lvime, a xxxiiii^{te} an qe ieo men party de noz pais.

'Si pri a toutz les lisauntz, si lour plest, qils voillent Dieu prier
pur moy, et ieo priera pur eux. Et toutz cils qi pur moy dirrount
vne *Paternoster* qe Dieu me face remissioun de mes pecches, ieo
les face parteners et lour ottroie part dez toutz les bons pelrinages
et dez toutz les bienfaitz qe ieo feisse vnqes, et qe ieo ferray, si
Dieu plest, vncqore iusqes a ma fyn. Et pry a Dieu, de qy
toute bien et toute grace descent, qil toutz les lisantz et oyantz
Cristiens voille de sa grace reemplir, et lour corps et les almes
sauuer, a la glorie et loenge de ly qi est trinz et vns, et saunz
comencement et saunz fin, saunz qualite bons, saunz quantite
grantz, en toutz lieus present et toutz choses contenant, et qy nul
bien ne poet amender ne nul mal enpirer, qy en Trinite parfite
vit et regne par toutz siecles et par toutz temps.   Amen.'

274. *blamed*: The Old French verb *empescher* means both ' to
hinder, prevent ', and ' to accuse, impeach '. But here *empeschez*
should have been translated by ' prevented ', not ' blamed '.

284-306. This passage, which in one form or another appears
in nearly all the MSS. in English, has no equivalent in the
MSS. in French so far examined : and, as it conflicts with
ll. 313 ff., which—apart from the peculiarities of the Cotton
rendering—indicate that the *Travels* were written after Mandeville's return, it must be set down as an interpolation.

The art of forging credentials was well understood in the
Middle Ages, and the purpose of this addition was to silence
doubters by the *imprimatur* of the highest authority, just as the
marvel of the Dancers of Colbek is confirmed by the sponsorship
of Pope Leo IX (1 246-9).   The different interpretation of the
latest editor, Hamelius, who thinks it was intended as a sly hit
at the Papacy (*Quarterly Review* for April 1917, pp. 349 f.)
seems to rest on the erroneous assumption that the passage
belonged to the French text as originally written.

The anachronism by which the author is made to seek the
Pope *in Rome* gives a clue to the date of the interpolation.
From the beginning of the fourteenth century until 1377 Avignon,
and not Rome, was the seat of the Pope ; and for another thirty
years there was doubt as to the issue of the conflict between
the popes, who had their head-quarters at Rome and were
recognized by England, and the antipopes, who remained at
Avignon and had the support of the French.   The facts were
notorious, so that the anachronism would hardly be possible to

one who wrote much before the end of the century, even though he were a partisan of the Roman court.

From internal evidence it would seem that the interpolation first appeared in French. The style is the uniform style of translation, with the same tags—*and ȝee schull vndirstonde = et sachiez* ; *ȝif it lyke ȝou = si vous plest* ; and the same trick of double rendering, e.g. *of dyuerse secte and of beleeve* ; *wyse and discreet* ; *the auctour ne the persone.* More decisive is an example of the syntactical compromise explained in the note to l. 329 : be *the whiche the Mappa Mundi was made* after. With so many French MSS. of Mandeville in use in England, an interpolation in French would have more authority than one that could not be traced beyond English ; and it can hardly be an insuperable objection that no such French text exists to-day, since our knowledge of the Cotton and Egerton versions themselves depends in each case on the chance survival of a single MS.

The point has a bearing on the vexed question of the relations of the English texts one to another. For brevity we may denote by D the defective text of the early prints and most MSS., which is specially distinguished by a long gap near the beginning ; by C the Cotton text (ed. Halliwell, Pollard, Hamelius) ; by E the Egerton text (ed. Warner). Nicholson (in the *Encyclopaedia Britannica*) and Warner give priority to D, and consider that C and E are independent revisions and expansions of D by writers who had recourse to the French original. Their argument seems to be this : There is precise evidence just before the gap that D derives direct from a mutilated French text (see *Enc. Brit.*), and if it be granted that a single translation from the French is the base of C, D, and E, it follows that C and E are based on D.

A fuller study by Vogels (*Handschriftliche Untersuchungen über die Englische Version Mandeville's*, Crefeld 1891) brings to light a new fact : the two Bodleian MSS., E Museo 116 and Rawlinson D 99, contain an English translation (say L) made from a Latin text of the *Travels*. Vogels also shows that E is based on D, because the characteristic lacuna of D is filled in E by a passage which is borrowed from L and is not homogeneous with the rest of E. So far there is no conflict with the view of Nicholson and Warner. But, after adducing evidence in favour of the contention that C, D, and E are at base one translation, Vogels concludes that D derives from C, arguing thus : There is good evidence that C is a direct translation from the French, and if it be granted that a single translation from the French is the base of C and D, it follows that D derives from C.

In short, the one party maintains that C is an expansion of D, the other that D is an abridgement of C ; and this flat opposition results from the acceptance of common ground: that C and D represent in the main one translation and not two translations.

To return to our interpolation:

(1) Vogels's first piece of evidence that C, D, and E are at base one translation is the appearance in all of this interpolation, which is absent from the MSS. in French. But a passage so remarkable might spread from one to the other of two independent English texts; or if the interpolation originated in England in a MS. of the French text since lost, it might be twice translated.

(2) Vogels assumes that the interpolation first appeared in type C. But C is the form in which it would be least likely to originate, because here the contradiction of statement is sharpest owing to the rendering at ll. 313–14: *and now I am comen hom*, which is peculiar to C (see the French).

(3) If, in order to eliminate individual peculiarities, we take two MSS. of the D type — say Harley 2386 and Royal 17 C. xxxviii—we find that their text of the interpolation is identical with that of E. This is consistent with Vogels's finding that the body of E derives from D; and it confirms the evidence of all the defective MSS. that the interpolation in this particular form was an integral part of the D type.

(4) But between the text of the interpolation in D and that in C there are differences in matter, in sentence order, and in phrasing, which, while they do not exclude the possibility of interdependence, do not suggest such a relation. In D the passage is a naked attempt at authentication; in C it is more artfully though more shamelessly introduced by the touch of piety conventional in epilogues. And as the signs of a French original that appear in C are absent from D, it is unlikely that the text of the interpolation in C derives from D.

(5) Again, in D and E the addition follows the matter of ll. 307–20. Unfortunately, though the balance of probability is in favour of the order in C, the order intended by the interpolator is not certain enough to be made the basis of arguments. But such a difference in position is naturally explained from the stage when the interpolation stood in the margin of a MS., or on an inserted slip, so that it might be taken into the consecutive text at different points. And an examination of the possibilities will show that if the interpolation originated in French, the different placing is more simply explained on the assumption that C and D are independent translations than on the assumption that one of them derives from the other.

To sum up: the central problem for the history of the English texts is the relation of C and D. Taken by itself the evidence afforded by the text of the interpolation is against the derivation of C from D; it neither favours nor excludes the derivation of D from C; it rather favours independent translation in C and D

For the relations of the rest of the text these deductions afford no more than a clue. Against independent translation of C and D stands the evidence adduced by Vogels for basic unity. Much of this could be accounted for by the coincidences that are inevitable in literal prose translations from a language so near to English in vocabulary and word order ; and a few striking agreements might be due to the use of French MSS. having abnormal variants in common, or even to reference by a second translator to the first. The remainder must be weighed against a considerable body of evidence in the contrary sense, e. g. several places where the manuscripts of the French text have divergent readings, of which C translates one, and D another.

It is unlikely that any simple formula will be found to cover the whole web of relationships : but any way of reconciling the conclusions of the authorities should be explored ; and the first step is an impartial sifting of all the evidence, with the object of discovering to what extent C and D are interdependent, and to what extent independent translations. The chief obstacle is the difficulty of bringing the necessary texts together ; for an investigator who wished to clear the ground would have to face the labour of preparing a six-text *Mandeville*, in the order, French, C, D, E, L, Latin.

301. *Mappa Mundi*: OFr. and ME. *Mappemounde*, was the generic name for a chart of the world, and, by extension, for a descriptive geography of the world. It is not clear what particular *Mappa Mundi* is referred to here, or whether such a map was attached to the manuscript copy of the *Travels* in which this interpolation first appeared.

329. *fro whom all godenesse and grace cometh fro*: cp. 24–5 *the lond of the whiche on of the þre Kynges . . . was kyng offe*; 76–8 *þei . . . of whom all science . . . cometh from*; and 301–2 *be the whiche the* Mappa Mundi *was made after*. The pleonasm is explained by the divergence of French and ME. word order. In French, as in modern literary English, the preposition is placed at the beginning of the clause, before the relative (*de qui, dont*, &c.). ME. writers naturally use the relative *that*, and postpone the preposition to the end of the clause : e. g. *þat all godenesse cometh fro*. The translator compromises between his French original and his native habit by placing the preposition both at the beginning and at the end.

X

Dialect: Northern (Scots): the MS. copy was made in 1487 more than a century after the poem was composed.

Vocabulary: Note *till* 'to' 4, 77 (in rime); *syne* 'afterwards' 35, 112; the forms *sic* 'such' 135, *begouth* 94, and the

short verbal forms *ma* (in rime) 'make' 14, *tane* (in rime)
'taken' 19.

Inflexions :

VERB : pres. ind. **3 sg.** *has* 76.

　　　　　　　　　　3 pl. *has* 52, *mais* 72 ; but *thai haf* 16.

　　　　pres. p. *rynand* 17, *vyndland* 129 (in rime).

　　　　strong pp. *gane* 84, *drawyn* 124.

PRONOUN 3 PERS.: sg. fem. nom. *scho* (in rime) 80; pl. *thai* 1 ;
thair 28 ; *thame* 3.

Sounds : OE. *a* remains : *brynstane* (in rime) 20, *sare* 51.

OE. *ō* (close *ǭ*) appears as *u*(*ū* ?) : *gude* 36, *fut* 57, *tume* 143.

Unaccented -(*e*)*d* of weak pa. t. and pp. becomes -(*i*)*t* : *passit* 2,
&c.

Spelling: *i* (*y*) following a vowel indicates length : *weill* 10,
noyne ' noon' 67.

OE. *hw-* appears as *quh-* (indicating strong aspiration): *quhelis*
'wheels' 17, *quhar* 18.

v and *w* are interchanged : *vithall* 9, *behevin* 163, *in swndir*
106.

Book XVII of *The Bruce* begins with the capture of Berwick
by the Scots in March 1318. Walter Stewart undertakes to hold
the city, and is aided in preparing defences by a Flemish
engineer, John Crab. Next year King Edward II determines
to recapture the stronghold by an attack from both land and sea.
He entrenches his forces and makes the first assault unsuccess-
fully early in September 1319. In this battle the Scotch garrison
capture a clever engineer (see note to l. 71 below). King Robert
Bruce meanwhile orders a raid into England as a diversion, and
on 20 September 1319, an English army, led by the Archbishop
of York, is disastrously defeated by the invaders at Mitton.
Our extract gives the story of the second assault on Berwick,
which was also fruitless. The fortress fell into English hands
again as a result of the battle of Halidon Hill in 1333: see
XIV *a* 35–6.

5–6. 'They made a sow of great joists, which had a stout
covering over it.' The *sow* was essentially a roof on wheels.
The occupants, under shelter of the roof, pushed up to the walls
of the besieged place and tried to undermine them. For an
illustration see Cutts, *Scenes and Characters of the Middle Ages*,
Pt. VI, chap. vi, where other military engines of the time are
described.

15. *Crabbis consale*: John Crab was the engineer of the
garrison. He is no doubt the same as the John Crab who in
1332 brought Flemish ships round from Berwick to attack the
English vessels at Dundee. There was an important Flemish
colony at Berwick from early times.

36. *Schir Valter, the gude Steward* : Walter Steward, whose surname denotes his office as Steward of Scotland, was the father of Robert II, the first king of the Stuart line.

42. *Rude-evyn* : September 13, the eve of the feast of the Exaltation of the Cross.

49. *thame . . . of the toune,* 'the defenders of the town'.

51. *or than,* 'or else'.

71 ff. *The engynour* : an English engineer captured by the garrison in the previous assault and forced into their service.

80. *scho,* 'she', some engine of war not previously referred to : apparently a mechanical sling.

123 ff. The boats were filled with men and hoisted up the masts, so as to overtop the walls and allow the besiegers to shoot at the garrison from above. The same engine that proved fatal to the sow was used to break up the boats.

146. *thar wardane with him had,* 'their warden (who) had with him'; cp. note to XIII *a* 36.

158–61. A confused construction. The writer has in mind : (1) 'Of all the men he had there remained with him only one whom he had not left to relieve', &c.; and (2) 'There were no members of his company (except one) whom he had not left', &c.

192. for *ficht* (not *sicht*) cp. l. 115; see C. Sisam, *R.E.S.* N.S. xiii (1962).

XI

Dialect : South Midland.

Inflexions : *u* for inflexional *e*, as in *knowun a* 2, *seun a* 51, *azenus a* 29, *mannus b* 114 is found chiefly in West Midland.

    VERB : pres. ind. 2 sg. *madist b* 214.

                3 sg. *groundiþ a* 4.

                3 pl. *seyn a* 1, *techen b* 5.

        pres. p. *brennynge b* 67.

        strong pp. *knowun a* 2, *zouen b* 264, *take b* 271.

    PRONOUN 3 PERS. : pl. *þey, þei, a* 3, *b* 9; possessive usually *þer* in *a* 1, 23, &c.; but *her a* 52, and regularly *here* in *b* 25, 36, &c.; objective *hem a* 4, *b* 3.

Sounds : OE. *ā* appears regularly as *o, oo* : *more a* 7, *Hooly a* 10, *toolde a* 65.

OE. *y* appears as *y, i* : *synne a* 61, *stiren b* 93.

The form *þouþ* (= *þouʒ*) *b* 190 probably indicates sound-substitution ; and in *ynowbʒ* (= *ynouʒ*) *b* 149 there is wavering between the two forms.

a 12. *Wit Sunday* : the first element is OE. *hwīt* 'white', not ' wit '.

a 25 ff. Translations of the Bible were common in France at this time. No less than six fine copies survive from the library of John, Duke of Berry (d. 1416). About the middle of the fourteenth century King John of France ordered a new translation and commentary to be made at the expense of the Jews, but it was never finished, although several scholars were still engaged on it at the end of the century. The early French verse renderings, which incorporate a good deal of mediaeval legend, are described by J. Bonnard, *Les Traductions de la Bible en Vers Français au Moyen Âge* (Paris 1884); the prose by S. Berger, *La Bible Française au Moyen Âge* (Paris 1884). Of the surviving manuscripts mentioned in these excellent monographs several were written in England.

a 28 ff. In earlier times, when most of those who could read at all were schooled in Latin, the need for English translations of the Scriptures was not so pressing, and the partial translations that were made were intended rather for the use of the clergy and their noble patrons than for the people. Bede (d. 735) completed a rendering of St. John's Gospel on his death-bed. Old English versions of the Gospels and the Psalms still survive. Abbot Aelfric (about A.D. 1000) translated the first five books of the Old Testament; and more than one Middle English version of the Psalms is known. Wiclif was perhaps unaware of the Old English precedents because French renderings became fashionable in England from the twelfth century onwards, and he would probably think of the Psalter more as a separate service book than as an integral part of the Bible. But the prologue to the Wiclifite version attributed to John Purvey quotes the example of Bede and King Alfred; and the Dialogue on Translation which, in Caxton's print, serves as preface to Trevisa's translation of Higden, emphasizes the Old English precedents. Both may be read in *Fifteenth Century Prose and Verse*, ed. A. W. Pollard, London 1903, pp. 193 ff. The attitude of the mediaeval Church towards vernacular translations of the Bible has been studied very fully by Miss M. Deanesly, *The Lollard Bible and other Medieval Biblical Versions*, Cambridge 1920.

a 34. *þe pley of Jork.* The York Paternoster Play has not survived, but there are records from 1389 of a Guild of the Lord's Prayer at York, whose main object was the production of the play. It seems to have been an early example of the moral play, holding up 'the vices to scorn and the virtues to praise', and it probably consisted of several scenes, each exhibiting one of the Seven Deadly Sins. The last recorded representation was in 1572. See Chambers, *The Mediaeval Stage*, vol. ii, p. 154. The association of the friars with the production of religious plays is confirmed by other writings of the time. They were quick to realize the value of dramatic representation as a means of gaining favour with the people, and their encouragement must be reckoned an important factor in the development of the Miracle Play.

a 51. *wher*, 'whether'; cp. *b* 207. In ll. 197, 266, 274, it introduces a direct question; see note to v 118.

b 20. *Gregory*, Gregory the Great. See his work *In Primum Regum Expositiones*, Bk. iii, c. 28: *praedicatores autem Sanctae Ecclesiae ... prophetae ministerio utuntur* (Migne, *Patrologia*, vol. lxxix, col. 158).

b 44. ⟨*God*⟩. Such omissions from the Corpus MS. are supplied throughout from the copy in Trinity College, Dublin, MS. C. III. 12.

b 79–80. Cp. Luke xxi. 36 and 1 Thessalonians v. 17.

b 89–91. Proverbs xxviii. 9.

b 126. *as Ambrose*: In 386 St. Ambrose, besieged in the Portian Church at Milan by Arian sectaries, kept his followers occupied and in good heart by introducing the Eastern practice of singing hymns and antiphons. See St. Augustine's *Confessions* Bk. ix, c. 7.

b 131–2. *placebo*. Vespers of the Dead, named from the first word of the antiphon, *Placebo Domino in regione vivorum* (Psalm cxiv. 9).

dirige. Matins of the Dead, named from the first word of the antiphon, *Dirige, Domine, Deus meus, in conspectu tuo viam meam* (Psalm v. 9). Hence our word *dirge*.

comendacion: an office in which the souls of the dead are commended to God.

matynes of Oure Lady: one of the services in honour of the Virgin introduced in the Middle Ages.

The whole question of these accretions to the Church services is dealt with by our English master in liturgical study, the late Mr. Edmund Bishop, in his essay introductory to the Early English Text Society's edition of the *Prymer*, since reprinted with additional notes in his *Liturgica Historica* (Oxford 1918), pp. 211 ff.

b 137 f. *deschaunt, countre note, and orgon, and smale brekynge*. The elaboration of the Church services in mediaeval times was accompanied by a corresponding enrichment of the music. To the plain chant additional parts were joined, sung in harmony either above or below the plain chant. *Descant* usually means the addition of a part above, *organ* and *countre-note* (= counterpoint) the addition of parts either above or below. All these could be composed note for note with the plain chant. But *smale brekyng* represents a further complication, whereby the single note in the plain chant was represented by two or more notes in the accompanying parts.

b 140 f. The abuse is referred to in *Piers Plowman*:

Persones and parsheprestes pleynede to the bisshop
That hure parshens ben poore sitthe the pestelence tyme,
To haue licence and leue in Londone to dwelle,
And synge ther for symonye, for seluer ys swete.

Prologue ll. 81–4.

and by Chaucer in his description of the Parson :

> *He sette nat his benefice to hyre,*
> *And leet his sheepe encombred in the myre,*
> *And ran to Londoun, unto Seint Poules,*
> *To seken hym a chaunterie for soules.*

Prologue ll. 507–10.

b 183. *Ordynalle of Salisbury.* An 'ordinal' is a book showing the order of church services and ceremonies. In mediaeval times there was considerable divergence in the usage of different churches. But after the Conquest, and more especially in the thirteenth century, there was developed at Salisbury Cathedral an elaborate order and form of service which spread to most of the English churches of any pretensions. This was called 'Sarum' or 'Salisbury' use.

b 209. *þei demen it dedly synne a prest to fulfille,* &c. For this construction, cp. Chaucer, *Prologue* 502 *No wonder is a lewed man to ruste* ; Shakespeare, *Two Gentlemen of Verona,* v. iv. 108 f. *It is the lesser blot . . . Women to change their shapes,* &c. The same construction, where we now insert *for*, is seen in *Gawayne* (v. 352–3) *hit were a wynne huge . . . a leude, þat coupe, to luf hom wel,* &c.

b 221–3. 'They say that a priest may be excused from saying mass, to be the substance of which God gave Himself, provided that he hears one.'

b 228 f. *newe costy portos, antifeners, graielis, and alle opere bokis.* *Portos*, French *porte hors,* represents Latin *portiforium*, a breviary convenient for 'carrying out of doors'. The *antifener* contained the antiphons, responses, &c., necessary for the musical service of the canonical hours. The *graiel,* or *gradual,* was so called from the gradual responses, sung at the steps of the altar, or while the deacon ascended the steps of the pulpit : but the book actually contained all the choral service of the Mass.

b 230. *makynge of biblis.* Wiclif in his *Office of Curates* (ed. Matthew, p. 145) complains of the scarcity of bibles. *But fewe curatis han þe Bible and exposiciouns of þe Gospelis, and litel studien on hem, and lesse donne after hem. But wolde God þat euery parische chirche in þis lond hadde a good Bible !* &c.

b 234. At this time books, especially illuminated books, were very dear. The Missal of Westminster Abbey, which is now shown in the Chapter-house, was written in 1382–4 at a cost of £34 14s. 7d.—a great sum in those days, for the scribe, Thomas Preston, who took two years to write it, received only

£4 for his labour, 20s. for his livery, and board at the rate of 21s. 8d. the half year. The inscription in British Museum MS. Royal 19 D. 11, a magnificently illustrated Bible with commentary, shows that it was captured at Poitiers with King John of France, and bought by the Earl of Salisbury for 100 marks (about £66). Edward III gave the same sum to a nun of Amesbury for a rich book of romance. In France John, Duke of Berry, paid as much as £200 for a breviary, and the appraisement of his library in 1416 shows a surprisingly high level of values (L. Delisle, *Le Cabinet des Manuscrits*, vol. iii, pp. 171 ff.). These were luxurious books. The books from the chapel of Archbishop Bowet of York (d. 1423) sold more reasonably : £8 for a great antiphonar and £6 13s. 4d. *pro uno libro vocato 'Bibill'*, were the highest prices paid; and from his library there were some fascinating bargains : 4s. for a small copy of Gregory's *Cura Pastoralis* ; 5s. *pro uno libro vocato 'Johannes Andrewe'*, *vetere et debili*, which would probably turn out to be a dry work on the Decretals; and 3s. 4d. for a nameless codex, *vetere et caduco*, 'old and falling to pieces'. (*Historians of the Church of York*, ed. J. Raine, vol. iii, pp. 311, 315.)

But the failing activity of the monastic scriptoria, and the formation of libraries by the friars and by rich private collectors, made study difficult for students at the universities, where at this time a shilling per week—a third of the price of Bowet's most dilapidated volume—was reckoned enough to cover the expenses of a scholar living plainly. The college libraries were scantily supplied: books were lent only in exchange for a valuable pledge; or even pawned, in hard times, by the colleges themselves.

These conditions were not greatly improved until printing gave an easy means of duplication, and for a time caused the humble manuscripts in which most of the mediaeval vernacular literature was preserved to be treated as waste paper. As late as the eighteenth century Martène found the superb illuminated manuscripts left by John, Duke of Berry, to the Sainte Chapelle at Bourges serving as roosting places to their keeper's hens (*Voyage Littéraire*, Paris 1717, pt. i, p. 29).

b 261-3. The reference is to Acts vi. 2, 'It is not reason that we should leave the word of God, and serve tables.'

b 266. *wisere þan*. After these words the Corpus MS. (p. 170, col. i, l. 34 mid.), without any warning, goes on to the closing passage of an entirely unrelated 'Petition to the King and Parliament'. By way of compensation, the end of our sermon appears at the close of the Petition. Clearly the scribe (or some one of his predecessors) copied without any regard for the sense from a MS. of which the leaves had become disarranged.

b 285. Cp. Acts iii. 6.

XII

Dialect: London (SE. Midland) with Kentish features.
Inflexions:

VERB: pres. ind. 3 sg. *loveth a* 5; contracted *stant a* 74.

     3 pl. *schewen a* 136, *halsen a* 148, *be* (in rime) *a* 92.

   pres. p. *growende a* 80.

   strong pp. *schape* (in rime) *a* 130, beside *schapen a* 169.

PRONOUN 3 PERS.: sg. fem. nom. *sche a* 32; pl. *thei a* 148; *here a* 144; *hem a* 112.

Unaccented final *-e* is treated as in Chaucer, having its full value in the verse when it represents an inflexion or final vowel in Old English or Old French, e. g.

> *And for he scholdè slepè softè* *a* 93
> *An apè, which at thilkè throwè* *b* 5

Sounds: *e* appears as in Kentish for OE. *y*: *hell* 'hill' *a* 65, 79, 86; *keste* 'kissed' *a* 178; note the rimes *unschette : lette a* 71-2; *pet* 'pit' : *let b* 9-10; and less decisive *pet : knet* (OE. *knyttan*) *b* 29-30, 53-4; *dreie : beie b* 23-4.

Spelling: *ie* represents close *ę̄* : *fliestende a* 157, *hier b* 34; *diemed b* 216.

Syntax: The elaborate machinery of sentence connexion deserves special attention; and many turns of phrase are explained by Gower's fluency in French.

a 1. Gower follows Ovid, *Metamorphoses*, Bk. xi. Chaucer tells the story of Ceix and Alcyone in his *Death of Blanche the Duchess*, ll. 62 ff. This is presumably the early work to which the Man of Law refers:

> *I kan right now no thrifty tale seyn*
> *But Chaucer, thogh he kan but lewedly*
> *On metres and on rymyng craftily,*
> *Hath seyd hem, in swich Englissh as he kan,*
> *Of olde tyme, as knoweth many a man;*
> *And if he have noght seyd hem, leve brother,*
> *In o book, he hath seyd hem in another;*
> *For he hath toold of loveris up and doun*
> *Mo than Ovide made of mencioun*
> *In his* Epistelles, *that been ful olde.*
> *What sholde I tellen hem, syn they ben tolde?*
> *In youthe he made of Ceys and Alcione*, &c.
>   (Link to *Man of Law's Tale*, ll. 46 ff.)

Gower's rendering is the more poetical.

a 2. *Trocinie*. Ovid's *Trachinia tellus*, so called from the city of Trachis, north-west of Thermopylae.

a 23. *As he which wolde go :* otiose, or at best meaning no more than 'desiring to go'. Cp. *b* 25 *As he which hadde* = 'having' simply ; and similarly *b* 37, 203. It is an imitation of a contemporary French idiom *comme celui qui.*

a 26. *and* : the displacement of the conjunction from its natural position at the beginning of the clause is characteristic of Gower's verse. Cp. l. 152 *Upon the morwe and up sche sterte* = 'and in the morning she got up', and *a* 45, 49, *b* 121, 124, 135, 160, 182. See notes to ll. 32, 78 f.

a 32. Editors put a comma after *wepende,* and no stop after *seileth* : but it is Alceoun who weeps. The displacement of *and* is exemplified in the notes to l. 26 and ll. 78 f.

a 37. 'One had not to look for grief' ; a regular formula of understatement, meaning 'her grief was great'.

a 53. *Hire reyny cope,* &c. : the rainbow, which was the sign or manifestation of Iris.

a 59 ff.   *Prope Cimmerios longo spelunca recessu,*
          Mons cavus, ignavi domus et penetralia Somni.
                    (*Metamorphoses* xi. 592–3.)
Much of the poetry of Gower's description is due to Ovid.

a 78 f. Editors put no stop after *may* and a comma after *hell.* Hence *The New English Dictionary* quotes this passage as an isolated instance of *noise,* transitive, meaning 'disturb with noise'. But *noise* is intransitive, *hell* is governed by *aboute round,* and the position of *bot* is abnormal as in l. 105. Cp. notes to ll. 26, 32, and render ' But all round about the hill '.

a 105. For the word order see notes to ll. 26, 32, 78 f.

a 117. *The lif,* 'the man', cp. IV *a* 43.

a 118. *Ithecus* : for Icelos. According to Ovid 'Icelos' was the name by which he was known to the gods, but men called him ' Phobetor'.

a 123. *Panthasas* : Ovid's *Phantasos.*

a 152. See note to l. 26.

a 197. The halcyon, usually identified with the kingfisher, was supposed to build a floating nest on the sea in midwinter, and to have power to calm the winds and waves at that season, bringing 'halcyon weather'.

b 2. *I finde.* Matthew Paris in his *Chronica Maiora* (ed. Luard, Rolls Series, vol. ii, pp. 413 ff.) gives a similar story, which, he says, King Richard the First often told to rebuke ingratitude. In this version, Vitalis of Venice falls into a pit dug as a trap for wild beasts. The rescued animals are a lion and a serpent ; the rescuer is nameless, and the gem given to him by the serpent has not the magic virtue of returning when-ever sold. Nearer to Gower is the story told in Nigel Wireker's *Speculum Stultorum,* a late twelfth-century satire in Latin verse, which, from the name of its principal character Burnellus the

Ass, who is ambitious to have a longer tail, is sometimes called *Burnellus*; cp. Chaucer, *Nun's Priest's Tale*, l. 492:

I have wel rad in Daun Burnel the Asse
Among his vers, &c.

The poem is printed in T. Wright's *Anglo-Latin Satirical Poets and Epigrammatists of the Twelfth Century* (Rolls Series, 1872), vol. i. At the end the Ass returns disappointed to his master Bernardus (= Bardus). Bernardus, when gathering wood, hears Dryanus (= Adrian), a rich citizen of Cremona, call from a pit for help. The rescued animals are a lion, a serpent, and an ape. The gem given by the serpent in token of gratitude always returns to Bernardus, who, with more honesty than Gower's poor man shows, takes it back to the buyer. The fame of the marvellous stone reaches the king; his inquiries bring to light the whole story; and Dryanus is ordered to give half his goods to Bernardus.

Gower probably worked on a later modification of Nigel's story.

b 86. *blessed*, ' crossed (himself) '.

b 89. *Betwen him and his asse*, i.e. pulling together with the ass. The ass is, of course, the distinguished Burnellus.

b 116. *his ape*: for *this ape* (?).

b 191. *Justinian*, Emperor of the Eastern Roman Empire (d. 565), was best known for his codification of the Roman Law, and so is named here as the type of a lawgiver.

XIII

Dialect: South-Western, with some Midland forms.
Inflexions:
VERB: pres. ind. 3 sg. *bloweþ a* 7, *casteþ a* 8.
3 pl. *buþ a* 10, *habbeþ a* 15.
pres. p. *slyttyng, frotyng b* 59.
strong pp. *yknowe a* 12, *ysode a* 30.
NOUN: Note the plural in -(*e*)*n*, *tren* ' trees ' *a* 44, 51, 53 : *chyldern b* 16 is a double plural.
PRONOUN 3 PERS.: pl. *hy a* 17; *here a* 61 ; *ham a* 23.
Note the unstressed 3 sg. and 3 pl. form *a*, e.g. at *a* 13, 27.

Sounds : There is no instance of *v* for initial *f*, which is evidenced in the spelling of early South-Western writers like Robert of Gloucester (about 1300), or of *z* for initial *s*, which is less commonly shown in spelling. *u* for OE. *y* occurs in *hulles* ' hills ' *a* 18 (beside *bysynes b* 24, where Modern English has *u* in spelling but *i* in pronunciation ; and *lift* (OE. *lyft*) *b* 39, where Modern English has the South-Eastern form *left*).

a 2–3. *Mayster* ... *Minerua* ... *hys*: Trevisa appears to have understood ' Minerva ' as the name of a god.

a 6–49. Higden took all this passage from Book i of the twelfth-century Annals of Alfred of Beverley (ed. Hearne, pp. 6–7). The *Polychronicon* is a patchwork of quotations from earlier writers.

a 7. *Pectoun.* Higden has *ad Peccum*, and Alfred of Beverley *in monte qui vocatur Pec*, i.e. The Peak of Derbyshire. *cc* and *ct* are not distinguishable in some hands of the time, and Trevisa has made *Peccum* into *Pectoun.*

a 14. *Cherdhol.* Hearne's text of Alfred of Beverley has *Cherole*; Henry of Huntingdon (about 1150), who gives the same four marvels in his *Historia Anglorum*, has *Chederhole*; and on this evidence the place has been identified with Cheddar in Somerset, where there are famous caves.

a 22. *an egle hys nest*: cp. *b* 23 *a child hys brouch.* This construction has two origins: (1) It is a periphrasis for the genitive, especially in the case of masculine and neuter proper names which had no regular genitive in English; (2) It is an error arising from false manuscript division of the genitive suffix *-es*, *-is*, from its stem.

a 36. ⟨*þat*⟩ here and in l. 52 is inserted on the evidence of the other MSS. Syntactically its omission is defensible, for the suppressed relative is a common source of difficulty in Middle English; see the notes to v 4–6, 278–9; x 146; xiv *e* 54; xvii 66.

a 50. *Wynburney.* Wimborne in Dorset. Here St. Cuthburga founded a nunnery, which is mentioned in one of Aldhelm's letters as early as A.D. 705. The information that it is ' not far from Bath ', which is hardly accurate, was added by Higden to the account of the marvel he found in the *Topographia Hibernica* of Giraldus Cambrensis (vol. v, p. 86 of the Rolls Series edition of his works).

a 54–64. Higden took this passage from Giraldus, *Itinerarium Cambriae*, Bk. ii, c. 11 (vol. vi, p. 139 of the Rolls edition).

a 60–1. *be at here aboue*, ' be over them ', ' have the upper hand '.

a 63. *Pimbilmere*: the English name for Lake Bala.

b 6–7. *þe Flemmynges.* The first settlement of Flemings in Pembrokeshire took place early in the twelfth century, and in 1154, Henry II, embarrassed alike by the turbulence of the Welsh, and of the new host of Flemish mercenaries who had come in under Stephen, encouraged a further settlement. They formed a colony still distinguishable from the surrounding Welsh population.

b 11–12. The threefold division of the English according to their Continental origin dates back to Bede's *Ecclesiastical*

History. But the areas settled by Bede's three tribes do not correspond to Southern, Northern, and Midland. The Jutes occupied Kent, whence the South-Eastern dialect; the Saxons occupied the rest of the South, whence the South-Western dialect; and the Angles settled in the Midlands and the North; so that the Midland and Northern dialects are both Anglian, and derive from the same Continental tribe or tribal group.

b 26. *þe furste moreyn*: the Black Death of 1349. There were fresh outbreaks of plague in 1362, 1369, 1376.

b 26–42. The bracketed passage is an addition by Trevisa himself, and is of primary importance for the history of English and of English education. See the valuable article by W. H. Stevenson in *An English Miscellany Presented to Dr. Furnivall*, pp. 421 ff.

b 27–8. *Iohan Cornwal, a mayster of gramere.* A 'master of grammar' was a licensed teacher of grammar. Mr. Stevenson points out that in 1347–8 John of Cornwall received payment from Merton College, Oxford, for teaching the boys of the founder's kin. His countryman Trevisa probably had personal knowledge of his methods of teaching.

b 39–40. *and a scholle passe þe se*, 'if they should cross the sea'.

b 47–8. The bracketed words are introduced by Trevisa.

b 50 f. *and ys gret wondur*: *and* is superfluous and should perhaps be deleted.

b 58–65. Though still often quoted as a fourteenth-century witness to the pronunciation of Northern English (e. g. by K. Luick, *Historische Grammatik der englischen Sprache*, 1914, pp. 40 f.), this passage, as Higden acknowledges, comes from the Prologue to Book iii of William of Malmesbury's *Gesta Pontificum*, completed in the year 1125: see the Rolls Series edition, p. 209.

XIV

a 2. *Bannokburn.* Minot's subject is not so much the defeat of the English at Bannockburn in 1314, as the English victory at Halidon Hill on 19 July 1333, which he regards as a vengeance for Bannockburn.

a 7. *Saint Iohnes toune*: Perth, so called from its church of St. John the Baptist. It was occupied by the English in 1332 after the defeat of the Scots at Dupplin Moor.

a 13. *Striflin*, 'Stirling'.

a 15. Hall suggests that this refers to Scotch raids on the North of England undertaken to distract Edward III from the siege of Berwick.

a 19 f. *Rughfute riueling ... Berebag*: nicknames for the Scots, the first because they wore brogues (*riuelings*) of rough hide; the second because, to allow of greater mobility, each man carried his own bag of provisions instead of relying on a baggage train.

a 22. *Brig* = *Burghes* l. 25, 'Bruges'. At this time Scots, English, and French had all close connexions with the Netherlands. Observe that John Crab, who aided the Scots in the defence of Berwick (note to X 15), was a Fleming.

a 35. *at Berwik*. Berwick fell as a result of the battle of Halidon Hill which the Scots fought with the object of raising the siege. For an earlier siege of Berwick, in 1319, see No. X.

a 36. *get*, 'watch', 'be on the look out' (ON. *gǽta*).

b 5–6. Calais was at this time a convenient base for piracy in the Channel.

b 19. *A bare*: Edward III, whom Minot often refers to as 'the boar'.

b 24–6. In preparation for the long siege Edward III had built a regular camp beside Calais.

b 32. *Sir Philip*. Philip de Valois, Philip VI of France (1293–1350). His son, John Duke of Normandy (1319–64), who succeeded him in 1350, is of good memory as a lover of fine books. Two are mentioned in the notes to XI *a* 25 ff. and XI *b* 234. A splendid copy of the *Miracles de Notre Dame*, preserved until recently in the Seminary Library at Soissons, seems also to have been captured with his baggage at Poitiers, for it was bought back from the English by King Charles V. Another famous book produced by his command was the translation of Livy by Bersuire, with magnificent illuminations. The spirit of the collector was not damped by his captivity in England from 1356–60, for his account books show that he continued to employ binders and miniaturists, to encourage original composition, and to buy books, especially books of romance. See *Notes et Documents relatifs à Jean, Roi de France*, &c., ed. by Henry of Orleans, Duc d'Aumale (Philobiblon Soc., London 1855–6).

b 40. *þe Cardinales*. Pope Clement VI had sent cardinals Annibale Ceccano bishop of Frascati, and Etienne Aubert, who became Pope Innocent VI in 1352, to arrange a peace between France and England. But the English were suspicious of the Papal court at Avignon, and accused the cardinals of favouring the French cause.

b 82. *Sir Iohn de Viene*. Jean de Vienne, seigneur de Pagny (d. 1351), a famous captain in the French wars.

c 5 f. 'They (friends) are so slippery when put to the test, so eager to have ⟨for themselves⟩, and so unwilling to give up ⟨to others⟩.'

c 14. *And,* 'if'.

c 47. King John of France was captured at Poitiers in 1356 and held in England as a prisoner until the Treaty of Bretigny in 1360. See note to XIV *b* 32.

c 54. Note the omission of the relative : 'which recked not a cleat for all France', and cp. ll. 43-4, XIII *a* 36 (note).

c 59. *his helm,* 'its helm '—the bar by which the rudder was moved.

c 61. 'The King sailed and rowed aright '; on *him,* see note to XV *g* 24.

c 83. *An ympe* : Richard II.

c 90. *sarri* : not in the dictionaries in this sense, is probably OFr. *serré, sarré,* in the developed meaning ' active ', ' vigorous ', seen in the adv. *sarréement.*

c 103-4. 'If we are disloyal and inactive, so that what is rarely seen is straightway forgotten.'

c 108. ' Who was the fountain of all courage.'

c 111. *los,* ' fame '.

d 1. SCHEP : here means 'shepherd ', ' pastor ', a name taken by Ball as appropriate to a priest.

Seynte Marie prest of 3ork, 'priest of St. Mary's of York' (cp. note to I 44), a great Benedictine abbey founded soon after the Conquest ; see Dugdale, *Monasticon Anglicanum,* vol. iii, pp. 529 ff. *Marie* does not take the *s* inflexion, because it has already the Latin genitive form, cp. *Mary-3et* X 163.

d 2. *Iohan Nameles,* ' John Nobody', for *nameless* has the sense ' obscure ', ' lowly '.

d 6. *Hobbe þe Robbere. Hob* is a familiar form for *Robert,* and it has been suggested that *Hobbe þe Robbere* may refer to Robert Hales, the Treasurer of England, who was executed by the rebels in 1381. But *Robert* was a conventional name for a robber, presumably owing to the similarity of sound. Already in the twelfth century, Mainerus, the Canterbury scribe of the magnificent Bible now in the library of Sainte-Geneviève at Paris, plays upon it in an etymological account of his family : *Secundus* (sc. *frater meus*) *dicebatur Robertus, quia a re nomen habuit : spoliator enim diu fuit et praedo.* From the fourteenth century lawless men were called *Roberts men.* In *Piers Plowman* Passus v (A- and B-texts) there is a confession of ' Robert the Robber '; and the literary fame of the prince of highwaymen, ' Robin Hood', belongs to this period.

d 14. *do wel and bettre* : note this further evidence of the popularity of *Piers Plowman,* with its visions of *Dowel, Dobet,* and *Dobest.*

XV

a 8. *Þe clot him clingge!* 'May the clay cling to him!' i. e. 'Would he were dead!'

a 12. *Þider*: MS. *Yider*, and conversely MS. *Þiif* 23 for *Yiif* 'if'. *y* and *Þ* are endlessly confused by scribes.

b 1. *Lenten ys come ... to toune.* In the Old English *Metrical Calendar* phrases like *cymeð ... us to tune Martius reðe*, 'fierce March comes to town', are regular. The meaning is 'to the dwellings of men', 'to the world'.

b 3. *Þat*: construe with *Lenten*.

b 7. *him preteÞ*, 'chides', 'wrangles' (ON. *Þræta*?). See the thirteenth-century debate of *The Thrush and the Nightingale* (*Reliquiae Antiquae*, vol. i, pp. 241 ff.), of which the opening lines are closely related to this poem.

b 11. *Ant wlyteÞ on huere wynter wele*, 'and look at their winter happiness (?)'. This conflicts with *huere wynter wo* above ; and the explanation that the birds have forgotten the hardships of the past winter and recall only its pleasures is forced. Holthausen's emendation *wynne wele* 'wealth of joys' (cp. l. 35) is good.

b 20. *Miles*: a crux. It has been suggested without much probability that *miles* means 'animals' from Welsh *mîl*.

b 28. *Deawes donkeÞ Þe dounes.* Of the suggestions made to improve the halting metre the best is *Þise* for *Þe*. The poet is thinking of the sparkle of dew in the morning sun; cp. *Sir Gawayne* 519 f.:

> When Þe donkande dewe droÞeȝ of Þe leueȝ
> To bide a blysful blusch of Þe bryȝt sunne.

b 29–30. 'Animals with their cries (*rounes*) unmeaning to us (*derne*), whereby they converse (*domes for te deme*).' For the weakened sense of *deme* (*domes*) see note to V 115.

c 30. *Wery so water in wore*: the restless lover (l. 21) has tossed all night like the troubled waters in a *wore*; cp. *I wake so water in wore* in another lyric of the same MS. It has been suggested that *wore* = Old High German *wuor* 'weir'; but the rimes in both passages show that the stem is OE. *wār*, not *wōr*.

d 2. *the holy londe*: because Ireland was *par excellence* 'the Land of the Saints'.

f. I am obliged to Professor Carleton Brown for the information that this poem is found, with three additional stanzas, in MS. 18. 7. 21 of the Advocates' Library, Edinburgh. The complete text is now available in his *Religious Poems of the Fourteenth Century*, Oxford 1924.

f 4. *bere* (OE. *bȳre*) riming with *fere* (OE. *(ge)fēra*) indicates a South-Eastern composition.

g 1. *Scere Þorsday*: Maundy Thursday, the Eve of Good Friday.

*g*1–2. *aros : Iudas :* the alternative form *aras* may have given the rime in the original, but it is not justifiable to accept this as certain and so to assume an early date of composition for the poem. Morsbach, *ME. Grammatik,* § 135, n. 4, quotes a number of parallel rimes with proper names, and the best explanation is that *o* in *aros* still represented a sound intermediate between *ā* and *ǭ*, and so served as an approximate rime to *ǎ* in proper names.

*g*6. *cunesmen :* as *c* and *t* are hard to distinguish in some ME. hands, and are often confused by copyists, this reading is more likely than *tunesmen* of the editors—Wright-Halliwell, Mätzner, Child, Cook (and *N. E. D.* s.v. *townsman*). For (1) *tunesman* is a technical, not a poetical word. (2) In a poem remarkable for its terseness, *tunesmen* reduces a whole line to inanity, unless the poet thinks of Judas quite precisely as a citizen of a town other than Jerusalem; and in the absence of any Biblical tradition it is unlikely that a writer who calls Pilate *þe riche Ieu* would gratuitously assume that Judas was not a citizen of Jerusalem, where his sister lived. (3) Christ's words are throughout vaguely prophetic, and as Judas forthwith *imette wid is soster* —one of his kin—*cunesmen* gives a pregnant sense. [I find the MS. actually has *cunesmen*, but leave the note, lest *tunesmen* might appear to be better established.]

*g*8. The repetition of ll. 8, 25, 30 is indicated in the MS. by 'ii' at the end of each of these lines, which is the regular sign for *bis.*

g 16. 'He tore his hair until it was bathed in blood.' The MS. has *top*, not *cop.*

g 24. *In him com ur Lord gon.* In the MS. *ėst = Crist* has been erased after *Lord.* Note (1) the reflexive use of *him*, which is very common in OE. and ME. with verbs of motion, e. g. *Up him stod* 27, 29 ; *Þau Pilatus him com* 30 ; *Als I me rode* XV *a* 4 ; *The Kyng him rod* XIV *c* 61 ; cp. the extended use *ar þe coc him crowe* 33, and notes to II 289, V 86 : (2) the use of the infinitive (*gon*) following, and usually defining the sense of, a verb of motion, where Modern English always, and ME. commonly (e. g. *ȝede karoland* I 117 ; *com daunceing* II 298), uses the pres. p. : 'Our Lord came walking in'.

g 27. *am I þat ?* 'Is it I?', the interrogative form of *ich hit am* or *ich am hit.* The editors who have proposed to complete the line by adding *wrech*, have missed the sense. The original rime was *þet : spec*, cp. note to I 240.

g 30. *cnistes :* for *cniste = cnihte* representing the OE. gen. pl. *cnihta.* On the forms *meist* 6, *heiste* 18, *eiste* 20, *bitaiste* 21, *iboust* 26, *miste* 29, *cnistes* 30, *fiste* 31, all with *st* for OE. *ht*, see Appendix § 6 end.

h 17–18. Difficult. Perhaps 'The master smith lengthens

a little piece [sc. of hot iron], and hammers a smaller piece, twines the two together, and strikes [with his hammer] a treble note'.

h 21–2. *clopemerys ... brenwaterys*: not in the dictionaries, but both apparently nonce names for the smiths : they 'clothe horses' (for by the end of the fourteenth century a charger carried a good deal of armour and harness), and 'burn water' (when they temper the red-hot metal).

i 4. *þat*: dat. rel. 'to whom'; cp. VI 64. But *lowte* is sometimes transitive 'to reverence'.

i 6. This line, at first sight irrelevant, supplies both rime and doctrine. See in Chaucer's Preface to his *Tale of Melibeus* the passage ending :

> *I meene of Marke, Mathew, Luc and John—*
> *Bot doutelees hir sentence is all oon.*

An erased *t* after *Awangelys* in the MS. shows that the scribe wavered between *Awangelys* 'Gospels' and *Awangelystes*.

i 7. *Sent Geretrude*: Abbess of Nivelle (d. 659), commemorated on March 17. She is appropriately invoked, for one or more rats make her emblem.

i 11. *Sent Kasi*. Professor Bruce Dickins kindly informs me that St. Nicasius (Dec. 12) was celebrated in Northern France as an enemy of rats. I cannot trace his acts against them, but parallels are not wanting. St. Ivor, an Irish saint, banished rats from his neighbourhood *per imprecationem* because they gnawed his books ; and the charm-harassed life of an Irish rat was still proverbial in Shakespeare's day : 'I was never so berhymed' says Rosalind (*As You Like It*, III. ii) 'since Pythagoras' time, that I was an Irish rat'. In the South of France the citizens of Autun trusted more to the processes of the law, and brought a suit against the rats which ended in a victory for the defendants because the plaintiffs were unable to guarantee them safe conduct to the court (see Chambers, *Book of Days*, under Jan. 17). Even in such little things the Normans showed their practical genius :— A friend chancing to meet St. Lanfranc by the way inquired the cause of the strange noises that came from a bag he was carrying : 'We are terribly plagued with mice and rats', explained the good man, 'and so, to put down their ravages, I am bringing along a cat' (*Mures et rati valde nobis sunt infesti, et idcirco nunc affero catum ad comprimendum furorem illorum*). *Acta Sanctorum* for May 28, p. 824.

XVI

Dialect: Yorkshire.

Inflexions:

VERB: pres. ind. 2 sg. *þou royis* 99, *þou is* 360; beside *þou hast* 69.

        3 sg. *bidis* 23, *comes* 57.

        1 pl. *we here* 169.

        2 pl. *ȝe haue* 124.

        3 pl. *þei make* 103, *þei crie* 107, *dwelle* (rime) 102; beside *musteres* 104, *sais* 108.

imper. pl. *harkens* 37, *beholdes* 195 ; but *vndo* 182.

pres. p. *walkand* 53 (in rime); beside *shynyng* 94.

strong pp. *stoken* 193, *brokynne* 195, &c.

Contracted verbal forms are *mase* pres. 3 pl. (in rime) 116, *bus* pres. 2 sg. 338, *tane* pp. 172.

PRONOUN 3 PERS.: pl. nom. *þei* 21 ; poss. *thare* 18, *þer* 20 ; obj. *þame* 9 ; but *hemselue* 307. The demonstrative *þer* 'these' 97, 399, is Northern.

Sounds: *ā* remains in rimes : *are* : *care* 345-7, *waa* : *gloria* 406-8, *lawe* : *knawe* 313-15, *moste* (for *māste*) : *taste* 358-60; but *ǭ* is also proved for the original in *restore* : *euermore* : *were* (for *wǭre*) : *before* 13 ff.

Spelling: In *fois* (= *fǭs*) 30, the spelling with *i* indicates vowel length.

17. *were* : rime requires the alternative form *wǭre*.

39. *Foure thowsande and sex hundereth ȝere*. I do not know on what calculation the writer changes 5,500, which is the figure in the Greek and Latin texts of the Gospel of Nicodemus, in the French verse renderings, and the ME. poem *Harrowing of Hell*. Cp. l. 354.

40. *in þis stedde*: the rimes *hadde* : *gladde* : *sadde* point to the Towneley MS. reading *in darknes stad*, 'set in darkness', as nearer the original, which possibly had *in þister(nes) stad*.

49. *we* : read *ȝe* (?). For what follows cp. Isaiah ix. 1-2.

59. *puplisshid*: the rime with *Criste* shows that the pronunciation was *puplist*. Similarly, *abasshed* : *traste* 177-9. In French these words have -*ss*-, which normally becomes -*sh*- in English. It is hard to say whether -*ss*- remained throughout in Northern dialects, or whether the development was OFr. -*ss*- > ME. -*sh*- > Northern -*ss*- (notes to I 128, VII 4).

62. *þis*: read *His*(?). *frendis*: here 'relatives', 'parents' (ON. *frǽndi*) ; see Luke ii. 27.

65-8. Luke ii. 29-32.

73-82. Matthew iii. 13-17, &c.

75. *hande*: the rime requires the Norse plural *hend* as at l. 400 ; cp. XVII 255, IV *a* 65 (foot-note).

86 ff. Cp. Matthew xvii. 3 ff., Mark ix. 2 ff.

113. *Astrotte* : cp. 2 Kings xxiii. 13 'Ashtoreth, the abomination of the Zidonians'. I cannot identify *Anaball* among the false gods.

115. *Bele-Berit* : Judges viii. 33 'the children of Israel ... made Baal-Berith their god '. For *Belial* see 2 Cor. vi. 15.

122–4. A common misrendering for 'Be ye lift up, ye everlasting doors', Psalm xxiv. 7.

125 ff. postulate a preceding *et introibit rex gloriẹ*, which the writer has not been able to work into the frame of his verse.

128. *a kyng of vertues clere* = *dominus virtutum*, rendered ' Lord of Hosts' in Psalm xxiv. 10.

154–6. *ware : ferre* : the rime indicates some corruption. *ware* probably stands for *werre* 'worse'. The Towneley MS. has *or it be war*.

162. John xi.

165. John xiii. 27.

171 ff. 'And know he won away Lazarus, who was given to us to take charge of, do you think that you can hinder him from showing the powers that he has purposed (to show)?' But it is doubtful whether *what* is a true relative. Rather ' from showing his powers—those he has purposed (to show)'.

188. *I prophicied* : MS. *of prophicie* breaks the rime scheme.

190. Psalm cvii. 16 'For he hath broken the gates of brass, and cut the bars of iron in sunder.'

205 ff. The rimes *saide : braide : ferde : grathed* are bad. For the last two read *flaide* = 'terrified', and *graid*, a shortened form of *graithed*.

208. *and we wer moo*, 'if we were more', 'even if there were more of us'.

220. *as my prisoune* might be taken closely with *here* : 'in this place as my prison '. The Towneley MS. has *in* for *as*. Better would be *prisoune⟨s⟩* 'prisoners '.

240. *wolle* : read *wille* for the rime.

241. *God⟨ys⟩ sonne* : MS. *God sonne* might be defended as parallel to the instances in the note to XVII 88.

256. Apparently, 'you argue his men in the mire', i.e. if Jesus is God's Son, the souls should remain in hell because God put them there. But the text may be corrupt.

267 ff. Cp. Ezekiel xxxi. 16, &c.

281 ff. *Salamon saide* : Proverbs ii. 18–19 taken with vii. 27 and ix. 18. It was hotly disputed in the Middle Ages whether Solomon himself was still in hell. Dante, *Paradiso*, x. 110, informs a world eager for tidings that he is in Paradise : but Langland declares *Ich leyue he be in helle* (C-text, iv. 330) ; and, more sweepingly, coupling him with Aristotle : *Al holy chirche holden hem in helle* (A-text, xi. 263).

285-8. Perhaps a gloss on Job xxxvi. 18 ' Because there is wrath, beware lest he take thee away with his stroke: then a great ransom cannot deliver thee.'

301. *menys*, the reading of the Towneley MS. is better than *mouys*, which appears to be a copyist's error due to the similarity of *n* and *u*, *e* and *o*, in the handwriting of the time.

308. Judas hanged himself, according to Matthew xxvii. 3–5; Acts i. 18 gives a different account of his end. *Archedefell*: Ahithophel who hanged himself (2 Samuel xvii. 23) after the failure of his plot against David.

309. *Datan and Abiron*: see Numbers xvi.

313-16. ' And all who do not care to learn my law (which I have left in the land newly, and which is to make known my Coming), and to go to my Sacrament, and those who will not believe in my Death and my Resurrection read in order—they are not true.'

338. *þou bus*, 'you ought'; *bus*, a Northern contracted form of *behoves*, is here used as a personal verb, where *þe bus*, 'it behoves thee', is normal. See note to XVII 196.

360. *moste*: read *maste* to rime with *taste*.

371. *Of þis comyng*: the Towneley MS. reading *of Thi commyng* is possible.

378-80: Corrupt. The copy from which the extant MS. was made seems to have been indistinct here. The Towneley MS. has:

> *Suffre thou neuer Thi sayntys to se*
> *The sorow of thaym that won in wo,*
> *Ay full of fylth, and may not fle,*

which is more intelligible and nearer Psalm xvi. 10:

> *Nec dabis sanctum tuum videre corruptionem.*

405. *louyng*: 'praise', cp. IV a 24 (note).

XVII

Dialect: Late Yorkshire.

Vocabulary: Northern are *then* 108 (note), and *at* 'to' 235.

Inflexions:

VERB: pres. ind. 2 sg. *thou spekis* 206.

        3 sg. *ligis he* 84; *he settis* 92; *(God) knowes* 202.

        1 pl. *we swete or swynk* 195.

        2 pl. *ye carp* (in rime) 360.

        3 pl. *thay ryn* (in rime) 277, 357; beside *has* 345, *renys* 351.

pres. p. *liffand* 73, *bowand* 76, *wirkand* 120 (all in rime); beside *lifyng* 47, 48; *standyng* 416; *taryyng* 497.

strong pp. *rysen* 442; *fon* 'found' 503 is a Northern short form.

PRONOUN 3 PERS.: sg. fem. nom. *she* 186; pl. *thay* 27; *thare* 75; *thaym* 31. (MS. *hame* 143 is miswritten for *thame*.)

Sounds: OE. *ā* appears as *ǭ* in rime: *old : cold : mold* (OE. *móld*) 60–2, and probably *dold : old* 266–70; *sore : store : therfor : more* 91–4; but elsewhere remains *ā*, e.g. *draw* (OE. *drăgan*) : *knaw* 245–6. The spelling with *o* is the commoner. See notes on *emong* 400; *grufe* 463.

Spelling: Note the Northern spellings with *i*, *y* following a vowel to indicate length: *moyne* 'moon' 6, *bayle* 'bale' 26, *leyde* = *lede* 48; and conversely *farest* 'fairest' 79, *fath* 'faith' 330.

The maritime associations of the play of *Noah* made it a special favourite with the Trinity House guild of master mariners and pilots at Hull; and some of their records of payments for acting and equipment are preserved, although the text of their play is lost (Chambers, *Mediaeval Stage*, vol. ii, pp. 370–1):

anno   To the minstrels, 6 d.

1485.   To Noah and his wife, 1 s. 6 d.

To Robert Brown playing God, 6 d.

To the Ship-child, 1 d.

To a shipwright for clinking Noah's ship, one day, 7 d.

22 kids for shoring Noah's ship, 2 d.

To a man clearing away the snow, 1 d.

Straw for Noah and his children, 1 d.

Mass, bellman, torches, minstrels, garland &c., 6 s.

For mending the ship, 2 d.

To Noah for playing, 1 s.

To straw and grease for wheels, ¼ d.

To the waits for going about with the ship, 6 d.

1494.   To Thomas Sawyr playing God, 10 d.

To Jenkin Smith playing Noah, 1 s.

To Noah's wife, 8 d.

The clerk and his children, 1 s. 6 d.

To the players of Barton, 8 d.

For a gallon of wine, 8 d.

For three skins for Noah's coat, making it, and a rope to hang the ship in the kirk, 7 s.

To dighting and gilding St. John's head, painting two tabernacles, beautifying the boat and over the table, 7 s. 2 d.

Making Noah's ship, £5. 8s.
Two wrights a day and a half, 1 s. 6 d.
A halser [i. e. hawser] 4 stone weight, 4 s. 8 d.
Rigging Noah's ship, 8 d.

10. *is*: read *es* for the rime. Cp. note to I 128–9.

42. *and sythen*: MS. *in sythen*. Cp. note to VI 36.

49. *syn*: 3 pl. because *euery liffyng leyde* is equivalent to a plural subject 'all men'.

52. *coueteis*: MS. *couetous*.

56. *alod*: 'wide-spread' (?). Apparently the same as *olod* in a poem ascribed to Rolle (ed. Horstman, vol. i, p. 73, l. 22) where it means 'dispersed'. But see Onions, *Medium Aevum*, i. 206.

57. *Sex hundreth yeris and od*: the *od* thrown in to rime, as Noah was exactly 600 years old according to Genesis vii. 6.

66. *and my fry shal with me fall*: 'and the children ⟨that⟩ I may have' (?).

88. *for syn sake*: 'because of sin'. Until modern times a genitive preceding *sake* usually has no *s*, e. g. *for goodness sake*. The genitive of *sin* historically had no *s* (OE. *synne*), but the omission in a Northern text is due rather to euphony than to survival of an old genitive form. Cp. *for tempest sake* I 177.

108. *then*: 'nor', a rare Northern usage, which is treated as an error here in England and Pollard's text, though it occurs again at l. 535. Conversely *nor* is used dialectally for *than*.

109. *Hym to mekill wyn*: 'to his great happiness'.

137 *take*: 'make', and so in l. 272.

167–71. *knowe: awe*. The rime requires *knāwe* or *ǭwe*.

191. 'The worse ⟨because⟩ I see thee.'

196. *what thou thynk*: 'what seems to you best', 'what you like'; *thou thynk* for *thee thynk*—the verb being properly impersonal; see notes to XVI 338 and VI 192.

200. *Stafford blew*: from the context this line might mean 'you are a scaremonger', for blue is the recognized colour of fear, and it might be supposed that 'Stafford blue' represents a material like 'Lincoln green'. But Mätzner is certainly right in interpreting the line 'you deserve a beating'. *Stafford blew* would then be the livid colour produced by blows. The reference, unless there is a play on *staff*, is obscure.

202. *led*: 'treated'.

211. *sory*: the rime requires *sary*.

220. *Mary*: the later *marry!* = 'by (the Virgin) Mary!' cp. l. 226. So *Peter!* 367 = 'by St. Peter!'

246. *to knaw*: 'to confess'.

247–8. *daw to ken*: 'to be recognized as stupid', 'a manifest fool'.

272. *castell*: note the rime with *sayll : nayll : fayll*, which

may be due to suffix substitution on the analogy of *catail* beside *catel* 'cattle'. For *take* see note to 137.

281. *chambre*: the rime points to a by-form *chamb(o)ur*, but the uninflected form is awkward. Cp. *thre chese chambres* 'three tiers of chambers' 129, where the construction is the same as the obsolete *three pair gloves*.

289–92. Read *lider, hider, togider*.

292. *must vs*: cp. l. 334 and note to VI 192.

298. 'There is other yarn on the reel', i. e. there is other business on hand.

320. *brether sam*: 'brothers both'. Some editors prefer to read *brother Sam* 'brother Shem'.

336 ff. Chaucer refers to the quarrels of Noah and his wife in the *Miller's Tale* (ll. 352 ff.) :—

> '*Hastou nat herd*', quod Nicholas, '*also*
> *The sorwe of Noe with his felaweshipe*
> *Er that he myghte brynge his wyf to shipe?*
> *Hym hadde be levere, I dar wel undertake,*
> *At thilke tyme, than alle his wetheres blake,*
> *That she hadde had a shipe hirself allone.*'

The tradition is old. In the splendid tenth-century Bodleian MS. Junius 11, which contains the so-called Caedmon poems, a picture of the Ark shows Noah's wife standing at the foot of the gangway, and one of her sons trying to persuade her to come in.

370. *Yei* is defensible; cp. l. 353. *Þe* 'the' has been suggested.

383. *Wat Wynk*: an alliterative nick-name like *Nicholl Nedy* in l. 405.

400. *emong*: OE. *gemang*, here rimes as in Modern English with *u* (OE. *iung : tunge : lungen*), cp. note to VI 109 ff.; but in ll. 244–7 it rimes with *lang : fang : gang*—all with original *a*.

417. ⟨*floodis*⟩. Some such word is missing in the MS. Cp. ll. 454 f. and 426.

461. *How*: MS. *Now*. The correction is due to Professor Child. Initial capitals are peculiarly liable to be miscopied.

463. *grufe*: a Northern and Scottish form of the verb *grow*. The sb. *ro* 'rest' 237 sometimes has a parallel form *rufe*.

525. *stold*: for *stalled* 'fixed'. Note the rime words, which all have alternative forms *behald : bald : wald*.

APPENDIX

THE ENGLISH LANGUAGE IN THE FOURTEENTH CENTURY

§ 1. GENERAL. Gower's work shows that at the end of the century Latin and French still shared with English the place of a literary language. But their hold was precarious.

Latin was steadily losing ground. The Wiclifite translation of the Bible threatened its hitherto unchallenged position as the language of the Church; and the Renaissance had not yet come to give it a new life among secular scholars.

French was still spoken at the court; but in 1387 Trevisa remarks (p. 149) that it was no longer considered an essential part of a gentleman's education : and he records a significant reform—the replacement of French by English as the medium of teaching in schools. After the end of the century Anglo-French, the native development of Norman, was practically confined to legal use, and French of Paris was the accepted standard French.

English gained wherever Latin and French lost ground. But though the work of Chaucer, Gower, and Wiclif foreshadows the coming supremacy of the East Midland, or, more particularly, the London dialect, there was as yet no recognized standard of literary English. The spoken language showed a multiplicity of local varieties, and a writer adopted the particular variety that was most familiar to him. Hence it is almost true to say that every considerable text requires a special grammar.

Confusion is increased by the scribes. Nowadays a book is issued in hundreds or thousands of uniform copies, and within a few months of publication it may be read in any part of the world. In the fourteenth century a book was made known to readers only by the slow and costly multiplication of manuscripts. The copyist might work long after the date of composition, and he would then be likely to modernize the language, which in its written form was not stable as it is at present: so of Barbour's *Bruce* the oldest extant copies were made nearly a century after Barbour's death. Again, if the dialect of the author were unfamiliar to the copyist, he might substitute familiar words and forms. Defective rimes often bear witness to these substitutions.

Nor have we to reckon only with copyists, who are as a rule careless rather than bold innovators. While books were scarce and many could not read them, professional minstrels and amateur reciters played a great part in the transmission of popular literature; and they, whether from defective memory or from belief in their own talents, treated the exact form and words of their author with scant respect. An extreme instance is given by the MSS. of *Sir Orfeo* at ll. 267–8:

Auchinleck MS.: *His harp, whereon was al his gle,*
　　　　　　　He hidde in an holwe tre;
Harley MS.: *He takeþ his harpe and makeþ hym gle,*
　　　　　　And lyþe al ny3t vnder a tre;
Ashmole MS.: *In a tre þat was holow*
　　　　　　Þer was hys haule euyn and morow.

If the Ashmole MS. alone had survived we should have no hint of the degree of corruption.

And so, before the extant MSS. recorded the text, copyists and reciters may have added change to change, jumbling the speech of different men, generations, and places, and producing those 'mixed' texts which are the will-o'-the-wisps of language study.

Faced with these perplexities, beginners might well echo the words of Langland's pilgrims in search of Truth:

　　This were a wikked way, but whoso hadde a gyde
　　　　That wolde folwen vs eche a fote.

There is no such complete guide, for the first parts of Morsbach's *Mittelenglische Grammatik*, Halle 1896, Richard Jordan's *Handbuch der Mittelenglischen Grammatik*, Heidelberg 1925 and Luick's *Historische Grammatik der englischen Sprache*, Leipzig 1914– , remain unfinished. Happily two distinguished scholars—Dr. Henry Bradley in *The Making of English* and his chapter in *The Cambridge*

History of English Literature, vol. i, Dr. O. Jespersen in *Growth and Structure of the English Language*—have given brief surveys of the whole early period which are at once elementary and authoritative. But for the details the student must rely on a mass of dissertations and articles of very unequal quality, supplemented by introductions to single texts, and, above all, by his own first-hand observations made on the texts themselves.

Some preliminary considerations will be helpful, though perhaps not altogether reassuring:

(i) A great part of the evidence necessary to a thorough knowledge of spoken Middle English has not come down to us, a considerable part remains unprinted, and the printed materials are so extensive and scattered that it is easy to overlook points of detail. For instance, it might be assumed from rimes in *Gawayne, Pearl,* and the Shropshire poet Myrc, that the falling together of OE. *-ang-, -ung-,* which is witnessed in NE. *among* (OE. *gemang*), *-monger* (OE. *mangere*), was specifically West Midland, if the occurrence of examples in Yorkshire (XVII 397–400) escaped notice. It follows that, unless a word or form is so common as to make the risk of error negligible, positive evidence—the certainty that it occurs in a given period or district—is immeasurably more important than negative evidence—the belief that it never did occur, or even the certainty that it is not recorded, in a period or district. For the same reason, the statement that a word or form is found 'in the early fourteenth century' or 'in Kent' should always be understood positively, and should not be taken to imply that it is unknown 'in the thirteenth century' or 'in Essex', as to which evidence may or may not exist.

(ii) It is necessary to clear the mind of the impression, derived from stereotyped written languages, that homogeneity and stability are natural states. Middle English texts represent a spoken language of many local varieties, all developing rapidly. So every linguistic fact should be thought of in terms of time, place, and circumstance, not because absolute precision in these points is attainable, but because the attempt to attain it helps to distinguish accurate knowledge from conclusions which are not free from doubt.

If the word or form under investigation can be proved to

belong to the author's original composition, exactness is often
possible. In the present book, we know nearly enough the date
of composition of extracts I, III, VIII, X, XI *a*, XII, XIII, XIV; the
place of composition of I, III, X, XI *a*, XII, XIII, XVI, XVII (see map).

But if, as commonly happens, a form cannot be proved to
have stood in the original, endless difficulties arise. It will
be necessary first to determine the date of the MS. copy.
This is exactly known for *The Bruce*, and there are few
Middle English MSS. which the palaeographer cannot date
absolutely within a half-century, and probably within a
generation. The place where the MS. copy was written is
known nearly enough for IV *b*, *c*, XII, XIV *e*, XV *b*, *c* (possibly
Leominster), XVI, XVII; and ME. studies have still much to
gain from a thorough inquiry into the provenance of MSS.
Yet, when the extant copy is placed and dated, it remains to
ask to what extent this MS. reproduces some lost intermediary
of different date and provenance; how many such inter-
mediaries there were between the author's original and our
MS.; what each has contributed to the form of the surviving
copy—questions usually unanswerable, the consideration of
which will show the exceptional linguistic value of the
Ayenbyte, where we have the author's own transcript exactly
dated and localized, so that every word and form is good
evidence.

Failing such ideal conditions, it becomes necessary to limit
doubt by segregating for special investigation the elements
that belong to the original composition. Hence the importance of rimes, alliteration, and rhythm, which a copyist or
reciter is least likely to alter without leaving a trace of his
activities.

§ 2. DIALECTS. At present any marked variation from the
practice of educated English speakers might, if it were
common to a considerable number of persons, be described
as dialectal. But as there was no such recognized standard
in the fourteenth century, it is most convenient to consider as
dialectal any linguistic feature which had a currency in some
English-speaking districts but not in all. For example, *þat*
as a relative is found everywhere in the fourteenth century
and is not dialectal; *þire* ' these ' is recorded only in Northern
districts, and so is dialectal. Again, $\bar{\varrho}$ represents OE. *ā* in

the South and Midlands, while the North retains $\bar{a}$ (§ 7 b i): since neither $\bar{\rho}$ nor $\bar{a}$ is general, both may be called dialectal.

If a few sporadic developments be excluded because they may turn up anywhere at any time, then, provided sufficient evidence were available,[1] it would be possible to mark the boundaries within which any given dialectal feature occurs at a particular period: we could draw the line south of which *þire* 'these' is not found, or the line bounding the district in which the Norse borrowing *kirke* occurs; just as French investigators in *L'Atlas linguistique de la France* have shown the distribution of single words and forms in the modern French dialects.

Of more general importance is the fixing of boundaries for sound changes or inflexions that affect a large number of words, a task to which interesting contributions have been made in recent years on the evidence of place-names (see especially A. Brandl, *Zur Geographie der altenglischen Dialekte*, Berlin 1915, which supplements the work of Pogatscher on the compounds of *street* and of Wyld on the ME. developments of OE. *y*).   For example, on the evidence available, which does not permit of more than rough indications, OE. *ā* remains *ā*, and does not develop to *ō̧*, north of a line drawn west from the Humber (§ 7 b i); *-and(e)* occurs in the ending of the pres. p. as far south as a line starting west from the Wash (§ 13 ii); farther south again, a line between Norwich

---

[1] Sufficient evidence is not available. If in the year 1340 at every religious house in the kingdom a native of the district had followed the example of Michael of Northgate, and if all their autograph copies had survived, we should have a very good knowledge of Middle English at that time.   If the process had been repeated about every ten years the precision of our knowledge would be greatly increased.   For the area in which any feature is found is not necessarily constant: we know that in the pres. p. the province of *-ing* was extending throughout the fourteenth century; that the inflexion *-es* in 3 sg. pres. ind. was a Northern and North-Midland feature in the fourteenth century, but had become general in London by Shakespeare's time.   And though less is known about the spread of sound changes as distinct from analogical substitutions, it cannot be assumed that their final boundaries were reached and fixed in a moment.   There is reason to regret the handicap that has been imposed on ME. studies by the old practice of writing in Latin or French the documents and records which would otherwise supply the exactly dated and localized specimens of English that are most necessary to progress.

and Birmingham gives the northern limit for *Stratton* forms as against *Stretton* (§ 8 iv, note).[1]　The direction of all these lines is roughly east and west, yet no two coincide　But if the developments of OE. *y* (§ 7 b ii) are mapped out, *u* appears below a line drawn athwart from Liverpool to London, and normal *e* east of a line drawn north and south from the western border of Kent.　Almost every important feature has thus its own limits, and the limits of one may cross the limits of another.

What then is a ME. dialect?　The accepted classification is

Southern	{	South-Western	= OE. West Saxon
		South-Eastern	= OE. Kentish
Midland	{	East Midland	} = OE. Mercian
		West Midland	
Northern			= OE. Northumbrian

with the Thames as boundary between Southern and Midland, and the Humber between Midland and Northern. And yet of five actual limiting lines taken at random, only the first coincides approximately with the line of Humber or Thames.

Still the classification rests on a practical truth.　Although each dialectal feature has its own boundaries, these are not set by pure chance.　Their position is to some extent governed by old tribal and political divisions, by the influence of large towns which served as commercial and administrative centres, and by relative ease of communication.　Consequently, linguistic features are roughly grouped, and it is *a priori* likely that London and Oxford would have more features in common than would London and York, or Oxford and Hull; and similarly it is likely that for a majority of phenomena York and Hull would stand together against London and Oxford.　Such a grouping was recognized in

---

[1] The evidence of place-names does not agree entirely with the evidence of texts.　*Havelok*, which is localized with reasonable certainty in North Lincolnshire, has (*a*)*dradd* in rimes that appear to be original, and these indicate a North-Eastern extension of the area in which OE. *strǣt*, *drǣdan* appear for normal Anglian *strēt*, *drēda*(*n*).　This evidence, supported by rimes in Robert of Brunne, is too early to be disposed of by the explanation of borrowing from other dialects, nor is the testimony of place-names so complete and unequivocal as to justify an exclusive reliance upon it.

the fourteenth century. Higden and his authorities distinguish Northern and Southern speech (XIII *b*); in the Towneley *Second Shepherds' Play*, ll. 201 ff., when Mak pretends to be a yeoman of the king, he adopts the appropriate accent, and is promptly told to 'take outt that Sothren tothe'. In the *Reeves Tale* Chaucer makes the clerks speak their own Northern dialect, so we may be sure that he thought of it as a unity.

But had Chaucer been asked exactly where this dialect was spoken, he would probably have replied, *Fer in the North,—I kan nat telle where.* A dialect has really no precise boundaries; its borders are nebulous; and throughout this book 'Southern', 'Northern', &c., are used vaguely, and not with any sharply defined limits in mind. The terms may, however, be applied to precise areas, so long as the boundaries of single dialect features are not violently made to conform. It is quite accurate to say that *-and*(*e*) is the normal ending of the pres. p. north of the Humber, and that *u* for OE. *y* is found south of the Thames and west of London, provided it is not implied that the one should not be found south of the Humber, or the other north of the Thames. Both in fact occur in *Gawayne* (Cheshire or Lancashire); and in general the language of the Midlands was characterized by the overlapping of features which distinguish the North from the South.

From what has been said it should be plain that the localization of a piece of Middle English on the evidence of language alone calls for an investigation of scope and delicacy. Where the facts are so complex the mechanical application of rules of thumb may give quick and specious results, but must in the end deaden the spirit of inquiry, which is the best gift a student can bring to the subject.

§ 3. VOCABULARY. The readiness of English speakers to adopt words from foreign languages becomes marked in fourteenth-century writings. But the classical element which is so pronounced in modern literary English is still unimportant. There are few direct borrowings from Latin, and these, like *obiite* XVI 269, are for the most part taken from the technical language of the Church. The chief sources of foreign words are Norse and French.

(a) **Norse.** Although many Norse words first appear in English in late texts, they must have come into the spoken language before the end of the eleventh century, because the Scandinavian settlements ceased after the Norman Conquest. The invaders spoke a dialect near enough to OE. to be intelligible to the Angles; and they had little to teach of literature or civilization. Hence the borrowings from Norse are all popular; they appear chiefly in the Midlands and North, where the invaders settled; and they witness the intimate fusion of two kindred languages. From Norse we get such common words as *anger, both, call, egg, hit, husband, ill, law, loose, low, meek, take, till* (prep.), *want, weak, wing, wrong*, and even the plural forms of the 3rd personal pronoun (§ 12).

It is not always easy to distinguish Norse from native words, because the two languages were so similar during the period of borrowing, and Norse words were adopted early enough to be affected by all ME. sound changes. But there were some dialectal differences between ON. and OE. in the ninth and tenth centuries, and these afford the best criteria of borrowing. For instance in ME. we have *þouȝ, þof* (ON. *þŏh* for *þauh) beside *þei(h)* (OE. *þē(a)h*) II 433; *ay* (ON. *ei*) 'ever' XVI 293 beside *oo* (OE. *ā*) XV *b* 7; *waik* (ON. *veik-r*) VIII *b* 23, where OE. *wāc* would yield *wǫk*; the forms *wǫre* XVI 17 (note) and *wāpin* XIV *b* 15 are from ON. *várum, vápn*, whereas *wēre(n)* and *wĕppen* V 154 represent OE. (Anglian) *wēron, wēpn*. So we have the pairs *awe* (ON. *agi*) I 83 and *ay* (OE. *ege*) II 571; *neuen* (ON. *nefna*) 'to name' XVII 12 and *nem(p)ne* (OE. *nemnan*) II 600; *rot* (ON. *rót*) II 256 and *wort* (OE. *wyrt*) VIII *a* 303; *sterne, starne* (ON. *stjarna*) XVII 8, 423 and native *sterre, starre* (OE. *steorra*); *systyr* (ON. *systir*) I 112 and *soster* (OE. *sweostor*) XV *g* 10; *werre, warre* (ON. *verri*) XVI 154 (note), 334 and native *werse, wars* (OE. *wyrsa*) XVI 200, XVII 191; *wylle* (ON. *vill-r*) V 16 and native *wylde* (OE. *wilde*) XV *b* 19.

Note that in Norse borrowings the consonants *g, k* remain stops where they are palatalized in English words: *garn* XVII 298, *giue, gete* (ON. *garn, gefa, geta*) beside *ȝarn, ȝiue, for-ȝete* (OE. *gearn, giefan, for-gietan*); *kirke* (ON. *kirkja*) beside *chirche* (OE. *cirice*). Similarly OE. initial *sc-* regularly becomes ME. *sh-*, so that most words beginning with *sk-*, like *sky*, *skin*, *skyfte* VI 209 (English *shift*), *skirte* (English *shirt*), are Norse; see the alliterating words in V 99.

There is an excellent monograph by E. Björkman: *Scandinavian Loan-Words in Middle English*, 1900.

(*b*) **French.** Most early borrowings from French were again due to invasion and settlement. But the conditions of contact were very different. Some were unfavourable to borrowing: the Normans, who were relatively few, were dispersed throughout the country, and not, like the Scandinavians, massed in colonies; and their language had little in common with English. So the number of French words in English texts is small before the late thirteenth and the fourteenth centuries. Other conditions made borrowing inevitable: the French speakers were the governing class; they gradually introduced a new system of administration and new standards of culture; and they had an important literature to which English writers turned for their subject-matter and their models of form. Fourteenth-century translators adopt words from their French originals so freely (see note at p. 234, foot), that written Middle English must give a rather exaggerated impression of the extent of French influence on the spoken language. But a few examples will show how many common words are early borrowings from French: nouns like *country*, *face*, *place*, *river*, *courtesy*, *honour*, *joy*, *justice*, *mercy*, *pity*, *reason*, *religion*, *war*; adjectives like *close*, *large*, *poor*; and verbs *cry*, *pay*, *please*, *save*, *serve*, *use*.

Anglo-French was never completely homogeneous, and it was constantly supplemented as a result of direct political, commercial, and literary relations with France. Hence words were sometimes adopted into ME. in more than one French dialectal form. For instance, Late Latin *ca-* became *cha-* in most French dialects, but remained *ca-* in the North of France: hence ME. *catch* and (*pur*)*chase*, *catel* and *chatel*, *kanel* 'neck' V 230 and *chanel* 'channel' XIII *a* 57. So Northern French preserves initial *w-*, for which other French dialects substitute *g(u)*: hence *Wowayn* V 121 beside *Gawayn* V 4, &c. (see note to V 121). Again, in Anglo-French, *a* before nasal + consonant alternates with *au*:—*dance* : *daunce*; *chance* : *chaunce*; *change* : *chaunge*; *chambre* XVII 281 : *chaum-*

ber II 100. English still has the verbs *launch* and *lance*, which are ultimately identical.

As borrowing extended over several centuries, the ME. form sometimes depends on the date of adoption. Thus Latin *fidem* becomes early French *feið*, later *fei*, and later still *foi*. ME. has both *feiþ* and *fay*, and by Spenser's time *foy* appears.

The best study of the French element in ME. is still that of D. Behrens: *Beiträge zur Geschichte der französischen Sprache in England*, 1886. A valuable supplement, dealing chiefly with Anglo-French as the language of the law, is the chapter by F. W. Maitland in *The Cambridge History of English Literature*, vol. i.

§ 4. HANDWRITING. In the ME. period two varieties of script were in use, both developed from the Caroline minuscule which has proved to be the most permanent contribution of the schools of Charlemagne. The one, cursive and flourished, is common in charters, records, and memoranda ; see C. H. Jenkinson and C. Johnson, *Court Hand*, 2 vols., Oxford 1915. The other, in which the letters are separately written, with few flourishes or adaptations of form in combination, is the 'book hand', so called because it is regularly used for literary texts. Between the extreme types there are many gradations ; and fifteenth-century copies, such as the Cambridge MS. of Barbour's *Bruce*, show an increasing use of cursive forms, which facilitate rapid writing.

The shapes of letters were not always so distinct as they are in print, so that copyists of the time, and even modern editors, are liable to mistake one letter for another. Each hand has its own weaknesses, but the letters most commonly misread are :—

e : *o* e. g. *Beuo* for *Bouo* I 59 ; *wroche* for *wreche* II 333 ; *teches* IV *b* 60, where *toches* (foot-note) is probably right ; *pesible* (MS. *posible*) XI *b* 67.

u : *n* (practically indistinguishable) e. g. *menys* (MS. *mouys*) XVI 301 ; *skayned* (edd. *skayued*) V 99 ; *ryue3* or *ryne3* V 222 (note). This is only a special case of the confusion of letters and combinations formed by repetition of the downstroke, e. g. *u*, *n*, *m*, and *i* (which is not always distinguished by a stroke above). Hence *dim* II 285 where modern editors have *dun*, although *i* has the distinguishing stroke.

y : *þ* e. g. *ye* (MS. *þe*) XIV *d* 11 ; see note to XV *a* 12. Confusion is increased by occasional transference to *þ* of the dot which historically may stand over *y*. *ȝ* for *þ* initially, as in XVI 170, is more often due to confusion of the letters *þ* : *y* and subsequent preference of *ȝ* for *y* in spelling (§ 5 i) than to direct confusion of *þ* : *ȝ*, which are not usually very similar in late Middle English script.

b : *h* e. g. *doþ* (MS. *doh*) XV *b* 22 ; and notes to XII *b* 116, XVI 62.

b : *v* e. g. *vousour* (edd. *bonsour*) II 363.

c : *t* e. g. *cunesmen* (edd. *tunesmen*) XV *g* 6 (note); *top* (edd. *cop*) ibid. 16 ; see note to XIII *a* 7.

f : *ſ* (= *s*) e. g. *slang* (variant *flang*) X 53.

l : *ſ* (= *s*) e. g. *al* (edd. *as*) II 108.

l : *k* e. g. *kyþeȝ* (MS. *lyþeȝ*) VI 9.

§ 5. SPECIAL LETTERS. Two letters now obsolete are common in fourteenth-century MSS. : *þ* and *ȝ*.

þ : 'thorn', is a rune, and stands for the voiced and voiceless sounds now represented by *th* in *this*, *thin*. The gradual displacement of *þ* by *th*, which had quite a different sound in classical Latin (note to VIII *a* 23), may be traced in the MSS. printed (except X, XII). *þ* remained longest in the initial position, but by the end of the fifteenth century was used chiefly in compendia like *þᵉ* 'the ', *þᵗ* 'that '.

ȝ : called ' *ȝoȝ* ' or ' *yogh* ', derives from *g*, the OE. script form of the letter *g*. It was retained in ME. after the Caroline form *g* had become established in vernacular texts, to represent a group of spirant sounds :

(i) The initial spirant in *ȝoked* IX 253 (OE. *geoc-*), *ȝere* I 151 (OE. *gēar*), where the sound was approximately the same as in our *yoke*, *year*. Except in texts specially influenced by the tradition of French spelling, *y* (which is ambiguous owing to its common use as a vowel = *i*) is less frequent than *ȝ* initially. Medially the palatal spirant is represented either by *ȝ* or *y*: *eȝe* (OE. *ē(a)ȝ-*) XV *c* 14 beside *eyen* VIII *a* 168 ; *iseȝe* (OE. *gesegen*) XIV *c* 88 beside *iseye* XIV *c* 16. The medial guttural spirant more commonly develops to *w* in the fourteenth century : *awe* (ON. *agi*) I 83, *felawe* (ON. *félagi*) XIV *d* 7, *halwes* (OE. *halg-*), beside *aȝ-* V 267, *felaȝ-* V 83, *halȝ-* V 54.

(ii) The medial or final spirant, guttural or palatal, which is lost in standard English, but still spelt in *nought, through, night, high* : ME. *noʒt, purʒ, nyʒt, hyʒ* : OE. *noht, purh, niht, hēh*. The ME. sound was probably like that in German *ich, ach*. The older spelling with *h* is occasionally found ; more often *ch* as in *mycht* x 17 ; but the French spelling *gh* gains ground throughout the century. Abnormal are *write* for *wrighte* xvi 230, *wytes, nytes* for *wyʒtes, nyʒtes* xv *i* 19 f.

(iii) As these sounds weakened in late Southern ME., *ʒ* was sometimes used without phonetic value, or at the most to reinforce a long *i* : e. g. *Engliʒsch* xi *a* 28, 37, &c. ; *kyʒn* 'kine' ix 256.

N.B.—Entirely distinct in origin and sound value, but identical in script form, is *ʒ*, the minuscule form of *z*, in *Aʒone* (= *Azone*) 1 105, *clyffeʒ* 'cliffs' v 10, &c. It would probably be better to print *z* in such words.

§ 6. SPELLING. Modern English spelling, which tolerates almost any inconsistency in the representation of sounds provided the same word is always spelt in the approved way, is the creation of printers, schools, and dictionaries. A Middle English writer was bound by no such arbitrary rules. Michael of Northgate, whose autograph MS. survives, writes *diaknen* iii 5 and *dyacne* 9 ; *vyf* 22, *uif* 23, *vif* 37 ; *bouzond* 30 and *pousend* 34. Yet his spelling is not irrational. The comparative regularity of his own speech, which he reproduced directly, had a normalizing influence ; and by natural habit he more often than not solved the same problem of representation in the same way. Scribes, too, like printers in later times, found a measure of consistency convenient, and the spelling of some transcripts, e. g. 1 and x, is very regular. If at first ME. spelling appears lawless to a modern reader, it is because of the variety of dialects represented in literature, the widely differing dates of the MSS. printed, and the tendency of copyists to mix their own spellings with those of their original.

The following points must be kept in mind :

(i) *i* : *y* as vowels are interchangeable. In some MSS. (for instance, 1) *y* is used almost exclusively ; in others (viii *a*) it is preferred for distinctness in the neighbourhood of *u, n, m*, so that the scribe writes *hym*, but *his*.

(ii) *ie* is found in later texts for long close *ẹ̄*: *chiere* XII *a* 120, *flietende* XII *a* 157, *diemed* XII *b* 216.

(iii) *ui* (*uy*), in the South-West and West Midlands, stands for *ū* (sounded as in French *amuser*): *puit* XIV *c* 12; *vnkuynde* XIV *c* 103. The corresponding short *ŭ* is spelt *u*: *hull* 'hill', &c.

(iv) Quite distinct is the late Northern addition of *i* (*y*), to indicate the long vowels *ā, ē, ō*: *neid* X 18, *noyne* 'noon' X 67.

(v) *ou* (*ow*) is the regular spelling of long *ū* (sounded as in *too*): *hous, now, founden*, &c.

(vi) *o* is the regular spelling for short *u* (sounded as in *put*) in the neighbourhood of *u, m, n*, because if *u* is written in combination with these letters an indistinct series of down-strokes results. Hence *loue* but *luf, come* infin., *sone* 'son', *dronken* 'drunk'. In *Ayenbyte o* for *ŭ* is general, e.g. *grochinge* III 10. In other texts it is common in *bote* 'but'.

(vii) *u* : *v* are not distinguished as consonant and vowel. *v* is preferred in initial position, *u* medially or finally: *valay* 'valley', *vnder* 'under', *vuel* (= *üvel*) 'evil', *loue* 'love'. (Note that in XII the MS. distinction of *v* and *u* is not reproduced.)

(viii) So *i*, and its longer form *j*, are not distinguished as vowel and consonant. In this book *i* is printed throughout, and so stands initially for the sound of our *j* in *ioy, iuggement*, &c.

(ix) *c* : *k* for the sounds in *kit, cot*, are often interchangeable; but *k* is preferred before palatal vowels *e, i* (*y*); and *c* before *o, u*. See the alliterating words in V 52, 107, 128, 153, 272, 283.

(x) *c* : *s* alternate for voiceless *s*, especially in French words: *sité* 'city' VII 66, *resayue* 'receive' V 8, *vyse* 'vice' V 307, *falce* V 314; but also in *race* (ON. *rás*) V 8 beside *rase* XVII 429.

(xi) *s* : *z* (*ȝ*) are both used for voiced *s*, the former predominating: *kyssedes* beside *raȝteȝ* V 283; *þouzond* III 30 beside *bousend* III 34. But *ȝ* occasionally appears for voiceless *s*: (*aȝ-*)*leȝ* 'awe-less' V 267, *forȝ* 'force' 'waterfall' V 105.

(xii) *sh* : *sch* : *ss* are all found for modern *sh*, OE. *sc*: *shuld* I 50; *schert* II 230; *sserte* III 40; but *sal* 'shall', *suld* 'should' in Northern texts represent the actual Northern pronunciation in weakly stressed words.

(xiii) *v* : *w*: In late Northern MSS. *v* is often found for initial *w*: *vithall* x 9, *Valter* x 36. The interchange is less common in medial positions: *in swndir* x 106.

(xiv) *wh*- : *qu*(*h*)- : *w*-:—*wh*- is a spelling for *hw*-. In the South the aspiration is weakened or lost, and *w* is commonly written, e. g. VIII *b*. In the North the aspiration is strong, and the sound is spelt *qu*(*h*)-, e. g. *quhelis* 'wheels' x 17. Both *qu*- and *wh*- are found in *Gawayne*. The development in later dialects is against the assumption that *hw*- became *kw*- in pronunciation.

See also § 5.

The whole system of ME. spelling was modelled on French, and some of the general features noted above (e. g. ii, iii, v, vi, x) are essentially French. But, particularly in early MSS., there are a number of exceptional imitations. Sometimes the spelling represents a French scribe's attempt at English pronunciation: *foret* in xv *g* 18 stands for *forþ*, where -*rþ* with strongly trilled *r* was difficult to a foreigner; and occasionally such distortions are found as *knith*, *knit*, and even *kint* (*Layamon*, *Havelok*) for *kniʒt*, which had two awkward consonant groups. More commonly the copyist, accustomed to write both French and English, chose a French representation for an English sound. So *st* for *ht* appears regularly in xv *e*: *seuenist* 'sennight', and xv *g*: *iboust* 'bought', &c. The explanation is that in French words like *beste* 'bête', *gist* 'gît', *s* became only a breathing before it disappeared; and *h* in ME. *ht* weakened to a similar sound, as is shown by the rimes with *Kryste* 'Christ' in VI 98–107. Hence the French spelling *st* is occasionally substituted for English *ht*. Again, in borrowings from French, *an* + consonant alternates with *aun*: *dance* or *daunce*; *change* or *chaunge* (p. 273); and by analogy we have *Irlande* or *Irlaunde* in xv *d*. Another exceptional French usage, -*tz* for final voiceless -*s*, is explained at p. 219, top.

§ 7. SOUND CHANGES. (*a*) **Vowel Quantity.** No fourteenth-century writer followed the early example of Orm. Marks of quantity are not used in fourteenth-century texts; doubling of long vowels is not an established rule; and there are no strictly quantitative metres, or treatises on pronunciation. Consequently it is not easy to determine how far the quantity of the vowels in any given text has been affected by the very considerable changes that occurred in the late OE. and ME. periods.

Of these the chief are:

(i) In unstressed syllables original long vowels tend to become short. Hence *ŭs* (OE. *ūs*), and *bŏte* (OE. *būtan*) 'but', which are usually unstressed.

(ii) All long vowels are shortened in stressed close syllables (i.e., *usually*, when they are followed by two consonants): e.g. *kēpen*, pa. t. *kĕpte*, pp. *kĕpt*; *hŭsband* beside *hous*; *wĭmmen* (from *wīf-men*) beside *wīf*.

Exception. Before the groups -*ld*, -*nd*, -*rd*, -*rð*, -*mb*, a short vowel is lengthened in OE. unless a third consonant immediately follows. Hence, before any of these combinations, length may be retained in ME.: e.g. *fēnd* 'fiend', *bīnden*, *chīld*; but *chĭldren*.

(iii) Short vowels *ă*, *ĕ*, *ŏ* are lengthened in stressed open syllables (i.e., *usually*, when they are followed by a single consonant with a following vowel): *tă|ke* > *táke*; *mĕ|te* > *méte* 'meat'; *brŏ|ken* > *bróken*. To what extent *ĭ* and *ŭ* were subject to the same lengthening in Northern districts is still disputed. Normally they remain short in South and S. Midlands, e.g. *drŭen* pp.; *lŏuen* = *lŭven* 'to love'.

There are many minor rules and many exceptions due to analogy; but roughly it may be taken that ME. vowels are:

short when unstressed;

short before two consonants, except -*ld*, -*nd*, -*rd*, -*rð*, -*mb*;

long (except *i*(*y*), *u*) before a single medial consonant;

otherwise of the quantity shown in the Glossary for the OE. or ON. etymon.

(*b*) **Vowel Quality.** The ME. sound-changes are so many and so obscure that it will be possible to deal only with a few that contribute most to the diversity of dialects, and it happens that the particular changes noticed all took effect before the fourteenth century.

(i) OE. and ON. *ā* develop to long open *ǭ* (sounded as in *broad*), first in the South and S. Midlands, later in the N. Midlands. In the North *ā* (sounded approximately as in *father*) remains: e.g. *bane* 'bone' IV *a* 54, *balde* 'bold' IV *a* 51.   The boundary seems to have been a line drawn west from the Humber, and this approximates to the dividing line in the modern dialects.   There are of course instances of $\bar{\rho}$ to the north and of $\bar{a}$ to the south of the Humber, since border speakers would be familiar with both $\bar{a}$ and $\bar{\rho}$, or would have intermediate pronunciations; and poets might use convenient rimes from neighbouring dialects.

(ii) OE. $\breve{y}$ (deriving from Germanic $\breve{u}$ followed by *i*) appears *normally* in E. Midlands and the North as $\breve{i}$ ($\breve{y}$): e.g. *ky̆n, hill* (OE. *cȳ, hyll*).   In the South-East, particularly Kent, it appears as $\breve{e}$: *kĕn, hell*.   In the South-West, and in W. Midlands, it commonly appears as *u, ui* (*uy*), with the sound of short or long $\breve{u}$.   London was apparently at a meeting point of the *u, i,* and *e* boundaries, because all the forms appear in fourteenth-century London texts, though $\breve{u}$ and $\breve{e}$ gradually give place to $\breve{i}$.   The extension of $\breve{u}$ forms to the North-West is shown by *Gawayne*, and a line drawn from London to Liverpool would give a rough idea of the boundary.   But within this area unrounding of $\breve{u}$ to $\breve{i}$ seems to have been progressive during the century.   N.B.—It is dangerous to jump to conclusions from isolated examples. Before *r* + consonant *e* is sometimes found in all dialects, e.g. *schert* II 230.   *Church*, spelt with *u, i,* or *e*, had by etymology OE. *i*, not *y*.   And in Northern texts there are a number of *e*-spellings in open syllables, both for OE. *y* and *i*.

(*c*) Consonants:

(i) *f* > *v* (initial): this change, which dates back to OE. times, is carried through in *Ayenbyte*: e.g. *uele uayre uorbisnen* = Midland '*fele fayre forbisnes*'.   In some degree it extended over the whole of the South.

(ii) *s* > *z* (initial), parallel to the change of *f* to *v*, is regularly represented in spelling in the *Ayenbyte*: *zome* 'some', &c.   Otherwise *z* is rare in spelling, but the voiced initial sound probably extended to most of the Southern districts where it survives in modern dialect.

§ 8. PRONUNCIATION.   One of the best ways of studying ME. pronunciation is to learn by heart a few lines of verse in a consistent dialect, and to correct their repetition as more precise knowledge is gained. The spelling can be relied on as very roughly phonetic if the exceptional usages noted in §6 are kept in mind. Supplementary and controlling information is provided by the study of rimes, of alliteration, and of the history of English and French sounds.

Consonants. Where a consonant is clearly pronounced in Modern English, its value is nearly enough the same for ME. But modern spelling preserves many consonants that have been lost in speech, and so is rather a hindrance than a help to the beginner in ME. For instance, the initial sounds in ME. *kniʒt* and *niʒt* were not the same, for *kniʒt* alliterates always with *k-* (v 43, 107) and *niʒt* with *n-* (vii 149); and initial *wr-* in *wringe, wriʒte* is distinct from initial *r-* in *ring, riʒt* (cp. alliteration in viii *a* 168, v 136). Nor can *wriʒte* rime with *write* in a careful fourteenth-century poem. In words like *lerne, doghter, r* was pronounced with some degree of trilling. And although there are signs of confusion in late MSS. (iv *a*, xvi, xvii), double consonants were generally distinguished from single: *sonne* 'sun' was pronounced *sŭn-ne*, and so differed from *sone* 'son', which was pronounced *sŭ-ne* (§ 6 vi).

Vowels. Short vowels *ă, ĕ, ĭ, ŏ, ŭ* (§ 6 vi) were pronounced respectively as in French *patte*, English *pet, pit, pot, put*. Final unstressed *-e* was generally syllabic, with a sound something like the final sound in *China* (§ 9).

The long vowels *ā, ī, ū* (§ 6 v) were pronounced approximately as in *father, machine, crude*. But *ē* and *ō* present special difficulties, because the spelling failed to make the broad distinction between open *ǭ* and close *ọ̄*, open *ę̄* and close *ę̄*— a distinction which, though relative only (depending on the greater or less opening of the mouth passage), is proved to have been considerable by ME. rimes, and by the earlier and subsequent history of the long sounds represented in ME. by *e, o*.

(i) Open *ǭ* (as in *broad*) derives:

   (*a*) from OE. *ā*, according to § 7 b i: OE. *brād, bāt, báld* > ME. *brǭd, bǭt, bǭld* > NE. *broad, boat, bold*. The characteristic modern spelling is thus *oa*.

   (*b*) from OE. *ŏ* in open syllables according to § 7 a iii: OE. *brŏcen* > ME. *brǫke(n)* > NE. *broken*.

NOTE.—In many texts the rimes indicate a distinction in pronunciation between $\bar{\varrho}$ derived from OE. $\bar{a}$ and $\bar{\varrho}$ derived from OE. $\check{o}$, and the distinction is still made in NW. Midland dialects.

(ii) Close ϱ (pronounced rather as in French *beau* than as in standard English *so* which has developed a diphthong ϱu), derives from OE. $\bar{o}$: OE. $g\bar{o}s$, $d\bar{o}m$, $g\acute{o}ld >$ ME. $g\bar{\varrho}s$, $d\bar{\varrho}m$, $g\bar{\varrho}ld >$ NE. *goose, doom, gold.* The characteristic modern spelling is *oo*.

NOTE.—(1) After consonant $+ w$, $\bar{\varrho}$ often develops in ME. to $\bar{\varrho}$: OE. $(al)sw\bar{a}$, $tw\bar{a} >$ ME. $(al)s\bar{\varrho}$, $tw\bar{\varrho} >$ later $(al)s\bar{\varrho}$, $tw\bar{\varrho}$.

(2) In Scotland and the North $\bar{\varrho}$ becomes regularly a sound (perhaps $\ddot{u}$) spelt u: $g\bar{o}d > gud$, $bl\bar{o}d > blud$, &c.

Whereas the distribution of $\bar{\varrho}$ and ϱ is practically the same for all ME. dialects, the distinction of open $\bar{\varrho}$ and close $\bar{\varrho}$ is not so regular, chiefly because the sounds from which they derive were not uniform in OE. dialects. For simplicity, attention will be confined to the London dialect, as the forerunner of modern Standard English.

(iii) South-East Midland open $\bar{\varrho}$ (pronounced as in *there*) derives:

(a) from OE. (Anglian) $\bar{æ}$: Anglian $d\bar{æ}l >$ SE. Midl. $d\bar{\varrho}l >$ NE. *deal*;

(b) from OE. $\bar{e}a$: OE. $b\bar{e}atan >$ ME. $b\bar{\varrho}te(n) >$ NE. *beat*;

(c) from OE. $\check{e}$ in open syllables according to § 7 a iii: OE. $m\check{e}te >$ ME. $m\bar{\varrho}te >$ NE. *meat*.

The characteristic modern spelling is *ea*.

(iv) South-East Midland close $\bar{\varrho}$ (pronounced as in French *été*) derives:

(a) from OE. (Anglian) $\bar{e}$ of various origins: Anglian $h\bar{e}r$, $m\bar{e}ta(n)$, $(ge)l\bar{e}fa(n) >$ SE. Midl. $h\bar{\varrho}re$, $m\bar{\varrho}te(n)$, $l\bar{\varrho}ue(n) >$ NE. *here, meet, (be)lieve.*

(b) from OE. $\bar{e}o$: OE. $d\bar{e}op$, $\not{p}\bar{e}of >$ ME. $d\bar{\varrho}p$, $b\bar{\varrho}f$ $(\not{p}ief) >$ NE. *deep, thief.*

The characteristic modern spellings are *ee*, and *ie* which already in ME. often distinguishes the close sound (§ 6 ii).

NOTE.—The distinction made above does not apply in South-Eastern (Kentish), because this dialect has ME. *ea, ia, ya* for OE. $\bar{e}a$ (iii b), and OE. $\bar{e}$ for Anglian $\bar{æ}$ (iii a). Nor does it hold for South-Western, because the West Saxon dialect of OE. had *gelīefan* for Anglian *gelēfa*(*n*) (iv a). West Saxon also had *strǣt*, *-drǣdan*, where normal Anglian had *strēt*, *-drēda*(*n*), but the distribution of the place-names *Stratton* beside *Stretton*, and of the pa. t. and pp. *dradd*(*e*) beside *dredd*(*e*) (p. 270 and n.), shows that the ǣ forms were common in the extreme South and the East of the Anglian area; so that in fourteenth-century London both *ẹ̄* and *ę̄* might occur in such words, as against regular West Midland and Northern *ẹ̄*.

In NE. Midland and Northern texts some *ē* sounds which we should expect to be distinguished as open and close rime together, especially before dental consonants, e. g. *ʒēde* (OE. *ēode*): *lēde* (Anglian *lǣda*(*n*)) 1 152–3.

§ 9. INFLEXIONS. Weakening and levelling of inflexions is continuous from the earliest period of English. The strong stress falling regularly on the first or the stem syllable produced as reflex a tendency to indistinctness in the unstressed endings. The disturbing influence of foreign conquest played a secondary but not a negligible part, as may be seen from a comparison of some verbal forms in the North and the N. Midlands, where Norse influence was strongest, with those of the South, where it was inconsiderable:

	Normal OE.	Early Sth. ME.	Early Nth. and N.Midl.	Old Norse
Infin. ...	*drīfan*	*driue*(*n*)	*driue*	*drífa*
Pres. p. ...	*drīfende*	*driuinde*	*driuande*	*drífandi*
Pp. strong .	*gedrifen*	*ydriue*	*driuen*	*drifenn*

and although tangible evidence of French influence on the flexional system is wanting (for occasional borrowings like *gowtes artetykes* IX 314 are mere literary curiosities), every considerable settlement of foreign speakers, especially when they come as conquerors, must shake the traditions of the language of the conquered. A third cause of uncertainty was the interaction of English dialects in different stages of development.

The practical sense of the speakers controlled and balanced these disruptive factors. There is no better field than Middle English for a study of the processes of vigorous growth: the regularizing of exceptional and inconvenient forms; the choice of the most distinctive among a group of alternatives ; the invention of new modes of expression ; the discarding of what has become useless.

At the beginning of the fourteenth century the inflexional endings are : *-e* ; *-en* ; *-ene* (weak gen. pl.); *-er* (comparative) ; *-es* ; *-est* ; with *-eþ*, *-ede* (*-de*, *-te*), *-ed* (*-d*, *-t*), *-ynge* (*-inde*, *-ende*, *-ande*), which are verbal only.

NOTE.—(*a*) Sometimes one of these inflexions may be substituted for another : e. g. when *-es* replaces *-e* as the Northern ending of the 1st sg. pres. ind. Such analogical substitutions must be distinguished from phonetic developments.

(*b*) In disyllabic inflexions like *-ede*, *-ynge* (*-ande*), final *-e* is lost early in the North. In polysyllables it is dropped everywhere during the century.

(*c*) The indistinct sound of flexional *-e-* covered by a consonant is shown by spellings with *-i-*, *-y-* : *woundis* x 51 ; *madist* xi *b* 214; *blyndiþ* xi *b* 7 ; *fulfillid* xvi 6; *etin* xiv *b* 76 ; *brokynne* xvi 195. And, especially in West Midland texts, *-us*, *-un* (*-on*) appear for *-es*, *-en* : *mannus* xi *b* 234 ; *foundun* xi *a* 47 ; *laghton* vii 119. Complete syncope sometimes occurs : *days* i 198, &c.

Otherwise all the inflexions except *-e*, *-en*, are fairly stable throughout the century.

-en: In the North *-en* is found chiefly in the strong pp., where it is stable. In the South (except in the strong pp.) it is better preserved, occurring rarely in the dat. sg. of adjectives, e. g. *onen* iii 4, dat. pl. of nouns, e. g. *diaknen* iii 5, and in the infinitive ; more commonly in the weak pl. of nouns, where it is stable, and in the pa. t. pl., where it alternates with *-e*. In the Midlands *-en*, alternating with *-e*, is also the characteristic ending of the pres. ind. pl. As a rule (where the reduced ending *-e* is found side by side with *-en*) *-e* is used before words beginning with a consonant, and *-en* before words beginning with a vowel or *h*, to avoid hiatus. But that the preservation of *-en* does not depend purely on phonetic considerations is proved by its regular retention in the Northern strong pp., and its regular reduction to *-e* in the corresponding Southern form.

-e : Wherever *-en* was reduced, it reinforced final *-e*, which so became the meeting point of all the inflexions that were to disappear before Elizabethan times.

-e was the ending of several verbal forms; of the weak adjective and the adjective pl.; of the dat. sg. of nouns; and of adverbs like *faste*, *deepe*, as distinguished from the corresponding adjectives *fast*, *deep*.

That *-e* was pronounced is clear from the metres of Chaucer, Gower, and most other Southern and Midland writers of the time. For centuries the rhythm of their verse was lost because later generations had become so used to final *-e* as a mere spelling that they did not suspect that it was once syllabic.

But already in fourteenth-century manuscripts there is evidence of uncertainty. Scribes often omit the final vowel where the rhythm shows that it was syllabic in the original (see the language notes to I, II). Conversely, in *Gawayne* forms like *burne* (OE. *beorn*), *race* (ON. *rás*), *hille* (OE. *hyll*) appear in nominative and accusative, where historically there should be no ending. The explanation is that, quite apart from the workings of analogy, which now extended and now curtailed its historical functions, *-e* was everywhere weakly pronounced, and was dropped at different rates in the various dialects. In the North it hardly survives the middle of the century (IV *a*, x). In the N. Midlands its survival is irregular. In the South and S. Midlands it is fairly well preserved till the end of the century. But everywhere the proportion of flexionless forms was increasing. It may be assumed that, in speech as in verse, final *-e* was lost phonetically first before words beginning with a vowel or *h*.

§ 10. NOUNS: Gender, which in standard West Saxon had been to a great extent grammatical (i. e. dependent on the forms of the noun), was by the fourteenth century natural (i.e. dependent on the meaning of the noun). This change had accompanied and in some degree facilitated the transfer of nearly all nouns to the strong masculine type, which was the commonest and best defined in late OE.:

	OE.	ME.			OE.	ME.
Sg. nom. acc.	*cniht*	*kniȝt*	Pl. nom. acc.		*cnihtas*	*kniȝtes*
gen.	*cnihtes*	*kniȝtes*		gen.	*cnihta*	*kniȝtes*
dat.	*cnihte*	*kniȝte*		dat.	*cnihtum*	*kniȝtes*

In the North final -*e* of the dat. sg. was regularly dropped early in the fourteenth century, and even in the South the dat. sg. is often uninflected, probably owing to the influence of the accusative. In the plural the inflexion of the nom. acc. spreads to all cases; but in early texts, and relatively late in the South, the historical forms are occasionally found, e. g. gen. pl. *cniste* (MS. *cnistes*) xv *g* 30 (note), dat. pl. *diaknen* III 5.

Survivals: (i) The common mutated plurals *man* : *men*, *fot* : *fet*, &c., are preserved, and in VIII *b* a gen. pl. *menne* (OE. *manna*) occurs; *ky* pl. of *cow* forms a new double pl. *kyn*, see (iii) below; *hend* pl. of *hand* is Norse, cp. XVI 75 (note).

(ii) Some OE. neuters like *shep* 'sheep' VIII *b* 18, *ʒer* 'year' II 492, *þing* II 218, *folk* II 389, resist the intrusion of the masculine pl. -*es* in nominative and accusative. Pl. *hors* II 304, XIII *a* 34 remains beside *horses* XIV *b* 73; but *deores* 'wild animals' occurs at xv *b* 29, where Modern English preserves *deer*.

(iii) In the South the old weak declension with pl. -*en* persists, though by the fourteenth century the predominance of the strong type is assured. The weak forms occur not only where they are historically justified, e. g. *eyʒen* (OE. *ēagan*) II 111, but also by analogy in words like *honden* (OE. pl. *honda*) II 79, *tren* (OE. pl. *trēo*) XIII *a* 51, *platen* (OFr. *plate*) xv *g* 4. The inflexion still survives in three double plural formations: *children* VIII *b* 70 beside *childer* (OE. pl. *cildru*); *bretheren* VIII *a* 201 beside *brether* XVII 320 (OE. pl. *brōþor*); and *kyʒn* IX 256 for *ky* (cp. (i) above). The OE. weak gen. pl. in -*ena* leaves its traces in the South, e. g. *knauene* VIII *b* 56, xv *h* 4, and unhistorical *lordene* VIII *b* 77.

(iv) The group *fader*, *moder*, *broþer*, *doghter* commonly show the historical flexionless gen. sg., e. g. *doghtyr arme* I 136; *moder wombe* XI *b* 29 f.; *brother hele* XII *a* 18; *Fadir voice* XVI 79.

(v) The historical gen. sg. of old strong feminines remains in *soule dede* (OE. *sāwle*) I 212; but *Lady day* (OE. *hlǣfdigan dæg*) I 242 is a survival of the weak fem. gen. sg.

§ 11. ADJECTIVES. Separate flexional forms for each gender

are not preserved in the fourteenth century; but until its
end the distinction of strong and weak declensions remains
in the South and South Midlands, and is well marked in the
careful verse of Chaucer and Gower. The strong is the
normal form. The weak form is used after demonstratives,
the, *his*, &c., and in the vocative. As types *god* (OE. *gōd*)
'good' and *grene* (OE. *grēne*) 'green' will serve, because in
OE. *grēne* had a vowel-ending in the strong nom. sg. masc.,
while *gōd* did not. The ME. paradigms are:

Singular.		Plural.
Strong	Weak	Strong and Weak
god	godè	godè
grenè	grenè	grenè

Examples: Strong sg. *a gret serpent* (OE. *grēat*) xii *b* 72;
an unkindè man (OE. *uncynde*) xii *b* 1; *a stillè water* (OE.
stille) xii *a* 83. Weak sg. *The gretè gastli serpent* xii *b* 126;
hire oghnè hertes lif xii *a* 4; *O lef liif* (where the metre
indicates *leuè* for the original) 11 102. Strong pl. *per wer
widè wones* 11 365. Weak pl. *the smalè stones* xii *a* 84.

Note that strong and weak forms are identical in the plural;
that even in the singular there is no formal distinction when
the OE. strong masc. nom. ended in a vowel (*grēne*); that
monosyllables ending in a vowel (e.g. *fre*), polysyllables, and
participles, are usually invariable; and that regular dropping
of final *-e* levels all distinctions, so that the North and N.
Midlands early reached the relatively flexionless stage of
Modern English.

Survivals. The *Ayenbyte* shows some living use of the
adjective inflexions. Otherwise the survivals are limited to
set phrases, e.g. gen. sg. *nones cunnes* 'of no kind', *enes cunnes*
'of any kind', xv *g* 20, 22. That the force of the inflexion was
lost is shown by the early wrong analysis *no skynnes*, *al
skynnes*, &c.

Definite Article. Parallel to the simplification of the
adjective, the full OE. declension *sē, sēo, þæt,* &c., is reduced
to invariable *þe*. The *Ayenbyte* alone of our specimens keeps
some of the older distinctions. Elsewhere traces appear in
set phrases, e.g. neut. sg. *þat, þet* in *þat on* 'the one', *þat oþer*
'the other' v 344, and, with wrong division, *þe ton* xi *b* 27,

the toþer IX 4; neut. sg. dat. *þen* (OE. *þ̄æm*), with wrong division, in *atte nale* (for *at þen ale*) VIII *a* 109.

§ 12. PRONOUNS. In a brilliant study (*Progress in Language*, London 1894) Jespersen exemplifies the economy and resources of English from the detailed history of the Pronoun. In the first and second persons fourteenth-century usage does not differ greatly from that of the Authorized Version of the Bible. But the pronoun of the third person shows a variety of developments. In the singular an objective case replaces, without practical disadvantages, the older accusative and dative: *him* (OE. *hine* and *him*), *her(e)* (OE. *hīe* and *hiere*), *(h)it* (OE. *hit* and *him*). The possessive *his* still serves for the neuter as well as the masculine, e.g. *þat ryuer ... chaungeþ hys fordes* XIII *a* 55 f.; though an uninflected neuter possessive *hit* occasionally appears in the fourteenth century. In the plural, where one would expect objective *him* from the regular OE. dat. pl. *him*, clearness is gained by the choice of unambiguous *hem*, from an OE. dat. pl. by-form *heom*.

But as we see from *Orfeo*, ll. 408, 446, 185, in some dialects the nom. sg. masc. (OE. *hē*), nom. sg. fem. (OE. *hēo*), and nom. pl. (OE. *hīe*), had all become ME. *he*. The disadvantages of such ambiguity increased as the flexional system of nouns and adjectives collapsed, and a remedy was found in the adoption of new forms. For the nom. sg. fem., *s(c)he*, *s(c)ho* (mostly Northern), come into use, which are probably derived from *sị̄e*, *sẹ̄ō*, the corresponding case of the definite article. The innovation was long resisted in the South, and *ho*, an unambiguous development of *hēo*, remains late in W. Midland texts like *Pearl*.

In the nom. pl. ambiguous *he* was replaced by *þei*, the nom. pl. of the Norse definite article. This is the regular form in all except the Southern specimens II (orig.), III, XIII. And although the full series of Norse forms *þei, þeir, þe(i)m* is found in Orm at the beginning of the thirteenth century, Chaucer and other Midland writers of the fourteenth century as a rule have only *þei*, with native English *her(e)*, *hem* in the oblique cases. (For details see the language note to each specimen.)

The poss. pl. *her(e)*, beside *hor(e)*, was still liable to confusion with the obj. sg. fem. *her(e)*, cp. II **92**. Consequently this was the next point to be gained by the Norse forms, e.g. in vii 181. In the Northern texts x, xvi, xvii, all from late MSS., the Norse forms *þai, þa(i)r, þa(i)me* are fully established; but (*h*)*em*, which was throughout unambiguous, survived into modern dialects in the South and Midlands.

Note the reduced nominative form *a* ' he ', ' they ' in xiii; and the objective *his(e)* 'her', 'them' in iii, which has not been satisfactorily explained.

Relative: The general ME. relative is *þat*, representing all genders and cases (note to xv *i* 4). Sometimes definition is gained by adding the personal pronoun: *þat . . . he (sche)* = 'who'; *þat . . . it* = 'which'; *þat . . . his* = 'whose'; *þat . . . him* = 'whom', &c.; e.g. *a well,* þat *in the day* it *is so cold* ix 5–6, cp. v 127 (note); *oon* That *with a spere was thirled* his *brest-boon* ' one whose breast-bone was pierced with a spear', *Knight's Tale* 1851. For the omission of *þat* see note to xiii *a* 36.

In later texts, *which,* properly an interrogative, appears commonly as a relative, both with personal and impersonal antecedents, e.g. *Alceone . . .* which *. . . him loveth* xii *a* 3 ff.; *þat steede . . . fro* whilke *þe feende fell* xvi 13 f. Under the influence of French *lequel,* &c., *which* is often compounded with the article *þe,* e.g. *a gret serpent . . .* the which *Bardus anon up drouh* xii *b* 72 f.; *no thing of newe, in* the whiche *the hereres myghten hauen . . . solace* ix 275 f. Further compounding with *þat* is not uncommon, e. g. *the queen of Amazoine,* the whiche þat *maketh hem to ben kept in cloos* ix 190 f.

More restricted is the relative use of *whos, whom,* which are originally interrogatives, though both are found very early in ME. as personal relatives. Examples of the objective after prepositions are: *my Lady, of* quom *. . .* vi 93; *God, fro* whom *. . .* ix 328 f.; *my Sone . . . in* whome xvi 81 f. The possessive occurs in *Seynt Magne . . . yn* whos *wurschyp* i 90 f.; *I am . . . the same,* whos *good* xii *b* 78 f.; and, compounded with the article, in *Morpheüs,* the whos *nature* xii *a* 113. The nominative *who* retains its interrogative meaning, e. g. *But* who *ben more heretikis ?* xi *b* 77 f.; or is used as an indefinite, e.g. *a tasse of grene stickes . . . to selle,* who that *wolde hem beie* xii *b* 22 ff.; but it is never used as a relative; and probably *what* in xvi 174 is better taken as in apposition to *myghtis* than as a true relative.

§ 13. VERB. Syntactically the most interesting point in the history of the ME. verb is the development of the compound tenses with *have, be, will, shall, may, might, mun, can, gan*. But the flexional forms of the simple tenses are most subject to local variation, and, being relatively common, afford good evidence of dialect. Throughout the period, despite the crossings and confusions that are to be expected in a time of uncertainty and experiment, the distinction between strong and weak verbs is maintained; and it will be convenient to deal first with the inflexions common to both classes, and then to notice the forms peculiar to one or the other.

(i) **The Infinitive** had already in Northumbrian OE. lost final *-n* : *drīſa* 'to drive'. Hence in ME. of the North and N. Midlands the ending is *-e*, which becomes silent at varying rates during the fourteenth century; e.g. *dryue* 1 171, *to luf* IV *a* 17. In the South and S. Midlands the common ending is *-e*, e.g. *telle* III 3, which usually remains syllabic to the end of the century; but *-(e)n* is also found, especially in verse to make a rime or to avoid hiatus: e.g. *sein* (: *aʒein*) XII *a* 27; *to parte and ʒiven half his good* XII *b* 201.

(ii) **The Present Participle** (OE. *drīfende*) in the North and N. Midlands ends in *-and(e)*, though *-yng(e)*, *-ing(e)* is beginning to appear in V, VII, XVI, XVII. In S. Midlands the historical ending *-ende* still prevails in Gower; but Chaucer has more commonly *-yng(e)*; and in IX, XI, both late texts, only *-yng(e)* appears. In the South *-yng(e)* is established as early as the beginning of the century, e.g. in II.

N.B. Carefully distinguish the verbal noun which always ends in *-yng(e)*. Early confusion resulted in the transference of this ending to the participle.

(iii) **Present Indicative.**

    (*a*) Singular: OE. 1 *drīfe*, 2 *drīf(e)s(t)*, 3 *drīf(e)ð*
    (late Northumbrian *drīfes*).

In ME. *-e, -est, -eþ* are still the regular endings for the South and most of the Midlands. Shortened forms like *fint = findeþ* II 239; *stant = standeþ* XII *a* 74 are commonest in the South, where in OE. they were a feature of West Saxon and Kentish as distinguished from Anglian. Distinct are the Northern and N. Midland *mas(e)* 'makes', *tas* 'takes', with contracted infinitives *ma, ta*; and *bus* 'behoves', which Chaucer uses in his imitation of Northern English, *Reeves Tale* 172.

In N. Midlands the modern 3rd sg. -(*e*)*s* is common (v, vi, but not in earlier 1). Farther North it is invariable (iv, x, xvi, xvii). The distribution of -*es* as the ending of the 2nd sg. is the same, and it is extended even to the 1st person.

(*b*) Plural: OE. *drīfað* (late Northumbrian *drīfas*).

Only Southern ME. retains the OE. inflexion as -*eþ* (ii, iii, xiii). The Midland ending, whence the modern form derives, is -*e(n)*; though in the N. Midlands -*es* occasionally appears. Northern has regularly -*es*, *unless the personal pronoun immediately precedes*, when the ending is -*e*, as in the Midlands, e.g. *þei make* xvi 103.

N.B. In applying this test, care must be taken to exclude inversions, which are subject to special rules; to distinguish the subjunctive (e.g. *falle* xiii *a* 52, *drawe* xiii *b* 6) from the indicative; and, generally, to choose examples that are syntactically free from doubt, because concord of number is not always logical in ME.

SUMMARY.

	OE.		ME.		
		South	S. Midl.	N. Midl.	North
1. sg.	*drīf-e*	-*e*	-*e*	-(*e*)	(*e*) or (*e*)*s*
2.	*drīf-es(t)*	-*est*	-*est*	-*es(t)*	-*es*
3.	*drīf-eð* (Nth. -*es*) -*eþ*	-*eþ*	-*eþ* or -*es*	-*es*	
pl.	*drīf-að* (Nth. -*as*) -*eþ*	-*e(n)*	-*e(n)* or -*es*	-*es* or -(*e*)	

(iv) **The Imperative Plural** might be expected to agree with the pres. ind. pl. In fact it has the ending -*eþ* not merely in the South, but in most of the Midlands, e.g. 1, viii, Gower and Chaucer. Northern and NW. Midland (v, vi, xiv *b*, xvi) have commonly -*es*. But Chaucer, Gower, and most late ME. texts have, beside the full inflexion, an uninflected form, e.g. *vndo* xvi 182.

(v) **Past Tense.**

(*a*) Strong: The historical distinctions of stem-vowel were often obscured in ME. by the rise of new analogical forms, the variety of which can best be judged from the detailed evidence presented in the *New English Dictionary* under each verb. But, for the common verbs or classes, the South and S. Midlands preserved fairly well the OE. vowel distinction of past tense singular and plural; while North and N. Midlands usually preferred the form proper to the singular for both singular and plural, e.g. *þey bygan* I 72; *þey ne blan* I 73; *thai slang* x 53, where OE. has sg. *gan* : *gunnon*; *blan* : *blunnon*; ON. *slǫng* : *slungu*.

(*b*) Weak: In the South and Midlands the weak pa. t. 2nd sg. usually ends in *-est* (N. Midland also *-es*): *hadest* II 573; *cursedest* I 130; *kyssedes, raȝteȝ* v 283. In the North, and sometimes in N. Midland, it ends in *-(e)*: *þou hadde* XVI 219. The full ending of the pa. t. pl. is fairly common in the South, S. Midlands, and NW. Midlands: *wenten* II 185, *hedden* III 42, *maden* XII *b* 196, *sayden* VI 174.

(vi) **Past Participle (Strong)**: OE. (*ge*)*drǐfen*.

In the North and N. Midlands the ending *-en* is usually preserved, but the prefix *y-* is dropped. In the South the type is *y-driue*, with prefix and without final *n*. S. Midland fluctuates—for example, Gower rarely, Chaucer commonly, uses the prefix *y-*.

(vii) **Weak Verbs with -i- suffix**: In OE. weak verbs of Class II formed the infinitive in *-ian*, e.g. *acsian, lufian*, and the *i* appeared also in the pres. ind. and imper. pl. *acsiaþ* and pres. p. *acsiende*. In ME. a certain number of French verbs with an *-i-* suffix reinforced this class. In the South and W. Midlands the *-i-* of the suffix is often preserved, e.g. *aski* II 467, *louy* v 27, and is sometimes extended to forms in which it has no historical justification, e.g. pp. *spuryed* v 25. In the North and the E. Midlands the forms without *i* are generalized.

A

MIDDLE ENGLISH
VOCABULARY

BY

J. R. R. TOLKIEN

ABBREVIATIONS

AFr.   Anglo-French.
allit.   alliterative; (in) alliterative verse, &c.
cf.   in etymologies indicates uncertain or indirect relation.
constr.   constructed with; construction.
Du.   Dutch.
E.; Mn.E.   (Modern) English.
E.D.D.   The English Dialect Dictionary.
Fr.   French.
Fris.   (Modern) Frisian (dialects).
from   is prefixed to etymologies when the word illustrated has additional suffixes, &c., not present in the etymon.
G.   German.
Goth.   Gothic.
Icel.   (Modern) Icelandic.
Kt.; OKt.   Kentish; Kentish dialect of Old English.
L.; Med.L.   Latin; Mediaeval Latin.
MDu.   Middle Dutch.
ME.   Middle English.
MHG.   Middle High German.
MLG.   Middle Low German.
N.E.D.   The Oxford (New) English Dictionary.
Nth.; ONth.   Northumbrian; Northumbrian dialect of Old English.
NWM.   North West Midland.
OE.   Old English.
OFr.   Old French.
OFris.   Old Frisian.
OHG.   Old High German.
OIr.   Old Irish.
ON.   Old Norse, especially Old Icelandic.
ONFr.   Northern dialects of Old French.
OS.   Old Saxon (Old Low German).
prec.   preceding word.
red.   reduced; reduction.
Swed.   Swedish.
WS; OWS.   West Saxon (dialect of Old English).
*   is prefixed where forms are theoretically reconstructed.
+   between the elements shows that a compound or derivative is first recorded in Middle English.

NOTE

THIS glossary does not aim at completeness, and it is not primarily a glossary of rare or 'hard' words. A good working knowledge of Middle English depends less on the possession of an abstruse vocabulary than on familiarity with the ordinary machinery of expression—with the precise forms and meanings that common words may assume; with the uses of such innocent-looking little words as the prepositions *of* and *for*; with idiomatic phrases, some fresh-minted and some worn thin, but all likely to recur again and again in an age whose authors took no pains to avoid usual or hackneyed turns of expression. These are the features of the older language which an English reader is predisposed to pass over, satisfied with a half-recognition : and space seldom permits of their adequate treatment in a compendious general dictionary or the word-list to a single text. So in making a glossary for use with a book itself designed to be a preparation for the reading of complete texts, I have given exceptionally full treatment to what may rightly be called the backbone of the language.

Brief indications of the etymology of each word are given, with references in difficult cases to the Oxford English Dictionary (*N.E.D.*). Apart from their usefulness as a basis for exercises in phonology and the analysis of vocabulary, these will serve to differentiate words distinct in origin which coincide in some of their forms or spellings. The Old English or Old French forms cited are those that best illustrate the Middle English; in consequence the Old English forms frequently differ from normal West-Saxon, and the Old French forms are especially those of the French current in England (Anglo-French is rarely specified). Old Norse words have usually been cited in the normal spelling (e.g. of Zoëga's *Old Icelandic Dictionary*). Accordingly, long vowels in Old Norse words are marked as in *bráðr*. In Old English words stable long vowels are marked as in *brād*; uncertain quantity or probable shortening in Old English times is marked as in *adrĕdd*; vowels that were lengthened in the Old English period (e.g. before *ld, mb, nd*) are marked as in *cáld, clímban, bíndan*.

For the convenience of beginners the glossary is liberally supplied with cross references, and the prefixed Table summarizes the principal variations of form or spelling. Particular attention should be given to the following points of arrangement : (i) ʒ has a separate alphabetical place following *G* ; cross-references to *gh* are not given: (ii) Þ has a separate alphabetical place following *T* ; variation between *þ* and *th* is disregarded, and initial *Th* is entered under *Þ* : (iii) *U*, *V* are alternative forms of the same letter ; variation between them is disregarded, and initial *U* is entered under *V*: (iv) *Y* initially has its usual place ; but medial or final *Y* will be found in the alphabetical position of *I*.

J. R. R. T.

PRINCIPAL VARIATIONS OF FORM OR SPELLING

1. a *varies with* o (*before* m, n); *as* land, lang, lamb—lond, long, lomb; man, name—(*Western*) mon, nome.
2. a (= ā) *varies in Northern texts with* (i) ai, ay; *as* (*a*) fare, fare—fayɪe (*b*) fayre—farest, *fairest* : (ii) *with Southern* o, oo; *see* 14.
3. ai, ay *varies with* (i) ei, ey; *as* mayntene—meyntene : (ii) a; *see* 2 : (iii) o, oo; *see* 2.
4. au (*before* m, n) *varies with* a (*chiefly in French words*); *as* daunce—dance.
5. be-, *prefix varies with* bi-; *as* begynne—biginne.
6. c *varies with* k; *as* bac, court—bak, kort.
7. des-, *prefix varies with* dis-; *as* des-, disavauntage.
8. e (= ẹ̄) *varies in Northern texts with* ei, ey; *as* wel(e)—weill, weyl; stele—steill. *See* 13, 20.
9. ei, ey *varies with* (i) ai, ay (*cf.* 3); *as* weie, wey(e)—way(e) : (ii) *hence in Northern texts with* a; *as* strat-ly—streyte : (iii) *with* e; *see* 8.
10. er *varies with later* ar; *as* fer, hertely—far, hartely.
11. f *varies with* u (= v) : (i) *initially* (*Southern*); *as* fader—uader : (ii) *finally* (*Northern*); *as* haf(e)—haue.
12. ght *varies with* ʒt, cht (*Scottish*), ht, st; *as* nyght—niʒt, nycht, nyht, seuenist.
13. i (*vowel*) *varies with* y, *passim* : i, y *varies with* (i) e *in Northern texts*; *as* hider, liuen, myddel—hedeᴦ, leue, medill : (ii) *with* e, (*South*) *Western* u; *as* hil, fyrst—hell, uerst—hul, furst.
14. o, oo (= ǭ) *varies in Northern texts with* (i) a; *as* hot, hoot—hate : (ii) *hence also with* ai (*see* 2) : (iii) *with* oi, oy; *see next*.
15. o, oo (= ọ̄) *varies in Northern texts with* (i) ou, u; *as* god, good—goud, gud(e) : (ii) oi, oy; *as* none, noon—noyne.
16. (s)sch *varies with* (s)sh, ss; *as* schewe—shewe, ssewe; fle(s)sch—flessh.
17. þ *varies with* th, *passim*.
18. u (*in* au, eu, ou) *varies with* w, *passim*; *see* 21.
19. u, v (= u) *varies with* o (*esp. before* m, n); *as* sun(ne)—sonne; but—bot(e); *see also* 15.
20. u, v (= ü) *varies in Western texts with* (i) e, eo; *as* erthe—(*Western*) eorþe, vrþe : (ii) *with* i, y, e; *see* 13.
21. w *varies medially with* gh, ʒ (u); *as* owen, *own*—oghne, oʒene, oune : *initially* (*Scottish*) *with* v; *as* woundit—voundit.
22. y (*consonant*) *varies initially with* ʒ; *as* ye—ʒe; *medially with* i, (i)gh, (i)ʒ; *as* say, se(i)gh, se(i)ʒe, *saw.*
23. *single consonant varies with double*; *as* sad—sadde.
24. *single vowel varies with double*; *as* breed—brede, *breadth*; wod—wood, *mad.*

GLOSSARY

A, *pron.* he, XIII *a* 27, 47, 48;
they, XIII *a* 13, *b* 22, 36, 39, 61,
64, 66. [Unaccented form of
ME. *ha. See* Hare, Ham.]

A, *v. inf.* have, I 127. [Reduced
unaccented form of *haue; see*
Habbe(n).]

A(n), *adj.* one, IV *b* 34; *indef. art.*
a(n), I 22, VIII *b* 7, &c. *See*
Ane, On(e).

A(n), *prep.* on, in, &c. II 137, III
introd., 22, VIII *a* 43, XIII *a* 11,
b 19, 34, &c. ; *a blode*, with
blood, XV *g* 16; *a nyghtes*, at
night (OE. *on niht, nihtes*),
VIII *b* 16; *a pre*, in three, XIII *b*
49 (*see* Ato, Atwynne); *a
Goddes half*, for God's sake,
XII *b* 80. [Weakened form of
On, *q.v.*; *an* in III is possibly
dialectal ; *a* is used only before
following consonant.] *See* Ane.

Abandoune, *v.* to abandon, resign, X 50. [OFr. *abandouner.*]

Abasshed, *pp.* perturbed, XVI 177
(note to XVI 59). [AFr. *abaiss-*;
OFr. *e(s)bair, e(s)baiss-.*]

Abate, *v.* to lessen, XIV *b* 19;
reduce, VIII *a* 209 (*imper. sg.*);
intr. XVII 445; Abatid (*of*),
pp. ceased, VII 104. [OFr. *abat-
re.*]

Abedde, *adv.* in bed, XII *a* 141.
[OE. *on bedde.*] *See* Bedd(e).

Abhomynable, *adj.* abominable,
XI *b* 90. [OFr. *abominable.*]

Abide, Abyde, Habide, *v.* (i)
intr. to wait, remain, stay, II 84,
IX 197, XVII 531; tarry, II 348;
imper. wait !, V 149; halt !, XVI
213; (ii) *trans.* to await, XVII
334; withstand, endure, XIV *b*
31; Abode, *pa. t.* XIV *c* 68,
XVII 373; Abyde, *pp.* in *ys
abyde*, has survived, XIII *b* 50.
[OE. *ā-bīdan.*] *See* Bide.

Abite, *n.* outward appearance,
XI *b* 99. [OFr. (*h*)*abit.*]

Able, *adj.* able, VI 239, XI *b* 92.
[OFr. (*h*)*able.*] *See* Vnable.

Abone, *adv.* above, XVII 146.
See Aboue(n).

Abosted, *pa. t. sg.* threatened
boastfully, VIII *a* 148. [ME. *a-*
+ Boste, q. v.]

Aboue(n), Abovin, Abuf, *adv.*
above, overhead, on top, V 149,
VII 105, 135, IX 56, X 61; on
the surface, VII 160; *prep.*
above, higher than, XI *b* 182,
XVII 83; *quasi-sb.* in *be at here
aboue*, get the upper hand of
them, XIII *a* 61. [OE. **on-bufan,
abufan.*] *See* Abone.

Aboueseyd, *adj.* aforesaid, IX 307.
[Prec. + *pp.* of Seie.]

Aboute(n), Abowte, Obout
(XIV *a*), (i) *adv.* about, round, on
all sides, here and there, to and
fro, I 233, V 165, VIII *a* 297,
XI *b* 270, XII *a* 143, *b* 117, XIV *a*
15, XV *i* 3, XVII 303, 351, &c. ;
round about, VII 83, &c. ; round
it, II 359; *al aboute round*, all
round about, XII *a* 79; (ii) *prep.*
about, round, &c. (often following *n.* or *pron.*), I 54, II 274,
284, V 95, XIV *b* 68, &c. ; on,
XI *b* 236; in, XI *b* 293, 296;
about al, in all directions, II 387;
aboute with *for to* (*vn-bynde*),
XVI 7. [OE. *onbūtan, ābūtan.*]

Abrod, *adv.* out wide, XII *a* 176.
[OE. *on* + *brād.*]

Abuf. *See* Aboue.

Abugge, *v.* to pay for (it), VIII *a*
75, 159. [OE. *ā-bycgan.*] *See*
Bigge.

Ac, *conj.* but, II 56, III 34, VIII 67,
&c. [OE. *ac.*]

Acheue, *v.* achieve, VI 115. [OFr.
achever.] *See* Cheue.

Accordandly, *adv.* accordingly, IV *b* 33. [From pres. p. of Acorde.]

Acord(e), Accord, *n.* agreement, VI 149, XI *a* 32; concurrence, united will, XVII 30; *made acorde of care and me*, associated me with, caused me to know, care, VI 11. [OFr. *acord(e)*.]

Acorde(n), *v. trans.* to reconcile, V 337; *to acorde me with*, to associate myself with, V 312; *intr.* agree, XI *b* 128, XII *b* 145, XIII *b* 52. [OFr. *acorder*.] *See* Corden.

Acountes, *n. pl.* settlement of accounts, VIII *a* 83. [OFr. *acont, acunt*.]

Acsede. *See* Axe(n).

Actif, Actyf, *adj.* active, VIII *a* 245, XI *b* 74, 102. [OFr. *actif*.]

Aday, *adv.* in *dyne aday*, eat at (mid-day) meal, VIII *a* 303. [OE. *on dæge*, by day.]

Ademand, *n.* loadstone (magnetic iron ore), IX 123, 125, &c. [OFr. *adema(u)nt*, L. *adamantem* (acc.), properly 'diamond'. The application to 'loadstone' was due to false association with L. *ad-amāre*. The mediaeval 'adamant' in consequence often combined the properties of diamond and loadstone.] *See* Dyamand.

Admytte, *v.* to admit XVII 551. [L. *admittere*.]

Adoun, Adown, *adv.* down, II 223, 435, VIII *a* 31, &c. [OE. *of-dūne, adūne*.] *See* Doun(e).

Adrad, *pp.* afraid, XII *b* 133; **Adred**, XVII 201. [OE. *of-drǽdd, ofdrédd*, pp.] *See* Drede(n).

Adreynt, *pp.* drowned, II 397. [OE. *ā-drencan*, pp. *ā-drenct*.]

Adresced, *pp.*; *therupon him hath adresced*, has fastened himself to it, XII *b* 85. *See* Dresse. [OFr. *adresser*.]

Aduersouris, *n. pl.* adversaries, X 144. [OFr. *adversier* with alteration of suffix.]

Afelde, *adv.* to the fields, VIII *a* 136, 283. [OE. *on félda*.] *See* Feld(e).

Aferd(e), *adj.* afraid, I 4, 67, 262, VIII *a* 115, XVII 316, &c. [OE. *ā-fǽred*.] *See* Ferde.

Affaite, *v.* train, tame, VIII *a* 32 (note). [OFr. *afait(i)er*.]

Affecoyon, *n.* affection, (worldly) desire, IV *b* 52, 71. [L. *affectiōn-em* through OFr.]

Af(f)erme, *v.* affirm, IX 77, XI *c* 50; confirm, IX 305. [OFr. *afermer*.]

Affie, *v.* to have (faith in), XVI 29. [OFr. *afier*.]

Afforces (*thame*), *pres. pl.* (*refl.*) endeavour, IV *b* 20. [OFr. *s'afforcer*.]

Affray, *n.* fear, XII *a* 142. [OFr. *e(s)frai*.]

Afine, *adv.* to the end, II 277. [OFr. *a fin*.]

Afore, *adv.* beforehand, XVII 164. [OE. *æt-foran*.]

Aforth, *v.* to afford, VIII *a* 192. [OE. (late) *ge-forðian*, to manage.]

Afright, *pp. Not afright*, undeterred, XVII 541. [OE. *ā-fyrht*.]

After (-ir, -yr, -ur), *adv.* after, behind, II 378, VII 24, XVI 376, &c.; afterwards, then, VII 46, VIII *a* 5, &c.; *be the whiche . . . after*, in accordance with which (mixed Fr. and E. constr.), IX 302; *prep.* after, next to, I 215, XI *b* 27, &c.; according to, IX 220, 291, XI *b* 189, &c.; for (after *desire, ask*, &c.), VII 20, VIII *a* 291, XV *h* 5, XVI 242, &c.; *conj.* after, XVII 148. *After þan*, afterwards, II 597. [OE. *æfter; æfter þām*.]

Afterward, Aftyrward(e), &c., *adv.* afterwards, II 164, IV *b* 59, XI *b* 147, &c.; **Efterward**, III 16, 35, 38, 48. [OE. *æfterweard* (Kt. *efter-*).]

Agayn(e), Agane, *adv.* back, again, IV *b* 83, XVI 11, XVII 180, 479, &c. *See* Aȝayn.

Agaynes, *prep.* against, IV *b* 18, 19. [Prec. + adv. *-es*.] *See* Aȝeines.

Agaynste, *prep.* against, XVI 280;
to loke a., to gaze on, XVI 92.
[Extended from prec.]

Agast, *pp.* afraid, XIV *c* 51, XVII
184, 297; astonished, XVII 449.
[*a-* + OE. *gæsted*, afflicted.]
See Gastli.

Age, *n.* age, time of life, VI 52,
XII *introd.*; mature age, IX 22;
old age, VII 6, XIV *c* 106, &c.
[OFr. *age*.]

Ago, *pp.* gone by, XII *a* 34. [OE.
ā-gān.]

Agrete, *adv.* collectively, as a
body, VI 200. [OE. *on* + *grēat*.]

Agreued (*for*), *pp.* weighed down
(with), V 302; annoyed (by),
I 88. [OFr. *agrever*.]

Aȝayn, *adv.* again, back, V 53,
257, 332; **Aȝe,** XIII *a* 8; **Aȝein,**
Aȝeyn, I 230, VIII *a* 44, XII *a* 28,
&c.; **Aȝen,** IX 132; **Oȝain,** II
141, 162. [OE. *ongēn, ongegn*.]

Aȝayn, Aȝen, Aȝein, Aye, Oȝain,
prep. against, III 58, V 48, IX 19;
towards (of time), II 497, XII *b*
18. [As prec.] *See* Agayn.

Aȝeines, *prep.* against, contrary to,
VIII *a* 309, 311, 315; **Aȝenes,**
XIII *b* 17; **Aȝens,** I 261, 264,
VIII *b* 78; **Aȝenus,** XI *a* 29.
[Prec. + adv. *-es*.] *See* Agaynes.

Aȝenst, *prep.* against, IX 92, 315,
XI *b* 43, 46, 97. [Extended from
prec.] *See* Agaynste.

Aȝleȝ, *adj.* without fear, V 267.
[ON. *agi* + OE. *-lēas*.] *See*
Awe.

A-hungrye, *adj.* hungry, XVII 499.
[*a-* + OE. *hungrig*.]

Ai, Ay, *adv.* always, ever, IV *a* 1,
14, VII 18, X 61, XV *a* 10, 17, &c.;
for ay, for ever, XVII 26. [ON.
ei.]

Ay, *n.* fear, in *for loue or ay*, in any
event, II 571. [OE. *ege*.]

Aye. *See* Aȝayn.

Ayenbyte, *n.* remorse. *See* III
introd. [OE. *ongēn* + *bite*.]

Ayere, Aire, *n.* air, IV *b* 5, VII
107, 110. [OFr. *air*.]

Aire, *n.* heir, VIII *b* 62. [OFr.
(*h*)*eir*.]

Ays. *See* Ese.

Aither, Ayþer, Athir, Eyþer,
adj. and *pron.* both, VII 65;
either, V 112; *eyþer oþer*, each
other, XIII *b* 57; *athir othir in*,
one in the other, X 22. [OE.
ǣgþer, both; *ā(w)þer*, either.]
See Euþer.

Ayther, Aþer, *conj.* or, VI 131;
ayther .. or, either .. or, XVII
477. [As prec.] *See* Or²; Oþer,
conj.

Aywhere, *adv.* on all sides, V 113.
[OE. *ǣghwǣr*.]

Aketh, *pres. pl.* ache, VIII *a* 253
(*see* Wombe). [OE. *acan*.]

Akyng, *n.* aching, XI *b* 136.

Al, *adj.* all, I 120, II 114, III 6,
&c.; **Alle,** I 19, &c.; *pl.* III 55,
&c.; *al*(*l*) *a*(*n*), a whole, VII 183,
VIII *a* 253, XIII *a* 32, 44, XIV *c* 4;
al(*le*) *maner*(*e*), all kinds of,
II 589, XI *a* 12 (*cf.* Alkyn);
al(*le*) *þing*(*e*), see þing; *all way,*
weys, see Alway, Way; *all it*
(*þei, we*), all of it (them, us),
XV *g* 16, IX 104, XVII 456, &c.;
here names of alle, the names of
them all, I 37; *of al and sum,*
in general and particular, in full,
VI 224; as *sb.* all, XVI 303, &c.;
every one (with *sg.* verb), VI 87.
[OE. *al*(*l*).] *See* Algate, Alkyn,
Alsaume, &c.

Al, All(**e**), *adv.* entirely, quite,
very, I 108, II 76, V 304, VIII
a 138, &c.; in comb. with To-
II 81, 106, 262, IV *a* 78, VII 147;
with For-, II 398, XV *c* 29. *Al*
away, quite away, IV *a* 75; *al*
one, alone, V 87, XII *a* 131, *b* 15;
al oon, all one (and the same
thing), XI *a* 41; *al to*, up to (the
number of), III 56; *all be* (*were*)
it þat, although, IX 50, 171, 302,
312; *all if*, although, XVII 231.
[OE. *al*(*l*).]

Al, All(**e**), *n.* all, everything, III
43, 51, &c.; *about al*, in all
directions, II 387; *ouer al*,
everywhere, II 208 (OE. *ofer*
all). [OE. *al*(*l*).]

Aldai, Al day, *adv.* all day, VI

166, XII *introd*. [OE. *alne dæg*.]

Alde. *See* Olde.

Alepy, *adj*. (a) single, I 159. [OE. *ănlĕpig*.]

Algate, *adv*. by all means, at any rate, I 107, II 231. [*Cf*. ON. *alla götu*, all along, always.] *See* Gate, *n²*.

Algatis, *adv*. continually, XI *a* 38. [Prec. + adv. *-es*.]

Aliens, *n. pl*. foreigners, XIII *b* 61. [OFr. *alien*.]

Aliȝt, Alihte, *v*. to alight, II 377, XII *a* 76. [OE. *ā-lihtan*.] *See* Liȝt, *v²*.

Aliri, *adv*. ⸮ across one another (of legs), VIII *a* 116. [⸮ Related to Lyre, *n²*.]

Alis, *v*. *See* Eyleþ.

Alyue, *adj*. living, VI 85. [OE. *on life*.]

Alkyn, *adj*. of all kinds, VIII *a* 70. [OE. **alra cynna*.] *See* Kyn.

Allas, *interj*. alas! II 107, &c. [OFr. *alas*.]

Alleg(g)e(n), *v*. to cite (in support of a contention), XI *b* 56, XVI 277; to contend, XI *b* 79. [OFr. *esligier, aligier*, associated with unrelated L. *allēgāre*.]

Allowe, *v*. approve, receive with approval, XVI 330; Alod, *pp*. XVII 56 (note). [OFr. *alouer*, from L. *allaudāre*.]

Allþough,⸰ Althogh, *conj*. (even) though, IX 110, XII *b* 196, &c. [Al, *adv*. + þogh, *q.v*.]

Allweldand, *adj*. almighty, XVII 494. [Cf. OE. *alwäldende*.]

Almes(se), *n. sg*. an act, or works, of charity, charitable gift or offering, VIII *a* 121, 140, XI *b* 2, 163, 270, &c.; **Elmesses** *pl*. (OKt. *elmessan*), III 17. [OE. *ælmesse*.]

Almyȝt, *adj*. almighty, VI 138. [OE. *æl-miht*.]

Almyty, -myghty, *adj*. almighty, VIII *b* 105, XV *i* 12. [OE. *æl-mihtig*.]

Alofte, *adv*. in the air, aloft, V 220,

XII *a* 94, &c. [ON. *ā loft*.] *See* Lofte.

Alod, *pp*. *See* Allowe.

Alone, *adj*. alone, XVII 489; *see* Al, *adv*.

Als, *adv*. also, as well, V 292, VIII *a* 148, X 8, 11, XVII 126, 127. [Reduced form of Also, *q.v*.]

Als, Alss, *conj*. as (*esp*. in *als . . as*, as . . as), like, IV *a* 2, 63, 84, *b* 86, VIII *a* 37, &c.; as for instance, like, XVI 306, 308, 311; as, while, IV *b* 43, XV *a* 4; *als . . þat*, so . . that, IX 151; *als b(i)liue*, as quickly (as possible), straightway, II 531, 584. [As prec.] *See* As.

Alsaume, *adv*. (all) together, I 98. [Cf. ON. *allir saman*.] *See* Sam(e), *adv*.

Also, Alsua (X), *adv*. also, as well, I 35, II 144, X 33, &c.; *conj*. like, II 508; *also bliue, also spac, also swiþe*, as quickly (as possible), straightway, II 142, 343, 574. [OE. *al-swā*.] *See* Als, As.

Al(1)way,-wey, *adv*. always, (for) ever, continually, XIII *a* 3, *b* 63, XVI 150, 168, &c; in any case, certainly, XVI 164. [OE. *alne weg*.] *See* Algate(s).

Am, I *sg. pres. ind*. am, V 90, &c.; coalescing with prec. pron. in Icham, Ycham (*q.v*.). [OE. *am*.] *See* Ar, Art, Is, &c.

Amaistrien, *v*. to master, control, VIII *a* 205. [OFr. *amaistrier*.]

Amang, *adv*. in the meanwhile, XVII 247; **Emang,** at times, from time to time, XVI 262, 301. [OE. *on-(ge)máng*.] *See* Amonge.

Ame, *v*. to guess; *as y kan ame*, I guess, I 45. [OFr. *aesmer, amer*.]

Amend(e), *v*. to make better, reform, set right, VIII *a* 268, IX 338, XI *a* 48, XVII 256. [OFr. *amender*.] *See* Mend(e).

Amendement, *n*. improvement, cure, I 238, II 200, VIII *a* 132. [OFr. *amendement*.]

Amercy, *v.* to fine, VIII *a* 40.
[OFr. *amercier.*]

Amidde, *prep.* in the middle of,
II 355. [OE. *on-middan.*]

Amiddes, *adv.* in the midst, XII *a*
170; *prep.* (from) among, II 191.
[Prec. + adv. *-es.*]

Amys, *adv.* amiss, VIII *a* 322.
[ON. *á miss.*] *See* Mysse.

Amoner, *n.* almoner, alms-giver,
III 16. [OFr. *aumoner.*]

Among(e), *prep.* among, II 220,
VIII *a* 89, &c.; Emang, Emong,
XVII 112; (follows noun) XVII
400. [OE. *on-(ge)máng.*] *See*
Amang, Mong.

Amonges, *prep.* amongst, II 306,
VII 37, &c. [Prec. + adv. *-es.*]

Amorwe, *adv.* on the next day,
II 181, 497. [OE. *on morgene.*]

An, And, Ant, *conj.* and, I 254,
VIII *a* 205, XI *a* 1, XV *b* 11, *d* 2,
e 6, *g* 25, 26, *i* 5, &c.; *an te,* and
the, XV *e* 19; if, II 43, VI 200,
238, VIII *a* 250, XIII *a* 44, *b* 39,
XIV *c* 14, 103, XVI 208 (even if),
XVII 297, 502. On postpone-
ment of *and* in Gower see note
to XII *a* 26. [OE. *and.*]

Ancres, *n. pl.* anchorites, religious
recluses, VIII *a* 139. [OE. *áncra.*]

Andzuerede. *See* Ansuere.

Ane, *indef. art.* a, X 5, 16, 31, &c.;
representing older inflected
forms, III 11 (first), 13, 49;
adj. one, a single, IV *a* 58, X 157;
(predicatively) one, united, IV *a*
56; *pron.* one, IV *b* 1, 43; a
certain person, IV *a* 69, X 169.
See A(n), On(e).

Ane, *prep.* on; *ane his lhordes
haf,* on his master's behalf, III
11. [From OE. *on, an,* on anal.
of *in, inne.*]

Anely, *adv.* only, IV *b* 81. [OE.
ánlic, adj.] *See* Onely.

Anewe, *adv.* once more, XV *a* 22.
[*a-* + OE. *níowe.*]

Angelis. *See* Aungel.

Anger, *n.* grief, V 276. [ON.
angr, grief.]

Angré, *adj.* angry, XVII 187.
[From prec.]

Angwys, *n.* grief, IV *b* 28. [OFr.
anguisse.]

Ani, Any, *adj.* any, I 2, 18, II 528,
&c. [OE. *ǽnig.*] *See* Eny,
Ony.

Animal, *n.* II 364, a misreading
for aumal *q.v.*

Anodir. *See* Anoþire.

Anoynt, *v.* to smear, XVII 127.
[Formed on OFr. *enoint* pp. of
enoindre.]

Anon(e), *adv.* at once, straightway,
next, II 385, 499, VI 224, XVII
490, 526, &c.; Onone, VII 149,
XVII 275. [OE *on án.*]

Anothire, Anoþer, *adj.* and *pron.*
another, IV *b* 3, 34, IX 37, &c.;
Anoþur, XIV *c* 27; Anouþer,
I 140; Anodir, XVI 87. [OE.
án + óþer.]

Anouȝ. *See* Ynoȝ.

*****Anowrned,** *pp.* adorned, II 363
(MS. anowed). [OFr. *aourner*;
? *a-* to *an-* on anal. of E. alternation *a-, an-.*]

Ansuer(e), Answere, *v.* to
answer, III 5, 25, IX 178, XII *b*
76; Andzuerede, *pa. t.* III 33.
[OE. *an(d)swerian.*]

Answar, *n.* answer, VI 158. [OE.
an(d)swaru.]

Ant. *See* An, *conj.*

Antifeners, *n. pl.* antiphonaries,
XI *b* 229 (note). [OFr. *anti-
phonier.*]

Apayed, *pp.* pleased, satisfied,
VIII *a* 102, 189. [OFr. *apaier.*]
See Paie.

Apassed, *pp.* as *prep.* past, VI 180.
[OFr. *apasser.*]

Ap(p)ere, Appiere, *v.* to appear,
VI 45, XII *a* 132, XVI 368, XVII
173. [OFr. *aper-*; *apareir.*]

Ap(p)eyre, *v.* to do harm to,
injure, impair, VIII *a* 126, 164,
212, XIII *b* 14; Apeyryng, *n.*
impairing, XIII *b* 15. [OFr. *empeirer.*] *See* Empeyre.

Apert, *adj.* plain, V 324; *adv.*
openly, plainly, I 200, VI 229;
for all to see, II 586. [OFr.
apert.]

Apon. *See* Vpon.

Aposede, *pa. t.* put a (hard) question to, VIII *b* 10. [OFr. *oposer, aposer.*]

Apostel, *n.* apostle, XI *a* 12, *b* 15, ·99, 273, &c. [OE. *apostol.*] *See* Posteles.

Apparaille, *v.* to dress, VIII *a* 59. [OFr. *aparailler.*]

Apparale, *n.* preparations, apparatus, gear, X 3, 14, 44, 119. [OFr. *aparail.*]

Apparence, *n.* appearance, XII *a* 127. [OFr. *ap(p)arence.*]

Appetit (*to*), *n.* desire, appetite (for), VIII *a* 261, IX 15, XII *a* 87. [OFr. *apetit.*]

Appiereth. *See* Ap(p)ere.

Approprid, *pp.* assigned as personal property, XI *b* 97. [OFr. *aproprier.*]

Aquit, *pp.* requited, XII *b* 138, 197. [OFr. *aquiter.*]

Ar, *conj.* before (usually with *subj.*), VIII *a* 93, 196, 258, 261, 269, XV *g* 33, &c. [OE. *ār*, and with weak stress *ĕr*(!).] *See* Are; Er(e), *adv.*; Or.

Ar(e), *pres. ind. pl.* are, IV *b* 18, V 9, 27, &c.; Aren, VIII *a* 268, 270, &c.; Arn(e), II 13, VI 24, 42, &c. [OE. (Nth.) *aron.*] *See* Art, Er(e), Ben, &c.

Aray, *n.* array, X 68; rank, estate, VI 131; *of aray*, stately, XVII 539 (or *grete of aray*, great in magnificence). [OFr. *arei.*]

Arayed, *pp.* arranged, XIII *a* 1. [OFr. *areyer.*]

Aratede, *pa. t.* rebuked, VIII *b* 11. [Unknown.]

Archidekenes, *n. pl.* archdeacons, VIII *b* 75. [OE. *ærce-diacon*, OFr. *archedekne.*] *See* Dyacne.

Are, *adv.* before, I 93, XVI 38, 98, 345. [ON. *ár* (! late Nth. *ar*); but see Ar, *conj.*]

Arered, *pp.* raised, set up, XIII *a* 11, 13, &c. [OE. *ā-rǣran.*]

Arȝe (*wyth*), *v.* to be terrified, quail (at), V 203, 209, 233. [OE. *eargian.*]

Aryȝt, *adv.* rightly, right well, XIII *b* 46; **Ariht**, XII *a* 67,

XIV *c* 61. [OE. *on-riht, ariht.*]

Arise, Aryse, *v.* to arise, rise, get up, come to pass, II 311, VIII *a* 112, 261, 319, *b* 15; Aros, *pa t. sg.* II 318, XV *g* 1 (note). [OE. *ā-rīsan.*]

Arm(e), *n.* arm, I 112, VII 162, &c.; embrace, XII *a* 161. [OE. *earm.*]

Armes, *n. pl.* arms, weapons, (knightly) warfare, II 182, IX 109, &c. [OFr. *armes.*]

Armyt, Armed, *pp.* armed, II 395, X 7, 37, &c.; Y-armed, II 136, 184, 292. [OFr. *armer.*]

Arn(e). *See* Ar(e), *v.*

Arryuen, Aryue, *v.* to come to land, IX 184; to come (to a destination), VI 87. [OFr. *arriver.*]

Art, 2 *sg. pres. ind.* art, I 202, 204, II 422, &c.; Artow, art thou, II 421 (*see* Þou); Ert, VIII *b* 34. [OE. *eart.*]

Artetykes, *adj. pl.* arthritic, accompanied with inflammation of the joints, IX 314. *See* Gowtes. [OFr. *artetique*, corruptly from L. *arthrīticus.*]

Arwes, *n. pl.* arrows, IX 258. [OE. *earh.*]

As(e), *conj.* as, I 24, II 290, III 48, &c.; *as . . . as* (foll. by accus.), XVII 19; *as that*, as, XVII 182; *as hys desserte*, according to his deserts, VI 235; even as, seeing that, XVII 427, 552; *as euer*, as sure as ever, XVII 237, 395; so (in oaths, &c.), V 55, &c.; as if (usually with *subj.*) I 31, 121, 195, II 108, 402, V 106, 133, 134, 189, 194, 221, 326, VII 45; as relative particle, I *introd.*, XVII 325; *as swyþe, tyte*, straightway, I 111, XVII 219. [Further reduced from Als, *q.v.*]

Asalis. *See* Assaylle.

Askes, *n. pl.* ashes, XIII *a* 4. [OE. *axe.*]

Aske(n), Aski (II), *v.* to ask for, demand, I 131, II 450, 467, VI 220, &c.; require, VIII *b* 71;

inquire, I 132, IX 176. [OE.
āxian.] *See* Axe(n).

Aspien, Asspye, *v.* to detect,
observe, VIII *a* 123, 217, XI *a*
60; Aspide, *pa. t.* III 42. [OFr.
espier.] *See* Spie.

Assai, Assay, *n.* test, trial; *at*
assai, when put to the test,
XIV *c* 5; *set in, till, hard(e)*
assay, place in sore straits, X 62,
170, 188. [OFr. *essai, assai*.]

Assaie, Assay(e), Asay, *v.* to
test, prove, make trial, II 452,
568, V 294, IX 61, 102, 121, XIV *c*
66, XVII 219, 249, 433; to endeavour, VIII *a* 24, XII *b* 81.
[OFr. *essayer*.] *See* Saye.

Assaylle, As(s)ale, Assa(i)lȝe
(X), *v.* to assail, attack, IX 88, X 4,
12, 43, 114, 132, 144, XVII 295,
&c.; Assaling, *n.* assault, X 41,
60. [OFr. *as(s)aillir*.]

Asse, *n.* ass, XV *f* 5, &c. [OE.
assa.]

Assemblid (*to*), *pa. t.* assembled
(at), VII 85. [OFr. *assembler*.]

Assembly, *n.* joining of battle,
VII 57. [OFr. *assemblee*.]

Assende, *v.* to ascend, XVI 32.
[OFr. *ascendre*.]

Assent, *pp.* sent for, XII *b* 208.
See Of-sende.

As(s)ente, *n.* agreement; compliance, VI 31; *of þare assente*,
of like mind with them, XVI 310.
[OFr. *asente*.]

Assent(e), *v.* to agree, VIII *a* 39,
57; *pp.* XVI 170. [OFr.
asentir.]

Assoylled, *pp.* absolved, IX 286.
[OFr. *assoillir*.]

Asspye. *See* Aspien.

As(s)tate, *n.* estate, (high) rank,
VI 33, 130, VII 21. [OFr.
estat.] *See* State.

Astrangled, *pp.* choked, II 396.
[OFr. *estrangler*.]

Asunder, -yr, *adv.* apart, I 224;
pleon. with *parte*, I 103. [OE.
on-sundran.] *See* Sonder.

Aswon(e), *adj.* in a swoon, I 195
(note), II 549. [OE. *geswōgen*.]
See Falle(n); Swone.

At, *prep.* at, I 13, 74, &c.; in,
VII 66, VIII *a* 63; IX 253; *at*
wordes, in words, II 139; (of
time) V 23, 100, IX 284, XI *a*
12; to, V 108, VII 13; with
infin. (*at do*), *see* Do; according
to, I 82, II 271, XIV *b* 56, XVI
258, XVII 4, 322; at the value
of, VIII *a* 162, *b* 101, XVII 364;
at the hands of, from, I 239, 240.
245, II 179, III 4. 31 (*see* Atte).
At on, at one, in accord, VI 18;
at þe full, completely XI *b* 198;
haue at þe, *see* Habbe(n). [OE.
æt.] *See* Atte; Þare.

At, *rel. particle*; *þat at*, that
which, what, VI 176 (note);
quhar at, *see* Whar. [ON. *at*;
þat at is possibly for *þat tat* (cf.
Atte, Þou, &c.).]

Ate. *See* Atte.

Atempree, *adj.* temperate, IX 29.
[OFr. *atempré*.]

Aþer, Athir. *See* Aither, Ayther.

At-hold, *v.* to restrain, II 88.
[OE. *æt-* + *háldan*.]

Atire, *n.* apparel, II 299. [From
next.]

Atire, *v.*; Atird, *pp.* equipped,
II 158. [OFr. *atir(i)er*.] *See*
Tired.

Atled, *pa. t.* intended, V 195.
[ON. *ætla*.]

Ato, *adv.* in two, apart, II 125,
IX 140; Atwo, VIII *a* 97.
[OE. *on twā*.] *See* A(n) *prep*.;
Tuo.

Atour, *n.* apparatus, equipment,
X 125. [OFr. *atour(n)*.]

Atourned, *pp.* equipped, II 291.
[OFr. *atourner*.]

Atrete, *adv.* straight out, plainly,
XIV *c* 78. [OFr. *a trait*.]

Atslyke, *v.* to slip away; *atsly-*
keȝ, is spent, VI 215. [OE. *æt-*
+ *slícan*.]

Atte, Ate, at the, II 232, 379,
III 4, VIII *a* 96, *b* 29; of the,
III 31; in fixed expressions
where Mn. E. has 'at', as:
atte chirche, VIII *a* 50; *at(t)e*
firste, last(e), mete, *see* Furste,
Laste, Mete; *atte nale* = *atten*

(OE. *æt þam*) *ale*, over the ale, VIII *a* 109. *See* At.

Atteynte, *v.* to convict, prove guilty, XVI 278. [From *ateint*, convicted, pp. of OFr. *ateindre*.]

Atteny, *v.* to reach, VI 188. [OFr. *ateign-*, stem of *ateindre*.]

Atwynne, *adv.* in two, I 189, 191. [OE. *on* + *twinn*.]

Atwo, Avay. *See* Ato, Awai.

Avayll, Avale, *v.* to be of use to, XVII 154; *it avalis you*, (it) is your best course, XVII 296. [*a-* + OFr. *vail-*, *valeir*.]

Avale, Availl (X), *v. intr.* to descend, IX 195; *trans.* to let down, X 28. [OFr. *avaler*.]

Avauntage, *n.* advantage, XIII *b* 35, 36. [OFr. *avantage*.]

Auctorité, *n.* authority, XI *b* 61. [OFr. *au(c)torité*.]

Auctour, *n.* original authority, author, IX 304; Autours, *pl.* XI *a* 23. [OFr. *autour*, and (from 14th c.) *auctour*, &c.]

Audience, *n.* formal hearing, audience, XII *b* 209. [OFr.]

Aue Maria, an Ave, Hail Mary, IX 323. [First two words of Latin prayer.]

Auentur(e), Auentour, *n.* chance, (notable) occurrence, feat, II 15, 18, 32, &c.; risk, X 118; *an auenture*, (as *conj.*) in case, VIII *a* 43; *at auentur*, as chance directed, recklessly, XIV *c* 34. [OFr. *aventure*.] *See* Aunter.

Aueril, *n.* April, XV *c* 1. [OFr. *avril*.]

Auȝt. *See* Owe, *v.*

Avys, *n.* deliberation, IX 295, 297. [OFr. *avis*.]

Avised, *pp.*; *wel avised*, judicious, XII *b* 217. [OFr. *aviser*.]

Aumal, *n.* enamel, II 364. [OFr. *aumail*.]

Aungel(l), *n.* angel, IV *a* 46, XI *b* 23, XVI 339, 389; Angel, XI *b* 152, &c. [OFr. *a(u)ngel*.]

Aunsetris, *n. pl.* ancestors, men of former days, VII 5. [OFr. *ancestre*, nom. sg.]

Aunter, *n.* chance, event, VII 5, 67, 155. [As Auentur; but due to older and more popular borrowing.]

Auter(e), *n.* altar, I 74, 76. [OFr. *auter*.]

Autours. *See* Auctour.

Auþer. *See* Oþer, *adv.* and *conj.*

Awai, Away(e), Awei(e), Awey(e), *adv.* away, VIII *a* 184, XII *b* 132, &c.; Avay, X 58, 187; Oway, II 192, 261, 329; Owy (in rime), II 96, 491, 561; *don awei*, abolished, XI *b* 206; *wanne awaye*, rescued, XVI 171; *predic.*, gone, over, II 59 (*oway*), XVII 537. [OE. *on-weg*, *aweg*; ‖ with *owy*, cf. rare OE. *wig*.]

Awake, *v. intr.* to be aroused, wake up, II 77, VIII *a* 318, *b* 1, &c.; *trans.* to wake, II 73; Awake, *pp.* wakened, XV *g* 14. [OE. *ā-wæcnan*, str.; *ā-wacian*, wk.; both intr.] *See* Forwake, Wackenet, Wake.

Awangelys, *n. pl.* gospels, XV *i* 6. [L. *ēvangelium*.] *See* Euaungelistis.

Awe. *See* Owe, *v.*

Awe, *n.* fear; *for Crystys awe*, for fear of Christ, I 83. [ON. *agi*.] *See* Aȝleȝ.

Awede, *v.* go mad, II 87; Awedde, *pp.* (gone) mad, II 400. [OE. *ā-wēdan*.] *See* Wode, *adj.*

Aweyward, *adv.* (turned) in the opposite direction, XIII *a* 35. [OE. *onweg* + adv. *-ward*.]

Awen, Awne. *See* Owen, *adj.*

Awenden, *pa. t. pl.* thought, XV *g* 17. [*a-* + OE. *wēnan*.] *See* Wene(n).

Awharf, *pa. t. sg.* turned aside, V 152. [OE. *ā-hweorfan*.]

Aworthe. *See* Yworth.

Awreke (*of*), *v.* to avenge (on), VIII *a* 166; Awroke, *pp.* VIII *a* 195. [OE. *ā-wrecan*.] *See* Wreke.

Ax, *n.* axe, V 155, XIV *e* 1, &c. [OE. *æx*.]

Axe(n), v. to ask, demand, inquire (of), VIII *a* 291, XI *b* 207, XII *a* 145, &c. ; **Acsede,** *pa. t.* III 4, 25, 31. [OE. *áxian.*] *See* Aske(n).

Babelynge, *n.* babbling, XI *b* 84. [Echoic; *cf.* Blabre.]
Bad(de). *See* Bidde.
Bagge, *n.* wallet (for food), VIII *b* 54. [ON. *baggi.*]
Bayarde, *n.* bay horse (as typical horse name); *þat was bake for B.* = coarse horse-bread, VIII *a* 187. [OFr. *baiard.*] *See* Bred.
Bayle, Bayll. *See* Bale.
Bayly, *n.* dominion, VI 82. [OFr. *baillie.*]
Bailyues, *n. pl.* bailiffs, managers of estates, XI *b* 288. [OFr. *baillif.*]
Baill, *n.*[1] wall (of the outer court in a feudal castle), XVI 195; Bale, prison, custody, XVI 161 (but this may belong to Bale, *q.v.*). [OFr. *bail.*]
Baill, *n.*[2] bundle, X 27. [OFr. *bale.*]
Bayn, *adj.* obedient, V 90, XVII 308. [ON. *bein -n,* direct.]
Bair. *See* Bare.
Bak, Bac (II), **Backe,** *n.* back, II 344, VII 126, XVII 264, &c. ; *bak and bone,* all over the body, XVII 407. [OE. *bæc.*]
Bake(n), *pp.* baked, VIII *a* 187, 288, 305; Ybake(n), VIII *a* 175, 278. [OE. *bacan.*]
Bakoun, Bacoun, *n.* bacon, VIII *a* 279, 304. [OFr. *bacun.*]
Balde. *See* Bold.
Bale ; Bayle, Bayll (XVII); *n.* torment, misery, sorrow, IV *a* 77, V 351, VI 13, XIV *a* 28, XVI 275, XVII 26, 311, 552, &c. ; at XVI 161 'torment' is possible, but *see* Bail, *n.*[1] [OE. *balu*].
Balȝ, *adj.* rounded, or ? with level surface, V 104 (*cf.* Sir Gaw. 2032, and Prompt. Parv. *balwe,* planus).
Balkes, *n. pl.* (unploughed) ridges

in a field, VIII *a* 101. [OE. *balc(a).*]
Ban, *v.* to curse, XIV *b* 94, XVII 94; Banned (*MS.*) I 188, ! read Bende (*q.v.*). [OE. *bannan,* proclaim ; ON. *banna,* forbid, curse.]
Bandis. *See* Bond.
Bane. *See* Bon.
Baner, *n.* banner, II 294, XIV *a* 8. [OFr. *banere.*]
Bank(k)es. *See* Bonk(e).
Baptiste, *pa. t.* baptizeȝ, XVI 75. [OFr. *baptiser*]
Barbe, *n.* cutting edge, V 242. [OFr. *barbe,* beard, barb (of arrow, spear, &c.).]
Bard, *pp.* penned, XVII 328. [OFr. *barrer.*] *See* Barres, Vnbarred.
Bare, Bair (x), *adj.* bare, naked, V 9, 188, VII 164, X 190, &c.; *on bonkes bare,* XIV *b* 20; despoiled, XIV *a* 20; bald (in style), VII 74; mere, V 284, X 113. [OE. *bær.*]
Bar(e), Bare(n). *See* Bore, *n.*; Bere, *v.*
Barely, *adv.* openly, XIV *b* 94; summarily, VII 68. [OE. *bærlíce.*]
Baret, *n.* strife, V 47 (*see* Bend). [OFr. *barat.*]
Barfot, *adj.* barefoot, II 232. [OE. *bær-fōt.*]
Barga(y)n, *n.* bargain, VIII *b* 100, XVII 94. [OFr. *bargaine.*]
Barge, *n.* a smaller sea-going ship belonging to a larger vessel, XIV *c* 53, 65 ; ship, VII 90. [OFr. *barge.*]
Barly, *n.* (as *adj.*) barley, VIII *a* 129. [OE. *bærlíc.*]
Barm, *n.* lap, XV *g* 13. [OE. *bearm.*]
Barm-fellys, *n. pl.* leather aprons, XV *h* 11. [OE. *bearm + fell* ; *cf. bearm-cláþ,* &c.]
Barne, *n.* child, VI 66, XVII 308, 419 ; *barnes bastardes,* bastards, VIII *b* 75. [OE. *bearn.*]
Barouns, *n. pl.* barons, II 201, 503, 550. [OFr. *barun.*]
Barras, *n.* defensive outwork, X 164. [OFr. *barras.*]

Barres, *n. pl.* bars, XVI 190.
[OFr. *barre.*]

Barste. *See* Brest(e).

Bastardes, *n. pl.* bastards; as
adj., VIII *b* 75. [OFr. *bastard.*]

Baston, *n.* stave, stanza, Introduction xv. [OFr. *baston.*]

Batail(e), Bataill, Batayl,
Batel(l), *n.* embattled host,
XIV *b* 52; battle, VII 56, 91,
*XI *b* 154, XIV *b* 31, XVI 131,
&c. [OFr. *bataille.*]

Bataild, *adj.* embattled, with
battlements, II 360. [Modelled
on OFr. *bataillé.*]

Bath. *See* Boþe.

Batis, *n. pl.* boats X 123. [OE.
bāt.]

Baþe, *v.* to bathe (*trans.* and
intr.), II 585, XIII *a* 25. [OE.
baþian.]

Baundoun, *n.* control; *in hire
baundoun*, at her disposal, XV *c*
8. [OFr. *bandun.*]

Be, *conj.* by the time (that), X 157.
Cf. *bi þat. See* next.

Be, Beo (XIV *c* 44), *prep.* by (way
of), IX 179, 192, 198; through,
IX 112, 136, 137; (of *time*)
by, at, in, VI 163, IX 204, 339,
XII *a* 117, 131, XV *i* 15, 20;
by (means of), through, III 22,
VII 23, IX 67, 130, XII *a* 23,
b 199, XVI 355, &c.; by (of
agent), III 30, IX 112 (first), 298,
305, XII *b* 217, &c.; by (in
oaths, &c.), XII *b* 45, 164.
Counted . . beo, set value on, XIV
c 44; for idiomatic expressions
see the nouns. [OE. *be.*] *See* Bi.

Be-. *See also* Bi-, By-.

Becam, Becomen. *See* Bicome.

Beclipte, *pa. t.* embraced, XII
a 178; Byclypped, *pp.* en-
circled, XIII *a* 21. [OE. *be-
clyppan.*]

Bede, *v.* to bid, offer, V 254, XIV *a*
9; Bede, *pa. t. sg.* (bade), V 22;
offered, 180, 284. [OE. *bēodan*,
early confused with *biddan.*]
See Bidde, Forbede.

Bed(e). *See* Bidde.

Bedd(e), Bede (IV), *n.* bed, II
93, 242, XII *a* 99, &c.; *dat. sg.*
in *to bedde*, to bed, VIII *a* 93,
XII *b* 105; *þe bede of blysse*, ? the
joyful bridal bed (of Christ and
the soul), IV *a* 11. [OE. *bedd.*]
See Abedde.

Bedes, *n. pl.* prayers, I 16. [OE.
ge-bed.]

Bedeyn. *See* Bidene.

Bedele, *n.* herald, one who delivers
the message of an authority, XI *b*
48. [OE. *bydel*; OFr. *bedel.*]

Bedreden, *n. pl.* the bedridden,
VIII *a* 185, *b* 21. [OE. *bedd-
reda.*]

Bee, Bees. *See* Ben.

Beest. *See* Best(e), *n.*

Befalle, *v.* to happen, chance,
IX 129, &c.; to befall, XVII
514; *pa. t. sg.* Befell(e), VII
67, 155; Bevil, Bifel, it
chanced, II 57, III 41; Be-
falle(n), *pp.* II 21, IX 194.
[OE. *be-fallan.*] *See* Falle(n).

Begge, to beg, VIII *a* 186, 233,
b 29, &c. [? OE. *bedecian*; see
N.E.D.]

Begger(e), *n.* beggar, II 483, 499,
VIII *a* 188, 197, &c. [See
N.E.D.]

Begyn(ne), Bigin(ne), By-
gyn(ne), &c., *v.* to begin, act,
do, come about, I 69, IV *b* 57,
VI 187, VIII *a* 160, XIV *b* 25,
c 83, XVI 268, 280, XVII 267,
&c.; *begyn of*, b. with, XVII
253; Be-, Bi-, Bygan, *pa. t.
sg.* began, I 154, &c.; did, XV
a 7; came to pass, II 598;
made (it) in the beginning,
XVII 29; Bygan, *pa. t. pl.* I 7;
Bygonne, VI 189; Begouth,
X 94; Begonne, *pp.* IX 171;
Be-, Bygynnyng(e), *n.* IV
b 58, IX 334, XIII *b* 9. [OE. *be-
ginnan; begouth* is due to confusion of *gan* with *can* (*couþe*);
See Gan; Can, *auxil.*]

Begynnar, Bygynner, *n.* beginner, causer, VI 76, XVII 406.
[From prec.]

Begon, *pp.* adorned, XII *a* 54
[OE. *be-gān.*]

Begonne, Begouth. *See* Begynne.

Bezonde, *adv.* beyond, further on, IX 263, 280. [OE. *be-geóndan*.]

Bezonde, Bezounde (1), Bizonde (V), *prep.* across, beyond, I 252, V 132, IX 8, 76, 135, &c.; *see* See. [As prec.]

Behald(e). *See* Bihold.

Behalue, *n.* behalf; *on Goddes b.*, in God's name, I 78. [Originally *be* prep. and *halfe* dat. sg.; *cf.* Half.]

Beheste, *n.* promise, XII *b* 196. [OE. (late) *be-hǽs*.] *See* Heste.

Behete. *See* Bihote.

Behevin, *pp.* hewn down, X 163. [OE. *be-héawan*.]

Behielde, -helde. *See* Bihold.

Behihtest. *See* Bihote.

Behynd, *prep.* behind, X 85; as *sb.*, XVII 331. [OE. *be-hindan*.]

Behufit. *See* Bihoue.

Beie. *See* Bigge, *v.*

Beyn, Beyng. *See* Be(n).

Beytter, *n.* healer, XVII 311. [From Bete, *v.*²]

Belamy, Bellamy, *n.* good friend (ironically), XVI 213, 338. [OFr. *bel ami.*]

Beleeve, *n.* belief, IX 289. [OE. *ge-léafa*, with change of prefix.]

Beleue, Bileue, *v.* to believe, I 89, VIII *a* 82, IX 120, XV *g* 9. [OE. *ge-léfan*, (late) *be-léfan*.] *See* Leue, *v.*³; Ylefde.

Belyue, *adv.* quickly, at once, straightway, VII 161, XVI 211; Belife, XVII 192; Bilyue, V 3; Blyue, IX 18; Bliue, in *also bliue*, II 142, *als bliue*, II 531, 584, as quickly as possible, immediately. [OE. **be lĩfe.*]

Bellewys, *n. pl.* bellows, XV *h* 6. [OE. *belgas*, pl.]

Ben, *v.* to be, II 207, VIII *a* 96, &c.; Be(e), I 4, XVI 7, &c.; Buen, XV *c* 18; *future*, 2 *sg.* Best, II 173; 3 *sg.* Bees, IV *a* 35, XVII 373, Botʒ, VI 251; *pl.* Be, V 43, XVI 331; *pres. pl.* Be(n), are, II 3, 4, 12, &c.; Beo, XIV *c* 5; Beoþ, XIV *c* 103; Beth, Beþ, II 59, 110, 273, 582,

VIII *a* 199, XV *f* 5; Buþ, XIII *a* 1, 6, 10, 13, &c.; Be(e), Beo, *pres. subj.*, II 165, 433, XIV *c* 98, *d* 3, &c.; Ben, XI *b* 73, 218, &c.; Be(o), *imper.* 2 *sg.* XV *g* 10, *f* 7, &c.; 3 *sg.* IV *a* 55; *pl.* VIII *a* 118, XIV *d* 11 (first); Be, *pp.* I 195, VIII *b* 74, XI *a* 44, XII *a* 20, XVII 192, &c.; Ben, II 103, V 196, &c.; Bene, V 275, XVI 40; Beyn, XVII 445, 532; Ybe, XIII *a* 16; Beyng, *pres. p.* in *in hytself beyng*, inherent, VI 86. *Ben (drepit, &c.)*, have been (smitten, &c.), VII 9, 11; *be(e) war*, see War(e); *lete ben*, &c., cease from, II 114, XVI 234. [OE. *béon*.] *See* Ar(e), Es, Was, &c.

Bend, *v.* X 90, 98, XVII 253; Bende, *pa. t.* XII *a* 58, **I 188 (MS. banned); Bende, *pp.* V 47, 156; Bendit, X 80. The divergent senses are all derived from the original one of stringing, bending, a bow: ❦ to bind, **I 188 (note); to set ready for discharging, X 80, 90, 98; to make curve, bend, V 156, XII *a* 58, XVII 253: ❦ to make bow, bring low, beat down, in *hatʒ … on bent much baret bende*, ❦ has upon the field overcome much strife (many opponents), V 47. [OE. *bendan*.]

Bene, *adv.* pleasantly, V 334. [Not known.]

Bene, *n.* bean, VIII *a* 175, 188, 209, 278, 288, 298, IX 54; as something of no value (cf. *pees*), XIV *c* 43. [OE. *béan*.]

Benedicite (L. *imper. pl.*) bless (me, us); as exclamation of amazement, XVII 163.

Benethe(n), Beneyth (XVII), *adv.* underneath, IX 56, XVII 137; in the lower part, IX 247. [OE. *beneoþan*.]

Benome. *See* Binam.

Bent, *n.* grass-slope, field, V 165; esp. in the allit. tag *on bent*, on the field (of battle), or (as variant of *vpon grounde*, &c.)

on earth, V 47, 80, VII 91; *on
þis bent*, here, V 270. [Perhaps
a special use of *bent*, bent-grass,
OE. *beonet*.]

Beo, Beoþ. *See* Ben; Beo, *prep.*

Berd(e), *n.* beard, II 265, 507,
585, V 160. [OE. *bĕard*.]

Ber(e), *v.* to bear, carry, wear, lift,
take; to hold, possess, keep; to
give birth to, produce; V 83,
VIII *a* 136, IX 69, 109, XII *a* 197,
XIII *a* 51, XVII 318, &c.; 2 *sg.
subj.* VI 106; Berth, 3 *sg. pres.
ind.* XII *a* 81; Bar(e), *pa. t. sg.* I
146, VIII *a* 93, XIV *c* 23, 59, XV *i*
3; Ber, V 193, VI 66; Baren,
pl. IX 148; Bere, II 307; Bore,
pp. I 85, II 210; Born(e), II 41,
V 252, 326, XIV *b* 12, &c.;
Ybore, II 546; Yborn, II 174.
Bar þe flour, see Flour; *b. þe
fela3schip,* keep thee company,
V 83; *the depnes ... we bere,* the
depth (of water) we have, XVII
434, 460; *born open,* laid open,
V 2 (cf. OE. *beran ūþ*). [OE.
beran.] *See* Forbere.

Bere, *n.*[1] clamour, outcry, I 75,
II 78, XVI 214. [OE. *ge-bǣre*.]

Bere, *n.*[2] byre, cattle-stall, XV *f* 4.
[OE. *bȳre*.]

Bere-bag, *n.* bag-carrier, a con-
temptuous nickname for Scots,
XIV *a* 20 (note). [Stem of Bere *v.*
+ ON. *baggi*.] *See* Bagge.

Ber3(e), *n.* mound, V 104, 110.
[OE. *be(o)rg*.]

Ber3e, *v.* to protect, III *introd.*
[OE. *be(o)rgan*.]

Berien, *n. pl.* berries, II 258 (note).
[OE. *beri(g)e*.]

Beringe, *n.* birth, III *introd.*
[From Bere, *v.*]

Berking, *pres. p.* barking, II 286.
[OE. *be(o)rcan*.]

Bernakes, *n. pl.* barnacle-geese
IX 147 (note). [Anglo-L. *ber-
naca,* OFr. *bernaque*.]

Bernes, *n. pl.* barns, VIII *a* 177.
[OE. *ber(e)n*.]

Berth. *See* Bere, *v.*

Beselé, *adv.* earnestly, XVII 240.
[OE. *bisig* + *-līce*.] *See* Bysy.

Besy(nes). *See* Bysy(nes).

Besyde. *See* Bisyde.

Beso(u)ghte. *See* Biseche.

Best e), *adj. superl.* best, IV *a* 84,
VIII *a* 197, IX 42, &c.; as *sb.,*
best (food), VIII *a* 295; *do þi
(doþ 3our) best, see* Don; *wyth
þe beste,* among the best (people),
with the saints, IV *a* 4; *adv.* best,
most readily, most, VIII *a* 81,
107, XVII 472, &c.; *þe best,*
VIII *a* 22. [OE. *betst*.]

Best, *v. See* Ben.

Best(e), *n.* animal, creature, II
214, 280, VIII *a* 134, IX 88,
XII *a* 78, &c.; Beest, XVII 3,
135, &c. [OFr. *beste*.]

Beswyke, Byswyke, *v.* to cheat,
IV *a* 13, VI 208. [OE. *be-swīcan*.]

Bet, *adv. compar.; predic.* in he
was þe bet, he was better off
on that account, VIII *b* 100.
[OE. *bet*.] *See* Best(e), Betre.

Bete, *v.*[1] to beat, I 6, VIII *a* 73,
XVII 407; *betes the stretes,* fre-
quents the streets, XIV *a* 25;
Bette, *pa. t. sg.* VIII *a* 171;
Byete, *pa. t. subj. sg.* III 40
(OE. *bēote*); Bet, *pp.* XVII 413;
Betin, Betyn, XIV *a* 8, XVII
381. [OE. *bēatan*.] *See* For-
bette.

Bete, *v.*[2] to assuage, remedy, IV *a*
77, VIII *a* 233, XIV *a* 28, 29.
[OE. *bētan*.] *See* Beytter.

Bet3, Betidde. *See* Ben, Bitide.

Betraied, *pp.* betrayed, XVI 331.
[*be-* + OFr. *traïr*.]

Bet(e)re, Better(e), Bettre, *adj.
compar.* better, II 40, XI *b* 37,
XIII *a* 60, XV *c* 33, &c.; *him
were betre,* it would be b. for
him, XII *b* 101; *þat war better,*
for whom it would be b., XIV *a*
32; *adv.* better, XI *b* 275, XIV *d*
14, &c.; rather, XI *b* 288; *þe
better,* all the better (for it), V 28,
XVII 353; as *conj.,* so that ...
(the) better, VIII *a* 46, XVII 175
[OE. *betera, bet(t)ra,* adj.]

Bette. *See* Bete, *v.*[1]

Betweohe, *v.* ! to commit (to protection of God), XV *i* 18. Only

GLOSSARY

in this passage; perhaps an error for *becwethe* (bequeath, commit), or *beteche* (*see* Bitaiste).

Betwen(e`,   Bytuene   (xv),
Bytwene *prep.* between, among, IX 162, 166, XII a 68, b 89, XV c 1, &c.; (follows case), V 174, VII 91. [OE. *betwēon(an)*.]

Betwix, Bitwixe, *prep.* between, XI a 32, XVII 185. [OE. *be-twix*.]

Beþ, Beth. *See* Ben.

Bevil. *See* Befalle.

Beuore. *See* Bifor.

Beweile, *v. refl.* to lament, XII a 32. [*be-* + ON. **veila*; cf. *veilan*, lamentation.]

Bewycche, *v.* to bewitch, IX 86. [OE. *be* + *wiccian*.]

Bewounde, *pp.*; *it hath b.*, wound (itself) about it, XII b 72. [OE. *be-windan*.]

Bewty, *n.* beauty, XVII 20. [OFr. *beauté*.]

By, *adv.* at the side, by; alongside (without coming on board), XVII 373; *þat ... by*, by which, IX 300. [OE. *bi*.] *See* Þer(e).

Bi, By, *prep.* (i) On, at, by, II 156, 470, VIII a 167, XV g 16, XVII 75, &c.; *bi ... side*, beside, II 66, V 76; by (way of), over, through, I 62, V 10, 16, 52, 93, X 11, XVII 477; along (with), beside, II 280, 308, V 9, VIII a 4, &c.; (following its case) II 301, V 21, XVII 18; against, touching, V 242; past, II 252, 290, V 36, 39. (ii) In, on, for (of *time*), II 8, 15, VIII a 95, 274, XV a 24, &c.'; *see* Dai, While. (iii) Measured by, compared with, according to, &c., V 28, 158, 296, 297, VIII a 35, 58, 159, 248, b 57, XI b 5, &c. (iv) By (means of), through, &c., II 408, VII 6, &c.; by virtue of, XI b 20; *lyue by*, &c., live on, II 257, VIII a 284, b 26; by (of *agent*), XI a 59, &c. (v) By (in oaths, &c.), II 316, V 54, &c. *Bi al þing*, by every token, II 321, 375; *by so*, provided that, VIII b 40; *bi þan*, thereby, *or* thereupon (cf. *after*

þan), II 553; *bi þat*, thereupon, V 84; by that time, VIII a 285; as *conj.*, by the time that, VIII a 294. [OE. *bi*.] *See* Be.

By. *See* Bigge.

Bi-, By-. *See* Be-.

Bible, *n.* bible, VIII a 227, XI b 230, &c. [OFr. *bible*.]

Bycause (*of*), *prep.* because (of), XIII b 16; *bycause, because þat*, (conj.) because, XIII b 61, 62, IX 114, 226. [Be, Bi + Cause, *q.v.*]

Biche, *n.* bitch, XIV b 78. [OE. *bicce*.]

Byclypped. *See* Beclipte.

Bicome, Become, *v.* to arrive; become; befit; *hyt bycomeþ for*, it befits, VIII b 65; **Becam,** *pa. t. sg.* XII b 13; **Becomen,** *pl.* IX 148; **Bicome,** II 288; **Bicome,** *pp.* II 194; *wher sche was bicome, whider þai bicome, wher he becam*, what had become (became) of her (them, him), II 194, 288, XII b 13. [OE. *be-cuman*.]

Bidde, Bydde, Bid, *v.* to pray, beg, VIII a 233; to bid, I 265, VI 160, VIII a 210, XI b 79, XII a 48, XIV d 3, XVI 118, XVII 418, &c.; **Bad(de),** *pa. t. sg.* bade, XII a 46, XV i 16, XVI 201, XVII 309, &c.; *bad to*, bade, XII b 87; **Bed,** prayed to, III 46 (OKt. *bed*); **Bad,** *pl.* II 88, 137; **Bede,** *pp.* XII a 42 (prayed), 101 (commanded). [OE. *biddan*; the confusion with *bēodan* began in OE.] *See* Bede.

Bidderes, *n. pl.* beggars, mendicants, VIII a 197. [OE. *biddere*.]

Byd(d)yng, Bidding, *n.* bidding, commands, I 86, XVI 257, XVII 76, 121, 375. [From Bidde.]

Bide, Byde, *v.* to abide (*intr.* remain, *trans.* await, face, endure), V 224, VI 39, XIV c 21, 47, XVI 23, 207, &c. [OE. *bidan*.] *See* Abide.

Bidene, Bydene, Bedeyn (XVII), *adv.* forthwith, withal (often meaningless), VII 79, 127, XIV b

74, XVII 442; *al bidene*, XIV *b*
11. [See *N.E.D.*]

Bye, Byete. *See* Bigge, Bete, *v.*[1]

Bifel. *See* Befalle.

**Bifor(e), Byforn, Befor(e), Be-
uore**, &c., *adv.* before (hand),
II 147, VII 121, &c.; *eir befor*,
X 140; as *sb.*, XVII 331; *prep.*
before, in presence of, &c., II 42,
III 58, V 4, IX 126, &c.; (of
time) VI 238, XI *b* 48, &c.;
bifore þat, before (*conj.*), XI *b*
195; Byfore, *conj.* (with *subj.*),
before, VI 170. [OE. *be-foran*.]

Big, Bigge, *v.* to take up one's
abode ; *to big his boure*, to
establish his dwelling, XIV *b* 26 ;
bigges him. settles himself, XIV *b*
24. [ON. *byggja*.] *See* Biging.

Bigan, Began, &c. *See* Begynne.

Bigge, Bygge, *adj.* strong, lusty,
big, IV *a* 51, V 33, VI 14, VII
139, VIII *a* 207. [See *N.E.D.*]

Bigge, *v.* to buy, purchase, pay
for, redeem, VIII *a* 275 ; Beie,
XII *b* 24 ; By(e), IV *a* 65, IX
113 ; Byye, VI 118 ; Bugge,
XV *g* 3 ; *pa. t.* Boght, IV *a* 38 ;
Bouȝte, VIII *a* 201 ; Bouhte,
VIII *b* 100 ; Boght, *pp.* IV *a* 80,
XII *b* 153, XVII 373 ; Bought(e),
XVI 8, 275 ; Iboust, XV *g* 26 (*see*
App. p. 278) ; *it bees boght full
dere*, you will pay for it dearly,
XVII 373. [OE. *bycgan*, (Kt.)
becgan.] *See* Abugge.

Byggynge, *n.* buying, IX 90.
[From prec.] *See* Bying.

Bigile, Bygyle, *v.* to deceive,
V 345, 348, 359, XIV *b* 44. [OE.
be- + OFr. *guiler*.] *See* Gile.

Biging, *n.* dwelling, XIV *a* 20.
[From Big, *v.*]

Bygonne, &c. *See* Begynne.

Bigrucccheth, 3 *sg. pres.* grumbles
at, VIII *a* 69. [OE. *be-* + OFr.
groucher.] *See* Grucche.

Byȝe, *n.* ring, VI 106. [OE. *bēg*.]

Bihold, Behald(e), *v.* to behold,
look, II 387, 502, IV *a* 81, XVII
509, 534, &c. ; *bihold on, behold
to*, look at, II 367, XVII 343 ;
Beholdes, *imper. pl.*, XVI 195 ;

Behelde, *pa. t. sg.* VII 64 ;
Biheld, II 101, 320, 323, 530 ;
Behielde, *pl.* XII *a* 164 ; Bi-
hold, -holde(n), *pp.* II 409, 417,
XII *b* 116. [OE. *be-háldan*.]
See Holde(n).

Bihote, Byhote, *v.* to promise,
vow, VIII *a* 227 ; *byhote God*, I
vow to God, VIII *a* 273 ; Behihtest, 2 *sg. pa. t.* XII *b* 43 ;
Behete, *pp.* XVII 430 ; Bihot,
XV *a* 20. [OE. *be-hātan*.] *See*
Hote.

Bihoue, *v.* to need ; *impers.* in
me bihoues, I must, it is time for
me to, V 228 ; *pers.* in Bus,
2 *sg. pres.* ; *þou bus be*, you
ought to be, XVI 338 ; Behuſt,
pa. t. had need (to), X 156.
[OE. *be-hōfian*; with the reduced
form *bus* cf. *has, hast*, &c.]

Byye. *See* Bigge.

Bying, *n.* redemption, XVI 12.
[From By, to buy. *See* Bigge,
v.; Byggynge.]

Biis, *adj.* dark, rich, II 242. [OFr.
bise.]

Biknowe, Byknowe, *v.* to confess,
V 317 (*I b. yow*, I confess to you),
VIII *b* 96 ; Beknowen, *pp.* ir
þou art b. of, you have confessed,
V 323. [OE. *be-cnāwan*, only
recorded in sense ' know '.]

Bile, Bill (XVII), *n.* beak, XII *a*
182, XVII 508. [OE. *bile.*]

Byled, *pa. t.* boiled, bubbled,
V 14 ; Boyled, *pp.* V 106.
[OFr. *boillir*; for similar de-
velopment of vowel in V, *see*
Nye, Disstryeȝ.]

Bylyue, *n.* food, VIII *b* 21, 29.
[OE. *bi-leofa.*]

Bylongeth, *v. impers.* it belongs
to, befits, VIII *b* 70. [Be- +
Longe, *v.*[2]]

Bilow, *v.* to humble, VIII *a* 223.
[Formed on Lowe *adj.*]

Bilt, *n.* dwelling, *11 483 (MS.
ybilt, but required sense 'lodged'
is unexampled). [Obscurely rel.
to ME. *bilden*, build ; see
N.E.D.]

Binam, *pa. t. sg.* in *b.* [*hym*] *his*

mnam, deprived him of his talent, VIII *a* 237 ; Benome, in *b. þe poure ane peny*, deprived the poor of a penny, III 13. [OE. *be-niman*.] *See* Nyme.

Bynde, *v.* to bind, unite, IV *a* 54, XVI 97 ; Bond, *pa. t. sg.* XII *b* 120 (but *sb.* = *trosse* is possible ; see Bonde, *n.*) ; Ybounde, *pp.* II 394. [OE. *bindan*.] *See* Vnbynde.

Biqueste, *n.* (bequest), will, VIII *a* 79. [OE. **be-cwiss*, related to *be-cweþan*, bequeath ; *cf.* Heste.]

Bir, Byr, Bur (v), *n.* a following wind, VII 126 ; speed (in *with a byr*, speedily) XVII 371 ; violence, V 254 ; strength, V 193. [ON. *byr-r*.]

Byrd. *See* Brid(d).

Bireue, *v.* to deprive ; *I wil it hym b.*, I will deprive him of it, VIII *a* 242. [OE. *be-rēafian*, *be-rēfan*.]

Byrye, *v.* to bury, I 137, 140, 142, 144. [OE. *byrigan*.]

Byrne, Burne, *v. trans.* and *intr.* to burn, X 21 (rime with *in* requires Brin, *q. v.*), X 181, &c. ; Byrnand, *pres. p.* IV *a* 26, X 27, 30. [OE. *birnan, byrnan*, &c., *intr.*] *See* Bren, Brin.

Byrthen, *n.* burden, IV *a* 49. [OE. *byrþen*.]

Biseche, Bysech, Beseche, *v.* to implore, II 113, 453, VI 30, IX 269, 328, XII *a* 38 ; Besoghte, *pa. t.* XII *a* 26 ; Besoughte, IX 294. [OE. *be* + *sēcan*.] *See* Seche.

Bisemeȝ, *v. impers.* it suits, V 123. [Be- + Seme, *q.v.*]

Bisyde, Besyde, *adv.* at the side, at one's side, hard by, I 209, V 20, 162, XII *b* 125. [OE. *be sīdan*, at the side.]

Biside(n), Be-, Bysyde, *prep.* beside, XI *b* 57 ; (following its case) I 243, II 303, V 197, XIV *b* 28, &c. *See* prec.

Bisides, Bisydeȝ, *adv.* at the side(s), round about, II 401, V 96. [Prec. + adv. -*es*.]

Bisides, Bysydes, *prep.* beside,

near, XIII *a* 10 ; (following pron.) II 281. [As prec.]

Bysy(e), Bysie, Besy (*aboute*), *adj.* busy, occupied (with, in), XI *b* 252, 287, 289, 293, 297. [OE. *bisig*.]

Bysynes(se), Besynes (IV), *n.* restlessness, IV *b* 28 ; industry, XIII *b* 24 ; *worldly b.* attention to worldly affairs, XI *b* 2, 309 ; *b. of worldly occupacion*, pre-occupation with w. affairs, XI *b* 251. [OE. *bisig* + *-nes*.]

Bis(s)chop, Bysshop(p)e , Bissoppe, *n.* bishop, I 246, III 58 (*dat. sg.*), VIII *a* 143, *b* 74, XI *a* 66, &c. [OE. *biscop*.]

Byswykeȝ. *See* Beswyke.

Biswynke, *v.* to earn with toil, VIII *a* 207. [OE. *be-swincan*.]

Bitaiste (= bitaihte), *pa. t.* entrusted, XV *g* 21. [OE. *betǣcan*, *pa. t.* betǣhte ; on spelling *see* App. p. 278.]

Byte, *v.* to bite, XVII 229 ; *apon the bone shal it byte*, it shall cut to the bone, XVII 220. [OE. *bītan*.]

Bitide, Bytyde, &c., *v.* to happen ; to happen to, befall, VI 37 ; *pres. subj.* V 127, 315, 341, XIV *a* 12 ; Betidde, *pp.* XVI 100 ; *tide wat bitide*, come what may, II 339. [OE. *be* + *tīdan*.] *See* Tide.

Bityme, *adv.* in *all bityme*, in good time, XIV *b* 27. [From *bi tyme*, in time ; cf. OE. *tō tīman*.] *See* Tyme.

Bitte, Bytte, *n.* cutting edge, V 242 ; blade V 156. [ON. *bit*, cutting edge ; OE. *bite*, a cut.]

Bittir, Bytter, *adj.* bitter, IV *b* 27 ; salt (of water), IX 244 ; grievous, XIV *c* 68, XVI 207, &c. [OE. *bitter*.]

Bytuene. *See* Betwene.

Bytwyste, *prep.* between (following its noun), VI 104. [A form of ME. *be-twixt(e)*, extended from Betwix, *q.v.*]

Biwyled, *pp.* deluded, V 357. [OE. *be* + *wiglian* ; cf. *be-*

wi3elien, Layamon 969.] *See* Wiles.

Blabre, *v.* to babble, XI *b* 248. [Echoic; *cf.* Babelynge, Blubre.]

Blac, Blak, *adj.* black, II 265, IX 23. XII *a* 99; *rowe and blac,* with shaggy black hair, II 459; Blake, *oblique* and *pl.* IX 4, XII *a* 137, XV *c* 14. [OE. *blæc.*]

Blame, *n.* blame; scolding, XVII 299; *v.* to blame, V 300, IX 274 (mistranslation; *see* note), &c.; *to blame,* in the wrong, XIV *b* 85. [OFr. *bla(s)me; bla(s)mer.*]

Blan. *See* Blynne.

Blasphemye *(to), n.* blasphemy (against), XI *b* 110. [OFr. *blasfemie.*]

Blawene. *See* Blowe.

Ble, Bleo (XV), *n.* hue, complexion, in *bri3t on ble,* fair of face, II 455; radiance, XV *b* 16. [OE. *bleo.*]

Blede, *v.* to bleed, XIV *c* 13; Bled(de), *pa. t.* I 119, II 80. [OE. *blēdan.*]

Blefte. *See* Bleue.

Blende, *pa. t.* mingled, in *blende in his face,* rose to his cheeks, V 303; **Blent,** *pp.* in *blent ... in blysse,* set amidst joy, VI 25. [ME. *blenden* obscurely related to OE. *blándan,* or ON. *blanda.*] *See* Vnblendyde.

Blended, *pp.* deluded, V 351. [OE. *bléndan.*] *See* Blyndiþ.

Blenk, *v.* to gleam, V 247. [OE. **blencan,* possibly identical with recorded *blencan,* to cheat; for ME. *blenchen, blenken,* &c. = to gleam, look at, glance aside, blench, cheat. Compare Glent, Glyfte.]

Blent, Bleo. *See* Blende, Ble.

Bleþeliche, *adv.* gladly, III 53. [? Obscure alteration of OE. *blīþelīce.*]

Bleue, *v.* to remain; *pres. subj.* III *introd.;* Blefte, *pa. t.* III 18. [OE. *belǽfan.*] *See* Leue, *v.*[1]

Bleu3, Blew. *See* Blowe.

Blew, *n.* blue (stuff), XVII 200

(note); *cled in Stafford blew,* beaten black and blue; cf. *clothe here well yn Stafford blewe,* Rel. Ant., I, p. 29. [OFr. *bleu.*] *See* Blwe.

Blynde, *adj. pl.* blind, deluded, XI *b* 79; as *sb.,* the blind, VIII *a* 115, 185. [OE. *blind.*]

Blyndiþ, 3 *sg. pres.* (blinds), deludes, XI *b* 7, 107. [OE. *bléndan* infl. by *blind,* adj.] *See* Blended.

Blyndnesse, *n.* blindness, XI *b* 221. [OE. *blindnes.*]

Blyn(ne) *(of), v.* to cease (from), IV *a* 39, V 254, XVI 16, 236, XVII 110 *(or I blyn* = without stopping); Blan, *pa. t. pl.* I 73. [OE. *blinnan.*]

Blis(se), Blys(se), *n.* happiness, joy, IV *a* 11, 40, VI 12, XIV *b* 19, XV *b* 3, &c.; *as haue I blys,* so may I have (eternal) joy, XVII 402. [OE. *bliss.*]

Bliss(e), Blesse, *v.* to bless, I *introd.,* VI 76, XVI 400, 404, XVII 174, 256, 300, 467; bless with sign of the cross, V 3, XII *b* 86; Blist, *pp.* XVII 514. [OE. *blētsian,* already infl. by *blītsian, blissian,* to gladden.]

Blisseful, Blysful, *adj.* joyous, II 412, 438, VI 49; as *sb.,* blissful one, VI 61; *Blissefulest (MS. blifulest), *superl.* II 527. [OE *bliss + ful.*]

Blissing, -yng, *n.* blessing, XVI 401, XVII 178. [OE. *blētsing.*] *See* Blis(se).

Bliþe, Blyþe, Blith (XIV *b*), *adj.* happy, glad, V 253, XIV *b* 49; *bliþe of,* glad at, II 573; *þatow be bliþe of hir,* that you may have joy of her, II 471. [OE. *blīþe.*]

Blyþely, happily, VI 25. [OE. *blīþelīce.*] *See* Bleþeliche.

Bliue, Blyue. *See* Belyue.

Blo, *adj.* black and blue, XVII 413. [ON. *blá-r.*]

Blod(e), Bloode, *n.* blood, I 119, V 246, IX 141, XV *g* 16, XVI 12, &c.; creature, XII *b* 220; *byndes blode and bane,* keeps the

body together, IV _a_ 54. [OE. _blŏd._]

Blodi, Blody, _adj._ bloody, II 110, IV _a_ 80, 86, &c.; _blody bretheren,_ brothers in blood, fellow men, VIII _a_ 201. [OE. _blŏdig._]

Blom, _n._ flower, perfection, VI 218. [ON. _blóm, blómi._]

Blosme(n), _n. pl._ flowers, blossoms, II 61, XV _b_ 2. [OE. _blŏsma._]

Blowe(n), _v._ to blow, VII 106, XIII _a_ 7, XV _h_ 6, &c.; to brag, XIV _c_ 101; Bleuȝ, _pa. t. sg._ XIV _c_ 77; Blew, VII 130, (sounded the trumpet) X 43; Blawene, _pp._ IV _b_ 13. [OE. _blāwan._]

Bloweing, _n._ blowing (of horns), II 285. [OE. _blāwung._]

Blubred, _pa. t._ bubbled, V 106. [Echoic; _cf._ Blabre.]

Blunder, _n._ trouble, confusion, XVII 406. [Not known.]

Blwe, _adj._ blue, VI 63. [OFr. _bleu._] _See_ Blew.

Bo, _adv._ as well, too, II 27. [OE. _bā,_ adj. neut.] _See_ Bope.

Boc-house, _n. dat. sg._ library, III _introd._ [OE. _bŏc-hŭs._] _See_ Bok(e).

Bodeþ, 3 _sg. pres._ predicts, portends, XIII _a_ 62. [OE. _bodian._]

Bodi(e), Body, _n._ body, I 113, II 105, XVI 23, &c.; _gon on bodi and bones,_ be in the flesh, live, II 54. [OE. _bodig._]

Bodyly, Bodely, _adj._ of (the) body, bodily (opposed to ‘spiritual’), VI 118, XI _b_ 147, 158, &c.; _bodely almes,_ (giving of) charitable gifts for the needs of the body, XI _b_ 2, 270, 301, 303. [From prec.]

Boffet, _n._ buffet, V 275. [OFr. _buffet._]

Bogh, Boȝeȝ (_pl._ v), **Bouȝ** (11), _n._ bough, branch, II 61, V 9, XV _a_ 14, XVII 535. [OE. _bōg._]

Boght. _See_ Bigge, _v._

Boȝe, _v._ to bend, bow; turn, go, V 110; Boȝen, _pa. t. pl._ turned, went their way, V 9; Bowand, _pres. p._ (bowing), obedient, XVII

76 (_cf._ Buxome, and Lowte). [OE. _bŭgan._]

Boyes, _n. pl._ fellows, knaves, XVI 97, 145. [Obscure.]

Boyled. _See_ Byled.

Bok(e), Boc, _n._ book, III _introd.,_ VII 14, 65, IX 294, XI _b_ 229, &c.; Bible, VIII _a_ 248, _b_ 39; Bible, or other book (as a book of the Gospels, a psalter, &c.) on which an oath could be taken, XII _b_ 165. [OE. _bŏc._]

Bold(e), Balde, _adj._ bold, II 139, IV _a_ 51, 83, &c.; _and that be ye bold,_ and be sure of that, XVII 524; Boldely, _adv._ XVI 178. [OE. _báld._]

Boldyng, _n._ encouragement, VII 14. [From prec.; cf. OE. _báldian,_ intr.]

Bole, _n._ bull; in _bole-hyde,_ bull’s hide, XV _h_ 11. [ON. _boli._]

Bollyng, _n._ swelling; _for b. of her wombe,_ to prevent the swelling of their bellies, VIII _a_ 209. [ME. _bolle-n, bolne-n,_ ON. _bolgna._]

Bolted, _pp._ bolted, shackled, VIII _a_ 130. [From OE. _bolt,_ n.]

Bon(e), Bane, _n._ bone, II 54, IV _a_ 54, VIII _a_ 85, IX 141, XVII 220, 253, &c.; _see_ Bak, Blod(e), Bodi, Flesch. [OE. _bān._]

Bond. _See_ Bynde.

Bond(e), _n._ bond; _bond to sheues,_ the straw binding for sheaves, VIII _b_ 14; _her bonde,_ the bondage they imposed, XIV _c_ 47; Bandis, _pl._ bonds, XVI 190, 196; Our Lady’s bonds, pregnancy, XVII 209 (see _N.E.D._, s.v. _Band, Bond_). [ON. _band._]

Bond(e)men, _n. pl._ bondmen, serfs, VIII _a_ 46, _b_ 69; Bondemenne, _gen. pl._ VIII _b_ 74. [OE. _bōnda_ (from ON. _bóndi_) + _mann,_ influenced in sense by prec. (etymol. unconnected).]

Bone, _n._ boon, request. I 131. [ON. _bón._]

Bonk(e), Bonkke, Bank(k)e, _n._ bank, XIII _a_ 40; shore, VII 126; hill-side, V 9, 14, 94, 97,

104, 132, 149, **XIV** *b* 20. [ON. *bakki,* older **banke.*]

Bood-worde, *n.* tidings, XVI 366. [Stem of OE. *bodian + word* ; cf. ON. *boð-orð,* command.]

Booste. *See* Boste.

Bord(e), *n.* board, XII *a* 92, XVII 119, 279 ; table, II 578, VIII *a* 262. [OE. *bórd.*]

Bore, Bare (XIV), *n.* boar, VIII *a* 31, XIV *b* 19, 25, 49, 87. [OE. *bár.*]

Bore ; Born(e). *See* Bere, *v.*

Borelych, *adj.* stout, V 80 ; massive, V 156. [Obscure.]

Borgh, Borugh, *n.* town, VIII *a* 301 ; *in borugh,* among townsfolk, XIV*d* 4. [OE. *burg, buruh.*]

Borne, Burn, *n.* stream, V 106, XIV *a* 2 ; **Buerne,** flood, sea (an allit. use), VII 159. [OE. *búrne.*]

Borow, *n.* surety ; *I dar be thi b.,* I'll go bail (for you), XVII 204. [OE. *borg.*]

Borwed, *pa. t.* borrowed, II 499, VIII *a* 93. [OE. *borgian.*]

Boste, Booste (XVI), *n.* boasting, XIV *a* 20 ; pride, XIV *a* 8 ; arrogance, XIV *b* 85, XVI 214. [Obscure.]

Boste, *v.* to boast, XIV *c* 101 ; **Bosting,** *n.* boasting, XIV *a* 9. [Obscure.]

Bot(e), But, *adv.* only, but, II 228, IV *a* 32, V 97, VI 22, VIII *a* 276, IX 17, X 159, XIII *a* 38, &c. [OE. *bútan.*] *See* next, and Boute.

Bot(e), But, *conj.* (i) Except, but, VI 136, VIII *b* 9, IX 198, &c. ; *ne .. bote,* only, III 6, 22, &c. (*cf.* Bote, *adv.*) ; *no3t deop bote to þe kneo,* only knee deep, XIII *a* 39 ; *bote 3ef,* except that, XIII *b* 5. (ii) Unless (with *subj.*), VI 68, VIII *a* 1, 39, 112, 143, *b* 95, X 73, XV *c* 17, *g* 21, XVII 44, 386, 550 ; *bot(e) if,* &c., unless, VIII *a* 17, 53, X 78, XVII 247, &c. ; *bot þat,* unless, II 428. (iii) But, however, yet, I 21, II 74, IV *a* 57, V 61, VI 14, &c. ;

(misplaced) XII *a* 79 (note), 105 ; *bot yit (3eit),* and yet, **X** 95, XVII 35, 64, 213. [OE. *bútan, búte.*]

Bot(e), *n.* cure, redress, salvation, IV *a* 7, VIII *a* 187, XIV *c* 84 ; *bote of,* cure for, II 552. [OE. *bót.*]

Botel, *n.* bottle, VIII *b* 54. [OFr. *botel.*]

Botened, *pp.* cured, I 241, VIII *a* 185. [Formed on Bot(e), *n.*]

Boþ(e), Both, Bath (IV, X), *adj.* and *pron.* both, IV *a* 56, V 315, VI 13 ; *in hem boþe* (after negative), in either of them, XI *b* 27 ; *vs both,* us two, XVII 185 ; *on bath halfis,* on both sides, X 198 ; *vpon boþe halue,* on either side, V 2, 97 ; *a3 adv.* (originally *pron.* in apposition), as well, too, V 306, VIII *a* 119, 162, 252, 274, *b* 46 ; *boþ(e) .. and, bath .. and,* both .. and, I 52, II 86, IV *a* 66, &c. [ON. *báði-r.*] *See* Bo.

Boþem, *n.* bottom, V 77. [OE. *botm,* **boþm* (still NWM.) ; cf. *bytme, byþme.*]

Bou3. *See* Bogh.

Bou3te, Bouhte, &c. *See* Bigge, *v.*

Boun(e), Bowne, *adj.* ready, IV *a* 81, XIV *a* 9, XVI 201 ; prompt, XVI 257 ; *make youe b.,* prepare yourselves, arm, XVI 178 ; *make þe b.,* hasten, XVI 339 ; *wat3 nawhere b.,* was not to be found anywhere, VI 174. [ON. *búin-n, bún-.*] *See* Busk.

Bounté, excellence, XV *c* 26. [OFr. *bonté.*]

Bour(e), Bower, *n.* abode, XIV *b* 26, XV *e* 17, 18 ; *pl.* bowers, chambers, XVII 348. [OE. *búr.*]

Bourde, *n.* entertainment, II 445 ; **Bourdys,** *pl.* jests, II 9. [OFr. *bourde.*]

Boute, *prep.* without, V 285. [OE. *bútan.*] *See* Bot(e).

Bowand. *See* Bo3e.

Bowe, *n.* bow, IX 258, XII *a* 57. [OE. *boga.*]

Bowers. *See* Bour(e).

Braggere, *n.* braggart, VIII *a* 148.

[From ME. *braggen*, of unknown origin.]

Braid. *See* Brode.

Braide, Brayd, Brade, *n.* a sudden movement; *in a brade*, in a trice, XVII 21 ; *bittir braide*, grievous onslaught, XIV *c* 68, XVI 207. [OE. *brægd.*]

Brayde, *v.* to move quickly; draw, V 251 ; Brayde, *pa. t.* threw, V 309 ; Brayde, *pp.* in *brayde down*, lowered, V I. [OE. *bregdan.*]

Brayn, *n.* brain, XV *h* 6 (*distrib. sg.* ; *see* Hert). [OE. *brægn.*]

Brak. *See* Breke(n).

Brandis, *n. pl.* pieces of burnt wood, X 113. [OE. *bránd.*]

Bras, *n.* brass, XVI 196. [OE. *bræs.*]

Brast. *See* Brest(e).

Braunche, Branch, *n.* branch, I 121, V 109, XVII 511. [OFr. *branche.*]

Bre, *n.* foaming sea, VII 152. [App. a curious allit. use of OE. *brīw*, **brēo*, broth.]

Bred(e), *n.* bread, VIII *a* 18, 129, 131, 207, 298; *as euer ete I brede* = so may I live, on my life, XVII 395 ; *hors bred, houndes bred*, bread of beans, bran, &c., for the food of horses and dogs, VIII *a* 208. [OE. *brēad.*]

Bred-corne, *n.* grain for bread, VIII *a* 64. [Prec. + OE. *corn.*]

Brede, Breed, *n.* breadth, XVII 126; *of breed*, in breadth, XVII 259. [OE. *brǣdu.*]

Brede, *v. intr.* (to expand), grow, VI 55. [OE. *brǣdan.*]

Brede3, *n. pl.* planks, V 3. [OE. *bred.*]

Breff, *adj.* brief, meagre, VII 74. [OFr. *bref.*]

Breke(n), *v.* to break, violate, VIII *a* 31, IX 46, XI *b* 187, XVI 257, XVII 387, &c.; *intr.* II 338, IX 118 ; Brak, *pa. t. sg.* X 106; Broke, *pa. t. pl.* V 14 ; Broke, *pp.* injured, VIII *b* 34 (*see* Broke-legged, VIII *a* 130); Brokynne, broken, XVI 195. [OE. *brecan.*]

Brekynge, *n.* breaking ; *smale b* breaking a long note into *a* number of short ones. fine trilling, XI *b* 138. [OE. *brecung.*]

Brem(e), *adj.* fierce, violent, V 132, VII 139, 152, &c.; threatening, wild, V 77; passionate, VII 104; glorious, II 61; *adv.* gloriously, XV *b* 27. [OE. *brēme*, adj. and adv.]

Brem(e)ly, *adv.* fiercely, violently, V 251, VII 106 ; exceedingly, V 165. [From prec.]

Bren, Bran, *n.* bran, VIII *a* 175, 278. [OFr. *bren.*]

Bren, *v.* to burn ; Brent, *pp.* VII 152, 159 ; Brennynge, *pres. p.* fervent, XI *b* 67 ; Brennynge, *n.* burning, IX 10. [ON. *brenna.*] *See* Byrne, Brin.

Brent, *adj.* steep, V 97. [Cf. OE. *brant.*]

Bren-waterys, *n. pl.* XV *h* 22, 'water-burners', *i.e.* blacksmiths (from the hiss of the hot iron when plunged in water). Compare *burn-the-wind*, a nickname for blacksmiths. [Bren, *v.* + Watter.]

Brere, *n.* briar, II 276. [OE. *brǣr, brēr.*]

Brest, *n.* breast, V 303. [OE. *brēost.*]

Brest(e), Brast (XVII), *v. trans.* and *intr.* to burst, IV *a* 81, XV *h* 6, XVII 264; Barste, *pa. t. sg.* VIII *a* 171 ; Brosten, *pp.* XVI 196. [OE. *berstan* ; ON. *bresta.*]

Bretfull, *adj.* full to the brim, VII 164. [OE., ME. *brerd-full*, prob. with substitution of ON. cognate form **bredd-* ; cf. Swed. *bräddfull.*]

Brether(en). *See* Broþer.

Breue, *v.* to set down in writing ; Breuyt, *pa. t. sg.* VII 65 ; *pp.* VII 14. [Med. L. *breviāre*, OE. *brēfan.*]

Brid(d), Byrd (XVII), *n.* young bird, XII *a* 196; (small) bird, II 305, VII 104, XII *a* 169, 172, XVII 514, &c. [OE. *bridd*, young bird (late Nth. pl. *birdas*).]

Brydel, *n.* bridle, v 84. [OE. *brídel.*]

Brygge, *n.* (draw)bridge, v 1. [OE. *brycg.*] *See* Draw-brig.

Bryght(e), Briȝt, Bryȝt, Briht (XII), Bryht (XV), &c., *adj.* and *adv.* bright, II 152, 269, 455, IV *a* 72, *b* 6, v 158, XII *b* 130, XV *b* 26, XVII 9, &c. [OE. *berht, byrht.*]

Brightnes, *n.* splendour, XVII 15, 20. [OE. *berht-nes.*]

Brimme, Brymme, *n.* water's edge, v 104; brink, XII *b* 32. [OE. *brymme.*]

Brin, Bryn, *v. trans.* to burn, X 21 (implied by rime); **Brynt, Brint, *pa. t.*** X 113; *pp.* X 32, 165. [ON. *brinna.*] *See* Bren, Byrne.

Bring(e), Bryng(e), *v.* to bring, take, escort; cause to be; IV *a* 7, *b* 46, VIII *a* 64, IX 60, X 17, XI *a* 3 (adduce), XII *a* 193, XIV *b* 68, &c.; **Broght(e), Broȝt(e), Brought, Brouȝt(e), *pa. t.*** I 123, II 93, III 11, VIII *a* 288, XII *a* 25, *b* 47 (*subj.*), XVI 161, &c.; *pp.* v 77, VII 90, XIV *b* 72, &c.; **Ybrouȝt,** II 389, 563; *bryng it to an ende,* accomplish it, IX 169; *bringen forth,* bring forth, produce, IX 60, XII *a* 193; *to thay bryng,* until they bring (something), XVII 499; *broughte oute of,* rescued from, XVI 161; *brought it so breff,* made it so meagre, VII 74; *broght dede,* brought to death, I 213. [OE. *bringan.*]

Brynstane, *n.* sulphur, X 20. [OE. *bryn-stän.*]

Brytouns, *n. pl.* men of Brittany, II 16. [OFr. *Breton*; L. *Brit(t)ō-nem,* Briton.]

Britoner, Brytonere, *n.* a man of Brittany, VIII *a* 148, 169. [From prec.]

Brockes, *n. pl.* badgers, VIII *a* 31. [OE. *brocc.*]

Brode, *adj.* broad, v 1, 165, VII 106, XV *g* 5; **Brood,** XIII *a* 39; **Braid,** X 24. [OE. *brād.*]

Broght(e), Broȝt(e). *See* Bring(e).

Broke, *n.* brook, stream, v 14, 132, VIII *a* 129. [OE. *brōc.*]

Broke, Brokynne. *See* Breke(n).

Broke-legged, *adj.* broken-legged, crippled, VIII *a* 130. *See* Breke(n), Legges.

Brood. *See* Brode.

Brosten. *See* Brest(e).

Broþe, *adj.* fierce, v 165. [ON. *brāð-r.*]

Broþely, *adv.* fiercely, v 309. [ON. *brāð-liga.*]

Broþer, *n.* brother, I 210, XII *a* 6; **Brother, *gen. sg.*** XII *a* 18; **Brether, *pl.*** XVII 318, 320 (*see* note); **Breþeren,** brethren, VIII *a* 201, XI *b* 243, &c. [OE. *brōþor*; ON. *brǣðr,* pl.]

Brouch, *n.* trinket, XIII *b* 23 (translates L. *crepundia*). [OFr. *broche.*]

Brouȝt(e), &c. *See* Bring(e).

Broun(e), Browne, *adj.* brown, VIII *a* 301, XV *c* 14; dull-hued, IX 38, 98; dark, VI 177. [OE. *brūn.*]

Browe, *n. pl.* eyebrows, XV *c* 14; forehead, v 238. [OE. *brū.*]

Buen. *See* Ben.

Buerne(s). *See* Borne, Burne.

Bugge. *See* Bigge, *v.*

Bugles, *n. pl.* bullocks, IX 256. [OFr. *bugle.*]

Bur. *See* Bir.

Burde, *pa. t. subj. impers.* (it would befit) in *me burde,* I had better, ought to, v 210, 360. [OE. *ge-byrian.*]

Burgase, Buriays, *n. pl.* burgesses, citizens, II 504, XIV *b* 65. [OFr. *burgeis,* sg. and pl.]

Buriel, Buryel, *n.* tomb, XIII *a* 46. [OE. *byrgels.*]

Burne. *See* Byrne.

Burne, *n.* warrior, knight, man, v 3, 21, 210, 247, 252, 270, 309, VI 37; *voc.* sir (knight), v 216, 254; **Buernes,** *pl.* VII 90, 91. [OE. *beorn.*]

Burnist, *pp.* polished, II 368. [OFr. *burnir, burniss-.*]

Burþ-tonge, *n.* native speech,

XIII *b* 16, 43. [OE. *byrþ* + *túnge*.]

Bus. *See* Bihoue.

Busk, *v.* (to prepare oneself); make haste, v 216 ; *refl.* in *busk þe*, hasten, XIV *a* 22 ; *trans.* (prepare), make, v 180. [ON. *búa-sk*, refl.] *See* Boune.

Busshel, *n.* bushel (a measure of volume varying very greatly at different times and places), VIII *a* 64. [OFr. *buissiel*.]

But. *See* Bot(e).

Butras, *n.* (? *pl.*) buttress, II 361. [? OFr. *bouterez*, nom. sg., or pl., of *bouteret*.]

Buþ. *See* Ben.

Buxome, *adj.* obedient, willing, VIII *a* 188. [Stem of OE. *búgan* + *-sum*.] *See* Boȝe.

Caas. *See* Cas(e).

Cagge(n), *v.* to tie up, VI 152. [Not known ; only allit.]

Cayre, *v.* to ride, v 52. [ON. *keyra*.]

Calabre, *n.* calaber (a squirrel fur), VIII *a* 265. [OFr. *Calabre*, Calabria.]

Calde. *See* Colde.

Call(e), *v.* to call (cry, summon, name), I 32, IV *b* 47, VI 182, X 70, XVI 126, XVII 432, &c.; *subj. sg.* XVI 141 ; Cald, *pp.* named, VII 70, XVII 513. [OE. (late) *ceallian*, from ON. *kalla*.]

Cam. *See* Com.

Cammede, *adj.* XV *h* 5 ; ? snub-nosed (cf. *Reeve's Tale*, 14) ; ? crooked (fits context better, but see etym.). [Cf. OFr., ME. *camus*, snub-nosed ; *cammed*, bent (from Welsh *cam*), is not else recorded till later.]

Can, *v.*[1] I know, know how to, can. *Pres. ind.* I, 3 *sg.* Can, II 22, 437, XIII *b* 38 (knows), &c. ; Con, V 70, 215, XV *c* 26 ; Kan(ne), I 45, IV *a* 11, 90, XVI 74 ; 2 *sg.* Can(ne), XVI 100, XVII 229 ; Canstow (*see* þou), VIII *b* 12 ; *pl.* Can, IX 208 ; Con, VI 21 ; Conen, know, IX

185, 208 ; Conne, VI 161 ; Conneþ, VIII *a* 116, XIII *a* 17, *b* 22, 38 (know) ; Cunne, XIV *c* 101 ; Kan(e), IV *b* 21, 41, 44, 86 ; Konne, VIII *a* 70 ; Kunnen, XI *b* 153 (know), 275 ; *pres. subj.* Conne, VIII *a* 143 ; Kun(ne), XIV *b* 90, VIII *a* 250 ; *pa. t.* Couþe, Cowþe, I *introd.*, V 115, 205, XII *introd.*, *b* 200, &c. ; *cowþeȝ* (2 sg.) with double constr., VI 124 (note); *pa. t. subj.* could, might (have), Coude, XI *b* 271, XVII 286 ; Couþe, V 276, 353 ; Cowth, XVII 473. *Can no other red*, XII *b* 102, *see* Red ; *how I can of*, what I can do in the way of, XVII 250. It is sometimes difficult to distinguish this verb from the next (*e.g.* at V 205, VI 139, XVII 468). [OE. *can, con* ; *cúþe*.]

Can, Con, *v.*[2] *auxil.* used with infin. as equivalent of simple pa. t. (*con calle* = called, V 144), and also, by confusion with prec., of a present (*con dresse* = brings about, VI 135) ; 1, 3 *sg.* Con, V 167, 227, VI 51, 77, 93, 181, 221, 223, &c. ; 2 *sg.* Coneȝ, VI 122 ; *pl.* Can, X 50, 66, 108, 112; Con, VI 149, 191 ; *pa. t.* did, ? V 205 (*see* prec.). [Due to confusion in form, and partly also in sense, between Gan (*q.v.*) and prec.; cf. *begouth* (*s.v.* Begynne).]

Canell, *n.* cinnamon, IX 158. [OFr. *canelle*.]

Caple, *n.* horse, V 107. [Cf. ON. *kapall*; see *N.E.D.*]

Cardinales, *n. pl.* cardinals, XIV *b* 40, 41. [OFr. *cardinal*.]

Care, Kare, *n.* woe, misery, IV *a* 18, 44, 60, V 316, VI 11, &c.; *care (of)*, anxiety (concerning), V 311. [OE. *caru*.]

Care, *v.* to have sorrow, XIV *b* 1. [OE. *carian*.]

Carie, *v.* to carry, XII *b* 27. [ONFr. *carier*.]

Caroigne, Caryou, *n.* dead body, carrion, VIII *a* 85, XVII 502.

[ONFr. *caroigne*; the phonology of the second form is
obscure.]

Carp, *v.* to converse, VI 21 ; prate,
XVII 360. [ON. *karpa*, brag.]

Carpyng, *n.* narration, X *introd.*
[From prec.]

Cart, *n.* cart, VIII *b* 13, XVII 534 ;
v. to cart, VIII *b* 66 ; Cartere,
n. carter (as a name), XIV *d* 3 ;
Cart-mare, *n.* draught-mare,
VIII *a* 282. [ON. *kart-r*, OE.
cræt.]

Cas, Case, *n.* chance, general run
of events, circumstances, plight,
II 175, III 20, VII 25, 73, XII *a*
49, *b* 194, &c.; Caas, *pl.* XIII *b*
40 ; *in cas*, it may be, XI 101,
105, 216 ; *per cas*, by chance, XII
a 7, *b* 4. [OFr. *cas.*]

Cast(e), *v.* ; Cast(e), *pa. t.* V 249,
XII *b* 70, &c. ; Kest, V 207 ;
Casten, *pp.* IV *a* 60 ; Icast,
XIV *c* 79 ; Kast, I 143 ; Kest,
V 174 ; to cast, throw, put, I 143,
IV *b* 3, VIII *a* 61, X 33, XII *b*
103, &c. ; (in charity), VIII *a* 16 ;
to cast off, XVII 262 ; *icast out*,
abandoned, XIV *c* 79 ; to offer,
propose, V 174, 207 ; to scheme,
XI *b* 306. [ON. *kasta* ; for *e*
forms before *st* cf. Morsbach,
ME. Gram. § 87, n. 2.] *See* Kest,
n. ; Vpcaste.

Castel(l), *n.* castle, II 159, X 173,
XVII 349, 538 ; a tower or raised
structure on the deck of a ship
(*see* Topcastell), XVII 272. [OE.
(late) *castel* from ONFr. *castel.*]

Catel, Catayll, Catall, *n. sg. collect.*, goods, property, VIII *a* 86,
141, 214, XIV *c* 75, XVI 242,
XVII 156 (cattle), 326. [ONFr.
catel.]

Cateractes, *n. pl.* flood-gates,
XVII 343, 451 (*see* Genesis, vii.
11, viii. 2 ; Vulgate *cataractæ*,
sluices).

Caue, *n.* cave, V 114, XII *a* 65.
[OFr. *cave.*]

Cause (*of*), *n.* cause, reason (of),
XI *a* 17. 54, XIII *b* 66, XIV *c* 9 ;
cause perto, cause for it, XVII

102 ; cause, side in a quarrel, &c.,
IX 82, XI *a* 50. [OFr. *cause.*]

Cawht. *See* Kache.

Cerched. *See* Serche.

Certayn(e), Certeyn(e), Sar-
teyn(e) (XVI), *adj.* certain, sure;
fixed, definite, XI *b* 113, XVI
225 ; some particular, IX 268 ;
come to no certeyn, came to
nothing, I 179 ; *nou3t of certeyne*,
no definite rule, VIII *a* 145 ; *adv.*
assuredly, indeed, I 231, XVI 94,
XVII 176, &c. [OFr. *certain.*]

Certes, Certis, *adv.* certainly,
truly, VIII *b* 22, X 134, XI *b* 42,
293. [OFr. *certes.*]

Cesse, Sesse, *v.* to cease, leave
off, come to an end, VIII *a* 172,
XI *b* 205, XVI 44, 294 ; Cest,
pp. XVII 451 ; Cessynge, *n.*
ceasing, XI *b* 85. [OFr. *cesser.*]

Chace, *n.* quarry (in hunting),
XII *b* 7. [OFr. *chace.*]

Chace(n), to pursue, drive, IX 167,
229 ; *chace of*, drive, oust from,
VI 83. [OFr. *chacier.*]

Chaffare, *v.* to engage in trade,
VIII *a* 235, *b* 98. [From ME.
chapfare, chaffare, n. ; *see* Chapuare.]

Chayngede. *See* Chaunge.

Chambre(s). *See* Chaumber.

Chanel, *n.* channel, river-bed,
XIII *a* 57. [OFr. *chanel.*] *Cf.*
Karel.

Chapel(le), *n.* chapel, private
oratory (attached to a castle,
&c.), V 35, 118, &c. ; Schapellis,
pl. XI *b* 234. [OFr. *chapelle.*]

Chapelleyn, Chaplayn, *n.* chap-
lain (a priest serving a ' chapel ' ;
see prec.), VIII *a* 12, V 39.
[OFr. *chapelain.*]

Chapman, *n.* merchant, XII *b* 179.
[OE. *cēap-man.*]

Chapuare, *n.* trading, bargain,
III 60. [OE. *cēap + faru* ; cf.
ON. *kaup-för.*] *See* Chaffare, *v.*

Charde, *pa. t. sg.* turned back,
ceased to flow, VI 248. [OE.
cerran.]

Charge, *n.* burden ; weight, IV *b*
48 ; *a ping of charge*, a weighty,

important matter, XIV *c* 52. [OFr. *charge*.] *See* next.

Charge(n), *v.* to burden, IV *b* 51; *charge*(*n*) *with*, to burden with, to impose as an obligation, XI *b* 150, 198, 199, &c.; to enjoin, order (a person), XI *b* 15, 31, 71, 120, 193; to attach weight, importance, to, XI *b* 104, 106, 184, 188, 225. [OFr. *charger*.]

Charious, *adj.* burdensome, XI *b* 204. [OFr. *chargeous*, *charjous*.]

Charité, Charyté, *n.* charity, christian love (for God or one's fellows), IV *b* 15, VI 110, XI *b* 25, &c.; *out of ch.*, not in a state of ch., XI *b* 26, 89; *I will kepe ch.*, I will not lose my temper, XVII 235; *par charité, for ch.*, *for of saynte ch.*, (formulæ used in prayers, or requests), in the name of (holy) charity, VIII *a* 250, XV *d* 5, XVII 165, 174; *amen tor ch.*, a formula of conclusion, XVII 558. [OFr. *charité*; (*de*) *par* (*sainte*) *charité*.]

Charke, *v.* to creak, XII *a* 70. [OE. *cearcian*.]

Charnel, *n.* cemetery, VIII *a* 50. [OFr. *charnel*.]

Chaste, *v.* to rebuke, punish, VIII *a* 53, 318. [OFr. *chastier*.]

Chastice, Chastis(e), Chastyse, *v.* to punish, chastise, curb, XIV *c* 70, *d* 5, XVII 398, 403. [OFr. (rare) *chastiser*.]

Chaud(e), *adj.* hot, VIII *a* 306; (Fr. word indicating affectation of manners above labourers' station.)

Chaumber, Chambre (XVII), *n.* room (usually a smaller private room or bedroom), II 100, 196, 584, XVII 129, 281 (*see* Ches, and note), &c. [OFr. *chambre*.]

Chaunce, Chance, *n.* chance, fortune, adventure, event, I 22, 25, 28, 135, 221, V 331, VII 16; *for ch. þat may falle*, whatever may happen, V 64; *he cheueʒ þat chaunce*, he contrives that event, brings it to pass, V 35; *per*

chance, XII *b* 18, 57. [OFr. *ch*(*e*)*ance*.]

Chaunge, Change, *v.* to alter, change, *trans.* and *intr.*, IV *a* 2, 42, XII *a* 125, XIII *a* 4, 56, XV *a* 22, &c.; Chayngede, *pa. t.* XIII *b* 28; Ychaunged, *pp.* VIII *b* 85, XIII *b* 27. *Chaunged his cher*, V 101, see Chere. [OFr. *changier*; *chaingier*.]

Chaungyng, *n.* vicissitudes, VII 16; *ch. of wit*, alteration of sense, mistranslation, XI *a* 47.

Chees. *See* Chese, *v.*

Cheyne, *n.* chain, X 31. [OFr. *chaine*.]

Chekes, *n. pl.* cheeks, VIII *a* 169; *maugré Medes* (*thi*) *chekes*, in Meed's (thy) despite, VIII *a* 41, 151; *see* Maugré. [OE. *cēace*, *cēce*.]

Chekke, *n.* ill-luck, V 127. [OFr *eschec*, checkmate.]

Chelde, *adj.* cold, XV *e* 16. [OE. (WS.) *cēald*.] *See* Colde.

Chenes, *n. pl.* fissures, XIII *a* 8. [OE. *cine*, *cion-*.]

Chepynge, *n.* market, VIII *a* 294. [OE. *cēping*.]

Cher(e), Chiere (XII), *n.* face, XV *c* 15; looks, XII *a* 120; demeanour, VI 47; *mery chere*, gladness, XVII 463. *Chaunged his cher*, V 101; †altered the direction in which he faced, turned this way and that (cf. *Sir Gaw.*, 711); but the phrase elsewhere always refers to colour or expression of face. [OFr. *chiere*, *chere*.]

Cherche, Chirche, Churche, *n.* church, Church, I 3, 21, VIII *a* 12, 50, *b* 12, 63 (note), XI *a* 62, *b* 178, &c. [OE. *cirice*, *circe*.] *See* Kirke.

Chercheʒerd, *n.* churchyard, I 3, 66, 263; Cherche porche, church porch, I 77. [Prec. + OE. *ʒeard*; OFr. *porche*.]

Cherles. *See* Chorle.

Cheruelles, *n. pl.* chervils (a garden pot-herb), VIII *a* 289. [OE. *cerfille*.]

Ohes, Chese (MS. chefe), *n.* in *thre ches(e)*, three tiers or rows of, XVII 129, 281 (followed by sg. noun). [Perhaps a use of ME. *ches*, chess, as 'rows of squares' (OFr. *eschez*, pl. of *eschec*, *see* Chekke).]

Ohese, *v.* to choose; *chese you*, choose (for) yourselves, II 217; **Chees, Ches**, *pa. t. sg.* XI *b* 56, XII *a* 110; for past pple. *see* Ycore. [OE. *cēosan*.]

Cheses, *n. pl.* cheeses, VIII *a* 276. [OE. *cēse*.]

Chesible, *n.* chasuble (the outer vestment of a priest when celebrating Mass), VIII *a* 12. [OFr. *chesible*.]

Chesouns, *n. pl.* reasons, XI *a* 50. [Shortened from OFr. *ache(i)son*; *see* Enchesone.]

Cheualrous, *adj.* chivalrous, V 331. [OFr. *chevalerous*.] *See* Chiualrye.

Cheue, *v.* (to acquire), control, bring about; *cheuez þat chaunce*, brings that event to pass, V 35; **Cheuyt**, *pp.* brought about, VII 16. [OFr. *chevir* and *achever*.] *See* Acheue.

Cheuentayn, *n.* chieftain, Lord, VI 245. [OFr. *chevetaine*.]

Chibolles, *n. pl.* chibols, a variety of small onion, VIII *a* 289. [ONFr. **chiboule*, OFr. *ciboule*.]

Chyche, *n.* niggard, VI 245. [OFr. *chiche*, adj.]

Chyde, *v. intr.* to complain, find fault, VI 43, VIII *a* 307, 314. [OE. *cīdan*.]

Chiere. *See* Cher(e).

Child, Chylde, *n.* child, III 39, IV *a* 73, &c., *child hys*, child's, XIII *b* 23; **Childer, Chylder**, *pl.* XVII 327, 527; **Childern, Chyldern**, XIII *b* 16, 33, 37, &c.; **Children**, VIII *a* 91, &c. [OE. *cild*; *cildru*, pl.]

Child-bedde, *n.*; *on child-bedde*, in travail, II 399. [OE. *cīld + bedd*.]

Chillyng, *n.* becoming cold, in *for chillyng of here mawe*, to prevent their stomachs getting cold, VIII *a* 306. [OE. *cīlian*; but see *N.E.D.*]

Chirche. *See* Cherche.

Chiries, *n. pl.* cherries, VIII *a* 289. [ONFr. *cherise*, sg.; cf. OE. *cires-bēam*.]

Chyteryng, *n.* chattering, XIII *b* 14. [Echoic.]

Chiualrye, *n.* knighthood, the knights as a body, XIV *c* 42. [OFr. *chev-*, *chivalerie*.] *See* Cheualrous.

Chorle, *n.* common man, V 39; **Cherles**, *pl.* VIII *a* 50. [OE. *ceorl*.]

Cité, Cyté, Cytee, Citie, Sité, *n.* city, II 48, 479, VII 66, 85, VIII *b* 94, IX 23, XIII *b* 67, &c. [OFr. *cité*.]

Cytryne, *adj.* lemon-yellow, IX 115. [OFr. *citrin*.]

Clanly, *adv.* elegantly, VII 53. [OE. *clǣn-līce*.] *See* Clene.

Clatere, *v.* to clatter, resound, V 133, VII 137. [OE. *clatrian*.]

Clateryng, *n.* clattering, XV *h* 4. [OE. *clatrung*.]

Clause, *n.* clause (in grammar), XIV *c* 11 (*see* Construwe).[Med.L. *clausa*, OFr. *clause*.]

Cled, *pp.* clad; *cled in Stafford blew*, beaten black and blue, XVII 200; *see* Blew. [OE. *clǣþan* (rare).]

Cleket, *n.* trigger, X 82. [OFr. *cliquet*.]

Clene, *adj.* clean, IV *b* 6, V 323, 325; unmixed, VIII *a* 299; pure, VII 179, XI *b* 295, XV *i* 7; elegant, VII 77; splendid, VII 150 (or *adv.*). [OE. *clǣne*.] *See* Clanly, Clense.

Clen(e), *adv.* entirely, VII 150 (or *adj.*), XIV *b* 77, *c* 56, 80. [OE. *clǣne*.]

Clengeȝ, 3 *sg. pres.* clings, V 10. [OE. **clengan*.] *See* Clingge.

Clense, *v.* to cleanse, clear out, IV *a* 7, VIII *a* 98. [OE. *clǣnsian*.]

Clepe(n), Clepyn, *v.* to call (cry, summon, name), I *intred.*, II

201, III 12, 24, IX 27, XII *a* 76, *b* 16 ; Cleped, Clept, *pp.* II 49, IX 3, XII *a* 6, &c. ; Ycleped, II 52, III 17, 32. [OE. *cleopian.*]

Clere, *adj.* clear, bright, glorious, fair, II 269, 358, V 283, VII 107, 123, XVI 128, 389 ; free (from guilt), *XVI 356 (MS. clene) ; *adv.* clearly, VII 77 ; Clerlych, *adv.* clearly, XIII *a* 12. [OFr. *cler.*]

Clerematyn, *n.* (? *lit.* 'fine morning') appar. name of a fine flour, or bread made from it, VIII *a* 299. [? OFr. *cler matin.*]

Clerk(e), *n.* one in holy orders, ecclesiastic (opp. to 'lay'), scholar, writer, II 2, VII 53, VIII *b* 56, 58, XI *a* 36, 59, *b* 55, 177, XVI 283, &c. ; Clerkus, *pl.* VIII *b* 65. [OE. *cler(i)c* ; OFr. *clerc.*]

Clete, *n.* cleat, small (wedge-shaped) piece of wood ; *jaf nouʒt a cl. of* = cared not a rap for, XIV *c* 54. [OE. **clēat* ; cf. OHG. *chlōʒ*, MDu. *cloot.*]

Cleue, *v.* to split, V 133. [OE. *clēofan.*]

Clyff, *n.* cliff, rock, V 10, 133. [OE. *clif.*]

Clingge, *v.* XV *a* 8 ; *the clot him clingge,* may the earth of the grave cling to him (*or* waste him ; cf. *alþaʒ oure corses in clotteʒ clynge,* Pearl 857) ; Yclongen, *pp.* withered, II 508. [OE. *clingan,* shrivel, shrink.] *See* Clengeʒ.

Clipte, *pa. t. sg.* clasped, XII *b* 62. [OE. *clyppan.*]

Cloise. *See* Clos.

Cloistre, *n.* monastery, III *introd.*, VIII *a* 141. [OFr. *cloistre.*]

Cloke, *n.* cloak, VIII *a* 265. [OFr. *cloque.*]

Clomben, *pa. t. pl.* climbed, V 10. [OE. *clímban* ; pa. t. pl. *clúmbon.*]

Cloos, *n.* enclosure ; *in cloos*, enclosed, IX 191. [OFr. *clos.*]

Clos, Cloise (oi = ō, cf. Coyll), *adj.* closed ; secluded, forbidden, VII 179 ; close, VI 152 (*man hit cl.,* make it secure) ; *adv.* (or

predic. adj.) close, near, VII 137. [OFr. *clos.*]

Close, *v.* to close, enclose, IX 172, XI *b* 39 ; Yclosed, *pp.* XIII *a* 24, 40. [From prec.] *See* Enclose.

Clot, *n.* clod, XV *a* 8 (*see* Clingge) ; Clottes, *pl.* lumps, XIII *a* 5. [OE. *clott.*]

Clop, *n.* a cloth, XV *f* 8 ; cloth, VIII *a* 14 ; Clopes, &c., *pl.* clothes, I 165, 236, II 408, VII 175, VIII *b* 18, XI *b* 257, XIII *a* 9, &c. [OE. *cláþ.*]

Cloped, *pp.* clothed, VIII *b* 2. [OE. (late) *cláþian.*]

Clope-merys, *n. pl.* ? mare-clothers, (? contemptuous reference to blacksmiths as fashioning pieces of horse-armour ; for similar compound *see* Brenwaterys), XV *h* 21. [Prec. + OE. *mēre.*]

Cloude, *n.*[1] clod of earth ; *under cloude*, in the ground, XV *b* 31. [OE. *clūd*, mass of earth, or rock.]

Cloud(e), Clowde, *n.*[2] cloud, VII 107, 137, XII *a* 137. [Prob. same as prec.]

Clout, *n.* piece of cloth, XV *f* 8, 11. [OE. *clūt.*]

Cloute, *v.* to patch ; *cloute more to*, stick more on to it, XI *b* 200 ; *go cloute thi shone*, go and cobble your shoes, 'run away and play', XVII 353 ; Yclouted, *pp.* patched, VIII *a* 61. [OE. *clūtian.*]

**Clowe ; *clowe gylofres,* cloves, IX 157. [OFr. *clou* (nail) *de girofle (gilofre).*]

Clustre, *n.* bunch, IX 153, 160. [OE. *cluster.*]

Cnistes. *See* Knyght(e).

Cnowe. *See* Knowe.

Coo, Cok, *n.* cock, XII *a* 77, XV *g* 33. [OE. *cocc.*]

Coffes, *n. pl.* mittens, gloves, VIII *a* 62. [Unknown ; *cf.* Prompt. Parv., '*cuffe,* glove or meteyne'.]

Coyll, n. *lit.* cabbage ; pottage, cabbage or vegetable soup, XVII 389. [OE. *cāl* ; *oy* = ō (see the rimes).] *See* Koleplantes.

Coke, *v.* to put hay into cocks, VIII *b* 13. [From (obscure) ME. *cocke,* hay-cock; see *N.E.D.*]

Coker, *n.* a labourer (at hay-making or harvest), VIII *b* 13. [From prec.; *cf.* Cath. Angl., ' *coker,* autumnarius '.]

Cokeres, *n. pl.* leggings, VIII *a* 62. [OE. *coxor,* quiver; *cf.* Prompt. Parv., ' *cocur,* cothurnus '.]

Coket, *n.* very fine flour next in grade to the finest (*wastell*), VIII *a* 299. [*Panis de coket* occurs in 14th c. legal Latin; connexion between this and AFr. *cokkette,* Anglo-L. *coketa,* cocket, seal of King's Custom-house, has been suggested, but not proved.]

Cold(e), *adj.* cold, I 119, VII 115, &c.; **Calde,** IV *a* 82. [OE. *cáld.*] *See* Chelde.

Cold(e), *n.* cold, I 163, IX 31, XV *f* 13; *for colde of,* to keep the cold from (*see* For. *prep.*), VIII *a* 62. [OE. *cáld.*]

Col(e), *n.* live coal, IV *a* 13; coal, XV *h* 5. [OE. *col,* live coal.]

Coloppes, *n. pl.* ' collops', eggs fried on bacon, VIII *a* 280. [See *N.E.D.,* s.v. *Collop,* and *Cockney.*]

Colour, *n.* colour, IX 34, XII *a* 55, &c.; outward appearance, XI *b* 217. [OFr. *colour.*]

Com, Come(n), **Cum** (X), *v.* to come, I 80, 176, II 137, V 43, X 45, 173, XVII 241, &c.; **Comest,** 2 *sg.* wilt come, XV *g* 5; **Commys,** 3 *sg.* XVII 507; **Cam,** *pa. t.* I 77, II 153, VIII *a* 294, &c.; **Com**(e), I 32, II 91, III 3, V 107, VI 222, VII 83, &c.; *pa. t. subj.* (should come, &c.), VI 214, 238, VIII *a* 108, X 29, XV *g* 30; **Come**(n), *pp.* I 161, II 29, 181, IX 314, &c.; **Comyn,** VII 40, 102; **Comne,** IV *a* 23; **Cumen,** XIV *b* 8, 87; **Ycome**(n), II 203, 319, 404, 422, 478, 592. With *dat. refl. pron.* in: *foret hym com,* forth

came, XV *g* 18; *in him com .. gvn,* came (walking) in (cf. OE. *cóm inn gán*), XV *g* 24; *him com,* III 19. *Comen of,* descended from, II 29. [OE. *cuman, cóm, cumen.*]

Coma(u)nde, Comawnde, Commaund, *v.* to command, I 105, VIII *a* 16, XI *b* 66, XV *i* 1, XVI 341, XVII 118, &c.; with *to,* XI *b* 40; to commend, V 343; to entrust, give, XI *b* 222. [OFr. *comander.*]

Com(m)**aundement,** &c., *n.* commandment, IV *b* 15, XI *b* 63, 86, 226; *gaf in comm.,* commanded, XVII 32. [OFr. *comandement.*] *See* Maundement.

Comenci (II), **Comse** (VIII), *v.* to begin, VIII *a* 34, 309; *pres. subj.* II 247 (note to l. 57). [OFr. *comencer.*] *See* Comessing.

Comendacion, *n.* ' Commendation of Souls ', an office for the dead (made a part of daily office) which originally ended with the prayer *Tibi, Domine, commendamus,* XI *b* 132.

Comessing, *n.* beginning, II 57. *See* Comenci.

Comford, &c. *See* Conforte, *v.*

Comyng(e), *n.* coming, advent, XII *a* 35, XVI 315, 363, &c.; *hom comynge,* homecoming, IX 285. *See* Com.

Comyn(s). *See* Com, Comun.

Comly(ch), *adj.* fair, beautiful, V 343, XVII 71. [OE. *cӯmlic,* influ. in ME. by assoc. with *becomen.*]

Comlyng, *n.* stranger, foreigner, XIII *b* 45. [OE. *cuma + -ling.*]

Commys. *See* Com.

Commyxstion, *n.* intermingling, XIII *b* 12. [L. *commixtiōnem.*]

Comne. *See* Com.

Comounly, *adv.* usually, IX 51; in common, IX 60. *See* Comun.

Compayni, *n.* company, II 462; **Company(e),** VII 150, IX 312, &c.; **Cumpany(e),** X 147, &c.; *in cumpanye,* in the society of men, I *introd.*, IX 288. [OFr. *compai(g)nie.*]

Comparison, *n.* comparison; *wiþoute comparison*, XI *b* 237. [OFr. *comparaison, -eson.*]

Compelle, *v.* to compel, XI *b* 51, XIII *b* 18. [OFr. *compeller.*]

Compilet, *pp.* compiled, put together, VII 53. [OFr. *compiler.*]

Comprehended, *pa. t. sg.* comprised, embraced, IX 300. [L. *comprehendere.*]

Compuncoion, *n.* repentance, XI *b* 180. [OFr. *compunction.*]

Comse. *See* Comenci.

Comun(e), *adj.* common (people), XIV *b* 67; as *sb.*, the community, VIII *b* 20, 79; Comunes, Comyns, *pl.* the common people; the Commons (as an estate of the realm), XIV *b* 67, *c* 73; lay men, XI *a* 39, 59. [OFr. *comun*; and direct from L. *commūnis.*]

Con(en), Coneȝ. *See* Can, *v.*[1] and *v.*[2]

Concyens, Conscience, *n.* conscience, IV *b* 15, VIII *b* 87, &c.; (personified) VIII *b* 6, &c. [OFr. *conscience.*]

Condicioun, *n.* nature, quality, XII *a* 120. [OFr. *condicion.*]

Confederat, *adj.* allied, XIII *b* 5. [L. *con-fœderātus.*]

Confesse, *v.* to confess, XI *b* 143; *confessed clene*, made clean by confession, V 323. [OFr. *confesser.*]

Conforme, *v.* (*refl.*), to suit (oneself), make (oneself) suitable, XII *a* 184. [OFr. *conformer.*]

Confort, Coumforde, *n.* support, comfort, consolation, VI 9, VIII *b* 79, XII *a* 151. [OFr. *con-, cunfort.*]

Conforte, Com-, *v.* to comfort, succour, support, IV *a* 15, VIII *a* 214; Comford, *pa. t. pl.* VII 173. [OFr. *conforter.*]

Confusyun, *n.* putting to shame, I 203. [OFr. *confusion.*]

Congele, *v.* to congeal, IX 64. [OFr. *congeler.*]

Conig, *n.* rabbit, XIV *b* 75. [OFr. *conin, coning.*]

Conne, Conneþ, &c. *See* Can, *v.*[1]

Connynge, *n.* intelligence, IV *b* 56, 79. [From *cunn-*, old infin. stem of Can, *v.*[1]]

Conquerour, *n.* conqueror, XIV *c* 92. [OFr. *conquerour.*]

Conquest, *n.* the (Norman) Conquest, XIII *b* 32. [OFr. *conqueste.*]

Consaile (-sale, -seyl, -seille), Counsail(le), (-sayle, -sayll), *n.* counsel, deliberation, advice, II 179, VIII *a* 309, X 15, XIV *b* 40, 43, XVI 114, 163, XVII 157; prudence, IV *b* 56, 57, 61; council, VIII *a* 312, IX 296, 298. [OFr. *conseil, c(o)unseil,* counsel, council.]

Conseille, to advise, VIII *a* 14; Counsell, *imper. sg.* XVII 472. [OFr. *conseillier.*]

Consente, *v.* to agree; *consented to o wyl*, was agreed, I 49. [OFr. *consentir.*]

Consider, *v.* to reflect, XVII 291. [OFr. *considerer.*]

Constreyne, *v.* to force, VIII *b* 56, XI *b* 248. [OFr. *constreign-*, stem of *constreindre.*]

Construccion, *n.* construing, XIII *b* 28. [L. *constructiōnem*; *see* next.]

Constru(w)e, *v.* to construe, interpret, XIII *b* 18, 34; *pres. subj. pl.* in *ȝif ȝe c. wel þis clause*, if you see the point of what I say, XIV *c* 11. [L. *construere.*]

Conteyne, *v.* to contain, IX 337, XIII *a* 20. [OFr. *contenir, conteign-*, stem of subj.]

Contemplacio(u)n, Contemplacyone, *n.* contemplation (of God), IV *b* 51, XI *b* 11, 308. [OFr. *contemplacion.*]

Contemplatyf, -if, *adj.* contemplative, devoted to prayer and contemplation of God, VIII *a* 245, XI *b* 1, 8, &c. [OFr. *contemplatif.*]

Continue, *v.* to persevere, VIII *b* 40, 110. [OFr. *continuer.*]

Contynuell, *adj.* continual, IX 32. [OFr. *continuel.*]

Contray (XIII), **Contré**, -ee, -ey, (IX), **Countré** (XVII), **Cuntray** (II), **Cuntré** (I), **Cuntrey** (XI), *n.* country, land, region, I 253, II 351, IX 4, 9, 26, 134, 138, XI *a* 35, XIII *a* 41, *b* 63, XVII 487 (*see* Sere), &c., as *adj.* in *contray longage*, language of the land, XIII *b* 13. [OFr. *contrée, c(o)untrée.*]

Contrarie (*to*), *adj.* opposed (to), XI *b* 54. [OFr. *contrarie.*]

Contrefetes, *n. pl.* imitations, IX 117. [OFr. *contrefet*, pp., made like.] *See* Counterfete, *v.*

Cop, *n.* top, XIII *a* 45. [OE. *copp.*]

Cope, *n.* long cloak, XII *a* 53; *esp.* the out-door cloak of an ecclesiastic, VIII *a* 182. [OE. *cápe, from Med.L. *cápa.*]

Cope, *v.* to provide with 'copes', VIII *a* 141. [From prec.]

Copuls, 3 *sg. pres.* links, IV *a* 12; **Coppled**, *pp.* linked (in rime), Introduction xv; *see* Kowe. [OFr. *copler.*] *See* Couple, *n.*

Corage, *n.* heart, XII *a* 11; gallantry, XIV *c* 108. [OFr. *corage.*]

Corde, *n.* cord, XII *b* 53, 60, &c. [OFr. *corde.*]

Corde(n), *v.*; *corden into on*, agree together, XV *i* 6. [Shortened from Acorde, *q.v.*]

Cormerant, *n.* cormorant, II 310. [OFr. *cormoran.*]

Coround(e), *pa. t.* crowned, VI 55; *pp.* II 593, VI 120. [OFr. *corouner.*] *See* Crouned(e).

Corounez, *n. pl.* crowns, VI 91. [OFr. *coroune.*] *See* Croun(e).

Corsed(est). *See* Curse.

Corseynt, *n.* shrine of a saint, I 239. [OFr. *cors saint*, holy body.]

Cortays(e), **Curteys** (II), *adj.* gracious, II 28, VI 73; as *sb.*, gracious lady, V 343. [OFr. *corteis, curteis.*] *See* Kort.

Cortaysye, **Cortaysé**, **Courtaysye**, *n.* courtesy, grace, VI 72, 84, 96, 109, 121 (*of cortaysye* prob. only equivalent to *cortayse*, adj.); *of courtaysye, by cortaysye*, &c. by especial favour, VI 97, 108, 120. [OFr. *corteisie, curteisie.*]

Cortaysly, **Curteisly**, -lich, *adv.* courteously, VI 21, VIII *a* 34, 157. *See* Cortays.

Cossez, **Cosses**, *n. pl.* kisses, V 283, 292. [OE. *coss.*] *See* Kysse.

Cost, *n.*[1] border, IX 192; **Costes**, *pl.* coasts, regions, VII 83, 146. [OFr. *coste.*]

Cost, *n.*[2] expenditure, cost, XI *b* 169; ? means (to meet expense), XI *b* 141. [OFr. *cost.*]

Costen (*in*), *v.* to expend (on), XI *b* 234. [OFr. *coster.*]

Costes, *n. pl.* manners, disposition, V 292. [OE. (Nth.) *cost* from ON. *kost-r.*]

Costy, *adj.* costly, XI *b* 228, 234. [From Cost, *n.*[2]]

Cote, *n.*[1] cot, mean dwelling, II 489, VIII *b* 2. [OE. *cot.*]

Cote, *n.*[2] coat; here a tunic (*cf.* 'waistcoat') worn beneath the outer gown, XVII 262. [OFr. *cote.*]

Coth, *n.* pestilence, XVII 417. [OE. *copu.*]

Cou, **Cow**, *n.* cow, III 49, 52, 54, VIII *a* 282; *pl.* **Ken**, III 56; **Kyzn**, IX 256; **Kyn**(e), VIII *a* 134, *b* 18. [OE. *cú*; pl. *cý* (Kt. *cé).]

Couaytyng, **Coueytynge**, *n.* coveting, IX 90; object of coveting (cf. *louyng*, &c.), IV *a* 23. [From OFr. *coveit(i)er.*]

Couaytise (III), **Coueitise** (XI), **Couetyse**, (v), **Coueteis** (XVII), *n.* covetousness, avarice, III 22, V 306, 312, XI *b* 55, 256, XVII 52. [OFr. *coveitise.*]

Couche, *n.* bed, XII *a* 89. [OFr. *couche.*]

Coude. *See* Can, *v.*

Coueyne, *n.* band (of conspirators), I 41. [OFr. *cov(a)ine.*]

Coueitous, *adj.* covetous, XI *b* 196. [OFr. *coveitous*.]

Couenable, *adj.* suitable, XIII *a* 20. [OFr. *covenable*.]

Covenant, Couenaunde, -aunt, *n.* covenant, agreement, V 260, 272, VI 202, 203, VIII *a* 153, XII *b* 41, 96, 199 ; *pl.* terms of the agreement, V 174 ; *in c. þat*, on condition that, VIII *a* 28. [OFr. *covenant*.]

Coueryng, *n.* covering, I 177, 184. [From OFr. *covrir*.]

Coumforde; Counsail(le), &c. *See* Confort; Consaile (-seille).

Counted, *pa. t.* reckoned on (*or* heeded), VII 115 ; *counted nouȝt a bene beo*, gave not a bean for, XIV *c* 43. [OFr. *cunter*.]

Counterfete, *v.* to imitate (fraudulently), IX 114 ; to resemble, VI 196 (bad connotation often absent in this use, but possibly here present—'make them unjustly resemble us'). [Formed from ME. *counterfete*, imitated, OFr. *contrefet*.] *See* Contrefetes.

Countes, *n.* countess, VI 129. [OFr. *cuntesse*.]

Countré. *See* Contray.

Countre note, *n.* counterpoint, a melody added as an accompaniment to another, XI *b* 137 (note). [OFr. *countre + note*.]

Couple, *n.* match, pair, II 458 (note) ; **Copple**, couplet (in verse), Introduction xxxiii. [OFr. *couple*.]

Cours(e), *n.* course, VII 102, XIII *a* 61, &c.; *cours...about*, circuit, X 157 ; flow, VII 123 ; force, rushing, VII 115 ; *by course*, in due order, VII 73. [OFr. *cours*.]

Court(aysye). *See* Cortaysye, Kort.

Courtpies, *n. pl.* short jackets, VIII *a* 182. [Current in 14th and 15th centuries ; cf. MDu. *korte pie*, short coat of coarse woollen stuff.]

Coupe, Couthe. *See* Can, *v.*

Couwee, *adj.* tailed, in (*ryme*) *couwee*, rime in pairs followed by a shorter line, or 'tail', tail-rime, Introduction xv. [OFr. *rime couée*.] *See* Kowe.

Cowardise, Coward(d)yse, *n.* cowardice, V 205, 306, 311. [OFr. *couardise*.] *See* Kowarde.

Cowth, Cowþe(ȝ). *See* Can, *v.*

Crache, *v.* to scratch, II 80. [Obscure ; cf. MDu., MLG. *kratsen*.]

Cradel, *n.* cradle, XIII *b* 22, XV *f* 4. [OE. *cradol*.]

Craft(e), *n.* craft ; industry, VIII *b* 20; knowledge, in *to ken all the cr.*, to know the whole story, VII 25. [OE. *cræft*.]

Crafty, *adj.* skilled in a craft, VIII *a* 70. [OE. *cræftig*.]

Cragge, *n.* crag, V 115, 153. [Obscure.]

Crak, *v.* to crack, XIV *a* 10; **Crakked**, *pp.* XIV *a* 11. [OE. *cracian*, to crack (sound).]

Craue, Crafe (XVII), *v.* to demand, VIII *a* 86 ; to plead for, XVII 174 ; *craue aftir*, ask for, XVI 242. [OE. *crafian*, demand.]

Creatoure, Creatur, *n.* creature, XV *i* 4, XVII 78. [OFr. *creature*.]

Crede, *n.* the Creed, VI 125 ; *sall ken ȝow ȝowre crede* = will teach you what you ought to know, a lesson, XIV *b* 4. [OE. *crēda*, from L. *crēdo*, I believe (cf. VIII *a* 83).]

Credence, *n.* credence, IX 303. [OFr. *credence*.]

Creem, *n.* cream, VIII *a* 277. [OFr. *cresme*.]

Cren, *n.* crane (machine), X 16, 28. [OE. *cran* (bird) ; the above are the earliest recorded instances of the transferred sense.]

Crepe, *v.* to creep, XII *b* 173. [OE. *crēopan*.]

Creuisse, *n.* fissure, V 115. [OFr. *crevasse*.]

Cri(e), Cry, *n.* lamentation, II 114, 220 ; *held in o cri*, lamented in the same strain, II 195 ; shouting, clamour, II 285, XV *h* 4; a cry, appeal, II 511 (*see* Sette) [OFr. *cri*.]

Crie(n), Crye(n), Cry, to cry out (shout, call, lament), proclaim, XI *b* 48, XII *a* 76, 140, XVI 186, 363, XVII 384, &c. ; *pres. subj.* XVI 141 ; Crid(e), *pa. t.* II 78, XII *b* 31, 69 ; Cryit, X 86 ; Criand, -ende, *pres. p.* XVI 73, XII *b* 16. *Cryen after*, shout for, XV *k* 5 ; *crie on*, appeal to XVI 107 ; *cry me mercy*, cry to me for mercy, XVII 384 (the earliest recorded sense in E.). [OFr. *crier*.]

Criere, *n.* crier, herald, XI *b* 48. [OFr. *crier*.]

Criing, Criyng(e), *n.* (loud) shouting, XI *b* 133, 249 ; *at o criing*, with one voice, II 581 (cf. *at one cri*, Havelok 2773) ; lamentation, II 195. [From Crie(n).]

Cristal(l), *n.* crystal, II 358, IX 32, 103, &c. [OFr. *cristal.*]

Crystemesse, *n.* Christmas, I 29. [OE. *crīstmesse.*]

Cristen(e), Crystene, Crystyn (I), Krysten (VI), *adj.* Christian, I *introd.*, 82, VI 101, IX 211, XI *a* 37, &c. ; as *sb. pl.* VIII *a* 89. [OE. *crīsten.*]

Cristendom, -dam, *n.* Christian lands, IX 214, XIV *c* 19. [OE. *crīsten-dōm*, Christianity.]

Croft, *n.* small field, VIII *a* 33, 285, *b* 17. [OE. *croft.*]

Croppeth, 3 *pl. pres.* nibble, VIII *a* 33. [ON. *kroppa.*]

Crouders, *n. pl.* fiddlers, II 522. [From ME. *croud, crouþ* (Welsh *crwth*), fiddle.]

Croun(e), Crowne, *n.* crown, II 235, 415, VI 67, &c. ; crown of the head, XIV *a* 10, 11. [OFr. *coroune* ; cf. ON. *krúna.* In the sense 'crown of head' only the cr- forms appear.] *See* Coroune3.

Crouned(e), *pp.* tonsured, admitted to holy orders, VIII *b* 58, 62, 67. [OFr. *corouner.*] *See* prec. (which also in ME. had sense 'tonsure'), and Corounde, Vncrouned.

Crowe, *n.* a crow, XII *a* 75. [OE. *crāwe.*]

Crowe, *v.* to crow, XV *g* 33 (with pleonastic reflex. pron.) ; to announce by crowing, XII *a* 77. [OE. *crāwan.*]

Cruddes, *n. pl.* curds, VIII *a* 277. [Obscure.]

Cruell, *adj.* cruel, IX 237. [OFr. *cruel.*]

Cubite, (Cubettis, *pl.*), *n.* cubit (Biblical length measure = ell), XVII 124, 136, 258, 261, 443. [OE. *cubit*, L. *cubitus.*]

Cultur, *n.* coulter, iron blade fixed in front of the share in a plough, VIII *a* 98. [OE. (from L.) *culter.*]

Cum, Cumen. *See* Com.

Cumbrit, *pp.* hampered, VII 183. [OFr. *(en)combrer.*]

Cunesmen, *n. pl.* kinsfolk, XV *g* 6. [OE. *cynnes*, gen. + *mann.*]

Cunne(s). *See* Can, Kyn.

Cuntek, *n.* contest ; *yn cuntek*, vying with one another, I 31. [OFr. (only AFr.) *contek*, of unknown origin.]

Cuntenaunce, *n.* bearing, II 293. [OFr. *cuntenance.*]

Cuntray, -6, -ey. *See* Contray.

Cuppes, *n.* cups, IX 256. [OE. *cuppe.*]

Curse, *v.* to curse, I 98, 130, &c.; Corsed, Cursed, *pp.* and *adj.* v 128, 306, IX 85, &c. ; *cursed shrewe*, VII 183, VIII *a* 153. [OE. (late) *cūrsian*, from OIr. *cúrsagim.*]

Cursyng, *n.* cursing, I 128, 154, 261. [OE. (late) *cūrsung.*]

Curteis, -eys. *See* Cortays.

Custome, *n.* custom, IX 292, XI *b* 204, 206. [OFr. *custume.*]

Dai, Day(e), *n.* day, I 138, VI 56 XII *a* 68, &c. ; dawn, XII *a* 77 ; life-time, II 572, &c. (also *pl.* VI 56, VII 39) ; *daies olde*, old age, XII introd.; time, in *withinne tuo monthe day*, in two months' time, XII *a* 29 ; *þise daye3* (gen. sg.) *longe*, all (this) day long, VI 173 (*see* Longe) ; *by dayes*, once upon a time, II 15 ; *bi this dai*, (for) this day, VIII *a* 274; but an oath at XV *a* 24, XVII 386; *on a day*, one day, II 303; *þis othir daye*, the other day, XVI 148; *þis endre dai*, a day or two ago (*see* Endre), XV *a* 4. [OE. *dæg*.]

Dayeseȝes, *n. pl.* daisies, XV *b* 4. [OE. *dæges éage*.]

Dalf; Dalt. *See* Deluen; Delen.

Dam(e), *n.* dame, lady, queen, II 63, 113, 322, VIII *a* 72, XVII 298, &c.; mother, VIII *a* 73, XVII 324. [OFr. *dame*.]

Damisel, Damysel(le), *n.* damsel (*esp.* young lady-in-waiting), II 90, 144, VI 1, 129. [OFr. *damisele*.]

Dampne, *v.* to damn, condemn, XI *b* 197, 306; Dampnet, *pa. t. pl.* VII 50; Dampned, *pp.* XVI 272; as *sb.* XVI 377. [OFr. *dam(p)ner*.]

Dan(e), Danȝ, Master, Dom, an honourable title esp. prefixed to names of members of religious orders, I *introd.*, III *introd.* [OFr. *Dan* (nom. *Danz, Dans*); L. *Dom(i)nus*.]

Danes, *n. pl.* Danes, XIII *b* 13. [Med. L. *Dani.* (cf. ON. *Danir*).]

Dang. *See* Dynge(n).

Dar, *v.* dare, 1 *sg. pres.* II 336, VIII *a* 263, &c.; 3 *sg.* IX 88, &c.; Dare, *pres. pl.* XVI 145; Dore(n), XI *b* 36, 199; Dorst(e), *pa. t. sg.* dared, XII *b* 109, XIV *c* 21; Durst, II 140, 427, 482; *pl.* II 73, 84, X 130; Durst, *pa. t. subj.* (would) dare, XVII 479. [OE. *dearr, durron*; *dorste*.]

Dare, *v.* to cower, V 190; ? Dard, *pa. t. sg.* VI 249 (*see* note). [OE. *darian*.]

Dase, *v.* to be dumbfounded, XVII 314. [OE. **dasian*; cf. *darian*, and ON. *dasa-sk*.]

Dastard, *n.* wretch, vile fellow, XVI 180, 203. [Perhaps formed with Fr. suffix *-ard* from *dased*, *dast*, pp. of prec.]

Date, *n.* date, used in VI in various senses, some strained; point of time, hour, VI 169, 181; season, 144 (*see* Dere), 145; limit (beginning or end), 133, 156, 157, 168, 180; *to dere a date*, ? too soon, 132 (*cf.* 126). [OFr. *date*.]

Daunce, Dance, *n.* dance, I 134, 227; *fig.* plight, XIV *b* 72. [OFr. *dance, daunce*.]

Daunce, Daunse, *v.* to dance, I 21, 72, 87, II 298, XV *d* 6; **Daunsynge**, *n.* dancing, XI *b* 139. [OFr. *dancer*.]

Daw, *n.* (jackdaw), fool, XVII 247. [OE. **dawe*.]

Dawing, Dawyng, *n.* daybreak, first signs of dawn, IV *a* 94, X 42. [OE. *dagung*.]

De. *See* Deye.

Deaw, Dew, *n. pl.* dew, IX 59, XV *b* 28, &c.; *May dew*, dew gathered in May (believed to have medicinal and magical properties), IX 63. [OE. *déaw*.]

Debate, *n.* parleying, wrangling, V 180, XVI 142; *wythouten debate*, putting aside contention, VI 30. [OFr. *debat*.]

Debate, *v.* to contend, XII *b* 225; Debatande, *pres. p.* debating, V 111. [OFr. *debat-re*.]

Declare, *v.* to set out, declare, VII 77, XII *b* 210. [OFr. *declarer*.]

Declyne, *v.* (to decline), fall; *con d. into acorde*, came to an agreement (*cf.* ME. *fall at* (or *of*) *accorde*), VI 149. [OFr. *decliner*.]

Ded(e), *adj.* dead, I 195, 209, II 108, &c.; used as pp. of 'slay', VII 92, XVI 148; *was broght dede*, was brought to death, died, I 213. [OE. *déad*.] *See* next, and Deþ.

Ded(e), *n.*[1] death, I 212, IV *a* 48, *b* 71, X 51, 77, 118, XVI 317, XVII 193, 543. [A variant, usually Northern, of Deþ, *q.v.*]

Ded(e), *n.*[2] deed, act, feat, event, III 45, VII 38, 88, IX 312, XI *b*

255, XVI 24, &c.; as obj. to *do*,
I 79, VIII *b* 9, XII *a* 111; behaviour, way of acting, IV *a* 62,
XI *b* 62; *Dedis of Apostlis*, Acts
of the Apostles, XI *b* 285; *in
dede*, in the actual performance,
VII 23, XVI 72; *to fre of dede*,
too lavish in its action, VI 121;
in dede and poʒte, in performance
and intention, VI 164. [OE. *dēd*.]

Ded-day, *n.* death-day, VIII
introd. [OE. *dēaþ-dæg*; see Dede
(death), but here assimilation of
þd to *dd* is possible.]

Ded(e), Deden, *v.* *See* Don.

Dedir, *v.* to tremble, XVII 314.
[Cf. MnE. *dither*.]

Dedly, *adj.* mortal, XI *b* 208, 209,
211. [OE. *dēadlic*.]

Defaced, *pp.* effaced, erased, III
36. [OFr. *de(s)facier, defacer*.]

Defaute, *n.* defect, XI *a* 43, 44,
57; lack, in *for defaute of*, for
lack of, VIII *a* 200, XI *b* 250.
[OFr. *defaute*.]

Defence, Defens (of), *n.* defence
(against), IX 332, X 64, 135; *of
noble defens*, nobly fortified, II
48. [OFr. *defense*.]

Defend(e), *v.* to defend, V 49,
VIII *a* 82, X 52, &c.; to make
defence, X 61, 191; make de-
fence against, ward off, VII 85;
Defending, *n.* defence, X 194.
[OFr. *defend-re*.]

Defensouris, *n. pl.* defenders, X
153. [OFr. *defensour*.]

Deffie, *v.* to defy, XVI 158. [OFr.
de(s)fier.]

Degiselich, *adj.* strange, wonderful, II 360. [From OFr. *de(s)-
guis(i)é*.] *See* Gisely.

Degrade (rime-form of), *pa. t. sg.*
degraded, XVII 20. [OFr.
degrader.]

Degré, Degree, *n.* position, rank,
VIII *b* 71, XVII 21, 489; state
(of preparedness), X 40. [OFr.
degré.]

Deye (VIII), De (X), Dye(n),
v. to die, II 189, VIII *a* 269, 325,
IX 150, X 73, &c.; Deye, *pres.
subj.* VIII *a* 92, 114; Deyd, *pa.*

t. sg. I 215; Dyʒede, XIV *c* 106;
Deyden, *pa. t. pl.* VIII *b* 41;
do .. deye, garre .. dye, kill, VIII
a 269, XVI 164. [ON. *deyja*.]

Deill, Deyll. *See* Dele, *n.*

Deyned, *pa. t. pl.* deigned, VIII *a*
303. [OFr. *deigner*.]

Deynté, *n.* delicacy, II 254.
[OFr. *deinté*.]

Delaiement, *n.* delay, XII *b* 152.
[OFr. *delaiement*.]

Dele, Deill, Deyll, *n.* part,
quantity, in *a grete dele*, a great
deal, XVII 450; *ich a deyll*, all,
XVII 299; *ylk a dele, ilke deill*,
altogether, IV *a* 27, X 75. [OE.
dǣl.] *See* Euerydel, Halvendel,
Somdel, &c.

Dele(n), *v.* to divide, distribute,
deal, mete out, perform, V 124,
217, VI 246, VIII *a* 91, XI *b* 270,
272; Dalt, *pa. t. sg.* V 350;
Deled, *pp.* XIII *b* 49; *dele with*,
have to do with, XVI 63; with
cognate obj. *dele penny doyll*,
XVII 390 (*see* Doyll); *delen ato*,
part (*intr.*), II 125. [OE.
dǣlan.]

Dele. *See* Deuel.

Delit(e), Delyte, *n.* delight, IV *b*
39, XII *a* 88, XVI 63; *delytes of*,
delight in, IV *b* 62. [OFr. *delit*.]

Delitabill, *adj.* delightful, X *introd.* [OFr. *delitable*.]

Delytte, *v.* in *delyttes þaym* (*in*),
3 *pl. refl.*, take delight (in), IV *b*
42. [OFr. *delit(i)er*.]

Deliuer, *adj.* nimble, V 275;
Deliuerly, *adv.* nimbly, quickly,
X 58, 89. [OFr. *de(s)livre*.]

Deliverance, *n.* deliverance, XII *b*
17. [OFr. *delivrance*.]

Deluen, *v.* to dig; to bury; VIII *a*
135; Dalf, *pa. t. sg.* XIV *introd.*;
Doluen, *pa. t. pl.* VIII *a* 184;
Doluen, *pp.* (dead and) buried,
VIII *a* 173. [OE. *delfan*.]

Delueres, *n. pl.* diggers, VIII *a*
101. [OE. *delfere*.]

Deluynge, *n.* digging, VIII *a* 244.
[OE. *delfing*.]

Deme, Dieme, *v.* to judge, sentence, XII *b* 216, XVI 34; criti-

elze, VIII *a* 75 ; consider, deem, XI *b* 190, 209, 211 ; *ne deme thow non other*, imagine nothing different, VIII *a* 173 ; speak, say, V 115 (note), VI 1 ; with cognate obj. *domes for te deme*, to tell their tales, XV *b* 30. [OE. *dēman*.]

Den, *n.* cave, XIII *a* 41, 42, 43. [OE. *denn*.]

Den. *See* Dynne.

Dene3, *adj.* Danish ; *Dene3ax*, an axe with a long blade and usually without a spike at the back, V 155 (note). [OE. *denisc* ; OFr. *daneis*.]

Deop. *See* Dep.

Deores, *n. pl.* wild animals, XV *b* 29. [OE. *dēor*.]

Departed(e), **Depertid**, *pa. t.* separated, VI 18 (*intr.*), VII 145 (*trans.*); departed, IX 308, 320; *pp.* divided, IX 1. [OFr. *de(s)partir*.]

Dep(e), **Deop** (XIII), *adj.* deep, XII *b* 11, XIII *a* 39, XVI 377 ; as *sb.*, the deep (sea), VII 154, XII *a* 160 ; *adv.* deeply, VI 46. [OE. *dēop*; adv. *dēope*.]

Depely, *adv.* deeply, greatly, VII 114. [OE. *dēop-līce*.]

Depertid. *See* Departed.

Depnes, *n.* depth, XVII 434, 460, 520. [OE. *dēop-nes*.]

Depriue, -**pryue**, *v.* to deprive, VI 89, XVI 175. [OFr. *depriver*.]

Dere, *adj.* dear; prized, I 258 ; beloved, I 125, VI 8, VIII *a* 91, XIV *c* 1, XVf 1, XVII 172, 190, 419, 527; *my dere*, my friend, VIII *a* 251 ; pleasing, VI 40 ; good, &c. (vaguely applied in allit. poems), VI 132, 144, VII 61 ; **Derrist**, *superl.* best, VII 39. [OE. *dēore ; dēorra*, compar. (whence also stem of ME. superl.).]

Dere, *n.* harm, I 166, XVII 317 ; *maken þe worlde dere*, do injury to mankind (! *or* 'make the world dear to live in'; but *cf.* 166), VIII *a* 154. [OE. *daru*, influenced by *derian*.]

Dere, *v.* to afflict, XIV *b* 10. [OE. *derian.*] *See* prec.

Dere, *adv.* dearly, at great cost, IV *a* 80, VIII *a* 75, XVII 373 ; *as me dere liketh*, to my liking, VIII *a* 286. [OE. *dēore.*]

Derffe, *adj.* doughty, VII 84. [ON. *djarf-r*, older, **dearf-*.] *See* Deruely.

Derke, *n.* darkness, VII 167. [OE. *de(o)rc*, adj.] *See* þerk.

Derlyng, *n.* darling, IV *a* 54. [OE. *dēor-ling*.]

Derne, *adj.* secret, XV *b* 29 (note). [OE. *derne*.]

Derrist. *See* Dere, *adj.*

Derthe, *n.* dearth, famine (personified), VIII *a* 324. [OE. *dēorþu.*] *See* Dere *adj.*

Deruely, *adv.* boldly, V 266. [ON. *djarf-liga*.] *See* Derffe.

Des, *n.* seat, throne, XVII 17. [OFr. *deis* ; see *N.E.D.*, s.v. *Dais.*]

Des-, **Dis-avauntage**, *n.* disadvantage, XIII *b* 35, 37. [OFr. *desavantage.*]

Deschaunt, *n.* descant, XI *b* 137 (note). [OFr. *deschant.*]

Desert, *adj.* uncultivated and desolate, IX 200; *n.* desert, uninhabited land, IX 179, XI *b* 24. [OFr. *desert.*]

Deserue(n), *v.* to deserve, VIII *a* 43, *b* 32 ; to earn, VIII *a* 211, *b* 43, 47. [OFr. *deservir*.] *See* Serue(n).

Desyre, *n.* desire, IV *a* 5, XI *b* 295. [OFr. *desir.*] *See* Dissiret.

Desplaid, *pp.* unfurled, II 294. [OFr. *despleier.*]

Desport, *n.* amusement, IX 276 ; *do desport*, play, make merry, XII *a* 174. [OFr. *desport.*]

Desserte, *n.* deserts, merit, VI 235. [OFr. *desserte.*]

Desspendoure, *n.* steward, almoner, III 21. [OFr. *despendour.*] *See* Spendere.

Destiné, *n.* fate, V 217, Fate, VIII *a* 269. [OFr. *destinée.*]

Destresse, *n.* distress, II 514. [OFr. *destresse.*]

Det, *n.* debt, XVII 222; Dettes, *pl.* VIII *a* 92. [OFr. *dette.*]

Determynable, *adj.* decisive, authoritative, VI 234. [OFr. *determinable.*]

Determinacion, *n.* authoritative decision, XI *b* 263. [OFr. *determinacion.*]

Deþ, *v.* *See* Don.

Deþ(e), Deth, *n.* death, II 332, V 37, VII 9, VIII *a* 324 (the Plague), &c. [OE. *déaþ.*] *See* Ded(e), *adj.* and *n.*

Deuel(l), Deuelle, Deuyl(l), Dele (v), *n.* devil, Devil, IV *b* 20, 26, V 120, VIII *a* 56, 114, XI *b* 105, XV *h* 16, XVI 341, 399, &c.; *what deuel,* what the devil, XVI 223. [OE. *déofol.*]

Deuelway; *in þe d.,* in the Devil's name, XVI 133. [See *N.E.D.,* s.v. *Devil* 19.]

Deuere, *n.* duty, XVII 319. [OFr. *deveir.*]

Devyded (*in*), *pp.* divided (into), IX 28. [L. *dividere.*]

Deuise, -yse, Devise, *v.* to descry, II 312; to describe, relate, IX 267, 268, 271. [OFr. *deviser;* see *N.E.D.,* s.v. *Devise.*]

Deuocio(un), Deuocyun, *n.* devotion, devoutness, pious practice, I 18, V 124, XI *b* 110, 120, XII *a* 14, &c. [OFr. *devocion.*]

Deuote, Deuout, *adj.* devout, VI 46, XI *b* 58, &c. [OFr. *devot.*]

Deuoutnes, *n.* devoutness, XIV *c* 79. [From prec.]

Dew, Dewly, *See* Du, Duly.

Dyacne, *n.* deacon, III 9, 12; Diaknen, *dat. pl.,* III 5. [OE. *diacon,* OFr. *diacne.*] *See* Archidekenes.

Dyamand, Dyamaund, *n.* diamond, IX 33, 36, &c. [OFr. *diamant,* altered form of *ademant;* see Ademand.]

Diche, Dyche, *n.* moat, dike, II 361, VI 247; notion in VI appar. releasing of water pent up by a dam. [OE. *dic.*]

Dyd, Dide(n). *See* Do(n).

Dye(n). *See* Deye.

Diemed. *See* Deme.

Diete, *v.* *refl.* to diet (oneself), VIII *a* 263. [From OFr. *diete,* n.]

Diffynen, *pres. pl.* determine, fix, IX 315. [OFr. *definer.*]

Digge, Dyggen, *v.* to dig, II 255, IX 231; Digged, *pa. t. pl.* VIII *a* 101. [? OFr. *diguer;* see *N.E.D.*]

Dyggynge, *n.* digging, IX 201.

Dignyté, *n.* dignity; *of dignyte,* worshipful, XVII 166. [OFr. *dignete.*]

Dyȝede. *See* Deye.

Diȝte, Dighte, Dyȝte, Dyghte, *v.* to arrange, prepare, make, I 30, V 155, VIII *a* 286; *diȝte,* arrayed for battle, XIV *b* 34; *dyght to dede,* put to death, XVII 543. [OE. *dihtan.*]

Diken, Dyken, *v.* to dig, VIII *a* 135, 184. [OE. *dician.*]

Diker(e), Dyker, *n.* digger, ditcher, VIII *a* 101, 325. [OE. *dicere.*]

Dykynge, digging, ditching, VIII *a* 244. [OE. *dicung.*]

Diligently, *adv.* watchfully, IX 191. [From OFr. *diligent.*]

Dim, *adj.* faint, II 285; Dimme, *adv.* faintly, XII *b* 31. [OE. *dimm.*]

Dymes, *n. pl.* tithes, XI *b* 300. [OFr. *di(s)me,* from L. *decima.*]

Dimuir, *adj.* calm, XIV *c* 37. [OFr. **demeur,* in *demeurement,* soberly.]

Dyne, *v. trans.* to eat (at dinner), VIII *a* 303; 2 *sg. pres. subj.* VIII *a* 257; Dyned, *pp. intr.* had dinner, VIII *a* 274. [OFr. *di(s)ner.*]

Dyner, *n.* dinner, VIII *a* 286. [OFr. *di(s)ner.*]

Dynge(n), *v.* to strike, smite, beat, V 37 (MS. dynneȝ), VIII *a* 135, XVI 180, 203; Dang, *pa. t. pl.* X 54. [OE. **dingan;* cf. *dencgan,* ON. *dengja.*]

Dynne, *n.* noise, XVI 234, 284; Den, XV *h* 2. [OE. *dyne.*]

Dynt, *n.* stroke, blow, V 48, 155,

196, XV *h* 2; *dynt of honde*, a blow (with a weapon), V 37, VII 92. [OE. *dynt.*]

Diol. See Dole.

Dirige, *n.* (dirge), matins in the office for the dead, VIII *b* 48, XI *b* 132 (note). [L. *dirige.*]

Disceit, *n.* deception, wile, XI *b* 171, 311. [OFr. *deceite.*]

Disceyue(n), *v.* to deceive, IX 112, XI *b* 92. [OFr. *deceiv-re, decev-eir.*]

Discende, *pa. t.* descended, XVI 77. [OFr. *descend-re.*]

Disciple, *n.* disciple, XI *b* 15, XII *introd.* [OFr. *disciple.*]

Discord, *n.* discord; *without discord*, in peace (*or* incontestably; *cf.* Distance), XVII 31. [OFr. *discord.*]

Discrecyone (*of*), *n.* ! separation (from), IV *b* 69. [OFr. *discrecion.*]

Discre(e)t, *adj.* judicious, discerning, VIII *b* 88, IX 295. [OFr. *discret.*]

Disour(e)s, *n.* *pl.* professional story-tellers, jesters, I *introd.*, VIII *a* 56. [OFr. *disour.*]

Dispisen, *v.* to despise, XI *b* 93, 179. [OFr. *despire, despis-.*]

Dysplese3, Displeases, *v.* 3 *sg. pres.* displeases, VI 95, XVII 85; *imper. pl.* (*intr.*) be displeased, VI 62. [OFr. *desplaisir.*]

Dysseuer, *v.* depart, XVII 27. [OFr. *dessevrer.*]

Dissiret, *pa. t.* desired, VII 114. [OFr. *desirer.*] See Desyre.

Disstrye3. See Distroie.

Distance, *n.* quarrelling; *without distance*, indisputably, XVII 57. [OFr. *destance.*]

Distreynen, *v.* to afflict, IX 315. [OFr. *destreindre, destreign-.*]

Distroie, -oy(e), Destroye, *v.* to destroy, VII 28, IX 215, XI *b* 215, XVII 93; **Disstrye3,** *pres. pl.* V 307. [OFr. *destrui-re*; with *disstrye3* cf. Byled, Nye.]

Distroiynge, *n.* destruction, XI *b* 100. [From prec.]

Dysturble, *v.* to disturb, I 16. [OFr. *destourbler.*]

Ditees, *n.* *pl.* poems, XII *introd.* [OFr. *dité.*]

Diuers(e), Dyuers(e), *adj.* varying, divergent, XIII *b* 44; different, various, IX 16, 287, 289, XII *a* 55, &c.; *dyuers maner(e)*, different kinds of, XIII *b* 47, 48; *ich maner diuers animal*, every kind of different animal, II 364. [OFr. *divers.*]

Dyuersitees, -ee3, *n.* *pl.* (strange) varieties, IX 266, 280. [OFr. *diversité.*]

Do(n), Doo, *v.* I 219, IV *b* 65, IX 169, &c. to do; *to done* (OE. *tō dōnne*), VIII *a* 104, 197, IX 160; 2 *sg.* Dos, XVII 196; **Doste,** VIII *a* 75; Dot3, VI 196; 3 *sg.* Dep (OE. *dēþ*), III 60; **Dose,** IV *a* 57, &c.; Dot3, V 143; Doþ, II 112, &c.; *pl.* **Don(e),** II 2, VIII *a* 220, &c.; Dos, I 157; Doþ (MS. doh), *XV *b* 22; *imper. pl.* Dot3, VI 161, 176; Doþ, I 82, II 218. *Pa. t. sg.* Ded(e), I 176, II 232, III 17, &c.; Dyd I 166, &c.; Did(e), XI *b* 13, XVII 11 (2 *sg.*), &c.; *pl.* Dede(n), II 32, XV *i* 13; **Diden,** XI *b* 247. *Pres. p.* Doande, IV *b* 9; *pp.* Do, XI *b* 271, XII *a* 107, &c.; Doyne, XVII 139; Don(e), IX 326, XIV *a* 24, &c.; Ydo, II 381; Ydone, II 76. (i) To act, do, make, perform, work, II 32, III 17, IV *b* 9, 25, VI 161, XIV *b* 38, &c.; to exert, XI *b* 6; representing any verb understood, I 157, II 112, &c.; *be to done, es to doo*, is to be done, IV *b* 65, VIII *a* 197; *doþ at*, act according to, I 82; *don gret pyne*, toil hard, VI 151; *don him felaschipe*, bear him company, XII *a* 24; *doþ 3our best*, do your best, II 218; *do þi best*, get on as best you can, II 126; *made hymself to done*, set himself to work, VIII *a* 104. (ii) To make, cause to, III 60, VI 196; *ded come*, fetched, I 176;

do deye, kill, VIII *a* 269; *dot‡ me drede*, makes me afraid, V 143; *do(n) to wyte*, to *vnderstande*, give (one) to understand, inform, II 2, VIII *a* 56; followed by *infin.* (without expressed subj., as *did it wryte*, had it written), I *introd.*, 218, VIII *a* 79 (note), and (merging into mere auxil. as in Mn.E.) I 167, XVI 203, XVII 326, &c. (*cf.* Gar). (iii) To put, I 219, VI 6; *dede on* (*upon*), donned, II 343, XII *a* 53; *don awei*, set aside, abolished, XI *b* 206. (iv) *Refl.* in *dede him out*, went out, II 232, 474. (v) *Pp.* finished, I 68, XVII 139; at an end, XIV *a* 24; past, over, II 76, VII 167, XVII 148; *haue done*, (get it done), be quick, XVII 316, 352, 480. *I haue at do*, I have something to do, XVII 235 (*see* At); *do way!*, enough!, II 226. [OE. *dōn*; *dyde* (*dēde*, *dǣde*), pa. t.; *see* Morsbach, ME. Gram., § 130, *n.* 6.] *See* Vndo.

Docke, *v.* to curtail, mutilate, XI *a* 57. [Obscure.]

Doctours, *n. pl.* doctors (of the Church), XI *a* 27. [OFr. *doctour*.]

Do‡ty, Doughty, Douhti, *adj.* doughty, V 196, VII 84, XIV *c* 106; as *sb.*, V 266. [OE. *dohtig*.]

Do‡tyr, Doghter, -yr, Dou‡ter (VIII), Dowhter (XII), *n.* daughter, I 44, 47, 215, VIII *a* 14, 73, XII *a* 192, &c.; Doghtyr, *gen. sg.* I 136; [OE. *dohtor*.]

Doyne. *See* Do(n).

Doyll, *n.* dole, what is distributed in charity; *penny doyll*, masspenny, the offering for a mass for the soul of one dead, XVII 390. [OE. (*ge-*)*dāl*.] *See* Dele(n).

Doynge, *n.*; *d. awaye of*, putting away, IV *b* 61; *doyngis*, affairs, XI *b* 290. [OE. *dōung*.]

Dold, *adj.* stupid, XVII 266. [? Related (as *dulled* to *dull*) to OE. *dol*.] *See* Dull.

Dole, Diol (II), *n.* lamentation,

grief, misery, II 198, VIII *a* 114, XIV *b* 10, XVI 347. [OFr. *dol*, *doel*, *deol*, *diol*, &c.]

Dol(e)ful, *adj.* doleful, XIV *b* 72, XV *h* 16. [Prec. + -*ful*.]

Doluen. *See* Deluen.

Dome, *n.* judgement, XVI 319; doom, I 173; award, VI 220; *domes for te deme*, to converse, XV *b* 30 (*see* Deme). [OE. *dōm*.]

Domesday(e), Domysday, *n.* Doomsday, IV *a* 35, XI *b* 48, XVII 25. [OE. *dōmes dæg*.]

Donge, *n.* dung, manure, VIII *a* 283. [OE. *dung*.]

Donke‡, *pres. pl.* moisten, XV *b* 28. [Unknown; *cf.* Mn.E. *dank*.]

Dore, Doore (XVII), *n.* door, XII *a* 70, XVII 137, 280, 376. [OE. *duru*; *dor*.]

Dore(n), Dorste. *See* Dar.

Dosnyt, *pp.* dazed, stunned, X 129 [Obscure.]

Dote, *n.* dotard, fool, XVII 265 [? From next.]

Dote, *v.* to talk folly, XVII 367. [Cf. MDu. *doten*; ? OFr. *redoter*.]

Dot‡, Do‡. *See* Do(n).

Doubill, Double, *adj.* double, X *introd.*, XII *a* 162. [OFr. *double*.]

Doufe; Dou‡ter; Douhti. *See* Dowue; Do‡tyr; Do‡ty.

Doumbe, *adj.* dumb, XI *b* 175. [OE. *dumb*.]

Doun, *n.* down (feathers), XII *a* 95. [ON. *dún-n*.]

Doun(e), Down(e), *adv.* down, I 76, 194, II 69, X 101, &c. *See* Adoun.

Dounes, *n. pl.* hills, XV *b* 28. [OE. *dūn*.]

Dousour, *n.* sweetness, VI 69. [OFr. *dousur*.]

Dout(e), *n.* fear, I 147, XII *a* 144, XIV *a* 14; (fear of) danger, X 38, [OFr. *doute*.]

Doute, *v.* to fear, VII 114; Dutte, *pa. t. sg.* V 189. [OFr. *douter*.]

Dowhter. *See* Do‡tyr.

Dowid, *pp.* endowed, XI *b* 140. [OFr. *do*(*u*)*er*.]

Dowue, Dowfe, Doufe, *n.* dove,

XVI 78, XVII 484, 505, 514.
[OE. ! *dúfe*; ON. *dúfa*.]

Drad, Dradde. *See* Drede(n).

Dragounes, *n. pl.* dragons, IX
203. [OFr. *dragon*.]

Dray(e), *n.* commotion, XIV *b* 34,
XVI 146. [OFr. *de(s)rai*.]

Draught, *n.* (a move in chess), an
artful trick, XVI 399 (*see* Drawe).
[OE. **draeht*, related to next.]

Draw(e), *v. trans.* to draw, drag,
pull, bring, &c., IV *b* 19, IX 124,
X 82, XIII *a* 33, XVI 319; to
cart, VIII *a* 283; *intr.* move,
proceed, &c., XVII, 245; Drogh,
pa. t. sg. XV *a* 12; Drou, XV *g*
16; Drouh, Drowh, XII *a*
155, *b* 73, 124; Droghe, *pa.
t. pl.* VII 88; Drew, X 58;
Drawe, *pp.* XII *b* 90, XIII *a* 35;
Drawyn, X 124; Ydrawe, II
295. *þou drawes to wittenesse,*
thou citest, XVI 279; *drawe vs
no draught*, make no move
against us, play us no trick
(a chess metaphor; cf. Chaucer,
Bk. Duchesse, 682), XVI 399;
drou hymselue bi þe top, tore his
hair, XV *g* 16; *drawe to, toward,*
approach, XII *b* 124, XIII *a* 57;
draweth (to) colour lyke, ap-
proaches the colour of, IX 34
(note); *drawe after*, take after,
resemble, XIII *b* 6. [OE.
dragan.] *See* Vp-, With-drawe.

Draw-brig, *n.* drawbridge, X 165.
[Prec. + ON. *bryggja*.] *See*
Brygge.

Drawynge (*intill*), *n.* coming (to),
IV *b* 63.

Drede, *n.* fear, I 147, 211, &c.;
doubt (cf. Dredles), in *I puit ȝou
holly out of d.*, I assure you,
XIV *c* 12; *ensample and drede
aȝens*, a fearful caution against,
I 261; *for drede*, in fear, V 190,
XVII 212; in spite of their
fear (of me), XVI 146. [From
next.]

Drede(n), Dred, *v. trans.* to fear,
IV *b* 85, V 287, XI *b* 141, XVII 47,
55; *intr.* to be afraid, IV *a* 31
(with *of*), 61, V 143; *refl.* to be

afraid, XI *a* 61, XII *b* 67, 108
(*dradde him vnto*, was afraid of).
Dradde, *pa. t.* XII *b* 67, 108;
Dredde, I 145, XIV *c* 30, 62;
Drad, *pp.* XIV *c* 19. [OE. (on)-
drēdan, *-drædan*.] *See* Adrad.

Dredles, Dreid(les), *adj.* fearless,
V 266; (parenthetic) without
doubt, X 88. [From Drede, *n.*]

Dreed, *pp.* endured, XVII 533.
[OE. *drēogan*, str. v.]

Dregh, Dreȝ, *adj.* heavy; tedious,
IV *a* 12; *adv.* heavily, forcibly,
V 195. [ON. *drjúg-r*, older
*dreog-.]

Dreie. *See* Druyȝe.

Dreynte, *pa. t.* drowned (*intr.*),
XII *a* 135; Dreinte, *pp.* XII *a*
167. [OE. *drencan, drencte.*]

Dreme, *n.* noise, XV *h* 16. [OE.
drēam.]

Dremys, *n. pl.* dreams, XI *b* 73.
[ON. *draum-r*, appar. identified
in form with OE. *drēam*, noise,
music; *see* prec.]

Drepit, *pp.* smitten, VII 9. [OE.
drepan.]

Dresse, Dres, *v.* (to direct); to
arrange, ordain, VI 135; to set
(up), X 16; *I will dres me to*,
I will get ready to, XVII 238.
[OFr. *dresser.*]

Drife, Dryfe. *See* Dryue.

Dryȝtyn, *n.* God, V 70. [OE.
dryhten.]

Drink, Drynk(e), Dryng, *n.*
drink, XV *e* 14, 15; *esp.* in *mete
and drink*, &c., *see* Mete; *pl.*
potions, VIII *a* 269. [From
next.]

Drynke(n), *v.* to drink, IX 6, 256,
&c.; drink strong drink, VIII *a*
257; *fig.* pay the penalty, pay
for it, XVII 380 (*or* drown; but
cf. *N.E.D.*, s.v. *Drink* 16);
Drank, *pa. t. pl.* I 158; Dronken, *pp.* in *ben lyghtly d.*, easily
get drunk, IX 14; Ydronke,
VIII *a* 274. [OE. *drincan.*]

Dryue, Driue; Dryfe, Drife
(XVII), *v. trans.* to drive, VIII *a*
128, 184, *b* 19, XV *h* 2, XVII
273; *intr.* to hasten, I 171, XVII

193; *as þai miȝt driue*, as fast as they could go, II 141; **Dryuen**, *pp. (intr.)* hurtled, v 195. [OE. *drīfan*.] *See* To-dryue.

Drogh(e). *See* Draw(e).

Drone, Drowne, *v.* to drown, VII 154, XVII 372. [See *N.E.D.*]

Dronke-lewe, *adj.* given to drunkenness, XI *b* 197. [OE. *druncen-lǣwe*.]

Dronken. *See* Drynke(n).

Drou(h), Drowh. *See* Draw(e).

Drought, *n.* dry weather, VIII *a* 283 [OE. *drūgoþ, *drūhþ-.*]

Druyȝe, Dreie (XII), **Dry(e),** *adj.* dry, I 120, XII *b* 23, XVII 370; as *sb.,* XIV *c* 30. [OE. *drȳge* (Kt. *drēge*).]

Du, Dew, *adj.* belonging; *was dew to,* belonged to, VII 61; *hor du nyghtis,* the nights belonging to them, VII 127; **Duly, Dewly** (XVI), *adv.* correctly, rightly, as is due, VII 60, 64, XVI 248. [OFr. *deü, du.*]

Duell(e). *See* Dwelle(n).

Duine, *pp.* wasted, II 261. [OE. *dwīnan; dwīnen,* pp.]

Duk(e), *n.* duke, VII 84, 92, XIV *c* 65, &c. [OFr. *duc.*]

Dull, *adj.* stupid, foolish, VII 50. [OE. ! *dylle,* rel. to *dol.*]

Dulle, *v.* to make dull, stupefy, XII *introd.* [From prec.]

Dure, Duyre, *v.* to endure, last, remain, VIII *a* 58, *b* 25, XIII *a* 3, XIV *c* 4. [OFr. *durer.*]

Durst. *See* Dar.

Dusche, *n.* crash, X 106. [Echoic.]

Duschit, *pa. t. sg.* crashed, X 101. [As prec.]

Dutte. *See* Doute.

Dwelle(n), Duell(e), *v.* to linger, tarry, XII *b* 146; *to dwelle in,* to dwell on, XI *b* 130; to remain, abide, IV *a* 90, IX 173, XII *b* 172, XVI 304, &c.; to live, dwell, IX 10, 165, 288, &c. **Dwelling,** *n.* XIV *a* 24. [OE. *dwellan.*]

Ebreu, *n.* Hebrew (language), XI *a* 44; **Ebrew,** IX 208, 212. [OFr. *(h)ebreu.*]

Eche, *adj.* each, VIII *a* 104, XI *b* 6, 19, &c.; *eche a.* every, VIII *a* 2, 189, 243; *pron.* each one, II 403, XI *b* 47. [OE. *ǣlc.*] *See* Ich, Ilk, Vch.

Echone, *pron.* each one, I 51, 196; **Echoune,** I 49. [Prec. + OE. *ān.*]

Een; Eest; Eet. *See* Eiȝe; Est; Ete(n).

Eft(e), *adv.* afterwards, again, once more, thereupon, I 141, 143, 229, 235, II 211, V 227, 320, XVII 241, 448. [OE. *eft.*]

Eftsone, *adv.* (soon) afterwards, VIII *a* 163; immediately, XII *b* 68, 70. [Prec. + OE. *sōna.*]

Eftsoneȝ, *adv.* soon afterwards; moreover, V 349; **Eftsonis,** X 4. [Prec. + adv. *-es.*]

Efterward. *See* Afterward.

Egge, *n.* (edge, cutting weapon), axe, V 324. [OE. *ecg.*]

Eggyng, *n.* incitement, IV *b* 84. [From ON. *eggja,* to egg on.]

Egyrly, *adv.* fiercely, X 133. [From OFr. *aigre, egre.*]

Egle, *n.* eagle, IX 247, 251; *egle hys* for *egles* (gen. sg.), XIII *a* 22. [OFr. *aigle, egle.*]

Eiȝe, *n.* eye; *sg.* **Eye,** IX 304; **Ye,** I 149, 192; **Yȝe,** VI 207; **Yhe,** XII *a* 71; *pl.* **Een,** VII 57; **Eȝe,** XV *c* 14; **Eyen,** VIII *a* 168; **Eiȝe,** II 327, 591; **Eyȝen,** II 111; **Yhen,** XII *a* 106. [OE. *ēage, ēge.*]

Eir. *See* Er, *adv.*

Eyleþ, 3 *sg. pres. ind.* ails, troubles, VIII *a* 122, 254; **Alis,** XVII 294. [OE. *eglan,* to molest.]

Eiste, *n.* goods, XV *g* 20. [OE. *ǣht.* On *st* for *ht, see* App., p. 278.]

Eyþer. *See* Aither.

Ek(e), *adv.* also, II 323, VIII *a* 282, XII *b* 195. [OE. *ē(a)c.*]

Elles, -eȝ, -is, Els (XVII), **Ell** (IX), *adv.* otherwise, else, if not, VI 131, VIII *a* 175, 227, IX 132,

XI *l* 25, 241, 246, XVI 305, &c.;
pleonastic in apodosis to *bote*,
but if, I *introd.*, VIII *a* 307;
(any one)else, V 40; (introducing
threat), or (else), XVII 299. [OE.
elles.]

Elleswhere, *adv.* elsewhere,
away, XII *b* 180. [OE. *elles-
hwǣr.*]

Elmesses. *See* Almes.

Emang, Emong. *See* Amang,
Amonge.

Emell, *prep.* among (following
pron.) XVI 104. [ON. *á* (or *í*)
milli.]

Empeyre, *v.* to impair, IX 338.
[OFr. *empeirer.*] *See* Apeyre.

Emperise, *n.* empress, VI 81.
[OFr. *emperesse*, with substitution of fem. suffix *-ice.*]

Emperour(e), *n.* emperor, IX 260,
XII *b* 191, 211. [OFr. *empe-
r(e)our.*]

Empyre, *n.* imperial sway, VI 94.
[OFr. *empire.*]

En, *prep.* in Fr. phrase, *en exile*,
in exile, II 493. [OFr. *en.*]

Enarmede, *pp.* armed, VII 87.
[OFr. *enarmer.*] *See* Armyt.

Encerche, *v.* to explore, IX 273.
[OFr. *encerchier.*] *See* Serche.

Enchauntements, *n. pl.* spells,
IX 84. [OFr. *enchantement.*]

Enchauntour, *n.* sorcerer, IX 86.
[OFr. *enchant(e)our.*]

Enchesone, Enchesun, *n.* cause,
occasion, I 202; *for þat enchesone
of*, on account of, I 43. [OFr.
acheso(u)n, encheso(u)n, &c.
For a similar alteration, *see*
Endorde.] *See* Chesouns.

Enclose, *v.* to shut up, enclose,
IX 165, 168, 174, 227. [*en* +
Close; cf. *in cloos*, s. v. Cloos, *n.*]

Encrees, *v.* to increase (*intr.*),
XVI 292. [OFr. *encreis-* (AFr.
encres(s)-), stem of *encreistre.*]

Ende, *n.* (i) end, limit I 95, 187,
V 112, VII 98, &c.; *at þe ende*,
on the end, XII *b* 54; *sette an
e. of*, put finishing touch to,
XII *introd.*; *withouten e.*, for
ever, XVI 300, 404; *the vttire-

meste e. of all þi kynne, the
furthest point (to which one can
go back) in your ancestry, XVI
232; *see* Fer, Laste, Partener,
Toune, Tweluemonth; (ii) borders, confines, IX 180; (iii)
object, XII *a* 21; *to þat e. þat*,
&c., in order that, IX 111, 281;
(iv) result, success; *[ben] triet
in þe e.*, turn out trustworthy,
VII 17; *bryng to an e.*, accomplish, IX 169; *make an e.*, bring
it about, XII *a* 48; *betre (wors)
ende*, advantage, disadvantage,
XIII *a* 59, 60; (v) fate, death,
VII 180; *make e. of*, destroy,
XVII 104. [OE. *ènde.*]

Ende, *v. trans.* to end, I 206; to
complete, VII 4; *intr.* to come
to an end, VII 29; to continue
to the end, XI *b* 110. [OE.
èndian.]

Endyng, *n.*; *withowten e.*, for
ever, eternally, IV *a* 96, IX 335.
[OE. *endung.*]

Endyte, *v.* to suggest or dictate
(the form of words to be said or
sung), I 56. [OFr. *endit(t̮)er.*]

Endles(se), *adj.* endless, eternal,
IV *a* 90, VII 2, XVI 35, &c.;
Yendles, XVI 124. [OE. *ende-
lēas*; *ènde-*; with *Yend-* cf.
3ederly (and see *N.E.D.*, s. v.
End).]

Endorde, *pp.* as *sb.* adored (one),
VI 8. [OFr. *adorer*; confusion
of prefix is probably English,
but *cf.* Enchesone.]

Endre, *adj.* latter, just passed;
þis endre dai, a day or two ago,
XV *a* 4, Introduction xii. [ON.
endr adv., formerly.]

Enduir, -dure, Induyr, *v.* to
last, VII 39, XIV *c* 36, XVII 148,
283; to bear, have the strength
(to), XIII *a* 42; *endured in
worlde stronge*, suffered severely
in the world (*or* ? remained
strong in this world), VI 116.
[OFr. *endurer.*]

Enemy(e). *See* Enmy.

Enes ounnes. *See* Eny.

Enew. *See* Ynow.

Engendren, *v.* to beget offspring, IX 59. [OFr. *engendrer*.]

Engendroure, *n.* parentage, origin, VIII *a* 228. [OFr. *engendrure*.]

Engynys, *n. pl.* machines, X 33. [OFr. *engin*.] *See* Gyn(e).

Engynour, *n.* engineer (contriver of machines), X 71, 89. [OFr. *engigneor*.] *See* Gynour.

Engliȝsch, *n.* English (language), XI *a* 30, 37, 64, 65; Englysch, XIII *b* 29, 34. &c.; English, XI *a* 2; Englis(s), III *introd.*; Englysshe, VII *introd.*; Inglis, I *introd.* [OE. *englisc.*]

Engliȝsch, *adj.* English, XI *a* 34; Englisch, XIV *c* 17; Englyssh, I *introd.*; Inglis, X 43, XIV *a* 26, *b* 10. [OE. *englisc.*]

Engliȝsch(e)men, **Englyschmen**, *n. pl.* Englishmen, XI *a* 28, 40, 52, XIII *b* 9, 43, &c. [OE. *englisc + mann.*]

Eny, *adj.* any, III 5, VIII *a* 251, XIII *a* 48; *eny wyle*, any length of time, VIII *b* 25; *in eny weie*, by any means, XII *a* 16; **Enes cunnes**, XV *g* 22, **Eny kyns**, VIII *b* 20, of any kind, any kind of (OE. **æniges cynnes*). [OE. *ænig*, Kt. *æni(g)*.] *See* Ani, Ony.

Enmy, **Enemy(e)**, *n.* enemy, IV *a* 92, V 338, VIII *b* 78, IX 81, &c. [OFr. *enemi*.]

Enogh. *See* Ynoȝ, Ynow.

Enquestes, *n. pl.* inquests (inquiries into matters of public or state interest), VIII *b* 59. [OFr. *enqueste*.]

Ensa(u)mple, *n.* example, instance, I 202, XI *b* 298, 301; cautionary instance, warning, I 261 (*see* Drede; *cf.* next). [AFr. *ensample* altered, by confusion of prefixes, from OFr. *essample*.] *See* Sample.

Ensamplen, *v. refl.*; *wherof* [*he*] *may ensamplen him*, from which he may take warning, XII *b* 223 (*cf.* prec.). [From prec.]

Entaille, *n.* fashion, XII *a* 64. [OFr. *entaille*.]

Entent(e), *n.* purpose, VII 27; *to what e.*, for what reason, XII *b* 168; *to þat e. to*, *to þat e. and ende þat*, in order to, that, IX 120, 280; mind, X 184; will, desire, IV *a* 22; *with all thare e.*, with their whole minds, XVII 113. [OFr. *entent*, *entente*.]

Enterlacé, *adj.* interlaced, (verse) with alternate rime, Introduction xv. [OFr. *entrelacé*.]

Entyrludes, *n. pl.* comic dramatic pieces, farces, I 5. [AFr. **entrelude*, Anglo-L. *interlūdium*.]

Entysyd, *pa. t.* enticed, XVII 37. [OFr. *enticier*.]

Entre, **Entere**, *v.* to enter, XVI 270, 282; *entered in Iudas*, inspired Judas, XVI 165. [OFr. *entrer*.]

Entrike, *v.* to deceive, XII *a* 116. [OFr. *entriquer*.]

Enveremyt, *pa. t.* surrounded, X 46. [OFr. *environner*; the forms *enverom-* &c. first appear in English in 14th c.]

Enuy, *n.* envy, XVII 51. [OFr. *envie*.]

Eorne, *v.* to run; to flow, XIII *a* 23, 37, 54, 62; **Yarn**, *pa. t. sg.* ran, III 43; **Ourn**, *pl.* II 85; **Vrn**, II 89. [OE. *iornan*; pa. t. *iarn*, *urnon*.] *See* Ryn.

Eorþe. *See* Erth(e).

Erbeȝ, **Herbes**, *n. pl.* (green) plants, V 122, XII *a* 82. [OFr. (*h*)*erbe*.]

Erde, *n.* dwelling-place, own land, VIII *a* 194; in tag *in erde* (on earth, among men), V 348, it is perh. a form of Erth(e). [OE. *eard*. The frequent ME. (Northern) form *erd(e)*, earth, may, in part, be due to this; but *cf.* Dede *n.*[1]]

Er(e), **Eir** (X), *adv.* before, V 209, XII *b* 113; ere now, XVII 328; formerly, VI 12; earlier (with *befor*) X 140; *conj.* before (usually with *subj.*), II 190, 256, V 152, 204, 223, XII *a* 104, *b* 19; *prep.* before (in time), VIII *a* 140. [OE. *ær*.] *See* Ar, Are, Or.

Er(e), *pres. ind. pl.* are, I *introd.*, IV *a* 60, *b* 8, 53, 54, XIV *a* 6, 7, 12, 18, *b* 85, &c. [ON. *eru.*] *See* Ar(e), Es, &c.

Ere, *n.* ear, II 528, VIII *a* 263, XII *a* 104, *b* 32; Eris, *pl.* XI *b* 159. [OE. *ēare.*]

Erie, Erye, *v.* to plough, VIII *a* 4, 5, 67, 100, 110. [OE. *erian.*]

Erles, Erls, *n. pl.* earls, II 202, 503, VII 84. [OE. *eorl*, infl. in sense by cognate ON. *jarl.*]

Erliche, *adv.* early, VIII *b* 15; **Erly**, VI 146; *e. and late*, at all times, VI 32. [OE. *ǣr-līce.*] *See* Er(e)n, Ar.

Ernde, *n.* the business (on which one has come), V 235. [OE. *ǣrende*, message; ON. *erindi*, &c. message, business.]

Erre, *v.* to err, XI *b* 14. [OFr. *errer.*]

Errour, *n.* error, falsehood, heretical opinion, VII 46, XI *b* 44, 77, 215; *speke errour*, say what is mistaken, VI 62. [OFr. *errour.*]

Ert. *See* Art.

Erth(e), Eorþe (XIII, XIV *c*), **Vrþe** (VI), *n.* earth, soil, IV *b* 4, 12; the ground, IV *b* 36, V 161, IX 149, XIII *a* 8, 15; the world, VI 82, XI *a* 8, XVII 180; *in erth(e)*, on earth, in the world, IV *a* 47, IX 332, XVI 363, XVII 42, &c.; *in eorþe*, XIV *c* 110; *vpon erthe*, V 30; *in erth* (sc. *lufe in erth*), earthly (love), IV *a* 10. [OE. *eorþe, ȝorþe.*] *See* Erde.

Erth(e)ly, *adj.* earthly, IV *a* 29, *b* 12, 29, XVI 134, &c. [OE. *eorþ-lic.*]

Erytage, Herytage, *n.* inheritance, VI 57, 83. [OFr. *(h)eritage.*]

Es, 3 *sg. pres. ind.* is, I 7, *128 (note), IV *a* 1, 5, 10, &c., *b* 65, XIV *a* 5, 20, *b* 8, 9, XV *a* 9. [A Northern form. ON. *es.*] *See* Is, &c.

Eschue, Eschuie, *v.* to avoid, escape, VIII *a* 55, XII *b* 8. [OFr. *eschiwer, eschuer.*]

Ese, Ays, *n.* comfort, pleasure, in

him is ays, gives him pleasure or comfort, II 239; *at ese*, comfortable, VIII *a* 144; well off, XVII 388. [OFr. *aise, eise.*] *See* Malais, Missays.

Esely, Esily, *adv.* without discomfort, XII *b* 91; easily, IX 119. [From ME. *esē*, OFr. *aisié* (related to prec.).]

Est(e), Eest (XVII), east; *adj.* IX 2; *adv.* XVI 333; *n.* IX 73, XIII *b* 51, XVII 453. [OE. *ēast*, adv., *ēaste*, n.]

Ete(n), *v.* to eat, VIII *a* 129, 258, 298, IX 142, 242, XV *g* 25, XVII 395 (*see* Bred), &c.; Eet, *pa. t. sg.* VIII *a* 291; Ete, *pa. t. pl.* I 158, II 396; Eten, *pp.* VIII *a* 261, IX 144; Etin, XIV *b* 74, 76, 77. [OE. *etan.*]

Euaungelistis, *n. pl.* evangelists, XI *b* 306. [L. *ēvangelista.*] *See* Awangelys.

Euel(1). *See* Yuel.

Euen, Eve, *n.* evening, III 54, VIII *a* 178, XII *b* 18, XVII 205; *see* Morwe. [OE. *ǣfen, ēfen.*]

Euen(e), Euyn, Evin, *adv.* equally, exactly, just, quite, indeed, I *introd.*, VII 27, XII *b* 49, XVII 125, 290, 379, 462, &c.; also, too, VII 51, 154; *evin (till)*, just opposite, X 81; *euene ryȝt*, exactly, XIII *a* 47; *euen Hym by*, on a level with Him, XVII 18; *ful(l) euen*, equally, as well, quite, XVI 280, XVII 10, 344. [OE. *efen, efne.*]

Euenly, *adv.* exactly, XVII 258. [OE. *efen-līce.*]

Euensong(e), *n.* evensong, vespers, VI 169, XI *b* 131, 189, 224, 241. [OE. *ēfen-sáng, -sóng.*]

Euentyde, *n.* evening, VI 222. [OE. *ēfen-tīd.*]

Euer(e), *adv.* ever; always, continually, for ever, I 94, VII 2, VIII *a* 271, *b* 100, &c.; at any time, II 42, V 57, IX 327, &c.; added to indef. relatives (*q.v.*), I 2, XVII 210, &c. [OE. *ǣfre.*]

Euerich, Eueryche), Eueri, *adj.* every, each, I 9, II 60, 517,

580, IX 63, XIII *a* 22, 26, &c. ; *euerich a*, every, II 490, XVII 544. [OE. *æfre-ylc*.] *See* Eche, Ich, &c.

Euerichon, *pron.* every one, II 189 ; **Euerilkone**, XVI 311 (in apposition to prec. noun). [Prec. + OE. *ān*.]

Everydel, *adv.* in every detail, XII *a* 147. [Eueri + Dele, *q.v.*] *See* Somdel.

Euermare, Euermore, *adv.* (for) evermore, ever after, I 97, II 213, IV *a* 20, VIII *a* 236, XIV *b* 64, &c. ; now and always, VI 231. [OE. *æfre + māre*.] *See* Mor(e).

Euermo, *adv.* evermore, II 168. [OE. *æfre + mā*.] *See* Mo.

Euyll. *See* Yuel.

Evidence, *n.* evidence, indication (of what is to come), XII *a* 128. [OFr. *evidence*.]

Evin, Euyn. *See* Euen(e).

Euþer, *conj.* ; *euþer . . auþer . .* and, both . . and, VII 57. [OE. *æg-hwæþer, ægweþer*.] *See* Aither.

Examyne, *v.* to examine, test, IX 295, 297, 300. [OFr. *examiner*.]

Excellent, *adj.* surpassing, IX 270, 330 ; **Exellently**, *adv.* ; *exellently of alle þyse oþer*, conspicuously among all these others, V 355. [OFr. *excellent*.]

Excuse(n), *v.* to excuse, V 63, 360, XI *b* 8, 145, &c. [OFr. *excuser*.]

Exile, *n.* ; *en exile*, in exile, II 493. [OFr. *en exile*.]

Expownd, *v.* to expound ; *I expownd*, it is my opinion, XVII 440. [OFr. *expondre*.]

Expres, *v.* to express, XVII 13. [OFr. *expresser*.]

Expresse, *adv.* definitely, XI *b* 63. [OFr. *expres*, adj.]

Fabill, Fable, *n.* fable, fabulous tale, VI 232, VII 34, X *introd.* [OFr. *fable*.]

Face, *n.* face, V 303, &c. ; *distrib.* 59 (*see* Hert), XIII *a* 33 ; *in His face*, to His face, openly, XI *b*

179 ; *mannes face*, VIII *a* 234 (note). [OFr. *face*.]

Fader, Fadir, -yr, Uader (III), *n.* father, I 122, II 29, III *introd.*, VIII *b* 37, IX 286, &c. ; **Fadir**, *gen. sg.* XVI 79 ; **Fadris**, XVI 36. [OE. *fæder*.]

Fadirhode, *n.* fatherhood (as title), IX 294. [Prec. + OE. *hād*.]

Faggatis, *n. pl.* fagots, X 111. [OFr. *fagot*.] *See* **Flaggatis**.

Faght. *See* Fight.

Fai, Fay, *n.* faith, XIV *c* 7 ; in French formula *par ma fay*, By my troth, VI 129. [OFr. *fei*.] *See* Feith, Parfay.

Faierie. *See* Fairi.

Fayll, *n.* in *withoutten fayll*, without fail, XVII 149. [OFr. *faille*.]

Fail(l)e, Fayl, *v.* to fail, be wanting, VIII *a* 320, XI *b* 186, XIV *c* 35, XVII 274, &c. ; *faile (fayl) of*, to fail in, miss, XVI 157, XVII 492 ; **Fayled**, 2 *sg. pa. t.* were at fault, V 288 ; **Failet**, *pl.* in *f. hym*, he lacked, VII 175. [OFr. *faillir*.]

Fayn(e), *adj.* glad, VI 33, 90, VIII *a* 266, 295 ; *fayn I wold (that)*, I would be glad (if), XVII 526. [OE. *fægen*.]

Fayned. *See* Feynen.

Fair(e), Fayr(e), Feyre (I), **Uayre** (III), *adj.* fair, beautiful, I 63, II 70, XV *c* 13, &c. ; excellent, good, &c., I 260, III 2, V 250, VI 130, XIII *a* 30, &c. ; seemly, I 80 ; as *sb.* in *þat faire*, that fair being, IV *a* 81 ; *fayre myght the befall*, may good luck come to you, XVII 514 ; **Feyrest, Fairest, Farest**, *superl.* II 53, XV *c* 28, XVII 79, &c. ; as *sb.* the fairest (season), VII 99. [OE. *fæger*.]

Faire, Fayre, *adv.* fairly ; courteously, VIII *a* 25 ; well, V 161, XVII 255 ; deftly, V 241 ; properly (set out), VII 82. [OE. *fægre*.]

Fayre(s). *See* Fare, *v.*

Fairi, -y, Feyré, Faierie (XII), *n.* faëry, fairyland, II 10 (*the feyré*), II 283, 562; magic, II 193, 404, 492, XII *b* 67. [OFr. *faierie.*]

Fairnise, *n.* beauty, II 56. [OE. *fæger-nes.*]

Fais. *See* Foo, *n.*

Faitest, 2 *sg. pres.* beg under false pretences, VIII *b* 30. [Back-formation from Faitour.]

Fayth, &c. *See* Feith.

Faitour, *n.* impostor; beggar, or idler, feigning disease or injury, VIII *a* 115, 177; (as term of abuse), XVI 157, 209. [OFr. *faitour.*]

Falce *See* Fals.

Fall, *n.* fall, XII *b* 14. [OE. (*ge-*)*fall.*]

Falle(n), Fall, *v.* to fall; **Fel, Fell**(e), *pa. t. sg.* I 23, VII 25, XII *b* 28, &c.; **Fyl,** I *introd.*, 25, 28, 186; **Falled,** V 175; **Fell**(en), *pl.* VII 95, IX 149; **Fyl, Fillen,** I 194, II 15; **Fal, Falle**(n), *pp.* VII 93 (slain), XII *b* 57, XVII 521, &c.; *fal yn a swone* (corrupt. of *fallyn aswone*; *see* Aswone), I 195. To fall (down), I 194, II 327, &c.; *fel on slepe,* fell asleep, II 72; to happen, turn out, come to pass, I 23, II 8, V 183, 310 (*see* Foule), VII 25, XII *b* 18, &c.; (with *dat. pron.*) to happen to, befall, VII 171, XII *b* 28, 184; to fall to one's share, V 175, 259, VII 76; *hit fell hom of a foule ende,* an evil fate overtook them, VII 180; *as fell for the wintur,* for winter, VII 124. *And my fry shal with me fall,* my children who will share my fate (? *or* who I may happen to have) XVII 66; **Fallyng,** *n.* VII 109. [OE. *fallan.*] *See* Befalle.

Fals(e), **Falce,** *adj.* false, lying, dishonest, V 314, VII 18, VIII *a* 113, XI *a* 11, XVII 35, 201, &c.; as *sb.* VII 41; **Falsly,** *adv.* XI *b* 81. [OE. *fals,* from L. *falsus.*]

Falshed, *n.* lying, VII 34. [Prec. + OE. **hǣdu.*]

Falssyng, *n.* breaking of faith (applied to the girdle as the cause; *cf.* Kest), V 310. [From ME. *fals(i)en;* cf. OFr. *falser.*]

Fame, *n.* rumour, tale, XII *b* 189; *of good f.,* of good repute, XVII 141. [OFr. *fame.*]

Famyn, *n.* famine, VIII *a* 319. [OFr. *famine.*]

Fand(e). *See* Fynde(n)

Fang. *See* Fonge.

Fantasyes, *n. pl.* delusions, imaginings, IX 84, XI *b* 73. [OFr. *fantasie.*]

Fantosme, *n.* illusion, XII *b* 75. [OFr. *fantosme.*]

Fare, *n.* behaviour, practices, V 318, XVI 158; *his feynit fare pat he fore with,* the deceit he practised, VII 44. [OE. *faru.*] *See* Wel-fare.

Fare, Fayre (XVII), *v.* to go, fare, behave, II 604, XVII 190, 255, 415; *fare by, to, wip,* behave towards, treat, I 256, VI 107, XIV *c* 95; *fareȝ wel,* &c., farewell, V 81, XVII 238; **Fore,** *pa. t.* VII 93; *fore with,* practised, VII 44; dealt with, VII 176; **Faren,** *pp.* departed, gone (by), VII 29, VIII *a* 99. [OE. *faran*]. *See* Ferde, *pa. t.*

Farest. *See* Faire.

Farleis. *See* Ferly, *n.*

Fasor, *n.* appearance, VI 71. [OFr. *faisure.*]

Fast(e), *adv.* securely, I 101, II 94, IX 173, XII *b* 30, &c.; as intensive adv. varying with context, II 118, V 335, VIII *a* 102, XI *b* 187, XII *b* 69, XVI 107, XVII 488, &c.; quickly, V 147, XI *b* 274, XII *b* 104, &c.; *fast by,* hard by, XIII *a* 50. [OE. *fæste.*]

Fastes, 3 *pl. pres.* fast, IV *b* 49. [OE. *fæstan.*]

Fath. *See* Feith.

Fauco(u)n, *n.* falcon, II 307, 312, VIII *a* 32, &c. [OFr. *fauco(u)n.*]

Fauntis, *n. pl.* children, VIII *a*

278. [Shortened from OFr. *enfa(u)nt.*]

Fauour(e), *n.* grace, beauty, VI 68, XVII 79. [OFr. *favour.*]

Fautlest, *adj. superl.* in *on þe f.,* the (one) most faultless, V 295. [Error for, or red. of, *fautlesest;* OFr. *faute* + OE. *-lēas.*]

Fautours, *n. pl.* supporters, XI *a* 1, 49. [L. *fautor.*]

Fawty, *adj.* faulty, V 314, 318. [From ME., OFr. *faute,* n.]

Fe. *See* Fee, *n.*[1]

Feaw, Few(e), *adj. pl.* few, VI 212, VII 52, XIII *b* 50, XV *a* 19, &c. [OE. *fēawe.*] *See* Fone.

Fecche, *v.* to fetch, VIII *a* 150; **Fette(n),** *pa. t.* VIII *a* 287, XII *b* 150, XVI 382; **Yfet,** *pp.* II 170. [OE. *fetian, feccan.*]

Fede, *v.* to feed, VIII *a* 247, XI *b* 281; **Fedde,** *pa. t.* VIII *a* 292, XI *b* 278, &c.; **Uedde,** *subj.* would feed, III 8; **Fedde,** *pp.* IV *b* 39. [OE. *fēdan.*]

Fedynge, *n.* feeding; *in f. of,* for feeding, XI *b* 258. [OE. *fēding.*]

Fee, Fe, *n.*[1] goods, XVII 309, 326. [OE. *fe(o)h, fēo-.*] Distinguish next.

Fee, *n.*[2] fee (as a term of venery, the share given to the dog, falcon, &c.); some small gain in their hunting, XVII 490. [OFr. *feu, fe,* &c.]

Feeldes ; Feele ; Feende ; Feere ; Feest. *See* Feld(e); Fele, *adj.* ; Fende; Fere *n.*[1,2]; Fest.

Feghtande. *See* Fight.

Feye, *adj.* doomed to die, XV *c* 20. [OE. *fǣge.*]

Feill. *See* Fele, *adj.*

Feynd(is). *See* Fend(e).

Feyne(n), Fayne (VII), *v.* to feign, pretend, invent, VII 41, XI *b* 1, 81, &c.; *feyned hem,* pretended to be, VIII *a* 115; to falsify, VII 34; **Feynit,** *pp.* false, VII 18 ; *feynit fare,* deceit, VII 44. [OFr. *feindre, feign-.*]

Feyré ; Feyre(st). *See* Fairi; Faire.

Feith, Fayth, Fath (XVII), &c., *n.* faith. XI *b* 13, 171, XVI 364, &c. ; plighted word, troth, V 216; *bi my feith, in (god) fayth,* &c., upon my word, V 297, VIII *a* 266, XVII 228, 330, &c. [OFr. *feid,* later *fei.*] *See* Fai.

Feythful, *adj.* honest, VIII *a* 247 ; **Feithfulliche,** *adv.* honestly, VIII *a* 71 ; **Faithfully,** accurately, VII 78. [Prec. + OE. *-ful.*]

Fel. *See* Falle(n).

Felaȝschip, Felaschipe (XII), **Felaushepe** (I), **Felowship** (XVII), *n.* community, I *introd.*; company, in *bere, don f.* (with *dat. pron.*), keep (one) company, V 83, XII *a* 24; friendship, XVII 363. [Next + OE. *-scipe.*]

Felawe, Felowe, *n.* fellow, I *introd.,* XIV *d* 7, 16 ; (contemptuous), XVI 284. [OE. *fēo-laga,* from ON. *fé-lagi.*]

Feld(e), Filde, Fylde, *n.* field, II 60, VIII *a* 134, 232 ; field of battle, VII 45, 93 ; **Feeldes,** *pl.* XIII *a* 19. [OE. *féld.*] *See* Afelde.

Fele, Feele (XVI), **Feill** (X), **Uele** (III), *adj.* many, II 401, 522, III 2, V 349, VI 79, VII 29, X 55, 63, 141, XV *b* 10, XVI 61, &c. [OE. *fela,* adv.]

Fele, Feele, *v.* to feel, perceive, experience, IV *a* 25, *b* 45, V 125, XIII *a* 26, XVI 346 (*see* Fitte), XVII 121, &c.; *2 sg. subj.* V 204; **Felte,** *pa. t.* I 156, 163. [OE. *fēlan.*]

Fell, *v.* to fell ; to destroy, IV *a* 47. [OE. *fellan.*]

Fell(e), Fellen. *See* Falle(n).

Fell(e), *adj.* deadly, cruel, V 154, VI 7, VII 82, 109, XIV *b* 33 ; **Felly, Fellyche** (I), *adv.* cruelly, terribly, I 130; fiercely, V 234. [OFr. *fel.*]

Felloune, *adj.* grim, deadly, X 115, 192. [OFr. *feloun.*]

Femayll, Femele (IX), *adj.* female, IX 58, XVII 152. [OFr. *femelle.*]

Fend(e), *n.* devil, Devil, V 125, VIII *a* 82, IX 93, XI *b* 3, 220, XVI 340, &c.; Feende, XVI 9, 14, &c.; Feynd, XVII 35, 43. [OE. *fēond.*]

Fende, *v.* to defend, XVI 30. [Shortened from Defende, *q.v.*]

Fenyl, *n.* fennel, XV *b* 18. [OE. *finu(g)l.*]

Fenyx, *n.* Phœnix, VI 70. [OE. *fenix*, L. *phœnix.*]

Fer, Ferre, Far, *adj.* and *adv.* far, IV *b* 36, V 24, XIII *a* 27, XV *g* 5, XVII 439, &c.; *as fer as*, in so far as, IX 293; *(vn)to the fer(re) ende*, to the very end, VII 78, 95. Fer(re), Fyrre (V, VI), *compar.* farther, V 83, XIV *b* 18; away, XVI 156, 336; further, VII 97; moreover, V 53, VI 184; *fyrre þen*, beyond, VI 203. [OE. *feorr*; *feorr, firr* compar.] *See* Ferforth, Fyrþer.

Ferde, *n.* fear, in *for ferde*, in fear, V 62, 204, XVII 315. [Prob. false division of *forfer(e)d*, pp., terrified; OE. **forfǣran, -fēran.*] *See* next.

Ferd(e), *pp.* afraid, V 314, XIV *b* 93, XVII 102; at XVI 209 rime requires *flaide* (*see* Flay and note). [OE. *fǣran, fēran.*]

Ferd(e), *pa. t.* fared, XII *a* 43, 145; *ferd with*, dealt with, X 172. [OE. *fēran.*] *See* Fare, *v.*

Fere, Feere (XVI), *n.*[1] companion, XV *f* 5; wife, V 343, XVI 352. [OE. *fēra.*]

Fere, Feere, *n.*[2] company, in *in fere*, &c., all together, collectively, XVI 126, 364, 385. [OE. *ge-fēre*; but this use is prob. partly developed from ME. *y-fere(n)*, OE. *ge-fēran*, pl., (as) companions.] *See* Yfere.

Fere, *n.*[3] fear, VIII *a* 177, 292. [OE. *fǣr, fēr.*]

Fere, *n.*[4] outward appearance, VII 18. [Shortened from OFr. *afe(i)re.*]

Fere-flunderys, *n. pl.* fiery sparks, XV *h* 12. [*See* Fyr; *cf.* Mn.E. and dial. *flinders*, splinters.]

Ferforth, *adv.* far, XII *b* 190. [OE. *feorr + forþ.*] *See* Fer.

Ferked, *pa. t. sg.* flowed, V 105. [OE. *fer(e)cian*, go.]

Ferly, *adj.* wonderful, II 4 (note); *adv.* wondrously, extremely, I 145, XV *b* 10. [OE. *fǣr-līce*, suddenly, prob. infl. by ON. *ferliga* monstrously; *see* next.]

Ferly, *n.* a marvel, V 346, X 134; Farleis, Ferlies, *pl.* VII 95, XVI 61. [OE. *fǣr-lic*, sudden, prob. infl. by ON. *ferlíki* (ME. *ferlike*) monster.] *See* prec.

Ferre. *See* Fer.

Ferryit, *pp.; f. wes*, had farrowed, X 109. [Formed on *farrow*, *ferry*; OE. *færh, ferh*, young pig.]

Fers(e), *adj.* fierce, bold, II 293, XIV *b* 33, XVI 131. [OFr. *fers*, nom. sg.] *See* Fuersly.

Fersch, *adj.* fresh, XIII *a* 29, 49. [OE. *fersc.*] *See* Fresch.

Ferste, Uerst. *See* Furst.

Feruent, *adj.* hot, IX 10; burning bright, XVII 8; eager, XVII 77. [OFr. *fervent.*]

Fost, Feest (XVII), *n.* feast, festival, V 333, XVII 454 (? with topical allusion to the Corpus Christi festivities). [OFr. *feste.*]

Feste-dayes, *n.* feast-days (of the Church), VIII *b* 30. [From prec.]

Fest(e), *v.* make fast, confirm, XVI 340; *pa. t.* V 279; *pp.* fixed, made fast, IV *a* 1, 82, XVI 335, 337. [OE. *fæstan*; on the vowel *see* Cast.]

Festnyt, *pp.* fastened, X 124. [OE. *fæstnian*; see prec.]

Fet(e). *See* Fote.

Fethre-bed, *n.* feather-bed, XII *a* 94. [OE. *feþer-bedd.*]

Fette(n). *See* Fecche, Fote.

Feurþe, *adj.* fourth, XIII *a* 18. [OE. *feorþa, fēowerþa.*] *See* Fowre.

Fewe. *See* Feaw.

Ficht. *See* Fight.

Fift, Fyft, *adj.* fifth, VII 129, X 2. [OE. *fīfta.*]

Fyfteyn ; Uyf-, Vif-, Vyftene (III) ; *adj.* fifteen, III 21, 26, 29, XVII 443. [OE. *fíftēne.*]

Fight, Fyght(e), Fi3te, *v.* to fight, IV *b* 26, VIII *a* 36, XVI 131, &c. ; **Ficht,** X 66 ; **Fiste,** XV *g* 31 (*see* Appendix, p. 278); *fyght with,* oppose, XVII 138 ; **Faght,** *pa. t. sg.* XIV *b* 48 ; **Foght,** *pl.* VII 45 ; **Feghtande,** *pres. p.* in *are f.,* fight, IV *b* 18 ; **Yfou3te,** *pp.* VIII *a* 146. [OE. *fe(o)htan.*]

Fight, Fiht, *n.* fighting, battle, VII 29, 52, XIV *c* 60 ; **Ficht,** X 115, 198. [OE. *fe(o)hte.*]

Figure, *n.* shape, XII *a* 114. [OFr. *figure.*]

Fyked, *pa. t. sg.* flinched, V 206. [OE. **fician;* cf. *be-fician,* and next.]

Fikel, *adj.* fickle, XIV *c* 7. [OE. *ficol.*]

Fyl. *See* Falle(n).

Filde, Fylde. *See* Feld.

File, *n.* worthless creature, XIV *b* 47. [ON. *fýla.*]

Fyled, *pp.* sharpened, V 157. [OE. *fílian* to file ; or OFr. *afiler.*] *See* Fylor.

Fill, *v.* to fill, XVII 180. [OE. *fyllan.*]

Fill(e), Fulle, *n.* one's fill, II 256, VIII *a* 261, XVII 207. [OE. *fyllo.*]

Fille, *n.* chervil (*see* Cheruelles), *or* wild-thyme, XV *b* 18. [OE. *fille;* in glosses *fil, cerfille = cerpillum* (i.e. *serpyllum* thyme, but perhaps confused with *chærephyllum,* chervil).]

Fillen. *See* Falle(n).

Fylor, *n.* whet-stone, V 157. [Cf. OFr. *afiloir.*] *See* Fyled.

Filthe, *n.* filth, IV *a* 37, *b* 16 ; corruption, XVI 380 (*see* note). [OE. *fylþ.*]

Fyn(e), *adj.* fine, VII 175, IX 64. [OFr. *fin.*] *See* Fine.

Finaly, *adv.* in the end, XII *b* 107. [From OFr. *final.*]

Fynde(n), Finde, Fynd, *v.* to find, discover, II 1, 256 (*subj.*), VI 148, VII 82, IX 75, XIII *a* 17,
XVI 6, XVII 330, &c. ; to get, XII *a* 17, XVI 288 ; to invent, devise, II 4, 14, XI *b* 137 ; to provide for, VIII *b* 80 ; to provide one with (as *fynden hem tode*), VIII *a* 71, *b* 21, 27, 51, 92 ; *founden me to scole,* provided the means to put me to school, VIII *b* 37 ; *founden with,* provided with, XI *b* 140. **Fint, Fynt,** 3 *sg. pres.* (OWS. *fint*) II 239, VIII *b* 92 ; **Fand,** *pa. t. sg.* X 182, 186; **Fond(e),** I 37, II 426, VIII *b* 41, XII *a* 59, XV *a* 13, &c.; **Founde,** II 537, 569 (*subj.*) ; **Fande,** *pl.* XVI 62; **Found, Founde(n),** II 309, VII 172, VIII *b* 37 ; **Fon,** *pp.* XVII 503; **Fonden,** IV *a* 63; **Founde(n),** I 229, VII 66, XI *b* 140, &c.; **Fun,** XIV *b* 93; **Funden,** XIV *b* 47, 50 ; **Yfounde,** II 4, 14, XIII *a* 64. [OE. *fíndan.*]

Fyndynge, *n.* finding, IX 234 ; invention, XI *b* 226. [From prec.]

Fine, *adv.* extremely, very, II 94. [Cf. Afine, Fyn; *see* Zupitza, (15th c.) *Guy of Warwick,* l. 9086 (note).]

Fynen, *pres. pl.* refine, IX 45. [OFr. *finer.*]

Fynger, Finger, *n.* finger, II 109, VI 106, VIII *a* 10. [OE. *finger.*]

Fint, Fynt. *See* Fynde(n).

Fyr(e), Fire, Fuyr, *n.* fire, II 398, IV *a* 6, XII *a* 69, XIII *a* 3, 4, &c. ; **Fere,** in *fere-flunderys* (q.v.), XV *h* 12. [OE. *fýr* (Kt. *fér*).]

Firmament, *n.* firmament, heavens, VII 124, 134, XVII 7, 422. [(Christian) L. *firmāmentum;* first appears in E. *c.* 1050.]

Fyrre. *See* Fer.

Firste, Fyrst(e). *See* Furst(e).

Fyrþer, *adv.* further, I 255. [OE. *furþor,* ? infl. by *firr.*] *See* Fer, Forþer.

Fysch, Fische, Fysh, *n.* fish, VIII *a* 305, XIII *a* 37, XVII 3. [OE. *fisc.*]

Fiste. *See* Fight.

Fitte, *n.*; *fele þi fitte*, undergo your turn of woe, XVI 346. [ME. *fit*, terrible or violent experience, &c.; ! OE. (once) *fitt*, contest.]

Fyue; **Uif**, **Vif**, **Vyf** (III); *adj.* five, III 22, 23, 27, V 125, VI 91 (*see* þo, *adv.*), VIII *a* 319, XIII *b* 32, &c. [OE. *fíf.*]

Flaggatis. *n. pl.* fagots, X 23, 25, 27. [! Alteration of Faggatis, *q.v.*; another reading is *fagaldis*.]

Fla3(e). *See* Fle(n), Flye.

Flay, *v.* to put to flight; terrify, XVII 380; **Flaide**, *pp.* *XVI 209 (required by rime; MS. ferde). [OE. *flégan.*]

Flayles, *n. pl.* flails, VIII *a* 178. [OE. **flegel,fligel*; OFr. *flaiel.*]

Flapten, *pa. t. pl.* lashed, laid on, VIII *a* 178. [Cf. Du., G., *flappen.*]

Flasshet, *pa. t. sg.* flashed, VII 134. [Obscure.]

Flaw. *See* Flye.

Flawme, *n.* flame, IV *a* 14, 66. [OFr. *flaume.*]

Fle(n), *v.* to flee, V 57, 62, XV *i* 16, XVII 292, 296; **Fles**, 2 *sg. pres.* V 204; **Flese**, *pres. pl.* IV *b* 86; **Fleth**, *imper. pl.* XIV *d* 14; **Fla3(e)**, *pa. t. sg.* V 206, 208 (second); **Fley**, XI *b* 273; **Flowen**, *pl.* VIII *a* 177; **Fled**, *pa. t.* and *pp.* XIV *b* 48, 51, 80. [OE. *fléon*, str.] *See* Flye.

Flee, **Fle(e)ynge**; **Fle3e**; *see* Flye. **Fley**; *see* Fle(n).

Fleme, *n.* a fugitive, XV *b* 36. [OE. *fléma.*]

Flemmynges, *n. pl.* Flemings, people from Flanders, XIII *b* 7. [OE. **fléming*; cf. ON. *flǽming-r*, MDu. *vláming.*]

Fles(e). *See* Fle(n).

Flesch(e), **Flessche**, **Flessh(e)**, *n.* flesh, meat, I 129 (note), V 245, VIII *a* 18, 150, 305, IX 141; *flesshe* or *bone*, a limb, I 197. [OE. *flǽsc.*]

Flesch(e)ly, *adj.* carnal, of the body, IV *a* 57, *b* 71; **Flecshly**, carnal-minded, worldly, XI *b* 158. [OE. *flǽsc-lic.*]

Flete, *v.* to float; **Flietende**, *pres. p.* XII *a* 157; **Flett**, *pp.* XVII 436. [OE. *fléotan*, str.]

Fleth. *See* Fle(n).

Flett, *n.* floor, XVII 223. [OE. *flett.*]

Flex, *n.* flax, VIII *a* 13. [OE. *flex.*]

Flye, **Flyghe**, **Flee** (IV), *v.* to fly, I 193, IV *b* 4, 30, 38, 41, &c.; **Fla3**, *pa. t. sg.* V 208 (first); **Flaw**, X 92; **Fle3e**, was, VI 71 (note); **Fle(e)ynge**, *pres. p.* IX 148, 252; **Flone**, *pp.* XVII 487. [OE. *flé(o)gan.*] *See* Fle(n).

Flyeghynge, **Flyghyng(e)**, *n.* flying; *of gude* (*ill*) *fl.*, strong (weak) in flight, IV *b* 34, 35, 38. [From prec.]

Flietende. *See* Flete.

Flyt, **Flitte**, *v. trans.* and *intr.* to move, remove, escape, depart, XVI 210, 336, 340 (*subj.*), XVII 223, 263; **Flyt**, *pa. t.* XVII 17; **Flyt**, **Flit(t)**, *pp.* XVII 454, 540; *in synder flit*, separated, XIV *c* 31. [ON. *flytja.*]

Flo, **Floo**, *v.* to flow, XVII 101, 115. [OE. *flówan*, ON. *flóa.*]

Flone. *See* Flye.

Flood(e), **Flod(e)**, *n.* flood, water, stream, V 105, VII 160, XII *a* 166, XVI 76; (in pl.) waters, waves, VII 123, 142, 171; floods, VII 109, VIII *a* 320, XVII 101, &c. [OE. *flód.*]

Floterand, *pres. p.* weltering, tossing, VII 160. [OE. *floterian.*]

Flour, **Flowre**, *n.* flower, II 60, 67, IV *a* 57, XV *e* 19, &c.; *in the floures*, in the bloom, XII *introd.*; excellence, in *bar þe flour*, excelled (all), XIV *c* 23; flour, VIII *a* 150. [OFr. *flour*; the sense in VIII was not differentiated in spelling until end of 18th cent.]

Flowen. *See* Fle(n).

Flowyng, *n.* flood, XVII 540. [From OE. *flówan.*] *See* Flo.

Flume, n. ; *flume Iordanne*, River Jordan, XVI 76. [OFr. *flum*.]

Fo. *See* Foo.

Fode, Foode, n. food, VII 175, VIII *a* 21, 71, 200, 264, XVI 10 (*see* Frute), &c. [OE. *fōda*.] *See* Fede.

Foght ; **Fois.** *See* Fight ; Foo.

Foysoune, n. abundance, great number, X 166. [OFr. *foison*.]

Fold(e), n. earth, in (*vp*)*on folde*, allit. tag of little meaning, V 305, XIV *b* 18. [OE. *folde*.]

Fold(e), quasi-sb. (variety, repetition) in *many oþer folde*, manifold other things, I 20 ; *other wise many fold*, in manifold other fashions, XVII 54 ; *hi foldis seuen*, seven times, XVII 13. [False division of OE. *manigfáld, seofon-fáld*, &c., where *-fáld* is adj. suffix.]

Folde, v. to fold ; enfold, XV *f* 9, 10 ; **Folde, pp.** (? or *pa. t.*) in *folde vp*, ? covered with her hands, *or* upturned, VI 74. [OE. *fáldan*.]

Fole, Folys, &c. *See* Fool.

Folehardi, adj. foolhardy, II 426. [OFr. *fol-hardi*.] *See* Fool.

Folȝed. *See* Folwen.

Foly, n. folly, I 67, XI *b* 123. [OFr. *folie*.]

Folk(e), n. people, II 389, VIII *a* 292, 295, &c. ; mortals, VII 45 ; **Folkes, pl.** peoples, XVI 70. [OE. *folc*.]

Folwen, v. to accompany, VIII *a* 2 ; **Folȝed, pa. t.** V 354 (*see* note). [OE. *folgian*.]

Fome, n. foam, VII 172. [OE. *fám*.]

Fomen, n. pl. foemen, XIV *c* 85. [OE. *fáh mann*.] *See* Foo.

Fon, Fond(e), Fonden. *See* Fynde(n).

Fonde, v. to endeavour, seek (to), VIII *a* 213, XII *a* 183, XII *b* 171, XIII *b* 24 ; **Fondet, pa. t.** V 57. [OE. *fándian, fóndian*.]

Fone, Fune, adj. and pron. few, XIV *a* 28, 29, XVII 99. [ME. also *fo* ; ? obscurely rel to Feaw, *q.v.*]

Fonge, v. to get, take, VI 79, 119 ; **Fang,** XVII 245. [OE. *fón, ge-fángen* ; cf. ON. *fanga*.] *See* Onderuonge.

Fonnyd, (pp.) adj. infatuated, XI *b* 37, 38, 76, 167, 215. [From ME. *fon(ne)*, fool ; obscure.]

Foo, adv. as an enemy, fiercely, V 258. [OE. *fáh, fá-*.]

Foo, n. foe, XIV *d* 12 ; Fo, II 112, VIII *b* 60 ; *frende nor foo*, nobody, XVI 287 ; *ichon other fo*, each hostile to the other, every man against his neighbour, XVII 112 ; **Fais, pl.** X 55, 65, 197, **Fois,** XVI 30 ; **Fooes,** XVI 386. [OE. *ge-fá*.]

Fool, Fol(e), n. fool, I 30, V 346, XI *b* 42, 184, &c. [OFr. *fol*.]

For, conj. for, I 109, XVII 231, &c. ; Uor, III 6, 8, &c. ; because, V 300, VII 178, VIII *a* 235, 237, XIII *b* 16, XVI 258, 295 ; so that, XII *a* 93, 194, XVI 251 ; *for that*, so that, XII *b* 133. [OE. *for þam (þe)*, for, because ; *for þý þæt*, so that.] *See* Forþi.

For ; Uor, Vor (III) ; prep. for (i.) *Cause* : because of, on account of, through, I 134, II 32, III 17, IV *b* 35, V 279, VII 183, IX 130, X 136, XI *a* 32, *b* 28, 256, XV *b* 24, &c. ; *for of* (OFr. *de par*) for sake of, XV *d* 5 ; *for why (whi)* ?, and why ?, XVII 14, 284, 518 ; for (fear of), V 57, 199, XVII 102, &c. ; (as precaution) against, VIII *a* 9, 62, 87, 209, 306, XIV *a* 36, XV *h* 12. (ii.) *Indir. object* : for (benefit of), III *introd.*, VIII *a* 278, &c. ; for sake, on behalf, of, I 90, III 40, IV *a* 88, &c. (iii.) *Dir. object* : for (purpose of), with a view to, to get, &c., IV *a* 69, VII 32, 88, VIII *a* 230, X 41, XI *b* 126, 182, 235, XVI 220, &c. ; *for (uor) to, for te*, in order to, so as to, I 81, II 568, III *introd.*, 44, XV *b* 30, *c* 18, &c. ; *for till*, X 149, 169 ; as equiv. of *for* with vbl. sb., X 8, 33, 105 ; merely equiv. of *to, till*, I 21,

II 37, X 143, &c. (iv) *Equiva-
lence* : in favour of, VII 13, XI *b*
215 ; (in exchange, return, &c.)
for, IV *a* 42, ▼ 284, VIII *b* 76,
IX 190, XI *b* 162, XV *g* 20,
&c. ; as result of, IX 201 ; for,
as, VII 49, 50, VIII *a* 206, XII *a*
180, XIV *c* 92, &c. (v) *Reference* : with regard to, III 9,
&c. ; *for the*, for all you care,
XVII 193 ; in spite of, II 571,
▼ 64, XIV *a* 24, XVI 146 ; *for
all*(*e*), despite (all), I 73, 86,
XIV *b* 23, XVI 158. (vi) *Time*:
during, VI 226, VIII *a* 236, &c.
See Maystrie, Nones, Soþe ;
Þar(e), þere(fore), &c. [OE
for(*e*).]

Forbede, *v.* to forbid, VI 19 ;
forbede þat (with neg.), forbid to,
I 78 ; **Forbodyn,** *pp.* I 7. [OE.
for-bēodan.] *See* Bede, *v.*

Forbere, *v.* to spare, XIV *b* 12.
[OE. *for-beran*.] *See* Bere, *v.*

Forbette, *pp.* cruelly beaten, IV *a*
86. [OE. *for-* + *bēatan*, str.] *See*
Bete, *v.*[1]

Force, *n.* strength, XVI 210. [OFr.
force.]

Fordo, *v.* to destroy, XVII 100,
114 ; **Fordon**(**e**), *pp.* XVII 145 ;
ben fordon, come to grief, Introduction xv. [OE. *for-dōn*.] *See*
Do(n).

Fore. *See* Fare, *v.*

Forest, *n.* forest ; wild, unen-
closed, and partly wooded, land,
II 160, 246. [OFr. *forest*.]

Foret. *See* Forþ.

Forfete, *v.* to transgress, ▼ 326 ;
Forfette, *pa. t.* XVI 352. [From
OFr. *forfait, -fet*, n.]

Forgaa. *See* Forgon.

Forgete, *v.* to forget, IV *a* 79 ;
Forgetynge, *n.* IV *b* 68. [OE.
for- +ON. *geta*; cf. OE. *for-
getan*.] *See* Gete, Forȝete.

Forgon, *v.* to give up, XV *b* 35 ;
Forgoo, V 142 : **Forgaa,** IV *b*
31. [OE. *for-gān*.]

Forȝ, *n.* force, waterfall, V 105
(the earliest recorded instance in
E.). [ON. *fors*.]

Forȝelde, *v.* to repay, VIII *a* 272.
[OE. *for-gĕldan*.] *See* ȝelde.

Forȝete, *v.* to forget, XI *b* 157 ;
Forȝete, *pp.* XII *b* 202, XIV *c* 8,
&c. [OE. *for-getan*.] *See* Forgete, Vnderȝete.

Forȝeue, *v.* to forgive, IX 324.
[OE. *for-gefan*.] *See* ȝeue.

Forloyne, *v.* to go astray, VI 8.
[OFr. *forloignier*.]

Forlorn, (*pp.*) *adj.* ruined, in pitiful plight, I 136, II 127. [OE.
for-loren, pp.] *See* Lese, *v.*[1]

Forme, *adj. superl.* first, V 305.
[OE. *forma*.]

Forme. *See* Fourme.

Forne, *adv.* of old, V 354. [OE.
foran, forne.]

Forsake, Fursake (xv), *v.* to
deny, XV *g* 33 ; forsake, V 312 ;
(foll. by *infin*.) to refuse to,
neglect to, XV *c* 19, XVII 273 ;
Forsoke, *pa. t. sg.* forsook, II
227. [OE. *for-sacan*.]

Forschape, *pp.* transformed (to
something worse), XII *a* 8. [OE.
for-scapen, pp.] *See* Schap(e).

Forschreynt, *pp.* withered (by
fire), II 398. [OE. *for-screncan*,
oppress, rel. to *forscrincan*,
wither.]

Forseyde, *pp.* aforesaid, XIII *b* 49 ;
Uore-yzede, Uorzede, III 19,
23. [OE. *fore-sægd* (Kt. *-sēd*).]

Forsworn, *adj.* perjured, XIV *a* 21.
[OE. *for-sworen*.] *See* Swere.

Forto, *prep.* until, XIII *a* 28, 29.
[OE. *forþ tō*.]

Fortune, *n.* ; *by* (*be*) *f.* by chance,
VII 99, 180, IX 207 ; by good
fortune, VII 171. [OFr. *fortune*.]

Forþ(**e**), **Forth,** *adv.* forth, away,
out, on, forward, II 193, V 248,
&c.; **Foret,** XV *g* 18 (*see* Appendix
§ 6) ; **Fourth**(**e**), XVI 298, 386 ;
Furþ(**e**), **Furth**(**e**), I 72, 87,
X 87, XVI 140, XVII 480, &c. ;
forþe ygete, produced, II 14 ; *fra
thine furth*, thenceforward, X
130. [OE. *forþ, fórþ*.]

Forþer, *adv.* further, II 481. [OE.
furþor, forþor.] *See* Fyrþer.

Forþered, *pp.* furthered, advanced, XI *b* 231. [From prec.; *cf.* OE. *fyrþr(i)an, forþian.*]

Forþi (-þy, -thi, -thy), *adv.* and *conj.* wherefore, and so, therefore, II 461, IV *b* 35, V 42, 50, VIII *a* 79, 88, *b* 86, XII *introd.*, *b* 170, XV *c* 22; because, IV *b* 26. [OE. *for-þi, for-þi þe.*]

Forwake, *pp.* worn out with lying awake, XV *c* 29. [OE. *for-* + *wacen,* pp. of *wæcnan.*] *See* Awake.

Forward(e), *n.* agreement, covenant, V 279, VIII *a* 36, XVI 5, 166, 238. [OE. *fore-weard,* n.]

Forwes, *n. pl.* furrows, VIII *a* 98. [OE. *furh.*]

Fote, Foot(e), Fut (X), *n.* foot, V 248 (*see* Spenne), IX 17, &c.; *collect.* (*dat.*) *sg.* in *on fote* (*fut*), on foot, V 295; on their legs, X 57; *vnder fote,* XIV *c* 85; foot's length, V 83, VIII *a* 2, XVII 263, 366; **Feet, Fet(e),** *pl.* II 79, 441, IX 255, &c.; **Fette,** IV *b* 4; **Fote, Foot,** orig. *gen. pl.* in *two fote long,* &c., V 157, IX 155, XIII *a* 38, &c.; orig. *dat. pl.*, in *on his, to (my) fote,* V 161, 208, VII 174. [OE. *fōt.*]

Foul(e), *n.* bird, II 68, VIII *a* 32, XV *b* 6, 10, *c* 3, &c.; **Fowhel(e),** IV *b* 33; **Fowle,** IV *b* 47, XVII 3, 487, &c.; **Fowll,** XVII 472; **Foull,** *pl.* XVII 156. [OE. *fugol.*]

Foule, *adj.* foul, loathsome, bad, II 464, VII 180, VIII *a* 320, XVI 337, &c.; **Uoul,** III *introd.*; *adv.*, in *foule mot hit falle,* evilly may it fare, V 310. [OE. *fūl.*]

Founde, *v.* to hasten, V 62, 161. [OE. *fúndian.*]

Founde(n), &c. *See* Fynde(n).

Fourme, Forme, *n.* manner, fashion, V 62, IX 305. [OFr. *fo(u)rme.*]

Fourth(e). *See* Forþ(e).

Fourty, Forty, *adj.* forty, XVII 148, 445, &c. [OE. *fēowertig.*]

Fowe, *adj.* streaked or variegated (fur), vair, in *fowe and griis*

(partial transl. of ME., OFr. *vair & gris*), II 241. [OE. *fāg.*]

Fowheles, Fowle(s), Fowll. *See* Foul(e), *n.*

Fowre, Four e), *adj.* four, I 232, V 33, 157, XIII *a* 37, &c. [OE. *fēower.*] *See* Feurþe, Fourty.

Fra. *See* Fro, *prep.*

Fray, *n.* strife, XVII 184. [Shortened from Affray, *q.v.*]

Frayne, *v.* to inquire, VII 97. [OE. *(ge)frægnian.*]

Fraist, Frast (XVII), *v.* to question, inquire of, XVII 183; *fraist of,* investigate, VII 97. [ON. *freista.*]

Fram; Uram. *See* From.

Franche, *adj.* French, XIV *b* 33, 46; **Frensche,** XIV *c* 101; **Frankys,** *n.* French language, I *introd.*; **Freynsch,** XI *a* 27, XIII *b* 19, &c.; **Frensch,** XIII *b* 34, &c. [OE. *frencisc;* the forms show infl. of OE. *Francan,* OFr. *France,* &c.]

Franklens, *n. pl.* franklins (men of free, but not noble birth, holding land by freehold), VIII *b* 68. [OFr. *franclein.*]

Frast. *See* Fraist.

Fraunchyse, *n.* privilege, *or* liberality. VI 249; the interpretation depends on that of Dard, Rescoghe (*q.v.* and note). [OFr. *franchise.*]

Fredom, *n.* freedom, XI *b* 150, 205, 206, &c. [OE. *frēo-dōm.*]

Free, Fre, *adj.* free, VIII *b* 68, XVI 295; lavish, VI 121; noble, good, XVI 5, XVII 327; as *sb.*, noble one, XVII 310; **Freest,** *superl.* noblest, V 354. [OE. *frēo.*]

Freend. *See* Frende.

Freike(s). *See* Freke.

Freynsch. *See* Franche.

Freke, *n.* man, knight, V 57, 206, VIII *a* 212, &c.; **Freike,** VII 160, 172. [OE. *freca.*]

Freles, *adj.* without reproach, VI 71. [ON. *frýja* + OE. *-lēas.*]

Frely, *adj.* pleasant, II 4 (note). [OE. *frēolic.*]

Frely, *adv.* freely, IX 90, XI *b* 201, 245, 258. [OE. *fréo-líce.*]

Fremmede, *adj.* not akin, IV *b* 22. [OE. *fremede.*]

Frenchype. *See* Frendschip.

Frende, Freend, *n.* friend, VI 198, XIV *d* 12, XVII 118; *fr. nor foo,* nobody, XVI 287; **Frendes,** &c. *pl.* friends, IV *b* 22, XIV *a* 28, XVI 29, 385; kinsfolk, VIII *b* 37, 41, XVI 62. [OE. *fréond,* friend; ON. *frǽndi,* kinsman.]

Frendschip, -ship, *n.* friendship, love, XIV *c* 3, XVII 121; **Frenchype,** IV *b* 29; **Frenship,** XVII 362. [OE. *fréond-scipe.*]

Frensch. *See* Franche.

Freris, *n. pl.* friars, XI *a* 1, 33, 49, 55. [OFr. *frere.*]

Fresch, *adj.* fresh, VIII *a* 305. [Prob. OFr. *freis, fresche* (fem.), rather than OE. *fersc.*] *See* Fersch.

Frese, *n.* danger, in *no frese,* doubtless, XVII 391. [MDu. *vreese* (OFris. *frês,* OS. *frêsa*).]

Frese, *v.* to freeze, II 247. [OE. *fréosan.*]

Frete, *pa. t. pl.* devoured, II 539. [OE. *fretan,* pa. t. pl. *frǽton.*]

Frewte. *See* Frut(e).

Fry, *n.* offspring, XVII 66, 177. [ON. *frǽ, frjó,* seed.]

Frydays, *n. pl.* Fridays, VIII *b* 30. [OE. *frig(e)dæg.*]

Fryed, *pp.* fried, VIII *a* 305. [OFr. *fri-re.*]

Friþ, Fryth, *n.* woodland, park, II 160, 246, V 83. [OE. *fyr(h)þ, gefyrhþe,* wood.]

Fro, Froo, *adv.* away, XVI 210; *to and fro,* to and fro, on all sides, XVII 111. [ON. *frá.*]

Fro, *conj.* from the time when, since, VI 15 (cf. *fra þat*). [As prec.]

Fro, *prep.* (away) from, I 76, V 263 (follows pron.), VI 15, VII 90, VIII *a* 29, IX 26, &c.; **Fra,** IV *a* 18, *b* 34, X 130, &c.; *fra þat,* from when first, IV *a* 25; *þat ...fro,* whence, IX 230; *ther...*

fro, to where . . . from, XII *a* 33; *fro whom . . . fro,* from whom (mixed Fr. and E. constr.), IX 329 (*see* next). [ON. *frá.*]

From, Fram, *prep.* from, II 190, 225, VIII *a* 51, XIII *a* 27, &c.; **Uram,** III *introd.,* 4; *uram þet,* from the time that, III 38; *adv.* in *of whom . . . from,* from whom (mixed E. and Fr. constr.), IX 78 (*see* prec.). [OE. *from, fram.*] *See* Þere, Þare.

Frote, *v.* to rub; wring, tear at, II 79; **Frotyng,** *pres. p.* grating, XIII *b* 59. [OFr. *froter.*]

Frounse, *v.* to pucker, V 238. [OFr. *fronci(e)r.*]

Frut(e), *n.* fruit, II 257, VIII *a* 320, IX 143; **Fruyt,** IX 139, 148, XIII *a* 51; **Frewte,** in *f. of erthely foode,* ? the fruit of the tree, which was earthly food, XVI 10. [OFr. *fruit.*]

Fuersly, *adv.* fiercely; *fuersly fell,* turned out stormy, VII 129. *See* Fers(e).

Fuyr. *See* Fyr.

Ful, II 388; *see* note.

Ful, Full(e), *adj.* full, complete, II 60, XV *e* 3, 6, &c.; **Uol,** III 47; as *sb.,* in *at þe full,* completely, XI *b* 198; *his fulle, see* Fille. [OE. *full.*]

Ful, Full(e), *adv.* full, quite, very, I 22, II 443, 559, IV *b* 27, V 19, IX 244, &c. [OE. *ful.*]

Fulfille(n), Fulfylle, *v.* to fill, IX 331, XII *introd.*; to fulfil, finish, perform, accomplish, IV *b* 15, 73, VIII *a* 36, 319, IX 317, XI *b* 86, 88, XVI 6, &c.; **Uolueld,** *pp.* III *introd.* [OE. *fulfyllan* (Kt. *-fellan*).]

Fun, Funden. *See* Fynde(n).

Fune. *See* Fone.

Furred, *pp.* fur-trimmed, VIII *a* 264. [OFr. *fo(u)rrer.*]

Fursake. *See* Forsake.

Furst, *adv.* first, II 14, XIII *b* 12, 20; **Fyrst, First,** I 154, II 121, XVII 42, &c.; at first, I 226, 228, V 159; firstly, XI *a* 6, *b* 5, &c.; **Uerst,** at first, III 33; *boþ* *furst and last*, throughout, XIV *c* 76. [As next.]

Furste, *adj.* first, original, XIII *a* 7, *b* 4, 26; Ferste, XII *a* 112; Fyrst(e), I 214, VI 188, &c.; Firste, in *atte firste*, at once, VIII *a* 165. [OE. *fyr(e)st*, (Kt. *ferst*).]

Furth(e). *See* Forþ(e).

Fut. *See* Fote.

Ga, Gaa. *See* Go(n).

Gabberes, *n. pl.* swindlers, IX 112. [From ON. *gabba*, to mock.]

Gadre, *v.* to gather, pick up, assemble, XII *b* 22, 113, 117; Ged(e)re, Gedyr, IV *b* 81, V 192, VII 86; Ygadered, *pp.* III 44; *gedereʒ þe rake*, ! picks up the path, V 92. [OE. *gæderian*.]

Gaf, Gaffe. *See* Giffe.

Gay(e), *adj.* gay, gallant, V 297, VII 111; as *sb.*, fair one, VI 73. [OFr. *gai*.]

Gayne, *n.* gain (*i.e.* the three kisses), V 281. [OFr. *gaigne*.]

Gaynesay, *v.* to speak against, IV *b* 75. [ON. *gegn* + OE. *secgan*.] *See* Agayn, Seie.

Gam(e), Gaume (I), *n.* game, play, I 1 (*see* Somer), 99; sport, II 315; game (birds), II 309; trickery, XVII 214; merriment, XVII 529; *wiþ game*, merrily, II 19; Gamys, *pl.* rejoicings, XVI 20. [OE. *gamen*.]

Gan, *pa. t. sg.*; Gune, XVI 47, &c.; Gan, *pl.* II 504; Gonne, II 371; Gun, I 193: began, II 118, VIII *a* 146; (without *to*) II 425; made, II 438; did (without *to*, as equiv. of simple past) I 193, II 77, 78, 272, 371, 495, 504, 510, 530, XVI 47, 286. [OE. *ginnan*.] *See* Begyn(ne); Can, *auxil.*

Gane. *See* Go(n).

Gang, *v.* to go, depart, fare, X 4, XVI 144, 303, XVII 246. [OE. *gángan*.]

Garn, *n.* yarn, thread; *ther is garn on the reyll other*, there is other thread on the reel, other business on hand, XVII 298. [ON. *garn*.]

Garre, Gar, *v.* to make, cause to, IV *a* 26 (*subj.*), XVI 20, 144, 199, 334, XVII 346; Gert(e), *pa. t.* and *pp.* VIII *a* 296, X 198; caused (men to), X 16, 70, 82, 90, 98, 185; *garre dye*, kill, XVI 164; *gert ga, cum*, sent, brought, X 168, 173. [ON. *gøra*; the *a* forms are difficult to explain.]

Garryng, *adj.* grating, harsh, XIII *b* 15. [Cf. MDu., MLG. *garren*, v.]

Gase; Gast(e), &c. *See* Go(n); Gost(e), &c.

Gastli, *adj.* terrible, XII *b* 126. [OE. (once) *gǣst-lic*; cf. *gǣstan*, v.] *See* Agast; *distinguish* Gostly.

Gate, *n.*[1] gate, II 379. [OE. *gæt*, pl. *gatu*.] *See* ʒate.

Gate, *n.*[2] way, V 51; *hyʒe gate* (figuratively) highway, VI 35; *gang (ʒede) his gate*, go (went) his way, VI 166, XVI 144; Gatis, *pl.* in *many gatis*, in many ways, XI *b* 117. [ON. *gata*.] *See* Algate, Sogat, þus-gate.

Gate. *See* Gete, *v.*[1]

Gaud, *n.* trick, in *gaudes and gile*, XIV *a* 18, 30; *gaudis and gilery*, XVI 160. [! Cf. AFr. *gaudir*, to jest.]

Gaume. *See* Gam(e).

Gawle, *n.* gall; rancour, VI 103. The spelling and rimes are noteworthy at so early a date. [OE. *galla*.]

Ged(e)re, Gedyr. *See* Gadre.

Gedlyng, *n.* fellow (contemptuous), XVI 212. [OE. *gædeling*.]

Gees, *n. pl.* geese, VIII *a* 276, *b* 19. [OE. *gōs*, pl. *gēs*.]

Gef. *See* Giffe.

Geynest, *adj. superl.* most gracious, XV *c* 35. [ON. *gegn*.]

Gentil(l), Gentyl(e), Ientil (III), *adj.* of gentle birth, III 18, 23, VIII *b* 82, XIII *b* 20, &c.; noble, II 463, V 117, VI 245;

gentle, graceful, &c., II 305;
docile, XVII 505; *þat gentyl,*
that gentle lady, VI 242; *ientilman, gentleman,* III 18, XIV *introd.* [OFr. *gentil.*]

Gere, Geir (X), *n. sg.* tools,
apparatus, necessary things, X
110, XVII 245, 316, 326; arms,
XVI 211; contrivance (the ark),
XVII 274; affair, business, V 137.
[ON. *gervi.*]

Gered, *pp.* attired, V 159. [From
prec. in frequent sense 'apparel'.]

Gernier(e), *n.* garner, storehouse
(for corn), III 43, 46. [OFr.
gernier.]

Gert(e). *See* Garre.

Gesse(n), *v.* to be of opinion; to
expect, XI *b* 167; to conceive,
form an idea, V 139 (note).
[Cf. MLG. *gissen.*]

Geste, *n.* tale, VII *introd.*, Introduction xxxiii. [OFr. *geste.*]

Gestis, *n. pl.* joists, frame-timbers,
X 5. [OFr. *giste.*]

Get(e), *v.*[1] to get, find, XIV *c* 38,
110, XVII 184 (*subj.*); *pres.* as
fut. XIV *b* 3, XVII 299; lay hold
of, catch, XVII 339; *do get in,*
get in (*trans.*), XVII 326; Gate,
pa. t. sg. VII 176; Getyn, Ygete,
pp. in *getyn agayne,* won back,
XVI 11; *forþe ygete,* set forth,
produced, II 14. [ON. *geta.*]
See Forgete.

Get, *v.*[2] to guard; *get for,* look
out for, XIV *a* 36. [ON. *gæta.*]

Geþ. *See* Go(n).

Gyaunt, *n.* giant, VIII *a* 228.
[OFr. *geant.*]

Gyde, *n.* guide, VIII *a* 1. [OFr.
guide.]

Gif, Gyf, *conj.* if, IV *a* 85; *bot
gif,* unless X 78, 180. [Northern
variant of ʒif; the *g* (where not
graphic for ʒ) is difficult to
explain.]

Gif(fe), Gyf(fe), *v.* to give, IV *a*
18, *b* 66, V 327, VI 183, XVI
114, &c.; Gyue, XV *h* 21;
Gaf(fe), *pa. t. sg.* XVI 163, XVII
16; Gef, V 5 (wished), 281

(2 *sg.*); Gifen, *pp.* XIV *b* 88
(surrendered); Gyf(f)ene, IV *b*
53, 66; *gaf in commaundement,*
gave orders, XVII 33. [ON.
gefa, OSwed. *gifa;* see *N.E.D.*]
See ʒeue.

Gyfte, *n.* gift, IV *b* 53, 59, 69, VI
247; giving (? or privilege), VI
205. [ON. *gift.*] *See* ʒiftis.

Gile, Gyle, *n.* guile, treachery.
II 7, XIV *a* 6, *d* 4, XVII 214, &c.
[OFr. *guile.*] *See* Wiles, Bi-
gile.

Gilery, *n.* fraud, XVI 160. [OFr.
gilerie, from prec.]

Gill, *woman's name,* Jill, XVII
219; *for Iak nor for Gill,* for
nobody, XVII 336. [Shortened
from *Gillian,* OFr. *Juliane.*]

Gylofres, *n. pl.* in *clowe gylofres,*
cloves, IX 157. [OFr. *gilofre.*]
See Clowe.

Gyn(e), *n.* engine, machine, X 90,
99; contrivance, XVII 128, 276.
[Shortened from OFr. *engin.*]
See Engynys.

Gyng, *n.* troop, company, VI 95.
[OE. *genge;* ? infl. by *gang.*]

Gynour, *n.* engineer (contriver of
machines), X 98, 126. [Shorten-
ed from OFr. *engigneor.*] *See*
Gyn(e), Engynour.

Girdelstede, *n.* waist, II 266.
[OE. *gyrdel + stede.*] *See* Gurdel.

Gyrde, *v.* to strike; *gyrdeʒ he to,*
strikes spurs into, V 92. [? Same
as next.]

Gyrdit, *pp.* girt, X 24. [OE.
gyrdan.]

Gisely, *adv.* skilfully, II 299.
[From OFr. *guise,* n.] *See*
Degiselich.

Giserne, *n.* battle-axe, V 197.
[OFr. *guiserne.*]

Gyue. *See* Gif(fe).

Glad(e), *v.* to make glad, VIII *a*
113, XVII 491; Gladde, IV *a*
49. [OE. *gladian.*]

Gladde, Glad(e) (*of*), *adj.* happy,
glad (at), II 583, XII *introd.*,
XVI 42, 241, &c.; Gladly, *adv.*
XII *b* 37; *beren gladly,* are glad

to wear, IX 109. [OE. *glæd*, *glæd-līce*.]

Gle, Glew (I, IV), *n.* mirth, pleasure, play, II 34, 267, IV *a* 44, 72, XVII 529; (skill in) making music, minstrelsy, II 383, 434, 444, 529, &c.; *made hem glew*, directed their singing, I 39. [OE. *glēo*(*w*).]

Gleme, *n.* radiance, XVI 42. [OE. *glǣm*.]

Glent, *pa. t.* started aside, V 224. [Obscure; ME. *glenten* (mod. *glint*) has same senses as Blenk, *q.v.*]

Glew. *See* Gle.

Glyde, *v.* to glide, V 198, XII *b* 126. [OE. *glīdan*.]

Glyfte (*on*), *pa. t.* glanced sideways (at), V 197. [Obscure; ME. *gliffen*, and *gliften*, with same senses as Blenk, *q.v.*]

Glode, *n.* ? glade, open space, V 113; *on glode*, appar. a variant of *on bent* (q.v.), on earth, where he stood, V 198. [Unknown.]

Glorius, -ous, *adj.* glorious, XVI 42, XVII 166. [OFr. *glori*(*o*)*us*.]

Glotyny, Glotony, *n.* gluttony, XVII 37, 52. [OFr. *gloutonie*.]

Glotoun, *n.* Glutton (personified), VIII *a* 296. [OFr. *glouton*.]

Gloue, *n.* glove, VIII *a* 147. [OE. *glōfe*.]

Gnacchen, *v.* to gnash the teeth, XV *h* 9. [Echoic, on model of next.]

Gnauen, to gnaw, grind the teeth, XV *h* 9. [OE. *gnagan*.]

Go(n), *v.* VIII *a* 296, XV *g* 24, &c.; Goo, XI *b* 41, &c.; Ga, X 168; *pres. 2 sg.* Gost, II 129; 3 *sg.* Gase, IV *a* 11, XIV *a* 25; Geþ (OE. *gǣþ*), II 238, 551; Gotʒ, VI 5; Goth, IX 178, &c.; *pl.* Gaa, IV *b* 43; Goo, Go(n), IX 18, 177, XI *b* 15, &c.; Gotʒ, VI 150; Goþ, XIII *b* 64, 65; *subj.* Go, VI 170, XVI 156; *imper. pl.* Gos, VI 161; Gotʒ, V 51, 175; *pp.* Gane, X 84, 100, &c.; Go, I 222, II 196; Gon(e), I 161, II 492 (ago), VI 16, XVII 408 (done

for), &c.; Ygo, II 349, 541 (ago), Goande, *pres. p.* V 146. To walk, V 146, IX 18, XIV *a* 25; *in him com . . . gon* (OE. *cōm inn gān*), came walking in, XV *g* 24; to be (alive), V 41; *gon on bodi and bones, see* Bodi; to go, II 190, 345, XV *g* 12, &c.; *gon* (*be*), travel (about), IX 112; *go hunte*, &c., go and hunt, &c., VIII *a* 30, 32; *go slepe*, go to sleep, VIII *a* 296; *hadde go*, had gone on, I 222; *hou it geþ*, what is the (inevitable) course of things, II 551; *is go*(*n*), &c., went, II 196, X 176, XII *b* 176; *war tharin gane*, were in it, X 128; to come, get, IX 164, 186, &c.; *gotʒ* (*goth*) *out*, issues, VI 5, IX 178. [OE. *gān*.] *See* ʒede.

Gobet, *n.* small share, VIII *b* 106. [OFr. *gobet*.]

God, *n.* God, I 89, V 81, VI 241, &c.; Godd(e), I 78, V 51, 137, &c.; Godys (MS. God; *see* XVII 88, note), *gen. sg.* XVI 241; Godes, Goddes, *pl.* gods, II 31, VII 45, 176, 181, &c.; *gef hym God and goud day*, wished him Godspeed and good day, V 5. [OE. *god*.] *See* Goddesse.

God(e), *adj.* good, I 9, II 35, V 281, &c.; Good(e), VIII *b* 71, XI *b* 121, &c.; Goud(e), V 50, 202, VI 208; Gud(e), IV *b* 15, X 47, XIV *a* 14, &c.; Guod, III 59 (*guode*, wk., III 30, 31, &c.); *goud day, see* God. [OE. *gōd*.]

God(e), Good(e), Guode (III), Gude (IV, XIV *b*), *n. sg.* good, IV *b* 9, V 59, XII *a* 149; good thing, II 230; *collective*, goods, wealth, III 8 (*dat.*), IV *b* 81, VIII *a* 225, XII *b* 35, XIV *c* 75, &c.; Godes (and forms as above) *pl.*, goods, III 1, VII 122, VIII *a* 218, XI *b* 272, XII *b* 48, XIV *b* 11, &c. [OE. *gōd*, n.]

Goddesse, *n.* goddess, XII *a* 44. [OE *god* + OFr. -*esse*.]

Godenisse, God(e)nesse, Goodnesse, *n.* goodness, bounty, II

55, VI 133, VIII *a* 132, IX 329, &c. [OE. *gŏd-nes.*]

Godhede, *n.* divinity, VI 53, XI *b* 280, XVI 249. [OE. *god* + *-hēdu* ; cf. OE. *god-hād.*]

Godspelle, *n.* (*dat. sg.*) gospel, III 57 ; Gospel(l), VI 138, XI *a* 23, *b* 20, &c. [OE. *god-spell.*]

Goyng, *n.* ; *for goyng,* as a result of moving about, I 157. [From *Go*(*n*).]

Gold(e), *n.* gold, II 150, XV *g* 22 (*dat. sg.*), &c. [OE. *gŏld.*]

Golde-hemmed, *adj.* bordered with gold, V 327. [Prec. and OE. *hemm,* border.]

Golf, *n.* abyss (of water), VI 248. [OFr. *golfe.*]

Gome, *n.* man, V 50, 159, 171, 191, 202, VII 54, VIII *a* 210. [OE. *guma.*]

Gon(*e*), **Goo.** *See* Go(n).

Gonne. *See* Gan.

Gore, *n.* triangular strip (of cloth), gore ; by synecdoche for 'gown', in *under gore,* in gown (among women, alive), XV *c* 35. [OE. *gāra.*]

Gos, Gost. *See* Go(n).

Goshauk, *n.* goshawk (usually a large short-winged hawk), XII *a* 9. [OE. *gŏs-hafoc.*]

Gost, *n.* spirit, soul, V 182 ; **Haly Gast(e), Hooly Gost(e),** &c., Holy Ghost, IV *b* 53, IX 331, XI *a* 11, XVI 77, XVII 162, &c. [OE. *gāst.*]

Gostly, *adj.* spiritual, IX 332, XI *b* 281, 289 ; Gast(e)ly, IV *a* 51, *b* 70, 85. [OE. *gāst-lic.*]

Gotez, *n. pl.* streams, VI 248. [OE. **got-* rel. to *gēotan.*]

Gotz, Goþ, &c. *See* Go(n).

Goud(e). *See* Gode.

Gouerned, *pa. t.* controlled, XIV *c* 26. [OFr. *governer.*]

Goune, Gowne, *n.* gown (outer robe), V 328, XVII 262. [OFr. *goune.*]

Gowrdes, *n. pl.* gourds, IX 139. [OFr. *gourde.*]

Gowtes, *n. pl.* ; *gowtes artetykes,*

attacks of arthritic gout, IX 314. [OFr. *goute.*] *See* Artetyke.

Grace, *n.* favour, IX 296, XIV *b* 46, &c. ; consideration, VIII *a* 117 ; grace, mercy (of God), I 186, VI 76, 252, VIII *a* 120, *b* 106, XV *i* 8, XVII 551, &c. ; personified in our Lord, VI 65 ; what God may send, XVII 334 ; favour of fortune, luck, VII 76, VIII *b* 102, XII *b* 169, 186 ; lot, II 547. [OFr. *grace.*]

Graciouse, -yous, Gracius, *adj.* pleasing, VIII *a* 222 ; gracious, XVII 28, 165. [OFr. *gracious.*]

Gradde. *See* Grede.

Graidly. *See* Graythely.

Graielis, *n. pl.* books containing the 'gradual' (part of the Mass), XI *b* 229 (*see* note). [OFr. *graël.*]

Grayne. *See* Greyne.

Grayþed, *pa. t.* ; *grayþed hym,* got ready, V 191 ; **Graþhed,** *pp.* made ready, XVI 211 (rime requires Graide). [ON. *greiða.*]

Grayþely, Graþhely (XVI), **Graidly** (VII), *adv.* readily ; ready, V 224 ; aptly, VI 139 ; carefully, VII 54 ; directly, XVI 92. [ON. *greið-liga.*] *See* prec., and Grath.

Grame, *n.* wrath, XVII 89. [OE. *grama.*] *See* Greme.

Gramer(e), *n.* grammar, XIII *b* 36 ; *mayster of gr.,* (title of) a licensed teacher of grammar, XIII *b* 28. [OFr. *gramaire.*]

Gramerscole, *n.* grammar-school, XIII *b* 28, 33, 38. [Prec. + OE. *scōl.*]

Grant merci, gramercy, thank you (*lit.* great thanks), V 58, XII *b* 92. [OFr.]

Grapes, *n. pl.* grapes, IX 159, 160. [OFr. *grape.*]

Grases. *See* Gresse.

Grath, *n.* readiness, in *with grath,* promptly, XVII 482. [ON. *greiði.*] *See* Grayþed, &c.

Graue, *n.* grave, I 139, XVI 23, 393. [OE. *græf.*]

Graunt(e), Grante, *v.* to consent,

151 ; to grant, VII 3, VIII *a* 326, XIV *b* 46, XV *i* 8, XVII 178, &c. ; (with *infin.*) I 199, II 604. [OFr. *graanter*, AFr. *graunter.*]

Grece, *n.* fat, V 245. [OFr.*gresse.*]

Grede, *v.* to cry out, II 104 ; Graddde, *pa. t.* XII *b* 68. [OE. *grǣdan.*]

Greyn. *See* Grene.

Greyne, Grayne, *n.* grain, corn, VIII *a* 113, 120. [OFr.*grain.*]

Grekes, Grekys, *n. pl.* Greeks, VII 40, 61, 86, 111, 176. [OE. *Grē(a)cas,* L. *Grǣci.*]

Grem(e), *n.* anger ; resentment, VI 105 ; mortification, V 302 ; cause for anger, harm, V 183 ; *with greme,* wrathfully, V 231. [ON. *gremi* ; OE. *gremian,* v.] *See* Grame.

Gremþ, *n.* wrath, VII 176. [OE. **gremð.*]

Grene, Greyn (XVII), *adj.* green, II 353, V 35, VIII *a* 276, &c. ; *n.* green, V 123, 159, 191, 227 ; green sward, II 72 ; earth, XVII 534. [OE. *grēne.*]

Gresse, *n.* grass, II 244, V 113 ; Grases, *pl.* herbs, II 260. [OE. *gærs, græs.*]

Gret(e), Greate (III), *adj.* great, large, I 22, 210, II 101, 240, III 9, 17, &c. ; greatly esteemed, VII 40 ; big, boastful, XVII 379 ; *many grete,* many important people, XI *b* 207 ; *smale and grete, grete and small,* all, XIV *c* 22, XVII 90, 344 ; Grettere, *compar.* IX 70, 91 ; Grettest, *superl.* IX 182. [OE. *grēat* ; *grēttra,* compar.]

Gret(e), *v.*[1] to greet, XII *introd.,* XIV *d* 2. [OE. *grētan.*]

Grete, *v.*[2] to weep, V 89 ; Grette, *pa. t.* IV *a* 87. [OE. *grētan* (**grǣtan*), or *grēotan.*]

Gretnesse, *n.* size, IX 54. [OE. *grēat-nes.*]

Greu, *n.* Greek (language), XI *a* 45. [OFr. *greu.*]

Grevance, *n.* offence, sin (*or* affliction), XVII 58. [OFr. *grevance.*]

Greue, *v.* to grieve, offend, VI 111, VIII *a* 225, XV *f* 3 ; oppress, VIII *a* 313 ; injure, VIII *b* 60 ; *greueth hym a3eines,* voices a grievance against, VIII *a* 311 ; Greuyng, *n.* offending, insulting, VII 181. [OFr. *grever.*]

Greuous, *adj.* grave, IX 287 ; Greuously, *adv.* gravely, XI *b* 144. [OFr. *grevous.*]

Grew(e). *See* Growe(n).

Gryed, *pa. t.* sorrowed (inwardly), V 302. [Not known ; *cf.* XI Pains of Hell (OE. Miscell.) l. 160, *gryd and wept.*]

Griffoun, *n.* griffin, IX 245, 248, 251. [OFr. *griffon.*]

Griis, *n.* grey (fur), II 241 (*see* Fowe). [OFr. *gris.*]

Grymme, Grim, *adj.* fearsome, grim, II 184, V 192. [OE. *grimm.*]

Gryndel, *adj.* wrathful, V 270 ; Gryndelly, *adv.* wrathfully, V 231. [? Back-formation from **grindlaik (gryndellayk* Sir Gaw. 312), ON. *grimmd + leik-r* ; cf. ON. *grimm-leikr.*]

Gryndel-ston, *n.* grindstone, V 134. [OE. **grindel* (from *grindan*) + *stān.*]

Grys, *n. pl.* young pigs, VIII *a* 276. [ON. *gríss-s.*]

Grisbittyng, *n.* gnashing of the teeth, XIII *b* 15. [OE. *grist-bitung.*]

Gryste, *n.* resentment (? *lit.* grinding of the teeth), VI 105. [OE. *grist,* grinding.]

Grochinge, *n.* reluctance, III 10. *See* Grucche.

Gron(e), *v.* to lament, complain, V 89, XVII 409 ; groan, VIII *a* 255, XV *h* 9. [OE. *grānian.*]

Gronyngys, *n. pl.* lamentations (as a sign of repentance), XI *b* 99. [OE. *grānung.*]

Grot, *n.* small bit ; *euerich a grot,* every detail, II 490. [OE. *grot.*]

Ground(e), Grownd (XVII), *n.* ground, XII *a* 80, &c. ; bottom, XII *b* 71 ; bottom of the sea, XVII 439, 462 ; the soil, XIII *a*

52; land, XVII 465; foundation, cause, VI 12, 24, 36, 48, 60, VII 80; (*vp*)*on grounde*, on earth, V 82, VIII *a* 225; *to grounde*, on the ground, II 549, VI 74. [OE. *grúnd*.]

Grounde, *v.* in *nouȝt groundiþ hem*, they have no foundation, XI *a* 4; *groundid* (*in*), based (on), XI *b* 52; *ben not gr. in God*, have no divine sanction, XI *a* 62. [From prec.]

Grounden, *pp.* ground, V 134; **Ygrounde**, XIV *d* 9. [OE. *grindan, ge-grúnden*.]

Grow, *v.* to feel terror, X 94. [Cf. MLG. *grüwen*.]

Growe(n), Grufe, *v.* to grow, VIII *a* 113, IX 33, 53, XII *a* 80, &c.; to come into being, in *begynnys to grufe to vs*, is about to begin for us, XVII 463; **Grew(e)**, *pa. t.* I 164, 236, VI 65, VII 80; **Growe**, *pp.* II 266, XIV *c* 89, 98; **Growynge**, *n.* growth, IX 71. [OE. *grówan*; *grufe* is freq. Northern form.]

Grucche, Gruch, *v.* to grumble, VIII *a* 210, 311; grumble at, V 183; **Gruchyng**, *pres. p.* reluctant, V 58. [OFr. *gr(o)ucher*.] *See* Grochinge, Bigruccheth.

Grufe. *See* Growe(n).

Grwe, *n.* jot, in *no grwe*, not a jot, not at all, V 183. [? OFr. *gru*, grain; *cf.* Grot.]

Gud(e), Guod(e), &c. *See* Gode.

Gun(e). *See* Gan.

Gurdel, *n.* girdle, V 327; **Girdel**, V 290. [OE. *gyrdel*.]

Guttes, *n. pl.* entrails, VIII *a* 171. [OE. *guttas*.]

Ȝa, Ȝaa, *adv.* yea, yes, XVI 109, 305. [OE. *gēā*.] *See* Ȝe, Yei.

Ȝaf. *See* Ȝeue.

Ȝalow, *adj.* yellow, IX 34, 115, 116; fair (-haired), IX 22. [OE. *geolu, geolw-*.]

Ȝalownesse, *n.* fairness (of hair), IX 22. [From prec.]

Ȝar, *adj.* ready, X 110. [OE. *gearo*.]

Ȝare, *adv.* fully, V 342. [OE. *gear(w)e*.]

Ȝarkke, *v.* to ordain, decree, V 342; **Yȝarked**, *pp.* II 547. [OE. *gearcian*.]

Ȝate, *n.* gate, II 232 (*dat.*), 385; **Ȝet**, X 167, 181, &c.; **Ȝateȝ, -es, -iis**, *pl.* V 2, IX 223, XVI 124, &c. [OE. *ge(a)t, gæt* (pl. *gatu*); the pls. above show infl. of sg.] *See* Gate, *n.*[1]

Ȝe, *adv.* yea, yes, VIII *a* 38, 227, *b* 110. [OE. *gēa.*] *See* Ȝa, Yei.

Ȝe, *pron.* 2 *pl. nom.* you, I 38, II 215, &c.; **Ȝee**, IX 187, 219, 284; **Ȝe**, XV *g* 25, &c.; **Yee**, XVII 397. **Ou**, *acc.* and *dat.* (to) you, XIV *c* 97; **Ȝou**, II 24, 204, &c.; **Ȝow**, I 22, VIII *a* 6, 14, &c.; **You(e)**, XVI 402, XVII 294, &c.; **Yow**, V 23, 26, &c.; *refl.* (*acc.*) yourselves, VIII *a* 112, XIV *b* 7, XVI 178; yourself, V 49, VIII *a* 25; (*dat.*) for yourselves, II 216, 217; *ȝif ȝou lyke, it lyke ȝou*, if it please you, IX 74, 284; *ȝou to*, for yourselves, XIV *d* 7. **Ȝor**, *poss. adj.* XIV *c* 13, 106; **Ȝour(e)**, I 84, II 218, &c.; **Ȝowre**, VIII *a* 14, 21, XIV *a* 8, 10, *b* 4, &c. The plural forms are often used to a superior, as: II 582, VIII *a* 118, ff., &c.; but also without special reason and intermingled with *þou*, &c., as: II 466, V 42, 256-7, &c. [OE. *gē, ēow, ēower*.]

Ȝede (*pa. t.* of Gon, *q.v.*), fared, went, &c., I 53, 104, II 301, 476, VIII *a* 93, &c.; walked, II 509; was, V 265; *ȝede atwynne*, broke apart, separated, I 191; *ȝede on fote* = lived, V 295; *ȝede his gate*, went his way, VI 166. [OE. *ēode*; see *N.E.D.*, s.v. *Yede*, and Luick, Hist. Gramm. d. engl. Sprache § 261 n. 3; § 360.]

Ȝederly, *adv.* † promptly, † fully, V 257. [† OE. *ǣdre, ēdre*, quickly, fully; *cf.* Yendles.]

Ȝeer, *n.* year, IX 61, 63, &c.; **Ȝer(e)**, I 151, V 332, VIII *a* 44,

XIII *a* 44, &c.; **Yeare** (*dat.*),
III *introd.*; **Yer**(**e**), III 44,
VII 12, 99, XIV *e* 2, XVII 57;
Зer(**e**), *pl.* I *introd.*, II 264, 492,
541, VI 123, VIII *a* 319, *b* 36,
XVI 39, 354; **Зeres**, I *introd.*
[OE. *gēr, gēar.*] *See* Toзere.

Зef, **Yef**; **Зif**, **Зyf**, *conj.* (usually
with *subj.*) if, I 17, II 169, III 13,
28, V 230, VI 122, VIII *a* 163,
XIII *a* 35, 48, XV *b* 34, &c.;
whether, I 17, III 5, &c.; **Hyf**,
VIII *b* 43; **If**(**f**), VIII *a* 123,
XVI 331, &c.; **Iif**, V 275; **Yf**,
IV *b* 24; **Yiif**, XV *a* 23; *Зif* (*if*)
þat, if, IV *a* 24, 88, IX 219, 271,
XII *a* 16, *b* 46, XIV *c* 69; whether,
XII *a* 184; *all if*, although, XVII
231; *see* also Bote. [OE. *gef,
gi*(*e*)*f.*] *See* Gif.

Зeit. *See* Зet(e), *adv.*

Зelde(**n**), *v.* to yield, give (back),
pay, repay, V 155, 257, VIII *a*
44, IX 189; **Yelde**, III 510;
Зelde, *subj.* (*imper.*) in *з. hit
зow*, requite you for it, V 342;
з. зow (*of*), reward you (for),
VIII *a* 121; **Зolden**, *pp.* surrendered, XIV *b* 89; **Yolde**,
restored, III 58 (*see* the French).
[OE. *gěldan.*] *See* Forзelde.

Зemen, *n. pl.* yeomen, hired
labourers, VI 175. [? OE.
geong-man, ME. *зengman, зem-
man, зēman*; see *N.E.D.*, s.v.
Yeoman.]

Зeply, *adv.* cunningly; (allit. only)
quickly, promptly, V 176. [OE.
gēap-līce.]

Зer(**e**). *See* Зeer.

Зern(**e**), *adv.* eagerly, readily, II
323, VIII *a* 103, 292. [OE.
gěorne.]

Зerne, *v.* to desire, long for;
Yзyrned, *pp.* XV *c* 32 (the relative before *ychabbe* is omitted);
Зhernyng, *n.* (the object of)
desire, IV *a* 22 (*cf.* Couaytyng,
Lufyng). [OE. *gěornan, girnan;
gěorning.*]

Зet. *See* Зate.

Зet(**e**), **Зeit** (X), **Yet**; **Зit**(**t**), **Зyt**,
Yit; **Зut** (VIII *b*); *adv.* yet; up

to now, even now, XI *b* 243,
XII *a* 196, XIV *c* 84, XVI 373,
XVII 359, &c.; strengthening
(*n*)*euere*, II 103, 147, VI 89,
VIII *b* 41, XVI 136; still, once
more, in addition, moreover,
II 464, VI 14, VIII *a* 38, 250,
IX 40, 200, XII *b* 75, &c.; *all*
the same, none the less, I 225,
II 174, V 151, VI 83, VIII *b* 98,
XI *b* 119, XV *g* 31, XVII 12, &c.;
conj. and yet, but, XVII 17, 197;
ac зete, but зit, bot yit (*зeit*), &c.,
and yet, II 191, IX 99, X 95,
XI *b* 239, XVII 35, &c. [OE.
gēt(*a*), *gett, gī*(*e*)*t, gȳt*, &c.]

Зete, *v.* to grant, give; *no waning
I wyl þe зete*, I wish to give you
no curtailment (of what is due),
VI 198. [OE. (late) *gēatan*,
prob. modelled on ON *játa.*]

Зeue, **Yeue** (III), *v.* to give, grant,
III 7, IX 79, 293, XI *b* 162, &c.;
Зiue(**n**), II 454, VIII *a* 121
(*subj.*), XII *b* 35, 42, &c.; **Зyue**,
XI *b* 300; **Зifth**, 3 *sg. pres.* XII *a*
87. **Зaf**, **Yaf**, *pa. t. sg.* III 39,
44, VIII *a* 192, 238, XI *a* 11;
Yeaf, III 10, 22, 52; **Зaf**, *pa. t.
pl.* II 20; **Yeaue**, *pa. subj.* III
21, 51. **Зouen**, *pp.* IX 90, XI *b*
264; **Yeue**, III 7, 14; **Y-yeue**,
III 25, 29; *зaf of*, gave (cared)
for, XIV *c* 54. [OE. *gefan,
giefan, gyfan.*] *See* Giffe, For-
зeue.

Зhernyng. *See* Зerne, *v.*

Зif (**Зyf**); **Зifth.** *See* Зef; Зeue.

Зiftis, *n. pl.* gifts, VIII *a* 42, XI *b*
265. [OE. *gift*; see *N.E.D.*,
s.v. *Gift.*] *See* Gyfte.

Зit(**t**), **Зyt**, **Yit.** *See* Зet(e), *adv.*

Зiue(**n**), **Зyue.** *See* Зeue.

Зoked, *pp.* yoked, IX 253. [OE.
geocian.]

Зolden. *See* Зelde(n).

Зole, *n.* Yule, Christmas; *зole
nyзt*, Christmas night, I 187.
[OE. *gēol*; cf. ON. *jól*, n. pl.
Yule; *jóla-nátt*, Yule-night.]

Зon. *See* Yone.

Зong(**e**), **Yong** (XVII), *adj.* young,
VI 52, 114, 175, VIII *b* 36, IX 21,

XVII 397 ; *old or ȝong*, any one,
II 221 ; *ȝong and alde*, every one,
IV *a* 49. [OE. *geong*.]
Ȝor. *See* Ȝe, *pron.*
Ȝore, *adv.* (since long ago), a long
while, II 559, V 46, VI 226, XV *c*
32. [OE. *geāra*.]
Ȝou, Ȝour(e), Ȝow(re). *See* Ȝe.
Ȝouen. *See* Ȝeue.
Ȝut. *See* Ȝet(e), *adv.*

Haade. *See* next.
Habbe(n), *v.* to have, possess,
get, take, put, and *auxil.*, XIII *a*
59, 60, XV *g* 23 ; A, I 127 ;
Haf(e), IV *a* 64, V 150, &c. ;
Haif, XVII 286 ; Han, XIV *c* 6 ;
XV *h* 22 ; Haue(n), I 107, VIII *a*
74, XII *a* 66, &c. ; Hawe, X *introd.*
Haf, Haue, I *sg. pres.* V 23, IX
289, &c. ; *see* Ichabbe, Ichaue ;
Has(e), 2 *sg.* XVI 243, XVII
430, &c. ; Hast(e), I 131, XVI
223, &c ; Hatȝ, V 173, 228,
273, 324 ; Hauest, VIII *b* 26 ;
Habbeȝ, 3 *sg.* *V 271 (note) ;
Hase, IV *a* 39, XVII 550, &c. ;
Haþ, Hath, I 11, XVI 356,
&c. ; Hatȝ, V 46, 126, 340 ;
Haues, XV *a* 20 ; Haueþ, VIII *b*
98 ; Habbeþ, *pl.* III 2, XIII *a*
15, &c. ; Haf(e) (with *pron.*),
IV *b* 16, VI 159, X 16, &c. ;
Han (the commonest form), II
21, V 25, &c. ; Has(e) (sep.
from *pron.*), IV *a* 2, X 52, XIV *b*
71, XVII 95, &c. Haue, *pres.*
subj. V 219, VIII *a* 114, 261 ;
as haue I (thou), so may I (you)
have, XVII 237, 333, 402. Haf,
Haue, *imper. sg.* V 75, I 124,
&c. ; Haueth, *pl.* XIV *d* 13.
Hadde, *pa. t.* I 100, II 51, XI *b*
265, &c. ; Had(e), I 116, V 13,
XI *b* 202, &c. ; Hedde, III 5,
42, &c. (OKt. *hefde*) ; Hadde,
2 *sg.* XVI 219 ; Hadestow, II
533 (*see* Þou) ; Hadyn, *pl.* VII
126. Haade, *pa. t. subj.* had,
would (should) have, XI *b* 270 ;
Hadde, Had(e), II 559, I 195,
V 196, &c. ; Hed(d)e, III 13,
30, &c. ; Hadeȝ, Hadest, 2 *sg.*

subj. II 573, V 326. Yhad, *pp.*
II 249, 253. Haf (*haue*) *at* þe,
have (*i. e.* let me get) at thee,
V 220, XVII 219 ; *haue done*, be
quick, XVII 316, 352, 480 ; *his
lyf hade*, preserved his life, VII
163. [OE. *habban*.]
Habide. *See* Abide.
Habundant, *adj.* abundant, IX
330. [OFr. *abundant*.]
Hacches, *n. pl.* hatches ; of a
buttery, or kitchen, VIII *b* 29 ;
of a ship, VII 147. [OE.
hæcc.]
Hade, *see* Habbe(n), Heued ;
Hadestow, *see* Habbe(n).
Haf(e). *See* Habbe(n), Half.
Hafyng, *n.* possession, VI 90.
[From stem of Habben ; cf. OE.
hæfen.]
Hay(e), *n.* hay, XVII 159 ; mow-
ing grass, IV *a* 33. [OE. *hēg*.]
Haif. *See* Habbe(n).
Hayle, *n.* hail, I 162. [OE.
hægl.]
Hayroun, *n.* (*collective*), herons,
II 310. [OFr. *hairon*.]
Haithill. *See* Hapel.
Haywarde, *n.* hayward (who had
charge of fences, enclosures, &c.,
and was sometimes keeper of
the cattle on the common land),
VIII *b* 16 (*see* note). [OE. *hæg-
weard*.]
Hald(e), &c. *See* Holde(n).
Haldynge, *n.* ; *haldynge vp*, main-
taining, XI *b* 168. *See* Holde(n).
Hale, *v.* to draw, pull, XII *b* 87 ;
Halt, *pp.* in *vp halt*, uplifted,
high, V 11. [OE. *halian*
(OFris. *halia*), or OFr. *haler*.]
Half, Halue, Haf (III), *n.* side,
X 198 ; *vpon boþe halue*, on both
sides, V 2, 97 ; *o this half*, on
this side (of the world), IX 250 ;
behalf, in *ane ... haf* (with intervening *gen.*) on behalf of, III 11 ;
(*vp)on Goddeȝ halue, a (on)
Goddes half*, &c., in God's name,
for God's sake, V 51, 81, XI *a* 15,
XII *b* 80 ; *adj.* and *adv.* half,
IX 241, XII *b* 35, 79, &c. [OE.
half.] *See* Behalue.

Halʒeʒ, *n. pl.* saints, V 54. [OE. *hálga.*] *See* Holi.

Haly. *See* Holi.

Halydam, *n.* halidom, holy thing (such as relics of the saints, but frequent coupling with *God,* and *help,* seems to show word to imply the saints as a body; *cf.* prec. line),V 55. [OE. *háligdóm.*]

Hall(e), *n.* mansion, hall, home, II 219, V 261, XVI 136, XVII 67, 348, 516, &c. [OE. *hall.*]

Halme, *n.* shaft, V 156. [OE. *halm,* stalk; *cf.* Stele.]

Halpeny, *n.* halfpenny in *halpeny ale,* ale at a halfpenny a gallon, small beer, VIII *a* 300. [OE. *half-penig.*] *See* Pené.

Hals, *n.* neck, VIII *a* 63. [OE. *hals.*]

Halsed, *pa. t.* embraced, greeted, XVI 64. [OE. *h(e)alsian,* *embrace, implore, usually confused with next. Cf. ON. *heilsa* (= next), greet; *hálsa,* embrace.]

Halsen, *v.* to interpret (dream), XII *a* 148. [OE. *hǽlsian, hálsian,* interpret omens, &c.]

Halt, *see* Hale; Halue, *see* Half.

Halue-acre, Half-acre, *n.* half-acre, small plot, VIII *a* 4, 5, 100, 110. [OE. *half + æcer.*]

Halvendel, *n.* half, XII *b* 49, 218. [OE. *halfan dǽl,* accus.] *See* Dele.

Halwid, *pp.* consecrated, XI *b* 29. [OE. *hálgian.*] *See* Halʒeʒ Holi.

Ham, Hamsylf. *See* Hi, *pron. pl.*

Hame. *See* Hom, *adv.*

Hamerys, Hamers, *n. pl.* hammers, XV *h* 10, 13. [OE. *hamor.*] *See* Homered.

Hamese, *n. pl.* alleged oriental name for diamonds, IX 37 (so in French original).

Han, *see* Habbe(n); Hand(e), *see* Hond.

Handled, *pp.* wielded, XV *h* 13. [OE. *handlian.*]

Hange, *v.* to hang (*trans.* and *intr.*), I 219, VIII *a* 63, XVI 307;

Hongeþ, 3 *sg. pres.* II 506, 507; Heng(e), *pa. t. sg.* II 344, 500; Yhonged, *pp.* XIII *a* 14. [OE. *hōn* (pa. t. *héng*). trans.; *hángian,* intr.; *cf.* ON. *hanga* (str.) intr.]

Hap, Happ, *n.* chance, fortune, XII *b* 8, XV *c* 9; Happes, *pl.* happenings, II 8, XIII *a* 62. [ON. *happ.*] *See* Myshap.

Happe, *v. impers.* happen, VIII *a* 47; Happed, Happit, *pa. t.* it befell, VII 117, VIII *b* 99. [From prec.]

Happene, Happyn, *v.* to happen, IX 47, 207, XVII 481; Hapneth, 3 *sg. pres.* XII *b* 6. [Extended from prec.]

Hard. *See* Here, *v.*

Hard(e), *adj.* hard, harsh, cruel, I 28, 135, II 243, &c.; strong, immovable, IV *a* 48; as *sb.,* what is hard, VI 246; *adv.* hard, V 85, XV *h* 13; grievously, VII 117; closely, X 150, XVI 151. [OE. *heard; hearde.*]

Hardely, Hardily, Hardiliche, *adv.* boldly, VIII *a* 30, XVI 143; (parenthetic), certainly, I may say, V 322, XVII 522. [From next.]

Hardi, Hardy, *adj.* bold, II 27, VIII *a* 179, &c. [OFr. *hardi.*]

Hardyment, *n.* (act of) daring, X 183. [OFr. *hardement.*]

Hardynesse, *n.* hardihood, boldness, IX 79. [OFr. *hardi + -ness;* cf. OFr. *hardiesse.*]

Hardis, *n. pl.* hards (coarser part of flax), X 20. [OE. *heordan,* pl.]

Hare. *See* Hi, *pron. pl.,* and *fem.*

Harkens, &c. *See* Herkne.

Harlot, *n.* rascal, scurrilous fellow, VIII *a* 54, [XVI 185]. [OFr. *harlot.*]

Harm(e), *n.* grief, misfortune, injury, detriment, I 147, V 204, 209, VI 28, XII *a* 162, XIII *b* 39, XIV *a* 26, XVI 323, &c. [OE. *hearm.*]

Harp, *n.* harp, II 19, 231, &c. [OE. *hearp.*]

Harpe, *v.* to harp, II 37, 271, &c. [OE. *hearpian.*]

Harpour(e), Harper, *n.* harper, minstrel, II 35, 40, 513, 522, &c. [OE. *hearpere*; OFr. *harpour*.]

Harpyng, *n.* harping, minstrelsy, II 3, 43, 277, &c. [OE. *hearpung*.]

Harryng, *n.* snarling, XIII *b* 15. [Echoic.]

Harrowe, Herrowe, *interj.* a cry for help, XVI 185, 343; as *sb.*, uproar, XVI 98. [OFr. *harou*.]

Harrowing, *n.* despoiling, XVI *title.* [OE. *hergung*.]

Hartely. See Hertely.

Harwen, *v.* to harrow, VIII *b* 19. [Cf. ON. *herfi*, OSwed. *harva*, a harrow.]

Hasell-note, *n.* hazel-nut, IX 55. [OE. *hæsel-hnutu*.]

Hast(e), *n.* violence, haste, VIII *a* 291, XVII 411, &c; *an haste,* III 22, 43, 47; *in hast(e),* V 150, VIII *a* 167, XVII 158, 293, 447, speedily, immediately. [OFr. *haste*; cf. Heste, *n.*²]

Hast(e), *v. intr.* and *refl.* to hasten, VIII *a* 317, XVII 182; *hastis hemselue to hange,* rashly (precipitately) hang themselves, XVI 307. [OFr. *haster*.]

Hast(e)ly, *adv.* speedily, XVII 39, 109. [From Haste, *n.*; cf. OE. *hæstlice*.]

Hate. See Hoot.

Hate, *n.* hatred, VI 103, &c. [Stem of next.]

Hate, Hatie, 2 *sg. pres. subj.* (you should) hate, IV *a* 47, VIII *a* 52. [OE. *hatian*.]

Hat3, Hab, &c. See Habbe(n).

Hatte, *n.* hat, V 13, XIV *b* 41. [OE. *hætt*.]

Hatte, see Hote, *v.*; **Hatter, see** Hoot.

Habel, Haithill (VII), *adj.* noble, VII 38; *n.* knight, V 263, 340. [OE. *æbele*, adj., and *hæleþ*, warrior; see Björkman, *Morte Arthure,* 358 (note, and refs.).]

Hauenes, *n. pl.* harbours, XIII *b* 68, XIV *c* 38. [OE. *hæfen(e)*.]

Hauer-cake, *n.* oat-cake, VIII *a* 277. [ON. *hafri* + ME. *cake* (cf. Icel., Swed. *kaka*).]

Haukin, *n.*; *on haukin,* a-hawking, II 308. [OE. *hafoc*, ON. *hauk-r*, a hawk.]

Haunche, *n.* haunch; app. = shoulder, I 120. [OFr. *hanche*.]

Haunt, *n.* frequentation; *wel gode haunt,* great plenty, II 309. [OFr. *hant*, from next.]

Hauntep, 3 *sg. pres.* frequents, I 2. [OFr. *hanter*.]

Hawe. See Habbe(n).

He, *pron.* 3 *sg. masc.* he, I 4, 10, &c.; Hee, XVI 185; A, XIII *a* 27, &c. (*see* A); *indef.* one, VIII *a* 130, 131, 211; *as he which,* as (being) one who, XII *a* 23 (note), *b* 37, &c. Him, Hym(e), *acc.* and *dat.* I 63, II 51, &c.; *refl.* (for) himself, I 10, 70, II 244, 485, IV *b* 78, 80, V 191, VI 118, XVI 126; often pleonastic (*dat.*) with verbs of bodily action, II 289 (note), XV *b* 7 (note), *g* 33; esp. of motion, III 19, V 86, XIV *c* 61, XV *g* 18, 24 (note), 27, 29, 30; orig. *refl. accus.* II 475, 501. Himself, Hymself(e), -selue(n), -seluyn, -sylf, *nom.* himself, IV *b* 82, V 41, VII 69, XI *b* 225, XIII *a* 27, &c.; he himself, II 37, VII 161; *acc. refl.* XI *b* 223, XV *g* 16, &c. Hiis, *poss. adj.* (orig. *gen.*) XIV *d* 7; Hys, His, I 46, II 29, &c.; Hysse, VI 58; Hus, VIII *b* 60, 101, 102; Is, XV *g* 7, 24, 29; Us, VIII *b* 106; Hise, *pl.* XII *a* 156, &c.; as *sb.*, his folk, I 135, XVII 553; written for genitive inflexion, XIII *a* 22 (*see* note), *b* 23. [OE. *hē*, nom.; *his*, gen.; *him*, dat.] See Hi, Hit.

He, *pron. fem.* she, II 408, 446, XV *c* 7, 15, 17, &c. (*see* Hi, *pron. fem.*); *pl.* they, II 185 (*see* Hi, *pron. pl.*). [OE. *hēo*.]

He. See Heigh(e).

Hebenus, *n.* ebony, XII *a* 91. [L. *ebenus*.]

Hed(e), *see* Habbe(n), Heued;
Hedde(n), *see* Habbe(n).

Hede, *n.* heed, notice, VIII *a* 15,
XIV *c* 10; *take hede*, look you,
XVII 424. [Stem of OE. *hēdan*.]

Heder, -ir. *See* Hider.

Hee. *See* He, *masc.*; Heie, *adv.*

Heele, *n.* heel, XIII *b* 39; Hele3,
pl. v 85. [OE. *hēla*.]

Heele. *See* Hele, *n.*

Heep, **Hep**, *n.* host, VIII *a* 181;
an hep (without *of*), a host of,
XII *a* 82. [OE. *hēap*.]

Heere. *See* Her(e), *adv.* and *n.*

Heggen, *v.* to make and trim
hedges, *VIII *b* 19 (MS. eggen).
[From next.]

Hegges, *n. pl.* hedges, VIII *a* 31.
[OE. *hecg*.]

Heght. *See* Hight.

Heie, **Hye** (X), **Hy3(e)**, **Hee**
(IV); *adv.* high, IV *a* 9, VI 113,
X 16, 124, XV *g* 12; loudly, v
144, X 86. [OE. *hēh*.]

Heigh(e), **Hei3(e)**, **Heih**, *adj.*
high, noble; loud; II 26, 205, 326,
356, VIII *a* 4, XI *b* 133, XIV *c* 18,
100, 109, &c.; also **He**, XVII
469; **Hegh**, VII 142; **He3e**,
V 129; **Hye**, IX 196, XVII 553;
Hy3e, V 19, VI 35, XIII *a* 40,
&c.; **High(e)**, **Hygh**, I 113, VII
101, IX 137, &c.; **Hihe**, XII *a*
51; *an hy3*, *on hegh*, on high,
VII 142, XIII *a* 11; *hy3e gate*,
see Gate, *n.*[2]; *heighe pryme*, full
prime, the end of the period
'prime' (6–9 a.m.), VIII *a* 106;
hygh tymes, festivals, I 13;
heigh way, highway, VIII *a* 4;
Hyar, *compar.* taller, X 10.
[OE. *hēh*.]

Heighliche, *adv.* at a high rate,
VIII *a* 307. [From prec.; cf.
OE. *hēa-līce*.]

Hei3ing, *n.* haste; *an hei3ing*, in
haste, II 137. [From Hy, *v.*]

Heiste; **Heite**; **Held(e)**. *See*
Hote; Hete, *n.*; Holde(n).

Helde, *v. intr.* to incline, turn, v
263; Heldand, *pres. p.* inclined,
IV *a* 28. [OE. *hēldan*.]

Hele, **Heele** (XVI), *n.* health,

VIII *a* 256, *b* 7, 10; restoration,
XII *a* 18; salvation, XVI 38, 67,
106. [OE. *hǣlu*.] *See* Hol(e).

Hele, *v.* to heal, VIII *a* 186, IX
92. [OE. *hǣlan*.]

Hele3. *See* Heele.

Heling, *n.* covering, X 6. [From
OE. *hel(i)an*.]

Hell. *See* Hil.

Hell(e), **Hel**, *n.* hell, IV *a* 48, 64,
VI 82, &c.; originally *gen.*, in
helle pitte, the abyss of hell, XVI
348; *fendis in h.*, hell-fiends,
XI *b* 216 (*cf.* OE. *fēond on helle*).
[OE. *hell*.]

Helme, *n.*[1] helm(et), V 75, 129,
&c. [OE. *helm*.]

Helm(e), *n.*[2] helm (of rudder),
XIV *c* 59, XVII 272, 420. [OE.
helma.]

Help(e), *n.* help, reinforcements,
VII 3, VIII *a* 240, X 180, &c.;
forces, XIII *b* 65. [OE. *help*.]

Helpe(n), **Help(pe)**, *v.* to help,
avail, II 116, V 141 (note), VIII *a*
21, 241, &c.; *pres. subj.* V 55, XVII
247; **Holpyn**, *pa. t. pl.* VIII *a*
100; **Hulpen**, VIII *a* 110; **Help-
ing**, *n.* X 18. [OE. *helpan*.]

Hemself, **-selue**. *See* Hi, *pl.*

Hende, *adj.* courteous, gracious,
II 563, XVI 45; as *sb.*, good
sir, V 262; **Hendely**, *adv.* courteously, V 340. [OE. (*ge-*)*hēnde*,
convenient, at hand.]

Hendy, *adj.* gracious, fair, XV *c* 9,
37, &c. [Extended from prec.]

Henge. *See* Hange.

Hennes; **Hence**, **Hens** (XVII),
adv. from here, VIII *a* 273, *b* 84,
XVII 292, 507; from now, ago,
VIII *b* 36, XVII 25. [ME.
henen(e), *henne* (OE. *heonane*)
+ adv. *-es*.]

Hent(e), *v.* to catch, seize, get,
receive, I 112, V 249, VI 28
(*pres. subj.*), VIII *a* 167, 181;
hent to, lay hold of, XVII 420;
Hent, *pp.* IV *a* 24, V 209, 255;
Yhent, XV *c* 9, 37, &c. [OE.
hentan.]

Hep; **Heore**. *See* Heep; Hi, *pl.*

Her(e), **Heere**, **Hier(e)**, (III,

XII), *adv.* here, at this point,
III 2, VI 159, XI *a* 1, *b* 82, XII *b*
34, 118, XVI 40, &c.; here is,
XII *b* 161, XVI 325; *here abowte,*
hereabouts, XV *i* 1.   Her(e)-,
Hyer-, used for *neut. pron.*
(this &c.) in : Her(e)fore, for
this reason, XI *a* 22, 33, *b* 139 ;
Hereinne, VI 217 ; Her(e)of,
Hyerof, at, of this, III 1, VIII *a*
177, IX 150, XI *a* 54. [OE. *hĕr.*]
Her(e), Heere (1), *n.* hair, I 164,
237, II 265, 506, XV *c* 13.   [OE.
hǣr, hĕr.]
Her(e), *see* Hi, *pron. fem.* and *pl.*;
Hereself, *see* Hi, *fem.*
Herbarwe, Herberowe, *n.* lodg-
ing, II 434, XVI 136. [OE.
here-beorg.]
Herber, *n.* arbour (grassy place
with trees), XV *a* 13.   [OFr.
herbier.]
Here, *n.* host (of foes), V 203.
[OE. *here.*]
Here, *v.* to hear, listen to, hear of,
I 81, II 43, V 136, 205, VIII *a*
54, 206, XI *b* 223 (*subj.*), &c.;
Heryn, II 117; **Heris,** 2 *sg. pres.*
XVI 101 ; **Herd(e),** *pa. t.* I 75,
239, &c. ; **Hard,** *pp.* XVII 46;
Herd(e), IV *a* 24, IX 172, XVI
98.   *For likyng to here,* VII 71,
see Likeing. [OE. *hĕran.*] *See*
Yhere.
Heremites, Heremytes, *n. pl.*
hermits, VIII *a* 139, 181, *b* 4.
[Med.L. (*h*)*erĕmīta*; OFr. (*h*)*er-
mite.*]
Hereres, *n. pl.* hearers, IX 276,
321. [From Here, *v.*]
Heresye, *n.* heresy, XI *a* 1, 64.
[OFr. *heresie.*]
Heretik, *n.* heretic, XI *a* 4; **Here-
tikis, -ys,** *pl.* XI *b* 37, 45, &c.
[L. *hǣreticus.*]
Heryen, *v.* to praise, XI *b* 152.
[OE. *herian.*]
Heryng(e) (*of*), *n.* hearing (of),
listening (to), IX 277, X *introd.*,
XI *b* 59, &c.   [OE. *hĕring.*]
Herkne, Herken, *v.* to listen, II
443, 525 ; *imper. sg.* II 557,
XV *c* 36; *pl.* II 23; **Harke,**

imper. sg. XVI 137 ; **Harkens,**
pl. XVI 37.   [OE. *hercnian; cf.*
O.Fr. *herkia.*]
Herrowe. *See* Harrowe.
Hert(e), *n.* heart, II 338, IV *a* 8,
VI 4, VIII *a* 208, &c. ; *distrib.*
sg. for *pl.* (usual ME. idiom in
similar contexts, *cf.* Kne, &c.),
IV *a* 16, *b* 41 ; *hertes lif,* life,
XII *a* 4.   [OE. *heorte.*]
Hertely, Hartely, *adj.* heartfelt,
XVI 245 ; *adv.* in heart, XVII
388.   [Prec. + OE. *-lic(e).*]
Heruest, *n.* autumn, harvest, VII
101, VIII *a* 68, 285, 294, *b* 7.
[OE. *hærfest.*]
Heruest-tyme, *n.* harvest-time,
VIII *a* 108. [OE. *hærfest-tīma.*]
Hespyne, *n.* boat, X 127.   [ON.
esping-r, a ship's boat.]
Heste, *n.*[1] command(ment), XI *b*
106; **Hestis,** *pl.* XI *b* 70, 187,
191, &c. [Extended from OE.
hǣs ; *cf.* Beheste, Biqueste.]
Heste, *n.*[2] violence, VII 142. [OE.
hǣst (allit.).   This form has
hitherto escaped record(!); prob.
distinct from Hast(e), *q.v.*]
Het(e), Hette, &c.   *See* Hote, *v.*
Hete, *n.* heat, I 163, VI 194, VII
138, IX 13 ; **Heite,** VII 101.
[OE. *hǣtu.*]
Heterly, *adv.* bitterly, violently,
suddenly, V 223, 243, 249, VI
42.   [Blend of OE. *hete-līce,*
and ON. *hatr-liga.*]
Hethen, *adv.* hence, IV *a* 17.
[ON. *hēðan.*]
Hep(e), *n.* heath, II 237, 243.
[OE. *hǣþ.*]
Hepenisse, *n.* pagan lands, II
513. [OE. *hǣþen-nes.*]
Heu. *See* Hew(e).
Heue, *v.* to raise, exalt, V 220,
VI 113 (2 *sg.*).   [OE. *hebban,*
hef-.]
Heued, *n.* head, VI 99, 105, XV *g*
13 ; ? leader, XIV *d* 8; **Hade,** II
391 ; **Hed(e),** V 75, 249, VIII *a*
322, XI *b* 136, &c.; *on hed,* on
his head, II 149.   [OE. *hĕafod,*
hĕafd-.]
Heuen(e), Heuyn, *n.* sky, heaven,

Heaven, IV *a* 9, *b* 10, V 11, VII 137, 153, XIII *b* 52, &c.; **Heuenez**, *pl.* the heavens, VI 63, 81; *Crystes (þe Lordes,&c.) loue of heuene*, love of Christ (&c.) in heaven, VIII *a* 19, 214, XIV *d* 10. [OE. *heofon.*]

Heuenly, *adj.* heavenly, XI *b* 291. [OE. *heofon-lic.*]

Heuenryche, Heuenryke, *n.* Heaven, IV *a* 15; *vnder heuenryche*, on earth, V 355. [OE. *heofon-rice.*] *See* Ryche.

Heuy, *adj.* heavy, XV *h* 13; *heuy in*, laden with, IV *b* 29. [OE. *hefig.*]

Heuynes, Hevynesse, *n.* heaviness, IV *b* 35; sorrow, XII *a* 10. [OE *hefig-nes.*]

Hew(e), Heu (XV), *n.* hue, complexion, beauty, I 165, 237, IV *a* 69, XV *c* 13; shade (of colour), XII *a* 55. [OE. *hēow.*]

Hi, *pron.* 3 *sg. fem.* she, III 32, 33, 55, 60 (it, ref. to *fem. noun.*), &c.; Hy(e), II 81, 337, III 45; He, II 408, 446, XV *c* 7, 15, 17; Ho, VI 68, 77, 83, 84, 94, 96. Hare, *acc.* and *dat.* III 55; Her(e), I 53, II 92; Hir(e) (the most usual form), II 73, VI 68, X 30, XII *a* 27, 44, 107, 145, XV *c* 17 (*refl.*), &c.; Hyr, VI 67, 70; Hure, VIII *b* 53. *Poss. adj.* (orig. *gen.*) Hare, III 33, 35, 45; Her(e), I 210, 243, II 565; Hir(e) (the most usual form), II 56, IV *b* 6, &c.; Hyr(e), IV *b* 4, VI 69, XV *c* 4, &c. Hereself, Hirself, *refl. acc.* herself, XI *b* 57, XII *a* 32, 184. [OE. *hēo* (*hēō*), also *hē*, *hie*, *hī*, nom. and acc.; *heore*, *hire*, &c., gen. and dat. On vowel of *hare* see next.]

Hi, *pron.* 3 *pl.* they, III 58; Hy(e), II 91, XIII *a* 17, *b* 9, II; Hii, VIII *a* 15; also He, II 185, III 57 (second); A, XIII *a* 13, &c. (*see* A). *Acc.* and *dat.* Ham (to, for) them, III *introd.*, XIII *a* 23, *b* 39; Hem (the most usual form), I 39, II 88, &c.; Hom,

V 353, VII 24, 35, &c.; *refl.* (to, for) themselves, I 200, II 69, VI 191, VII 33, VIII *a* 69, 181, 182, XI *b* 40, XV *h* 10, &c.; pleonastic (*dat.*), XI *a* 61; *cf.* He. Hamsylf (XIII); Hemself, -selue, *nom.* themselves, XI *b* 190; *acc.* and *dat.*, XI *b* 198; (*refl.*) VIII *a* 144, XI *b* 93, 109, XIII *b* 24, XVI 307; *of hemself*, by themselves, XI *b* 73. *Poss. adj.* (orig. *gen.*) Hare, their, III *introd.*; Heore, XIV *c* 7, 45, &c.; Her(e) (the most usual form), I 39, II 16, &c.; Hire, IX 165, 185, &c.; Hor, V 345, VII 8, 181, &c.; Huere, XV *b* 8, 11, 29; Hure, VIII *b* 50; (pronom.) here, theirs, XI *b* 129; *here names of alle*, the names of all of them, I 37; *at here aboue*, *see* Aboue(n). [OE. *hī*, *hie* (*hē*, *hēō*), &c., nom., acc.; *heora*, *hira*, &c. gen.; *heom*, *him*, dat. The vowel of *a*, *hare*, *ham*, is prob. due to infl. of OE. *þā*, *þāra*, *þām*.] *See* þai, His(e).

Hy, Hyʒ (V), Hie, *v.* to hasten; *intr.* XI *b* 274, XII *b* 104, XVII 371; *refl.* V 53, XVII 289, 312 (1 *pl. imper.*). [OE. *hīgian.*]

Hy(e), *n.* haste, in *in hy(e)*, in haste, swiftly, X 46, 82, XVI 367, &c.; *in (full) gret hy*, X 80, 90, &c. *Cf.* Heiʒing. [From *prec.*]

Hy(e). *See* Heie, Heigh(e); Hi, *pron. fem.* and *pl.*

Hyar. *See* Heiʒ(e).

Hide, *v.* to hide, keep secret, XI *b* 57; *refl.* XIV *b* 22; Hidde, *pa. t.* II 268, XVI 249 (*intr.*); Hidd, *pp.* XII *b* 187. [OE. *hȳdan.*]

Hyde, *n.* skin, V 244; hide, XV *h* 11. [OE. *hȳd.*]

Hydel. *See* Ydel.

Hider, *adv.* hither, II 422, V 23, XIV *c* 47, &c.; Heder, XVII 290; Hedir, to me, XVII 291. [OE. *hider.*]

Hiderward, *adv.* hither, VIII *a* 317. [OE. *hiderweard.*]

Hidous, Hidus, *adj.* awful, XVII

101, 417; Hydously, *adv*. terribly, XVI 138. [OFr. *hidous*.]

Hiere, Hyerof, *see* Her(e), *adv*.; Hyf, *see* ȝef; Hyȝ(e), *see* Heie, Heigh(e); Hy, *v*.

Hight, Hyȝt (VI), Heght (XVII), *n*. height, XVII 260; *of h*., in height, XVII 125; *on h*., on high, above, up, VI 141, XVI 88, 235, XVII 136. [OE. *hēhþu*.] *See* Heigh(e).

Hiȝt(e) (Hyght, Hihte, &c.); Hihe. *See* Hote, *v*.; Heigh(e).

Hii, *see* Hi, *pl*.; Hiis, *see* He, *masc*.

Hyle, *v*. to protect, I 184. [ON. *hylja*.]

Hil, Hill(e), Hyll(e), *n*. hill, II 354, V 13, 131, XVII 337, 442, 466, &c.; Hell, XII *a* 65, 79, 86; Hul (Hulles, *pl*.), XIII *a* 18, 45; *by hylle ne be vale*, nowhere, under no circumstances, V 203. [OE. *hyll* (Kt. *hell*).]

Him, Hym(e). *See* He, *masc*.; Hit. Himself; Hymself, -selue, -sylf, &c. *See* He, *masc*.

Hyndrid, *pp*. hindered, XI *b* 232. [OE. *hindrian*.]

Hyne, *n*. servant, VIII *a* 125; *pl*. labourers, VI 145. [OE. *hīga*, gen. pl. *hīgna*.]

Hypped, *pa. t*. hopped, V 164. [OE. **hyppan*; cf. *hoppian*.] *See* Hoppit.

Hir(e), Hyr(e). *See* Hi, *prons*.

Hyre, Hire, Huyre (VIII), *n*. hire, pay, reward, VI 163, 223, VIII *a* 133, 189, 192, &c.; (in bad sense) XIV *b* 66, XVI 167, 260. [OE. *hȳr*.]

Hyre, *v*. to hire, VI 147; Huyred, *pp*. VIII *a* 108, 307. [OE. *hȳr(i)an*.]

Hirself. *See* Hi, *pron. fem*.

Hys, His(e). *See* He, *masc*.; Hit; Is.

His(e), *pron. acc. sg. fem*. her, III 32, 53; *acc. pl*. them, III 7, 8, 28 (*see* note). [See *N.E.D.*, s.v. *His*.]

Hysse. *See* He, *masc*.

Hystoriale, *adj*. historical, VII

title and *introd*. [OFr. *historial*.]

Hit, *pron*. 3 *sg. neut*. (*nom*. and *acc*.) it, III 27, IV *a* 52, &c.; Hyt, I 19, XIII *a* 12, &c.; It, II 132, &c.; pleonastic, XII *a* 56; as anticipated subject, *it is* (*ere*), there is (are), I *introd*., II 552; *it* (with pl. verb, ref. to prec. or following plural), they, VIII *a* 56, *b* 62, IX 139, XIII *a* 11; them, VIII *a* 43, 44. *Dat*. Him, (to) it, IX 124, 127; It, IV *a* 16, II 20 (*indef*. or *pl*.). *Poss. adj*. His, Hys, IX 130, 132, XIII *a* 61, XIV *c* 59; Hytself, *refl*. itself, VI 86. [OE. *hit, him, his*.]

Hitte, *v*. to strike, to hit (a mark), V 228; Hit, Hyt, *pa. t*. V 85, X 103, 127; Hitte, *pp*. V 219. [OE. (late) *hittan* from ON. *hitta*.]

Ho, Hoo, *interj*. ho !, esp. used to call a pause, V 262 (or *imper*. of next), XIV *d* 13, XVII 229. [Cf. OFr. *ho* !]

Ho, *v*. to pause, XVII 411. [From prec.]

Ho, *pron*. she; *see* Hi, *fem*.

Hobbe: familiar form of Robert (used contemptuously), XI *b* 176; *Hobbe þe Robbere*, XIV *d* 6 (*see* note).

Hode, *n*. hood, II 229, V 229, VIII *a* 264. [OE. *hōd*.]

Hogges, *n. pl*. hogs, VIII *a* 174. [OE. *hogg*.]

Hoylle. *See* Hol(e), *adj*.

Hoyne (= hōne), *v*. to delay, XVII 319. [? Related to Ho, *v*.]

Hol(e), *adj*. whole, sound, entire, (a)mended, V 322, VI 46, VIII *a* 61, IX 80; Hoylle, XVII 388; Holle, V 228. [OE. *hāl*.] *See* Hele, *v*.

Hold(e), *n*. stronghold, XII *a* 98; captivity, XVI 151. [OE. (*ge-*) *hǎld*.]

Holde, *adv*. loyally, V 61. [OE. *hólde*.]

Holde(n), Hold, Hald(e), *v*. *trans*. to hold, keep, guard;

possess, have ; regard as, think ; II 295 (inf. dep. on *se* 289), 495, IV *a* 52, 95, V 145, 280, 322, VI 94, 130, X 31, XI *b* 186, XIV *b* 37, &c ; *refl.* keep (oneself), remain, VIII *a* 194, IX 279, XIV *d* 15, XV *h* 10 (*holdyn*, pres. pl.) ; think oneself, IV *b* 12, V 273, XVI 325 ; *intr.* keep, remain, II 95, X 57. Held(e), *pa. t.* II 94, VII 21, &c. ; *2 sg. subj.* if you kept, V 61 ; Holdyn, *pa. t. pl.* VII 50 ; Halden, *pp.* V 29, 209 ; Holde(n), VII 38, XI *b* 45, XII *introd.*, &c. ; Yhold, II 31. *Held in hond*, ruled, II 488 ; *holde vp her hertis*, keep up their spirits, (*or* sustain them), VIII *a* 208 ; *holde with*, have to do with, VIII *a* 54 ; *holde it for*, treasure it as, VIII *a* 206 ; *hold none slyke*, reckon none like (her), XVII 233 ; *holde (to\)*, beholden (to), XII *introd.*; *holden*, bound, under obligation, VIII *a* 88, XI *b* 298, 300. [OE. *háldan*.] *See* Bihold.

Hole, *n.* hole, V 112, IX 222, XIV *b* 22, &c. [OE. *hol*.]

Hol3. *See* Holwe.

Holi, Holy, *adj.* holy, I 12, XI *b* 299, &c. ; **Hooly**, XI *a* 10, 11 ; **Haly**, IV *a* 84, *b* 50, 53, 75 ; **Holyere**, *compar.* XI *b* 28. [OE. *hálig*.] *See* Hal3e3, Halwid.

Holy. *See* Holliche.

Holicherche, *n.* Holy Church (personified), VIII *a* 239 ; **Holikirke**, VIII *a* 28. *See* Holi, Cherche, Kirke.

Holynesse, *n.* sanctity, XI *b* 100. [OE. *hálig-nes.*]

Holle. *See* Hol(e).

Holliche, Holly, Holy (VI), *adv.* wholly, altogether, VI 58, XIV *c* 12, 97. [From Hol(e).]

Holpyn. *See* Helpen.

Holtes, *n. pl.* woods, II 214. [OE. *holt.*]

Holwe, Hol3, *adj.* hollow, II 268, V 114. [OE. *holh*, n.]

Holwenes, *n.* cavity, XIII *a* 15. [From prec.]

Hom. *See* Hi, *pron. pl.*

Hom(e), *n.* home, XII *b* 181 ; *long home*, eternal home (after death), I 207. [OE. *hám* ; cf. *langne hám gesēcean*, Fates of Apost., 92.]

Hom(e), Hame (XVII), *adv.* home (-wards), II 162, III 54, V 53, VIII *a* 194, IX 285, 314, XVII 143, &c. ; back, VIII *a* 92. [OE. *hám.*]

Homely, *adv.* familiarly, XVI 64. [OE. **hám-líce.*]

Homered, *pa. t.* (hammered), struck, V 243. [From OE. *hamor, homor*, n.] *See* Hamerys.

Homward, *adv.* homewards, XII *b* 104, 154, XVII 182. [OE. *hámweard.*]

Hond(e), Hand(e), *n.* hand, I 101, II 470, IV *a* 27, V 37, XIV *c* 45 (*pl.* or *distrib. sg.* ; *see* Hert), &c. ; **Hend(e)**, *pl.* IV *a* 65, 80, XVI **75, 400, XVII 34, 255 ; **Honden**, *pl.* II 79. *Held in hond*, ruled, II 488 ; *at our h.*, at hand, VII 13 ; *hand yn h.*, I 151, 223 ; *on hond*, on the wrist, II 307 ; *out of honde*, straight away, V 217 ; *tak vpon hand* (without *to*), undertake to, X 130. [OE. *hónd, hánd* ; pl. *hánda* ; ON. pl. *hend-r*.]

Hondqwile, *n.* moment, VII 117. [OE. *hónd-hwīl*.]

Hondred, Hundred, *adj.* and *n.* (orig. foll. by *gen. pl.*), II 143, 291, III 12, 15, XIII *b* 31, XV *g* 30 (*see* note), &c. ; (as ordinal) hundredth, IX 301. [OE. *hundred*.] *See* Hund(e)reth ; Part.

Hondreduald, *adj.* hundredfold, III 50. [From prec. ; cf. OE. *hund(tēontig)fáld*.]

Hongeþ. *See* Hange.

Hony, *n.* honey, IV *b* 19, 20, 26. [OE. *hunig*.]

Honnoure, Honour(e), *n.* honour, II 36, VI 64, XVI 132, 133, &c. [OFr. *honour*.]

Honoure, *v.* to honour, adorn, VIII *a* 12 ; *pp.* as *adj.* V 344. [OFr. *honourer*.]

Honourable, *adj.* worthy (of

honour), IX 311. [OFr. *hon-ourable.*]

Hoo, *see* Ho, *interj.*; Hooly, *see* Holi.

Hoot, Hot(e), Hate (IV, VI), *adj.* hot, burning, II 58, VI 28, VIII *b* 7, IX 7, 11, XIII *a* 1, XV *h* 10, &c.; grievous, bitter, IV *a* 31; Hatter, *compar.* IV *a* 13. [OE. *hāt*; *hāttra,* compar.]

Hope, *v.* to hope, expect, imagine, V 233, VIII *introd., a* 88, XIV *c* 91, XVI 43, &c.; *hoped of,* hoped for, V 240. [OE. *hopian.*]

Hoper, *n.* sower's seed-basket, VIII *a* 63. [See *N.E.D.,* s.v. *Hopper.*]

Hoppit, *pa. t.* leapt, VII 142; Hoppyng, *pres. p.* dancing, I 233; *verbal n.* I 226. [OE. *hoppian.*] *See* Hypped.

Hor. *See* Hi, *pron. pl.*

Hore, *adj.* hoar, grey, II 214, VIII *a* 77. [OE. *hār.*]

Hors, *n.* horse, V 85, &c.; *pl.* XIII *a* 34 (beside *horses,* XIV *b* 73); *on hors,* on horseback, II 304, 395; *gen.* in *hors bred* (*see* Bred). [OE. *hors.*]

Hose, *n. pl.* hose, long stockings, XVII 225. [OE. *hosa, hose.*]

Hospitalité, *n.* hospitality, XI *b* 254. [OFr. *hospitalité.*]

Host. *See* Ost.

Hote, *v.* to bid; promise, assure, VIII *a* 256, 258; Hete, V 53, VI 42, XIV *a* 26. *Pa. t.* (*act.*) Het, bade, III 7, 20; Hyȝt(e), Hiȝte, promised, V 150, 273, VIII *a* 125, 230. *Passive* (*pres.* and *pa. t.*), is (was) called, Hatte, III *introd.,* VIII *a* 45, XIII *a* 63; Heiste (= heihte; *see* Appendix § 6, end), XV *g* 18; Hette, XV *g* 19; Hyȝt(e), Hyght, Hiȝte, Hight, I 27, 40, 45, VIII *a* 72, XVI 231, &c.; Hihte, XII *a* 85, *b* 20, &c. [Het], *pp.* promised, XVII 301; Hight(e), XVI 351, 396, XVII 46; Yhote, called, II 601; commanded, III 29. [OE. *hātan*; *hēt, heht,* pa. t.; *hātte,*

pass. *Hette, hiȝte,* &c., are due to blending in form and function of the *pa. t.* forms with *pass.* (taken as *wk. pa. t.*). *Hete,* pres., is prob. back-formation from *hette.*]

Hote. *See* Hoot.

Hou, *adv. interrog.* (*dir.* and *indir.*), how, in what way, that, II 132, 507, III 1, XI *a* 62, 233, &c.; Houȝ, XI *b* 281, XIII *a* 13, *b* 1, 42; How(e), XVI 3, &c.; *hou euere,* however, XI *b* 255; *how þat,* how (*indir.*), IX 220, XII *a* 43, &c.; *hou,* how (it happened), II 115. [OE. *hū.*] *See* Wou.

Houed; Houndes. *See* Hufe; Hund.

Houped, *pa. t. sg.* shouted, VIII *a* 165. [OFr. *houper.*]

Houreȝ. *See* Oure, *n.*

Hous(e), *n.* house, II 432, III 54 (*dat.*), XII *a* 47, XVI 136, &c.; *houses of offyce,* XVII 134; *see* Office. [OE. *hūs.*]

Housebonde, *n.* husband, XII *a* 133; Husband, XVI 45, XVII 208, &c. [OE. *hūsbunda,* from ON. *húsbóndi.*]

How(e), *interj.* ho!, VIII *a* 110, XVI 213. *Cf.* Ho.

Huanne; Huere; Huerof. *See* Whan(ne); Hi, *pron. pl.*; Wher(e).

Hufe, *v.* to tarry, XVII 461; Houed, *pa. t.* halted, V 100. [ME. *hōve(n)*; obscure.]

Huge, *adj.* great, V 13, 352, IX 233, XIII *a* 10. [Cf. OFr. *ahuge.*]

Huyre(d); Hul(les); Hulpen. *See* Hyre; Hil; Helpen.

Hund, Hound, *n.* dog, II 286, XIV *b* 21, 76; *houndes bred, see* Bred(e). [OE. *húnd.*]

Hund(e)reth, *adj.* and *n.* hundred, V 226, X 147, XVI 39, XVII 57, &c. [ON. *hundrað.*] *See* Hondred.

Hungre, Hunger, *n.* hunger, VIII *a* 233, XVII 155, &c.; Famine (personified), VIII *a* 165,

&c. [OE. *hungor*.] *See* A-
hungrye.

Hunt(e) (*to*), *v.* to hunt (after),
II 284, VIII *a* 30; Huntinge,
n. XII *b* 5. [OE. *huntian*; *hun-
tung.*]

Hure. *See* Hi, *pron. fem.* and *pl.*

Hurt, *v. trans.* to hurt, V 223;
pp. and *pa. t.* V 243, X 56.
[OFr. *hurter.*]

Hus. *See* He, *masc.*; We.

Hw-. *See* Wh-.

I. *See* Ich; In, *prep.*

Iacke, Iak. Jack, XI *b* 176; *Iak
nor Gill*, nobody, XVII 336.
[ME. *Iakke*, &c., pet-name
assoc. with 'John'.]

Iaies, *n. pl.* jays, XI *b* 249. [OFr.
jai.]

Iangle, *v.* to quarrel, VIII *a* 309.
[OFr. *jangler.*]

Iape, *n.* trick, delusion, XI *b* 137,
XII *a* 129, *b* 66. [Not known.]

Iboust. *See* Bigge, *v.*

Io; Icast. *See* Ich, *pron.*; Cast.

Ioh, *adj.*¹ (after *þis* or *þat*), same,
very, II 63, 455, 540; Yche,
I 208, 216. [OE. *ilca.*] *See*
Ilk(e), *adj.*¹

Ich, Yche, *adj.*² each, every, II
179, 254, 364 (*see* Manere),
VII 19, XVII 151 (*see* Kinde),
170, &c.; Vch, V 13, VI 243,
XV *b* 6; *ich a*, every, II 187,
276 (*not* 307); each, XVII 273;
vch a, VI 15, 76, 101, XIV *c* 20,
99; *ich a deyll*, *ylk a dele*, see
Dele, *n.*; *in ich ways*, see Way,
Wise; Ich, *pron.* each (one),
II 184, 292, 295, 307. [OE.
ylc.] *See* Eche; Euerich;
Ichon; Ilke, *adj.*²; Þe.

Ich, *pron.* I *sg.* I, II 113, III 2,
VIII *b* 1, XV *c* 5, *d* 4, *f* 6, &c.; Io,
XV *g* 26, 31; Icche, XV *a* 2, 11; I,
Y, *passim*; coalescing with foll.
word in Ichabbe, Icham, Ichaue,
Ichil, Ichim, Ichot, Ichulle, *q.v.*
Me, *acc.* and *dat.* (to, for) me, V
138, 145, VI 205, XV *a* 20, *c* 10, 31
(*see* Reue), and *passim*; Mee,
XVI 274; *ethic dat.* (I beg), V

76; in impers. constr. (where
Mn.E. has 'I'), II 177, IV *a* 10,
XV *b* 34; *me is wo*, woe is me,
II 331; *refl. acc.* myself, IX 279,
XVI 325, XVII 238, &c.; *dat.*
(pleonastic with verb of motion)
XV *a* 4. Mi, *poss. adj.* II 120,
124, &c.; My, *passim*; Min,
Myn(e), I 126, II 205, VIII *a*
31, XV *g* 11, &c.; as *sb.* (my
property, people, &c.), VI 206,
VIII *a* 142, XVI 217, 312, XVII
226 (*see* Þat, *pron.*). Miself(f)e,
Myselue(n), *nom.* myself, II
566, V 293, VIII *a* 80, IX 292,
&c.; I myself, VIII *a* 252, XVI 67,
212; *acc.* and *dat.* (me) myself
(not *refl.*), VIII *a* 28, 131. [OE.
ic, mē, mīn, mē selfan, &c.] *See*
Self.

Ichabbe, I *sg. pres. ind.* I have,
XV *c* 9; Yohabbe, XV *c* 32;
Iohaue, II 209, 516. [OE. *ic
hæbbe* (*hafo*, but not WS.).] *See*
Habbe.

Icham, I *sg. pres. ind.* I am, II
127, 382, 513, XV *c* 8, 29, *d* 1;
Ycham, XV *b* 23. [OE. *ic
am.*]

Ichil, I *sg. pres. ind.* I will,
intend to, II 132, 212, 341, 451;
(with ellipse of verb of motion)
I will go, II 129, 316; Iohulle,
XV *c* 19; *ichil þatow be*, may
you be, II 471. [OE. *ic wile*,
wylle.] *See* Wille, *v.*

Ichim = Ich him (*acc.*), II 428.

Ichon, Vohon (VI, VIII), *pron.*
each one, every one, II 161, VI
90, VIII *a* 202, &c.; in apposition with pl. noun, XVII 279.
[OE. *ylc + ān.*] *See* Ich, *adj.*²;
Echone, Euerichon, Ilkane.

Iohot, I *sg. pres. ind.* I know,
XV *b* 23, *c* 10. [OE. *ic wāt.*]
See Wite(n).

Iohulle. *See* Ichil.

Ionowe, *v.* to know, XV *g* 32.
[OE. *ge-cnāwan.*] *See* Knowe(n).

Ientilman. *See* Gentil.

Ieu, Iewe, *n.* Jew, IX 163, XI *b*
201, XV *g* 18, XVI 147, &c.
[OFr. *giu*, older *ju(ʃ)eu.*]

If(f), Yf, Iif. *See* 3ef.

Ile, *n.* island, IX 40 ; Yle, IX 134, 261 (note), 310. [OFr. *ile.*]

Ileid, Ileyd. *See* Lay.

Ilyche (MS. inlyche), *adv.* equally, alike, VI 186, 242. [OE. *ge-līce.*] *See* Lyke.

Ilyke, *adj.* equal, the same, IV *a* 14. [OE. *ge-līc.*] *See* Lyke.

Ilkane, Ilkone, *pron.* each one, every one, X 160 (note), XIV *b* 74. [OE. *ylc + ān.*] *See* Ilk, *adj.*[2]; Ichon ; Echone.

Ilk(e), *adj.*[1] (only after *þe, þis, þat*) very, same, III 45, V 65, VIII *a* 155 (*see* While), XII *a* 190, *b* 29, &c.; *þe ilke selue,* (namely) that same man, III 27. [OE. *ilca.*] See Ich, *adj.*[1]; Thilke; *þe.*

Ilk(e), Ylk (IV), *adj.*[2] each, every, X 35, XVI 273; *ilk(e) a,* every, IV *a* 27 (*see* Dele, *n.*), X 133, XVI 130, 253. [OE. *ylc.*] *See* Ich, *adj.*[2]; Eche.

Ill, Yll, *adj.* bad, IV *b* 35; grievous, IV *a* 31 ; evil, wicked, IV *b* 84, XVII 208 ; as *sb.* (*pl.*), the wicked, XVI 34; Ill(e), *adv.* ill, XV *b* 24 (*see* Like); badly, evilly, cruelly, unluckily, VIII *a* 198, XIV *a* 31, XVI 139, XVII 203, 220, 246, &c. [ON. *ill-r* ; *illa,* adv.]

Illusiouns, *n. pl.* deceptions, IX 85. [OFr. *illusion.*]

Imete, *v.* to meet, XV *g* 6 ; *imette wid,* he met, XV *g* 7. [OE. *ge-mētan.*] *See* Mete(n).

Impe. *See* Ympe.

In, Yn, *adv.* in (of motion), I 80, II 347, XIII *a* 9, XV *g* 24, XVI 270, &c.; Inne, V 128. [OE. *inn.*] *See* Into, Intill; Inne ; Þare.

In, *n.* lodging, II 565 ; *pl.* in *takes he his ines,* takes up his quarters, XIV *b* 27. [OE. *inn,* n.]

In, Yn, I (XV *a, g*), *prep.* (i) In, I 3, II 13, XIII *a* 3, XV *a* 9, *g* 5, 13, &c.; into, II 349, XII *a* 125, &c.; according to, as regards, with respect to, &c., VI 239, IX 141, XI *b* 26, 204, &c.; *in all his myghte,* with &c., IV *b* 77.

(ii) On, IV *b* 41, V 157, 279 (of time), IX 122, 286, XIII *a* 45, &c. *In cas, in feere (fere), see* Cas, Yfere (Fere). [OE. *in.*] *See* In, Inne, *advs.*

Incontynence, *n.* unchastity, IX 130. [OFr. *incontinence.*]

Indede, *adv.* indeed, XI *b* 108, &c. [OE. *in + dǣde,* dat. sg.]

Induyr. *See* Enduir.

Informacioun, *n.* information, IX 291. [OFr. *informacion.*]

Infortune, *n.* evil fortune, XII *a* 162. [OFr. *infortune.*]

Inglis. *See* Engli3sch.

Inne, Ynne, *adv.* in (inside), IX 188, XIII *a* 21; after rel. in *þat . . in(ne),* in which, I 190, VIII *a* 298, XV *i* 10; Ine, *prep.* in, III *introd.* 16, 33, 35, 49, 50 ; on (of time) III *introd.* [OE. *innan,* prep., adv.; *inne,* adv.] *See* In, *adv., prep.*; Þare; Þer(e).

Innoghe, Inogh(e). *See* Yno3.

Inpossible, *adj.*; *inpossible . . . to be,* impossible, IX 152. [OFr. *impossible.*]

Inspiracioun, *n.* inspiration, IX 331. [OFr. *inspiracion.*]

Instrumentis, *n. pl.* appliances, X 8. [OFr. *instrument.*]

Insuffisance, *n.* inability, IX 313. [OFr. *insuffisance.*] *See* Suffise.

Intil(l), Intyl(l), *prep.* into, IV *a* 3, 9, 16, 21, *b* 30, &c.; in, X 118, 122. [OE. *inn + ON. til.*] *See* In, *adv.*; Til, *prep.*

Into, Yntɑ, *prep.* into, I 146, II 163, &c.; onto, in *putten hem into,* embark on, IX 183; up to, until (*cf.* To), XII *a* 190, 221; (un)to, XIV *c* 25. [OE. *inn tō, intō.*] *See* In, *adv.*

Inward, *adv.* inside, XII *a* 72. [OE. *in(nan)-weard.*]

Inwardly, *adv.* heartily, earnestly, XVI 361. [OE. *in weard-līce.*]

Inwyt, Inwytte, *n.* conscience, III *title* and *introd.* [OE. *in + witt*; cf. *in gewitnes,* conscience.]

Inwith, *adv.* within, V 114. [OE. *in + wiþ.*]

Iohan, Iohon. John, XIV *d* 2, 3, 6, 9, 16. [L. *Iōhannēs*; cf. OFr. *Jehan*.] *See* Iacke.

Ioie, Ioy(e), *n.* joy, II 6, 45, IV *b* 54, XII *a* 175, &c.; *makes ioie*, rejoice, XVI 383. [OFr. *joie*.]

Iolif, *adj.* gay, joyous, II 305. [OFr. *jolif*.]

Iolité, *n.* riotous mirth, levity, XI *b* 116, 129, 182. [OFr. *joli(ve)té*.]

Ioparde, *n.* hazard; *lys no ioparde of*, there is no question of, VI 242. [OFr. *ju (jeu) parti*, even game, doubtful chance.]

Iourneyes, *n. pl.* day's journeys, IX 259 [OFr. *journée*.]

Ipotayne, *n.* hippopotamus, IX 240. [*Ipotaine*, mistake (*in* for *m*) for OFr. *ypotame*, convenient corruption of L. *hippopotamus*.]

Ire. *See* Yre, *n.*³

Irnebandis, *n. pl.* iron bands, X 24. [OE. *īren* + ON. *band*; cf. OE. *īren-bend*.]. *See* Bond; Yre, *n.*¹

Is, Ys, His (XI), 3 *sg. pres. ind.* is, I 9, 19, VIII *b* 105, XI *b* 256, &c.; exists, IX 146; (without *pron.*) it is, I 253, 254, V 121, &c.; 2 *sg.* art, XVI 360; *pl.* are, VIII *b* 48, X 124, XVII 10, &c.; rime requires Es (*q.v.*) at I 128 (note), XVII 10. [OE. *is*.] *See* Es, Nis.

Is, *gen. sg.* *See* He.

Iseʒe, -seye, -seiʒe. *See* Se(n).

Isold. *See* Selle(n).

Issue, *n.* way out, IX 198, 235. [OFr. *issue*.]

Ist, is it, XVII 517. *See* Is.

It; Itake. *See* Hit; Take(n).

Iueler, *n.* jeweller, XII *b* 150. [OFr. *juel(i)er*.]

Iuelis, *n. pl.* jewels, XI *b* 283. [OFr. *juel*.]

Iuge, *v.* to judge, XVI 320. [OFr. *jugier*.]

Iuggement, *n.* judgement, XII *b* 207. [OFr. *jugement*.]

Iuntly, *adv* close, X 97. [From OFr. *joint, juint*, pp.]

Iustice, *n.* justice, VIII *a* 324. [OFr. *justice*.]

Iwis, Iwysse, *adv.* certainly, indeed (often, *esp.* in rime, practically meaningless), V 121, 172, VI 34, XIV *b* 17, XVII 550. [OE. *ge-wiss*, adj.; cf. *mid (te) gewisse*.]

K-. *See* also C.

Kache, *v.* to chase, catch; *kacheʒ his caple*, urges on his horse, V 107; **Kaʒt** (*to*), *pa. t.* took hold (of), V 308; **Cawht.** *pp.* caught, XII *a* 161. [ONFr. *cachier*, conjugated on anal. of ME. *la(c)chen*.]

Kaies, Kayes, *n. pl.* keys, XIV *a* 36, *b* 88, 89. [OE. *cǣg*.]

Kalf, *n.* calf, VIII *a* 282. [OE. *calf*.]

Kanel, *n.* (wind-pipe), neck, V 230. [ONFr. *canel*.] *See* Chanel.

Karol(l)e, *v.* to perform a 'carol' (*see* next), I 54, 83, &c.; **Karol-lyng,** *n.* I 55. [OFr. *carol(l)er*.]

Karolle, *n.* a carol, a dance accompanied with song (often used with ref. to song only), I 1, 14, &c. [OFr. *carolle*.]

Kauelacion, *n.* cavilling, quibbling objection, V 207. [OFr. *cavillacion*.]

Keyng(es). *See* Kyng.

Kele, Keill, Keyle, *v.* to cool, IV *a* 26 (*intr.*); *to kele (keill) cares*, to assuage sorrows, XVI 84, XVII 300; with person as dir. obj., *from cares the to keyle*, to preserve thee from grief, XVII 118. [OE. *cēlan*.]

Ken, Kenne, *v.* to make known, VII 25 (*see* note); to teach, VIII *a* 14, 22, 24, XIV *b* 4 (*see* Crede), XVI 50, &c.; to know, in *daw to ken*, to be known for a fool, XVII 248; *will ʒe it ken*, if you will recognize the fact, XIV *b* 8; understand, I *introd.*; *pp.* (well) known, XIV *b* 9. [OE. *cennan*, prob. infl. by senses of ON. *kenna*.] Cf. Knowe(n).

Ken. *See* Cou, Kyn.

Kene, *adj.* keen, bold, eager, XIV *a* 2, *b* 9, 76; bitter (enemy), V 338. [OE. *cēne.*]

Kepe, *n.* heed; in *tok no kepe of,* XII *a* 159. [From next.]

Kepe, *v.* to guard, preserve, keep, tend, II 208, V 80, 230, VIII *a* 85, 134, 153, IX 206, XI *b* 146, XVII 235 (*see* Charité), &c.; *kepe seyntewarie,* minister in the sanctuary, VIII *b* 83; to care to, in *þe lette I ne kepe,* I have no wish to stop you, V 74; Kepynge, *n.* XI *b* 70. [OE. *cēpan.*] *See* Vnkept.

Kertel. *See* Kirtel.

Keruе(n), *v.* to cut, VIII *a* 98; prune, VI 152. [OE. *ceorfan.*]

Kest, *n.* a 'cast' (*see* Cast, *v.*); a blow, V 230; plot, treachery, V 345; used as 'treacherous thing' (*cf.* Falssyng), V 308. [ON. *kast.*]

Kest(e). *See* Cast, Kysse.

Ketten. *See* Kutten.

Keuer(e), *v.* to (re)gain, recover; *intr.* recover, survive, V 230; *keuereʒ,* 'gets', makes his way, V 153. [OE. *ā-cofrian,* intr., and OFr. (*re-*)*covrer,* 3 sg. -*keuvre,* trans.] *See* Recoueren.

Kidde, Kyd; Kyend; Kyʒn, Kyn(e). *See* Kyþe; Kinde; Cou.

Kille, Kylle, *v.* to kill, VIII *a* 32, V 43. [! OE. **cyllan*; earliest ME. sense appar. 'beat'.]

Kyn, Kynne, Ken (III), *n. sg.* kindred, relatives, III *introd.,* VIII *b* 81, XVI 232 (*see* Ende); kind, sort: Cunnes, Kyns, *gen. sg.* in *enes cunnes,* (of any kind), any sort of, XV *g* 22; *eny kyns,* VIII *b* 20; *nones cunnes,* (of no kind), no sort of, XV *g* 20; (with loss of inflexions) *na kyn,* X 59 (*see* þing); *nor … no kyn,* nor … any (sort of), XVII 138; *cf.* Alkyn, Wolues-kynnes. [OE. *cynn* (Kt. *cenn*).] *See* Eny, No(ne).

Kinde, Xynd(e), Kyend (IV), *n.* nature, natural character (of body or mind), kind, IV *a* 41, 44 (*see* note), V 312, VIII *a* 157, IX 56, XII *a* 8, 125, &c.; *in hir kinde,* in her own way, XII *b* 128; species, in *ich kynd* (without *of*), every kind of, XVII 151; Kyndis, *pl.* characteristics, IV *b* 1. [OE. (*ge-*)*cýnd.*]

Kynde, *adj.* inborn, naturally belonging to one, VIII *a* 243, *b* 58; *to his kynde name,* as his proper name, VII 70; *Kynde Witt,* natural intelligence, common sense, VIII *a* 243 (personif.). [OE. (*ge-*)*cýnde.*] *See* Vnkinde.

Kynd(e)ly, *adv.* kindly, VI 9, VII 173, &c. [From prec. in developed sense 'having natural feeling'; OE. *ge-cýnde-līce,* naturally.]

Kindel, *v.* to kindle; *trans.* to cause (sorrow), XIV *a* 10; *intr.* to begin, XIV *a* 19. *Cf.* Kele. [Rel. to ON. *kynda* (cf. *kyndill,* torch); distinct from ME. *kindlen,* beget.]

Kyndom, *n.* kingdom, VI 85. [OE. *cyne-dōm.*] *See* Kyngdome.

Kyng, King, Keyng (IV), *n.* king, I 27, II 25, IV *a* 8, 66, V 207 (note), XIV *d* 10 (note), &c.; Kynggis, *pl.* XI *b* 284. [OE. *cyning, cyng,* &c.]

Kyngdome, Kingdome, *n.* kingship, XI *b* 268, XVI 186; kingdom, II 206, &c. [OE. *cyning-dōm.*]

Kirke, Kyrk, *n.* church, Church, V 128, VIII *a* 85; *see* note to VIII *b* 63. [ON. *kirkja.*] *See* Cherche.

Kirtel(l), Kertel (III), *n.* kirtle (a short coat reaching about to the knees, worn under an outer garment), II 229, III 39, XIV *b* 61. [OE. *cyrtel,* Kt. **certel.*]

Kysse, *v.* to kiss; Kyssedes, 2 *sg. pa. t.* V 283; Keste, 3 *sg.* XII *a* 178. [OE. *cyssan* (Kt. *cessan*).] *See* Cosseʒ.

Kiþ, Kyth, *n.* country, people, V 52, XIV *c* 92. [OE. *cýþþu.*]

Kyþe, *v.* to make known, reveal;

*Kyþeȝ (MS. lyþeȝ), *imper. pl.*
show, VI 9; **Kidde**, *pp.* revealed,
XII *b* 188, XVI 251; **Kyd**,
shown, offered, V 272; acknowledged, VII 173; Kud, famed,
XIV *c* 91. [OE. *cȳþan*, pp. (*ge-*)
cȳdd.]

Knacke(n), *v.* to sing in a lively
or ornate manner (ref. esp. to
the breaking up of simple notes
into runs and trills; cf. *smale*
brekynge), XI *b* 161, 173, 177;
Knackynge, *n.* trilling, XI *b*
159, 182. [Prob. same as ME.
knacken, to crack, snap, &c.]

Knackeris, *n. pl.* trill-singers,
XI *b* 145. [From prec.]

Knape, *n.* fellow, V 68. [OE.
cnapa.]

Knappes, *n. pl.* studs, bosses,
VIII *a* 265. [OE. *cnæpp.*]

Knarreȝ, *n. pl.* ? crags, ? gnarled
boulders, v 98. [? Cf. LG.
knarre, knot.]

Knaue, Knafe (XVII), *n.* a low-
born man, servant, VIII *a* 51,
b 66, XVI 244, XVII 173;
Knauene, *gen. plur.* VIII *b* 56,
XV *h* 4. [OE. *cnafa.*]

Knaw(e). *See* Knowe.

Kne, Kneo (XIII), *n.* knee, II
507, XIII *a* 39, XVII 488 (*distrib.*
sg.; *see* Herte). [OE. *cnēo.*]

Knele, Kneole (XIII), *v.* to
kneel, II 223, 418, 472, V 4,
XIII *a* 48; Kneland(e), *pres. p.*
II 250, VI 74, XVII 488. [OE.
cnēowlian.]

Knet; Knew(e). *See* Knit;
Knowe.

**Knight(e), Knyght(e), Kniȝt,
Knyȝt(e), Kniht** (XIV), *n.*
knight, II 86, III 14, V 63, VII
87, VIII *a* 22, IX 108, XIV *c* 58,
&c.; Kniȝte, *dat. sg.* III 11,
25; Cnistes (for Cniste, *gen.*
pl.), XV *g* 30 (note). [OE.
cniht, servant; on *cnistes*, see
Appendix, p. 278.]

Knyght-fees, *n. pl.* estates of land
(held by a knight under obligation of armed service), VIII *b* 81.
[Prec. + OFr. *fé.*]

Knit, Knyt, Knet (XII), *pp.* tied,
bound, closed together, XII *b* 30,
54, XIV *c* 29, XVII 451. [OE.
cnyttan.]

Knok(ke), Knock(e), *n.* knock,
blow, V 311, XV *h* 4, XVII 342.
[From next.]

Knokkeþ, 3 *sg. pres.* knocks, II
379. [OE. *cnocian.*]

Knokled, *adj.* knobbed, rugged,
V 98. [From ME. *knok(e)le*,
knob, knuckle; cf. OFris.
knok(e)le.]

Knorned, *adj.* ? gnarled, V 98.
[Unknown.]

Knowe(n), *v.* to know, V 26, IX
75, &c.; Cnowe, VIII *a* 213;
Knaw(e), I, IV, VI, XVI, XVII;
Knewe(n), Knew, *pa. t.* II
408, IV *a* 43, IX 291, &c.;
Knowe(n), *pp.* VII 46, XI *b* 231,
XIV *c* 91; Knowun, XI *a* 2, 7,
&c.; Yknowe, XIII *a* 12, *b* 1:
to know, understand, recognize,
I 220, IV *b* 86, V 174, VI 50,
VIII *a* 51, IX 75, 114 (*subj.*),
XI *a* 40, &c.; *knowe* (*fro,*
fram), distinguish (from), VIII *a*
50, XIV *d* 12; to experience, in
vnrid to knowe, grievous to endure, XVII 41; to confess, ac-
knowledge (*cf.* Biknowe), XVI
315; *the soth for to knaw*, to
tell the truth, XVII 246; to
make known, declare, XVI 283.
[OE. (*ge-*)*cnāwan.*] *See* Icnowe,
Ken.

Knowing, *n.* knowledge, XI *a* 41,
66. [From prec.]

Knoweleche, Knowlage, *n.*
knowledge, VII 73; *for knowe-*
leche, for fear of recognition, II
482. [? Stem of ME. *knowe-*
lechen, OE. **(ge-)cnāwlǣcan*;
but the noun is recorded first.]

Koyntly. *See* Queynt.

Kokeney, *n.* (*lit.* cocks' egg),
small egg, VIII *a* 280. [ME.
cokken(e), gen. pl. (OE. *cocc*) +
ey (OE. *ǣg*); *see N.E.D.*, s.v.
Cockney.]

Kole-plantes, *n. pl.* cabbages
(and similar vegetables), VIII *a*

281. [OE. *cāl+plante.*] *See* Coyll.

Kongons, *n. pl.* changelings, misshapen creatures, XV *h* 5. [ME. *conjoun* (frequent) ; from ONFr. **ca(u`ngiŭn,* OFr. *changon* (very rare).]

Konne. *See* Can, *v.*

Kort, *n.* court, V 272 ; Court(e), I 232, II 376, &c. [OFr. *co(u)rt.*]

Kowarde, *adj.* coward(ly), V 63. [OFr. *couard.*] *See* Cowardyse.

Kowe, *n.* tail, (verse in) tail-rime; *couthe not haf coppled a k.,* could have made nothing of an intricately rimed verse, Introduction xv. [OFr. *cous.*] *See* Couwee.

Kronykeles, *n.* chronicles, I 251. [OFr. *cronicle.*]

Kud. *See* Kyþe.

Kun, Kunne(n). *See* Can, *v.*

Kutten, *v.* to cut, IX 140 ; Cut, VII 146; **Ketten,** *pa. t. pl.* VIII *a* 182. [† OE. *cyttan ; see *N.E.D.*]

Labour(e), *n.* labour, VIII *a* 27, 247, *b* 44, &c. [OFr. *labour.*]

Labor(e), Labour(e), *v.* to labour, VIII *a* 118, *b* 8, 70, &c.; *laboure with londe,* till the soil, VIII *a* 267 ; *trans.* to labour upon, cultivate, VI 144. [OFr. *labo(u)rer.*]

Laborer(e), *n.* labourer, VIII *a* 302, 313, *b* 77, XI *b* 296. [From prec.; cf. OFr. *laboreor.*]

Lac, *n.* blemish, flaw, II 460. [Cf. MLG. *lak.*] *See* Lakke.

Lacche, *v.* to catch ; to get, VIII *a* 223 ; Laghton, *pa. t. pl.* in *laghton þe watur,* put to sea, VII 119. [OE. *læccan, læhte.*]

Lace, *n.* thong, V 158 (*see* note).

Lacyd, *pp.* ensnared, caught, IV *a* 79. [OFr. *lac(i)er.*]

Ladde, *n.* low-born fellow, XVI 243. [Obscure.]

Ladde. *See* Lede(n).

Ladyschyp, *n.* queenly state, VI 218. [OE. *hlǣfdige + -scipe.*] *See* Leuedi.

Laghton. *See* Lacche.

Lay, Legge (VIII), **Lei, Ley(e),**

Leyn, *v.* to lay, set, put, I 217, IX 125, XV *f* 12, *g* 13, XVII 461 ; *lay on,* smite, XVI 143 ; *leid to wedde,* deposited in pledge, mortgaged, VIII *b* 77 ; to wager, VIII *a* 263, XVII 479 ; lay down, establish (law), XVI 329. Layde, *pa. t.* in *layde þeron,* applied to it, II 38 ; Leyde, VIII *a* 116; Ileyd, Ileid, *pp.* in *ileid . . . lowe,* laid low, XIV *c* 71, 81 ; Layd, Laide, I *introd.,* XVI 83, XVII 282, &c. ; Leyd, Leid(e), I 109, XII *b* 33, 119, &c. [OE. *lecgan, leg-; legde.*] *See* Ligge(n).

Lay, Layʒ. *See* Ligge(n).

Lay(e), *n.* lay, II 3, 13, 599, &c.; *see* note to II 12. [OFr. *lai.*]

Layf, Laiff, *n.* remainder, rest, X 132, 142. [OE. *lāf.*]

Layne, *v.* to conceal ; *layne yow (me),* keep your (my) secret, V 56, 60. [ON. *leyna.*]

Laite, *n.* lightning, VII 135, 153. [OE. *lēget(u).*]

Laited, *pa. t.* searched for, VII 170. [ON. *leita.*]

Lake, *n.* lake, IX 182, XIII *a* 63, 64. [OE. *lacu,* stream infl. by unrelated OFr. *lac,* lake.]

Lakke, *v. intr.* with *dat.* to be lacking (to) ; *yow lakked a lyttel,* you were somewhat at fault, V 298 ; *trans.* to find fault with, VIII *a* 219. [From Lac, *n.*; cf. M.Du. *laken.*]

Lammasse, *n.* Lammas (August 1st), VIII *a* 284 (note). [OE. *hlāf-mæsse, hlāmmæsse.*]

Lance, *v.* to utter, V 56. [OFr. *lanc(i)er,* cast.] *See* Launchet.

Land(e) ; Lang-. *See* Lond ; Long-.

Langage, Longage (XIII), language, VII 59, IX 185, XI *a* 12, XIII *b* 2, 4, &c. [OFr. *langage.*]

Langett, *n.* thong (for tying hose, shoes, &c.), XVII 224. [OFr. *languette.*]

Lante. *See* Lene, *v.*[1]

Lanterne, *n.* lantern, VIII *a* 170. [OFr. *lanterne.*]

Lapidarye, *n.* treatise on precious

stones, IX 75 (*see* note). [L. *lapidārium*.]

Lappe, *n.* loose end, or fold, of a garment, VIII *a* 288, XV *f* 11. [OE. *læppa*.]

Large, *adj.* generous, II 28; ample, VI 249; broad, large, V 157, IX 18, 155, 254 &c.; Largelich, *adv.* generously, II 451. [OFr. *large*.]

Larges, *n.* generosity, V 313. [OFr. *largesse*.]

Lascheth, 3 *sg. pres.* ? belabours, XV *h* 17. [See *N.E.D.*, s.v. *Lash*.]

Lasse, Les(se), *adj. compar.* less, smaller, IV *a* 92, V 158, VI 131, IX 29, 48, XIII *b* 36, &c.; *quasi-sb.*, less, VI 241, &c.; ? a smaller piece, XV *h* 17; *þe lasse in werke*, those who have worked less, VI 239, 240 (*see* Longe, *adv.*); *more and les(se)*, *les and more*, *see* More; *adv.* less, V 300, VIII *a* 161, XI *a* 58, &c.; *neuer þe lesse*, nevertheless, I 71. Leest, Leste, *superl.* least, IV *b* 85; *both the most and the leest*, all, XVII 452. [OE. *lǣssa* (*lǣs*, adv.); *lǣst*.]

Last, Lest, *conj.* lest, XI *b* 242, XV *c* 31, XVII 55. [OE. *þe lǣs-þe*.]

Last(e), *superl. adj.* last, VI 187, 211, &c.; *quasi-sb.* in *at þe*, *atte*, *ate last(e)*, at last, in the end, II 93, VIII *b* 99 (MS. latiste), XII *a* 105, *b* 188, &c.; *at þe laste ende*, in the end, VIII *b* 101. [OE. *latost*, *lætest*.] *See* Atte, Late, Furst.

Last(e), *v.* to endure, last, extend, IV *a* 1, 25, IX 199, XVI 66, XVII 265, &c.; Last (OE. *lǣst*), 3 *sg. pres.* II 335; Last, *pa. t. sg.* VII 56; *be lastand*, endure, IV *a* 58; *euer to last*, everlasting, VII 2; Lastynge, *n.* endurance, perseverance, IV *b* 73, XI *b* 122. [OE. *lǣstan*.]

Lat(e) *See* Lete.

Late, *adv.* late, I 108, VI 178, XIV *b* 91, &c.; lately, recently,

XVII 442; *erly and late*, at all times, VI 32; *nowe late*, just lately, XVI 162, 329. [OE. *late*.] *See* Laste.

Lateyn, Latyn(e), *n.* and *adj.* Latin, I 58, 96, XI *a* 18, &c. [OFr. *latin*.]

Latte. *See* Lete.

Laped, *pa. t.* invited, V 335. [OE. *laþian*.]

Laude (*of*), *v.* to praise (for), XVI 384. [L. *laudāre*.]

Laue, *v. trans.* and *intr.* to pour, VI 247, XV *g* 16. [OE. *lafian*.]

Launce, *n.* lance, V 129. [OFr. *lance*.]

Launchet, -it, *pa. t.* darted, leapt, VII 135, 153; *launchet to*, reached, VII 163. [ONFr. *lancher*.] *See* Lance.

Launde, *n.* glade, grassy space, V 78, 86, 103, 265. [OFr. *la(u)nde*.]

Laund-syde, *n.* shore, VII 170. [OE. *land + sīde*.] *See* Lond(e).

Law. *See* Lowe, *adj.*

Law(e), *n.*[1] law, VIII *a* 159, 313, XI *a* 2, 22, XIV *b* 63, XVI 313, &c.; practice, customary behaviour, in *doþ at Crystyn mennys l.*, behave as Christians, I 82. [OE. *lagu*, from ON.]

Lawe, *n.*[2] mound, knoll, V 103, 107. [OE. *hlǣw*.]

Lawse, *v.* to loose(n), undo, V 308; Lowsyd, *pa. t.* delivered, XVII 209. [From ME. *laus*, *lous*, adj.; ON. *laus-s*.]

Leche, *n.* physician, VIII *a* 268. [OE. *lǣce*.]

Lechecraft, *n.* (art of) medicine, VIII *a* 251. [OE. *lǣce-crǣft*.]

Lechery(e), *n.* sensuality, VIII *a* 137, XVII 53. [OFr. *lecherie*.]

Ledderis, *n. pl.* ladders, X 53. [OE. *hlǣdder*.]

Lede, *n.*[1] man, knight, V 27, VII 62, 75; *voc.* my good man, VI 182; Leyde, XVII 48, in *euery liffyng l.*, everybody; Leude, V 265, 321, 353. [OE. (allit.) *lēod*, prince.]

Lede, Leede, *n.*[2] people, country,

in *þurgh land and lede*, over the
earth, I 227 ; *in leede*, on earth,
XVI 70, 135. [OE. *líode*, pl.,
and *léod*, fem.]

Lede(n), Ledyn, Leyd (XVII),
v. to lead, bring, I 153, IX 214,
XVI 391 ; guide, direct, XI *a* 55 ;
to pass, lead (life), IV *a* 49, 63, VI
32, XV *h* 20, XVII 393. Ledys,
pres. pl. IV *b* 55 ; Ladde, *pa. t.*
II 584 ; Ledde, I 63, III 55 ;
Led, *pp.* treated, XVII 202.
[OE. *lǽdan*.]

Ledeing, *n.* ; *at his l.*, under his
control, XIV *b* 54. [From prec.]

Leder. *See* Lyþer.

Leders, *n. pl.* leaders, XIV *b* 94.
[From Lede(n).]

Leede. *See* Lede, *n.*³

Leef, Lef, *n.* leaf ; item (with ref.
to books), VIII *a* 251 ; *sette . . .
at a lef*, made light of, VIII *b*
101 ; Leues, Leves, *pl.* II 244,
VII 103, IX 154, XV *b* 14. [OE.
léaf.]

Leel ; Leere. *See* Lele ; Lere.

Lees, Lese, *n.* falsehood ; *with-
out(en) lees*, &c., truly, XVI 127,
XVII 390. [OE. *léas.*] *See*
Lesing.

Leest ; Leet ; Leeue. *See*
Lasse ; Lete ; Leue, *v.*³

Lef, Leof (XIV), *adj.* dear, II 102,
*406 ; eager, XIV *c* 6 ; Leue
(*wk.* in *voc.*), XV *g* 10 ; as *sb.*,
dear one, VI 58. Leuer, *com-
par.* in *l. me were to*, I would
rather, II 177 ; Leueste, most
pleasing (to God), VIII *b* 89.
[OE. *léof.*]

Lef, *see* Leef ; Lef(f)e, Lefte,
see Leue, *v.*¹

Leggaunce, *n.* (performance of)
duty to his liege lord, XIV *c* 67.
[OFr. *legiance*.]

Legg, *n.* leg, VI 99, V 160, VIII *a*
116. [ON. *legg-r*.]

Legge, Lei, Ley(e), &c. *See*
Lay, *v.*

Leid(e), Leyd(e). *See* Lay, *v.* ;
Lede, *n.*¹ ; Lede(n).

Leif(f), Leyf, Leyue. *See* Leue,
*v.*¹ and *v.*²

Leymonde. *See* Leme.

Lele, Leel, *adj.* lawful, VIII *b* 109;
faithful, XVI 65 ; according to
covenant, XVII 446. [OFr.
leël.]

Lelly, *adv.* loyally, faithfully, V
56, 60, XVI 403. [From prec.]

Leme, *v.* to shine, flash, V 158 ;
Leymonde, *pres. p.* VII 153.
[OE. **léomian* ; ON. *ljóma.*]

Lemes. *See* Lym(e).

Lemman, *n.* lover, XV *a* 20.
[OE. **léof-man* ; early ME.
leofmon.]

Lende, *v. trans.* and *intr.* to
' land' ; *lende (on)*, to come,
fall (upon), XVI 47, 54 ; *lendes
(in)* brings (into), IV *a* 44 ;
Lended, *pa. t.* remained, XIV *b*
45 ; Lent, *pp.* gone, taken
away, XV *c* 11, 39 ; Ylent (*on*),
come (upon), XV *c* 24. [OE.
lendan, go, arrive ; the ME.
sense development is obscured
by confusion with Lene, *v.*¹]

Lene, *adj.* lean, II 459. [OE.
hlǽne.]

Lene, *v.*¹ to grant, give, VIII *a* 17,
(*absolutely*) VIII *a* 215 ; Lante,
pa. t. V 182 ; Lent, *pp.* IV *a* 21.
[OE. *lǽnan*.]

Lene, *v.*² to lean ; *lened (with)*,
inclined, V 187 : *lened (to)*,
leant (on), V 264. [OE. *hleo-
nian.*]

Leng ; Lengar, -er. *See* Long(e),
adv.

Lenghe, *n.* length, VI 56. [OE.
lengu.]

Lent. *See* Lende, Lene, *v.*¹

Lenten, *n.* spring, XV *b* 1 ; Len-
ten-tyde, Lent, I 242. [OE.
lencten, lencten-tíd.]

Lenþe, Lennthe, Lenght, *n.*
length, V 248, XVII 123, 257.
[OE. *lengþu.*]

Leof. *See* Lef.

Lepe, *v.* to leap, run ; *lepeʒ hym*,
gallops, V 86 ; Lepte, *pa. t.*
leapt, XII *a* 160. [OE. *hléapan*,
str.]

Lepys, *n. pl.* leaps ; *wyth sundyr
lepys*, †dancing separately, I

234 (but *see* Sonder, and note).
[OE. *hlēp*.]

Lere, *n*. face, VI 38. [OE. *hlēor*.]
See Lyre.

Lere, Leere, *v. trans.* to teach,
instruct, VIII *a* 251, XVI 55,
127, 330, 391; *intr.* to learn,
IV *a* 17, XIV *b* 57, XVI 313, 321;
Lerid, *pp.* educated (*i. e.* clergy),
XI *a* 38. [OE. *lǣran*, teach.]

Lerne(n), *v.* to learn, II 39, VII
20, &c. Lurne(n), XIII *b* 29,
34, 36. [OE. *lĕornian*.]

Lernyng(e), *n*. learning, XI *b* 169;
instruction, in *for l. of us*, for
our instruction, VII 32; knowledge, XVI 85. [OE. *lĕornung*,
intr.]

Les(e). *See* Lasse, Lees.

Lese, *v.*[1] to lose, II 178, V 74,
IX 130; Lose, XVII 363; Lore,
pp. XII *a* 187; Lorne, XVI 198;
Lost, VII 148, VIII *b* 99; Ylore,
II 209, 545. [OE. (*be-, for-*)
lĕosan, *pp. -loren*; cf. *losian*,
be lost.] *See* Forlorn.

Lese, *v.*[2] to glean, VIII *a* 68. [OE.
lesan.]

Lesing, *n.* a lie, II 465; **Lesyngis**,
pl. XI *b* 39; *lesyngis on*, lies
against, XI *b* 98. [OE. *lēasing*.]
See Lees.

Lesse. *See* Lasse.

Lesso(u)n, *n*. lesson, VIII *a* 272,
XIII *b* 19. [OFr. *leço(u)n*.]

Lest(e). *See* Lasse; Last, *conj.*

Lete, Lette (IV *a* 88), *v.* to let,
&c.; Lat(e), IV *b* 41, X 30;
Lat(e), Latte, *imper. sg.* VIII *a*
40, 262, XVI 194, &c.; Let(e),
II 114, V 140, &c.; Lete3, *pl.*
V 319. Leet, *pa. t. sg.* IX 223,
232; Let(e), II 386, III 34,
&c.; Lette, V 189; Lete, *pl.*
II 74; Ylete, *pp.* III 32, *VIII *b*
3. (i) To let, allow, II 74,
IV *b* 41, &c.; bequeathe, III 32,
34; cause to (as *leet make*,
caused men to make, had it
made), IX 223, 232, XII *b* 192;
let untrusse, unloaded, XII *b* 52;
forming periphrastic imper.,
XIV *b* 90; *lete ben, latte be*,

cease, stop, II 114, XVI 234:
let be, left unheeded, XII *b* 94.
(ii) To give up, abandon, IV *a*
88, VIII *a* 266, XIV *c* 6; lose,
II 177; cease, II 279; neglect
(to), XIV *c* 70. (iii) *Lette as*,
behaved as if, V 189; *lete li3te
of*, make (made) light of, give
little thought to, VIII *a* 161,
XIV *c* 63; *lytel ylete by*, held
in small esteem, *VIII *b* 3. [OE.
lǣtan, *lētan*; forms with *a*
perhaps due partly to ON. *láta*,
and partly to early shortening
(? orig. in imper. sg.).]

Lette, *n*. hindrance, obstacle, XII *a*
72; delay, XII *a* 154. [From
next.] *See* Ylet.

Lette(n), Let (*of*, *fro*), *v.* to
hinder, prevent, keep (from),
V 74, 235, XI *a* 41, *b* 3, 155, 179,
XVII 341 (*subj.*), 470; Let, *pp.*
XII *b* 10; Lettid, XI *b* 181;
lette to sue (*studie*), prevent
from following (studying), XI *a*
41, *b* 112. [OE. *lettan*.] Distinguish Lete.

Lettynge, -ing (*to*), *n.* hindering
(from), hindrance, XI *a* 26, *b* 307;
delay, interruption, VIII *a* 7, XI *b*
80. [OE. *letting*.]

Lettres, *n. pl.* letters, III *introd.*;
Letturs, writings, VII 26, 59
[OFr. *lettre*.]

Leþe3, 3 *sg. pres.* softens, is
assuaged, VI 17. [OE. (*ge-*)
liþian, *-leoþian*, distinct from
liþian.]

Leude. *See* Lede, *n.*[1]

Leue, *n*. permission, VIII *a* 68;
leave, in *tok his leve*, XII *a* 31.
[OE. *lēaf*, fem.]

Leue(n), *v.*[1] to leave (alone, behind, off), abandon, neglect,
cease (to), V 86, XI *b* 10, 50,
301, XIII *a* 56, XVI 284, &c.;
Lef(f)e, IV *b* 66, XVI 376;
Leif(f), X 156, 198; Leueþ,
imper. pl. stop, I 265. Left(e),
pa. t. and *pp.* I 71, IV *b* 74, VII
26, XI *b* 261, XII *b* 179, XVI 314,
&c.; Leuid, Leuyt, Levit,
VII 74, 126, X 159, XIV *b* 78;

Yleft, *pp.* XIII *b* 8, 41. *For to leue for to*, that you may cease to, I 21 ; *to lefe*, to be left undone, avoided, IV *b* 66. [OE. *lǣfan*.] *See* Bleue.

Leue(n), Leeue, *v.*² to grant, in *Crist leue*, Christ grant, XIV *c* 87, 95. [OE. *lēfan*.] *See* Leue, *n.*

Leue(n), *v.*³ to believe, V 60, 353, VI 65, 109, VIII *a* 84 ; **Leyf, Leyue,** *imper.*, VIII *b* 3, 24. [OE. *(ge-)lēfan*.] *See* Beleue, Ylefde.

Leue, Leu-, &c. *See* Leef, Lef, Liue(n).

Leued, *adj.* leafy, I 62. [From Leef.]

Leuedi, *n.* lady, mistress, II 53, 89, 347, 455, XV *c* 23, &c. ; **Ladi,** XII *a* 50, 144, &c. ; **Lady,** *gen. sg.* in *oure Lady day*, I 242. [OE. *hlǣfdige*.]

Levyn, *n.* lightning, XVII 346. [? OE. **lēfn-* < **lau(h)mni-* (cf. Goth. *lauhmuni*).]

Levyr, *n.* liver ; *l. and long*, allit. elaboration of *hert*, XVII 399. [OE. *lifer*.]

Lew. *See* Lo.

Lewed(e), Lewid, *adj.* lay, ignorant, uneducated, III *introd.*, VIII *b* 4, XI *a* 3, XII *b* 144 ; *lerid and lewid*, XI *a* 38. [OE. *lǣwede*.]

Lewté, *n.* loyalty, fidelity, V 298, 313. [OFr. *le(a)uté*.] *See* Lele.

Lhord, &c. *See* Louerd.

Lyand. *See* Ligge(n).

Libben, *v.* to live, XV *a* 10 ; **Libbe,** I *sg. pres.* XV *c* 5 ; **Libbeth, Lybbeth,** *pres. pl.* VIII *a* 20, 71. [OE. *libban, libbe, libbaþ*.] *See* Liue(n).

Lich(e) ; Lyckend. *See* Lyk ; Likne.

Lie, *v.* to tell lies, VIII *a* 227. [OE. *lē(o)gan*.]

Lye. *See* Ligge(n).

Lif, Lyfe (obl. stem **Lif-**, and **Lyu-** &c.), *n.* life, manner of life, lifetime, I 199, V 44, VI 32, VIII *a* 170, XI *a* 57, *b* 40, XVII 398, &c. ; **Liffe,** XVI 66 ; **Liif,**

II 124, &c. ; living being, IV *a* 43, XII *a* 117, 121 ; *lef liif*, beloved (one), II 102, *406. **Lyfes,** *gen. sg.* IX 328 ; **Lyue3,** VI 117 (*see* Longe, *adv.*), 218 ; **Liue, Lyue,** *dat. sg.* II 583 (being still alive), III 16, XII *a* 168 ; *bi my lyue*, during my life, VIII *a* 95 ; *yn þys lyue*, in this world, I 170 ; *vpon lyue*, alive (*lede vpon l.* = man), V 27. [OE. *līf*.] *See* Liue(n).

Lyf-holynesse, *n.* holiness of life, VIII *b* 84. [OE. *līf + hālignes*.]

Lyflich, *adj.* active, XIV *c* 93. [OE. *līf-līc*.]

Liflode, Lyflode, *n.* (means of) living, sustenance, food, VIII *a* 17, 230, 267, 284, *b* 43, 47, XII *b* 25. [OE. *līf-lād*.]

Lift, Lyfte, Left, *adj.* left (hand, &c.), V 78, IX 69, XIII *b* 39, &c. [OE. *lyft*.]

Lift, *n.* sky, X 100. [OE. *lyft*.] *See* Loft(e).

Lyfte, *v.* to raise, IV *a* 15, V 241 ; **Lyft(e),** *pp.* IV *a* 9, VI 207 (*see* Lyþer). [ON. *lyfta*.]

Lyf-tyme, *n.* lifetime, VIII *a* 27. [OE. *līf + tīma*.]

Ligge(n), Lygge, Lig, *v.* to lie (down, idle, &c.), be (lodged, situated, &c.), II 74, VIII *b* 16, XIII *a* 53 (*subj.*), XVII 409 ; **Lye,** VII 172, IX 19 ; **List** (OE. *list*), 2 *sg. pres.* XV *f* 2 ; **Lyeþ,** 3 *sg.* is to the point, is admissible, VIII *b* 93 ; **Liggeth,** lies idle, VIII *a* 156 ; **Ligis,** XVII 84 ; **Lys,** exists, VI 242 ; **Liþ** (OE. *līþ*), II 243, XII *a* 95 ; **Liggeþ,** *pl.* II 441, VIII *a* 15 ; **Lyse,** IV *a* 61. **Lay,** *pa. t. sg.* I 181, II 133, IX 286, &c. ; *pl.* II 394, 399, X 1 (were encamped), &c.; **Lay3,** *subj.* XI *a* 52. **Lyand,** *pres. p.* X 55 ; **Ligand,** XIV *b* 71 ; **Liggeand,** II 388 (*see* note). **Lyggyng,** I 139. *Liggen oute*, be abroad, out of doors, VIII *b* 16. [OE. *licgan* ; the *g(g)* forms in I, XIV *b*, XVII prob. represent dial. *lig* from ON. *liggja*.]

Lightnes, *n.*[1] splendour, XVII 16. [OE. *lĭht-nes.*]

Lightnes, Liȝtnesse, *n.*[2] lightness; gladness, VII 15; ease, unburdensomeness, XI *b* 151. [OE. *lĭht*[2] + *-nes.*]

Lyȝt, Light, Lyht, *n.* light, VII 135, XI *b* 291, XV *b* 25, &c. [OE. *lĕ(o)ht.*]

Liȝt, *v.*[1] to shine, II 371. [OE. *lĭhtan.*[1]]

Lyȝt, Liȝte, Light, *v.*[2] *trans.* to lighten, relieve, IV *a* 70; *intr.* to alight, V 108; come down, V 152; **Lyht** (*on*), *pp.* lit (on), settled (on), XV *c* 12. [OE. *lĭhtan*[2]]

Lyȝte, Liȝt, Lyhte, *adj.*[1] light, bright, II 369, VI 140, XV *b* 14. [OE. *lĕ(o)ht, lĭ(o)ht,* adj.[1]]

Liȝte, Lyght, Liht, *adj.*[2] light, slight, easy, I *introd.,* IV *a* 49; *lete liȝte* (*liht*) *of,* make (made) light of, give little thought to, VIII *a* 161, XIV *c* 63; **Lyȝttere,** *compar.* easier, XI *b* 238. [OE. *lĕ(o)ht, lĭ(o)ht,* adj.[2]]

Liȝtly, Lightly, Lyghtly, *adv.* lightly, easily, IV *b* 5, V 241, IX 14, 118. [OE. *lĭht-lice.*]

Lyȝtnyng, *n.* lightning, I 166. [From ME. *liȝtne(n)*, extended from Liȝt, *v.*[1]]

Liif. *See* Lif.

Lik, *v.* to sup, taste; *lik on,* have a taste of, XVII 378; *cf.* Drynk. [OE. *liccian.*]

Lyk(e), Like, Lich(e), *adj.* and *adv.* usually foll. by (*un*)*to,* like, IV *a* 16, VI 72, 141, IX 35, 98, XII *a* 57, XVII 506. [OE. (*ge-*)*lic*; (*ge-*)*lice,* adv.] *See* Ilyche.

Like, Lyke, *v.* to please, II 251, 449, 529, VI 206, VIII *b* 42, XI *b* 142; *impers.* with *dat.* (as *vs liketh,* it pleases us, we please), V 66, 178, VIII *a* 150, 286, IX 177, XII *a* 115, XVI 321 (or *pers. pl.* 'like', as below), &c. ; *ȝif ȝou lyke,* if it pleases you, IX 74 (*cf. ȝif it lyke ȝou,* 284); *for ioue þat likes ille,* that are wretched bec. of love (*or* bec. of

love that is painful), XV *b* 24; *quasi-pers.* (with *it*) V 267, IX 284; *pers.* to like, XVII 361. [OE. *lician.*]

Likeing, Likyng, Lykyng(e), *n.* delight, pleasure, IV *a* 30, VII 20, 75, XI *b* 158, XVII 75, &c. ; *for likyng to here,* to be heard with delight, to give pleasure in the hearing, VII 71; *of gode likeing,* well-pleasing, II 599. [OE. *licung.*]

Likne, Lykne, Lyken, *v.* to make like, XIII *b* 23; to compare, IV *a* 6, VI 140, XIV *c* 74; **Lyckend,** *pp.* (to be) compared, IV *a* 33. [From Lyk, *adj.*]

Liknes(se), *n.* likeness, appearance, XII *a* 9, 133, 172, XVII 28. [OE. *lic-nes.*]

Lilie, *n.* lily, XV *b* 17; **Lilie-flour,** lily, XV *e* 19. [OE. *lilie; see* Flour.]

Lym(e), *n.* limb, member, VI 102, XIV *c* 93; **Lemes,** *pl.* IX 80; **Limes, Lymes,** II 171, VIII *a* 118, *b* 8; **Lymmeȝ,** VI 104. [OE. *lim*; pl. *leomu, limu.*]

Lymbo, Lymbus, *n.* limbo; the 'border' (of hell) where the souls of the just who died before Christ awaited His coming, XVI 102, 198. [L. *limbus (patrum)*; *in limbo.*]

Lymp(e), *v.* ! to limp; *lympit of the sothe,* ! stumbled from, fell short of, the truth, VII 36. [Cf. OE. *lemp-healt,* limping; MHG. *limphin,* to limp. Not recorded otherwise in E. until much later.]

Lynage, *n.* kindred, VIII *b* 26; tribe, IX 163. [OFr. *li(g)nage.*]

Lynde, *n.* lime-tree; (allit.) tree, V 108. [OE. *lind(e).*]

Lyne, *n.* sounding-line, XVII 461. [OE. *line*; OFr. *ligne.*]

Lynt, *n.* lint, refuse of flax used as an inflammable stuff, X 20. [ME. *lin(e)t,* obscurely rel. to OE. *lin* (OFr. *lin*), flax.]

Lyoun, *n.* lion, II 538, IX 247, 249. [OFr. *lioun.*]

Lippe, Lyppe, *n.* lip, V 238,

VIII *a* 259, XI *b* 84, XII *a* 181, &c. [OE. *lippa*.]

Lyre, *n.*[1] face, XVI 119. [ON. *hlýr*.] *See* Lere.

Lyre, *n.*[2] flesh, calves, V 160. [OE. *líra*.]

Lys(e), List. *See* Ligge(n).

List(e), Lyst(e), *v. impers.* to desire, wish (as *me list*, I desire), IV *a* 77, V 65, 74, XVI 68, 277; prob. *pers.* at IX 302, XVI 313; *þat hym list after*, what he has a desire for, VII 20; List, *pa. t.* VII 166. [OE. *lystan*.]

Lyste, *n.* joy, VI 107. [Alteration of Lust, under infl. of prec. ; or ON. *lyst*.]

Lystens, *imper. pl.* listen, XIV *b* 57. [OE. **hlysnan* (ONth. *lysna*) infl. by *hlystan*.]

Lite, *adv.* little; *bot gode lite*, of but little worth, II 258. [OE. *lȳt*.]

Lyte, *n.* waiting; *on lyte*, in delay, V 235. [From ME. *líten*, to expect, await, tarry; ON. *hlíta*, to trust.]

Litel, -ill, Lytill, Littel, Lyttel, Lutel (XV *c*), &c., *adj.* little, small, slight, unimportant, IV *b* 45, VI 214 (or *adv.* ' little time there '), 244, IX 14, 21, 141, XV *a* 6, *c* 3, &c.; *quasi-sb.* in *a lityl*(*l*), &c., a little, V 298, IX 62; ? a small piece, XV *h* 17; somewhat (*adv.*), V 199, IX 103, 110; a little way (*adv.*), V 78, 103, XVII 507; *for litill*, for little cause, XVII 187; *litel or nouȝt*, little or nothing, XI *b* 188 (*adv.*), 258; *wyth lyttel*, with little result (*or* ? soon), VI 215; Litel, Litle, Lyttill, *adv.* little, IV *b* 24, VII 36, VIII *b* 3, XI *b* 253, &c. [OE. *lȳtel*, adj.] *See* Lite.

Liþ₄ Lyth, *n.* limb, VI 38, XIV *c* 93. [OE. *liþ*.]

Liþ, Lith. *See* Ligge(n).

Lyþer, Leder, *adj.* bad ; sluggish, XVII 289; as *sb.*, in *to lyþer is lyfte*, ? is turned towards evil, VI 207. [OE. *lȳþre*.]

Liue(n), Lyue(n), *v.* to live, II 168, VI 117, VIII *a* 70, &c.; Lif(fe), Lyf(e), IV *a* 17, 73, XVI 68, 70, XVII 4, 58, 145, &c.; Leue, XVI 243, 322, 353, &c.; Lyfed, 2 *sg.pa. t.* VI 123 ; *pres.p.* living, (while) alive, IV *b* 31, XII *a* 171, XVI 55, XVII 47, 48, 73, &c.; *lyue men*, let men live, XI *a* 46; *liuen bi*, &c., live on, II 257, VIII *b* 26 (but *lyue on*, VIII *b* 46, &c.) ; *lyue* (*leue*) *with*, live by, VIII *b* 44, XVI 160. [OE. *lifian, leofian*.] *See* Libben, Lif.

Lo, Loo, *interj.* lo ! II 381, 556, XVII 239; look, see, II 505, 507; Lew, XVII 507 ; *we loo*, alas ! V 140 (*see* We, *interj.*). [OE. *lā* ; ME. vowel and usage show infl. of Loken.]

Lode, *n.* load, XII *b* 26. [OE. *lād*.]

Lodesman, *n.* leader, I 39. [Cf. OE. *lād-mann.*]

Lofers, *n. pl.* lovers, IV *a* 50. [From Louye.]

Lofte, *n.* air, in *on lofte*, aloft, V 193. [ON. *loft, á loft*.] *See* Alofte, Lyft.

Logede, *pa. t.* dwelt, VII 62. [OFr. *logier*.]

Loȝe, Loh. *See* Louȝ.

Loke, *pp.* locked, I 101. [OE. *lūcan*, pp. *locen*.] *See* Vnlokynne.

Loke(n), Look, *v.* to look, I 124, XVII 129, &c.; Lokyt, *pa. t.* VII 36 ; Yloked, *pp.* III 58. *Intr.* (i) to look, gaze, I 124, II 112, III 34, V 78, &c.; have an expression, VIII *a* 315 ; appear, VIII *a* 170; *loken* (*app*)*on*, look at, VIII *a* 179, XI *b* 175 ; read, VII 75 ; *on lusti to loke*, pleasant to read, VII 15 ; *loke agaynste*, gaze (straight) at, XVI 92 ; *loke to*, look at, V 265; (ii) to make investigations, VII 36 ; (iii) to see to it, take care ; foll. by *þat* and *subj.*, II 165, XVI 152, 211 ; without conj., IV *a* 19, 46, VIII *a* 39, XIV *d* 7, XVII 129. *Trans.* to watch over, in

God þe mot loke, may God have you in his keeping, V 171 ; adjudicate, III 58 ; ordain, decree, VIII *a* 313. *Loke what*, consider what (*i.e.* whatever, *interrog.*), VI 103 (cf. OE. *lōc*(*a*) *hwæt*, indef.). [OE. *lōcian*.]

Lokyng, *n.* examination, VII 26. [From prec.]

Lokkeჳ, *n. pl.* locks (of hair), V 160. [OE. *locc*.]

Lollare,-ere, *n.* idler, vagabond, VIII *b* 2, 4 ; **Lollarene**, *gen. pl.* VIII *b* 31. [From ME. *lollen*, to lounge ; see Piers Pl. C x 215.]

Lomb(e), **Lamb**, *n.* lamb, IX 142 ; used of Our Lord, VI 47, 53. [OE. *lómb*, *lámb*.]

Lome, *n.* tool, weapon, V 241, VIII *b* 47. [OE. *lóma*.]

Lond(e), **Land**(e), *n.* land, country, soil, I 25, II 208, 355, VII 163, VIII *a* 267, IX 179, XIV *b* 63, &c. ; *in land*(*e*), on earth, XVI 68, 314, XVII 145 ; *þurgh land and lede*, I 227 (see Lede, *n.*²). [OE. *lónd*, *lánd*.]

Long, *n.* lung (see Levyr), XVII 399. [OE. *lungen*.]

Longage. *See* Langage.

Long(e), *adj.* long, II 506, IX 152, 155, &c. ; *longe clothes*, clerical garb, VIII *b* 42 ; tall, VIII *b* 24 ; lasting long, I 203, VIII *a* 7 ; *þy long home*, your eternal home (after death), I 207 (OE. *lang hām*) ; *for long ჳore*, a long while, VI 226 ; *þe long day, the l. night ouer, al þe woke l.*, all day (&c.) long, VI 237, VII 166, XIII *a* 28 (*cf.* next) ; tedious, IX 267. [OE. *láng, lóng*.]

Long(e), **Lang**, *adv.* a long while, II 335, V 232, VIII *a* 19, *b* 84, XV *c* 19, XVII 244, &c. ; after an *advb. gen.*, in *hys lyueჳ longe, þise dayeჳ longe*, all his life (this day) long, VI 117, 173 (*cf.* prec.) ; **Leng**, *compar.* longer, II 84 ; **Lenger**(e), **Lengar**, I 79, II 330, V 235, XI *b* 130, XII *b* 146, XVI 68, 193 ; *euer þe lenger þe lasse þe more*, the further (you pursue the argument) the less (work) the more (pay), VI 240 ; **Longer**, XVII 531. [OE. *lónge, lánge*; compar. *léng* (adv.), *lengra* (adj.).]

Long(e), *v.*¹ to long, VII 113 ; **Langand**, *pres. p.* in *langand es*, longs, IV *a* 91. [OE. *lóngian, lángian*.]

Long(e), *v.*² ; *longe to* (*into*), to belong (to), befit, V 313, XIV *c* 25, 53 ; **Longande**, *pres. p.* that belongs, VI 102. [From ME. (*i*)*long*, adj.; OE. *ge-láng* (*on*), dependent (on).] *See* Bylongeth.

Longinge, -yng, *n.* longing, VII 119, XV *c* 24 ; **Langyng** (*til*), longing (for), IV *a* 93. [OE. *lóngung, lángung*.] *See* Louelonginge.

Longith, 3 *sg. pres.* lengthens, ? beats out long, XV *h* 17. [From Long, *adj.*]

Lording, -yng, *n.* man of high rank, II 26, 520 ; sir (as a polite address, *esp.* of minstrel to his audience), II 23, 204. [OE. *hláfording*.] *See* Loued.

Lordischipes, -is, *n. pl.* lordships, estates, XI *b* 97, 141. [OE. *hláford-scipe*.]

Lore, *n.* (method of) teaching, XI *a* 39, XIII *b* 28. [OE. *lár*.]

Lore, Lorne, *pp.* of Lese, *v.*¹

Lorel(l)**is**, *n. pl.* good-for-nothings, wastrels, XI *b* 140, 161, 173. [Prob. from prec.] *See* Loseles.

Los, *n.* fame, XIV *c* 111. [OFr. *los*.]

Loseles, *n. pl.* wastrels, VIII *a* 116. [Prob. from ME. *lose*(*n*), variant of *lore*(*n*) pp. of Lese, *v.*¹] *See* Lorel(l)is.

Losengerye, *n.* lying flattery (of a parasite), VIII *a* 137. [OFr. *losengerie*.]

Lossom, Lossum. *See* Louesum.

Lost, *n.* loss, VIII *b* 101. [Rel. to Lese, *v.*¹ ; cf. OE., ME. *los*.]

Lote, *n.* noise, V 143. [ON. *lá* (pl.), behaviour, noise ; *cf.* Bere *n.*¹]

Loþ, Lothe, *adj.* hateful, I 9; loath, unwilling, XIV *c* 6. [OE. *lāþ*, adj.]

Loþe, *n.* grief, VI 17. [OE. *lāþ*, n.]

Loþli, Loþlich, *adj.* horrible, II 78; unpleasing, II 461. [OE. *lāþ-lic*.]

Loud(e), *adj.* loud, II 511, XII *a* 138; *loud or still,* under all circumstances, XIV *b* 54. [OE. *hlūd*.]

Loue, *n.* love, II *12, 55, &c.; Louue, XV *a* 21; Luf(e), I *introd.*, IV *a* 1, 5, XVII 82; with *object. gen.* (as *mi lordes loue,* love for my master), II 518 (note), VIII *a* 19, 214; *þi loue,* love of thee, VIII *a* 27; *for loue or ay,* in any event, II 571. [OE. *lufu*.] *See* Louye.

Louely, *adj.* gracious, beautiful, pleasant, VIII *a* 10, 272, XVI 119. [OE. *luf(e)lic*.] *See* Luflyly.

Lou(u)e- longinge, *n.* unsatisfied love, XV *a* 9, *c* 5. [OE. *lufu* + *lóngung*.] *See* Longinge.

Louerd, *n.* lord, (the) Lord, master, husband, XV *g* 1, 11, &c.; Lhord, III *introd.*, 11, 29, 46; Lord(e), II 120, 518, VIII *a* 19, 272, XII *a* 157, &c.; Lordene, *gen. pl.* VIII *b* 77. [OE. *hláford*.]

Loues, *n. pl.* loaves, VIII *a* 278. [OE. *hláf*.] *See* Pese-lof.

Louesum, -som, *adj.* beautiful, lovely, II 111, 460; Lossom, -sum, XV *b* 17, *c* 15; Lufsoum, as *sb.*, lovely one, VI 38. [OE. *lufsum*.]

Louȝ, *pa. t. sg.* laughed, II 314; Loȝe, V 321; Loh (*on*), smiled (upon), XV *c* 15. [OE. *hlæhhan*, pa. t. *hlōh*.]

Louy(e), Louie, *v.* to love, like, V 27, 31, VIII *a* 202; Loue(n), II 34, IX 100, 101, XII *a* 5, &c.; Luf(e), Luffe, IV *a* 4, *b* 7, V 300, XVI 403, XVII 47, &c.; Yloued, *pp.* II 123. [OE. *lufian*.]

Louyly, *adj.* ? lawful, VI 205

(note). [OE. *lah-lic*.] *See* Lawe, *n.*[1]

Louyng, Lufyng, *n.*[1] love; beloved (one), IV *a* 5 (note), 56. [From Louye.] *Distinguish* next.

Louyng, *n.*[2] praise, IV *a* 24, XVI 405. [OE. *lofung*.] *Distinguish* prec.

Loupe, *n.* any jewel of imperfect brilliance (*esp.* sapphire, with which it is often joined), IX 116. [OFr. *loupe.*]

Lowable, *adj.* praiseworthy, VIII *b* 109. [OFr. *louable.*]

Low(e), Law, *adj.* low, VII 102, X 137, XVII 21; near the bottom, VI 187; lowly, VIII *a* 223, &c.; *heiȝe and lowe,* all men, XIV *c* 100; *adv.* low, V 168, XII *b* 11, &c.; *thus low,* here below, in so lowly a place, XVII 173. [ON. *lág-r*.]

Low(e), *n.* flame, VII 136, 152, 159. [ON. *logi*.]

Lowe, *v.* to praise; *to lowe,* praiseworthy, II 12 (MS. Harl.); *cf. Sir Gaw.* 1399, and (for idiom) Wale. [OFr. *louer*.] *See* Allowe.

Lowsyd. *See* Lawse.

Lowte, *v.* to bow; *trans.* (but *see* þat, *rel.*) bow before, reverence, XV *i* 4; Lutte, *pa. t. sg.* bowed, V 187; *refl.* V. 168. [OE. *lūtan*, str.]

Lud, *n.,* in *on hyre lud,* ? in her own language, XV *c* 4. [? OE. *léoden, lýden,* language.]

Lufe, *n.* kind of rudder, XVII 462; see C. Sisam, *R.E.S.* N.S. xiii (1962).

Luf(f)-. *See* Loue-; Louy(e); Louyng, *n.*[1]

Luflyly, *adv.* courteously, V 321; in seemly manner, V 108. [From Louely.]

Lunatyk, *adj.* suffering from recurrent fits of insanity (thought to depend on the changes of the moon), IX 93. [L. *lūnāticus*.]

Lurdans, *n. pl.* rascals, XVI 102. [OFr. *lourdein,* lazy fellow.]

Lurnede, Lurneþ. *See* Lerne.

Lust, *n.* pleasure, desire, IV *a* 16, 59 ; lust, IV *b* 17, IX 277. [OE. *lust.*] *See* Lyste.

Lustful, *adj.* pleasure-loving, XI *b* 256. [OE. *lust-ful.*]

Lusti, *adj.* pleasant, VII 15. [From Lust.]

Lutel; **Lutte.** *See* Litel; Lowte.

Ma. *See* Make(n), Fai.

Maad(e), **Mad(e)**, &c. *See* Make(n).

Madde, *adj.* mad, XVI 247. [OE. (*ge-*)*mĕdd*, pp.]

Madde, *v.* to act madly, V 346. [From prec.]

Magesté, *n.* majesty, VII 1. [OFr. *majesté.*]

Magré. *See* Maugré, *prep.*

Maȝtyly, *adv.* powerfully, forcibly, V 194, 222. [OE. *mæhtig-lice.*] *See* Myȝt(e).

Mai, *v.* 1 & 3 *pres.* (*ind.* and *subj.*), am able to, can, may, may well, have reason to, &c., IV *a* 31, XII *a* 66, XIV *c* 1, &c. ; May(e), IV *a* 6, 36, &c. ; May(e), 2 *sg.* IV *a* 20, XVI 173, &c. ; Meist (= meiht ; *see* Appendix, p. 278), XV *g* 6 ; Miȝt, Myȝt(e), II 452, VIII *a* 217, *b* 35. Mai, May, *pl.* IV *a* 61, IX 213, &c. ; Moun, VI 176 ; Mowe, I 115, VIII *a* 40, IX 164, &c. Micht, Mycht, *pa. t.* (*ind.* and *subj.*), was able to, could, might, &c., X 17, 139, &c., Miȝt(e), Myȝt(e), I 16, II 221, VIII *a* 133, XI *a* 44, *b* 283, &c. ; Myȝtte, XI *b* 30, 103 ; Myght(e), I 184, IX 276, &c. ; Mihte, Myhte, XII *a* 16, 75, XIV *c* 36, &c. ; Moȝt(e), VI 67, 115, 119, Moghte, IV *b* 31. [OE. *mæg* (*meaht, miht*, 2 sg.) ; late pl. *mugon*, subj. *muge*; pa. t. *mihte* (late *muhte*).]

Mai, **May**, *n.*[1] maiden, VI 75, XV *a* 6, 16, *c* 28, Introduction xii. [ON. *mæ-r*, gen. *meyj-ar*; cf. OE. *mæg*, woman (in verse).]

May, *n.*[2] May, II 57, IV *a* 57 ; May dew, dew gathered in May (thought to have special pro-

perties), IX 63. [OFr. *mai.*] *See* Deaw.

Maid(e). *See* Make(n).

Mayde(n), **Maiden**, *n.* maiden, virgin, I 41, II 64, VIII *a* 323, XV *i* 7, &c. [OE. *mægden.*]

Mayll, **Male**, *adj.* male, IX 58, XVII 152. [OFr. *ma(s)le.*]

Mayn, *n.* might, XVII 310. [OE. *mægen.*]

Mais; **Maister.** *See* Make(n) ; Mister.

Maysterful, *adj.* arrogant, VI 41. [From next.]

Maistre (-er, -ur), **Mayster**, *n.* lord, Lord, II 413, VI 102, VII 1, XIII *a* 2 ; master, V 22, VIII *a* 41, 236, 314, XV *h* 17 ; *mayster of gramere*, a title, XIII *b* 27 (*see* note). [OFr. *maistre*; OE. *mægester.*]

Maistrie, **Maystrie**, *n.* mastery, VIII *a* 323 ; *for the maystrie* (OFr. *pour la maistrie*), to the utmost possible degree, IX 233 ; *pl.* (partly due to OFr. *maistrise*, sg.) in *make maistries*, do a wonderful, mighty (*here* masterful, high handed) deed, XVI 116, 202, 216, 217. [OFr. *maistrie.*]

Make, *n.* mate, XV *b* 20, *c* 18, 31, XVII 139. [OE. (*ge*)*maca.*]

Make(n), **Mak**, *v.* to make, do ; (with or without *to*) cause, compel; VIII *a* 205, 280, IX 120, 206, XIV *b* 87, &c. ; Ma, X 14, 167 ; Mase, 3 *sg.* IV *a* 15 ; Matȝ, VI 250 ; Mais, *pl.* X 72 ; Man, VI 152 ; Mase, XIV *b* 34, XVI 116 ; Makes, Maketh, *imper. pl.* VIII *a* 14, XVI 383. Mad, Made(n), *pa. t.* I 39, II 20, VI 179, &c. ; Maid(e), X 5, XVII 3 (2 *sg.*), 28, &c. ; Maked, II 329, 498, &c. Maad(e), *pp.* XI *b* 101, 196, &c.; Mad, VI 126, VIII *b* 74, &c. ; Maid(e), X 3, XVII 73, &c. ; Ymad, III *introd.* ; Ymaked, VIII *a* 180. *Mad sumoun*, caused (men) to summon (them), VI 179 ; *makes ioie*, rejoice, XVI 383 : *it maketh*, brings it about (that), VIII *a* 199;

ich made of, I summed up (as Mn. E. idiom), VIII *b* 5; *see also* Dere, Qwart, Ylet, &c. [OE. *macian*; with the reduced forms cf. Taken.]

Makeleȝ, *adj.* matchless, VI 75. [OE. *ge-maca + -lēas.*]

Maker, *n.* maker, causer, I 204; Creator, VII 1, XVI 2, XVII 1. [From Maken.]

Makyng(*e*), *n.* building, work, I 183; making, XI *b* 230. [OE. *macung.*]

Malais, *n.* hardship, II 240. [OFr. *malaise.*] *See* Ese.

Malice, Malis, *n.* evil purpose, ill-will, VII 177, IX 119, XVI 302. [OFr. *malice.*]

Malt, *pa. t. sg.* melted, V 12. [OE. *mieltan, mæltan.*]

Man. *See* Make(n).

Man(e), Manne, *n.* man, mankind, (any) body, one, I 102, II 27, IV *a* 12, *b* 62, XVII 236, &c.; Mon, V 32, 170, 271 (note), VI 160, &c. *Gen. sg.* (often generic, equiv. to 'human', &c.), Manes(se), II 55², XV *i* 16; Mannes, -is, -ys, -us, III 54, VIII *a* 234 (note), XI *b* 113, 114, XII *b* 139, XVI 246, &c.; Mans, in *mans wonder*, monster, XVII 408. Manne, *dat. sg.* III 19. Men(e), *pl.* I 32, IV *b* 9, &c.; Men(ne), Mene, *gen. pl.* men's, people's, &c., IV *b* 69 (footnote), VIII *b* 29, XIII *b* 20; Mennes, -ys, -us, I 82, VIII *a* 96, XI *b* 119, 192; Mens, IV *b* 50, *69 (footnote). [OE. *man(n), mon(n).*] *See* Men, Noman.

Manaced, *pa. t.* threatened, VIII *a* 163; Mansed, V 277. [OFr. *manecier, manasser*; cf. Comsed, for the reduction.]

Manans, *n.* threat, X 72. [OFr. *manace*, with confusion of suffix.]

Mandeþ, 3 *sg. pres.* sends forth, XV *b* 16, 25. [OFr. *mander.*]

Maner(e), Manyere (III), *n.* (a) manner, way, I 80, X 103, XI *a* 11, XIII *b* 30 (without foll. *of*), &c.; *in his manere*, after his fashion, VIII *a* 104; custom, II 431, XIII *b* 17, 26; kind, sort, IX 102, 139, &c.; *any (ich) maner*, any (every) kind of, II 364, VIII *a* 213; with *sg.* form after *al(le)*, *meny*, and numerals (usually without *of*, II 302, III *introd.*, VIII *a* 20, XIII *a* 37, *b* 1, 9, &c.; *deuyse, tell, the maner (of)*, describe, IX 264, 268; Manereȝ, *pl.* courtesy, * VI 22 (MS. marereȝ). [OFr. *man(i)ere.*]

Manes(se). *See* Man(e).

Manfully, *adv.* manfully, X 117. [From OE. *mann + -full.*]

Manhode, *n.* virility, IX 80. [OE. *mann + hād.*]

Mani(e), Many(e), *adj.* many, I 133, II 294, III 41, VIII *a* 100, &c.; Meny(e), VIII *b* 36, XIII *a* 6, &c.; Moni, Mony, V 201, VI 212, &c.; *mani (moni) a*, &c., many a, II 432, XIV *c* 68, 92, &c.; (without *a*), I 157 (note), II 520, XVII 355, 436; *many ... fold(e)*, *see* Fold(e). [OE. *manig, menig, monig.*]

Manyere. *See* Maner(e).

Manyfold, *adj.* many times multiplied, great, XII *b* 154. [OE. *manig-fáld.*] *See* Fold.

Mankyn, *n.* mankind, XVII 71. [OE. *man-cyn(n).*]

Mankunde, Mankynde, *n.* mankind, XIII *a* 2, XVI 15. [OE. *mann + cýnd*; cf. prec.]

Mannus, &c.; Mansed. *See* Man(e); Manaced.

Mappa Mundi, *n.* map, *or* descriptive geography, of the world, IX 301. [Latin; also appears in ME. in Fr. form *mappemounde.*]

Mar, Marre, *v.* to hinder, stop, XVI 116, XVII 129 (*subj.*); *marre .. to*, prevent from, XVI 173; to destroy, V 194, XVI 208. [OE. *merran*, hinder, spoil.]

Marchant, *n.* merchant, XII *b* 166. [OFr. *marchand.*]

Marchaundise, *n.* commercial dealings, XI *b* 290. [OFr. *marchandise.*]

Marches, *n. pl.* (frontiers), regions, IX 273. [OFr. *marche*.]

Marche, *v.*; **marcheth** (*to, upon*), borders on, IX 193, XII *a* 61. [OFr. *marchir*, from prec.]

Mare. *See* Mor(e).

Maryage, *n.* marriage; *to Hys m.*, as His spouse, VI 54. [OFr. *mariage*.]

Mark, *n.* a mark (about ⅔ of a pound, 13*s.* 4*d.*), XI *b* 162. [OE. *marc*, a borrowed word of disputed origin.]

Marked, *n.* market-place, VI 153. [Late OE. *marcet*, from ONFr. *market*.]

Martyrdome, *n.* martyrdom, I 34. [OE. *martyr-dōm*.]

Mase. *See* Make(n).

Mased, *adj.* bewildered, XVI 247. [Cf. OE. *ā-masod*.]

Masse, *n.*[1] Mass, VIII *a* 88, XI *b* 131, &c.; **Messe,** I 8, 69, VI 137, &c. [OE. *mæsse, messe*; OFr. *messe*.]

Masse, *n.*[2] conglomerate mass, IX 44, 46. [OFr. *masse*.]

Masse-prest, *n.* (secular) priest, V 40. [OE. *mæsse-prēost*.]

Mast. *See* More, Mor(e).

Mast, *n.* mast, X 123, XIV *c* 49, &c. [OE. *mæst*.]

Mate, *adj.* dejected, VI 26. [OFr. *mat*, orig. 'mated' in chess.]

Mater(e), Matiere, *n.* matter, subject, VII 35, 98, IX 111, XII *a* 45, XIV *c* 14. [OFr. *mat(i)ere*.]

Matȝ. *See* Make(n).

Matyn(n)es, -ys, *n. pl.* matins (first of the canonical 'hours', properly recited at midnight or before daybreak), V 120, XI *b* 131, 189, &c.; applied to all the morning office preceding public Mass, I 68, ! XI *b* 208; *matynes of Oure Lady*, matins proper to Our Lady (made a part of daily morning office), XI *b* 132. [OFr. *matines*.]

Maugré, *n.* displeasure, ill-will, VIII *a* 236. [OFr. *maugré*.]

Maugré (-ee), Mawgree, *prep.* in spite of, VIII *a* 69, IX 197, 314;

Magré, X 197; *m. Medes* (*þi*) *chekes,* in spite of Meed (you), VIII *a* 41, 151 (an extension of ME. *maugré þin, his,* &c. where *þin,* &c., are orig. *gen.*). [OFr. *maugré.*]

Maulardes, *n. pl.* mallards, wildduck, II 310. [OFr. *mallart.*]

Maundementis, *n. pl.* commandments, XI *b* 184. [OFr. *mandement.*]

Maunged, *pp.* eaten, VIII *a* 255. [OFr. *mangier.*]

Mawe, *n.* belly, VIII *a* 167, 306 (*pl.* or *distrib. sg.*; *see* Herte). [OE. *maga.*]

Me. *See* Men; and Ich, *pron.*

Measse, *n.* mess, portion (of food), XVII 389. [OFr. *mes.*]

Mecull. *See* Mekill, *adj.*

Mede, *n.* reward; Lady Meed (personif. of bribery, &c.), VIII *a* 41; *to mede,* in payment, as reward, IV *a* 64, XIV *b* 2, XVII 122; *qwite hym his m.,* pay him out, XVII 216. [OE. *mēd.*]

Medeful, *adj.* profitable, XI *b* 247. [From prec.]

Medycyne, *n.* cure, I 244. [OFr. *medicine.*]

Medill-erd. *See* Myddel-erde.

Medyn, ! *n. pl.* meadows, XV *i* 14 (such a pl. form is remarkable in this text, if genuine). [OE. *mǣd, mēd.*]

Meditacioun (*of*), *n.* meditation (upon), XI *b* 295. [OFr. *meditacion.*]

Meete, *n.* measure(ment), XIII *a* 47. [OE. *ge-met.*] *See* Meteth.

Meyny, *n.* household, body (of servants, &c.), retinue, company, VI 182; **Meneye,** XVII 290; **Menȝhe,** X 39; **Menye,** VII 37, XVII 22. [OFr. *mai(s)nee.*]

Meyntene(n), Mayntene, *v.* to maintain, defend, support, keep up, VIII *a* 37, XI *b* 43, 55, 166, XIV *c* 76; *subj.,* XIV *c* 100; **Meyntenynge,** *n.* upholding, XI *b* 170. [OFr. *maintenir.*]

Meist. *See* Mai, *v.*

Meke, *adj.* meek, humble, sub-

missive, IV *a* 74, VI 44, VIII *a*
199, XI *b* 58, XVI 1. [ON.
mjúk-r, earlier **meuk-*.]

Mekenesse, *n.* meekness, gentle-
ness, VI 46, VIII *a* 41 (personified), XI *b* 118, 122. [From
prec.]

Mekill, *adj.* great, X 116, XIV *b*
84, XVI 129, XVII 109, &c. ;
Mecull, VII 10. [OE. *micel*.]
See Miche, Mochel, More.

Mekill, *adv.* greatly, much, IV *b*
23. [OE. *micel, micle*.] *See*
Moche, Mor(e), Mo.

Mekis, 2 *sg. pres.* in *mekis þiselffe*,
humblest thyself, XVI 350.
[From Meke, *adj.*]

Mele, *v.* to speak, say, V 227,
268, 305, VI 137, 229, ? *XV *b* 20
(MS. miles). [OE. *mǣlan*.]

Melke, Milke, *n.* milk, II 146,
VIII *a* 176. [OE. *me(o)lc, milc*.]

Mell, *v.*[1] to announce, declare ;
? grant, XVII 44 (*or* from next,
in vague use extended from that
seen in XVI). [OE. *meðlan*.]
Cf. Mele.

Melle, *v.*[2] to mix, mingle, XVI
302 ; Mellit, *pp.* X 22 ; Ymelled, XIII *b* 3 ; Mellyng, *n.*
mingling, XIII *b* 12. [OFr.
mesler, meller.]

Melody, *n.* melody, (sweet) music,
II 46, 278, 442, 523, 590, IV *a*
67. [OFr. *melodie*.]

Membre, *n.* limb, member, V 224,
VIII *b* 34 ; *fig.* VI 98. [OFr.
membre.]

Memoire, Memorye, *n.* memory,
XII *b* 221 ; commemoration (of
the faithful departed), VIII *a* 89.
[OFr. *memoire, memorie*.]

Men, *impers. subject sg.* one, IX
69 ; also freq. (esp. in *men may*)
in syntactically doubtful cases
prob. apprehended as pl., as IX
75 (first), 118, XV *h* 3, &c. ; Me,
III 3, 16, 48, 51, XIII *a* 9, XV *g*
8, 28. [OE. *man*, reduced under
wk. stress.] *See* Man (*esp.* V 170).

Mencioun, *n.* mention, IX 267.
[OFr. *mencion*.]

Mend(e), *v.* to improve ; make

better (free from fault), XVI 359,
increase (joy), XVI 79 ; *mend
ȝow of ȝoure misdede*, reform
your evil ways, XIV *b* 7 ; Mendyng, *n.* improvement, VI 92.
[Shortened from Amend.]

Mendinauns, *n. pl.* beggars, VIII *b*
80. [OFr. *mendinant*.]

Men(e). *See* Man e).

Mene, *adj.* common, thin (ale),
VIII *a* 176. [OE. *(ge-)mǣne*.]

Mene(n), *v.*[1] to mean ; signify,
I introd., VIII *b* 38, XVI 46;
declare (as one's intention), XVI
174 ; to intend, *XVI 301 (MS.
mouys) ; to imagine, suppose
XI *b* 74 (*or* imply) ; *impers.* in
me menys, I call to mind, XVI
231 ; Menede, *pa. t.* VIII *b* 38 ;
Mente, *pa. t.* I introd.; *pp.* XVI
174 ; Ymende, *pp.* noted, III
introd. [OE. *mǣnan*.]

Mene, *v.*[2] to complain, XV *b* 22 ;
refl. in *mened hem*, made their
complaint, VIII *a* 2. [OE.
mǣnan, v.[2] ; prob. distinct from
prec., and rel. to Mon(e), *q.v.*]

Meneye. *See* Meyny.

Mengen, *v.* to remember, VIII *a*
89. [OE. *myn(d)gian*.]

Menȝhe. *See* Meyny.

Meny(e). *See* Mani, Meyny.

Menyng, *n.* mention, XVI 103.
[From Mene, *v.*[1]]

Menne(s), -ys, -us. *See* Man(e).

Menskes, *n. pl.* honours, V 342.
[ON. *mennska*, humanity, kind-
ness, ?hence in ME. grace,
courtesy, honour ; cf. senses of
OE. *ār*.]

Menstraci, *n.* minstrelsy, music,
II 302, 420, 589. [OFr. *mene-
stralsie*.]

Menstrel, *n.* minstrel, II 430,
449, 532 ; Minstrel, II 382,
486. [OFr. *menestral, -el*.]

Mente. *See* Mene, *v.*[1]

Merci, Mercy(e), Mersy, *n.*
mercy, I 167, II 113, III 1, VI 23,
VIII *a* 40 (personified), XVI 359,
&c. ; *grant merci*, thank you, V
58, XII *b* 92 (*see* Grant). [OFr.
merci.]

Mercii, *n. pl.* Mercians, men of the Midlands, XIII *b* 54. [Med.L. *Mercii*; OE. *Merce*.]

Mery. *See* Miri(e).

Meridionall, *adj.* Southern, IX 2, 3. [L. *meridionālis.*]

Merke(nes). *See* Mirke, Myrknes.

Mersh, *n.* March, XV *c* I. [AFr., ONFr. *march*(*e*).]

Merþe. *See* Mirthe.

Meruayl(l)e, -uail(e), -ueyl(l)e, &c. (*of*), *n.* amazement, wonder (at), I 211, IX 151, 226; marvel, II 409, 598, IX 143, 146, 292, &c.; a marvel (without *a*), I 115, 205, IX 18; *no meruayle þaȝ* (with *subj.*), no wonder (if), V 239. [OFr. *merveille.*]

Merueyl(l)ous, *adj.* marvellous, I 247, IX 145; Merveilous, XII *a* 64; Mervelus, XVII 12, 164. [OFr. *merveillous.*]

Meschaunce; Meschief. *See* Myschance; Myschefe.

Mese, *n.* moss, II 248. [OE. *mēos.*]

Message, *n.* errand, XII *a* 52, 102; message, XII *introd.* [OFr. *message.*]

Messagere, *n.* messenger, XII *a* 46; Messengere, XVI 362. [OFr. *messager.*]

Messais. *See* Missays.

Messe. *See* Masse, *n.*[1]

Mesurable, *adj.* moderate, reasonable, VIII *a* 192. [OFr. *mesurable.*]

Mesure, *n.* capacity, XI *b* 113; moderation, XVI 302. [OFr. *mesure.*]

Mesurit, *pp.* measured, X 25. [OFr. *mesurer.*]

Mete, *n.* food, VIII *a* 133, IX 15, XV *e* 7, *g* 3, XVII 160, &c.; Mette, XVI 230; *esp.* joined with *drink*, I 158, II 254, VIII *a* 20, XI *b* 257, XVII 197; *at*(*te*) *mete,* at table, II 519, VIII *a* 55, XV *g* 24. [OE. *mete.*]

Mete(n), *v.* to meet, II 510, V 138, 167, VI 20, XIV *a* 27; Mette, *pa. t.,* VIII *a* 163, *b* 6. [OE. *mētan.*] *See* Imete.

Meteþ, 3 *sg. pres.* measures, XIII *a* 46. [OE. *metan.*] *See* Meete.

Methles, *adj.* immoderate. violent, v 38. [OE. *mǣþ-lēas.*]

Mette, *pa. t.* dreamt, XII *a* 139, 153. [OE. *mǣtan,* impers.]

Meue, Moue, *v.* to move; *trans.* (inspire), XI *a* 66, *b* 246; *intr.* proceed, pass on, VII 98; Meuyt, *pa. t.* passed, VII 30; Mevid, *pp.* carried away, XVII 542. [OFr. *moveir;* accented stem *moev-, meuv-,* &c.]

Mezeyse. *See* Missays.

Mi, My. *See* Ich, *pron.*

Miche, Myche, *adj.* great, much, II 278, 523, 560, VII 41, 122. [OE. *micel.*] *See* Mekill, Mochel, More.

Micht, Mycht. *See* Mai, *v.*; Myȝt(e).

Mid, Midde (XV), *prep.* with, III *introd.,* 9, 51, 55, XV *a* 19. [OE. *mid.*] *See* Þer(e).

Myddel, *adj.* central, Midland, XIII *b* 10, 54. [OE. *middel.*]

Middel, Myddel, *n.* middle, XIII *b* II; waist, XV *c* 16. [OE. *middel.*]

Myddel-erde, Medill-erd, *n.* the world, v 32, XVII 100, 234. [Altered by assoc. with prec. from OE. *middan-(g)eard.*]

Mydyng, *n.* midden, dunghill, XVII 376. [Cf. Danish *mög-dynge, mödding* (ON. **myk(i)-dyngja*) muck-heap.]

Mydnyȝt, *n.* midnight, V 119. [OE. *mid-niht.*]

Myghtfull, *adj.* mighty, XVII I. [OE. *miht + -ful.*]

Mighty, Myghty, *adj.* mighty, VII 177, &c.; *was so myghty to,* had the power to, XVI 91; *quasi-sb.* mighty princes, VII 118. [OE. *mihtig.*]

Myȝt(e), *n.* might, power, strength, capacity, I 84, 186, VIII *a* 195, XI *b* 114; Mycht, X 48, 65, &c.; Myght, IX 197, XVI 233, &c.; Miste, Myste (*see* App. p. 278), XV *g* 29; *of myste,* mighty, VI 102; *pl.* deeds of power, XVI

174; *do (all) his my3t*, &c., do all in his power, X 79, XI *b* 6; *with thair mychtis all*, with all their might, X 95; *at my myght*, as far as I can, XVII 322. [OE. *miht*.]

Mi3te, Mihte, &c. *See* Mai, *v*.

Myke3, *n. pl.* ? favourites, VI 212 (note); *see* Mike, *n.* in *N.E.D.* [Unknown.]

Milde, Mylde, *adj.* gentle, kindly, IV *a* 74, *b* 75, XV *g* 2, &c. [OE. *mild*.]

Mile, Myle, *n.* mile; *sg.* for *pl.* after numerals, II 350, XIV *b* 42; *wel a four grete myle*, fully (a distance of) four 'long miles', IX 200 (*see* note). [OE. *mil*.]

Miles, ? *n. pl.* XV *b* 20; ? read *meles murge (wi)þ*, call lovingly to; *see* Mele, *v*.

Myn, *adj.* smaller, in *more and myn*, all, XVII 112, 278. [ON. *minni; meiri ok minni*.]

Myn, Mynne, *v.* to remember, recall, mention, VII 30, 37; *myn(ne) of*, be mindful of, VI 223, XVII 551. [ON. *minna*, remind; *minna-sk*, remember.]

Min, Myn(e). *See* Ich, *pron*.

Mynd(e), *n.* mind, memory, VII 10, 11, 30, IX 319, XVI 2; *take in m.*, recollect, XII *a* 194, *b* 223. [OE. *(ge-)mynd*.]

Myne, *n.* ore, IX 46, 52. [OFr. *mine*.]

Myne(n), *v.* to mine, tunnel, IX 222, 224, 231, X 8. [OFr. *miner*.]

Mynestres, *n. pl.* servants, VIII *b* 63. [OFr. *ministre*.]

Ministre, Mynstre, *n.* monastery, VIII *b* 95, XIII *a* 50. [OE. *mynster*.]

Mynget, -it, *pa. t.* mingled, VII 131; *pp.* VII 108. [OE. *mĕngan*.]

Mynt, Munt, *n.* aim; feint, pretence at a blow, V 277, 282, 284. [From next.]

Mynte, *v.* to aim, swing (an axe), V 222; **Mynte**, Munt, *pa. t. sg.* V 194, 206. [OE. *myntan*.]

Miracle, *n.* miracle, XI *b* 280. [OFr. *miracle*.]

Mire, Myre, mire; *fig.* a desperate situation, XIV *b* 71, XVI 256. [ON. *mýr-r*.]

Miri(e), Myrie, *adj.* merry, joyous, gay, II 58, 436, VIII *a* 151, XV *a* 11, 16, &c.; **Mery**, VIII *a* 69, XVII 463; **Myryest**, *superl.* VI 75; **Muryly**, *adv.* pleasantly, playfully, V 227, 268, 277. [OE. *myrge*.] *See* Mirth(e), Murgeþ.

Mirke, Mørke, *adj.* dark, VII 108; *n.* darkness, XVI 53. [OE. *myrce*, ON. *myrk-r*, adj.]

Myrknes, *n.* darkness, IV *a* 64; **Merkenes**, VII 131. [From prec.]

Mirth(e), Myrth, *n.* joy, mirth, IV *a* 44, XIV *b* 3, XVI 79, &c.; **Merþe**, II 6. [OE. *myrgþ*.]

Mys. *See* Misse, Mysse.

Mysbede, *v.* to ill-use, VIII *a* 46; **Mysboden**, *pp.* V 271. [OE. *mis-bēodan*.]

Myschance, Meschaunce, *n.* disaster, misfortune, V 127, IX 87, XIV *b* 30. [OFr. *mescha(u)nce*.]

Myschefe, -cheif, -chief, *n.* distress, damage, misfortune, I 175, VIII *a* 199, X 136, 178; **Meschief**, XII *b* 14. [OFr. *mesch(i)ef*.]

Misdede, *n.* wrong-doing, XIV *b* 7. [OE. *mis-dēd*.]

Miself(f)e, Myselue(n). *See* Ich, *pron*.

Myserecorde, *n.* mercy, VI 6. [OFr. *misericorde*.]

Myshap, *n.* accident, VIII *b* 35. [OE. *mis-* + Hap, *q. v.*]

Myslyke, *v. impers.* it displeases, is unpleasant to; *subj.* IV *b* 58, V 239. [OE. *mis-līcian*.]

Missays, Messais, *n.* hardship, suffering, II 262, 325; **Mezeyse**, III 42. [OFr. *mesaise, -eise*.] *See* Ese.

Mysse, Mys, *n.* (sense of) loss, VI 4; misery, XVII 551; **Mysses**, *pl.* offences, faults, V

323. [OE. *miss*, and *mis*-prefix.] *See* Amys.

Misse, Mys(se), *v.* to miss ; *misse (of)*, fail (in), VII 118, XVII 404 ; to do without, XVII 237 ; lack, VI 22. [OE. *missan.*]

Mysspended, *pp.* misspent, VIII *b* 97. [OE. *mis-* + *spēndan.*] *See* Spende.

Myste, Mist, *n.* mist, ▼ 12, VII 108, &c. [OE. *mist.*]

Miste, Myste. *See* My3t(e).

Mister, Myster, *n.* need, IV *b* 58, 67, X 151, 161 ; Maister, in *hom maister were*, was their duty, VII 35. [OFr. *mest(i)er, meistier.*]

Myst-hakel, *n.* cloak of mist, ▼ 13. [OE. *mist* + *hacele.*]

Mnam, *n.* (mina), talent, VIII *a* 237, 238 ; Nam, VII *a* 235. [L. *m(i)nam*, accus.]

Mo, *adj.* and *quasi-pron.* more (in number), others, I 133, II 90, 350, V 254, IX 153, XIV *d* 7, XV *b* 22, XVI 358, XVII 134, &c. ; Moo, XVI 208, 328. [OE. *mā*, compar. adv.]

Moche, *adv.* greatly, much, IX 101, 300, XI *b* 107, 183, &c. ; to a great extent, XIII *b* 41 ; Much(e), VI 14, XI *b* 297, &c. [OE. *mycel, mycle.*] *See* Mekill, Mor(e), Mo.

Mochel, *adj.* (and *quasi-sb.*), great, much, XII *a* 105, *b* 212 ; Moche, II 36, III 25, 32, XIII *a* 51, &c. ; Much, V 72, 268, VI 244, &c. ; *in so moche*, to the corresponding extent, XI *b* 232 ; *in so moche þat*, in as much as, IX 299. [OE. *mycel.*] *See* Mekill, Miche, More.

Mod, *n.* mood, temper, VI 41. [OE. *mōd.*]

Mody, *adj.* as *sb.* the passionate (lover), XV *b* 22. [OE. *mōdig.*]

Moder, -ir, *n.* mother, II 30, III 40, V 252, XVI 250, &c. ; Moder, *gen. sg.* XI *b* 29 ; as *adj.* in *modir tunge*, XI *a* 40. [OE. *mōdor.*]

Mo3t(e) Moghte. *See* Mai, *v.*

Moyne. *See* Mone.

Moyst, *adj.* moist, IX 95. [OFr. *moiste.*]

Mol, *n.* dust, VI 22 (cf. *mul*, Pearl 905). [OE. *myl.*]

Mold(e), *n.* earth, in tag *(ap)on mold(e)*, on earth, alive, XIV *b* 3, XVI 1, 91, XVII 62. [OE. *mōlde.*]

Mon. *See* Man(e).

Mon(e), *n.* complaint, lamentation, grief, II 198, VI 14, VIII *a* 117, XIV *a* 27. [OE. **mān*, rel. to Mene, *v.*[2]]

Mone, *n.* moon, XV *b* 16, 25, XVII 355 ; Moyne, XVII 6 ; lunar month, 478 ; *abouen þe m.*, to the skies, ridiculously high, XI *b* 182. [OE. *mōna.*]

Moneday, *n.* Monday, XIII *a* 29. [OE. *mōnan-dæg.*]

Mong, *prep.* among, VII 120. [Shortened from Amonge, *q. v.*]

Moni, -y. *See* Mani.

Moniales, *n. pl.* nuns, VIII *b* 80. [Med.L. *moniālis.*]

Monk(e), *n.* monk, V 40, VIII *a* 322, *b* 80. [OE. *munuc.*]

Monthe, *n.* month, VIII *b* 52, XII *a* 34, &c. ; *pl.* (orig. *gen.*) in *tuo monthe day*, two months' time, XII *a* 29 (*see* Day). [OE. *mōn(a)þ.*] *See* Tweluemonth(e).

Moo ; Moost. *See* Mo ; Mor(e).

Mor, *n.* moor, V 12, XV *e* 1, &c. [OE. *mōr.*]

More, *adj. compar.* greater, V 32, IX 28, 245, &c. ; more, further, &c. (easily passing into *adv.*, as XIV *b* 3, &c.), II 264, V 180, XVI 106, &c. ; *quasi-sb.* a greater amount, more, VI 193, 217, 240 (*see* Longe *adv.*), &c. ; *more and les(se)*, les and more, all, XVI 383, XVII 11, 94 ; *more and myn*, all, XVII 112, 278 (*see* Myn). Mast, *superl.* greatest, most, X 18, 38, 104 ; Most(e), XI *b* 25, XIV *c* 15, XVI 360 ; *both the m. and the leest*, all, XVII 452 ; *þe most*, (the) most (part), I 23. [OE. *māra*, *mǣst* (late Nth. *māst*, with vowel of compar.).] *See* Mekill, &c.

Mor(e), Mare (IV, XIV), *adv. compar.* more, VI 193, &c.; forming *compar.*, VI 239, IX 248, XII *b* 130, &c.; longer, further, in the future, again, &c. (*esp.* in *no more, na mare,* &c.), I 83, 144, IV *a* 58, XIV *b* 3 (or *adj.*), &c.; moreover, VI 205; *no3t . . . more,* not . . . either, VI 228; *no more bot,* none the more except that, V 243. Mast (IV), Moost, Most(e), *superl.* most(ly), for the most part, II 12, 33 (*see* Ony), IV *a* 77, VII 10, XI *a* 20, &c.; forming *superl.,* IX 42, &c. [As prec.; for older compar. adv. *see* Mo.] *See* Mekill, &c.; Nomore.

Moreyn, *n.* plague; *þe furste moreyn,* the Black Death (1349), XIII *b* 26. [OFr. *morine.*]

Morn(e), *n.* morning, morrow, I 137, V 282. [OE. *morne* dat. sg.] *See* Morwe.

Mornyf, *adj.* mournful, VI 26. [Stem of Mournen + OFr. *-if*; cf. OFr. *morni.*]

Mornyng, *n.* morning, XVII 498. [From Morne.]

Mornynge. *See* Mournen.

Morter, *n.* mortar, VIII *a* 136. [OFr. *mortier.*]

Morthereres, *n. pl.* murderers, VIII *a* 268. [Cf. OE. *myrþra,* OFr. *mordreour.*]

Morwe, Morow, *n.* morning, morrow, VIII *a* 140, XII *a* 152, *b* 176, &c.; *fram m. til euen,* all day, VIII *a* 178, (reversed for rime) XVII 205. [OE. *morgen.*] *See* Morn(e).

Most(e), &c. *See* Mor(e), and next.

Mot(e), *v.* may, II 532, V 52, XI *b* 115, XIV *c* 87, &c.; must, II 125, 248, VIII *a* 284, XI *a* 38, &c.; Most (*to*), 2 *sg. pres.* must go (to), XV *g* 3; Most(e), *pa. t.* might, II 233, 330; must, is (was) bound to, II 468, IX 197, 287, XI *b* 205; Must(e), XVI 274, XVII 130 (2 *sg.*); *impers.* in *must vs,* we must, XVII 292, 334. [OE. *mōt,* pa. t. *mōste.*]

Mote, *n.* a whit, V 141. [OE. *mot.*]

Mote, *v.* to argue, XVI 256 (*see* note). [OE. *mōtian.*]

Mournen, *v.* to mourn, XV *c* 34; Mournyng, *n.* mourning, sorrow, IV *a* 72; Murning, XIV *b* 2; Mornynge, XI *b* 118, 125, 130, &c. [OE. *múrnan.*]

Moun. *See* Mai, *v.*

Mountayne, *n.* mountain, IX 161, 162, &c. [OFr. *muntai(g)ne.*]

Mounte3, *n. pl.* hills, V 12. [OE. *munt*; OFr. *munt.*]

Mo.thed, *pa. t.* uttered, VIII *a* 234. [From next.]

Mouþe, *n.* (*dat. sg.*) mouth, II 465; *be mouthe,* by word of m., XII *b* 199. [OE. *múþ.*]

Mowe. *See* Mai, *v.*

Mowe(n), *v.*[1] to mow, VIII *b* 14 (first). [OE. *māwan.*]

Mowe(n), *v.*[2] to stack (in mows), VIII *b* 14 (second). [OE. *múga, múwa,* a mow, heap.]

Mowres, *n. pl.* Moors, IX 5. [OFr. *Maure, More.*]

M·roh(e). *See* Moche(l).

Muged, *pa. t.* drizzled, was damp, V 12. [Cf. Norw. *mugga,* drizzle, and *Mug*[4] in *E.D.D.*]

Muk, Mukke, *n.* dung, VIII *a* 136, XVII 62. [Cf. ON. *myki.*]

Mullere, *n.* Miller, XIV *d* 3, 9. [OE. **mylnere.*]

Mulne, *n.* mill, V 135. [OE. *mylen.*]

Multiplye(n), *v.* to multiply, increase; *trans.* III 1, VIII *a* 120, 323; *intr.* IX 60, XVII 31, 179. [OFr. *multiplier.*]

Multitude, *n.* multitude, XI *b* 228. [OFr. *multitude.*]

Mun, *v. auxil.* will (*fut.*), XIV *b* 2. [ON. *munu.*]

Munt. *See* Mynt(e).

Murgeþ, *pres. pl.* gladden, XV *b* 20 (*see* Miles). [OE. (*ā-*)*myrgian.*] *See* Miri(e).

Muryly. *See* Miri(e).

Murning. *See* Mournen.

Mused, *pa. t.* mused; existed, were, V 356 (characteristic

action of '*homo rationalis*' standing for verb 'to be'; cf. *flaʒe*, VI 71). [OFr. *muser*.]

Muster, -ir, *v.* to show, manifest, XVI 86, 104, 174. [OFr. *moustrer*.]

Na. *See* No, Non(e).

Nabbe, I *sg. pres. ind.* have not, XV *f* 8, 11 ; **Nade,** *pa. t.* had not (with another neg.), II 392. [OE. *nabban*, *næfde*.] *See* Habbe, Ne.

Nacion, *n.* race, nation, XIII *b* 4, 17. [OFr. *nacion*.]

Naʒt, *n.* night ; *be naʒt*, by night, by the time night has come, VI 163. [OE. *næht*.] *See* Nyght.

Naʒt, nothing (with neg. adv.), III 18; Naʒt, Nauʒte, *adv.* not, VIII *a* 43; (with neg. verb) III 42. [OE. *nā-wiht, nā(u)ht*. *See* Nat, Noʒt.

Nay(e), *adv.* nay, II 131, III 26, XVI 335, &c.; as sb., in *withoutten nay*, undeniably, XVII 2 (*cf.* No). [ON. *nei*.]

Nail(e), Nayle, Naill(e), Nayll, *n.* nail, XVII 119, 273, 277; finger-nail, I 164, 236, II 106, VIII *a* 62. [OE. *nægel*.] *See* Naule.

Nayled, *pp.* nailed, IV *a* 86. [OE. *nægl(i)an*.]

Nale; *atte nale* = *atten ale*, at the ale, over their ale, VIII *a* 109. [OE. *alu*.] *See* Atte.

Nam, I *sg. pres. ind.* am not; *nam bot*, am only, II 430. [OE. *nam*.] *See* Ne.

Nam. *See* Mnam, Nyme.

Name, *n.* name, I 37, VII 60, XV *i* 10, &c.; good name, praise, XI *b* 257; Nome, VII *introd.*; *be name* (*nome*), by name, individually, I *introd.*, 46, VII 37; *by name*, especially, XVI 190; *bi Godes name* (oath), II 316. [OE. *nama, noma*.]

Nameles, *adj.* (as a name) Nameless, Nobody, XIV *d* 2. [OE. *nama + -lēas*.]

Namely, -liche, *adv.* namely, especially, I 264, VIII *a* 55, XI *b* 253. [OE. *nama + -līce*.]

Namore ; Nane. *See* Nomore; Non(e), *pron.*

Nar(e), *pres. ind. pl.* are not (with neg.), II 390, V 24. [OE. *naron*.] *See* Ne.

Narwe, *adj.* narrow, mean (dwelling), II 483. [OE. *nearu*.]

Nas, Nes (III), *pa. t. sg.* (usually with neg.) was not, II 98, 150, 354, III 42, XV *g* 28; **Nere,** *pl.* II 123; *subj.* would be, II 457. [OE. *næs* (Kt. *nes*); *næron, nære*.]

Nat, *neg. adv.* not, I 12, 97, 132, VIII *b* 93. [Reduced form of Naʒt, *q.v.*]

Natheles. *See* Noþeles.

Nature, *n.* nature, XII *a* 113. [OFr. *nature*.]

Nauʒte. *See* Naʒt.

Nauʒty, *adj.* (worth nought), penniless, VIII *a* 218. [Cf. OE. *næht-lic*.] *See* Naʒt.

Nauy, *n.* navy, VII 111, 143. [OFr. *navie*.]

Naule, *n.* finger-nail, VI 99. [ON. *nagl*, or OE. *nægl*, **naglas*.] *See* Naile.

Nauþer, Nawþer, V, VI; **Noþer,** I, VIII, XIII; **Nouþer,** -ur, XIV *c*; **Nowder,** XVII; **Nowþer, Nowther,** XIV *b*; **Nowthir,** XVI; *adv.* neither, either (after a neg.), V 299; *conj.* neither (foll. by *ne, nor*), I 118, V 206, XIV *b* 75, 78, *c* 57, 62, XVI 287, XVII 534, &c.; (foll. by *then*) XVII 535; nor, XIII *a* 13, 37. [OE. *nā-hwæþer, nō-hwæþer, nā(w)þor, nōþer*, &c.] *See* Neyther, Noiþer.

Nawhere. *See* Nowhar(e).

Ne, *adv.* not (preceding verb), I 73, V 74, VIII *a* 138, 172, &c.; (usually with another neg., esp. *noʒt*, &c.), I 71, 156, III 18, VI 2, &c.; coalescing with auxil. verbs, *see* Nabbe, Nam, Nar(e), Nas, Nil, Nis, Not; *conj.* nor, I 118, 160, IV *a* 2, &c.; *ne ... ne*, neither ... nor, nor ... nor,

I 158, IX 201; (foll. by another neg.) and, I 12, 153, VIII *a* 280, IX 181, &c. [OE. *ne.*]

Nede, Neid (x), *n.* need, IV *b* 67, X 18, XI *b* 259, XVII 426; *at nede*, in time of need, VIII *a* 113; *pl.* wants, business, V 148. [OE. *nēd.*]

Nedes, *adv.* needs, of necessity, II 468, IX 288, XI *b* 205. [OE. *nēdes.*]

Nedeth, Nudeþ, *pres.* (*impers.*) *sg.* (it) is necessary, VIII *a* 240, *b* 20; *hem nedeth*, they have need, VIII *a* 203; *Neyd*, with mixed constr. in *neyd thowe*, you need, XVI 242. [OE. *nēodian*; *cf.* next.]

Nedid, *pa. t.* compelled, XI *b* 75; *pp.* XI *b* 9, 35. [OE. *nēdan.*]

Nedeful(l), Nedfull, *adj.* necessary, IX 113, 131, XI *a* 51. [OE. *nēd + -ful.*]

Nedy, *adj.* needy, in want, VIII *a* 15, 218; as jocular name, XVII 405. [OE. *nēadig-*, **nēdig.*]

Nedle, *n.* needle (of compass), IX 124, &c. [OE. *nēdl.*]

Nee. See Ny3.

Negh (*nere*), *v. intr.* to approach, XVI 224; **Nyghys,** 3 *sg. pres.* XVII 370; **Neighed,** *pa. t.* VIII *a* 294. [From Ny3, *q.v.*]

Neid; Neyd; Nei3e; Neir. See Nede; Nedeth; Ny3; Ner(e).

Neyther, Neiþer, *adv.*; *ne neyther*, and neither, VIII *a* 276; *neiþer . . . ne*, neither . . . nor, XI *b* 190, 286. [OE. *ne + ǣgþer*; cf. *nāhwæþer.*] See Nauþer, Noiþer.

Nek, *n.* neck, V 187, 242. [OE. *hnecca.*]

Neltow. See Nil.

Nemeled, *pp.* named, mentioned, XV *i* 10. [OE. *nemnan*, with *mn > ml.*]

Nempned, *pa. t.* named, II 600. [OE. *nemnan.*] See Neuen(e).

Ner(e), Neir (x), *compar. adj.* and *adv.* nearer, I 255; as *pos.*, near, X 77, XII *b* 114, XVI 43, 224, XVII 370; *adv.* nearly,

VIII *a* 171, XVII 412; *prep.* near (to), VI 44, VIII *a* 294, X 67; **Nest,** *superl.* next, I 215; **Next(e),** nearest, VII 13; next, I 138, &c. [OE. *nēar(a)*, compar. (cf. ON. *nær*, compar. and pos.); *nēst(a)*, *nēxt(a).*] See Ny3.

Nere, Nes. See Nas.

Nesch, *adj.*; *quasi-sb.* (what is) soft, pleasant, VI 246. [OE. *hnesce.*]

Nest. See Ner(e).

Nest(e), *n.* nest, IV *b* 36, IX 252, XIII *a* 22. [OE. *nest.*]

Neuen(e), *v.* to name, mention, I *introd.*, XVII 12. [ON. *nefna.*]

Neuer(e), *adv.* never, I 152, VIII *a* 23 &c.; not at all, I *introd.*, XVII 313; *neuer sa, so*, no matter how, IV *a* 75, V 61, VI 211; *neuer þe lesse*, nevertheless, I 71. [OE. *nǣfre.*]

New(e), Nw(e) (V, VI), *adj.* new, II 217, V 176, 332, VI 167, VIII *a* 294, &c.; *quasi-sb.* IX 275; *na new*, no new thing, IV *a* 42; *for new*, in exchange for new (ones), VII 13; *adv.* anew, II 593; newly, V 155; *now newe* (OE. *nū nīowan*), just lately, XVI 314. [OE. *nīowe.*]

Next; Nye. See Ner(e); Noy(e).

Nyghys. See Negh.

Nyght, Ni3t, Ny3t; Nycht (x); **Nyht** (XII); *n.* night, I 29, II 370, VII 127, X 197, XII *a* 68, &c.; *be ny3t, nyhte* (dat.), at night, XII *a* 117, 131, XV *i* 15; *on nyght*, at night, XV *h* 22; *see* next. [OE. *niht.*] See Na3t.

Nyghtes, Nihtes, Nytes (xv), *adv.* at, by, night, XV *c* 21; with prep., *a nyghtes, be nytes*, VIII *b* 16, XV *i* 20. [OE. *nihtes.*]

Nyght-rest, *n.* rest at night, IV *a* 83. [OE. *niht + rest.*] See Ryste.

Nygromansye, *n.* necromancy, black magic; (used vaguely as) impious nonsense, XI *a* 5. [OFr. *nigromanc(i)e.*]

Ny3, Nyh, Nee (IV), **Nei3e** (II), *adv.* nigh, at hand, close (by), XII *a* 155, *b* 13, XIII *a* 52, *b* 61; *nyh aboute*, near at hand, XII *a* 74; almost, II 199; *prep.* near (to), IV *a* 11 (note), XII *b* 29. [OE. *nē(a)h*.] *See* Ner(e), Welne3.

Ny3t-olde, *adj.* kept over night, a day old, VIII *a* 303. [OE. *niht-dld*.]

Nyhte, *v.* to become night, grow dark, XII *b* 19. [From Nyght, *n.*]

Nyhtegales, *n. pl.* nightingales, XV *b* 5. [OE. *nihtegale*.]

Nil, 1, 3 *sg. pres. ind.* will not (usually with another neg.) II 211, 332, 338; **Nul**, XV *g* 20; **Neltow** (nelt + þow), 2 *sg.* VIII *a* 149; **Nule**, *pl.* XV *g* 25; **Nold(e)**, *pa. t.* would not, was unwilling to, II 140, 280, V 163, VIII *a* 232; *subj.* V 82; *wold ich nold ich*, whether I would or not, willy nilly, II 154. [OE. *nyllan, nellan*; *nōlde*.] *See* Ne.

Nym(e), *v.* to take, catch, seize; receive; take one's way, go (*cf. haþ þe way ynome*, II 477); VIII *a* 43; *nyme to þyseluen*, take upon yourself, be responsible for, V 73; **Nymmeth**, *imper. pl.* VIII *a* 15; **Nam**, *pa. t. sg.* I 76, II 154, XII *b* 84, 156; **Nom**, III 53; XII *b* 182; **Nom(e)**, *pl.* I 233, II 92, 287, VI 227; **Ynome**, *pp.* II 182, 193, 403, 477, 565 (note). [OE. *niman*.] *See* Vndernome.

Nyne, *adj.* nine, XIII *b* 33. [OE. *nigon*.]

Nis, Nys, 3 *sg. pres. ind.* is not (usually with another neg.), II 131, 306, 552, XII *b* 118, XIV *c* 27, XV *c* 25. [OE. *nis*.] *See* Ne.

Nist; Nytes. *See* Not, *v.*; Nyghtes.

No, Na (IV), *adj.* no, none, (with neg.) any, I 11, 156, IV *a* 16, 36, 4² (*see* Newe), &c.; **Non(e)** (before *h* or vowel, or sep. from noun) I 15, 160, II 354, 392,

v 38, VIII *a* 54, IX 182, &c.; *na* (*no*) *kyn*, *see* Kyn, þinge; *non oþer*, nothing different, *see* Oþer(e); *na thyng*, *no þing*, *see* þinge; **Nones**, *gen. sg.* in *n. cunnes*, *see* Kyn. [OE. *nān*.] *See* Non(e), *pron.*

No, Na, *adv.* not, no, I 79, II 84, IV *a* 58, &c.; *see* Mor(e), No-more. Used in II as equivalent of Ne (*q.v.*); *adv.* not, II 84, 147, 225, &c.; *conj.* nor, and (with neg.), II 140, 150, &c.; *no ... no*, neither ... nor, II 229. As *sb.* in *wiþouten no*, undeniably, II 50 (*cf.* Nay). [OE. *nā*.]

Noble, Nobel, -ill, -ull, *adj.* noble, excellent, II 48, VII 5, 49, XIII *b* 67, XIV *b* 65, *c* 18, XVII 128, 276, &c. [OFr. *noble*.]

Nobleie, *n.* splendour; *fame and n. of þe world*, ? reputation for splendour among men, XI *b* 235. [OFr. *nobleie*.]

Noblesse, *n.* nobility, in *youre ... noblesse* as form of address, IX 270. [OFr. *noblesse*.]

Nobot, *conj.* only, V 114. [OE. *nā* + *būtan*.]

No3t, Noght(e), Noth (XV *f*), **Nou3t(e), Nouht, Nout**, &c., and reduced **Not**, *adv.* not at all, not, I 64, 86, II 22, 73, 348, IV *b* 2, VIII *a* 46, *b* 94, XV *f* 7 (*see* App. p. 278), &c.; (with further neg.) I 15, II 306, 336, IX 196, &c. [OE. *nā-(wi)ht*, *nō-(wi)ht*.] *See* Na3t.

No3t, Noght(e), Nocht, Nou3t(e), *n.* nothing, VIII *a* 142, 241, X *introd.*, XI *a* 4, XVII 96, 287; (with addit. neg.), VI 160; *for no3t*, to no purpose, I 183, XIV *b* 55; no good, in *nou3t nis* (*nere*), is (would be) impossible, II 131, 457 (*cf.* OE. *nāht*, worthless). [As prec.]

Noy(e), Nuy, Nye (V), *n.* harm, distress, V 73, VII 149, XIII *a* 49; *noy for to here*, grievous to hear (*cf.* Pine, Reuþe), VII 133 [Shortened from OFr. *anoi*, *anui*; with Nye compare Byled, Strye.]

Noye, *v.* to do harm, XIII *a* 36. [Shortened from OFr. *anoier*.]

Noys(e), Noise, *n.* noise, I 75, VII 133, XV *h* 3, &c. [OFr. *noise*.]

Noise, *v. intr.* to make a noise, XII *a* 78 (note). [From prec.]

Noiþer, *pron.* neither, II 324; *conj.* in *noiþer . . . no*, neither . . . nor, II 346. [Nauþer, Noþer infl. by Neyþer.]

Nolde. *See* Nil.

Noman, *n.* nobody, XII *a* 67, *b* 8, &c. [OE. *nān + mann*.]

Nombre, Nowmber, *n.* number, VII 86, IX 195. [OFr. *numbre, nombre*.]

Nom(e). *See* Name, Nym(e).

Nomore, *n.* nothing more, VIII *a* 90; Namore, VIII *a* 140. [OE. *nā + māre*, neut.] *See* Mor(e).

Non(e), Nane (IV, X), *pron.* none, not one, I 197, V 101, X 143, XII *b* 13, XIII *a* 23, &c.; no one, (with neg.) any one; I 153, II 423, IV *a* 13, V 36, VI 83, X 130, &c. [OE. *nān*.] *See* No, *adj.*

None, Noyne (X), Noon, *n.* noon, mid-day hour, II 372, VII 129, X 67, XIII *a* 28, XVII 317, &c.; Nones, *pl.* mid-day meal, VIII *a* 139. [OE. *nōn*, L. *nōna* (*hōra*).]

Nonetide, *n.* noontide, II 497. [OE. *nōn-tīd*.]

Nones; *for þe nones*, for the nonce (practically meaningless tag), II 53, XII *a* 83. [For *for þen ones* (OE. **for þam ānum* + adv. *-es*) as regards that particular thing, occasion, &c.]

Norysscht, *pp.* nourished, IX 59. [OFr. *norrir, norriss-*.]

Normans, *n. pl.* Normans, XIII *b* 13, 20. [OFr. *Normant*, pl. *Normans*.]

Norþ, *n.* and *adj.* north, XIII *b* 53, 64, XVII 477, &c. [OE. *norþ*, adv.; *norþ-*.]

Norþeron, *adj.* northern, XIII *b* 10, 56. [OE. *norþerne*.]

Northumbres, *n. pl.* Northumbrians, XIII *b* 58. [Cf. OE. *Norþ-hymbre*.]

Not, I *sg. pres. ind.* know not, XII *b* 164, XIV *c* 110; Nist, *pa. t.* (with neg.) knew not, II 288, 296, 494. [OE. *nāt, nyste*.] *See* Ne, Wite(n).

Note, *adj.* ? useful, required; desired, V 24. [? Rel. to next.]

Note, *n.*[1] affair, business, XVI 268 (with pl. vb.), XVII 264; ado, XVII 368. [OE. *notu*.]

Note, *n.*[2] (musical) note, II 438, XI *b* 162, &c.; tune, II 602, XV *a* 11. [OFr. *note*, L. *nota*.] *See* Countre note.

Note, *n.*[3] nut, IX 157 (note). [OE. *hnutu*.]

Notemuges, *n. pl.* nutmegs, IX 157. [Prec. + OFr. *mug(u)e*, musk; *cf.* OFr. *nois mug(u)ede*, &c.]

Noth. *See* Noȝt, *adv.*

Notwiþstondinge, *prep.* in spite of, XI *a* 25. [Noȝt + *pres. p.* of ME. *wiþstonden*, OE. *wiþstándan*.]

Noþeles, *adv.* all the same, nevertheless, XIII *a* 6, *b* 3, &c.; Natheles, IX 51, XII *a* 130, &c. [OE. *nā-þe-lǣs*.]

Noþer, *adj.* no other; (*no*) *no noþer*, nor any other, II 230. [OE. *nān + ōþer*.]

Noþer; Noþynk. *See* Nauþer; þing(e).

Nouelrie, *n.* newfangledness, new invention, XI *b* 124, 164, 169, 200, 206, 210, 215. [OFr. *novelrie*.]

Novels, *n. pl.* news, something new, XVII 508. [OFr. *novel(l)e*.]

Nouȝt(e), Nou(h)t. *See* Noȝt.

Nouþe, Nouthe, *adv.* just now, II 466; at present, VIII *a* 199. [OE. *nū-þā*.] *See* Now(e).

Nouþer, -ur. *See* Nauþer.

Now(e), Nou, *adv.* now, I 128, IV *b* 43, XI *a* 21, &c.; *oþer now oþer neuer*, now or never, V 148;

see Late, New(ə); *conj.* since, now that, v 352, VI 29; *now ... now*, now that, VI 17. [OE. *nū.*]

Nowder. *See* Nauþer.

Nowhar(e), -where, Nawhere (VI), *adv.* nowhere, v 96, VI 174, XIII *a* 17; in no case, not at all, v 186. [OE. *nā-hwǣr.*] *See* Whar(e).

Nowmber; Nowþer, &c. *See* Nombre; Nauþer.

Nudeþ; Nuy; Nul(e); Nw(e). *See* Nedeth; Noy(e); Nil; New(e).

O. *See* Of, On, On(e).

Obediand, *adj.* obedient, XVII 121. [OFr. *obedient* with substitution of pres. p. -*and*.]

Obediencer, *n.* an obedientiary, one owning obedience (to a monastery, &c.); an administrative officer of a religious house, VIII *b* 95. [OFr. *obediencier*.]

Obitte, *adj.* dead, XVI 269. [Nonce-use of L. *obitus*, deceased.]

Obout. *See* Aboute(n).

Occean, *n.* Ocean (as name of Indian Ocean), IX 9. [OFr. *occean*.]

Occupacio(u)n, *n.* occupation, employment, XI *b* 156, 251, 288, &c. [OFr. *occupacion*.]

Occupied (*aboute, in*), *pp.* occupied (with, in), XI *b* 114, 218, 242, 262. [OFr. *occuper*, altered on anal. of verbs in -*fier*, -*plier*, &c.]

Od, *adj.* odd, (some) over, XVII 57. [ON. *odda-*, in *odda-maðr*; see *N.E.D.*, s.v. *Odd*.]

Oder. *See* Oþer(e), *adj.*

Of, Offe, *adv.* off, v 181, 340; of, out of, from (after *þat* relative), VI 65, IX 135, 282, &c.; (with infin.) IX 257, 282, &c.; *of the whiche ... offe, see* next. [OE. *of*.] *See* Her(e), þar(e), þer(e).

Of, Off, VII 5; O, II 12, 283, VI 69, VII 18; *prep.* of. (i) From, off,

out of, II 29, III 4, 36, v 131, 153, 179, VI 247, VII 169, VIII *a* 204, &c.; out of, (made) of, in, II 4, 362, IX 115, XVII 119, &c. (ii) By, III 18, IV *b* 5, v 99, IX 55, XI *b* 31, 204, &c.; by (means of), with, II 364, IX 65, &c. (iii) Of, about, concerning, I 160, II 5, 12, III 3, VIII *a* 197, IX 147, XI *b* 1, 295, &c. (iv) *Forming equiv. of gen.*: as *possess.*, I 34, 216, &c.; *adjectival*, II 3, IV *b* 34, &c. (*see* the nouns); in, as regards, &c., v 170, VI 71, VII 18, 38, 164 (first), VIII *a* 52, XII *a* 9, XVI 129, XVII 543, &c.; *of breed*, &c., in breadth, &c., XVII 123, 125, 259, 520; (introd. actual measurement), IX 155, XVII 126; *objective gen.*, at, for, on acc. of, &c., II 471, 573, VIII *a* 38, 117, XI *b* 10 (first), XII *a* 144, &c.; *grame . . . of*, wrath against, XVII 90; *partitive*, of, among, in, VII 43 (*see* Oþere), VIII *a* 259, IX 182, XI *a* 39, XVI 388 (*cf.* note to II 388); after Fr. idiom, IX 158, 227, 275, XII *a* 66; *see* Ony, Oþer(e), Owen; *adverbial* (of *time*), for VIII *a* 253; in, XI *b* 136. *Of the whiche ... offe, of whom ... from*, of which, from whom (mixed E. and Fr. constr.), IX 25, 77; *of preiere of holy lif* (XI *b* 83), *see* Vnderstonden; for other idiomatic uses see the nouns, &c., concerned. [OE. *of*.]

Offend, *v.* to offend, XVII 108. [OFr. *of(f)endre*.]

Office, *n.* duty, XI *b* 18, 21, 47, 60; *houses of offyce*, quarters, stables (orig. places set apart for menial duties), XVII 134. [OFr. *office*.]

Offringis, *n. pl.* offerings, offertories, XI *b* 300. [OE. *offring*.]

Of-hild, *pa. t. sg.* withheld, III 10. [OE. *of-hęaldan*, pa. t. -*hēold*.]

Of-sende, *v.* to send for, II 428. [OE. *of-séndan*.] *See* Assent.

Oft, Ofte(n), *adv.* often, II 1, 197,

III 39, &c.; *ofte(n) tyme(s)*, IX
61, 129, XVI 370. [OE. *oft.*]

Oftesithes, Oft(e)**sythes**, *adv.*
often, IV *b* 27, VII 182, IX 63.
[OE. *on oft-siþas.*] *See* Sithes.

Oghne. *See* Owen(e).

Oght(e), O3t, **Ought**, Ou3t, *pron.*
anything, IV *b* 45, V 147, XII *b*
99, 107, XVI 100; *adv.* in any
way, at all, XIV *c* 69. [OE.
ō(wi)ht.]

Oghte. *See* Owe.

O3ain; O3e; O3ene. *See* A3ayn;
Owe, *v.*; Owen(e).

Oyl(l)e, *n.* oil, IX 35; *fig.* XVII
46. [OFr. *oile.*]

Ok, *n.* oak, XIV *c* 57. [OE. *āc.*]

Old(e), **Alde**, *adj.* old, V 114,
VII 5, XII introd. (*see* Dai),
&c.; as *sb.*, in *old or 3ong*, *3ong
and alde*, any one, every one, II
221, IV *a* 49; *of olde*, of old, VII
26, 182. [OE. *ǎld.*]

Olif-tre, *n.* olive-tree, XVII 510.
[OFr. *olive*+Tre.]

On, *adv.* on, II 343 (*see* Do);
(still) V 232; (with *infin.* or *relative*), upon, at, in, I 89, II 367,
VII 15, XV *f* 9, 10, XVI 179.
[OE. *on.*] *See* þer(e).

On; **O**, VII 106, IX 250, XV *a* 5,
g 28; *prep.* on. (i) On, upon,
I 92, 194, II 303, XV *c* 24 (following pron.), &c.; *on him sei3e*,
saw he had, II 325; *on my frenship*, as you value my f., XVII
362. (ii) At, V 112 (first), XV *c*
15, *h* 3, 22, XVII 137, &c.;
(iii) In, I 99, XIV *b* 79, XV *a* 5,
XVII 422, &c.; *see* Bodi, Lyte,
Lud, &c.; after 'believe', I 89,
VI 65; with *manere*, *wise*, I 80,
V 124, VII 65, 77, XI *a* 11, XIV *b*
95, &c.; (reference) II 455,
XV *c* 13, &c.; *on Englyssh
tunge*, into English, I introd.
(iv) Of (after 'think') I 221, &c.
(v) A, in *on a day*, a day, VI 150
(OE. *on dæg*). (vi) A-, on (in
adv. expressions), as *on haukin*,
a- hawking, II 308; *see* Behalue,
Fote, Lofte, Slep, &c. [OE. *on.*]
See A-; A(n), *prep.*; Vpon.

Onderuonge, *pp.* received, III 28.
[OE. *under-fōn*, pp. *under-
fángen.*] *See* Fonge.

On(e); Oon(e), XI *a* 41, XVII 2,
&c.; Oo, I 180, 231; O, I 49,
&c.; *adj.* one, a single, II 306,
V 83, VI 170, IX 17, XI *a* 45,
XIII *b* 45, XIV *d* 8, XVII 136, &c.;
one (and the same), I 49, 231,
II 95 (*see* Cri); one (indivisible),
VII 2, IX 334, XVII 2, 169; one
(as opposed to 'other'), I 180,
IX 180, &c. (*see* þe, Ton); *o*, a
certain, II 308; *oone or two*,
one or two, some, XVII 133, 484;
quasi-sb. in *into one*, together,
XV *i* 6; *at on*, at one, in harmony, VI 18; *al oon*, (all) one
and the same thing, XI *a* 41.
[OE. *ān.*] *See* A(n), Ane,
One.

On(e), *pron.* one (thing *or* person),
V 348, VI 197, IX 24, XI *b* 223,
XIII *a* 24, XV *b* 23, 34, &c.;
Oone, XVII 209; Onen, *dat. sg.*
III 4; one (opposed to 'another'), IX 53, XIII *b* 16; *boþe
þat on and þat oþer*, both, V 344;
see þe, Ton; (some) one, a certain person, V 149, VII 54 (with
name). [As prec.]

One, *adj.* alone, only, V 6, VIII *b*
54, XIV *b* 61; strengthened with
al, V 87, XII *a* 131, *b* 15; *a . . .
one*, one . . . only, V 181, 277;
oure one, by ourselves, V 177
(note); *let . . . one*, leave alone,
avoid (*cf.* OE. *ān-forlǣtan*),
V 50. [OE. *āna.*]

Onehed, *n.* unity, *or* ! simplicity;
onehed of wit, the uniformity of
men's understanding (interpretation) of the Bible, *or* ! the ease
of understanding it, XI *a* 32.
[OE. *ān* + *-hēdu.*]

Onely, *adj.* in *onely alepy*, a single
solitary, I 159; Oon(e)**ly**, *adv.*
only, XVII 288, 307. [OE.
ān-lic, adj.] *See* Anely.

Ones, One3 (V), Onys (XVII),
adv. once, on a single occasion,
I 182, II 122, V 212, XII *b* 92;
formerly, V 150, VIII *a* 202; at

some (future) time or other, XVII
207, 389. [OE. *ānes*.]

Onest, *adj* trustworthy, VII 48.
[OFr. *honeste*.]

Ony, *adj.* any, IX 85, 245, XI *b*
300, &c.; *most of ony þing*,
above all things, more than anything, II 33; *pron.* any, IX 326,
XI *b* 147. [OE. *ǣnig*, infl. by
ān.] See Ani, Eny.

Onone. *See* Anon(e).

Oo, *adv.* ever, continually, XV *b* 7.
[OE. *ā.*]

Oo, Oon(e), &c. *See* On(e), &c.

Oostré, *n.* inn, lodging, XVII 329.
[OFr. *host(e)rie*.]

Opan, Opon. *See* Vpon.

Opyn, Open, *adj.* open, V 2,
XVII 344; manifest, XI *b* 42.
Opynly, *adv.* manifestly, XI *b*
52; publicly, XI *b* 62. [OE.
open, *open-līce.*]

Opynne, Oppen, *v.* to open, XVI
122, 194. [OE. *openian.*]

Oplondysch. *See* Vplondysch.

Or, *conj.*¹ or, I 1, &c.; *or . . . or*,
either . . . or, VIII *a* 244. [Re-
duced form of Oþer, *conj.*]

Or, *conj.*² before, ere (usually with
subj.), VIII *a* 79, X 2, XVI 154
(*see* Ware, *adj.*) 156, 278, XVII
110 (*see* Blyn), 153, 263, &c.;
(postponed) XVII 130; lest,
XIV *d* 11. [*See* next.]

Or, *prep.* before, ere, XVI 224,
XVII 317, 481. [?OE. *ǣr*, pos.
and compar. (once late Nth. *ar*)
infl. by ON. *ár*, pos.] *See*
Ar(e), Er(e).

Orchard, *n.* garden, orchard, II 166,
91, 163; Orchard-side, II 134.
[OE. *ort-geard*, *orceard*.]

Ordayn(e), Ordainy, *v.* to decree, establish, appoint, direct,
arrange, contrive, fashion, &c.,
II 205, XVII 309; Ordand,
XVII 119, 468; Ordeigne, XII *b*
216; Ordeyn(e), I 55, 148,
VIII *b* 57, XI *b* 125, 132, &c.;
Ordand, Ordanit, *pa. t.* X 11,
34, XVI 25, 226; *ordaynede to*,
destined to, IV *b* 54. [OFr.
ordener, 3 sg. *ordei(g)ne*, *-aine*.]

Ordynal(e), -alle, *n.* a book
setting out the order and manner
of church services and ceremonies,
XI *b* 1, 183, 186. [Med.L. *or-
dināle.*]

Ordenaunse, Ordynaunce, *n.*
ordinance, decree, law, XI *a* 15,
b 100, &c.; *preie oure . . . or-
dynàunce*, say the prayers we
have appointed, XI *b* 38. [OFr.
ordenance.]

Ordre, Order, -yre, *n.* order,
rank, VIII *a* 159, XI *b* 20; *pl.*
religious orders, XI *a* 61; the
(nine) orders of angels, XVII 10;
moderation, in *holde þe ordyre
of*, keep the rule of, observe
moderation in, IV *b* 22. [OFr.
ordre.]

Orgon, *n.* diaphony; singing in
two parts, XI *b* 138 (note). [OE.
organ, song, from L. *organum.*]

Orysun, *n.* praying; *yn orysun*,
at prayer, I 17. [OFr. *oreisoun.*]

Oritore, *n.* oratory, chapel, V 122.
[OFr. *oratour*, infl. by prec.]

Orpedly, actively, V 164. [OE.
orped-līce.]

Ost, Host, *n.* (armed) host, army,
II 290, X 43, 45; multitude,
XIII *a* 32. [OFr. (*h*)*ost*, army.]

Oþeȝ, Othes, *n. pl.* oaths, V 55,
XII *b* 44. [OE. *āþ.*]

Oþer(e), Other(e), -ir(e), -yre;
Oder, XVII 160; Ouþer, I, (i)
Adj., other, another, other kinds
of, I 18, 258, IV *b* 16, 45, V 274,
IX 227, XII *b* 170, XVII 298 (*see*
Garn), &c.; Othre, *pl.* XII *a* 82,
136; *many oþer folde*, see Folde;
othere gude, some other good
(thing), IV *b* 9; *oþer mani*, many
other, II 496; *þat oþer*, see þe;
þis othir daye, the other day,
XVI 148. (ii) *Pron. sg.* another,
some one (something) else, the
other, I 101, II 324, VI 89, X 22
(*see* Aither), &c.; Opereȝ, *gen.
sg.* VI 90; *ichon other*, each man
to his neighbour, XVII 112;
non other, nothing different (from
what has been said), VII 42,
VIII *introd.*, *a* 173; *oþer oþer*,

þat oþer, see next and þe; *pl.*
(uninflected), others, I 211, IV *b*
67, 78, V 355, VII 48, X 154, &c.;
Othre, *pl.* XII *introd., a* 41;
Oþren, *dat. pl.* III 53; *derrist
of other*, most excellent of (illo-
gically for 'more worthy than')
all others, VII 39. [OE. *ōþer.*]
See Anoþire. Toþer.

Oþer, Other; Auþer, V 225;
Ouþer, Outhire, Owthyre,
IV *b* 8, 23, IX 276; *adv.* and *conj.*
or, I 3, II 350, V 39, VIII *a* 305,
&c.; *oþer oþer*, or any one else,
V 34; *oþer . . . oþer*, either . . .
or, V 148; *oþer . . . or*, I 197,
IV *b* 8, 23, IX 276; introducing
alternative questions, VIII *b* 34,
35; *adv.* in *or oþer*, or else, I 6;
oþer . . . auþer, or else, V 225.
[OE. *ā-hwæþer*, *ā(w)þer*; *ō-
hwæþer*, *ōwþer*.] *See* Or²,
Ayther, Euþer.

Oþer-while, Other-while, Oþerwyle (VIII *b*), *adv.* on another
occasion, XVII 213; at other
times, II 289, 297; now and
again, VIII *b* 52; *other while
. . . other while*, sometimes . . .
sometimes, XII *a* 128. [Oþer,
adj. + While.]

Ou. *See* 3e.

Ouer(e), Our(e), *prep.* over,
I 177, V 246, X 84, 112, &c.;
over and above, XI *b* 150; (of
time) through, VII 166 (following noun); *adv.* over, II 578,
V 164, &c.; *all . . . ouer*, all
over, in all parts, VII 134 (*cf.*
next); too, I 130, IV *b* 23, 24,
VI 113, VII 36, &c. [OE. *ofer.*]

Oueral, *adv.* everywhere, II 62,
208, XII *introd., b* 184. [OE.
ofer all.]

Oueroast, *pp.* overcast, clouded,
VII 107, XVII 353. [OE. *ofer-
*+ON. *kasta.*]

Ouercoms, 3 *sg. pres.* overcomes,
IV *a* 68. [OE. *ofer-cuman.*]

Ouergrowen, *pp.* overgrown, V
113, 122. [OE. *ofer + grōwen,*
pp.]

Ouerheghede, *pp.* raised too high,

IV *b* 5. [Ouer, *adv.* + ME. *hei3en*
from Heigh.]

Ouerlaide, *pp.* covered over, sub-
merged, XVII 306. [OE. *ofer-
lecgan.*] *See* Lay.

Ouermoche, *adj.* and *n.* too much,
VIII *a* 255, XI *b* 219; *cf.* IV *b* 23.
[OE. *ofer-mycel.*] *See* Mochel.

Ouerraght, *pa. t.* revised, VII 69.
[OE. *ofer* + ? *ræcan* ? *reccan.*]

Ouersen, *v.* to supervise, VIII *a*
107. [OE. *ofer-sēon.*]

Ouerset, *pp.* overthrown, defeated,
XIII *a* 59. [OE. *ofer + settan.*]

Ouertake, *v.* to (re)gain, V 319
(note). [OE. *ofer* + ON. *taka.*]

Ouerte, *adj.* open, plain to see,
VI 233. [OFr. *overt.*]

Ouerturnyt, *pp.* overturned, VII
148. [OE. *ofer + túrnian* (see
Turne).]

Ought, Ou3t, Ouhte. *See* Oght,
Owe.

Oune. *See* Owen.

Oure, *n.* hour, time, I 188, 189,
VI 170, 191, &c.; Houre,
I 190, VI 195. [OFr. *(h)oure.*]

Our(e); Our(e), Ous, &c.; Ourn.
See Ouer(e); We; Eorne.

Out(e), Owt(e), *adv.* out, I 50,
IV *b* 3, XI *b* 26 (*see* Charité),
XVI 18, &c.; abroad, out of
doors, VIII *b* 16; *as* exclam. of
anger, dismay, &c., XVI 185, 195,
343; *out(e) apon the*, fie on thee,
XVII 229, 408. [OE. *ūt, ūte.*]

Outguoinge, *n. ate outguoinge
of*, on departing from, III 4.
[From OE. *ūt-gān.*] *See* Go(n).

Ouþer, Outhire. *See* Oþer(e),
adj. and *conj.*

Outraye, *v.* to transgress, XIV *c*
69 (*ou3t* is adv.). [OFr. *out-
reier.*]

Oway. *See* Awai.

Owe, Owyn, O3e, *v.* to have; to
have (to), be bound (to), ought,
XI *b* 6, XV *i* 4; with mixed *pers.*
and *impers.* constr., in *vus o3e*,
we ought, VI 192; to owe, VI
183; Awe, 2 *sg. pres.* XVII 171;
Oghte, *pa. t.* possessed, XII *b*
48; Ouhte, ought to, VIII *b* 73;

Auȝt, was bound to, II 555. [OE. *āgan*, pa. t. *ǎhte*.]

Owen(e), **Owne**, *adj*. own, I 126, V 291, VIII *b* 63, IX 185, &c.; **Oghne**, XII *a* 4; **Oȝene**, III *introd*.; **Oune**, XIII *a* 47, *b* 18, &c.; **Owhen**, II 163, &c.; **Awen**, V 73, 233; **Awne**, XVI 237, XVII 74; *quasi-sb.* in *of hire owne*, of their own, IX 188; *haue of myn owen*, have property of my own, VIII *a* 77. [OE. *āgen*.]

Owher, *adv*. anywhere, II 17. [OE. *ŏ-hwǣr*.]

Owy; **Owr(e)**; **Owte**. *See* Awai; We; Out(e).

Owth, *adv*. on top, X 6. [? Reduction of OE. *ufan*, *ufe-* + *wiþ*; cf ME. *out-wiþ*.]

Owthyre. *See* Oþer, *conj*.

Oxe, *n*. ox, XV *f* 5; **Oxen**, *pl.* IX 253, 255. [OE. *oxa*.]

Page, *n*. knave, fellow, XVI 125. [OFr. *page*.]

Pay, *n*. pay, V 179. [OFr. *paie*.]

Paie, **Pay(e)**, *v*. to please, satisfy, VIII *a* 304; *payes to*, is pleasing to, IV *a* 29; *impers.* in *me paies*, I am pleased, XVI 82; to pay, II 451, VI 164 (*fut.*), VIII *a* 87, XIV *d* 10; **Paied**, **Paid(e)**, &c., *pp.* satisfied, content, V 273, XVI 325, XVII 283; paid, VI 224, 243. [OFr. *payer*.] *See* Apayed.

Paiement, **Payment**, *n*. payment, VI 238, XII *b* 151. [OFr. *paiement*.]

Payn(e), **Peyne**, *n.*[1] pain, suffering, torment, I 163, XI *b* 32, XVI 4, 122, XVII 547, &c. [OFr. *peine*.] *See* Peynen.

Payne, *n.*[2] bread, VIII *a* 144. [OFr. *pain*.]

Payneme, *n*. pagan, IX 171. [OFr. *pai(e)nisme*, sg. collect., pagans.]

Palays, *n*. palace, II 85, 157 (*see* note), 439. [OFr. *palais*.]

Pale, *adj*. pale, II 110, IV *a* 10; wan, chill (connoting 'fatal', 'ill-omened'), VII 100, 116, 125. [OFr. *pale*.]

Palfray, *n*. palfrey, saddle-horse (*esp.* for use of women), II 156. [OFr. *palefrei*.]

Palmer, *n*. pilgrim (properly one that had been to the Holy Land and bore a palm-branch in token of this), VIII *a* 66. [OFr. *palm(i)er*.]

Pans. *See* Pené.

Panter, *n*. snare (for birds); *fig.* XI *b* 220. [OFr. *pantiere*.]

Pappe, *n*. breast, XV *f* 12. [Children's language.]

Par, **Per** (XII), *prep.* (with French words), by, through, for, VI 129, VIII *a* 250, XII *a* 7, *b* 18, &c. (*see* the nouns); transl. (in Fr. phrases) by *for*, *thurgh*, XII *b* 8, XV *d* 5, XVII 557, &c. [OFr. *par*, *per*.] *See* Paramoure, -aunter, -fay, Perdé.

Paradys, **Paradis(e)**, *n*. Paradise, II 45, 376, XVI 48, &c. [OFr. *paradis*.]

Parage, *n*. (noble) lineage, VI 59, XIV *c* 109. [OFr. *parage*.]

Paramoure, *adv*. with all (his) heart, XVII 80. [OFr. *par amour*.] *See* Par.

Paraunter, **Peraunter** (IX), **Peraventure** (XVII), *adv*. perhaps, V 275, VI 228, IX 272, XVII 503. [OFr. *par aventure*.] *See* Auentur(e), Par.

Parceyuet, **Persauit**, *pp.* perceived, X 76, XIII *a* 13. [OFr. *parceiv-re*.]

Pardoun, *n*. forgiveness of sins, VIII *a* 66. [OFr. *pardun*.]

Parfay, *interj.* by my troth, II 315, 339, 382. [OFr. *par fei* (*fai*).] *See* Fai.

Parfyt, **Perfyte**, -fite, *adj*. perfect, IV *b* 84, VIII *b* 88, IX 338. [OFr. *parfit(e)*.]

Parfytnesse, *n*. perfection, perfect conduct, VIII *b* 94. [From prec.]

Parforme, **Performe**, *v*. to complete, IX 170; to perform, XI *b* 194, 286. [OFr. *parfourmer*.]

Parische, **Parysshe**, *n*. parish; *attrib.* in *þ. prest*, *p. chirchis*,

I 201, XI *b* 97. [OFr. *paroche, paroisse.*]

Parlement, *n.* parliament, council, II 216. [OFr. *parlement.*]

Parloures, *n. pl.* parlours, living rooms, XVII 133. [OFr. *parlour.*]

Part, *n.* part, share, VI 213, IX 31, 325, XI *b* 57, &c.; *more be an hundred part,* more (by) a hundred times, IX 301 (*lit.* more by the hundredth part: the use seems modelled on that of ME. *dele*; see *N.E.D.,* s.v. *Deal,* I *e*). [OFr. *part.*]

Part(e), *v.* to divide, share, XII *b* 201; separate, I 103; *refl.* in *part me . . . with,* part with, leave, VII 96; Partinge, -yng, *n.* distribution, IV 275; separation, IV *a* 31. [OFr. *partir.*]

Partener(e), *n.* sharer, IX 325; *parteners of þe endes,* sharers (in their linguistic peculiarities) with the extremes, XIII *b* 55. [OFr. *parson(i)er,* infl. by Part.]

Party, Partie, *n.* part, IX 1, 2, X 156, XIII *b* 52, &c.; side, IX 72; party (in legal proceeding), XII *b* 215; *most party,* most (part) of, XVII 49. [OFr. *parti, partie.*]

Pas, *n.* pace, gait; *queynt pas* (as *adv.*), with skilful steps, II 300. [OFr. *pas.*]

Passage, *n.* passage, pass, IX 205, 206. [OFr. *passage.*]

Passe(n), Pas, Pasi (III), *v.*; **Passed, -it, Past(e),** *pa. t.* and *pp.* (i) *Intr.* to pass, proceed, go, get, IV *b* 34, VII 125, VIII *a* 78, XVI 296, &c.; go one's way, depart, pass on, V 61, VII 112, VIII *a* 196, XVI 66, 96, 152, 194, &c.; pass away, XI *a* 9; *passe bi (be),* pass (by), V 36, &c.; go over (through), IX 8, 137, &c.; *passe the see,* go abroad, IX 308, XIII *b* 39; *was past to,* had reached, VII 100; *pp.* past, gone by, over, VII 9, IX 317, XVI 105, XVII 181, &c. (ii) *Trans.* to cross, go over (through), pass

(safely), V 3, VII 116, 171, IX 308, XIII *b* 39, &c.; to surpass, VI 68; *passynge,* exceeding(ly), IX 11, 232; to pass (time), III 44. **Passed, Passit,** *pp.* as *prep.* past, VI 168, X 2. *Cf.* Apassed. [OFr. *passer.*]

Pater, Pater-noster, *n.* the 'Our Father', Lord's prayer, VI 125, VIII *b* 48, 91, IX 323, XI *a* 33, 35.

Patrones, *n. pl.* patrons, those holding advowson, or right of presentation to benefices (earliest use in E.), VIII *b* 82. [OFr. *patron.*]

Pauement, *n.* pavement, I 194. [OFr. *pavement.*]

Pece, *n.* piece, VIII *a* 304, IX 46. [OFr. *pece.*]

Pees, Pesse, *n.* peace, XIV *d* 15, XVI 66, 296. [OFr. *pais, pes.*]

Pees. *See* l'ese.

Peiere, *v.* to impair, damage, XI *b* 250; *peierid* imperfect, XI *b* 26. [Shortened from Ap(p)eyre, Empeyre.]

Peyne. *See* Payn(e), *n¹.*

Peynen, *v. refl.* to take pains, endeavour, IX 272. [OFr. *se pener,* 3 sg. *peine.*] *See* Payne, *n.¹*

Peler, *n.* robber, XIV *a* 15. [From ME. *pelen,* OFr. *peler,* rob.]

Pelrinage. *See* Pilgrimage.

Penaunce, *n.* penance, V 324, VI 117, VIII *a* 78, *b* 88. [OFr. *pen(e)ance.*]

Pené (VI), **Peny, Penny,** *n.* penny (a silver coin, a twelfth of the shilling), III 13, VI 150, 186, VIII *a* 275, &c.; *penny doyll, see* Dele, Doyll; **Pans,** *pl.* pence, III 6, 10, &c. (*cf.* ME. *paneyes,* and OFris. *panning*). [OE. *peni(n)g, pæn(n)ing.*] *See* Halpeny.

Peny-ale, *n.* ale at a penny a gallon, thin ale, VIII *a* 304 (*cf.* Halpeny-ale). [Prec. + OE. *alu.*]

Pennes, *n. pl.* quills, barrels of the feathers, IX 257. [OFr. *penne.*]

Peopull, People, *n.* people, VII 16, 82, XIII *b* 1, &c.; **Peple,** VIII *a* 287, IX 165, XI *b* 19, &c.,

Pepul(l), VII 145, XVI 194 ;
Poeple, VIII *a* 156 ; Puple,
XI *a* 13, 20, *b* 268, XIV *b* 67, &c.
[OFr. *people, poeple, puple,* &c.]

Peraventure, -aunter. *See* Paraunter.

Perce(n), *v.* to pierce, penetrate,
IX 224, XII *a* 104. [OFr. *percer.*]

Percil, *n.* parsley, VIII *a* 281.
[OFr. *persil.*]

Perdé, *interj.* (by God), indeed,
XVII 512. [OFr. *pardieu, -dé.*]
See Par.

Pereles, *adj.* peerless; unequalled,
XVI 4. [From ME., OFr. *per.*]

Perfite, -fyte. *See* Parfyt.

Peril, *n.* peril, VIII *a* 87, 111, &c. ;
Perellis, *pl.* VII 116. [OFr.
peril.]

Peril(l)ous, Perelous, Perlous,
adj. perilous, dangerous, par-
lous, V 29, VIII *a* 45, XI *b* 44,
XVII 431, &c. [OFr. *perillous.*]

Perish, *v.* to perish, XVII 94, 155.
[OFr. *perir, periss-.*]

Perl(e), *n.* pearl, V 296, VI 16,
IX 66, &c. [OFr. *perle.*]

Persauit. *See* Parceyuet.

Person(e), *n.* person, IX 304, XI *a*
46, XII *a* 115, XVII 2. [OFr.
persone.]

Pese, Pees, *n.* a pea, V 296, IX
48 ; *at a pees,* at nought, VIII *a*
162 ; Pesen, *pl.* peas, pease,
VIII *a* 189, 293 ; Peses, VIII *a*
180. [OE. *pise, peose.*]

Pese-coddes, *n. pl.* peascods,
pea-pods, VIII *a* 287 ; Pese-lof,
n. loaf made of pease-meal,
VIII *a* 172. [Prec. + OE. *codd,
hláf.*]

Pesible, *adj.* tranquil, **XI *b* 67
(MS. posible). [OFr. *paisible,
pesible.*]

Pesse ; Pet ; Peté. *See* Pees ;
Pyt ; Pité.

Philosophie, *n.* philosophy,
natural science, IX 77. [OFr.
philosophie.]

Phisik, *n.* (art, practice, of) medicine, VIII *a* 266 ; (personified)
VIII *a* 264. [OFr. *fisique,* L.
physica.]

Picche, *v.* ; *picche atwo,* ! to
thrust apart, divide (on the
sharp point of the *pyk-staf*),
VIII *a* 97 ; to pitch, load (hay,
in homing the crop), VIII *b* 13.
[Perh. distinct verbs ; see
N.E.D., s.v. *Pitch.*] *See* Pike.

Pictes, *n. pl.* Picts, XIII *b* 6. [L.
Picti ; cf. OE. *Pihtas.*]

Pie, *n.* magpie, XI *b* 249, XII *a*
75. [OFr. *pie.*]

Pik, Pyk, *n.* pitch, X 19, XVII
127, 282. [OE. *pic.*]

Pike, *v.* to pick ; *piked vp,* ! dug
out (with a pointed implement),
VIII *a* 105 ; Pyke3, 3 *pl.* ! pick
out, get, VI 213. [ME. *pi(k)ken,*
with variety of senses prob. due
to confusion of distinct words ;
see *N.E.D.,* s.v. *Pick, Pike,*
&c.]

Pykers, *n. pl.* pilferers, VIII *b* 17.
[! From prec.]

Pykstaf, *n.* pikestaff, staff with
a spike at lower end, VIII *a* 97.
[OE. *pic + stæf* ; cf. ON. (late)
pik-stafr.]

Piler, *n.* pillar, II 367. [OFr.
piler.]

Pylgrym, Pilgryme, *n.* pilgrim,
VIII *a* 59, 96, 99, XIII *a* 48.
[OFr. *pele(g)rin,* &c. ; cf. OHG.
(from Fr.) *piligrim.*]

Pilgrimage, Pylgrymage, &c.,
n. pilgrimage, VIII *a* 66, 78, IX
325 ; Pelrinage, XII *a* 12.
[OFr. *pel(e)rinage, pelrimage,
peligrinage,* &c.]

Pilwe, *n.* pillow, XII *a* 95. [OE.
pyle, (once in gloss.) *pylu.*]

Pyn, *n.* pin (as a something
valueless), XVII 364. [OE.
pinn.]

Pynd, *pp.* confined, penned, XVII
332. [ME. *pinne(n),* or *pin-
de(n)* ; OE. *pýndan.*]

Pine, Pyne, *n.* torment, suffering, grief, I 213, III 9, IV *a* 32,
50, 60, XVII 227, 437 ; toil,
VI 151 ; *pyne to behold,* (parenthetic), grievous to see, VII 145
(*cf.* Noy, Reuþe). [OE. **pín* ;
cf. next.]

Pyne, *v.* to torment, XVI 4, 219. [OE. *pīnian.*]

Pypynge, *n.* piping, playing on pipes, I 6. [OE. **pīpian,* from *pīpe,* pipe.]

Pyt, Pitte, Pet (XII), *n.* hole, pit, I 143, XII *b* 9, 11, 29, &c.; pit (of hell), XVI 271, 348. [OE. *pytt* (Kt. *pett*).]

Pité, Pyté, Peté, *n.* compassion, pity, II 101, &c.; piety, IV *b* 57, 75; *es . . . pyté,* is pitiful, IV *a* 87. [OFr. *pité.*]

Piteuous, *adj.* full of pity, III 39; Pytosly, *adv.* compassionately, VI 10. [OFr. *pitous; piteuous* is due to anal. of words like Plenteuous, *q.v.*]

Piþ, *n.* pith, XIV *c* 90. [OE. *piþa.*]

Placebo, *n.* Vespers of the Dead, VIII *b* 48, XI *b* 131 (*see* note).

Play(e), Pley, *n.* mirth, rejoicing, IV *a* 59, XVI 392; (dramatic) play, XI *a* 34. [OE. *plega.*]

Play(e), Pleie, *v.* to play, amuse oneself, II 66, XIII *b* 22; rejoice, XII *b* 159; **Playinge,** *n.* disport, XV *a* 5. [OE. *pleg(i)an.*]

Plain, Playne, *adj.* flat, level, II 353; plain, clear, XVI 48; **Playnly, Pleynly,** *adv.* plainly, clearly, XI *b* 43, 47, XVI 267, 326. [OFr. *plain.*]

Playni, Pleigne, Pleyne, Pleny, *v.* to complain, III 19, VI 189; *refl.* in *pleyned hym,* made complaint, VIII *a* 152; to sue (at law), XII *b* 215. [OFr. *plaindre, plaign-.*]

Planettis, *n. pl.* planets, XVII 345. [L. *plantēta.*] *See* Starne.

Plas, Place, *n.* place, I 155, II 40, X 152, &c. [OFr. *place.*]

Platen, *n. pl.* (plates), pieces of (silver) money, XV *g* 4, 15, 21, 23 (*cf.* 'plates' in Wiclifite version, Matt. xxvi 15, &c.). [OFr. *plate.*]

Plee, *n.* (plea, lawsuit), quarrel, IX 81. [OFr. *plai(d), plait, plet,* &c.] *See* Plete.

Pleigne, Pleny. *See* Playni.

Plenté, -ee, *n.* plenty, abundance, II 253, VIII *a* 156, XIII *a* 63, XVI 392; *quasi-adv.* in *plenté,* abundantly, XVII 146; *more plentee,* in greater abundance, IX 245. [OFr. *plenté.*]

Plenteuous, *adj.* abundant, XI *b* 265. [OFr. *plentivous, -evous.*]

Plese, *v.* to please, VI 124, VIII *a* 105, 290, *b* 89, IX 321; **Plesynge,** *n.* in *to pl. of,* so as to please, **XI *b* 108. [OFr. *plaisir, ple(i)sir.*]

Plesance, *n.* pleasure, liking, IX 327, X *introd.*; *do the plesance,* perform the pleasant office, XII *a* 185. [OFr. *plaisance, ples-.*]

Plesant, *adj.* pleasant, IX 278. [OFr. *plaisant, ples-.*]

Plete, *v.* to sue for; claim, VI 203. [OFr. *plaitier, pleder,* &c.] *See* Plee.

Ply3t, *n.* (liability), offence, V 325. [OE. *pliht.*]

Pli3te, *v.* to plight, pledge, VIII *a* 35. [OE. *plihtan.*]

Plom, *n.* plummet; as *adj.* vertical, straight down (measured by the plumb-line), XVII 520. [OFr. *plomb.*]

Plouman, Plou3man, Plowman, *n.* ploughman, VIII *a* 3, 147, 152, XIV *d* 5. [Next + OE. *mann.*]

Plow(e), *n.* plough, VIII *a* 96, 99, 156, &c.; **Plogh,** XVII 534; **Plowgh,** IX 254. [OE. *plōg* (a land-measure); ON. *plóg-r.*]

Plow-fote, *n.* a stave supporting the plough-beam and regulating furrow's depth, but here appar. ⁃ 'plough-staff' (*cf.* other readings 'plou-bat'), a staff ending in a small spade for clearing earth, &c., from mould-board, VIII *a* 97. [Prec. + OE. *fōt.*]

Plus, *adv.* (in French phrase) more, VIII *a* 306. *See* Chaude.

Poeple. *See* Peopull.

Poesie, *n.* poetry, poem, XII *a* 1, 62. [OFr. *poesie.*]

Poeuere. *See* Pouer(e).

Poyet, Poete, *n.* poet, VII 33, 47, XII *introd.* [OFr. *poete.*]

Poynt(e), Point, *n.* (i) (sharp) point, V 324, IX 118; (ii) point (of time or place), VII 100, XII *a* 68; *at the poynt,* to hand, IX 253; *bryng me to þe poynt,* come to the point with me, V 216; item, detail, instance, matter, &c., VI 234, VIII *a* 38, IX 287, XI *b* 106, XVI 105, 326, &c. [OFr. (i) *pointe,* (ii) *point.*]

Poynted, *adj.* pointed, IX 55, 105. [From prec. (i).]

Poysoun, *n.* poison, IX 94. [OFr. *poison.*]

Poysoun, *v.* to poison, VIII *a* 293. [OFr. *poisonner.*]

Poletes, *n. pl.* pullets, chickens, VIII *a* 275. [OFr. *polete.*]

Polyse (v), Pollis(s)che, Pollysch, *v.* to polish, IX 35, 41, 119, 121, &c.; to cleanse, V 325. [OFr. *polir, poliss-.*]

Pond, *n.*[1] pool, lake, XIII *a* 19, 31, 43, &c.; Pound, XIII *a* 21, 23, 24, 25. [OE. **púnd,* cf. *pyndan.*]

Pond, *n.*[2] *pl.* pounds, III 21, 24, &c.; Poundis, XI *b* 162. [OE. *púnd.*]

Pope, *n.* Pope, I 249, VIII *b* 82, IX 286, XI *b* 46. [OE. *pāpa.*]

Popi, *n.* poppy, XII *a* 81. [OE. *popig.*]

Por-. *See* Pur-.

Porche, *n.* porch, I 77. [OFr. *porche.*]

Pore. *See* Pouer(e).

Poret(te), *n.* (young) leek or onion, VIII *a* 281; *collect. sg.* VIII *a* 293. [OFr. *poret,* leek; *porette,* small onion.]

Porful, *adj.* poverty-stricken, XV *f* 2. [From Pouer(e), Pore.]

Porpos. *See* Purpos.

Porter, *n.* porter (at the gates), II 380, V 4, &c. [OFr. *port(i)er.*]

Portos, *n.* (*pl.* as *sg.*) breviary, XI *b* 228 (*see* note). [OFr. *portehors.*]

Possyble, *adj.* possible, VI 92. [OFr. *possible.*]

Post(e)les, *n. pl.* apostles, XV *g* 24, 25; itinerant preachers,

VIII *a* 143. [OE. *postol.*] *See* Apostel.

Potage, *n.* (vegetable) soup, VIII *a* 144. [OFr. *potage.*]

Potful, *n.* potful, VIII *a* 180. [OE. *pott* + *full* (properly adj. with prec. noun).]

Pound. *See* Pond.

Pouerlich, *adv.* in humble guise, II 236, 567. [From prec.]

Pouer(e), *adj.* poor, humble, II 430, 486, XII *b* 20, 36, &c.; Poeuere, XI *b* 272; Poure, III 48, IV *b* 20, VIII *b* 82; Pore, VI 213, VIII *a* 18, XI *b* 255, &c.; *adj. pl.* as *sb.,* poor (people), the poor, III 8, 41, VIII *a* 18, &c.; Pouren, *dat. pl.* III 7. [OFr. *pov(e)re, poure.*]

Pour-. *See* Pur-.

Power(e), Pouer, Poure, *n.* ability, power, VIII *a* 35, XII *a* 187, XVI 219; authority, VIII *a* 143; forces, XIV *c* 46. [OFr. *po(u)eir, pouer.*]

Pray(e), *n.* prey, II 313, XVI 175; *fig.* (of good things won as prize) VI 79. [OFr. *preie.*]

Prece, Pres(s), *v.* to press; thrust, force, X 49, 69, &c.; *intr.* and *refl.* to press forward, hasten, V 29, X 131; *pressit on,* assailed, X 190; *hardest pressit,* most hard pressed, X 150. *See* Prees. [OFr. *presser;* on forms *prece, pre(e)s,* see *N.E.D.*]

Preche, *v.* to preach, VIII *a* 143, XI *b* 7, 24, XVI 51, &c.; Prechinge, -ynge, *n.* preaching, III 49, XI *b* 3, &c. [OFr. *prech(i)er.*]

Precious, Precy(i)ous(e), *adj.* precious, costly, IX 42, 99, XI *b* 257; *precious ston,* II 151, 366, IX 123. [OFr. *precious.*]

Preef, *n.* test, IX 128. [OFr. *proeve.*] *See* Preue.

Prees, Press, *n.* press; crowd, XII *b* 213; uproar, commotion, XVI 125. [From Prece, *q.v.*]

Preeued. *See* Preue.

Preie, Preye(n), Prey, Pray(e), *v.* to pray, beg, II 534, IV *b* 8, VIII *a* 119, 250, XI *b* 37,

XVII 242, &c.; **Praid, Preide, Preyd(e)**, *pa. t.* I 89, II 224, VIII a 117, XII b 69; *pray*, pray to, VI 124, *preye of*, beg for, VIII a 38, 117; *preye to*, pray (to), IX 320, 322; **Preiynge**, *n.* in *p. of lippes*, prayer with lips (only), XI b 89. [OFr. *preier*.]

Preiere, Preyer(e), **Preȝer** (XIV c), *n.* prayer, VIII a 244, b 88, XI b 36, XIV c 78, &c.; *preiere in lippis*, p. with the lips (only), XI b 90. [OFr. *preiere*.]

Preise(n), Preyse, Prayse, *v.* to praise, esteem, V 4, VIII a 102, b 31, XI b 176, 182. [OFr. *preis(i)er*.] *See* Prese, Prys, Prist.

Preostes. *See* Prest(e), *n.*

Pres(s). *See* Prece, Prees.

Prese, *n.* praise, great worth, VI 59. [Stem of Preise(n) with AFr. monophthongization.]

Presence, *n.* presence, IX 94, XII b 127, &c. [OFr. *presence*.]

Present(e), *adj.* present, IX 128, 336; as *sb.* in *in your presente*, in your presence, VI 29. [OFr. *present*.]

Present, *n.* present, gift, I 123, VIII a 42, 290. [OFr. *present*.]

Presente, *v.* to give gifts to, IX 24. [OFr. *presenter*.]

Prest, *adj.* prompt, quick, VIII a 190, XIV b 67; **Prestly**, *adv.* promptly, VIII a 87. [OFr. *prest*.]

Prest(e), *n.* priest, I 8, 9, III 49 (*dat.*), 53, &c.; Preost, XI b 291. [OE. *prēost*.]

Presthod, *n.* priesthood, XI b 47. [OE. *prēost-hād*.]

Pretermynable, *adj.* who predetermines, fore-ordains, VI 236. [Appar. invented for rhyme from *pre + terminable* used actively.]

Preue, Preeue, *v.* to prove, show, VII 47, IX 298; to test, IX 297; to approve, IX 305. [OFr. *preuv-*, *proev-*, &c. accented stem of *prover*.] *See* Preef, Proue.

Pryde, Pride, *n.* pride, magni-

ficence, IV a 59, b 14, XI b 55, XVII 543, &c.; *of pryde*, proud, XVI 182. [OE. *prȳde*.] *See* Proude.

Priis. *See* Prys.

Prike, *v.* to spur; *intr.* gallop, II 141, XIV a 15. [OE. *prician*, to prick.]

Pryme, *n.* prime, first division of the day according to the sun (varying with the season), *or* a fixed period 6–9 a.m.; *heiȝe pryme*, fully prime, end of the period of prime, about 9 a.m., VIII a 106. [OE. *prīm*, from L. *prīma* (*hōra*).]

Prymer, *n.* devotional manual, VIII b 48 (note). [Origin of name doubtful; see *N.E.D.*]

Primerole, *n.* primrose, IV e 9, 10, 13. [OFr. *primerole*.]

Prynce, Prince, *n.* prince, V 4 (*i.e.* Sir Gawayne), XIV c 59, XVI 182, &c. [OFr. *prince*.]

Princypall, Principall, *adj.* and *n.* chief, IX 1, 28, XVI 111; **Principaly**, *adv.* in the first place, XI b 96. [OFr. *principal*, or L. *principālis*.]

Pryour, *n.* priory, VIII b 95. [OFr. *priorie*; with this form of the suffix *cf.* Oritore.]

Prys, Prise, Priis (II), *n.* worth, excellence, V 296, VI 59; *of priis*, &c., worthy, excellent, noble, II 51, 64, 249, V 330, VII 47. [OFr. *pris*, earlier *prieis*.] *See* Preise(n), Prist.

Prisoune, Prison, *n.* prison, XI b 126, XVI 220 (*or read prisounes*, prisoners; *see* note). [OFr. *priso(u)n*.]

Prist, *pp.* esteemed, VII 33. [OFr. *pris(i)er*.] *See* Preise(n).

Processioun, *n.* procession; pomp, II 587. [OFr. *procession*.]

Proferi, Profre, *v.* to offer, II 434, V 278, VIII a 25, XII b 122, &c. [OFr. *proffrir*; *proferer*.]

Profession, *n.* declaration; vows (on entering religious order), in *singular prof.*, special vows, as opposed to the regular vows taken by all priests, XI *b* 101. [OFr. *profession*.]

Profit, *n.* profit, VIII *b* 107. [OFr. *profit*.]

Profit-, Profytable, *adj.* profitable, advantageous, VIII *a* 270, XIII *b* 68. [OFr. *profitable*.]

Prologe, *n.* prologue, VII 96. [OFr. *prologue*.]

Property, *n.* property, special virtue, VI 86. [OFr. *propriete*.]

Prophet(t)e, *n.* prophet, XI *b* 18, XV *g* 9, XVI 267, &c. [OFr. *prophete*, L. *propheta*.]

Prophecye, Prophicye, *n.* prophecy, IX 216, XVI 27. [OFr. *prophecie*.]

Prophicied, *pa. t.* prophesied (MS. prophicie), XVI 188. [From prec.]

Propre, *adj.* proper, separate, IX 187 ; Propurly, *adv.* properly, rightly (*or* of my own knowledge, at first hand), IX 264. [OFr. *propre*.]

Proude, Prowd(e), *adj.* magnificent, glorious, II 376 ; proud, haughty, arrogant, V 36, 201, VIII *a* 191, XV *b* 32, &c. ; *prowdist of pryde*, greatest in pride (*or* splendour), XVII 543 ; Prowdly, *adv.* out of pride, XVII 17. [OE. *prūt* (rarely *prūd*), from OFr. *prout*, *prou(d)*, valiant.]

Proue, Prufe, *v.* to prove ; demonstrate, show, X 74, XVI 255 ; test, try, XVII 460. [OFr. *prover* ; cf. OE. *prōfian*.] *See* Preue.

Prow(e) (*to*), *n.* benefit, good (of), IV *b* 82, XVI 220, 326 ; *may to prow*, may be of benefit ('prow' prob. apprehended as infin.), I *introd.* [OFr. *prou*.]

Psalme, *n.* psalm, VIII *a* 246 ; *Seuene Psalmes*, the Seven Penitential Psalms, VIII *b* 49 ; note allit. with *s.* [OE. (*p*)*salm*, L. *psalmus*.]

Puire, Puit. *See* Pure, Putte(n).

Pull, *v.* ; Puld, *pa. t.* ; to drag,

VII 178 ; *pull up*, hoist, VII 125, XVII 153. [OE. *pullian*.]

Puple. *See* Peopull.

Puplisshid, *pp.* (rime requires *puplist*), openly declared, XVI 59. [OFr. *puplier* + -*is*(*h*) from other verbs of Fr. origin.]

Purchase, Porchase, Pourchace, *v.* to acquire, obtain, VI 79, VIII *b* 81, XII *a* 18. [OFr. *p*(*o*)*urchac*(*i*)*er*.]

Pure, Puire, *adj.* pure ; elegant, seemly (*cf.* Clene), V 330 ; utter, sheer, VIII *a* 111, IX 31, XIV *c* 13. [OFr. *pur*.]

Pure(n), *v.* to purify, V 325, IX 45. [OFr. *purer*.]

Purgatorie, *n.* Purgatory, VIII *a* 45. [L. *Purgātōrium*.]

Purge, *v.* to purge out, IV *b* 77. [OFr. *purg*(*i*)*er*.]

Purper, *n.* purple, red, II 242. [OFr. *purpre*.]

Purpos(e), Pourpos, Porpos, *n.* intention, purpose, resolve, IV *b* 73, VI 148, VII 118, XII *a* 21, XIV *b* 39 ; *put in a p.*, resolved, VII 112. [OFr. *po*(*u*)*rpos*.]

Purpose(n), *v.* to intend, XI *b* 110. [OFr. *po*(*u*)*rposer*.]

Purs, *n.* purse, XII *b* 157, 173, 182. [OE. *purs*.]

Pursewe, Pursuen, Poursuie, *v.* to follow, pursue, IX 229, XII *b* 7 ; persecute, torment, IX 93 ; *pursewe to*, go eagerly to, XVI 316. [OFr. *pursiwer*, *pursuer*.]

Purvaye, Purueye (*to*), to provide, prepare (for), XVI 69, XVII 553. [OFr. *po*(*u*)*rveier*.]

Putte(n), Puit (XIV *c*), *v.* ; Put(te), *pa. t.* and *pp.* ; to thrust, IV *b* 3, 10, X 187, XVI 259, XVII 39 ; to put, set, VII 112 (*see* Purpos), VIII *a* 191, XII *b* 141, XIV *c* 12, XVII 21 ; to impose, XI *a* 64 ; *putte awey*, do away with, XI *b* 127 ; *putten errour in*, impute error to, XI *b* 77 ; *put hom perto*, set themselves to the task, VII 33 ; *putten hem into*, put out on, IX 183 ;

put vnto payn, set in torment, XVII 547; *putte wryten*, set in writing, IX 318. [OE. *pûtian, pŷtan, potian*; see *N.E.D.*]

Qu(h)-. *See also* Wh-.

Qualitee, *n.* degree (of goodness), question of how good, IX 335. [OFr. *qualité.*]

Quantytee, Quantité, *n.* limitation of greatness, question of how great, IX 336; capacity, quantity, X 26. [OFr. *quantité.*]

Quarell, *n.* cross-bow bolt, IX 258. [OFr. *quar(r)el.*]

Quaþ, Quath, *pa. t. sg.* quoth, said, II 127, VIII *b* 26, &c.; Quatʒ, VIII *a* 3; Quod, V 58, VI 61, &c. [OE. *cwæþ.*]

Queer, *n.* choir, VIII *b* 63, XI *b* 172. [OFr. *cuer.*]

Queynt, *adj.* skilful, elegant, II 299, 300 (*see* Pas); Koyntly, *adv.* cunningly, V 345. [OFr. *cointe, queinte*, &c.]

Quelle, Qwell, *v.* to kill, destroy, IV *a* 92, V 41. [OE. *cwellan.*]

Queme, *adj.* pleasant, V 41. [OE. *cwême.*]

Quen. *See* Whan(ne).

Quen(e), Queen(e), *n.* queen, II 51, 71, VI 55, IX 190, XII *a* 195, &c. [OE. *cwên.*]

Querele, *n.* (legal) complaint, accusation, XII *b* 209. [OFr. *querel(l)e.*]

Questioun, *n.* question, IX 178. [OFr. *questioun.*]

Quhedirand, *pres. p.* whirling, *or* whirring, X 92. [Cf. Early ME. *to-hwideren, -hwiðeren*, whirl to pieces; OE. *hwaþerian*, make a rushing noise.]

Quhelis, *n. pl.* wheels, X 17. [OE. *hwê(o)l.*]

Quhen; Quhill. *See* Whan(ne), Whil.

Quyk, *adj.* alive, V 41. [OE. *cwic.*]

Quyte; Qwyte, Qwite (XVII); *v.* to pay, repay, V 176, 256, VI 235, XVII 216, 228; Quitte, *pp.* paid, VIII *a* 92. [OFr. *quiter.*]

Quite, Quyte. *See* Whyyt.

Quo(m); Quod. *See* Who; Quaþ.

Qwake, *v.* to tremble, IV *a* 61. [OE. *cwacian.*]

Qwart, *n.* health; *mase in qwart*, heals, IV *a* 15. [ON. *kvirt*, (neut. adj.) untroubled.]

Qwiles. *See* Whiles.

Race, Rase, *n.* headlong course, XVII 429; onslaught, violent blow, V 8. [ON. *rás* infl. by senses of related OE. *ræs.*]

Raʒt, Raid. *See* Reche; Ride.

Rayle, *v.* to order, array, XV *b* 13. [OFr. *reiller.*]

Rayn, *v.* to rain, XVII 147; Renys, *pl.* are raining down, XVII 351. [OE. *regnian.*]

Rayn(e), *n.*[1] rain, VII 109, 132, XVII 445; Reyn(e), I 162, XIII *a* 18. [OE. *regn.*]

Rayne, *n.*[2] rein, V 109. [OFr. *raigne, rainne*, &c.]

Raysede, *pp.* uplifted, IV *b* 71. [ON. *reisa.*]

Rake, *n.* path, V 76, 92. [OE. *racu*, water-course, or ON. *rák*, streak (Norw. dial *raak*, path).]

Ram-skyt, *n.* a term of abuse, XVII 217. [OE. *ramm*+ON. *skita.*]

Ran(ne). *See* Ryn.

Randoune, *n.*; *in a randoune*, with a rush, X 102. [OFr. *en un randon.*]

Ranke, *adj.* brave, fine, VII 122. [OE. *ranc.*]

Rape, *v. refl.* to hasten, VIII *a* 112, *b* 108. [ON. *hrapa.*]

Rapely, *adv.* hastily; quickly, V 151; rashly VI 3. [ON. *hrapalliga.*]

Rapes; Rase. *See* Ropis; Race.

Rather, *adv.* earlier, VIII *a* 112. [OE. *hraþor.*]

Rathly, *adv.* quickly, XIV *b* 6. [OE. *hræþ-lîce.*]

Raton, *n.* rat, XV *i* 1, 9, 18. [OFr. *raton.*]

Rapeled, *pp.* entwined, V 226. [See *N.E.D.* s.vv. Raddle, v[1]., Ratheled.]

Raue, *v.* rave, talk foolishly, VI 3. [OFr. *raver*.]

Ravyn, *n.* raven, XVII 479, 499. [OE. *hræfn*.]

Rauysche, *v.* to carry off captive, carry away, IV *a* 16; Reuey(se)d, *pp.* II 82. [OFr. *ravir*, *raviss-*.]

Rawe; Rawþe. *See* Rowe; Reuþe.

Real, *adj.* royal, II 356. [OFr. *real*.]

Reame, *n.* realm, kingdom, VIII *b* 78; Reume, XI *a* 25, 32, 52; Rem(e), VI 88, XIII *b* 47, 48; Roialme, IX 261. [OFr. *re(i)alme*, *re(a)ume*; later *roialme*.]

Reasoune. *See* Reson.

Rebalde, *n.* Rascal, XVI 99. [OFr. *ribauld*.] *See* Rybaudry.

Rebuke, *v.* to rebuke, VI 7, VIII *b* 86. [ONFr. *rebuk(i)er*.]

Receyue, *v.* to receive, take, VIII *b* 73; Res(s)ayue, V 8, XVI 390; Resceyued, *pp.* XI *b* 265. [OFr. *receiv-re*.]

Reche, Recche, *v.*[1] to reck, care, VIII *a* 114; *me no reche*, I care not (mixed *pers.* and *impers.* constr.), II 342. [OE. *reccan*.]

Reche, *v.*[2] to give, V 256; Raȝt, *pa. t.* V 229; Raȝteȝ, 2 *sg.* V 283. [OE. *ræcan*, *ræhte*, *rähte*.]

Reches, *n. sg.* riches, IV *b* 61. [OFr. *richesse*.]

Recorde, *v.* to ponder, go over in one's mind, IX 317; record, XII *introd.*, *b* 111. [OFr. *recorder*.]

Recoueren, *v.* to regain, IX 131. [OFr. *recovrer*.] *See* Keuer(e).

Recuyell, *n.* compilation, VII *introd.* [OFr. *recueil*.]

Red(e), *adj.* red, II 107, XIV *b* 41, XV *e* 19; *red(e) gold*, red gold, II 150, 362. [OE. *rēad*.]

Red e), *n.* advice, III 51 (*dat.*); counsel, plan, in *can no other red*, sees nothing else for it, XII *b* 102 (*cf.* Wane, *n.*). [OE. *rǣd*, *rēd*.]

Red(e), Redyn, Reede, *v.* to advise, counsel, IV *a* 45, V 43 (note), VIII *b* 108, XIV *c* 97, XVII 341, &c.; to read, II 1, IV *b* 9, X *in-*

trod., XII *a* 112, &c.; to read aloud, I 14; to reckon, VIII *b* 73; to think, XVII 427; *hard red* (inf.), heard read, XVII 46; Ret (OE. *rǣtt*, *rēt*), 3 *sg. pres.* reads, III 3, 16: Rede, *pp.* read, XVI 317. [OE. *rǣdan*, *rēdan*, str., later wk.]

Redere, *n.* reader, IX 321. [OE. *rǣdere*.]

Redi, Redy, *adj.* prompt, ready (to hand), II 380, VI 231, X 34, XII *b* 119, XVI 394; *al redy*, prompt(ly), XVI 120; Redyly, *adv.* promptly, V 256. [Extended from OE. (*ge-*)*rǣde*.]

Redresse, *v.* to redress, set right, XII *b* 206. [OFr. *re-dresser*.]

Reformed (*of*), *pp.* changed back to his proper form (from), XII *a* 19. [OFr. *reformer*.]

Refuseþ, *pres. pl.* reject, VIII *b* 82. [OFr. *refuser*.]

Reghtewysnes, Reghtwysely. *See* Ryghtwyse.

Regioun, *n.* region, IX 161, XII *a* 13. [OFr. *regioun*.]

Regne, *n.* kingdom, VI 141. [OFr. *regne*.]

Regni, Regne, *v.* to reign, II 425, IX 339. [OFr. *regner*.]

Reherce, Reherse, *v.* to repeat, XI *a* 4, XII *a* 103; Rehercyng(e), *n.* recounting, IX 274, 279. [OFr. *rehercer*.]

Reyll, *n.* reel, XVII 298 (*see* Garn). [OE. *hrēol*.]

Reynand. *See* Ren.

Reyny. *adj.* rainy, XII *a* 53. [OE. *regnig*.] *See* Rayn(e), *n.*[1]

Rele, *v.* to reel, behave wildly, sway (in combat); *rele as vs likeȝ*, let us fight as fiercely as we please, V 178. [Prob. related to Reyll.]

Relece, *v.* to release, V 274. [OFr. *relaissier*, *relesser*.]

Relees, Reles, *n.* release, discharge, VIII *a* 84, XVI 288, 290. [OFr. *reles*.]

Releif, Releue, *v.* to relieve, give relief to, X 151, 161, XI *b* 255. [OFr. *relever*.]

Religioun, *n.* religious rule, or order, VIII *a* 145. [OFr. *religion*.]

Relikes, *n. pl.* heirlooms, precious things, VII 122. [OFr. *relique*.]

Rem(e). *See* Reame.

Remembraunce, *n.* recollection, VIII *b* 11. [OFr. *remembra(u)nce*.]

Remene (*to*), *v.* to compare (to), interpret (as), XIV *c* 41. [?OFr. *remener*, bring back; senses seem due to assoc. with Mene, *v.*[1]]

Remissioun, *n.* discharge, pardon, VIII *a* 84. [OFr. *remissioun*.]

Remytte, *v.* to hand on, refer (for consideration), IX 296. [L. *remittere*.]

Remnaunt, Remenaunte, *n.* remainder, V 274, 333, VIII *a* 94. [OFr. *remenant*.]

Remorde, *pp.* afflicted, VI 4. [OFr. *remord-re*.]

Remwe, *v.* to take away, VI 67. [OFr. *remuer*.]

Ren, Renne, *v.* to run, XIV *b* 6; to flow, IX 179, XII *a* 84; ? Reynand, *pres. p.* XVII 111; *see* Ryn. [ON. *renna*.]

Renys. *See* Rayn, *v.*

Renk, *n.* knight, man, V 138 (*see* note), 178, 269. [OE. *rinc*.]

Renne-aboute, Gad-about, Vagabond, VIII *a* 142. [From Ren.]

Renoun, Renowne, *n.* renown, glorious name, in *of renoun*, *renouns* (*pl.* in Fr. constr., with ref. to several persons), I 248, II 202, XIV *b* 81. [OFr. *renoun*.]

Rent, *pp.* torn, VII 147. [OE. *rendan*.]

Rental, *n.* rent-book, VIII *a* 84 (*see* note). [OFr. *rental*.]

Rentes, *n.* revenues from property, VIII *b* 77, XI *b* 96. [OFr. *rente*.]

Reparde, *pp.* shut off, barred, VI 251. [OFr. *re-* + ME. *parren*.]

Repe, *v.* to reap, VIII *b* 15. [OE. *rĩpan* ; on stem-vowel *see* N.E.D. s.v. *Reap*.]

Repent(e), *v.* to repent, XVII 81, 91, 117. [OFr. *repentir*.]

Repentance, *n.* repentance, XVII 56. [OFr. *repentance*.]

Repereyue, *n.* head-reaper, harvest-overseer, VIII *b* 15. [OE. *rip*, harvest (or stem of prec.) + *rēfa*.] *See* Reue, *n.*

Repleye, *v.* XVI 380 (*see* note). [Cf. OFr. *repley(i)er*, &c. or *replevir* ; see N.E.D. s.vv. *Repledge, Replevy*, &c.]

Reprené, *v.* to reprehend, find fault with, VI 184. [OFr. *reprendre, preign-*.]

Reproue, Reprouen (*of*), *v.* to reprove (for), V 201, XI *b* 187. [OFr. *repro(u)ver, repreuv-*.]

Reprufe, *n.* disgrace, XVII 84. [OFr. *repro(u)ve*.]

Rerd, Rurde (v), *n.* loud voice V 269, XVII 230 ; noise, V 151 (*see* Rusche), XVII 101. [OE. *rĕord*.]

Rert, *pp.* (aroused), ready, VI 231. [OE. *rœ̄ran*.]

Res(s)ayue, Resceyued. *See* Receyue.

Rescowe, Rescoghe, *n.* rescue, V 240 ; *matჳ rescoghe*, ? comes to the rescue (cf. *make reschewes*, Morte Arthure 433), VI 250 (*see* note). [Stem of ME. *rescouen*, *v.*, OFr. *rescourre*.]

Resette, *n.* (place of) refuge, shelter, V 96. [OFr. *recet*.]

Residue, *n.* residue, VIII *a* 94. [OFr. *residu*.]

Reson, Resoun(e), Reasoune, *n.* reason, (good) sense, VIII *a* 311, XI *a* 30, 48, *b* 6, XII *b* 225, XVII 501, &c. ; (personified) VIII *b* 5, &c. ; what is reasonable, XVI 263 ; reasoning, XVI 255 ; argument, saying, XVI 337 ; *by reson*, as a logical consequence, XVII 81 ; motive, in *by þat resoune*, with that intent, XVI 248. [OFr. *raison, re(i)son*.]

Resonabele, *adj.* reasonable, VI 163. [OFr. *resonable*.] *See* Vnresounable.

Restay, *v.* to stop ; *intr.* to pause, VI 77. [OFr. *resteir* ; see N.E.D., s. v. *Stay*, v.]

Restor(e), v. to restore, V 215, XVI 13, XVII 29; *trwe mon trwe restore*, let an honest man honestly restore (another's property), V 286. [OFr. *restorer*.]

Ret. See Red(e), v.

Reue, n. reeve, manager of an estate, VI 182, XI b 288. [OE. (*ge-*)*rḗfa*.]

Reue, v. to rob, steal, IV b 20; constr. with *dat. pron.* of person deprived, IV a 83, XV c 31. [OE. *rḗafian*.]

Reuey(se)d. See Rauysche.

Reuel, v. revel, V 333. [OFr. *reveler*.]

Reuerence, n. reverence; *at þe r.*, out of respect, V 138; *do a r.*, make an obeisance, XII b 128. [OFr. *reverence*.]

Reuerse, v. to reverse, countermand, XI a 15. [OFr. *reverser*.]

Reuest, *pa. t.* (*refl.*) vested, robed (himself), I 70. [OFr. *revestir*.]

Reulis, n. pl. rules, XI b 203. [OFr. *reule*.] See Rewle.

Reume. See Reame.

Reuþe, Rawþe, n. (mental) pain, grief; *hedde r. þerof*, was grieved at that, III 20; *r. to here*, grievous to hear, V 136 (*cf.* Noy, Pine). [Extended with suffix *-þ* from OE. *hrēow*; cf. ON. *hrygð*.] See Rewe(ful).

Reward(e), n. regard, consideration, in *takeþ r. of* (*to*), give a thought (to), XIV c 105–7; reward, VI 244, XII b 42. [ONFr. *reward*.]

Rewardeþ, 3 *sg. pres.* gives reward, VIII b 32. [ONFr. *rewarder*.]

Rew(e), v. to rue, regret, II 570, XVII 202; *it shal him rewe*, he shall rue it, XV a 23. [OE. *hrēowan*, pers. and impers.]

Reweful, Ruful (V), *adj.* rueful; piteous, II 114; grievous, V 8. [OE. *hrēow* + *full*.]

Rewle, v. to guide, XVII 429. [OFr. *reuler*.] See Reulis.

Rybaudrye, n. ribaldry, coarse jesting, II 9. [OFr. *ribauderie*.] See Rebalde.

Ribbes, n. pl. ribs, IX 257. [OE. *ribb*.]

Riche, Ryche, adj. of high rank, noble, II 326, 446, VIII b 26, XV g 18, &c.; wealthy, III 52, &c.; splendid, costly, rich, II 81, 161, 356, &c.; high (feast), V 333; *quasi-sb.* noble (steed), V 109; adv. (or *predic. adj.*) richly, II 362. [OE. *rīce*; OFr. *riche*.]

Ryche, n. kingdom, VI 241. [OE. *rīce*.] See Heuenryche.

Ryched, pp. directed, intended, V 138. [OE. *reccan*, but form prob. due to confusion with ME. *richen*, *ruchen* (OE. **ryccan*), draw.]

Richt, Rycht. See Right.

Rydde, v. to separate (combatants), V 178. [Blend of OE. *hreddan*, rescue, and ON. *ryðja*, rid.]

Ride, Ryde, v. to ride, II 340 (*subj.*), 347, V 39, 76 (note), &c., Raid, *pa. t. sg.* X 149; Rod(e); I 62, V 21, XV a 4; *him rod*, sailed, XIV c 61; Riden, pl. II 308; Ryden, pp. gone on military service (as knights), VIII b 78. [OE. *rīdan*.]

Rifild, pp. despoiled, XIV a 16, 17. [OFr. *rifler*.]

Rife, adj. plentiful, VII 122. [Late OE. *rȳfe*, **rīfe*.]

Ryfis. See Ryue.

Rigge, n. back, II 500; Rugge, XV g 4. [OE. *hrycg*.]

Right, Ryght, Rihte (XII), adj. right, proper, true, XII a 124, XVI 255, XVII 471, &c.; right (hand), IX 70. [OE. *riht*.]

Right, Ryght, Riȝt(e), Ryȝt, Riht (XII, XIV c); Richt, Rycht (X); adv. straight, right, II 100, 186, V 94, &c.; *ful riȝt*, straight (away), II 85, 191; *ryght vprise* (cf. Vpperight), rise up, XVI 31; correctly, XVII 139; exactly, just, right, I 94, II 166, V 236, IX 64, X *introd.*,

102, XII *a* 146, XVII 513, &c.; *richt evin*, just, X 93; (with neg.) at all, VI 160, VIII *a* 145, *b* 86, XVII 524, &c.; very, IX 150, X 138, XIV *c* 10, &c. [OE. *rihte*.]

Right, Ryght, **Ry3t**, *n*. right, XIV *b* 37; justice, V 278, VI 136, 231; just cause, VIII *b* 78; *by þe way of ry3t to aske dome*, if they demand an award acc. to strict justice, VI 220; **Ry3tes, Bi3ttis**, *pl.* duties, XI *b* 203; obligations, V 274. [OE. *riht*.]

Right, *pa. t.* corrected, VII 69. [OE. *rihtan*.]

Rightfull, *adj.* just, IX 82; **Ri3t-fulleste**, *superl.* XI *b* 193. [OE. (late) *riht-ful*.]

Ryghtfulnesse, *n.* Justice, VIII *b* 32. [From prec.]

Ryghtwyse, *adj.* righteous, IV *b* 7; **Reghtwysely**, *adv.* righteously, IV *b* 55; **Reghtewysnes**, *n.* righteousness, IV *b* 80. [OE. *rihtwīs (rehtwīs), -līce, -nes*.]

Ri3tes; *al to ri3tes*, quite correctly, fittingly, II 136; *to his ri3tes*, as he should be, fittingly, II 292. [Extension of *to ri3t*, according to what is right (*see* Right, *n.*), with adv. *-es*.]

Ryme, *n.* riming poem, I *introd.*; **Rymys**, *pl.* (trivial) popular poems, I 14; **Ryme couwee**, *see* Couwee. [OFr. *rime*.]

Ryn, *v.* to run, flow, pass swiftly, X 17, XVII 101, 277, 305, 357; **Ran**(ne), *pa. t.* I 155, IV *a* 9 (note), X 107; **Runne**, *pp.* in *þe runne*, may have mounted up, VI 163. [OE. *rinnan*.] *See* Lorne, Ren(ne).

Rinde, *n.* bark, II 260. [OE. *rīnd*.]

Ryne, *v.* to touch, V 222 (*see* note). [OE. *hrīnan*.]

Rynge, *v.* to ring, resound, XV *b* 12; **Ronge**, *pa. t.* V 136; **Ry(n)kande**, *pres. p.* V 269 (confus. of *ng, nk*, freq. in this poem). [OE. *hringan*, wk.]

Ryot, *n.* strife, violence, IX 83. [OFr. *riot(e)*.]

Rype, Ripe, *adj.* ripe, VIII *a* 289, IX 140. [OE. *rīpe*.]

Ris, *n.* leafy spray, II 305. [OE. *krīs*.]

Rise, Ryse, *v.* to rise, IV *a* 62, V 17, XVI 394, &c.; **Ros**, *pa. t. sg.* VI 77, 146, 159; **Ryse**, *pl.* I 208; **Rysen**, *pp.* XVII 442; **Rysing**, *n.* resurrection, XVI 317. [OE. *ā-rīsan*.]

Ryste, *n.* repose, rest, IV *b* 10; **Rest**(e), II 74, IV *a* 3, &c. [OE. *rest*; on *y*-form see *N.E.D.* s.v. *Rest*.]

Ryste, Rest(e), *v.* to rest; *intr.* IV *b* 42, V 263; *refl.* IV *b* 38, IX 20. [OE. *restan*; see prec.]

Ryue, *v.* to tear (asunder), cleave, V 222 (note); **Ryfis**, 3 *sg. pres. intr.* is torn, XVII 399; **Roue**, *pa. t.* V 278; **Ryue**, *pp.* I 121. [ON. *rīfa*.]

Riueling, *n.* a rough shoe (as nickname for a Scot), XIV *a* 19. [OE. *rifeling*.]

Riuer(e), **Ryuer**(e), *n.* river, II 160, 308, IX 12, XIV *a* 85, XIII *a* 16, &c. [OFr. *rivere*.]

Ro, *n.* peace, XVII 237. [OE. *rōw*, ON. *rō*.]

Robbe, *v.* to rob; **Yrobbed**, *pp.* III 18; **Robbing**, *n.* XIV *b* 6. [OFr. *rob(b)er*.]

Robbere, *n.* robber, XIV *a* 6. [From prec.; OFr. *robbour*.]

Robe, *n.* robe, II 81. [OFr. *robe*.]

Roo, Rokke, *n.* rock, V 76, 130, XV *g* 12. [Cf. OE. gloss *stān-rocc*, scopulus; OFr. *ro(c)que*.]

Roche, *n.* rock, II 347, V 131, IX 33, 62, &c.; **Rooch**(e), XIII *a* 21, 22. [OFr. *roche*.]

Roché, *adj.* rocky, V 226. [From prec.]

Rod(e). *See* Ride.

Rode, *n.*[1] rood, cross, VIII *a* 94, XIV *c* 73. [OE. *rōd*.]

Rode, *n.*[2] rosy hue, fair face, II 107, XV *b* 13. [OE. *rudu*.]

Rof, *adj.* rough; grievous (with *sore*), or ↑ *n.* gash, V 278 (note). [(i) As next with alteration of final spirant (*cf.* þof), though this is not the usual form of 'rough' in this text. (ii) Related to Ryue, *v.*]

Ro3(e), *adj.* rough, rugged, V 94, 109, 130; Rouh, XIV *c* 37; Rowe, II 265, 459 (*see* Blac); Ru3e, V 98. [OE. *rūh, rūg-, rūw-.*]

Roialme. *See* Reame.

Royis, 2 *sg. pres.* talkest folly, XVI 99. [Unknown.]

Rok, *n.* distaff, XVII 338. [Cf. ON. *rokk-r,* MDu., MLG. *rocke(n).*]

Rokke. *See* Roc.

Romayn, *n.* a Roman, VII 69. [OFr. *romain.*]

Romance, *n.* (French) romance, story, XIV *b* heading. [OFr. *romans.*]

Rome, *v.* to wander, make one's way, V 130, VIII *b* 11. [ME. forms point to OE. **rāmian.*]

Rooch(es). *See* Roche.

Rooris, 2 *sg. pres.* roarest, XVI 99. [OE. *rārian.*]

Rooþur. *See* Roþur.

Ropis, Rapes, *n. pl.* ropes, VII 147, XIV *b* 68. [OE. *rāp.*]

Ros. *See* Rise.

Rose, *n.* rose, XV *b* 13, *e* 19. [OE. *rose* from L. *rosa.*]

Rote, *n.*[1] root, V 226, VI 60 (origin), VIII *a* 97, XIV *c* 82; Rote, *pl.* (or *collect. sg.*), II 256, 260. [ON *rōt.*]

Rote, *n.*[2] way, in *bi rote,* on the way, V 139. [OFr. *rote.*]

Roted, *pa. t.* rotted, I 236. [OE. *rotian.*]

Roþur, Rooþur, *n.* rudder, XIV *c* 25, 29, 36, 57. [OE. *rōþor.*]

Roue; Rouh. *See* Ryue; Ro3(e).

Roun(e), *n.* speech, voice, XV *b* 2, 29 (*see* note), *c* 36; [OE. *rūn.*]

Round, *adj.* round; *adv.* in *al aboute round* (as *prep.*) round, XII *a* 79; Roundnesse, *n.* roundness, IX 67. [OFr. *roönd, round.*]

Rout(e), *n.*[1] host, company, (great) number, II 283, X 176, XII *b* 118, XIV *a* 16; *en a route,*

in a mass, tumultuously, XVII 305. [OFr. *route.*]

Rout, *n.*[2] roar, loud noise, X 92. [Stem of OE. *hrūtan,* or ON. *rauta;* see Rowtyn.]

Rouwed, *pa. t.* rowed, XIV *c* 61. [OE. *rōwan,* str.]

Rowe, Rawe, *n.* row, VI 185; *be rowe (rawe), on rawe,* in (due) order, in turn, XV *h* 15, XVI 317, 401. [OE. *rāw.*]

Rowe. *See* Ro3(e).

Rowtyn, *pres. pl.* they crash, beat, XV *h* 15. [OE. *hrūtan;* but see *N.E.D.* for various sources and senses of *Rout,* n. and v.]

Rude-evyn, *n.* eve of the feast of the (Exaltation of the) Cross, X 42. [OE. *rōd + æfen.*] *See* Rode, *n.*[1]

Ruful. *See* Reweful.

Rugge; Ru3e. *See* Rigge; Ro3(e).

Rugh-fute, *n.* rough-footed, XIV *a* 19. [OE. *rūh + fōt.*] *See* Ro3(e), Fote.

Ruysand, *pres. p.* glorifying, in *r. hyme of,* glorying in, taking credit to himself for, IV *b* 80. [ON. *hrōsa sér.*]

Runne; Rurde. *See* Ryn; Rerd.

Rusche, *v.* to rush; make a loud rushing noise, V 136; *rusched on þat rurde,* ↑went on with that rushing noise, V 151. [Echoic, but app. based on OFr. *r(e)usser,* AFr. *russ(h)er;* cf. OE. *hrȳscan.*]

Sa, Saat. *See* So; Sitte(n).

Sacramente, *n.* sacrament, XVI 316. [L. *sacrāmentum.*]

Sacrifise, -ice, *n.* sacrifice XI *b* 202, XII *a* 15, 40. [OFr. *sacrifice.*]

Sacrylage, *n.* sacrilege, I 4, 19. [OFr. *sacrilege,* infl. by suffix *-age.*]

Sad(de), *adj.* steadfast, IX 92; heavy, grievous, XVI 44; *sette hym sadde,* give him sorrow, XVI 204; Sadly, *adv.* sufficiently, long enough, V 341. [OE. *sæd,*

sated, wearied; ME. shows also senses 'heavy, firm', &c.]

Sadel, *n.* saddle, V 42. [OE. *sadol.*]

Saf(e), *see* Saue ; **Sagh,** *see* Se(n) ; **Say, Sai-,** *see* Se(n), Sei(e).

Saye, *v.* to make trial of, explore, XIV *c* 34. [Shortened from Assaie.]

Sayf. *See* Saue, *prep.*

Sayl(1), Sail, *n.* sail, VII 125, XIV *c* 50, XVII 153, 271, &c. [OE. *segl.*] *See* Seile.

Sayn, Saytz, *see* Sei(e); **Saynte,** *see* Seynte.

Sake, *n.* in *for . . . sake* (with interven. *gen.* or *poss. adj.*), (i) for (one's) sake, VIII *a* 96, XII *introd.* ; (ii) on (one's) account, XV *c* 23 ; (with loss of prec. inflexion) I 177, XVII 88 (note). [OE. *sacu*; cf. ON. *fyrir sakir* because of.]

Sakke, *n.* sack, VIII *a* 9. [OE. *sacc.*]

Sakles, *adj.* innocent (*i. e.* against whom you had no just quarrel), XIV *a* 3. [OE. *sac-lēas*, from ON. *sak-lauss.*]

Sale, *n.* in *to the sale*, for sale, XII *b* 148. [OE. **salu* (once) *sala.*]

Sal(1), Saltou. *See* Schal.

Salt(e), *adj.* salt, VIII *a* 279, IX 13, XII *a* 166, &c. ; *n.* XIII *a* 30. [OE. *salt*, adj. and n.]

Salvacioun. *n.* salvation, IX 333. [OFr. *salvacioun.*]

Sam(e), Samen, Somyn (VII), *adv.* together, VII 66, XVI 170, 239, XVII 316; *brether sam*, brothers both, XVII 320; *al samen, all sam (togeder),* (all) together, XVII 292, 530; with one accord, VI 158; *see* Alsaume. [OE. *æt samne, somne* ; (late) *somen*; cf. ON. *allir saman.*]

Same, *adj.* same I 188, &c. ; *pron.* in *þe (þis) same*, the very one (*or* thing), XII *b* 78, XVI 56, 71, &c. [ON. *sam-r.*]

Samon, *n.* salmon, XIII *a* 64. [OFr. *saumon.*]

Sample, *n.* illustration, parable.

VI 139. [Shortened from OFr. *essample.*] *See* Ensample.

Sand, *n.* sand, shore; *bi see and bi sand*, everywhere, XVII 75. [OE. *sánd.*]

Sang, Santis. *See* Song(e), Seynte.

Sap, *n.* sap, XIV *c* 90. [OE. *sæp.*]

Saphire, *n.* sapphire, IX 115, 116 (*see* Loupe), 122. [OFr. *safir.*]

Sapience, *n.* Wisdom; personif. of the 'sapiential' books (Proverbs, Ecclesiastes, Canticles, Wisdom, Ecclesiasticus), VIII *a* 231 (the ref. is to Prov. xx. 4). [L. *sapientia.*]

Sare. *See* Sore.

Sarri, *adj.* ? vigorous, XIV *c* 90. [OFr. *serré*; see note.]

Sarteyne; Sat. *See* Certeyne; Sitte(n).

Sauce, *n.* sauce, VIII *a* 259. [OFr. *sauce.*]

Saue, Saf, *adj.* safe; *a saue*, have safe, save, I 127 (*see* Habben) ; *vochen saf*, VIII *b* 51, *see* Vouchesaf. [OFr. *sauf, sauve* (fem.).]

Saue, Saf, Sayf (XVII), *prep.* save, except, IX 174, 228, XVII 106; *saue þat* (conj.), V 161. [OFr. *sauf.*]

Saue, Safe (XVII), *v.* to preserve, keep safe, V 5 (*subj.*), 71, XV *i* 19, XVII 309, 517, &c.; rescue, bring to salvation, XI *a* 38, *b* 305, XVI 108, &c. **Sauynge,** *n.* preservation, XI *b* 304. [OFr. *sa(u)ver.*]

Saufly, *adv.* safely, XII *b* 174. [From Saue, *adj.*]

Saugh. *See* Se(n).

Saul(e), Saull, Sawl(e), Soule, *n.* soul, IV *a* 24, 32, 61, VIII *a* 81, XVI 272, XVII 390, &c.; *distrib. sg.* (*see* Herte), XI *b* 250; **Soule,** gen. sg. I 212. [OE. *sáwol.*]

Sauour (*to*), *n.* savour, IX 153 ; relish (for), XI *b* 254. [OFr. *savour.*]

Sauoure, *v.* to give a savour to, VIII *a* 259. [OFr. *savourer.*]

Sauter, Sawter, *n.* the Psalter,

Book of Psalms, VI 233, VIII *a* 246, *b* 49, XVI 187. [OFr. *saut(i)er*.]

Sawe, *n.* saying; *aftir þi sawe*, according to thy word, XVI 397; proverb, XVI 281. [OE. *sagu*.]

Saw(e). *See* Se(n).

Sawte, *n.* assault, VII 57, 85. [Shortened from OFr. *as(s)aut*.]

Saxon, *adj.* Saxon, XIII *b* 49; **Saxonlych, *adv.*** in the Saxon fashion, XIII *b* 8. [OFr. *saxon*.]

Scaffatis, *n. pl.* scaffoldings, temporary wooden structures for assailing walls, X 9. [Cf. OFr. *escadafaut, eschaffaut*.]

Scarslych, *adv.* scantily, scarcely, XIII *b* 50. [From ONFr. *escars*.]

Scape, Skathe, *n.* damage, injury, V 285, XV *i* 13. [ON. *skaði*.]

Scere, *adj.* bright, pure, in *Scere þorsday*, Sheer, Holy, or Maundy Thursday, XV *g* 1. [OE. **scēre*, rel. to *scīr*; cf. ON. *skǣr-r, skír-r*, and ON. *Skíri-þórsdagr*, OSwed. *Skǣr(a)-þorsdagher*] *See* Schyre, Skyre.

Schadewe (*aȝen*), *v.* to screen (from), IX 19. [OE. *sceadwian*.]

Schaft, *n.* handle, V 264. [OE. *sceaft*.]

Schaȝe, *n.* shaw, small wood, V 93 (*see* Side). [OE. *scaga*.]

Schakeled, *pp.* shackled; protected with greaves, XV *h* 12. [OE. *sceacul*, fetter.]

Schal, Schall(e), Shal(l), Sal(l), *v. auxil.* 1 and 3 *sg. pres.* am (is) to, must, shall, will. I 22, II 172, 207, IV *a* 7, 79, IX 69, XIV *a* 34, XV *a* 10, XVI 15, XVII 164, &c.; 2 *sg.* Sal(l), IV *a* 17, 40; Schal(l), Shal(l), V 79, XVI 299, XVII 121, 381, &c.; Schalt(e), Shalt, I 206, II 130, VI 204, &c.; (with suffixed pron.) Saltou, XIV *a* 23; Shaltow, VIII *a* 223; *pl.* Sal(l), IV *a* 62, XIV *b* 18, &c.; Schal, Schall(e), V 332, XVI 49, 192, &c.; Schyn, V 333; Scholle, XIII *b* 39; Schull, Schulle(n), Shul(en), I 38, VIII *a* 140, IX

63, 210, XI *a* 9, *b* 82, &c. *Pa. t.* (*ind.* and *subj.*), was going to, ought to, was (were) to, should, would : Schold(e), Shold(e), II 467, VIII *a* 36, *b* 67, 80, IX 89, XII *a* 111, &c.; Schuld(e), Shuld(e), I 50, 69, 106, II 44, 190, V 16, XI *a* 21, &c.; Ssolde, III 7; Suld(e), IV *a* 91, *b* 19, X 12, &c.; 2 *sg.* Schulde, XVI 241; Schust, II 420, 570, &c. Note ellipse of a foll. verb, as 'have', XVII 227; freq. 'go', 'come', II 130, IV *a* 91, V 16, 332. *Which slepe schal*, that may (at any time) sleep, XII *a* 117; *when it schuld be*, whenever it was, II 370. [OE. *sceal*; *sculon, scylon*; *scólde*, &c.]

Schalk, Shalke, *n.* man, V 200, 304, VII 72, 89. [OE. *scealc*, servant, (in verse) man.]

Scham(e), Schome (v), Shame, *n.* shame, XIV *c* 13; disgrace, XII *b* 224; disgraceful thing, V 304; ignominy, disaster, harm, XIV *a* 12, *b* 84, XV *i* 18, XVII 301; *pl.* shameful things, I 2. [OE. *scamu, scomu*.]

Schamfully, *adv.* ignominiously, IV *a* 66. [OE. *scamful-líce*.]

Schank(e), *n.* leg (below the knee), XV *h* 12. [OE. *scanca*.]

Schapellis. *See* Chapel(le).

**Schap(e), Schappe, Shappe, *v.*; Schop, Shope, *pa. t.* V 260, VII 72; Schaped, *pp.* V 272; Schape(n), XII *a* 130, 169, &c.; Yschape, XIII *a* 45. *Trans.* to fashion, make, V *261, 272, VII 72, VIII *b* 18, IX 107; te turn (into), XII *a* 169, XIII *a* 45; to contrive, bring (it) about, V 70, XII *a* 130; ordain, appoint, V 260; *schappe ȝou to*, appoint for yourselves, XIV *d* 7; *refl.* in *shappis hym*, designs, intends, XVI 155; *intr.* to prepare, be about (to), X 14. [OE. *sceppan, scōp, ge-scapen*.] *See* Forschape.

Schapp, *n.* shape, IX 248. [OE. *ge-sceap*.]

Scharp(e), Sharp(e), *adj.* keen, sharp, harsh, bitter, severe, II 38, 539, **V** 199, XI *b* 142, XIII *b* 59, XIV *c* 21, 33, XVII 350, 356, &c. ; as *sb.*, the sharp blade, **V** 245, 264. [OE. *scearp.*]

Schaterande, *pres. p. intr.* dashing, splashing, **V** 15. [OE. **scaterian*; cf. M.Du. *scheteren.*]

Schaued, *pa. t.* shaved, II 585. [OE. *scafan*, str.]

Schawys. *See* Schewe(n).

Sche, *pron. fem. sg.* she, II 75, 77, 323, &c.; **She,** I 48, &c.; **Scho,** IV *b* 1, 2, 4, 6, &c. ; ref. to inanimate thing (*gyne*), **X** 80. For obl. cases, &c., *see* Hi, *fem.* [See *N.E.D.* s.v. *She.*]

Schede, *v.* to spill; *intr.* fall, VI 51 (*cf.* Pearl 10); **Shedyng,** *n.* spilling, VIII *a* 9. [OE. *scādan, scēadan.*]

Scheep, Shep, *n. pl.* sheep, VIII *b* 18, IX 238. [OE. *scē(a)p.*] *See* Schep.

Schelde, *n.* shield, **V** 250. [OE. *sceld.*]

Scheltrom, *n.* rank of armed men, II 187. [OE. *sceld-truma.*]

Schene, Shene (VII), **Schine** (II), *adj.* fair, goodly, VII 89, 120, 151, 157; bright, II 358, **V** 246; as *sb.*, bright blade, **V** 200. [OE. *scēne, scȳne, scīne.*]

Schende, *v.* to ruin, destroy, **V** 198, VIII *a* 166, XVI 155; **Schente,** *pp.* brought to nothing, I *introd.* [OE. *scendan.*]

Schep, *n.* Shepherd, Pastor, XIV *d* 1. [OE. **scēpa.*] *See* Scheep.

Schere, *v.* to cut, score, IX 122. [OE. *sceran.*]

Schert, Sserte, *n.* shirt, II 230, III 40. [OE. *scyrte* (Kt. **scerte*); *see* Appendix p. 280.]

Schewe(n), Shewe, *v.* to show, reveal, declare, (make) manifest, II 159, IV *b* 10, **V** 188, IX 285, XI *a* 3, *b* 19, XII *a* 49, XVI 22, XVII 82; **Schawys,** 3 *sg.* **X** *introd.*; **Ssewep,** *pl.* III 59; **Shewyng,** *n.* in *of feyre sh.,* that puts the case plainly (*or* of

fair seeming, very presentable), I 260. [OE. *ge-scēawian.*]

Schylde, Sheld, *v.* to defend, protect, IV *a* 76, XVII 301; forfend, in *God schylde,* God forbid, IV *a* 91. [OE. *scildan, sceldan.*]

Schille, *adv.* shrilly, loudly, II 104, 526. [OE. **sciell, scyl,* adj.]

Schille, *v.* to shrill, resound, II 272. [OE. *sciellan.*]

Schyn; Schine. *See* Schal; Schene.

Schyne, Shyne, *v.* to shine, XVI 94, XVII 9, 453; to be conspicuous, IV *b* 70; **Schon,** *pa. t. sg.* II 152; **Schine,** *pa. t. pl.* II 415. [OE. *scīnan.*]

Schipman (-mannes, *gen. sg.*; -men, *pl.*), *n.* sailor, IX 124, **X** 119. [OE. *scip-mann.*]

Schip(pe), Ship(pe), *n.* ship, VII 89, 120, **X** 120, XIV *c* 17, &c. ; **Schipe,** *dat. sg.* XII *a* 23. [OE. *scip.*]

Schir. *See* Sir(e).

Schyre, Shire (VII), *adj.* bright, clear, fair, lovely, **V** 15, 245, VII 151, 157; *quasi-sb.* fair (flesh), **V** 188. [OE. *scīr.*] *See* Scere, Skyre.

Scho; S(c)hold-, Scholle; Schome; Schon; Schop (Shope). *See* Sche; Schal; Scham(e); Schyne; Schap(e).

Schore, *n.* (shore), bank, **V** 15, 93; *vpon schore* on the ground (by the river), **V** 264. [Cf. MDu., MLG. *schore.*]

Schort(e), Short, *adj.* short, brief, IV *b* 45, VII 72, XI *b* 136. [OE. *scort.*]

Schote, *v. trans.* to shoot, IX 258; *intr.* shot, sprang, in Schot, *pa. t. sg.* **V** 246, 250 ; Shotton, *pl.* VII 120. [OE. *scēotan.*]

Schoueles, *n. pl.* shovels, VIII *a* 183. [OE. *scofl.*]

Schour, Show(e)r, *n.* shower, VII 108, XVII 350; squall, XIV *c* 21. [OE. *scūr.*]

Schowue, *v. intr.* to thrust, make

one's way, **v** 15, 93. [OE. *scúfan.*]

Schranke, *pa. t. sg.* shrank; flinched, winced, **v** 199, 304; *schrank to,* penetrated into, **v** 245. [OE. *scrincan.*]

Schrifte, *n.* in *do thi schrifte,* made your confession, XII *introd.* [OE. *scrift.*]

Schulderez, -es, *n. pl.* shoulders, **v** 199, 246, 250. [OE. *sculdor.*]

S(o)hul-. *See* Schal.

S(o)hul-. *See* Schal.

Schunt, *n.* a sudden jerk and swerve, **v** 200. *See* next.

Schunt, *v.* to flinch; *pa. t.* **v** 212. [Prob. rel. to OE. *scunian.*]

Schust. *See* Schal.

Science, *n.* knowledge, learning, IX 77. [OFr. *science.*]

Sclauain, Sclauin, *n.* a pilgrim's mantle, II 228, 343. [OFr. *esclavine.*]

Sclaundre(n), *v.* to scandalize, XI *b* 242. [OFr. *esclandrer.*]

Scole, *n.* school, VIII *b* 37, XIII *b* 17. [OE. *scól.*]

Score, *n.* score, twenty, XIII *a* 20, 21, &c. [ON. *skor,* notch, twenty.]

Scornes, *n. pl.* taunts, XIV *c* 102. [OFr. (*e*)*scarn*; see *N.E.D.*]

Scottes, Skottes, *n. pl.* Scots, XIII *b* 3, XIV *a* 1, &c.; **Skot,** *sg.* XIV *a* 33. [OE. *Scottas.*]

Scoumfited, *pp.* defeated, XIV *c* 60. [ME. (*di*)*scomfite*(*n*), formed on OFr. *desconfit,* pp.]

Scowtes, *n. pl.* jutting rocks, **v** 99. [ON. *skúti.*]

Scrippe, *n.* pilgrim's wallet (for food), VIII *a* 63. [OFr. *escreppe*; ON. *skreppa.*]

Se. *See* See.

Se(n), See(n), Seo (XV *b*), *v.* to see, perceive, I 149, II 11, 462, VIII *b* 93, IX 225, XV *b* 17, &c.; **Sep,** 3 *sg.* II 251, 321. **Sagh,** *pa. t. sg.* I 175; **Say,** I 174; **Saugh,** IX 169; **Saw,** X 161, &c.; **Sez(e),** **v** 96, 102, &c.; **Seigh,** VIII *a* 231; **Seize,** II 147, &c.; **Seih,** XV *a* 6; **Size**

(riming *heize*), II 355; **Sih, Syh,** XII *a* 139, 146, &c.; **Saugh,** *pl.* IX 226; **Saw(e),** I 221, X 13; **See,** VII 57; **Segh,** VII 22; **Seize,** II 592. **Iseze, -seye,-seize,** *pp.* XIV *c* 8, 16, 88, &c.; **Yseye,** XIII *a* 16, 18; **Seze, Seyze,** XIV *c* 24, 32, &c.; **Seun,** in *wolden be seun,* would like to appear, XI *a* 51; **Seen(e),** **Sene,** (properly *adj.*; *see* Ysene), seen, visible, plain, IV *a* 33, VII 182, IX 102, XII *a* 196, XIV *a* 3, *b* 79, XVI 67, &c. [OE. *séon*; *se*(*a*)*h, sah*; *sáwon, ségon*; (*ge*)*-sewen, segen*; *ge-séne,* adj. (late pp.).]

Seasonable, *adj.* opportune, favourable, VII 128. [OFr. *seisonable.*] *See* Sesoun.

Seche, *v.* to seek, **v** 101, IX 108, &c.; to visit, II 432; to try, XII *b* 177; *intr.* to go (to), *see* the *pp.*; *for to seche,* absent, lacking, XII *a* 37; **Sekep,** *imper. pl.* XIV *d* 15; **Soght,** *pa. t.* IV *a* 39; **So3t, Soght,** *pp.* VII 54, XIV *b* 50, XVII 157; *so watz ... her answar so3t,* such was the answer they found (to give), VI 158; *were soght to,* had got to, VII 168. [OE. *sécan, sóhte.*]

Secound, Secunde, *adj.* second, XI *a* 54, XIII *a* 9, *b* 32. [OFr. *secund.*]

Secte, *n.* sect, IX 289. [OFr. *secte.*]

Securly. *See* Sikerlich.

Sed, *n.* seed, XII *a* 81. [OE. *sǽd, séd.*]

Sedgeyng, *n.* telling, narrating (as a 'Segger', *q.v.*), Introduction xxxiii.

See, *n.* sea, IX 9, XII *a* 25, XIV *c* 34, &c.; **Se,** VII 125, X 11, XIII *a* 28, &c.; **Sea,** VII 143, &c.; *bezo*(*u*)*nde pe see,* in foreign lands, I 252, IX 76, 128, 271; *bi see and bi sand, on se and bi side,* on sea and land, everywhere, XVII 75, 542. [OE. *sǽ.*]

Seede, XVI 48. A *pa. t.* is perh. concealed by corruption : ? *seeded,* was born (from

Sed; cf. *my moder of whom I dede sede*, Cov. Myst. 393); ! *deede*, died (from Deye, *q.v.*).

Seek; See(n); Seere. *See* Sike; Se(n); Ser(e).

Sege, *n.* siege, X. 1, XIV *b* heading. [OFr. *s(i)ege*.]

Segge, *n.* man, V. 339. [OE. *secg*.]

Seggers, *n. pl.* (professional) story-tellers, I *introd.* [From ME. *segge(n)* to tell (*see* Seie); cf. OE. *secgend*, and Disour.]

Segh, Seʒ(e). *See* Se(n).

Sei(e), Seye(n), Sein, Seyn(e), &c. *v.* to say, tell, mention, I 254, VIII *a* 123, 279, IX 76, 134, XI *a* 34, *b* 8, XII *a* 27, XIV *c* 9, &c.; *herd seye*, heard men relate, IX 221; Say(n), Sai(e), IV *a* 74, VII 182, XIV *b* heading, XVI 169, XVII 382, &c.; Zigge, in *yhyerde zigge of*, heard it said by, III 49. Seist, 2 *sg. pres.* VIII *a* 226; Sais, Says, VI 49, XVI 60, &c.; Seyt, 3 *sg.* II 556; Seiþ, &c., I 97, VIII *a* 246, &c.; Saytʒ, VI 97, 141; Zayþ, III 48; Sais, *pl.* XVI 108; Seith, *imper. pl.* XIV *d* 13. Seyd(e), Sayd(e), &c., *pa. t.* I 78, II 188, &c.; Zayde, Zede, III 12, 28; Seyd, Saide, *pp.* I 108, IX 297 (aforesaid), &c.; *þat is sone saide*, that is easily said, easier said than done, XVI 205. [OE. *secgan* (*segþ*); *sægde*, *sæde*.] *See* Aboueseyd, Forseyde.

Seigh, Seiʒe, Seih, &c. *See* Se(n).

Seiynge, *n.* saying, assertion, XI *b* 12, 222. [From Sei(e).]

Seile, Saile, Sayle, *v.* to sail, VII 128, XII *a* 31, XIV *c* 33. [OE. *segl(i)an*.] *See* Sayll.

Seyll; Seymland. *See* Sele; Sembland.

Seynt(e), Saint, Saynt(e), *adj.* holy, I 246, XV *d* 5; Saint, I 34, III *introd.*, 3, VIII *a* 3, XIV *d* 1, &c.; *n.* saint, XI *b* 87, 95, &c.; Sant, XVII 555; Sauynt,

III *introd.*; Sent, XV *i* 7, 11. [OFr. *saint.*]

Seyntewarie, *n.* sanctuary, VIII *b* 83. [OFr. *saintuaire.*]

Seyr, *see* Ser(e); Seist, Seyt, Seiþ, &c., *see* Sei(e); Seke, *see* Sike; Sekeþ, *see* Seche.

Selde(n), *adv.* seldom, VI 20, XIV *c* 8, 40, &c. [OE. *seldan.*]

Sele, Seyll (XVII), *n.* happiness, prosperity, V 341, 354 (*see* note), XVII 301. [OE. *sǣl.*]

Self(e), Selue, Seluen, Zelue (III), *adj.* same, very, II 341, V 79; *þe burne seluen*, Troy *selfe*, the knight himself, Troy itself, V 309, VII 63; *quasi-sb.* self, person, V 88, 233; *þe ilke zelue þet*, the very one who, III 27 (*see* note); *see* the personal prons. [OE. *self(a).*]

Selle, *n.* prison-cell, XVI 342. [OFr. *celle.*]

Selle(n), Sell, *v.* to sell, IV *a* 46, VIII *a* 264, IX 113, &c.; Sulle, XV *g* 19, 20, 22; Solde, *pa. t.* XVI 147; Sold, Isold, *pp.* in *boght and sold*, *iboust ant isold*, XII *b* 153, XV *g* 26; *to selle*, for sale, VIII *a* 301. [OE. *sellan* (late WS. *syllan*).]

Selly, *adj.* strange, curious, V 102. [OE. *sel(d)-lic.*]

Seluer. *See* Siluer.

Sembland, Seymland, *n.* looks, countenance, XIV *b* 79, XVII 211. [OFr. *semblant.*]

Seme(n), *v.* to beseem, suit, XV *b* 33; to seem fitting, XI *a* 6; to seem, appear, IV *b* 50, VIII *b* 27, 94, XI *b* 288, &c. [ON. *sóma* (*sǿmdi*, pa. t. subj.); cf. next.]

Semly, *adj.* seemly, fair, II 411, XIV *b* 28, XV *b* 26; Semlokest, *superl.* XV *c* 6. [ON. *sǿm-r* + OE. *-lic*, *-lucost*; cf. ON. *sǿmiligr.*]

Sen. *See* Siþen, Se(n).

Sendal, *n.* a kind of thin rich silk, VIII *a* 11. [OFr. *cendal.*]

Sende, *v.* to send, IV *a* 132, &c.; Sende, *pa. t.* V 294; Sent (*after*), sent (for), II 424; sent

word, VIII *a* 321; **Zente**, III
23, 37; **Send(e), Sent**, *pp.* I
92, XVI 56, 398, XVII 254,
&c.; **Yzent**, III 14, 30. [OE.
séndan.]

Sent. *See* Seynt(e).

Sentence, -ense, *n.* (considered)
opinion, authoritative pro-
nouncement, XI *b* 264; passages
from (authoritative) writings,
XI *a* 27; (subject) matter, XI *a*
30; meaning, sense (opp. to
words), XI *b* 134, 143, 174;
in þis sentense, as follows, XI *a*
55. [OFr. *sentence*.]

Septentrion, *n.* North, IX 31.
[OFr. *septentrion*.]

Serche, *v.* to search; to inquire
(of), VII 24; **Cerched**, *pp.* explored, IX 310. [OFr. *cerchier*.]
See Encerche.

Ser(e), Seere, Seyr (XVII), *adj.*
special, XVI 41, 387, 398;
various, different, manifold, IV *b*
42, 60, X 44, 152, XVI 122, 294;
into seyr countré, abroad, XVII
487; *fele sere*, many and various
(women), V 349. [ON. *sér*,
dat. sg., for (by) itself; separately.]

Serely, *adv.* individually, differ-
ently, IV *b* 60. [ON. *sér-liga*,
apart.]

Sergont, Ser(g)ant, *n.* servitor,
III 11; man-at-arms, XIV *b* 28.
[OFr. *serjant*.]

Serymonyes, *n. pl.* ceremonies,
XI *b* 202. [OFr. *cerimonie*.]

Serpent(e), *n.* serpent, IX 203,
XII *b* 72, 126. [OFr. *serpent*.]

Seruaunt(e), -ant, *n.* servant, V
71, XI *b* 170, XVI 65, XVII 65,
&c.; Seruand, XVII 110; Ser-
uauntz, *pl.* VIII *a* 252. [OFr.
servant.]

Serue(n), *v.*[1] to serve, be servant
to, do one's duty to, VIII *b* 65,
70, XI *b* 178, XII *a* 189; deal
with, treat, XVI 206; (without
obj.) to serve mass, VIII *b* 12.
[OFr. *servir*.]

Serue(n), *v.*[2] to deserve, VI
193 (*or* 'served', from prec.);

Yserued, *pp.* VIII *a* 81. [Short-
ened from Deseruen, *q. v.*]

Seruyce, -ys(e), Servise, *n.*
service, IV *b* 37, XI *b* 181, XII *b*
122; church-service, I 81, XI *b*
174. [Late OE. *serfise* from
OFr. *servise*.]

Sese, *v.* to seize, V 339; *sesed in*,
seised in, put in legal possession
of, VI 57. [OFr. *seisir*.]

Sesoun, *n.* season, time, V 17.
[OFr. *se(i)son*.]

Sesse. *See* Cesse.

Sete, *n.* seat, throne, XIV *c* 86.
[ON. *sæti*.]

Sete(n); **Seþ**; **Seþen, Seþþe(n)**,
&c. *See* Sitte(n); Se(n); Siþen.

Sett(e), Set, *v.* to set; **Yset**, *pp.*
XIII *a* 12. To seat, VIII *a* 48;
set in sete, enthroned, XIV *c* 86;
refl. to sit, I 200, II 69, XVII 340;
to set, put, place, IV *b* 23, V 162,
X 48, 62, XVI 140, 387, &c.; to
set up, erect, I 91, 180; fix
(time), XII *a* 35; to cause to be,
make, XVI 204, 205; to value,
XII *b* 149; *set(te) at*, set, value at
(the rate of), VIII *a* 162, *b* 101,
XVII 364. *Sette aboute*, occupied with, XI *b* 115; *sett a*
crie on, appealed to, II 511 (*see*
Crien, *v.*); *set his entent (apon)*,
determined (on), X 184; *seites* (1
sg.) *my ioy . . . when*, account it
happiness when, IV *a* 30; *settis*
no store bi, has no regard for, XVII
92; *set till*, trained on, X 81;
set vp, to open, X 185. [OE.
settan.]

Settel, *n.* throne, IV *a* 9. [OE.
setl.]

Seuen(e), *adj.* seven, IV *b* 53,
XVII 13, &c.; *see* Psalme, Starne.
[OE. *seofon*.]

Seuenyst (Seuenistes, &c.), *n.*
seven nights, a sennight, week,
XV *e* 3, 6. [OE. *seofon niht*
(pl.); *see* Appendix, p. 278.]

Seuered, *pa. t. intr.* severed, was
cut (*or trans.* with omitted *he*),
V 244. [OFr. *sev(e)rer*.]

Seun, Sewingly. *See* Se(n);
Sue(n).

Sex, Six, *adj.* six, IX 106 (*see* Squared), XVI 39, XVII 57, &c.; **Sexti**, sixty, II 90, 304. [OE. *sex, sextig.*]

Sh-. *See* Sch- (except as below).

Shaltow; Shep; Sheld. *See* Schal; Scheep; Schylde.

Sheues, *n. pl.* sheaves, VIII *a* 135, *b* 14. [OE. *scēaf.*]

Shlepe. *See* Slep(e), *n.*

Shon(e), *n. pl.* shoes, VIII *b* 18, XVII 353 (*see* Cloute). [OE. *sc(e)ō*, late gen. pl. *sceōna.*]

Shotton; Showr. *See* Schote; Schour.

Shrewe, *n.* a bad man, evil-doer, VII 183, VIII *a* 153. [OE. *scrēawa*, shrew - mouse; see *N.E.D.*]

Sybbe, *adj.* related, akin, IV *b* 22. [OE. *sibb.*]

Sic; Sich(e); Sicht. *See* Swilke; Swiche; Sight.

Side, Syde (Siddis, *pl.*), *n.* side, II 156, V 112, IX 69, XVII 542 (shore; *see* See), &c.; *bi (at) ... side*, (orig. with intervening *gen.*) beside, II 66, V 76, 93; *on the see syde*, in the direction of the sea, IX 177; *in (on) no syde*, in no direction, V 102, IX 164, 192; *in on syde*, in one respect, XIII *b* 35; *on alle siddis*, in all respects, XI *b* 238; *quasi-adj.* lying on either side, XIII *b* 55. [OE. *sīde.*]

Sygh(e), *v.* to sigh, IV *a* 69, 85; *trans.* to lament, regret, IV *a* 59. [Alteration of OE. *sīcan*, ME. *siken*, aided by ME. pa. t. *sihte.*]

Sight, Siȝt, Syght(e), Syȝt, Sicht (X), *n.* sight, view, II 334, IV *b* 50, X 192, XV *i* 16, XVII 555, &c.; *at a syght*, at one view, XVII 469; *be sight*, by sight, XVI 229; *to sight*, to look upon, XVI 90; *with sight*, by looking (reading), VII 24. [OE. *gesihþ, -siht.*]

Signe, Syngne (V), *n.* sign, token, evidence, V 96, XI *a* 3, XVI 19, 41, &c. [OFr. *signe.*]

Siȝe. *See* Se(n).

Sih, Syh. *See* Se(n).

Sike, *adj.* sick, ailing, morbid, XI *b* 242; **Seek**, XV *a* 2; **Soke**, XVII 61. [OE. *sēoc, sēc.*]

Sykel, *n.* sickle, VIII *b* 23. [OE. *sicol.*]

Sikenesse, Syke-, *n.* sickness, disease, VIII *a* 122, 254. [OE. *sē(o)c-nes.*]

Siker, Syker, *adj.* safe, sure, secure, II 35, VIII *b* 40, XI *a* 238, XIV *c* 49, 55. [OE. *sicor.*]

Sikerlich, Securly, *adv.* certainly, II 571, XVII 38, 372. [From prec.]

Sikernesse, *n.* security, XII *b* 40. [As prec.]

Silke, *n.* silk, VIII *a* 11. [OE. *seolc; silcen*, adj.]

Siluer, Syluer, Seluer, Zeluer (III), *n.* silver, money, II 150, III 5, VIII *a* 186, *b* 76, XV *g* 4, &c. [OE. *seolfor, silfor*, &c.]

Symented, *pp.* cemented, IX 233. [OFr. *cimenter.*]

Symonye, *n.* simony, XI *b* 98. [OFr. *simonie.*]

Symple, Simple, *adj.* simple, ignorant, XII *b* 95, XVII 173. [OFr. *simple.*]

Syn(e). *See* Synn(e), Siþen.

Synder, *adv.* in *in synder*, asunder, XIV *c* 31. [OE. *synder-*; *see* Sonder.]

Syndry, *adj.* sundry, various, X 3, 9, 152. [OE. *syndrig.*] *See* Sondri.

Synful, Synffull, *adj.* sinful, XI *b* 105, 133, &c.; *synffull care*, the woe due to sin, XVI 292. [OE. *synn-ful.*]

Synge(n), Sing(g)e, *v.* to sing, I 14, 56, II 68, VIII *b* 72, XV *a* 7, *b* 6, &c.; **Sinkestou**, singest thou, XV *a* 17. Songen, *pa. t. pl.* VIII *a* 109; **Sung(g)e**, I 57, 66, 168; **Songen**, *pp.* XI *b* 133, 135, 143; **Syngynge**, *n.* I 5. [OE. *singan.*]

Synglerty, *n.* uniqueness, VI 69. [OFr. *senglierté.*]

Syngne. *See* Signe.

Singuler, *adj.* individual; unusual,

irregular, XI *b* 101; **Singulerly**,
adv. uniquely, solely, XI *a* 52.
[OFr. *singuler*.]

Synke, *v.* to sink, XVI 348; **Sonkyn**, *pp.* having sunk, VII 161.
[OE. *sincan*.]

Sinkestou. *See* Synge(n).

Synn(e), **Syn(e)**, Zen (III), *n.*
sin, III *introd.*, IV *a* 7, *b* 16, 76,
VI 250, IX 324, &c.; **Syn**, *gen.
sg.* (before *sake*), XVII 88. [OE.
synn (Kt. *senn*).]

Synn(e), **Syn**, *v.* to sin, XI *b* 28,
144, XVII 37, 49. [From prec.]

Synnelees, *adj.* without sinning,
VIII *a* 226. [OE. *synn-lēas*.]

Sir(e), **Syr(e)**, **Schir** (X), *n.* lord,
master, XIV *b* 69, XVI 117; sire,
father, XVI 254; *oure syre*, the
master of our house, XVII 396;
(as polite form of address) sir,
II 131, 431, XIV *c* 105, XVII 294,
&c.; *sir swete*, my good sir,
V 169; (pref. to names and titles)
Sir; *e.g.* of knights, V 50, X 36,
&c.; but used also of kings,
II 24, XIV *a* 9, *b* 32, &c.; ecclesiastics, I 201, XI *b* 176; and
generally, II 512, VIII *a* 262,
b 55, XVI 169. [OFr. *sire*.]

Syster; **Sité**. *See* Suster; Cité.

Sythe, **Sype**, *n.* scythe, V 134,
VIII *b* 23. [OE. *sighe*.]

Sithes, *n. pl.* times, IX 244. [OE.
sīþ.] *See* Oftesithes.

Sitte(n), **Sytt**, **Sit**, *v.* to sit, sit
at table, V 42, VIII *a* 262, XV *g*
25, XVII 247, &c.; *I sit not dry*,
it isn't dry where I sit, XVII 370;
to dwell, remain, IV *a* 64, XVI
272, 342; **Sitt**, 3 *sg. pres.* (OE.
sitt), II 443; **Saat**, *pa. t. sg.*
XI *b* 57; **Sat**, II 42, 519, &c.;
Sete, II 413, 580; **Sete(n)**, *pl.*
II 276, 395, VIII *a* 109, XV *g* 24,
&c.; **Sete**, *pp.* seated, II 520;
Sittynge, *n.* XI *b* 58. [OE.
sittan.]

Sitthenes, *adv.* afterwards, VIII *a*
65. [OE. *siþþan* + adv. *-es*.]
See Sipen.

Sipen, **Sythen**, &c. *adv.* after
that, afterwards, next, then,

since, IV *a* 59, 85, V 153, VII 66,
&c.; **Seppe(n)**, I 248, II 162,
587, &c.; **Septhe**, XIII *b* 27;
Syne, X 22, 35, &c.; *ay syne*,
ever since, XVI 223; *or syne*, ere
long, XVII 228. [OE. *siþþa(n)*,
seoþþan; ON. *siðan*.]

Sipen, **Sypen**, *conj.* after, when,
since, seeing that, V 26, 326,
XI *a* 35, &c.; **Sytthen**, VIII *b*
41; **Sith**, **Sip**, VIII *b* 74, XI *b*
8, &c.; *sith þat*, IX 176;
Seþ(þ)en, I 116, II 121, 469;
seþþen þat, II 425; **Supthe**,
XIII *b* 19; **Syn**, VI 159, VII 29,
&c.; *syn þat*, V 252; **Sen**, XVI
169, 254, &c. [As prec.]

Sk-. *See* also Sc-.

Skayned (*of*), *pp.* grazed (by),
V 99 (*see* note). [ON. *skeina*.]

Skant, *n.* little, XVII 198. [ON.
skam(m)-t, neut. adj.]

Skelp, *n.* a smack, XVII 323.
[Unknown.]

Skewe, **Skwe** (v), *n.* cloud, V 99,
VII 132, 136. [ON. *ský*, earlier
*skiwj-.]

Skyfte, *v.* to apportion, arrange,
VI 209. [ON. *skifta*.]

Skill, *n.* discernment, reason; *as
it is skill*, as is reasonable, XVII
334. [ON. *skil*.]

Skipte, *pa. t.* leapt, XII *b* 61.
[Obscure.]

Skyre, *adj.* bright, VII 136. [ON.
skír-r.] *See* Scere, Schyre.

Skirmyt, *pa. t.* skirmished;
darted to and fro, VII 136.
[OFr. *eskirmir*.]

Sklayre, *n.* veil, VIII *a* 7. [MLG.
sleier.]

Skryke, *v.* to shriek, XVII 232.
[?OE. **scrīc(i)an*; cf. ON.
skrækja.]

Skunnyrrit, *pa. t.* shrank, were
dismayed, X 59. [Obscure; ? cf.
Schunt, and OE. *scunian*.]

Skweȝ. *See* Skewe.

Slade, *n.* valley, V 79. [OE.
slæd.]

Slayn. *See* Slo.

Slake, *v.* to slacken, die down,
XIII *a* 4. [OE. *slacian*.]

Slang, *pa. t. pl.* flung, **X** 53; **Slongyn**, *pp.* **VII** 165. [ON. *slyngva*.]

Sle, *adj.* cunning, **X** 15; working in secret, **IV** *a* 10 (*see* note). [ON. *slég-r*.] *See* Slyght.

Slep(e), **Sleep**, **Shlepe**, *n.* sleep, **XI** *b* 219, **XII** *a* 81, 88, **XV** *g* 14, &c.; (personified) **XII** *a* 47, 89, &c.; *on slepe*, asleep, **II** 72; *slydyn vppon shlepe*, fallen into oblivion, *or* fallen asleep, dead, **VII** 6. [OE. *slēp, slǣp*.]

Slepe(n), *v.* to sleep, **II** 407, 456, **XII** *a* 141, **XV** *a* 3, &c.; *refl.* in *slep þou þe*, go to sleep, **XV** *g* 13; *go slepe*, go to sleep, **VIII** *a* 296; **Slepe**, *pa. t.* **II** 75, 134, 402; **Slepte**, **I** 159, 243. [OE. *slēpan, slǣpan*, str. and wk.]

Slepi, *adj.* sleepy, drowsy, **XII** *a* 91, 104, 109. [OE. in *un-slēpig*.]

Sleuthe, **Sloth**, *n.* sloth, **VIII** *a* 137, **XVII** 53. [OE. *slǣwþ*.] *See* Slowe.

Slicche, mud **VII** 165. [OE. **slīc*.]

Slydyn, *pp.* slipped; fallen, **VII** 6. [OE. *slīdan*.]

Slyght, *n.* skill, **XVII** 137. [ON. *slǣgð*.] *See* Sle.

Slike, **Slyke**, *adj.* such, **XIV** *b* 35; *none slyke*, (that) no one (is) like her, **XVII** 233. [ON. *slīk-r*.] *See* Swilke.

Slip, *v.*; *slip this spyndill*, strip, spin off all that is on this spindle, **XVII** 364. [Cf. MLG. *slippen*; ON. *sleppa*.]

Sliper, *adj.* slippery, untrustworthy, **XIV** *c* 5. [OE. *slipor*.]

Slyttyng, *adj.* harsh, piercing, **XIII** *b* 59. [OE. *slītan*, ? *slittan*.]

Slo, *v.* to slay, **II** 332; **Slewe**, *pa. t.* **XVI** 306; **Slogh**, **XIV** *a* 3; **Slouȝ**, **II** 313, **XIV** *c* 45; **Slayn**, *pp.* **XVII** 307, 546. [OE. *slēan*; ON. *sld*.]

Slober, *n.* slime, ooze, **VII** 165. [Cf. ME. *slobere(n)*, *v.*, and similar forms in Du., Fris.]

Sloken, *v.* to extinguish, **IV** *a* 6. [ON. *slokna*, intr.]

Slombrende, *pres. p.* slumbering, drowsy, **XII** *a* 106. [OE. **slū-merian*; cf. *slūma*.]

Slomeryng, *n.* slumber, sleep, **VII** 6. [As prec.]

Slongyn. *See* Slang.

Slowe, **Slouȝ**, *adj.* sluggish, slothful, **XI** *b* 219; dull (unfeeling *or* spiritless), **XIV** *c* 103. [OE. *slāw*.]

Sluche, *n.* erroneous reading for *slicche*, **VII** 165.

Smal(e), *adj.* small, slender, fine, **II** 109, **IX** 46, **XI** *b* 138, **XIII** *a* 30, &c.; *adv.* fine, in small pieces, **II** 538, **XI** *b* 177, **XIV** *d* 9, &c. [OE. *smæl*; *smale*, adv.]

Smateryd, *pp.* be-grimed, **XV** *h* 1. [Cf. ME. *smoter-lich*, *bi-smoteren*.]

Smekyd, (*pp.*) *adj.* smoky, smoke-blackened, **XV** *h* 1. [OE. *smē(o)can*.]

Smertly, *adv.* suddenly, swiftly, **X** 83, 91, 168. [ME. *smert*, sharp; cf. OE. *smeart*.]

Smeþes, *n. pl.* smiths, **XV** *h* 1. [OE. *smiþ*.]

Smyle, *v.* to smile, **XVII** 215. [? OE. **smīlian*, rel. to MHG. *smielen*, Sw. *smila*, &c.]

Smyte, **Smytte**, *v.* to smite, **V** 192, **XVII** 215, 218, 220; to rebuke, **IV** *b* 76; **Smytte**, *pp.* **XVI** 338. [OE. *smītan*, smear.]

Smoþe, *adj.* smooth, level, **II** 353. [OE. *smōþ*.]

Snaw(e), **Snogh** (1), **Snowe**, snow, **I** 162, **V** 20, 166, 247, **XVI** 89; *snowe-white*, **II** 145. [OE. *snāw*; *snāw-hwīt*.]

Snewe, *v.* to snow, **II** 247. [OE. *snīwan*, **snēowan*.]

Snyrt, *pa. t.* touched, grazed, **V** 244. [Cf. ON. *snerta*, str.]

So, **Soo** (**XVI**), **Sa** (**IV**, **X**), *adv.* (i) *Demonstr.* so, thus, in this (that) way, **I** 90, 150, **IV** *a* 20, **XVI** 206, &c.; (in adjurations, &c.; *cf.* As) so, **II** 532, **VI** 127, &c.; in like manner, the same, **V** 213, **XV** *b* 22 (*or* as, *rel.*), **XVI** 373, **XVII** 391, &c.; so, to such a degree, &c., **II** 39, **IX** 11, 202,

XVI 99, XVII 357; (intensifying
adjs. and advs.) I 28, VI 20,
X 133, &c.; (before adjs. without a) such (a), II 148, 426,
IX 159, X 47, &c.; neuer sa,
(n)ever so, IV a 75; (giving
indef. sense to relatives, q.v.) so
ever, II 340, IV a 71, VI 206, &c.;
so ... till þat, so that, until, IX
223, 229, 231; so as, (in so far)
as, XII a 126, 174, 177, &c.; so
þat, so long as, provided, XI b
223. (ii) Relative as, II 112,
VIII a 215, XV b 33, c 30, g 14;
as ... so, as ... as, II 352; so
may be, may be, VIII b 34; by
so, provided that, VIII b 40. [OE.
swā.] See As(e), Swa.

Sobre, adj. earnest, serious, VI 31,
172. [OFr. sobre.] See Vnsober.

Socour(e), n. succour, help, XII b
17, XVII 157, 254. [OFr. sucurs,
infl. by related verb; see Succur.]

Sod, n. sod, clod, XVII 58. [MLG.,
MDu. sode.]

Sodeinli, Sodonly. See Soudein.

Soferan, n. sovereign lord, XVII
92; Souereynes, superiors,
VIII a 74. [OFr. soverain.]

Softe, adj. soft, tender, gentle,
VII 130, XII a 181; adv. softly,
gently, XII a 93, b 89; Softly,
adv. II 300. [OE. sōfte, adj.
and adv.]

Sogat, adv. in this way, XIV b 96.
[So + Gate, n.²] See Þusgate.

Soght, Soȝt; Soyne. See Seche;
Sone, adv.

Soio(u)rne, v. to dwell, II 47, XVI
221; stay, V 341. [OFr. so-
journer.]

Solace, Solas, n. consolation,
solace, IX 316, XVI 28, 41, 46;
enjoyment, VII 22, IX 276;
solace make, amuse themselves,
I introd.; joy, XVI 387, 398, 407.
[OFr. solas.]

Solas, v. to delight, II 383. [OFr.
solacier.]

Sole, n. (level) place, XVII 391.
[OFr. sole.]

Solempne, adj. awe-inspiring,
XVI 355. [OFr. solem(p)ne.]

Solitarie, adj. solitary, *XI b 36
(MS. solarie). [L. sŏlĭtārĭus.]

Solowe, v. to be soiled, sullied,
I 165, 237. [OE. *solgian, cf.
solian.]

**Som(e), Somme, Sum(me),
Zome** (III), adj. some, (a)
certain, V 51, VI 68, VII 33, IX
119, XVI 19, XVII 157, &c.;
pron. sg. one, I 135; some,
(a) part, II 516, XI a 56, &c.; pl.
some, II 5, III 2, VI 148, VIII a
9, &c.; Sum time, Som tyme,
&c., adv. once (upon a time),
II 31, XIII b 5, XIV c 17, 43,
d 1; sometimes, VIII b 49, IX
47, 240, XIV a 32. [OE. sum.]

Somdel(l), adv. somewhat, IX
13, XIII b 27. [OE. sume
dǣle.]

Somer, n. summer, II 257, 352;
Somour games, summer-games,
I 1. [OE. sumor.]

Somyn. See Sam(e), adv.

Somwhat, adv. somewhat, a little,
VIII a 257, XIII b 6. [OE. sum
+ hwæt indef.]

Son. See Sonne.

Son(e), adv. at once, straightway,
I 69, II 71, XIV b 7, XV a 16,
XVII 353, &c.; soon, II 153,
XVI 205 (see Seie), &c.; Soyn(e),
X 70, XVII 21, 28, 189; Sunner,
compar. I 10; conj. as soon as,
XV a 11 (cf. sone so, XV g 14).
[OE. sōna.] See Eftsone(3).

Sonder, Sundyr, Swndir, adv.
in in sonder, &c., asunder, X 106,
XVII 407 (cf. ON. í sundr);
Sundyrlepys, adv. separately,
(corruptly) in wyth s. l., I 234
(see Lepys, and note). [OE.
sundor, on-sundran, sundor-
lēpes.] See Asunder, Synder

Sondre, Sundir, v. to disperse,
VII 143; intr. to separate, XVI
240. [OE. (ā-)sundrian.]

Sondri, adj. (with sg.) sundry,
XII introd., b 185. [OE. syn-
drig under influence of sundor.]
See Syndry.

Sone, n. son, I 46, VIII a 74, b 76,
&c.; Sonne, XVI 241, XVII

GLOSSARY

141; Sun, XIV *b* 70, 92. [OE. *sunu*.]

Song(e), Songge, Sang (IV), *n.* song, singing, I 66, 168, IV *a* 24, VII 104, XI *b* I, 112, &c. [OE. *sáng, sóng*.]

Songen; Sonkyn. *See* Synge(n); Synke.

Sonne, *n.* sun, sunlight, II 152, VI 170, XII *a* 66, &c.; Son, XVII 6, 354, 453; Sunne, V 17, VI 159, &c.; Sun, VII 101, &c. [OE. *sunne*.]

Sonne(s); Soo; Soon. *See* Sone; So; Soun.

Sopers, *n. pl.* soap-dealers, VIII *b* 76. [From OE. *sápe*, soap.]

Sopertyme, *n.* supper-time, VIII *a* 260. [OFr. *so(u)per* + OE. *tíma*.]

Sore, Sare, *adj.* sore; in pain, XVI 204, 205; grievous, V 48, X 51; *n.* wound, V 278 (*see* Rof, and note); pain, grief, II 263, 560, XV *c* 33; *adv.* sore(ly), bitterly, exceedingly, I 88, IV *a* 59, VI 190, X 141, XIV *b* 60, &c. [OE. *sár*, n. and adj.; *sáre*, adv.]

Sori, Sory, *adj.* woeful, wretched, I 123, II 458 (note), XVII 61, 211, 264. [OE. *sárig*.]

Sorȝe, *n.* sorrow, pain, V 315, 347; Sorow(e), Sorwe, I 210, IV *a* 66, IX 84, XV *h* 21, &c. [OE. *sorg*.]

Sorowand (*of*), *pres. p.* sorrowing (for), IV *b* 80. [OE. *sorgian*.]

Sort, *n.* company, VII 168; kind, XII *a* 173. [OFr. *sorte*.]

Soster. *See* Suster.

Soth(e), Soþ(e), Suth (XIV *b*), *adj.* true, VI 122, VII 11, XI *a* 51, *b* 58, &c.; *n.* (the) truth, VII 36, VIII *a* 124, IX 247, XIV *b* 58, &c.; *in soth to me*, IX 100 (*see* note); *the soth for to knaw*, to tell the truth, XVII 246; *for soþe*, &c., (OE. *for soþ*) for a fact, with certainty, IV *a* 74, V 26, 291, VIII *b* 3; indeed, certainly, II 12, V 234, 339, VIII *b* 90, &c.; *adv.* actually, certainly, I 24, V

42. [OE. *soþ*, adj. and n.; *soþe*, adv.] *See* Suthfast.

Sothful, *adj.* truthful, VI 138. [OE. *soþ* + *full*.]

Sothlé, Sothly, *adv.* truly, V 294, XVII 496. [OE. *soþlíce*.]

Soudein, *adj.* sudden, XII *b* 6; Sodeinli, Sodonly, Suddan(d)ly, *adv.* suddenly, VII 130, X 179, 184, XII *b* 61. [OFr. *soudain*.]

Souereynes; Soule. *See* Soferan; Saul(e).

Soun, Soon (XIII), *n.* sound, II 272, 436, XII *a* 119; voice, VI 172; pronunciation, XIII *b* 44, 46. [OFr. *soun*; OE. *són*.]

Sounde, *adj.* unharmed, safe, II 592; Soundly, *adv.* without mishap, VII 128. [OE. *gesúnd, gesúnd-líce*.]

Sounyng, *n.* pronunciation, XIII *b* 52. [From ME. *soune(n)*, OFr. *souner*.]

Soupe, *v.* to sup, VIII *a* 211. [OFr. *souper*.]

Souþ, Southe, *n.* and *adj.* south, IX 8, XIII *b* 53, 64, XVII 477. [OE. *súþ*, adv.]

Souþeron, *adj.* southern, XIII *b* 10, 56, 60. [OE. *súþerne*.]

Sow, *n.* a sow; a movable structure with a strong roof, X 5 (note), 29, 109, &c. [OE. *sugu*; cf. Med.L. *sûs, scrôfa*, in this sense.]

Sowe, *v.*[1] to sew, VIII *a* 9, 11. [OE. *séow(i)an*.]

Sowe(n), *v.*[2] to sow, VIII *a* 26, 65, 67; Sowen, *pp.* VIII *a* 5. [OE. *sáwan*.]

Sownd, *v.* to sound (for depth), XVII 438. [OFr. *sonder*; cf. OE. *súnd-líne*.]

Spac, *adj.* quick; *adv.* in *also spac*, straightway, II 343 (*see* Also). [Cf. ME. *sprac-liche*, mod. dial. *sprack* (? rel. to ON. *spark-r*, *sprœk-r*); but see *N.E.D.*]

Spaoe, *n.* space; place, XVI 110; space of time, while, XVII 337;

in þat (*this*) *space*, then (now),
VI 78, XVII 552. [OFr.
(*e*)*space*.]

Spak(e); **Spar**, *v.* *See* Speke(n);
Spere.

Spar, *n.* piece of timber, XVII
130. [MLG., MDu. *spar*(*re*),
OFr. *esparre*.]

Spare, *v.* to abstain from; *trans.*
to spare, XVII 379; *intr.* to
hesitate to, XIV *b* 13; to desist,
stop, XIV *b* 23; Spard, *pa. t.* in
no sp. noiþer stub no ston (cf.
sparede he neyþer tos ne heles,
Havelok 898), stopped for nothing, went as fast as he could,
II 346. [OE. *sparian*.]

Sparke, *n.* spark, XII *a* 69. OE.
spearca.]

Spec. *See* Speke(n).

Speche, *n.* speech, talk(ing), language, what is said, VI 40, VII
34, XII *b* 212, XIII *b* 4, &c.
[OE. *sp*(*r*)*ǣc*.]

Special(l), *adj.* special, IX 296,
XVI 110; *in special*, especially,
particularly, in detail, XII *a* 110,
135, &c.; Specialych, Specyaly, Special(l)y, especially,
particularly, I 13, V 25, XI *a* 37,
XIII *b* 58. [OFr. (*e*)*special*.]

Spede, *n.* prosperity; (cause of)
success, asset, XIV *c* 15. [OE.
spēd.]

Spede, *v. intr.* to succeed, prosper, fare, I 110, VIII *a* 46;
Spedde, *pa. t.* XII *b* 106; *all
ill mot þou spede*, curse you, XVI
139; *trans.* to speed, make
prosperous, V 52, VI 127; to
further, V 148; *God spede*, God
speed thee (as greeting), XVII
190. [OE. *spēdan*.]

Speke(n), *v.* to speak, talk, tell,
say, II 138, V 234, IX 212, XI *b*
256, XIII *b* 8, XVII 206 (as *fut.*)
&c.; Spak(e), *pa. t. sg.* I 225,
XII *a* 100, &c.; *als I spake*,
according to my word, XVI 28;
Spec, XV *g* 2, 28, 29; Speke,
II 324, VI 78; Spak, *pl.* I 200;
Speke, *pp.* XII *b* 99; Spoke(n),
I 100, IX 135, &c.; Spekynge,

n. speaking, conversing, XI *b*
121, 160. [OE. *sp*(*r*)*ecan*.]

Spelle, *n.* tale, speech, talking,
V 116 (*see* Deme), VI 3, XV *h* 8;
gospel, III 50. [OE. *spell*.]

Spelle, *v.* to tell, declare, V 72,
XV *h* 8. [OE. *spellian*.]

Spend(e), *v.* to dispense, XVI 28;
to spend, VIII *b* 28, 73; use
(up), XVII 130; lose (life), V
45; *spende aboute*, spend on,
XI *b* 236; Spent, Yspent, *pp.*
ended, dead, II 199, 215. [OE.
spęndan.]

Spendere, *n.*[1] dispenser, steward,
III 22, 24, 28. [Shortened from
Desspendoure, *q.v.*]

Spendour, *n.*[2] spender, spend-
thrift, VIII *b* 28. [From Spende.]

Spennefote, *adv.* striking out with
the feet, V 248. [Stem of OE.
spinnan, kick + *fote*; cf. MDu.
spinnevoeten, Fris. *spinfoetsie*.]

Sper(e), *n.* spear, V 75, X 138,
XIV *b* 13; *spere lenþe*, spear's
length, V 248. [OE. *spere*.]

Spere, **Spar**, *v.* to bar, shut, XVI
139; *out to spar*, to keep out,
XVII 128; Sperde, *pp.* shut up,
XVI 110. [OE. *ge-sparrian*;
MDu. *sperren*.]

Sperhauke, *n.* sparrowhawk,
VIII *a* 190. [OE. *spear-hafoc*.]
See Haukin.

Spices, *n. pl.* spices, IX 158.
[OFr. *espice*.]

Spie, **Spy**, *v.* to spy; *spyde with*,
detected in, XVII 544; to search,
enquire (after), V 25 (cf. Sir
Gaw. 901). [OFr. (*e*)*spier*.]
See Aspien.

Spyll, **Spill**, *v.* to destroy, waste,
IV *a* 32, XIV *a* 33. [OE. *spil-
lan*.]

Spille-tyme, *n.* idler, VIII *b* 28.
[Prec. + OE. *tīma*.]

Spyndill, *n.* spindle, XVII 364.
[OE. *spinl*; OFris., MDu.
spindel.]

Spyn(ne), *v.* to spin, VIII *a* 13,
XVII 238, 359, 361; Span,
pa. t. sg. XIV *introd.*; Spon,
pp. XVII 337. [OE. *spinnan*.]

Spyryt, Spirit(e), *n.* spirit, IX 85, XI *b* 39, XIII *a* 2. [OFr. (*e*)*spirit*.]

Spyttyn, *pres. pl.* spit, XV *h* 8. [OE. *spitt*(*i*)*an*.]

Spitus, Spytus, *adj.* ill-tempered, XVII 416; cruel, XVII 455. [Shortened from OFr.*despitous*.]

Spoke(n); Spon. *See* Speke(n); Spyn(ne).

Spornande, *pres. p.* stumbling, VI 3. [OE. *spórnan*.]

Sprai, Spray, *n.* (leafy) spray, XV *a* 1, *c* 2, &c. [? OE. **spræg* (cf. *spræc*).]

Spraulyn, *pres. pl.* sprawl, move in ungainly fashion, XV *h* 8. [OE. *spréawlian*, move convulsively.]

Sprede(n), *v.* to spread, unfold ; *intr.* II 67, IX 217; **Spradde,** *pa. t.* (*trans.*) XII *a* 176; **Sprad,** *pp.* outspread, XII *a* 156. [OE. *sprǽdan*.]

Spring(e), Spryng, Sprinke, to spring; sprout, II 67, XV *a* 1, *b* 9, *c* 2, &c.; *con spryng,* was born, VI 93 ; **Sprang,** *pa. t. sg.* rose, broke (of day), VII 167 ; **Yspronge,** *pp.* scattered, XIII *a* 19. [OE. *springan*.]

Spryng, *n.* sunrise, early morning, IV *a* 94. [From prec. (cf. VII 167) ; cf. OE. *up-spring*.]

Sprit, *pa. t.* sprang, V 248. [? OE. *spryttan*, to sprout; cf. senses of *springan*.]

Spurye, *v.* to enquire (after), V 25. [OE. *spyrian* (*æfter*).]

Square, *adj.* square ; of regular geometric shape, IX 55, 105; **Squared,** in *six* (*&c.*) *squared,* with six (&c.) regular facets, IX 106 ; **Squarenesse,** geometric, crystalline, shape, IX 68. [OFr. *esquar*(*r*)*e*, n.; *esquarré,* adj. ; *esquarrer,* v.]

Squier, *n.* squire, II 86. [OFr. (*e*)*squier*.]

Sserte, Sseweþ, Ssolde. *See* Schert, Schewe, Schal.

Stabyl, *v.* to make steadfast, IV *a* 27. [OFr. (*e*)*stablir*.]

Stabylnes, *n.* steadfastness, constancy, IV *a* 42, *b* 46. [From next.]

Stable, *adj.* steadfast, VI 237, XI *b* 119. [OFr. (*e*)*stable*.]

Stad, Sted(de), *pp.* placed, **set ;** *stad, stratly stad, hard sted,* hard put to it, sore bested, VII 156, X 145, XVII 199 ; *stad with,* furnished with, V 69 ; *see* note XVI 40. [ON. *steðja,* pp. *stadd-r.*]

Staf, *n.* staff, stick, XII *b* 55, XVII 381 ; **Staue** (*dat.*), V 69. [OE. *stæf.*]

Staffing, *n.* hitting (with a staff) ; beating, X 193. [From prec.]

Stage, *n.* stage ; degree of advancement, VI 50 ; *the hihe stage,* the high places (of the gods), XII *a* 51. [OFr. (*e*)*stage.*]

Stalke, *v.* to stalk, stride, V 162. [OE. in *be-stealcian, stealcung.*]

Stall, *n.* (*distrib. sg.*) place, station, XVII 345. [OE. *stall.*] *See* Stold.

Stalward, -worþ, *adj.* valiant, strong, II 27, IV *a* 48, X 6 ; **Stalworthly,** *adv.* valiantly, XIV *b* 86. [OE. *stælwyrþe.*]

Stande(n), Stant ; Stane, &c. *See* Stonde ; Ston(e).

Stane-still, *adj.* perfectly silent, XIV *a* 32. [OE. *stān + stille.*] *See* Still(e), Ston(e).

Stark, *adj.* stiff, XVII 268 ; *stark ded,* stiff in death, XII *a* 156 ; hard, XV *h* 14 ; strong, X 31 ; **Starkast,** *superl.* X 105. [OE. *stearc.*]

Starne, Sterne, *n.* star, XVII 8 ; *the seven starnes,* the Seven Stars, usually the Pleiades (cf. OE. *seofon steorran, seofonstierre*), but here the seven ' planets ' (Jupiter, Mars, Mercury, Moon, Saturn, Sun, Venus), XVII 423 (*cf.* 345). [ON.*stjarna,* earlier **stern-.*]

Start, Sterte(n), *v.* to start ; flinch, V 218 ; *pa. t.* sprang, XII *a* 143, 152. [OE. *styrtan* (once), **stertan.*]

State, n. state, position; *in a higher state*, at a greater height, XVII 443. [OFr. *estat*; L. *status*.] *See* As(s)tate.

Statut, n. decree, ordinance, VIII a 315, XI b 105. [OFr. *statut*, L. *statūtum*.]

Staue; Sted. *See* Staf; Stad.

Sted(e), Stedde, Steed(e) n.¹ place, I 15, IV a 46, V 145, XVI 40 (*see* note), &c.; *in þis* (*other*) *stede*, here, elsewhere, V 255, XII b 177; town (or *distrib. sg.* posts), X 117; stead, in *in mi stede, in stede of*, II 207, VIII a 63; *pl.* estates, II 161. [OE. *stede*.] *See* Stude.

Stede, n.² steed, II 145. [OE. *stēda*.]

Stedfastly, adv. steadfastly, IV a 90. [OE. *stede-fæst*, adj.]

Steem, n. esteem (of men), Introduction, xxxiii. [OFr. *estime*.]

Steke, v. to fasten, shut, &c.; Stoken, *pp.* shut, XVI 193; *stoken vp*, hidden away, VII 11; *haþ stoken me þis steuen*, has 'stuck me with' this tryst, imposed it on me, V 126. [OE. in *be-stecan*; see *N.E.D.* s.v. *Steek*.]

Stele, n.¹ stem; shaft, handle, V 162. [OE. *stela*.]

Stele, Steill, n.² steel, X 122; *trew as stele*, XVII 120. [OE. *stēle*.]

Stele, v. to steal, XIV b 14; Stole, *pp.* II 491. [OE. *stelan*.]

Stelyd, pp. made of steel, XV h 14. [OE. *stēled*.]

Stende, pa. t. subj. should stone, XV g 8. [OE. *stǣnan*.]

Stere, Steer(e), v. to steer, XIV c 26, XVII 175. [OE. *stēoran*.]

Stereman, n. steersman, captain, XVII 427. [OE. *stēor-mann*.]

Steren. *See* Sturne.

Stere-tre, n. tiller, XVII 433. [OE. *stēor* + *trēo*.]

Steryd, see Stire(n); **Sterne, see** Starne, Sturne; **Sterte(n), see** Start.

Steuen, Stevyn, n.¹ voice, V 268, XVII 72. [OE. *stefn*, fem.]

Steuen, n.² tryst, appointed meeting, V 126, 145, 170. [OE. *stefn*, masc., time; ON. *stefna*, tryst.]

Steward, n. steward, master of (king's) household, II 205, 495, &c.; *cf.* X 36, 171. [OE. (late 11th c.) *stī-ward*.]

Stie, v. to mount, XI b 123. [OE. *stīgan*.]

Stif(fe), adj. unyielding, dauntless, V 31, 301, XIV c 20. [OE. *stíf*.]

Stiȝtel, Styȝtel, v. to control, govern; *stiȝtleȝ*, is master, V 145; *sturn .. to stiȝtel*, ill to deal with (*or* harsh in his rule), V 69; *refl.* in *styȝtel þe vpon*, limit yourself to, V 184. [Cf. OE. *stihtan*.]

Stik, v. to thrust through, XIV b 14. [OE. *stician*.]

Still, v. to quieten, XVII 217. [OE. *stillan*.]

Still(e), Styll(e), Styl, adj. still; motionless, I 196, II 117, V 184; quiet, silent, I 265, II 443, 525, XII a 83, XV g 10, 32, &c.; inactive, XI b 37; calm, II 103; *holde me stille*, hold my peace, IX 279; *stylle as þe ston, still as (a) stone*, firm as a rock, V 225, XVII 525; perfectly quiet, XVII 406; *adv.* quietly, XV b 21; without contention, V 317; secretly, II 567; perpetually, ever, IV a 42, XVI 168. *See* Loud(e). [OE. *stille*.]

Stynk, v. to stink; *to thou stynk*, until you stink, XVII 381; **Stynkynge, pres. p.** disgusting, XI b 99. [OE. *stincan*.]

Stynt, v. trans. to stop, check, X 65, 105; **Stint, pp.** ceased, II 447. [OE. *(ā)-styntan*.]

Stire(n), Stir(e), Styr(e), v. trans. and *intr.* to stir, move, I 197, XVII 366; to toss, VII 141; to rouse, incite, induce, XI b 39, 93, 129, 310, XVII 37, &c.; **Steryd, pa. t.** I 197. [OE. *styrian*.]

Stith(e), *adj.* stout, doughty, VII 7; violent, VII 141, 156; *quasi-sb.* doughty men, VII 21. [OE. *stīþ.*]

Stod(e); Stoken. *See* Stonde; Steke.

Stoking, *n.* stabbing, X 193. [OFr. *estoquer*; MLG. *stoken.*]

Stok(ke), *n.* stem, tree-trunk, I 121, XIV *c* 82; block, XIV *e* 1; anvil, XV *h* 14; *by stok oþer ston,* anywhere, VI 20; *nouþur stok nor strete* (rime-substitute for *ston*), nothing, XIV *c* 62; *cf.* Stub(be). [OE. *stocc.*]

Stold, *pp.* fixed, XVII 525 (for *Stald; *see* note). [OE. *stallian.*]

Stole. *See* Stele, *v.*

Ston(e), Stoon, Stane (X), *n.* stone, rock, precious stone, II 151, IX 88, X 54, 83, XI *b* 40, XII *b* 130, XIII *a* 53, XV *g* 12, &c.; stone floor, ground, II 197, V 162; *trew .. as ston in the wall,* XVII 515; for other phr. *see* Still(e), Stok(ke), Stub(be); *cf.* Stane-still. [OE. *stān.*]

Stony, *adj.* of stone, XIII *a* 5. [OE. *stānig.*]

Stonde, Stand(e), *v.*; Stant, 3 *sg. pres.* XII *a* 74, &c.; Stont, II 556; Stod(e), *pa. t.* I 74, II 391, V 301, &c.; Stood, XIII *a* 32; Stude, X 196; Standen, *pp.* VI 159. To stand, I 8, V 184, VI 154, &c.; *up him stod,* stood up, XV *g* 27, 29 (*see* He, *masc.*); to stand firm, endure, remain, IV *a* 42, X 196, XII *a* 188, *b* 221, XIV *d* 4; *to stonde for,* stand up for, XI *a* 66; *stonde þe a strok,* stand a blow from you, V 218; to stand still, I 64, 169; *lete .. stonde,* left, VIII *a* 106; to be, XII *a* 165, XVII 416; *hou that it stod(e),* how it had been settled, XII *b* 202; how matters stood, XII *a* 150; *how so euer it standis,* whatever the circumstances, XVII 210; *to stonde in,* consist of, XI *a* 55, 60; *upon hem stant,*

is based on, consists of, these. XII *a* 127. [OE. *stándan, stóndan.*]

Store, *n.* store, stock, in *settis no store bi,* has no regard for, XVII 92. [OFr. (*e*)*stor.*]

Storyis, Stories, *n. pl.* stories, VII 11, 21, X *introd.* [OFr. (*e*)*storie.*]

Storke, *n.* stork, IV *b* 47; *see* Strucyo. [OE. *storc.*]

Stounde, *n.* space of time; *in þat stounde,* thereupon, II 550. [OE. *stúnd.*]

Stoupe, *v.* to stoop, VIII *b* 24. [OE. *stúpian.*]

Stour(e), *n.* conflict, battle, VII 7, 28, XIV *c* 20, XVI 130. [OFr. (*e*)*stour.*]

Stout(e), *adj.* proud, II 293; fierce, II 184, XIV *a* 13, XVII 304, 347; *adv.* stoutly, II 360; Stoutly, *adv.* boldly, X 60. [OFr. (*e*)*stout.*]

Strak; Straught (Strauhte). *See* Strok(e); Strecche.

Strange, Straunge, *adj.* foreign, outlandish, strange, IX 274, 311, XII *a* 13, XIII *b* 14, 40, &c.; Strangelych, *adv.* in a foreign tongue, XIII *b* 62. [OFr. (*e*)*strange.*]

Strangere, Introduction xv; ! *n.* stranger, foreigner, as name of (unknown) variety of stanza; ! *adj. compar.* stranger (metre; *i.e.* than 'rime couée'). [OFr. *estrangier,* or *estrange.*]

Stratly, *adv.* straitly; *stratly stad,* hard put to it, X 145; *ferd . . . stratly with,* pressed sorely on, X 172. [From Streyte.]

Strecche, Streche, *v.* to stretch; *intr.* extend, IX 30, 180; to direct one's course, go, II 341; Strauhte, *pa. t.* (*refl.*) in *strauhte him to,* made for, XII *b* 93; Straught, *pp.* departed, VII 11; *see* Streght. [OE. *streccan; stræhte, strehte.*]

Streem, Strem, *n.* stream, XIII *a* 17, 37, XV *b* 21. [OE. *stréam.*]

Streght, *adj.* straight; *streght vp*, sheer, IX 197. [Pp. of Strecche.]

Streyt(e), *adj.* narrow, IX 205; *adv.* closely, IX 229. [OFr. (*e*)*streit*.] *See* Stratly.

Strenghe, *n.* strength, fortitude, IV *b* 56, 73. [OE. *stréngu*.]

Strenght, Strengthe; Strinth, Strynth (X); *n.* strength, force, IX 71, 199, X 187, 195, XIII *b* 65; *full strenght*, ? in full measure, fully, XVII 261. [OE. *strengþ(u)*.]

Streny (*hem*), *v. refl.* to exert (themselves), VI 191. [OFr. (*e*)*streindre*, (*e*)*streign-*.]

Stret(e), *n.* street, II 509, XIV *a* 25, *c* 62 (*see* Stokke), XV *g* 5. [OE. *strét, strǽt*.]

Streuyn. *See* Stryue.

Strydeʒ, 3 *sg. pres.* strides, V 164. [OE. *strīdan*.]

Strye. *See* Struye.

Strif, Stryf(fe), *n.* strife, quarrel, VII 28, IX 83, XVII 400; *withoute stryf*, unresisting, V 255. [OFr. (*e*)*strif*.] *See* Stryue.

Stryke(n), Strik(e), *v. trans.* to strike, V 31, 237, X 139, XV *h* 14, XVII 231 (*subj.*), &c.; *intr.* to glide, flow, II 252, XV *b* 21; *strykeʒ*, shall come (*i. e.* for his reward), VI 210. [OE. *strīcan*.]

Strinth, Strynth. *See* Strenght.

Strype, *n.* stance, firm position of the feet, V 237 (cf. *stryppe*, Sir Gaw. 846). [? Cf. OE. *stride*, stride.]

Stryue, Stryfe, *v.* to strive; *stryue aʒeines, with*, rebel against, disobey, VIII *a* 315, XVII 107; **Streuyn**, *pp.* striven, XIV *b* 86. [OFr. (*e*)*striver*.]

Strok(e), Strak (X), *n.* blow, stroke, V 184, 255, X 105, XVII 382, &c. [OE. **strāc*, rel. to *strīcan*, Stryken.]

Stronde, *n.* sea-shore, XII *a* 134. [OE. *strǻnd*.]

Strong(e), *adj.* strong, valiant, VI 171, VII 7, IX 92, XVI 130, &c.; violent, XIII *a* 7, 42; severe, IX 204; *adv.* severely,

VI 116 (*see* Enduir, and note); **Strongly**, *adv.* vigorously, IX 231. [OE. *strǻng, stróng*; *stránge, stránglīce*, adv.]

Strowed, *pp.* strewn, XII *a* 96. [OE. *stréowian*.]

Strucyo, *n.* ostrich (wrongly explained as 'Storke'), IV *b* 47. [L. *strūthio*, ostrich, stork.]

Struye, *v.* to destroy, VIII *a* 29; **Strye**, V 126. [Shortened from OFr. *destrui-re*; with vowel of *strye* cf. Nye, Byled.] *See* Distroie.

Strumpatis, *n. pl.* harlots, XI *b* 176. [Obscure.]

Stub(be), *n.* tree-trunk, stump, V 225; *noiþer stub no ston*, nothing, II 346 (*cf.* Stokke). [OE. *stybb, stubb*.]

Stude, *n.* place, XV *g* 28. [OE. *styde*.] *See* Sted(e).

Stude. *See* Stonde.

Study, Studie, *n.* deep thought, V 301; study, XI *b* 227. [OFr. (*e*)*studie*.]

Studie, *v.* to study, XI *b* 112, 135, &c.; *subj. pl.* let (many) study, XI *a* 46; **Studiynge**, &c., *n.* XI *b* 230, 293, &c. [OFr. (*e*)*studier*.] *See* Vnstudied.

Stuf, *v.* to furnish, provision, XVII 155; *refl.* to gorge, glut (oneself), XVII 85. [OFr. *estofer*, to furnish; ? infl. by *estoffer*, to choke.]

Sturdy, *adj.* obstinate, X 194; **Sturdely**, *adv.* resolutely, X 45. [OFr. (*e*)*stourdi*.]

Sturn(e), *adj.* grim, V 31, 68 (*see* Stiʒtel); **Steren**, XIV *a* 13; **Sterneliche**, *adv.* grimly, VIII *a* 315. [OE. *stýrne, *stéorne*.]

Subieccioun (*of*), *n.* subjection (to), IX 218, 219. [OFr. *subjection*.]

Substance,*n.*: *þat God comaundid Himself to þe s. þerof*, of which God gave Himself to be the substance, XI *b* 223. [OFr. *substance*.]

Succour, *v.* to bring help, X 39. [OFr. *succur-re*.] *See* Socour(e).

Such(e); Suddan(d)ly. *See*
Swiche; Soudein.

Sue(n), *v.* to follow, VII 24, XI *a*
38, *b* 65, &c.; Suiende, *pres. p.*
XII *a* 122; Sewyngly, *adv.* in
seye ȝou s., go on to tell you, IX
134. [OFr. *suir, sewir.*]

Suete. *See* Swete, *adj.*

Suffise (*to*), *v.* to be sufficient
(for), IX 270; to be able,
capable, XII *a* 177 (with pleon.
mai). [OFr. *suffire, suffis-.*]

Suffre, Suffer, *v.* to endure,
suffer, bear, I 34, II 264, IV *a*
88, IX 7, &c.; permit, let,
VIII *a* 74, 174, XVI 378;
Ysuffred, *pp.* II 559. [OFr.
suffrir.]

Suffrance, *n.* sufferance (of God),
VIII *a* 138. [OFr. *suffrance.*]

Suiende. *See* Sue(n).

Suir, *adj.* sure, XIV *c* 39; Sure,
adv. securely, well, XVII 282.
[OFr. *s(e)ur.*]

Suld(e); Sulle; Sum(me). *See*
Schal; Selle(n); Som(e).

Summer, *n.* (main) beam, X 104.
[OFr. *som(i)er, sumer.*]

Sumoun, *v.* to summon; *mad
sumoun,* made (men) summon
(them), VI 179. [OFr. *sumuner.*]

Sun; Sundir; Sung(g)e; Sun(ne);
Sunner. *See* Sone, *n.*; Sonder;
Synge(n); Sonne; Sone, *adv.*

Supplantorez, *n. pl.* usurpers,
VI 80. [OFr. *sousplanteor,* L.
supplantator.]

Suppos(e), *v.* to imagine, XVII
221; *suppos that,* even suppos-
ing that, X *introd.* [OFr. *sup-
poser.*]

Surfait, *n.* surfeit, excess (personified), VIII *a* 262. [OFr.
surfait.]

Sustenaunce, *n.* sustenance,
livelihood, XI *b* 297. [OFr.
sustena(u)nce.]

Suster, *n.* sister, I 36; Soster,
XV *g* 7, 10; Syster, -yr, I 112,
126. [OE. *s(w)uster, swoster;*
ON. *systir.*]

Sutelté, *n.* cunning, skill in invention, X 74. [OFr. *s(o)utilté.*]

Suth; Supthe. *See* Soth(e); Siþen.

Suthfast, *adj.* true, X *introd.*
[OE. *sōþ-fæst.*] *See* Soth(e).

Suthfastnes, *n.* truth, X *introd.*
[OE. *sōþfæst-nes.*]

Swa, Zuo (III), *adv.* demonstr.
thus, so, in this way, III 17, 39,
IV *b* 19, 45, X 13; thereupon,
III 28; therefore, III 36; in the
same way, IV *b* 49; so mightily,
X 144; *swa þat, zuo þet,* so that,
III 18, X 155, 157. [OE. *swā.*]
See So.

Swage, *v.* to become assuaged; to
grow less, XIV *c* 111. [Short-
ened from OFr. *asouagier.*]

Swalprit, *pa. t.* floundered, VII
162. [? Only recorded here; cf.
Du. *zwalpen*; G. (dial.) *schwal-
pen.*]

Swange. *See* Swynke.

Swappit, *pa. t.* let fly, X 83, 91, 99.
[? Altered form of OE. *swāpan.*]

Swarte, *adj.* black, XV *h* 1. [OE.
sweart.]

Swat. *See* Swete, *v.*

Swavnand, *pres. p.* swooning, X
56 (*v.r.* swonande). [Not a possible Scottish form of Swone,
q.v. Perh. scribal corruption of
swalmand, or *swemand*; see
N.E.D., s.vv. *Swalm, Sweam.*]

Swech. *See* Swiche.

Sweng, *n.* labour, VI 215. [OE.
(ge-)*swenc,* -*swinc,* occas.
-*swing.*] *See* Swynke.

Swerd, Sworde (v), *n.* sword,
II 295, V 251, XIV *b* 13, 61,
XVII 103. [OE. *sweord, swurd,*
&c.]

Swere, *v.* to swear, take one's
oath, V 54, VIII *b* 59, XII *b* 165,
XVII 227, &c.; Swor, *pa. t.*
XII *b* 200; Swoir, X 73;
Swore, *pp.* XII *b* 44. [OE.
swerian.] *See* Forsworn.

Swete, *adj.* sweet, II 414, 442,
IV *a* 73, V 169 (see Sire), XV *f*
1, &c.; Suete, XV *b* 5; *swete
wille,* good pleasure, II 384;
(*þat*) *swete,* (that) sweet one,
IV *a* 78, XV *f* 7; Swettere,
compar. (*adv.*) VIII *a* 211;

Suetest, Swettest, *superl.* IV *a* 53, Introduction xii. [OE. *swēte*; compar. *swēttra*.] *See* Swote.

Swete, *v.* to sweat, IX 96; (joined with allit. *swynke* or its translation *trauayle*), VIII *a* 26, 122, *b* 59, XIV *c* 94, XVII 195; Swat, *pa. t.* VI 226. [OE. *swǣtan*, pa. t. *swǣtte*.]

Swetnesse, Swettnes, *n.* sweetness, IV *a* 89, *b* 44. [OE. *swēt-nes.*]

Sweuene, *n.* dream, IX 83, XII *a* 49, 97, 127, 147. [OE. *swefn.*]

Swiche, Swych(e), *adj.* such, I 2, 92, II 198, 317, &c.; Swech, XV *h* 3; Sich(e), XI *a* 41, *b* 159, XVII 400, &c.; Such(e), II 46, IX 227, &c.; *swych, such,* such a, I 79, XII *a* 86; *swiche a,* what a!, II 505; *swech . . . a,* such a, XV *h* 16; *suche,* of like kind, XII *a* 82; *pron. pl.* VIII *a* 33, 213; *alle swyche* (with sg. verb), everything of the kind, I 9. [OE. *swelc, swilc, swylc, swulc.*] *See* Swilke, Slike.

Swyft, Swifte, *adj.* swift, VI 211, XIV *c* 65; Swiftenes, *n.* swiftness, swift passing, VII 12. [OE. *swift, swift-nes.*]

Swikele, *adj.* treacherous, XV *g* 7. [OE. *swicol.*]

Swilke, Swylk(e), *adj.* of this kind, such, IV *a* 35, XVI 38, 116; Sic, X 40, 66, 74, 103, 135; *pron. pl.* such folk, IV *b* 25. [Northern form of Swiche, *q.v.*]

Swym, *n.* dimness, oblivion, VII 12. [OE. *swīma*, swoon.]

Swimme, to swim; Swimmende, *pres. p.* XII *a* 170, 172; Swam, *pa. t.* VII 162. [OE. *swimman.*]

Swyn, *n. pl.* swine, VIII *b* 19. [OE. *swin.*]

Swyngyng, *n.* swinging, strokes, VII 162. [OE. *swingan.*]

Swynke, *n.* toil; *in sudore* (L.) *and swynke* (var. on usual *swete and swink*), VIII *a* 229. [OE. *(ge-)swinc.*] *See* Sweng.

Swynke, *v.* to toil (freq. allit.

with *swete*), VIII *a* 26, 122, 188, 210, *b* 59, XVII 195; Swange, *pa. t. pl.* VI 226. [OE. *swincan,* and occas. in same sense *swingan.*]

Swire, Swyre, *n.* neck, XIV *b* 68 (*distrib. sg.*; *see* Herte), XV *c* 27. [OE. *swira.*]

Swipe, Swype, Swith, *adv.* very, II 118; exceedingly, II 472; (very) quickly, I 106, II 474, V 191, XIV *b* 51; *also swipe, as swype,* at once, I 111, II 574 (*see* Also, Ase). [OE. *swiþe.*]

Swndir; Swoir. *See* Sonder; Swere.

Swolowet, *pp.* swallowed, VII 12. [OE. *swe(o)lgan.*]

Swon, *n.* swan, XV *c* 27. [OE. *swan, swon.*]

Swone, *n.* swoon, in *fal yn a swone,* fallen in a swoon, I 195 (note); orig. false analysis of *fallyn aswone,* fallen swooning (*cf.* II 549). [OE. *ge-swōgen,* ME. *(y)swowen,* &c., pp.] *See* Aswone.

Swone, *v.* to swoon, II 197. [ME. *swo(w)nen,* from prec.]

Swor(e). *See* Swere.

Swot(e), *adj.* pleasant, sweet, XV *a* 13, 18. [OE. *swōt.*] *See* Swete, *adj.*

Ta. *See* Take(n).

Tabernacle, *n.* high-seat under a canopy, II 412. [OFr. *tabernacle.*]

Tabourer, *n.* player on the tabour, II 521. [From next.]

Tabure, Tabour, *n.* tabour, small drum, I 6, II 301. [OFr. *tabour.*]

Tache, *v.* to fasten, V 108; *fig.,* to set, implant, VI 104. [Shortened from OFr. *atachier.*]

Taȝt. *See* Teche(n).

Tagyld, *pp.* entangled, encumbered, IV *b* 62. [Obscure; appar. peculiar to Rolle.]

Taile, *n.* tail, XVI 159 (*see* Top). [OE. *tægl.*]

Tayll. *See* Tale.

Takelles, *n. pl.* tackle, gear, VII 148. [MLG. *takel.*]

Take(n), Tak, Ta (v, X), *v.* (i) to catch, capture, VII 121, IX 243, X 71, XIII *a* 38, &c.; seize, fall upon, VIII *a* 138, 258; get, VI 192, VIII *a* 133, &c.; take, II 74, V 289, IX 123, X 130 (*see* Hond), 143, XIV *d* 6, &c.; see also In(e), Mynde, Reward(e), &c.; pick (up), II 550, XII *b* 136; assume, XII *a* 114; choose, VIII *b* 83, XI *b* 76, &c.; accept, receive, XI *b* 268, XVI 331; (ii) to commit, entrust, *see* pp.; (iii) to make, XVII 137, 272. **Takth,** 3 *sg. pres.* XII *b* 136; **Tas,** V 237; **Tot3,** goes, VI 153 (*cf.* Nyme; *see* note). **Tok(e),** **Took,** *pa. t.* I 136, II 19, 64, V 175 (2 *sg.*), XI *b* 273, XIV *c* 45, &c. **Take,** *pp.* XI *b* 271; *hath take,* has been stricken with, XII *a* 11; **Takyne,** X 71; **Tane,** X 19, XVI 172 (entrusted); *hase tane,* has (got), IV *a* 53; **Tone,** committed, V 91 (*see* VI 153, note); **Itake, Ytake,** XIII *a* 38, XV *g* 15. [ON. *taka.*]

Tald(e). *See* Telle.

Tale, Tayll (XVII), *n.* tale, story; talk; word(s), what one has said, I 247, V 56, VI 230, XII *b* 88, XVI 273, XVII 315, &c.; *upon the tale,* immed. after their talk, XII *b* 147; *pl.* idle tales, VIII *a* 52, 54; *see* Telle, and next. [OE. *talu.*]

Talk, *v.* to talk; speak of, V 304; with cognate obj. in *talk þe tale,* hold the converse, V 65. [Prob. OE. **talcian,* rel. to prec.]

Talouns, *n. pl.* talons, IX 254. [OFr. *taloun.*]

Tane. *See* Take(n).

Tappe, *n.* tap, knock, V 289. [Echoic; cf. OFris. *tap*; OFr. *taper,* v.]

Targe, *n.* (small) shield, XIV *c* 55. [OFr. *targe.*]

Tary(e), Tarie, *v.* to harass;

trans. to hinder, delay, keep (waiting), IX 111, XVII 236; *intr.* for *refl.* to be troubled (*or* as next, but *cf.* Tene, *v.*), XVII 210; to linger, tarry, XII *b* 28, XVII 244, 497, 499; **Taryy-(i)ng,** *n.* delay, XVII 377, 475. [OE. *tergan,* &c. annoy; OFr. *tarier,* torment; the sense-development is curious.]

Tas. *See* Take(n).

Tasse, *n.* pile, XII *b* 22. [OFr. *tas.*]

Tast(e), *v.* to test; to sound (water), XVII 448; to experience, XVI 358. [OFr. *taster.*]

Taterynge, *n.* tearing (long notes) to fragments (cf. *smale brekynge,* 138), *or* babbling, singing without regard to the sense, XI *b* 159. [ME. *tateren* (i) to tear to rags; cf. ON. *töturr,* tatters: (ii) to babble; cf. MDu. MLG. *tateren,* babble.]

Tau3te(n), Tauhte. *See* Teche(n).

Taxoure, *n.* assessor, VIII *a* 40. [OFr. *taxour.*]

Te, *prep.* in *for te* (with infin.), to, XV *b* 30, *c* 18. [Unaccented reduction of To.]

Te, *v.* to draw; *intr.* to go, II 212, 290, 318; **Teþ,** *pres. pl.* draw near, II 274. [OE. *tēon.*]

Te. *See* þe *def. art.*; þou.

Teche(n), *v.* to teach, show (the way), direct, *IV *b* 60 (*see* note), V 7, VIII *a* 6, 76, XI *b* 5, &c.; **Ta3t,** *pa. t.* V 311; **Tau3t(e),** VIII *a* 202, 296, XI *a* 20, *b* 12, &c.; **Tauhte,** VIII *b* 5; **Tau3t(e),** *pp.* VIII *a* 23, XI *a* 6, &c.; **Ytau3t,** XIII *b* 21; **Techinge, -ynge,** *n.* teaching, XI *a* 56, *b* 121, XIII *b* 30, &c. [OE. *tǣcan, tǣhte, tāhte.*]

Teyn. *See* Tene, *n.* and *v.*

Tell(e), Tel, *v.* to enumerate, recount, II 263, 373, XV *c* 26; to account, consider, I 19; to tell, relate, mention (foll. by *dat.* without *to*), I 22, 58, II 115, V 62, XVII 164, &c.; *herd slike tales tell,* heard such tales told,

XIV *b* 35; to recite, **V** 120.
Telp, 3 *sg. pres.* III 38 ; **Talde**,
pa. t. IV *a* 84 ; **Told**(e), I 262,
II 86, &c.; **Toolde**, XI *a* 65;
Tald(e), *pp.* IV *a* 50, **X** 140 ;
Told(e), XII *a* 147, **XVI** 149,
&c.; **Ytold** (*of*), highly thought
(of), XIII *b* 25. [OE. *tellan* ;
pa. t. *tálde*.]
Teme, *n.*¹ team (for ploughing),
VIII *a* 128. [OE. *téam*.]
Teme, *n.*² theme, subject, VIII *a* 23.
[OFr. *tesme*, **teme* ; L. *thema*.]
Teme(n) (*to*), *v.* to be attached
(in loyalty to), belong, **VI** 100.
[OE. *téman*, appeal (to an
authority).]
Temperal, *adj.* temporal, XI *b*
140, 272. [L. *temporālis*.]
Tempest(e), *n.* storm, tempest,
VII 103, XII *a* 137, &c. ; *gen. sg.*
(before *sake* ; *see* XVII 88, note),
I 177. [OFr. *tempeste*.]
Tempre, *v.* to tune, II 437, 526.
[OE. *temprian*, from L. *tem-
perāre*.]
Tenaunt, *n.* tenant, VIII *a* 39.
[OFr. *tenant*.]
Tendre, **Tender**, *adj.* soft, IX 39,
40 ; tender, VI 52 ; **Tenderly**,
adv. tenderly, IV *a* 87. [OFr.
tendre.]
Ten(e), *adj.* ten, II 99, 183, &c.
[OE. *tēn*(*e*).]
Tene, **Teyn** (XVII), *n.* suffering,
grief, IV *a* 36, *b* 28, VII 81, VIII *a*
127, XVII 533; anger, VIII *a*
111; injury, in *in tene*, wrong-
fully, VII 178 ; as *adj.* dismal,
ill, **V** 7. [OE. *téona*.]
Tene, **Teyn** (XVII), *v. trans.* to
injure, VIII *a* 39 ; *intr.* to feel
grief, XVII 210. [OE. *ténan*,
téonian.]
Tent, *adj.* tenth, XVII 478. [ME.
tenðe, *tend*(e), *tent* (*cf.* Fift) ;
ON. *tiundi*.]
Tente (*on*), *n.* notice (of), **VI** 27.
[Shortened from OFr. *atente*.]
Tent(e), *v.* to look after, XVI 172,
XVII 433 ; tent (*to, hedir*), pay
attention (to, to me), XVII 291,
421. [From prec.]

Teorneþ. *See* Turne.
Ter, *n.* tar, X 19 ; **Tar**, XVII 127,
282. [OE. *te*(*o*)*ru*.]
Teres, *n. pl.* tears, II 327. [OE.
tēar.]
Terme, *n.* appointed period, VI
143. [OFr. *terme*.]
Testament, *n.* testament, will,
III 33, 35, XII *introd.* [L. *tes-
tāmentum*.]
Teþ, *n. pl.* teeth, II 539. [OE.
tēþ, pl.]
Teþ. *See* Te, *v.*
Tethee, *adj.* touchy, irritable,
XVII 186. [Obscure; see
N.E.D., s.v. *Teethy*.]
Text, *n.* text; words or account
of the original authority, VII 51
(*cf.* Destr. Troy 407). [OFr.
texte.]
Th-. *See* þ-.
Tyde, *n.* time ; *þat yche tyde*, at the
same time, together, I 208 ; (*at,
in*) *þat tyde*, then, thereupon, **V**
18, 100, XVII 39 ; *þis tyde*, now,
XVI 184, 215. [OE. *tīd.*]
Tide, *v.* to happen, befall ; *tide
wat bitide*, come what may, II
339; **Tid**(e), *pa. t.* VII 81 ; *þat
tid for to*, chanced to, did, VII
178. [OE. *tīdan.*]
Tydely, *adv.* quickly, XVII 291.
[ON. *tíð-liga*, with ME. *ðl > dl*.]
See Tyte.
Tiding, **Tydinge**, **Tythyng**
(XVII), *n.* (piece of) news,
tidings, II 97, XII *a* 36 ; *pl.* news,
II 487; *newe tydynges*, *ty-
thyngis*, IX 278, XVII 199. [OE.
tīdung; ON. *tíðindi*.]
Tyʒe, **Tye**, *v.* to tie, XVII 225;
as an allit. synonym of Tache
(*q.v.*), VI 104. [OE. *tēgan*.]
Tyʒt, *pp.* come, arrived, VI 143.
[ME. *tihten* ; OE. *tyhtan*, draw.
Cf. Te, *v.*]
Tyyl, *n.* brick, XIII *a* 25. [OE.
tigele.]
Til, **Tyl**, **Till**(e), *conj.* until, VII
167, VIII *b* 38, XII *a* 150, XVI 24,
&c. [From next.]
Til, **Till**(e), **Tyl**(l), *prep.* (in
Northern texts synon. and inter-

changeable with To; *not* with
To- *prefix*, as scribal error at
X 75), to, towards, into, up to,
IV *a* 6, 18, 33, X 26, 81, XIV *b*
72, XVI 32, &c.; (postponed)
IV *a* 30, X 77, XVI 393; with
infin. X 4, 14, &c. (and *see* For);
for, IV *a* 93, *b* 25; until, I 185,
II 75, IV *a* 35. &c.; *till þat, tyl
. . . þat*, until (*conj.*), VI 188,
IX 224, 229, XIV *c* 98, &c.
[OE. (rare Nth.) *til*; ON. *til*.]
See Intil, Þar(e).

Tyl, *v.* to entice, I 50. [Cf. OE.
be-tillan, for-tyllan.]

Tilye, *v.* to labour for, earn, VIII *a*
229; to till, VIII *a* 232. [OE.
tilian.]

Tyme, Time, time, period, season,
occasion, I 142, VI 143, VII 19,
VIII *b* 106, XII *a* 27, &c.; *whan
tyme is*, when it is (the) time,
VIII *a* 11, 72; (life)time, day,
I 27, VII 8, VIII *b* 107, &c.;
pl. periods, hours, VIII *b* 107;
any tyme, at any time, IV *b* 44;
at þis tyme, (for) now, V 23,
IX 270; *for þe tyme*, for the
time being, XI *b* 128; *fram
tyme þat*, from the time (*conj.*),
XIII *b* 21; *in tyme*, opportunely,
XVI 149; *many tyme*, often, IX
44; *see* Heigh, Ofte(n), Som(e),
&c. [OE. *tīma*.]

Tymed, *pp.* timed, V 173. [From
prec.]

Timliche, *adj.* temporal, III 1,
60. [OE. *tīm-līc*.]

Tyne, *v.* to lose, IV *a* 52; *to tyne*,
for nothing, in vain, XVII 441;
Tynde, Tynt, *pp.* VII 103,
VIII *b* 97. [ON. *týna*.]

Tyrantis, *n. pl.* tyrants, XVI 311.
[OFr. *tyrant*.]

Tired, *pa. t.* attired, II 586.
[Shortened from Atire, *q.v.*]

Tyste, VI 100. Usually interpreted
as *tyȝte* (*see* App., p. 278), tight,
close; this is not else recorded
until early Mn.E. (where it is
obscure alteration of ME. *þiȝt*,
ON. *þéht-, þétt-r*). Read Tryste,
q.v.

Tyte, *adv.* quickly, XVI 332; *as
tyte*, at once, XVII 219. [ON.
titt, neut. of *tíð-r*.] *See* Tydely.

Tythe, *n.* tenth part, tithe, VIII *a*
86. [OE. *ti(o)goþa*, &c., tenth.]

Tythingis. *See* Tiding.

To, *adv.* too, I 108, II 335, V 232,
VI 121, VIII *a* 260, *b* 23, 24,
IX 267, XIV *a* 2, *b* 91. [OE. *tō*;
orig. same word as To, *prep.*]

To, *conj.* till, XVII 241, 381, 499;
cf. Til. [From next; cf. OE.
tō-þæs-þe.]

To, *prep.* to, I 9, &c.; (postponed)
II 119, 517; *to him was*, he had,
XI *b* 285–6; (hunt) after, VIII *a*
30, 31; at, II 441, 579, V 265,
VII 85, XVII 343 (*see* Biholde);
to my hend, in, under, my hands,
XVII 255; in, according to, XVII
28; (turn) into, IV *a* 94, *b* 26;
on, on to, II 549, V 264, VI 74,
VII 174, VIII *a* 66, IX 182; up to,
III 56; until, XI *b* 25; towards,
with regard to, VI 108 (*see* Fare,
v.); against, XI *b* 111; for, II
485, VI 147, VIII *b* 14, XI *b* 56,
59, XVII 109, &c.; *ȝou to*, for
yourselves, XIV *d* 7; *to me* (IX
100), *see* note; for, by way of,
as, in, VII 70, IX 150, XI *b* 223,
XII *a* 3; *see* Mede; *to plesynge*
(&c.) *of*, so as to please, &c., IX
333, XI *b* 108, &c. *Adv.* to it,
on, XI *b* 200; *go to*, get along,
XVII 236; *þat . . . to*, to which,
I 33, V 29; *to and fro*, XVII 111.
[OE. *tō*.] *See* Te, Þar(e).

To. *See* Tuo.

To-breke, *v. intr.* to burst, break,
IV *a* 78; *subj. sg.* in *þin herte þe*
(dat.) *tobreke*, may your heart
be stricken with remorse (*or
literally* break) within you, XV *g*
10. [OE. *tō-brecan*.]

To-chine, *pp.* cracked; *al to-
chine*, all scarred, II 262. [OE.
tō-cīnan.]

To-dele, *v.* to divide, XIII *a* 55.
[OE. *tō-dǣlan*.]

To-dryue, *v.* to dispel, destroy;
subj. sg. XV *h* 16. [OE. *tō-
drīfan*.]

To-for(e), *adv.* before, XII *a* 188; *nou tofore*, just now, XII *b* 43; *prep.* before, in front of, XII *b* 131, XIII *a* 43, *b* 26. [OE. *tō-foran*.]

To-fruschyt, *pa. t.* smashed to pieces, *x 75 (Ms. till frusche; *see* Til). [OE. *tō-* + OFr. *fruissier*.]

Toȝere, *adv.* this year; *noȝt toȝere*, not for a long time yet, VI 228. [OE. *tō gēare*.]

To-gidre, -**gider(e)**, -**gyd(e)re**, *adv.* together, II 121, IX 173, 253, XI *b* 9, XV *h* 9, &c.; **To-gedre**; -**geder**, -**yr**, -**ur**, I 229, VII 131, IX 53, XIV *c* 29, &c. [OE. *tō-gædere*.]

Togideres, *adv.* together, VIII *a* 175. [Prec. + adv. *-es*.]

Toȝt, *adj.* taut, firmly bound; *made hit toȝt*, ? made a compact of it, VI 162. *Maken hit tough(t)*, is a fixed expr. = raise objections, make conditions (see forms and senses in *N.E.D.*, s.v. *Tough*); but this would require *ne* for *and*. [OE. **toht*, rel. to *tēon*, draw.]

Toiþer. *See* Toþer.

Tok(e), **Token**. *See* Take(n).

Token, -**yn**, **Tokne**, *n.* token; sign, omen, XII *a* 149, XVII 471, 517; memento, V 330. [OE. *tācn*.]

Tokynyng, *n.* indication, proof, XVII 476. [OE. *tācnung*.]

Told(e). *See* Telle.

Tole, *n.* weapon, V 192, XVI 179. [OE. *tōl*.]

Tolled, *pa. t.* enticed, I 53. [OE. **tollian*, rel. to Tyl, *v.*]

Tom(e), **Tume** (x), *n.* leisure, opportunity, VII 43, X 143; time, VI 225. [ON. *tóm*.]

Tomorwe, *adv.* to-morrow, II 165, XII *b* 170. [OE. *tō morgen*.]

Ton, *pron.* in *þe ton*, the one, XI *b* 27, 104. [False division of *þet on*; on *þet* see *þe, def. art.*] *See* On(e), Toþer.

Tone. *See* Take(n).

Tong(e), **Tung(e)**, *n.* tongue,

II 222, IV *a* 89, XVII 398 (*distrib. sg.*; *see* Herte); speech, language, I 58, VIII *a* 52, XI *a* 7, XIII *b* 2, &c.; *hold þi tong*, XVII 217; (*spekynge*) *in tonge*, (words) on tongue, on our tongues, XI *b* 121. [OE. *túnge*.]

Toolde. *See* Telle.

Top, **Toppe**, *n.* hair on the crown of the head, XV *g* 16; top, XVII 469; (of a ship = Topcastell), XVII 271; *fro toppe to taile*, from top to bottom, beginning to end, XVI 159. [OE. *topp*.]

Topcastell, *n.* fighting top, embattled platform at mast-top for archers, &c., VII 148, X 121. [Prec. + Castell, *q.v.*]

To-rett, *pa. t.* rent in pieces, II 81 (riming *witt*). [OE. *tō* + ME. *ritten*, OE. **rittan*.]

Torfer, *n.* hardship, VII 81. [ON. *tor-fœri*.]

Torne. *See* Turne.

To-rochit, *pp.* torn to shreds, VII 147. [OE. *tō-* + **ryccan*, pull (*see* Ryched).]

Totȝ. *See* Take(n).

Toþer, -**ir**, **Toiþer**, **Touþer**, *adj.* and *pron.* in *þe toþer*, &c., the other, I 181, VII 63, IX 4, X *introd.*, XI *b* 104. [False division (not merely in spelling—*see* allit. at VII 63) of *þet oþer*; *see* þe, *def. art.*] *See* Oþer(e), Ton.

To-prete, *v.* to menace, XIV *c* 102. [OE. *tō-* + *þrēatian*.]

To-tore, **To-torn**, *pp.* torn (to pieces), II 106, 171, 173, 538. [OE. *tō-teran*, pp. *tō-toren*].

Tou, **Tow**. *See* þou.

Touche, **Toche**, **Towch**, *v.* to touch, reach, affect, *IV *b* 60 (note), XV *h* 18 (note), XVII 462; *toucheth to*, joins on to, IX 182; *touche of*, touch on, treat of, IX 282, XII *a* 90. [OFr. *toucher*.]

Toumbe, *n.* tomb, I 243. [OFr. *tumbe*.]

Toun(e), **Tounne**, **Town(e)**, *n.* town, I 32, II 588, VII 112,

121, **X** 12, 46, **XIV** *a* 7, *b* 83,
XVII 539, &c.; *out of toun*, out
of the town (*or* from the society
of men; *see* below), II 236; *to
toune*, to town, XII *b* 27; *þe
tounes ende*, end of the main
street, outskirts of the town,
II 481, 564; the dwellings of
men, the world, xv *b* 1, *c* 28
(cf. OE. *lencten gæþ to tūne*);
in ilke a toune, among all men,
XVI 253. [OE. *tūn*.]

Tour, Towre, *n.* tower, II 159,
245, 359, XVII 349; (of a ship
= Castell), XIV *c* 18. [Late
OE. *tūr* from OFr. *tour*.]

Tourne(s). *See* Turne.

Touper. *See* Toþer.

Toward(e), *prep.* towards, in the
direction of, IX 31, 71, 136, &c.;
me towarde, to me, VI 78;
with regard to, in the eyes of,
XII *a* 17; Towardes, *prep.* towards, IX 225. [OE. *tō-weard,
-weardes*.]

Towch(ith). *See* Touche.

Tray, *n.* misery, XVII 533. [OE.
trega.]

Trayne, *n.*[1] stratagem, guile, VII
94, XVI 9. [OFr. *traine*.]

Trayne, *n.*[2] error for *tayner*, burrow, fox's earth, IX 222. [OFr.
taignere.]

Trayst, *adj.* faithful, IV *a* 41.
[ON. *traust-r*, infl. by next.]
See Tryste, Trystyly.

Traist(e), Traste (*on, to*), *v.* to
trust (in), rely (on), IV *a* 68,
XVI 179; *tru for to traist*, to be
relied on, trustworthy, VII 17 (*cf.*
XVII 515). [ON. *treysta*.] *See*
Trist.

Traytoure, *n.* traitor, XVI 150.
[OFr. *traitre*, acc. sg. *traitour*.]

Transforme, *v.* transform, XII *a*
123; *of that he hadde be transformed*, from that (into which)
he had been changed, XII *a* 20.
[OFr. *transformer*.]

Translate, *v.* to translate, VII 71,
XI *a* 17, 19, 26; Translating, *n.* XI *a* 43. [OFr. *trans-
later*.]

Trantis, *n. pl.* tricks, XVI 159.
[? Cf. MDu. *trant*, step.]

Traste. *See* Traist(e).

Trauail(le), Trauayl(e), Traueile, Trauel, &c., *n.* labour,
toil, I 206, IV *a* 3, *b* 8, XI *b* 227,
XII *b* 197; *trauel and tene*, toil
and trouble, IV *a* 36, VIII *a* 127;
affliction, I 204; travel, journey,
V 173. [OFr. *travail(le)*.]

Trauail(l)e, Trauayl(l)e, Tra-
val(e), Trauele(n), *v.* to toil,
labour, IV *b* 11, VI 190, VIII *a*
133, X 142, XI *a* 17, 49, XII *b*
140, XIV *c* 94; travel, XIII *b* 40;
trans. subject to hardship, IX
272; afflict, IX 93; Trauaillynge (*in*), *n.* assiduity (in),
VIII *a* 244. [OFr. *travailler*.]

Traues, *v.* to thwart; 3 *sg. pres.*
XVI 150. [OFr. *traverser*.]

Traw(e); Trawþe. *See* Trow(e);
Treuthe.

Tre, Tree, *n.* tree, II 268, 508,
XII *a* 74, XVII 34, &c.; wood,
XIII *a* 44; piece of timber, XVII
253; cross, IV *a* 86; Trees, *pl.*
VII 103, &c.; Treis, logs, X 21;
Tren, trees, XIII *a* 51, 53; pieces
of wood, XIII *a* 44. [OE. *trēo*.]

Treble, *n.* ! treble note, xv *h* 18.
[OFr. *treble*.]

Trechery(e), *n.* treachery, II 7,
V 315. [OFr. *trecherie*.]

Treson, *n.*; *do him tr.*, work
treason against him, XIV *b* 38.
[OFr. *traison*, AFr. *treson*.]

Tresour, Tresowre, *n.* treasure,
VII 121, XI *b* 283. [OFr. *tresor*.]

Trete, *v.* to treat, consider, XIV *c*
14. [OFr. *traitier*, *tretier*.]

Tretys, *n.* treatise, IX 290. [AFr.
tretiz.]

Treuthe; Trouthe, Trowthe,
XII; Trawþe, V, VI; Truth(e),
VII; *n.* truth, VII 42, 51, 94;
(personified) VIII *a* 16, 39, &c.;
fidelity, XII *a* 164; faith,
(plighted) word, troth, V 219,
VIII *a* 35, XII *b* 164, 203; compact, V 280; honesty, VIII *a*
70, 90; equity, VI 135. [OE.
trēowþ.] *See* Vntrawþe.

Trew(e); Treue, XI *b* 51; Tru, VII 17; Truee, **v** 173; Trwe, v 286, VI 61; *adj.* faithful, loyal, II 554, IV *a* 41, XI *b* 51, XII *a* 195, XV *a* 21, &c.; trusty, honest, **v** 173, 286; (vaguely, as compliment), II 23; true, truthful, VIII *a* 52, IX 298, XI *a* 27, *b* 71, 121, XVI 273, &c.; true (in fact), VI 61, XVII 201; Trwe, *adv.* loyally VI 100; honestly, v 286. [OE. (*gé-*)*tréowe*.] *See* Vntrewe.

Trewe, *n.* truce, VIII *a* 326. [OE. *tréow*.] *See* Truse.

Trew(e)ly, Treuly (IX), Trw(e)ly (V), *adv.* loyally, faithfully, **v** 280; correctly, rightly, VIII *a* 23, XI *a* 37; indeed, IX 247; confidently, IV *a* 68, v 44, XVI 95. [OE. *tréow-līce.*]

Trewman, *n.* honest fellow; (as name), XIV *d* 6, 16.

Tribute, *n.* tribute, IX 190. [OFr. *tribut*, L. *tribūtum.*]

Triet, *pp.* proved (true), VII 17. [OFr. *trier.*]

Trifuls, *n. pl.* nonsense, foolish lies, VII 43. [Cf. OFr. *trufle.*]

Trinité, Trynyté, -tee, -ty, *n.* (the) Trinity, IX 338, XVII 30, 83, 169, &c. [OFr. *trinité.*]

Trist, Tryst, Trust, *v.* to trust, XVII 505; *trew for to trist*, to be relied on, trusty, XVII 515 (*cf.* VII 17); *trust ye non other*, believe nothing else, VII 42 (*cf.* Deme); *þerto ȝe tryst*, be sure of that, **v** 257. [OE. **trȳstan*, or ON. **trýsta*, rel. to Traist(e); cf. MHG. *trūst*.]

Tryste, *adj.* trusty; *adv.* faithfully, in *trwe and tryste*, ***VI 100 (MS. tyste). [Related to Traiste as prec.]

Trystyly, *adv.* faithfully, **v** 280. [From ME. *tristi*, &c., extended from prec.]

Trompour, *n.* trumpeter, II 521. [OFr. *trompour*.] *See* Trunpes.

Trosse. *See* Trusse.

Troteuale, *n.* idle tale, I 257. [Unknown (used several times

by Manning); *!* cf. *walt(e)rot*, Piers Pl. *B* XXI, 146.]

Trouble, *adj.* muddy, not clear, IX 12, 34, 104. [OFr. *trouble.*]

Trouthe, Trowthe. *See* Treuthe.

Trow(e), *v.* to believe (in), be sure, think, I 23, II 429, **v** 137, IX 151, XI *a* 31, XIII *b* 60, XVI 95, &c.; Traw(e), VI 127, XVII 45, 244, &c.; ***Trod, *pp.* I 254 (MS. trowed; riming *God—see* etym. and note); *trowe þe . . . of*, trust you in, **v** 170; (with double obj.) *trawe me þat*, believe me in that, **v** 44. [OE. *tréowan*, *trūwian*, and perh. OEast Scand. *tróa* (I 254).]

Tru(ee); Truth(e). *See* Trew(e); Treuthe.

Trunpes, *n. pl.* trumpets, II 301. [OFr. *trumpe.*] *See* Trompour.

Trus, *v.*; *trus sam*, pack up, XVII 316. [OFr. *tro(u)sser.*] *See* Vntrusse.

Truse, *n.* truce, VII 94. [Orig. pl.; OE. *tréow*, and **tréows* (cf. *tréowsian*).] *See* Trewe.

Trusse, Trosse, *n.* bundle, XII *b* 30, 104, 120. [OFr. *tro(u)sse.*]

Trust. *See* Trist.

Trwe, Trw(e)ly. *See* Trew-.

Tuaye, Twey(n), *adj.* two, I 41, III 10, XIII *b* 16, XV *h* 18. [OE. *twēgen*, masc.] *See* Tuo.

Tulk(e), *n.* man, **v** 65, VII 63. [*!* Cf. ON. *túlk-r*, spokesman.]

Tume; **Tunge.** *See* Tom(e); Tong(e).

Tuo, *adj.* (orig. *fem.* and *neut.* of Tuaye, and still so distinguished in use in III), two, II 83, III 12, XII *a* 29, 136, 180; Two, **v** 284, &c.; Twa, IV *b* 14; To, II 64, 111, 135; *in two*, (broken) in two, XVII 412; *oone or two*, one or two, several, XVII 133, 484. [OE. *twā.*] *See* Ato.

Turmente, *v.* to torment, persecute, XVI 312. [OFr. *turmenter.*]

Turmentis, *n. pl.* torments, XVI 358. [OFr. *turment.*]

Turn(e); Teorne, XIII *a* 53;
Torne, IV *a* 44 (*see* note), XII
passim; **Tourne**, IV *a* 3, V 7; *v.*
trans. to turn, IX 73, XIII *a* 32;
turned into, diverted to, XI *a*
229; with (*in*)*til*, (*in*)*to*, change,
turn (into), IV *a* 94, *b* 26, VIII *b*
107, XII *a* 168, XIII *a* 43, &c.;
pervert, VII 42, XVI 332; translate, XI *a* 36; *refl.* turn, IV *b* 37;
intr. turn (back), IV *b* 83, XII *a*
33, *b* 142; *turne vntill*, turn
upon, XVII 218; *turne to*, return
upon, IX 87; pass, proceed (to),
V 7, XIV *a* heading; (with *til*,
into) change, turn (into), IV *a* 72,
XIII *a* 30, 53; *turneth to ben*,
turns, becomes, IX 23. **Yturnd**
(*to*), inclined to, fond of, XIII *b*
64; **Turnyng**, *n.* translating,
XI *a* 44. [OE. *turnian, týrnan*;
OFr. *to*(*u*)*rner*.]

Turtill, *n.* turtle-dove, XVII 506.
[OE. *turtle*.]

Twa; **Twey(n)**. *See* Tuo; Tuaye.

Twelue, *adj.* twelve, I 30. [OE.
twelf(*e*).]

Twelvemonth(e), Twelmonyþ,
n. twelvemonth, year, I 97;
quasi-adv. a year ago, V 175;
þat twelvemonþe, all that year,
I 103; (*at þe*) *twelvemonth ende*,
at the end of a year, I 95, 187.
[OE. *twelf mōn*(*a*)*þ*, pl.]

Twyneth, 3 *sg. pres.* twines, joins,
XV *k* 18 (*see* note). [ME.
twīnen; ! from OE. *twīn*, twine,
n.]

Twynkelyng, *n.* twinkling, *in yn*
tw. of an ye, I 192. [OE. *twin-*
clian.]

Twyn(ne), *v. intr.* separate, part,
IV *a* 19, XVI 278. [Cf. OE.
(*ge-*)*twinn*, double.] *See* A-
twynne.

Twyys, *adv.* twice, I 182; for the
second time, XVII 362. [OE.
twi(*g*)*a* + adv. *-es*.]

Twnnys, *n. gen. sg.* tun's, great
cask's, X 26. [OE. *tunne.*]

Paȝ(e), þau (XV), *conj.* (with
subj.) though, even if, III 40,

v 44, 68, VI 8, XV *g* 30; if, that
(after 'no wonder'), V 239, 346.
[OE. unacc. form *þah*, or ON.
**þoh*; *see* Þogh, þei.]

Pai, þay, þei, þey, *adj. pl.* those,
X 25, 27, 135; *pron. pl.* those, IX
128, 149, 216 (second), X 13, 68,
&c.; they, I 32, II 32, 523, IV *b* 8,
VIII *a* 144, XVII 24, &c.; *alle*
þay, all of them, V 357, IX 104.
Acc. and *dat.* (to, for) them,
those: **þaym(e)**, IV *b* 2, 19, 23,
37, &c.; **þam(e)**, IV *b* 25, X 13,
XIV *b* 14, &c.; *refl.* (to, for)
themselves, IV *b* 20, 37, 39, X 3,
41, &c.; **þamselfe**, *acc.* themselves, IV *b* 12. *Poss. adj.* (*gen.*
pl.), their: **þair(e)**, IV *a* 61,
b 14, 19, X 28, &c.; **þar(e)**,
IV *a* 59, X 78, XVI 18, 310, &c.;
þeire, þeyre, IV *b* 27, 41;
þer(e), VII 9, XI *a* 1, XVI 20,
30, &c. [ON. *þei-r, þeim* (dat.),
þeira.] *See* Hi, *pron. pl.*

Thair. *See* þar(e), *adv.*

Þan(e). *See* Þanne, *conj.*; þat; þe,
def. art.

Þank, *n.* favour, XI *b* 167. [OE.
þanc.]

Thank(e), *v.* to thank, XVI 381,
XVII 172, &c.; **þonk(k)e**, II
472, V 340, XII *b* 135; **Thank-**
ynge, *n.* IX 334. [OE. *þan-*
cian, þoncian.]

Þan(ne), *adv.* then, thereupon,
afterwards, in that case, consequently, I 224, III 7, VII 169,
VIII *a* 34, XI *b* 16, 150, &c.;
þen(e), V 131, 191, 227, &c.;
þenn(e), V 78, 92, 268, 321,
&c.; *or than*, or else, X 51.
[OE. *þonne, þanne, þænne*.]

Þan(ne), þane, þen(n), *conj.*
than, I 11, IV *b* 82, V 32, VI 195,
IX 249, XVII 13, &c.; nor, XVII
108 (*see* note), 535. [As. prec.]

Thapparence = Þe + Apparence.

Þar, 3 *sg. pres.* need, V 287;
impers. in *ȝow* (acc.) *þar*, you
need, I 132. [OE. *þearf*.]

Þar(e), Thair, *adv.* there, IV *b* 39,
V 105, X 31, 156, XIII *a* 10, &c.;
anticipatory IV *a* 70, 89, &c.; *rel.*

(in cases) where, when, IV a 1,
41, 82, XIII a 4; combined with
prep. or *adv.*, there-, it, them :
Tharat, x 182, 186, &c.; Þar(e)-
for(e), on that account, &c.,
I 88, 254, xv f 6, &c. ; Þarfram, (after *Þat* rel.) from, XIII a
37 ; Þar(e)in, Þarynne, IV a
26, x 128. XIII a 38; Þar(e)-
of, IV b 57, x 23; Thartill, to
it, x 48; Þarto, IV a 68, x *97,
181 ; Tharwith, thereby, *IV b
63. [OE. *Þǽr*, *Þār(a)* ; and
prob. unaccented *Þǣr*, *Þara*.]
See Þer(e), Þore.

Þar(e). *See* Þai.

Þat, Þet (III), *conj.* (i) With *indic.*
that, I 30, II 333, III 5, &c. ; so
that (of *result*), II 439, v 246,
xv b 12, &c. ; until, II 76 ; after
Swa (So), Swych, &c., *passim* ;
(with *neg.*), without (with *vbl.*
sb.), I 156, 197, &c. (ii) With
subj. that, to (with *infin.* ; *esp.*
after verbs of commanding,
desiring, purposing, &c.), II 534,
III 7, 37, XI b 217, XIV c 99, &c.;
loosely connected with what precedes, VIII a 11 (note), 52, XI b
247; lest (after ' fear '), XI a 61,
XVII 184, 372, &c.; so that (of
purpose), in order that, lest (with
neg.), I 220, IV a 22, b 13, XVI
199, 399, &c.; *see* Forbede.
So that, in order that, XII a 19,
&c.; *wende . . . Þat*, go . . . and,
VIII a 271. *Indef.* where, if, IV b
75, 83, &c. (iii) Forming con-
junctions with preps. and advs.
(orig. a pro-nominal use as in
OE. *for Þam Þe*), *see* the preps.
&c.; subjoined to other conjs.
(as ʒif, &c.), *see* the conjs. ;
or to rel. and interrog. advs.
(*see* Þat, *rel.*), as *whan that*,
when, IX 22, &c.; hence used
to obviate repetition of a conj.,
in *whan (that) . . . and that*,
when . . . and when, XII a 36,
b 155–6, 180–2; similarly pleonastic in *Þe more Þat*, the more,
XI b 114. [OE. *Þǣt*, *Þǣtte*.]

Þat, Þet, *demonstr. adj.* (i) As

def. art. (orig. *neut.*), *see* Þe.
(ii) *Emphatic* that, I 93, 108,
&c. ; the same, that very, I 95,
190, 226, &c. Þane, *acc. sg.*
masc. that, III 9. For *pl. see* Þo,
Þos. [*See* next.]

Þat, Þet (III), *pron.* that, it, the
same, II 131, 543, III 56, v 44,
XIII b 49, &c.; even that, VIII a
306 ; *am I that*, is it I (you
mean), xv g 27 ; *that is myne*,
there's one from me, XVII 226 ;
that withoute, what is outside,
XII a 73 ; *quasi-adv.* (at) that,
too, XVII 146 ; as regards that,
XVII 524 (*see* Bold). Þan, *dat.*
sg. in *after (bi) Þan*, after (by)
that, II 553, 597 ; *see* Bi, Wiþ.
[OE. *Þǣt* (Kt. *Þet*), neut.; Þane,
acc. masc.; *Þǣm*, dat.]

Þat, Þet (III), *rel. pron. indecl.*
that, which, who(m), I 11, 16,
47, III 17. &c. ; for whom, XIV a
32 (*see* Betre; but here *Þat* is
perh. already felt as *nom.*); a
thing which, XI b 26, &c.; *Þat*
Þat, that which, what, IV b 65,
IX 70, &c.; *Þat at*, VI 176; *it . . .*
Þat, VIII a 242, &c.; (elliptically)
Þat, that which, I 178, 180, II
516, XVII 164, &c.; he who, IV
196; him that, VIII a 114 ;
those whom, XVI 8; *same Þat*, just
what, XVI 71, &c.; (loosely, or
with ellipse of prep.) *Þat*, to
whom, VI 64, xv i 4 ; (as that)
in which, I 188 ; (from that) in
which, IX 320; that into which,
XII a 20. Supplemented by
pers. prons., as *Þat . . . hym*,
whom, v 37; *Þat . . . hit*, which,
I 185, IV a 36, v 127, IX 6, x 6 ;
Þat Þai, which, XIV b 76; *that . . .*
thame ilkane, x 160 (*see* note);
similarly, *Þat . . . Þat tyde*
(= then), when, v 17; *Þat . . .*
Þerof, of which, XI b 222–3 ; *cf.*
XIII a 36–7. For use with separated preps. and advs. (as, *Þat*
. . . of, of whom, VI 65) *see*
the preps., &c.; note *Þat . . . after*,
that after which, VII 20, *same Þat*
. . . fro, same as that from which,

IX 230. Subjoined to other relatives, and indir. interrogatives, see Hou, Whan, What, &c.; cf. Þat, conj. [Substitution of prec. for OE. þe; þat, that which, may in part repres. OE. þæt-þe, þætte.] See App., p. 289.

Þatow, = þat þou, that thou, II 165, 454, 471; cf. þat tou, XV g 9. See Þou.

Þau. See Þaȝ(e).

Þe, adv.; demonstr. (by) so much, for that, the, V 300, VIII b 100; (pleonastic), VIII a 112; the wars I thee see, so much the worse for seeing you, XVII 191; rel. by which, in þe better, (so) that ... better, VIII a 46, XVII 175; correl. in þe ... þe (... þe), the ... the, I 255, VI 240 (see note). [OE. þȳ, þĕ.] See Forþi.

Þe, def. art. the, I 8, *XVI 170 (MS. 3e), &c.; generic, IX 109, &c.; see Whiche, Whilke, Who. Te, in an te, and the, XV e 19; Th- (before vowels), XII a 127, b 191, 211. Þane, acc. sg. masc. III 10, 14, 59; Þat, Þet, neut. sg. III 41, 44, 46, 57; with French masc. III 46; before vowels and merging into Þat demonstr., I 43; esp. in þat yche, ilk(e), the same, &c., I 208, V 65, &c.; but þe ilke, masc. and fem., III 27, 45; þat o(n), the one, V 244, 344, IX 176, XV h 7; þat oþer(-), the other, V 72, 169, 200, 344, XII a 118, XV h 7; see Ich, Ilke, Ton, Toþer, &c. [OE. se (late þe), &c.]

The, v. to prosper, in as euer myght I the, so may I prosper, on my life, XVII 328. [OE. þēon.]

Þe, The(e). See Þou.

Þede, n. (folk), land, II 475, 194, 535, VI 123. [OE. þēod.]

Þedyr, -ur, &c. See Þider.

Þeeues, n. pl. thieves, VIII b 17; Þeuys, XI b 176; Þieues, III 18. [OE. þēof (Kt. þīof).]

Þei, Þey, conj. though, even if, II

173, 247, 433, XIII a 32; Þeyȝ, Theigh, VIII a 220, XIII b 9. [OE. þē(a)h.] See Þogh.

Þeire; Þeise. See Þai; Þes.

Themperour = þe + Emperour.

Þen(e), Þenn(e). See Þan(ne), adv., conj.

Þenche, Þenk(en), v. to think, I 221, II 373, XI b 253, &c.; Þinke, Thynk(e), II 44, IV a 78, VII 30, &c.; Þoȝte, Thoghte, pa. t. III 57, XII a 11, &c.; Thoucht, X 28, &c.; Þouȝte, Thoughte, VIII a 293, IX 167; Thoȝht, þouȝt, pp. II 390, XIV b 53, &c.; to consider, XVI 3; þ. on (vpon), think, be mindful, of, IV a 78, 95, V 329, VI 10, &c.; intend to, be resolved to, VII 30, X 79; expect to, XII a 28; þ. to (for to, till), expect to, VIII a 293, X 28, XIV b 36, &c.; conceive, imagine, II 373, 390, XVII 286, &c; Thynkynge, n. IV b 68. [OE. þencan, þōhte.] See Þinke.

Þenne, adv. thence, I 153. [Cf. OE. þanone.] See Thine.

Þens, adv. thence, in from þens, IX 259, XVII 548. [Prec. + adv. -es.]

Þer(e), adv. demonstr. there, I 98, II 189, III 42, &c.; correl. in þere ... where, where, IX 222; indef. (unaccented; see Þyr), II 10, 39, XII a 75, &c.; rel. where, when, I 154, V 8, 52, 329, VIII a 240, XII a 141, &c.; equiv. to neut. pron. it, that, them, and occas. rel. which: Þer(e)aboute(n), (round) about it, IX 156, *XI b 252; Þerafter, afterwards, V 350, VIII a 108, &c.; according to it, XI b 244; Þerap(p)on, on it, &c., VII 75, XVII 282; Þerate, there, II 380, VI 154; Þerby(e), by that means, XI a 13, XVI 161; on that account, XIII b 35; according to it, XVI 322; Þer(e)for(e), Þeruore, &c., on that account. I 71, III 41, V 211 (pleonastic), 289, XVII 20, &c.; on account

of which, XVI 167; because, IX
108 (note); þerfro, XVI 295;
ther . . . fro, whence, XII *a* 33;
þerin(ne), -ynne, II 278, V
106, XIII *a* 16, &c.; *rel.* wherein,
II 413; Ther(e)myd(d)e, therewith. VIII *a* 69, 151; þer(e)of,
þereoffe, of it, from it, &c., III
20, IV *a* 39, VIII *a* 191, IX 6,
&c.; *rel.* of which, XIII *a* 31;
see þat, *rel.*; þeron, of it, VI 27;
þerto, to it (that), V 257, XVII
385; at it, XIII *a* 48; for it, XI *b*
254; in addition, XII *b* 200;
(after *rel.*) to, XI *b* 246, XIII *a* 37;
þer vnder, underneath (them),
V 11; þerupon, at it, XII *b*
162; þer(e)with, by that
means, VIII *a* 95, 102, &c.; with
it (after Part, *v.*), VII 96. [OE.
þǣr, þēr.] *See* þar(e) þyr, þore.
þer(e). *See* þai; Thire.
þerewhiles, *adv.* in the meantime, VIII *a* 8. [OE. (*on*) *þǣre
hwīle* + adv. -*es*.] *See* þerwhile.
þerk, *adj.* dark, II 370. [OE.
*þeorc (*þeorcung* = *deorcung*);
see Kluge, *Urgerm.* § 37 *d*.]
þerwhile, *conj.* while, VIII *a* 156;
see While. [OE. *on þǣre hwīle
þe*.] *See* þerewhiles.
þes, *demonstr. adj.* (and *pron.*) *sg.*
this, VIII *b* 78, XV *i* 18; þis(ē),
þys(se), I 20, II 47, VI 10, 173,
&c.; þhis, XVI 61; *this*, this
woman, XVII 403; þeise, *pl.*
these, IX 117, 318; þes, VIII *b*
42, XI *a* 61, &c.; *pron.* V 354,
VII 50, &c.; þese, I 43, 47, &c.;
þis, þys, II 13, 340, VI 145
(*note*), XVII 445, &c.; þise,
þyse, III 59, V 355, XVII 181,
&c.; þuse, VIII *b* 70. [OE. *þes,
þēos, þis*; see *N.E.D.*]
þet. *See* þat; þe, *def. art.*
þeuys. *See* þeeues.
þi, þy. *See* Forþi, þou.
Thicke, *adj.* dense, pouring (rain),
VII 107, 132. [OE. *þicce*.]
þider, *adv.* thither, II 316, 318,
&c.; þedyr, Thedir, -ur, I 43,
VII 88, XVII 312, &c. [OE.
þider.]

þyderward, Thederward, *adv.*
thither, in that direction, XIII *a*
33, XVII 245. [OE. *þider-
w(e)ard*.]
þieues. *See* þeeues.
Thilke, *adj.* that (same), XII *b* 59,
205, 220; þulke, those, XIII *a*
2. [OE. *þylc*, such; treated in
sense as a contraction of þe +
Ilk(e), *q.v.*]
Thine, *adv.* thence, in *fra thine
furth*, thenceforward, X 130.
[Obscure red. of ME. *þeþen* (cf.
ON. *þaðan*); cf. *sine* from
siþ(þ)en, seþen.]
þin(e), þyn(e). *See* þou.
þing(e), þyng, þynk (VI), *n.*
thing, II 33, IV *a* 29, &c.; *al
þat þing*, everything there, II
417; *al this thyng*, all this, XVII
154. *Na thyng, no þing* (*þynk*,
&c.), nothing, anything (with
neg.), II 172, IV *a* 6. VI 136, 227,
IX 275, &c.; as *adv.* no whit,
in no way, I 67, II 39, V 168,
XVII 289; *na kyn thing*, no
whit, X 59; *for no þing*, for any
(other) cause, II 98. þing, &c.,
pl. things, affairs, matters, I 7,
II 4, 218, 297, XI *b* 249; *al(le)
þing*, &c. (constr. as *sg.* or *pl.*)
everything, II 11, IV *a* 68, VIII *a*
203, IX 239, XIV *c* 2, XVII 73,
&c.; all things, XV *c* 6; *bi al
þing*, by every token, II 321,
375; þinges, Thyngeȝ, &c.,
II 496, IV *b* 62, &c.; compositions, tasks, XIII *b* 19. [OE.
þing.]
þink(e), þynk(e), þenk(e), *v.*
to seem to (with *dat. pron.*), II
442; þynkkeȝ, thou seemest,
V 294; *impers.* in *me þinkeþ,
thynkys me*, &c., it seems to
me, VIII *b* 55, XIV *c* 28, XVII
511, &c.; endingless form
in, *me* (*him, vs*) *þink*, &c., it
seems to me, I think, &c., II
375, IV *a* 10, 12, V 41, VI 192,
230, XVII 399, &c.; *þynk me*,
XVII 255; with *nom. pron.* in
thou thynk, (it) seems good to
you, XVII 196, 379. þoȝt,

Thoght(e), *pa. t.* (it) seemed to, V 95, XII *b* 74, XVII 82, 425 ; with *nom. pron.* in *þey þoȝt*, they thought good, I 87. [OE. *þyncan, þūhte*. The endingless forms prob. arose in I *sg.* by confusion with *þenche*, *q.v.* ; but *cf.* ON. *þykki mér*.]

Þyr, *adv. indef.* there I 170. [Reduced unaccented form of Þer(e) ; *y* repres. obscure vowel, as (*e.g.*) in *þedyr*, 171.]

Thire, *adj.* and *pron. pl.* these, IV *b* 55, 59 ; Þer, XVI 97, 399. [Obscure ; usually Northern.]

Thirté. See Þritti.

Þis(e), Þys(se), &c. See Þes.

Þiself(f)e, Þiselue(n). See Þou.

Þo, *demonstr. adj. pl.* those, V 130, VII 113, VIII *b* 5, IX 33, &c. ; *pron.* they, those, &c. II 575 (second), VI 197, VIII *a* 155, IX 48, XV *b* 23, XVI 279, XVII 228. [OE. *þā.*] See Þat.

Þo, *adv.* then, thereupon, II 49, 117, III 12, VIII *a* 22, XII *a* 6, &c. ; in addition, more, in *þo fyue*, five (times) more, VI 91 ; *rel.* when, III 3, 32, 44, 54, 56. [OE. *þā.*]

Þof, *conj.* though, even if, IV *a* 12, 75, VII 29. [As next, with alteration of final spirant ; *cf.* Þouþ ; Rof.]

Þogh, *conj.* though, (even) if, IX 207, XII *a* 187, &c. ; *þogh þat*, though, I 224 ; Þou, XV *f* 8 ; Þouȝ, Þough, IX 139, XIV *c* 37, &c. ; Þowȝ, Þowgh, VIII *a* 36, 40, &c. [ON. *þó*, earlier **þoh*.] See Þaȝe, Þei, Allthough.

Þoȝt(e), Thoght(e). See Þenche, Þinke, Þouȝt.

Þolien, Þole, *v.* to endure, IV *a* 14, V 351, XV *c* 33 ; *tholid . . . for to be*, suffered myself to be, XVI 3. [OE. *þolian.*]

Thoner ; Þonk(k)e. See Þundyr ; Thanke.

Þore, *adv.* there, then, I 96, 175, V 288, VI 202. [OE. *þāra*.] See Þar(e).

Þorgh, *prep.* through ; through-

out, over ; because of, out of ; by (means of) : IX 87, XV *i* 3, &c. ; Thoro, XVII 278 ; Þorw, VIII *a* 20, XIV *c* 19, &c. ; Thorwgh, VIII *a* 320 ; Þourgh, VIII *a* 320 ; Throu, X 15 ; Throughe, VII 16, 92 ; Þurch, II 237, &c. ; Þurȝ, V 83, VI 53, &c. ; Þurgh(e), I 186, IV *b* 71, VII 103, &c. ; *adv.* through, IX 224. [OE. *þurh, þorh.*]

Þorghout, *prep.* throughout, IX 217 ; Thurghout, *adv.* in every detail, XII *b* 219. [OE. *þurh-ūt*.]

Þorsday, *n.* Thursday, XV *g* 1 [OE. *þōresdæg*, from ON. *þórs-dag-r*.] See Scere.

Þos, *pron. pl.* those, VI 155 ; Those, XVII 45, &c. [OE. *þās.*] See Þat.

Þou, *pron.* thou, you, I 130, II 108, &c. ; Þow(e), IV *a* 22, V 256, XVI 242, &c. ; Þu, VII 94 ; Tou, Tow (after closely connected words ending in *d, t, s*), II 452, XV *a* 17, *g* 9 ; see also *artow, canstow, hadestow, neltow, saltou, shaltow, þatow, wiltou, wolte* (with further reduction). **Þe, The(e), Te** (after *is*), *acc.* thee, you, II 116, XVII 118, 407, &c. ; *dat.* (to, for) thee, II 132, V 175, 218, 291 ; XV *g* 10, &c. ; concerning thee, XV *g* 28 ; *what is te, what þe is*, what is the matter with thee, II 102, 115 ; *for the*, as far as you are concerned, XVII 193 ; *refl.* (to, for) thyself, yourself, V 184, 229 (first), 289, VIII *a* 32, 223, XV *f* 13, XVII 224, &c. **Þi, Þy** ; **Þin, Þyn(e)** (usually before vowels) ; *poss. adj.* thy, your, I 125, II 105, V 235, VI 207, &c. ; (*objective*) of thee, VIII *a* 27, XV *g* 31, &c. ; **Þine, Þyne**, *oblique* and *pl.* II 109, XV *c* 23, &c. ; *pron.* belonging to thee, XVI 221 ; thy folk, XVI 252. **Þiselffe, -selue** ; **Þyseluen, -self(e)**, *nom.* (thou) thyself, XVI 206, 261, 299 ; *refl.* thyself, V 73, VI 113, XVI 350, &c. [OE. *þū, -tū* ; *þē* ; *þīn*.]

þou, þouȝ, þough. *See* þogh.

Thoucht, þouȝt(e), &c. *See* þenche.

þouȝt, *n.* thought, mind, imagination, II 373; þoȝte, VI 164, *see* Dede; Thoght(e), IV *a* 5, *b* 23, XVII 156, &c. [OE. (ge-)-þōht.]

þourgh. *See* þorgh.

þousand(e), -end, -ond; þou-zond; Thowsande; *n. sg.* and *pl.* thousand, III 30, 34, VIII *a* 185, XI *b* 279, XIII *b* 31. XVI 39, &c. [OE. þūsend.]

Thousendfold, *adj.*; *many thousendfold*, in many thousands, XII *a* 97. [OE. þūsend-fáld.]

þouþ, *conj.* though, even if, XI *b* 190. [As þogh, with alteration of final spirant; *cf.* þof.]

þow(e); þowȝ, &c. *See* þou; þogh.

Thrall, *n.* slave; predic. as *adj.* in bondage, subject, XVI 134. [OE. þrǽll, from ON. þrǽl-l.]

þre(e), *adj.* three, I 196, II 70, IX 244, &c.; þri, III 6, 15; þre (*squared*), IX 106; *a* þre, in three, XIII *b* 49. [OE. þrēo, fem., neut.; þrī(e), masc.]

þrepe, *n.* contest, V 329. [Cf. OE. þrēapian, v.]

þresch, *v.* to thrash; smite, V 232. [OE. þerscan, late þrescan.]

þrestelcoo, *n.* (male) throstle, song-thrush, XV *b* 7. [OE. þrostle + cocc; on form see *N.E.D.*, s. v. *Throstle.*]

þrete, *v.* to threaten, V 232, XIV *a* 31; to wrangle, VI 201; *reft.* in *him þreteþ*, wrangles, chides, XV *b* 7 (note). [OE. þrēatian; ! ON. þrǽta (in sense 'wrangle').]

Threting, *n.* threatening (language), XIV *a* 30. [OE. þrēat-ung.]

Thretty. *See* þritti.

þrewe, *pa. t.*; *ouer . . . þrewe*, overturned, II 578. [OE. þrā-wan, twist; pa. t. þrēow.]

þri. *See* þre(e).

þrid(de), þryd(de), *adj.* third, III 10, IX 30, XII *a* 122, &c.

Thirde, Thyrde, IV *b* 6, XVI 31; *at þe þrid*, on the third occasion, V 288; *þe þryd(de) tyme*, for the third time, I 142, XII *b* 81, XVII 460. [OE. þridda, late Nth. þirda.]

þrien, *adv.* thrice, XV *g* 33. [OE. þri(g)a.] *See* þryys.

Thrife, Thryfe. *See* þriue.

Thryft, *n.* prosperity; in oath *by my thryft = as euer myght I thrife* (*see* The, þriue), XVII 218. [ON. þrift.]

Thrifty, *adj.* prosperous; goodly, fine, VII 158. [From prec.]

þryys, *adv.* thrice, I 182. [OE. þri(g)a + adv. -es.] *See* þrien.

þrynge, *v.* to press; *intr.* make one's way, V 329; Thringand, *pres. p.* pressing, X 166. [OE. þringan.]

þritti, *adj.* thirty, XV *g* 4, 15, 21; Thretty, VII 158; Thirtê, Thyrty, XVII 125, 260. [OE. þrit(t)ig.]

þriuaund, *pres. p.* prosperous; goodly, noble, VII 158. [From next.] *Cf.* Thrifty.

þriue, Thrife, Thryfe, *v.* to prosper; *I may not thryfe*, I can ill bear it, *or* may scarcely recover, XVII 414; in oaths: *so mot þou þriue, as euer myght I thrife*, &c., so may you (I) prosper, on your (my) life, II 532, XVII 191, 243 (*cf.* The, *v.*). [ON. þrífa-sk.]

þro, *adj.* fierce, V 232. [ON. þrá-r, stubborn.]

Throu, Throughe. *See* þorgh.

þrowe, *n.* time, moment, XII *b* 59; *a þrowe*, for a time, I *introd.*, V 151. [OE. þrāg.]

þrublet, *pa. t.* crowded, gathered (*intr.*), VII 132. [Obscure. In *N.E.D.* as var. of *Trouble*, grow dark; but cf. *Purity*, 504, 879.]

þu; þulke. *See* þou; Thilke.

þundyr, *n.* thunder(storm), I 166; Thonder, VII 132, XVII 346. [OE. þunor.]

þurch, þurȝ, &c. *See* þorgh.

Þus, *adv.* thus, so, I 37, XI *b* 270, XII *a* 88, XVI 283, &c.; therefore, XI *a* 40. [OE. *þus.*]

Þus(e). *See* Þes.

Þusgate, *adv.* in this way, VIII *b* 53. [Þus + Gate, *n.*[2]] *See* Sogat.

U-, V-; for init. *u, v* (in III) see also F.

Vayn(e), *adj.* frivolous, vain, worthless, IV *b* 28; Veyn, XI *b* 104, 124, 137, &c.; *yn veyn*, *in vayn*, in vain, I 178, XVII 360. [OFr. *vain.*]

Vale, *n.* vale, V 203 (*see* Hil). [OFr. *val.*]

Valay, Valeye, *n.* valley, V 77, 177, IX 195, XI *b* 155. [OFr. *valée.*]

Vald; Vall. *See* Wille, *v.*; Wal.

Value, *n.* value, X 132. [OFr. *value.*]

Vanyté, *n.* frivolity, vanity, vain thing, IV *b* 13, 52, XI *b* 181, 219, XIV *c* 3. [OFr. *vanité.*]

Vapnys; Var. *See* Weppen; Was.

Vauntwarde, *n.* vanguard, VIII *b* 60. [ONFr. *avant-warde.*]

Vch(eu). *See* Ich(on).

Velany. *See* Vylany.

Vedde. *See* Fede.

Veyn. *See* Vayn(e).

Venge (*on*), *v.* to take vengeance (on); *it schal ben venged ... so*, such vengeance shall be taken, XII *b* 100. [OFr. *venger.*]

Venia(u)nce, Vengaunce, *n.* vengeance, punishment, I 92, 129, VIII *a* 138, XI *b* 49, XVII 55, &c. [OFr. *venjance.*]

Venym(e), *n.* poison, IV *b* 86, IX 94. [OFr. *venim.*]

Venymous, *adj.* poisonous, IX 203. [OFr. *venimous.*]

Ver(r)ay, *adj.* true, IX 65, XVII 1; *adv.* truly, very, XVII 198; Verayly, *adv.* truly, V 177. [OF. *verai.*]

Verament, *adv.* assuredly, XVII 6. [OFr. *veirement, veraiment.*]

Verce, *n.* verse, VI 233. [OE. *fers*; OFr. *vers.*]

Verrit (*for*), *pp.* averred, declared (to be), VII 49. [Shortened from OFr. *averer.*]

Verst. *See* Furst.

Vertu(e), *n.* power, peculiar property, quality, IX 67, 70, 74, XII *b* 175, XV *i* 3, &c.; virtue, IV *b* 16, V 307; *kyng of vertues*, XVI 128 (*see* note). [OFr. *vertu.*]

Vertuous, Virtuus, *adj.* in possession of its proper qualities, IX 126; virtuous, VII 49. [OFr. *vertuous.*]

Ves. *See* Was.

Vessel(1), *n.* vessel, I 218, (ship) XVII 327. [OFr. *vessel.*]

Vggely, Vgly, *adj.* forbidding, horrible, V 11, 122, XVI 101. [ON. *ugg-ligr.*]

Vgsom, *adj.* horrible, VII 133. [Cf. ON. *uggsam-ligr.*]

Victorye (*of*), *n.* victory (over), IX 81, XI *b* 153. [OFr. *victorie.*]

Vif(tene), &c. *See* Fyue, Fyfteyn.

Vylany, Velany, *n.* unknightly conduct, V 307; ignominy, shameful fate, XVII 67. [OFr. *vilanie.*]

Vile, *adj.* worthless, IV *b* 12; miserable, II 548. [OFr. *vil.*]

Vilté, *n.* vileness, IV *b* 77. [OFr *vilté.*]

Vyndland, *pres. p.* turning over and over, X 129. [Cf. ON. *vindla*, wind.]

Vyne, *n.* vineyard, VI 142, 161, &c.; vine, IX 158. [OFr. *vi(g)ne.*]

Violastres, *n. pl.* as supposed name of a kind of diamonds of inferior lustre; due to mistransl. of French *violastres* (adj. pl.), purplish, IX 97 (note).

Vyolentlych, *adv.* violently, XIII *a* 33. [From OFr. *violent.*]

Vyolet, Violet(te), *n.* violet (flower), IX 99, XV *e* 13; (colour), IX 98; *see* IX 97 note. [OFr. *violet(te).*]

Vyrgyne, *n.* Virgin, virgin, I 85, 240, &c. [OFr. *virgine.*]

Vyrgynflour, *n.* perfect maiden-hood, VI 66. [Prec. + Flour.]

Virtuus. *See* Vertuous.

Visage, *n.* face, II 80. [OFr. *visage.*]

Vyse, *n.* vice, V 307. [OFr. *vice.*]

Vitayll, *n.* victuals, provisions, XVII 155. [OFr. *vitaille.*]

Vithall, -in. *See* Withal, -inne.

Vmbethoucht (*hym*), *pa. t.* be-thought (him), reflected, X 179. [OE. **ymb(e)-þencan* (cf. *ymbeþanc*); but prefix is influenced by ON. *umb.*]

Vmbreide (*of*), *pa. t. subj.* re-proached (with), XII *b* 98. [OE. *ŭp-gebregdan*, upbraid, with pre-fix assimilated to ME. *umb(e)* as in prec.]

Vnable, *adj.* incapable, IX 313; impossible, VII 46. [OE. *un-* + OFr. *hable.*] *See* Able.

Vnablen, *v.* to render incapable, XI *b* 109, 117. [From prec.]

Vnbarred, *pp.* unbarred, V 2. [OE. *on-(un-)* + OFr. *barrer.*] *See* Bard, Barres.

Vnbynde, *v.* to unbind, release, XVI 8; **Vnbounde,** *pp.* I 228. [OE. *on-bindan*, late *un-bindan.*]

Vnblendyde, *adj.* unpolluted, IV *b* 16. [From pp. of Blende, *q.v.*]

Vncessantlé, *adv.* unceasingly, XVII 147. [From OFr. *incessant.*]

Vnclene, *adj.* impure, IV *b* 17. [OE. *un-clǣne.*]

Vncouþe, Vnkowthe, *adj.* strange, unknown, II 535, VII 146. [OE. *un-cŭþ.*]

Vncrouned, *adj.* without the tonsure, lay, VIII *b* 66. *See* Crounede.

Vndede. *See* Vndo.

Vnder, -ur, *prep.* under, II 70, IX 179, XIII *a* 15; (postponed) V 250; *see* Gore, Heuenryche; *adv.* underneath, XVII 409; in reality (opposed to appearance on surface), VII 18, XIV *a* 18; *see* Þere. [OE. *under.*]

Vnder, *n.* 'the third hour', about the middle of the morning, VI 153. [OE. *undern.*] *See* Vnder-tide.

Vnderȝete, *pa. t. pl.* perceived, II 576. [OE. *under-getan*, pa. t. pl. *-gē(a)ton.*]

Vnderlynge, *n.* inferior, VIII *a* 47. [OE. *underling.*]

Vndernome, *pp.* taken in (men-tally), realized, II 320. [OE. *underniman*, pp. *-numen.*] *See* Nym(e).

Vnderstonde, Vndirstand(e), &c., *v.* to understand; compre-hend, I 12, IV *b* 76, IX 214, XI *b* 117, XIII *b* 55, &c.; learn, be told, I 26, II 215, IX 187, &c.; *vnderst. bi*, intend (to be under-stood) by, XI *a* 9; *vnderst. of preiere of holy lif*, mean by 'prayer' (that consisting in) holy living, XI *b* 82; **Vnder-stod,** *pa. t.* XII *b* 36, 88, &c. [OE. *understándan, -stóndan.*]

Vnderstondyng(e), **-standynge,** &c., *n.* comprehension, XI *b* 134; intelligence, IV *b* 49, 56, 65; *of kynde vnderst.*, it stands to ordinary reason, naturally, VIII *b* 58. [OE. *under-stánding.*]

Vndertake, *v.* to undertake, XIV *c* 52; warrant, XVII 274; **Vnder-take,** *pp.* XII *a* 52. [OE. *under-* + ON. *taka.*]

Vndertide, Vndrentide, *n.* (orig.) mid-morning, (*esp.* as time for a rest from work), but often vaguely applied and appar. nearly equiv. to 'noon', II 65, 76, 133, 181, 282; *slepe her undertides*, were taking a noon-tide sleep, II 402. [OE. *undern-tīd.*] *See* Vnder, *n.*

Vndisposid (*to*), *adj.* indisposed, disinclined (to), XI *b* 135. [From OFr. *disposer.*]

Vndo, *v.* to undo, open, XVI 182; **Vndede,** *pa. t.* II 385. [OE. *on-dōn, un-dōn.*] *See* Do(n).

Vnglad, *adj.* in misery, XVII 22. [OE. *un-glæd.*]

Vnité, *n.* coherence of mind,

sanity (? but this sense unexampled), VIII *b* 10. [OFr. *unité*, unity.]

Vnkept, *adj.* not kept, broken, XI *b* 233. *See* Kepe.

Vnkinde, Vnkuynde, *adj.* unnatural (in conduct, &c.); disloyal, XIV *c* 103 ; hard-hearted, XII *b* 1, 220, 224. [OE. *un-(ge)cýnde*.]

Vnkindenesse, Vnkyndnes, *n.* unnatural conduct, XII *b* 205, XVII 12. [From prec.]

Vnkowþe. *See* Vncouþe.

Vnlokynne, *pp.* opened, XVI 197. [OE. *on-lúcan*, *un-*; pp.-*locen*.] *See* Loke, *pp.*

Vnmanerly, *adv.* discourteously, V 271. [From ME. *maner-ly*, formed on Maner(e), *q.v.*]

Vnneþe, *adv.* with difficulty, hardly, II 221, 416, XIII *b* 60, XIV *c* 4. [OE. *un-éaþe*.]

Vnoccupied, *adj.* unoccupied, XI *b* 127. *See* Occupied.

Vnreso(u)nable, *adj.* unreasonable, VI 230, VIII *a* 145. [From OFr. *resonable*.] *See* Resonabele.

Vnrid, *adj.* hard, cruel, XVII 40. [OE. *un-gerýde*, rough.]

Vnryghtwysely, *adv.* unrighteously ; more than is right, IV *b* 24. [OE. *un-rihtwīs-līce*.]

Vnschape, *adj.* formless, XIII *b* 59. [OE. *un-gescapen*, unformed.]

Vnschette, *v.* to open, XII *a* 71. [OE. *on-(un-)+scyttan* (Kt. **scettan*).]

Vnsober, *adj.* violent, VII 143; **Vnsoberly**, *adv.* violently, VII 130. [From OFr. *sobre*.] *See* Sobre.

Vnsoght, *adj.* unexpiated, not atoned for, XVII 97. [ME. *un-sa(u)ght*, from ON. *ú-sáttr* (older **un-saht-*) ; cf. OE. *un-seht*. The orig. rimes were prob. *naght, saght, wraght* ; *see* Werche.]

Vnstudied, *adj.* not studied, XI *b* 165, 232. *See* Studie.

Vntil(l), *prep.* to, XII *a* 132, XVI 370, XVII 218 (*see* Turne); until, XVI 52. [As next with subst. of interchangeable *til.*]

Vnto ; Vntew, XVII 505 ; *prep.* to, I 111, II 186, XII *a* 25, XVI 319, XVII 241; towards, for, XVI 246 ; up to, until, I 95, VII 95, IX 328. [?OE. **untō*; cf. OS. *untō*, prep.; Goth. *untē*, conj.]

Vnto, *conj.* until, I 68. [As prec.] *See* To, *conj.*

Vntrawþe, *n.* perfidy, V 315. [OE. *un-tréowþ*.] *See* Treuthe.

Vntrew(e), *adj.* inaccurate, untrue, VII 47, XI *a* 43. [OE. *un-tréowe*.] *See* Trew(e).

Vntreweliere, *adv. compar.* less accurately, XI *a* 59. [OE. *un-tréow-līce*.]

Vntrusse, *v.* to unload, XII *b* 52. [OE. *on-* (*un-*)+OFr. *trusser.*] *See* Trus.

Vnwar, *adj.* (or *adv.*) unawares, XII *b* 9. [OE. *unwær*, adj. and adv.] *See* War(e).

Vnworthi, *adj.* unworthy, IX 308. [Extended from OE. *un-weorþ(e)*.] *See* Worþy.

Vochen saf. *See* Vouchesaf.

Voided, *pp.* ' cleared out ', been dismissed, II 574. [OFr. *(a)-voider.*]

Vois, *n.* voice, XII *a* 119, *b* 31, &c.; **Voyce**, Voice, XVI 73, 79. [OFr. *vois.*]

Vol(ueld). *See* Ful(fillen).

Vorbisne(n), *n. pl.* examples, illustrations, III 2, 59. [OE. *for(e)-bisen.*]

Vore-yzede, Vorzede. *See* Forseyde.

Vouche-saf, Vowch-sayf, *v.* to vouchsafe, deign, IX 330, XVII 172 ; **Vochen saf**, *pres. pl.* guarantee (*sc.* me), VIII *b* 51. [OFr. *vo(u)cher sauf.*]

Voundit. *See* Woundit.

Vousour, *n.* vaulting, II 363. [OFr. *vousure.*]

Vp, Vpp(e), *adv.* up, I 200, II 96, V 11, XVI 113, &c.; open, X

185; (open) wide, XVI 122, 194; *vp wiþ*, up with, lift up, hold high, XIV *c* 99. [OE. *úp*, *upp*(*e*).]

Vpcaste, *pa. t.* lifted up, XII *a* 106. [OE. *up*(*p*) + ON. *kasta*.] *See* Cast(e).

Vpdrawe, *pp.* drawn up, XII *b* 64. [OE. *up*(*p*) + *dragan*.]

Vplondysch, Oplondysch, *adj.* rustic, XIII *b* 23, 50. [Cf. OE. *úp-lendisc*.]

Vp(p)on; Vpo, XV *g* 4; Opan, II 506; Opon, II 72, &c.; Apon, IV *a* 86, X 123, &c.; *prep.* (i) (up)on, V 134, VIII *a* 135, IX 33, X 183, XII *a* 126 (*see* Stonde), XIII *a* 12, &c.; (postponed) II 500, 506; (of *time*) I 29, &c.; immediately after, XII *b* 147; (commenting) on, XI *b* 20; *upon this matiere*, on this business, XII *a* 45. (ii) in, VI 185, X 66, XII *introd.*, *a* 175; (believe) in, XV *g* 9; into, VII 6, 140; (iii) to, V 184 (*see* Stiʒtel); (iv) (think) of, V 329, VI 10. *See* Grounde, Half, Out(e), Þer(e), &c. [OE. *up*(*p*)-*on*.]

Vpon, *adv.* on; *dede upon*, put on, XII *a* 53. [As prec.]

Vpperight, *adv.* (straight) up, XVI 394. [OE. *úp-rihte*.]

Vprise, *v.* to rise up, XVI 31 (*see* prec.). [OE. *up*(*p*) *á-rīsan*.]

Vpward, *adv.* in the upper part, IX 246. [OE. *úp-weard*.]

Vr(e); Vrn; Vrþe. *See* We; Eorne; Erþe.

Vs. *See* He, We.

Vsage, *n.* usage, XIII *b* 17. [OFr. *usage*.]

Vse, Vss(e), *n.* use, XIII *a* 1; usage, ritual, XI *b* 189, 196, &c. (*see* note, XI *b* 183). [OFr. *us*, L. *ūsus*.]

Vse, *v.* to use, practise, have dealings with, V 38, 358, XIII *b* 14, XIV *a* 30; Y-vsed, *pp.* XIII *b* 26. [OFr. *user*.]

Vtmast, *adj.* outermost, II 357. [OE. *út*(*e*)*mest*.]

Vttiremeste, *adj.* extreme, furthest, XVI 232 (*see* Ende). [Formed on ME. *utter*(*e*), OE. *úttra*, on anal. of prec.]

Vus. *See* We.

Wa(a). *See* Wo.

Wack(e)net, *pa. t.* and *pp.* awoke, (was) aroused, VII 105, 110. [OE. *wæcn*(*i*)*an*.] *See* Wake.

Wage, *v.* to undertake, guarantee, pay (hire), &c.; *intr.* or *absol.* ‡ (used for) securely continue, *or* ‡ bring reward, VI 56. [ONFr. *wager*.]

Wagh(e), Wawe, Wawgh(e), *n.* wave, water (of the sea), VII 140, XII *a* 157, XIV *c* 33, XVII 426, &c. [ON. *vág-r*.]

Wai, Way, *interj.* woe! II 234, 546; *wai es him*, unhappy is one (who), XV *a* 9. [ON. *vei*.] *See* We, *interj.*; Wo.

Way(e), Wey(e), Weie, We (x), *n.* way, course, manner, distance, &c., II 476, VII 144, VIII *a* 6, IX 220, X 85, XII *a* 16, XVI 74, &c.; *all way, all weys*, continually, XVII 500; always, IX 212, 277; *by þe way of*, *see* Right, *n.*; *in þe waye*, on (by) the way, IV *b* 41; *in ich ways*, in every way, II 158 (*see* note); *adv.* away, in *do way*, have done, enough, II 226. [OE. *weg*.] *See* Alway, Awai, Heigh.

Waik, *adj.* weak, VIII *b* 23. [ON. *veik-r*.]

Waille, *v.* to bewail, VIII *a* 308. [ON. **veila* (cf. ON. *vǽla*, Swed. *veila*).]

Wayte, *v.* to look, V 95, 221. [ONFr. *wait*(*i*)*er*.]

Wake, *v.* to lie awake, keep vigil, IV *b* 49, XV *c* 21; *trans.* to arouse, kindle, XVII 89. [OE. *wacian*, *intr.*] *See* A-, Forwake.

Wal, Wall, *n.* wall, II 357, XI *b* 40, XIII *a* 24, XVII 515 (*see* Ston), &c.; Vall, X 131. [OE. *wall*.]

Wald(e). *See* Wille, *v.*

Wale, *v.* to choose; *to wale* (to

be chosen), conspicuous, excellent, VII 8. [ON. *val*, n.; *velja* (pa. t. *valdi*), v.]

Walk(e), *v.* to walk, wander, V 110, VI 39, XII *b* 21, XVI 53, 333; *walkes wide*, is spread abroad, XIV *b* 29 (*see* Word); Ywalked, *pp.* XIII *a* 16. [OE. *walc(i)an*, roll, go to and fro.]

Wallande, *pres. p.* welling, bubbling, VI 5. [OE. *wallan*.]

Walschmen, *n. pl.* Welshmen, XIII *b* 3. [OE. *wĕlisc, wǣlisc* + *mann*.]

Walt, *v.* to roll; *trans. pa. t.* rolled, VII 140 (*rel.* to *blastes* omitted); *intr. infin.* totter (and fall), VII 138; *pa. t.* was tossed, VII 144 (*rel.* to *nauy* omitted). [OE. (Nth.) *wælta*.]

Wan. *See* Wanne, Wynne(n).

Wan(e), *v.* to decrease, subside, XVII 450, 458, 493. [OE. *wanian*.]

Wane, *n.* dwelling-place (translating Latin *mansio*), in *I ne wate na better wane*, IV *a* 55. [? ON. *ván*, expectation.] *See* Wones.

Waudren, *v.* to wander, VIII *a* 297. [OE. *wandrian*.]

Wandreth, *n.* trouble, distress, IV *a* 19, XVII 40. [ON. *vandrǽði*.]

Waning, *n.* curtailment, VI 198 (*see* ȝete, *v.*). [OE. *wanung*.]

Wan(ne), **Won** (xv), *adj.* gloomy, VII 140; sickly, wan, II 108, IV *a* 10, XV *c* 22. [OE. *wann, wonn*, dark.]

Wanne. *See* Whan, Wynne(n).

Want, *n.* lack (*esp.* of food), XVII 194. [ON. *vant*, neut. adj.] *See* Wonte.

Wap, *n.* a blow, V 181. [Cf. ME. *wappen*, w(h)op, beat; echoic.]

Wapin. *See* Weppen.

War (*with*), *v. imper.* guard (against), beware (of), XIV *a* 6. [OE. *warian*, refl.]

War(e), *adj.* in *be war* (*of*), be on one's guard (against), beware

(of), take care, V 320, XI *b* 217, 311, XIV *d* 4; *be war or ye be wo*, look before you leap, XIV *d* 11 (*see* Wo). [OE. *wær*.] *See* Vnwar.

War(e). *See* Was.

Ward(e), *n.* custody, XVI 222; post (in the defence), X 35. [OE. *weard*.]

Warda(i)ne, *n.* warden, commander of the garrison, X 146, 169, XIV *b* 83. [ONFr. *wardein*.]

Ware, *adj.* XVI 154; *see* Werre, and note.

Ware, *v.* to lay out, spend, VII 19; Waret, *pp.* given (in exchange), dealt, V 276. [OE. *warian* (recorded once as 'treat with') rel. to *waru*, wares.]

Wary, *v.* to curse, XVII 208; Wery, XIV *a* 23. [OE. *wærgan, wergan*.]

Wark, *v.* to feel pain, ache, XVII 269. [OE. *wærcan*; cf. ON. *verkja*.]

Wark(e); **Warld**. *See* Werk(e); World(e).

Warn(e), *v.* to warn, inform, VIII *a* 125, 158, 316, 321, XVII 124; forewarn, XVII 110. [OE. *war(e)nian*.]

Warnist, *pp.* furnished, manned, X 121. [ONFr. *warnir, warniss-*.]

Warp, *v.* to cast; offer, V 185. [OE. *weorpan*; ON. *varpa*.]

Wars; **Warth**. *See* Wors; Worþe, *v.*

Was, *pa. t. sg.* was, I 28, &c.; have been, VIII *a* 160; 2 *sg.* XVII 120; Ves, X 15, 32; Watȝ, V 1, VI 4, &c.; 2 *sg.* V 326, VI 12, &c.; Wes, III 16, X 2, XV *g* 1, &c.; *subj.* was, were, might (would, &c.) be, Var, X 38; War(e), IV *a* 19, 23, &c.; Weor, XIV *c* 89; Wer(e), I 92, II 108, IV *a* 75, XV *g* 8, XVI 199, &c. *Pl. ind.* and *subj.* War(e), X 10, XIV *b* 93, &c.; Weir, X 137; Wer(e), Weren, Weryn, Wern(e),

I 41, II 18, III 58, V 354, VI 18, 225, &c.; **Wore**, I 114, VI 214, *****XVI** 17 (note). [OE. *wæs* (*wes*), *wǣron*, &c.; ON. pl. *várum*, &c.] *See* Nas.

Wassche, *v. intr.* to wash, XIII *a* 25. [OE. *wascan*.]

Waste, *n.* wild, uninhabited place, V 30. [ONFr. *wast*; OE. *wěste*.] *See* Wysty.

Waste(n), *v. trans.* to waste, VIII *a* 127, 155; *intr.* XIV *c* 2. [ONFr. *waster*.]

Wastour(e), *n.* waster, despoiler, rogue, VIII *a* 29, 124, 146, &c. [ONFr. *wastur*.]

Wat; **Wate**; **Wat3**. *See* What(e); Wite(n); Was.

Watches, *n. pl.* watches; watchmen, XVI 140. [OE. *wæcce*.]

Wape, *n.*[1] peril, V 287; **Wope**, VI 15; **Woth**, XVII 416. [ON. *váði*.]

Wathe, *n.*[2] (something gained in) hunting, XVII 486; *cf.* Fee, *n.*[2] [ON. *veið-r*.]

Watter; **Watur**, **-er**; *n.* water (sea, lake, flood), V 163, VII 119, VIII *a* 318, &c.; **Watres**, *pl.* IX 12, 243. [OE. *wæter*.]

Wattered, *pa. t. intr.* watered, VIII *a* 168. [OE. *wæterian*, trans.]

Wawe, Wawghes. *See* Wagh(e).

Waxe(n), **Wax**, *v.* to increase, grow, become, XV *b* 15, 32, *c* 22, XVII 60, 179; **Wexe(n)**, **Wex**, II 62, IX 22, 95, XVI 344, &c.; **Wax**, *pa. t.* I 237; **Wex**, VI 178. [OE. *we(a)xan*.]

We, *interj.* (of grief, consternation, surprise, &c.) alas, ah, &c.; II 176, V 117, XVI 139, 149, 301, XVII 217, 238; *we loo*, V 140. [OE. *wǣ* (*lā*).] *See* Wai, Wo.

We, *pron. pl.* we, I 64, &c. *Acc.* and *dat.* (to, for) us, Hus, XVII 46; Ous, II 167, 604, VIII *b* 92, &c.; Vs, IV *a* 7, VII 32, &c.; *vs must*, *see* Mot(e); Vus, V 174, VI 94, &c.; *vus þynk vus oȝe*, *see* Owe, þinke; **Vs** self, *refl.*

ourselves, XI *b* 157; **Our(e)**, **Owr(e)**, *poss. adj.* our, I 203, III 29, IV *a* 16, 55, XV *g* 26, &c.; **Vr(e)**, XIV *c* 15, 84, XV *g* 1, 24; *oure one*, alone by ourselves, V 177 (*see* note); **Oure**, *pron.* ours, XI *b* *128, 129; **Ouris**, X 88. [OE. *wě*, *ūs*, *ūre*.]

We. *See* Way(e).

Wecht, *n* weight, X 101. [ON. *vétt-r*, earlier *****weht**-.]

Wedde, *n.* pledge, in *leide to wedde*, pledged, assigned **as** security, mortgaged, VIII *b* 77. [OE. *wedd*; *lecgan to wedde*.]

Wede, *n.* garment, article of attire, II 146, V 290; *wight in wede*, valiant (in arms), XIV *b* 5. [OE. *wǣd*, *ge-wǣde*.]

Weder, **-ir**, **-ur**, *n.* weather, II 269, XVII 470; foul weather, storm, VII 114, VIII *a* 320, XIV *c* 35, XVII 451. [OE. *weder*.]

Wedes, *n. pl.* weeds (plants), VIII *a* 105. [OE. *wēod*.]

Wedmen, *n. pl.* wedded folk, XVII 400. [OE. *wedd* + *mann*.] *See* Wedde, Yweddede.

Wedows; **Wees**, **Wegh(es)**; **Weete**; **Weie**, **Wey(e)**; **Weyn**; **Weir**. *See* Wodewe; Wyȝe; Wete; Way(e); We-ne(n); Was.

Wel(e), **Well(e)**, **Weyl** (I), **Weill** (X), *adv.* well, I 110, II 136, X 12, XIV *d* 2, &c.; very, II 309, 345, XIII *a* 26, XIV *c* 39, &c.; *wel riȝt, wel sone*, &c. at once, II 71, 270, X 70; fully, quite, I 254, II 553, &c.; (*esp.* with numbers) II 183, IX 199, XIV *b* 42, &c.; (with *compar.*) a good deal, much, II 464, X 10, XVI 334; without disadvantage, IV *b* 31; easily, VIII *a* 47, XVII 5, &c.; *predic.* good, XV *e* 7, &c.; prosperous, VIII *a* 271; *well were he*, happy were he who, XVII 339; *well is vs*, happy are we, XVII 459; *wel worth þe*, may it go well with thee, V 59; *wele wurth þe while*, happy the occasion, XIV *a* 5,

&c.; *cf.* Wo. [OE. *wĕl.*] *See*
Welneȝ.

Wela, *adv.* very, in *wela wylle*
(*see* Wylle), v 16. [OE. *wel* + *lā*
(intensive).]

Welcom, Welcum, Wolcome,
adj. welcome, II 433, V 172,
VIII *b* 52; as *interj.* VI 39.
[OE. *wil-cuma* infl. by *wel-*
(*-cwĕme*) ; cf. ON. *vel-kominn.*]

Welde, *v.* to possess, IV *a* 20.
[OE. (*ge-*)*wĕldan.*]

Wele, Weole, *n.* (usually allit.
with Wo, *q.v.*) happiness, prosperity, wealth, II 5, IV *a* 2, *b* 74,
V 66, VI 34; *worldes wele*, good
things of this world, wealth,
IV *a* 28, XIV *b* 16; *wunne we(o)le*,
wealth of joy, XV *b* *11 (MS.
wynter), 35. [OE. *we(o)la.*]

Weleful, *adj.* prosperous, XIV *b*
17. [Prec. + OE. *-full.*]

Wel-fare, *n.* welfare, easy life,
VIII *b* 8. [Wel + Fare, *n.*]

Welkyn, *n.* sky, VII 138. [OE.
wolcen, weolcn.]

Well(e), *n.* spring, fount, VI 5,
IX 5, XIII *a* 1, &c.; *fig.* XIV *c*
108. [OE. *well(a).*]

Welle-spring, *n.* spring, XV *e* 16.
[Cf. OE. *well(e)-spryng.*]

Well-wirkand, *adj.* righteous in
deeds, XVII 120. [Cf. OE. *wel-
wyrcende.*] *See* Werche.

Welneȝ, Welnyȝ, Welnygh,
adv. almost, VI 168, XIII *b* 4;
welnygh now, but a moment ago,
VI 221. [OE. *wel-nē(a)h.*] *See*
Wel(e), *adv.*; Nyȝ.

Welth(e), *n.* happiness, IV *a* 32,
XVI 324. [Extended from Wele
with abstract *-þ.*]

Wen, *n.* blemish, diseased growth;
fig. III *introd.* [OE. *wenn*,
tumour.]

Wende, *v. trans.* to turn, v 84;
intr. to turn (and toss), XV *c* 21;
to return, I 199; go, come, I 94,
II 427, VIII *a* 6; depart, VIII *a*
67, 79, 271; *refl.* go, II 475,
501; Went(e), *pa. t.* I 113;
Wende, I *189 (*see* note), II 65,
185, &c.; Went(e), *pp.* gone,

departed, I 93, VIII *a* 198, &c.;
is went, went, X 178; Ywent,
come about, III *introd.* [OE.
wéndan.]

Wene(n), to think, imagine, ex-
pect, IV *a* 35, V 336, VIII *a* 242,
XI *b* 72, &c.; Weyn, XVII 444,
535; Wende, *pa. t.* I 110, 127,
XII *b* 66. [OE. *wénan.*] *See*
Awenden.

Wenges; Wenne. *See* Wyng;
Whan(ne).

Wente, *n.* turn(ing), XII *b* 6.
[From Wende, *v.*]

Weole; Weor. *See* Wele; Was.

Wepe, *n.* weeping, in *w. and wo*,
II 195, 234. [OE. *wōp*, assimilated to stem of next.]

Wepe, Weepe, *v.* to weep, II 118,
XII *a* 32, XIV *b* 60, XV *f* 6;
Wepte, *pa. t. sg.* I 174; Wepe,
pl. II 591; Wepeing, Wep-
yng(e), *n.* II 219, IV *a* 32, XI *b*
155, &c. [OE. *wépan*; pa. t.
wéop (ONth. *wǣpde*).]

Weppen, *n.* weapon, V 154;
Wapin, XIV *b* 15; Vapnys,
pl. X 190. [OE. *wépn*; ON.
vápn.]

Wer(e), *n.* war, VII 8, 88, XIV *b*
15; Werre, IX 81, XIV *c* 76.
[ONFr. *werre.*]

Wer(e), Weryn, &c. *See* Was.
Werby. *See* Wher(e), *adv.*

Werche, *v.* to work, labour;
make; bring about, cause; act,
do; I .90, 218, VIII *a* 297;
Werke, XVI 334; Wirk(e),
XIV *b* 20, XVI 265, XVII 116;
Wyrk(e), VI 176, XVII 262;
Worch(e), V 28, VI 151, VIII *a*
8, *b* 25, &c.; Werkis, 2 *sg.* XVI
264; Wroȝt(e), Wroght, *pa. t.*
I 65, 168, V 293, VI 165, XVII 4
(2 *sg.*), &c.; Wrouȝte, VIII *a*
103, 243 (*subj.*), &c.; Wrouhte,
VIII *b* 87 (*subj.*); Wroȝt,
Wroght, *pp.* V 276, VII 58,
&c.; Wrouȝt, II 374, VIII *a*
308: Wraght, *XVII 98 (MS.
wroght; *see* Vnsoght); *let God
worche*, let God do as He wills
(compare the phrases under

Yworth), v 140. [OE. *wyrcan*; pa. t. *worhte* (*warhte*, *wrohte*); with *er* forms *cf.* Scherte, Werse, and see App. p. 280.]

Were, *v.*[1] to ward (off), I 167. [OE. *werian.*[1]]

Were, *v.*[2] to wear (clothes), v 290; Ywerd, *pp.* II 241. [OE. *werian.*[2]]

Were, *v.*[3] to wear (out), decay, XIV *c* 2; *til hit be wered out*, until the present state has passed away, VIII *b* 85. [A sense-development of the prec. (cf. OE. *for-wered*, worn out); but the infl. of forms of quite distinct origin, such as OE. *for-weren*, *-woren*, worn out, decayed, (*for*)*weornian*, decay, was perh. ultimately responsible.]

Wery. *See* Wary, *v.*

Wery, *adj.* weary, XI *b* 135, XIII *a* 48, XV *c* 30. [OE. *wērig.*]

Werynes, *n.* weariness, I 156, XIII *a* 49. [OE. *wērig-nes.*]

Werk(e), Wark(e), *n.* work; labour, VI 239, VIII *a* 191, &c.; fabric, II 374; *werkis*, works, fortress, XVI 191; action, deed, IV *a* 65, 84, VII 58, XI *b* 106, &c.; task, VIII *b* 56, XVII 130, 244, 255, &c.; written work, VII 4, 55; in *sg.* deeds, doings, dealings, &c., II 317, V 299, XVI 17, 200. [OE. *we(o)rc.*]

Werke. *See* Werche.

Werkman, Workeman, labourer, craftsman, VIII *a* 308, *b* 25; Werk(e)men, *pl.* VI 147, VIII *a* 53, IX 119, &c.; *my werkemen*, doers of my will, XVI 17. [OE. *we(o)rc-mann.*]

Werldes; Wern(e). *See* World; Was.

Wernyng, *n.* refusal, v 185. [From OE. *wérnan.*]

Werre, *adj.* and *adv. compar.* in worse plight, worse, XVI *154 (MS. ware; *see* note), 334. [ON. *verri*; adv. *verr.*] *See* Wors(e).

Werre; Werse (Werst); Wes. *See* Wer(e); Wors(e); Was.

West(e), *adv.* and *n.* west, VII 105, XVI 333. [OE. *west*, adv.]

Wete, *adj.* and *n.* wet, II 80, VII 110, XIV *c* 30. [OE. *wǣt*; *wǣta*, *n.*]

Wete, Weete, *v.* to wet, IX 62, XIII *a* 34. [OE. *wǣtan.*]

Weþer. *See* Wheþer, *conj.*[1]

Weue(n), *v.* to weave; *pp.* Wouen, woven, v 290. [OE. *wefan*, pp. *wefen*; cf. ON. pp. (*v*)*ofinn.*]

Weued, *pa. t.* presented, v 291 (*see* note). [OE. *wǣfan.*]

Wexe(n). *See* Waxe(n).

Wha(m). *See* Who.

Whan(ne), *adv. interrog.* and *rel.* when, I 104, 161, v 163, IX 19, XI *a* 8, &c.; *whan that*, when, IX 22, XII *a* 28, 155, &c. (*see* þat); Huanne, III 27, 31; Quen, V 206, 247, VI 18, Quhen, X 40, 171; Wanne, VIII *b* 1, 52, &c.; Wenne, VIII *b* 7; When, I 221, &c.; Whon, XIV *c* 110. [OE. *hwonne*, *hwanne*, *hwænne.*]

Whar(e), Hwar, *adv. interrog.* and *rel.* where, XIV *a* 7, XV *a* 6, XVI 294; (with *subj.*) wherever, II 170; Quhar, to the place where, X 18; *quhar at*, *quhar that*, where, X 38 (*see* At *rel.*), 149. As *neut. pron.* in: Whar(e)fore, for what (which) reason, IV *b* 33, XIII *a* 13. [OE. *hwǣr*, *hwāra*, and prob. unacc. *hwær*, *hwara.*] *See* Nowhar(e); Wher(e), *adv.*; cf. þar(e)

Wharred, *pa. t.* whirred, v 135. [Echoic.]

What(e), Wat, Quat (V, VI), *pron. interrog.* what, II 102, XI *b* 195, XV *e* 8, XVII 163, &c.; *indir.* I 56, IV *b* 65, V 111, VIII *b* 38, &c.; *indef.* (with *subj.*) whatever, II 339, 450, 467; approaching *rel.* XII *b* 142 (*cf.* VIII *a* 242), XVI 174 (*see* note and App. p. 289); *exclam.* what!, XVI 101; lo! V 133-6; *quat so*, whatsoever, VI 206; *what with* .. *and* (as Mn.E

idiom), XVII 214. *Adj. interrog.*
what, VI 115, &c.; *indir.* VI
32, VII 83, &c.; *indef.* (with
subj.) whatever, VI 163; *exclam.*
what !, II 234; *loke what, see*
Loke; *what man (þing),* who,
what, II 421, 116, &c.; *what . . .
þat,* what, VII 92; whatever,
XII *a* 115, XIII *a* 58 (with *subj.*).
[OE. *hwæt.*]

Wheder; Whedir. *See* Wheþer;
Whider.

Whelp, *n.* whelp, pup, XIV *b* 78.
[OE. *hwelp.*]

Wher(e), Quere (VI), *adv. interrog.* and *rel.* where, whither, II
194, VI 16, XVI 272, 377;
wherever (with *subj.*), XVI 402;
wher(e) þat, (to the place)
where, IX 184, XII *a* 59, 153,
&c.; in a case where, when,
XII *b* 139; wherever, IX 177.
As *neut. pron.* in: Werby,
Wherby, on account of which,
VIII *b* 35; by which, XII *b* 55;
Wheriore, wherefore; why, IX
176, &c.; and so, V 210, IX 135,
202, &c.; Wher(e)of, Hueroff,
(out) of which, III 2, 8, IX 153,
238, XII *b* 120, &c.; on account
of which, XII *a* 10, 38, 71, 190,
b 159, &c.; concerning which,
II 16, XII *b* 212, &c.; *wherof
that,* whereby, wherefore, XII *a*
116, 140, *b* 222; Whereon, in
which, II 267. [OE. *hwǣr,
hwēr.*] *See* Whar(e).

Wher(e), *conj., interrog.* (introd.
a direct question), XI *b* 64, 171,
197, 266, 274; (indir.) whether,
XI *a* 51, *b* 207. [Reduction of
Wheþer [1], *q.v.*]

Whestones, *n. pl.* whetstones,
XIII *a* 45. [OE. *hwet-stān.*]

Whete, *n.* wheat, VIII *a* 9, 33,
299; *adj.* wheaten, VIII *a* 131.
[OE. *hwǣte*; adj. *hwǣten.*]

Wheþer, Whethire, Wheder
(XVII), Weþer (VI), *conj.[1] interrog.* with *ind.* or *subj.*; (introd.
a direct question) V 118, VI
205; (indir.) whether, XVII
363; (alternative condition)

whethire . . . or, whether . . . or,
IV *b* 76; Queþersoeuer, (with
subj.) whether, VI 246. [OE.
hwæþer.] *See* Wher(e), *conj.*

Wheþer, *conj.[2]* however, (and)
yet, VI 221. [OE. *hwæþere.*]

Whette, *pa. t.* ground; made a
grinding noise, V 135; Quettyng, *n.* sharpening, grinding,
V 152 (note). [OE. *hwettan.*]

Whi, Why, Hwi, *adv. interrog.*
why, I 64, II 332, XV *a* 17, XVII
294, &c.; *for whi,* XVII 14,
518; Quy, VI 201; Wi, XV *g*
25; Wy, VI 173, 204; *indirect*
in *þe cause why,* the reason why,
XIII *b* 66; *exclam.* why then,
V 232. [OE. *hwī.*]

Which(e), Wiche, *interrog. adj.*
which, what, II 494, &c.; *pron.*
which, who, VIII *a* 126, &c.;
rel. adj. in *the whiche,* which,
IX 2; *pron.* who, which, XII *a*
52, 61, 111, &c.; *the which(e)
(wiche),* which, whom, VIII *b* 31,
IX 276, 298, XII *a* 35, &c.; *the
whiche þat,* who(m), IX 190,
337; *of the whiche . . . offe,* of
which, IX 24; *as he which,* &c.,
see note XII *a* 23. *See* App.,
p. 289. [OE. *hwilc.*] *See*
Whilke.

Whider, Whedir (XVII), *adv.
interrog.* whither, II 128, 288,
296, XIV *a* 21, XVII 313; *indef.*
whithersoever, II 129, 130;
Whider so, (with *subj.*)
whithersoever, II 340. [OE.
hwider.]

Whyyt, *adj.* white, XIII *a* 31;
Whyte, White, II 105, XVI
89, &c.; Quyte, Quite, V 20,
296; Whittore, *compar.* XV *c*
27. [OE. *hwīt*; compar.
hwĭttra.]

Whil(e), Whyl(e), Wyl, Quhill (X), *conj.* while, I 8, VII
56, XIV *c* 29, 36, &c.; until, VI
168, X 32, 67, 197; *quhill þat,*
until, *x 63. [OE. *þā hwīle þe*;
see next.]

While, Whyle, Wyle, *n.* time,
while, V 301, XIV *a* 5 (*see* Wel),

23, &c. ; *by whyle,* from time to time, II 8 ; *eny wyle,* for any length of time, VIII *b* 25 ; *þat ilke while . . . þerwhile,* while (*conj.*), VIII *a* 155–6 ; *þe while,* while (*conj.*), VIII *a* 58, 283. [OE. *hwīl.*] See Hondqwile, Þerwhiles, Þerwhiles, &c.

Whyle, *adv.* for a while, XV *c* 33. [OE. *hwīle, hwīlum.*]

Whiles ; Whils, Whyls ; Qwiles (VII) ; *conj.* while, VII 39, VIII *a* 314, XVI 55, XVII 397. [Extended from While, *conj.,* with adv. *-es.*]

Whilke, Wylke, *rel. pron.* which, XVI 14 ; *þe wylke,* which, IV *b* 30. [OE. *hwilc.*] See Which(e).

Whilom, Whilum, *adv.* once, formerly, XII *a* 179, *b* 2, XIV *b* 5. [OE. *hwīlum.*]

Whyne, *v.* to scream, XVII 229. [OE. *hwīnan.*]

Whyp, *n.* whip, XVII 378. [Obscure.]

Whyrlande, *pres. p.* whirling, v 154. [OE. *hwyrf(t)lian* ; ON. *hvirfla.*]

White, Whittore. *See* Whyyt.

Who, Wha (IV), **Quo** (VI), *pron. interrog.* who, II 263, IV *a* 14, VI 67, &c. ; *who is,* who is it, XVII 295 ; *indir.* I 50, &c. ; *indef.* in *who that,* whoever, if any one, XII *b* 24. *Obl. case :* **Wham,** *interrog.* whom, II 128 ; **Quom, Whom(e),** *rel.* VI 93, IX 77, XVI 82, &c. ; **Whos,** *gen. sg. rel.* whose, I 91, XII *b* 79 ; *the whos,* whose, XII *a* 113. **Whasa, Whoso** (euer), *indef.* whoever, I 2, IV *a* 71, VIII *a* 67, &c. ; *but whoso,* unless one, VIII *a* 1. [OE. *hwā,* dat. *hwǎm.*]

Whon. *See* Whan(ne).

Wi, Wy. *See* Whi.

Wycche, *n.* wizard, IX 85. [OE. *wicca.*]

Wiche ; Wicht. *See* Which(e) ; Wight, *adj.*

Wid. *See* With.

Widder, *v.* to wither, XVII 63.

[OE. **widr(i)an,* expose, be exposed, to the weather.]

Wyde, Wide, *adj.* wide, spacious, II 365, XVII 541 ; *adv.* wide open, X 185 ; far and wide, XIV *b* 29. [OE. *wīd* ; adv. *wīd(e).*]

Wydwes. *See* Wodewe.

Wif(e), Wyf, Wiif (II), *n.* wife, II 178, V 283, XII *a* 3, XVII 106, &c. ; **Wyue,** *dat. sg.* III 52 ; **Wiues, Wyues, Wifis,** *pl.* II 399, VIII *a* 13, XVII 144, &c. [OE. *wīf.*]

Wyfman, *n.* woman, III 30, 31, 36 ; **Wymman,** III 23 ; **Wimon,** XV *g* 7 ; **Wom(m)an,** II 211, XI *b* 61, &c. ; **Wymmen(e),** *pl.* IV *b* 54, V 347, XV *b* 32, *c* 11, &c. ; **Wommen,** I 53, VIII *a* 8, &c. ; **Women(e),** IV *b* 42, XVII 208. [OE. *wīf-mann, wimman.*]

Wight, Wyht, Wicht (X), *adj.* valiant, X 122, 148, XIV *b* 5 (*see* Wede) : *adv.* quickly, straightway, XV *b* 36. [ON. *vīg-r,* neut. *vīg-t.*]

Wight, Wyght, *n.* creature, person, VIII *a* 243, XVII 47, &c. ; **Wyȝte,** VI 134 ; **Wiht,** XII *b* 77 ; **Wytes,** *pl.* XV *i* 19. [OE. *wiht.*]

Wyȝe, Wegh, *n.* knight, man, V 6, 30, VII 19, &c. ; *vocative,* Sir (knight), &c., V 23, 59, 172 ; **Wyȝeȝ, Weghes, Wees,** *pl.* VI 219, VII 23, 55. [OE. *wiga,* warrior.]

Wiȝtliche, *adv.* vigorously, VIII *a* 21. [From Wight, *adj.*]

Wiif. *See* Wif.

Wyke, *n.* week, VIII *a* 253. [OE. *wice.*] *See* Woke.

Wikid, Wikked, Wykked, Wicked, *adj.* bad, evil, wicked, IV *a* 65, VIII *a* 1, 29, IX 85, XVI 234, &c. [Extended from (obscure) ME. *wikke,* bad ; *cf.* Wrecched.]

Wil, Wyl(e). *See* Whil(e) ; Wille, *n.* and *v.*

Wild. *See* Wille, *v.*

Wild(e), Wylde, *adj.* wild, II

214, 257, V 95, &c.; unruly, self-willed, in *þof he wer neuer sa wylde*, however sinful were his life, IV a 75. [OE. *wilde*.] *See* Wylle, *adj*.

Wildernes, -nisse, *n*. wilderness, II 212, 560. [OE. *wildeornes* (in Sweet).]

Wiles, Wyles, *n. pl.* wiles, V 347, 352, XIV b 55. [OE. *wig(e)l* coalescing with ONFr. **wile* (OFr. *guile*); *see* Napier, *O. E. Glosses*, p. 159 (note).] *See* Gile, Biwyled.

Wylyde, *adj*. ! guileful, V 299. [From prec.]

Wylke. *See* Whilke.

Will(e), Wyll(e), Wil, Wyl, *n*. pleasure, desire, will, intent, purpose, I 49, II 224, 345, 568, IV a 29, V 90, X 47, XI b 7, XV b 34, c 3, &c.; good will, favour, V 319; *at his owhen w.*, at his pleasure, II 271; *at my (his) wille*, subject to my (his) will, VIII a 200, XIV b 56; *wiþ wille*, joyously, XV b 15; *with my wille*, with my consent, XVI 297; *lightnes of w.*, levity, VII 15; *swete w.*, good pleasure, II 384. [OE. *ge-will, willa*.]

Wylle, *adj*. bewildering, wandering (path), V 16. [ON. *vill-r*.] *See* Wild(e).

Wille, *v*. desire, wish, be willing; be likely, wont; intend, will, &c., and as auxil. of *fut*. 1 and 3 *sg. pres*. Wil, Wyl, I 10, V 89, 147, VIII a 24, 39, IX 252, &c.; Will(e), Wyll, III 2, IV a 31, 52, &c.; Wol(e), II 24, IX 279, XI a 48, &c.; Woll(e), VIII b 40, XV c 17, XVI 7, &c.; 2 *sg*. Wil, Wyl(1), IV a 4, 17, 88, VIII a 222, &c.; Wylt, V 73. Wolt, VIII a 271, XII b 42, XV g 33; (with suffixed pron.) Wiltou, -ow, II 128, XIV a 21, &c.; (further reduced) Wolte, XV g 19, 22; *pl*. Wyl, Wil(1), I 259, IV b 2, IX 118, &c.; Wol, Wole(n), VIII b 85, IX 64, XI b 64, 161, XIII b 23, &c.; Wolle, XVI 240 (rime—

fille); *wiltow or neltow*, whether you are willing or not, VIII a 149 (*cf*. II 154); (without expressed infin.) will go (come), V 64, XVII 504; *wilt thou so*, you'll do that, will you ! XVII 226. *Pa. t.* desired, wished, was willing; was likely, used; intended, would; *subj.* would (be willing), would (should) like, could wish, &c.; as auxil. of *condit.* or *pa. t. subj.* would, should, &c.: Vald, X 79; Wald(e), IV a 39, X 21, XIV b 12, &c.; Wild, I *introd.* (? ON. *vilda*); Wold(e), I 185 (rime *colde*), II 188, 279, III 37, IV b 25, V 28, VI 30, VIII a 204, XI a 51, XIV c 20, XVI 253, XVII 47, &c.; Wulde, I 47, 90, 171; 2 *sg*. Wold(e), Woldeჳ, -est, II 454, V 59, VI 50, XVI 362, XVII 172, &c.; *wold awede*, was like to go mad (*or* was going mad) II 87; *wold ich nold ich*, whether I would or no, II 154 (*cf*. VIII a 149); (without expressed infin.) *wold vp (in)*, desired to rise (enter), II 96, 378; *whider þai wold*, where they were going to, II 296; *walde away*, would depart, IV a 75. [OE. *willan, wyllan*; pa. t. *wólde, wálde*.] *See* Ichil, Ichulle.

Wilnest, 2 *sg. pres.* desirest, VIII a 256. [OE. *wilnian*.]

Wymman, Wimon, &c. *See* Wyfman.

Wind(e), Wynd(e), Wynt, *n*. wind, breath, IV b 5, VII 116, XIII a 8, XIV a 33, c 35, &c.; Wynd blast, blast of wind, XVII 355. [OE. *wind*.]

Wyndo(w), *n*. window, XVII 136, 280. [ON. *vind-auga*.]

Wyne, *n*. wine, IV a 51 (footnote). [OE. *win*.]

Wyng, Weng, *n*. wing, IV b 6, 48, IX 257, XII a 176, &c. [ON. *næng-r*.]

Wynke, *n*. a wink (of sleep), I 159. [From OE. *wincian*, v.]

Wynne, Wyn, *n*. gain, profit,

v 352; *hym to mekill wyn*, to
his great profit, XVII 109. [OE.
(*ge-*)*winn*.]

Wynne(n), Winne, Wyn, *v.* to
win; **Wan(ne),** *pa. t. sg.* VIII a
90, XVI 9, &c.; *pl.* VII 174;
Wonne(n), *pp.* V 23, VI 157,
&c.; **Wonen,** V 347, VII 169;
Won, XIV b 95, &c.; **Ywon,**
II 561; *trans.* to procure (with
toil), VIII a 21, 127; to win (in
contest, &c.), win over, IV a 8,
20, XIV b 16, 56, XVI 9, &c.; to
earn, VI 219, VIII a 90, XVI
230, &c.; to gain, get, XVI 132,
XVII 363, &c.; to (manage to)
bring, get, IV a 40, V 23, 347,
VII 174; *wynne (away)*, rescue,
II 561, XVI 18, 171, 266, 406;
intr. to labour profitably, earn
(something), VIII a 155, 316,
XII b 37; to win one's way, get
(to), V 163; get (away, from),
escape, XVII 24, 549, &c.; (*were*)
wonen to, had escaped, VII 169;
wyn to end, succeed in com-
pleting, XVII 130; to go, come,
V 147, VI 157. [OE. *ge-winnan*
and ON. *vinna*.]

Wynnynge, *n.* gain, profit, VIII b
102. [From prec.; ON. *vin-
ning-r*.]

Wynt. *See* Wind(e).

Wynter, Wintur, -er, *n.* winter,
II 259, VII 100; as *adj.* XV b 8,
11 (*see* note); Winter-schours,
-tyde, winter storms, winter
time, II 59, XIV b 26. [OE.
winter; *winter-scūr, -tīd*.]

Wypped, *pa. t.* sent flying, V 181.
[Cf. Fris., Du., LG. *wippen*.]

Wyrde, *n.* fate, V 66, 350 (*cf.*
217); *wyrdes*, chances, VIII b
102. [OE. *wȳrd*.]

Wyre, *v.* to turn; throw, X 112.
[OFr. *virer*.]

Wirk(e), Wyrk(e), &c. *See*
Werche.

Wis(e), Wys(e), *adj.* wise, IV a
2, VII 31, XI b 250, XII b 222,
&c. [OE. *wīs*.]

Wys(e)dome, Wisdome, *n.*
wisdom, IV b 56, 68, VIII a 53;

piece of wisdom, VIII a 206.
[OE. *wīs-dōm*.]

Wyse, Wise, *n.* manner, fashion,
guise, *II 158 (note), V 124, VII
65, 77, VIII a 59, XVI 25; *in
many wise*, in many ways, XII a
39; *in no(ne) wise*, at all, VIII a
300, IX 283; *in the wise as*,
just as, XII a 101; *other wise
many fold*, in many another
fashion, XVII 54. [OE. *wīse*.]

Wish, *n.* desire, will, XVII 4.
[Stem of OE. *wȳscan*, v.]

Wysli, Wysely, *adv.* thought-
fully, carefully, XIV c 14, XVII
435. [OE. *wīs-līce*.]

Wisse, Wysshe, *v.* to guide,
direct, VII 4 (note); *wissed hym
bettere*, directed him (to do)
better, VIII a 158. [OE.
wissian.]

Wist(e), &c. *See* Wite(n), *v.*[1]

Wysty, *adj.* lonely, deserted, v
121. [OE. *wēstig*; for vowel
cf. Ryste, and see Morsbach,
M.E. Gram., § 109.]

Wit, Witt(e), Wyt, Wytt(e),
n. sg. mind, senses, wits, II 82,
III 46 (*dat.*), XII b 137, XVI 344,
&c.; wisdom, XI a 10; intelligence, discernment, understanding, I 11, VI 4, VIII a 53, XI a 12,
32 (? interpretation), 52, XII b
198, &c.; sense, meaning, XI a 6,
47, 53, &c.; *pl.* intelligence, II
38, XI b 113; senses, wits, XII a
158; *fyue wytteȝ*, five senses,
V 125. *Bi my wytte (wit)*, as
I think, v 28, XVII 452; *do . . .
his wit*, apply his mind, XI b 6;
gode wyt, sound mind, IX 83;
Kynde Witt, (natural) good
sense, VIII a 243. [OE. *witt*.]

Wit, Wyt. *See* With.

Wite(n), Wyte, Witte, *v.*[1] to
know, learn, be aware, I 38,
VIII a 204, XI b 82, XII a 43,
&c.; **Wate,** I and 3 *sg. pres.*
IV a 16, VI 142, XVII 444, &c.;
Woot, XI a 43, 50; **Wote,** I
38, XVII a 124, XVII 313, &c.;
see Ichot, Not; **Wost,** 2 *sg.* VI
51; **Wote,** XVI 222; **Wate**

pl. I *introd.*; Wyte, I 250; Wotte, XVI 171. Wist(e), Wyst(e), *pa. t.* I 160, II 194, III 27, 45; VII 23, XV *g* 11 (*subj.*), &c.; would know (*subj.*), IX 184; *see* Nist. *Don to wyte*, inform, II 2; *We wille ʒe witte*, we intend that you should know (*i.e.* have full warning of the rescue of the souls), XVI 176; *witte þou wele*, be assured, XVI 305. [OE. *witan*; *wāt* pret. pres.; *wiste*, &c.] *See* Ywyte.

Wite, *v.²* to guard, keep, II 206, XV *f* 13. [OE. *witian*, but in ME. the senses and forms due to OE. *witan* (str.), *witan* (pret. pres.), and *witian* (wk.) were confused.]

Wyte, *v.³* fade, vanish, IV *a* 34. [OE. *ge-witan*.]

Wyter, *adj.* wise, XV *c* 25. [Late OE. *witter*, from ON. *vitr*.]

Wyterliche, *adv.* clearly, VIII *b* 38. [From prec. in ME. sense 'plain'.]

Wytes. *See* Wight, *n.*

With, Wyþ, Wid (XV *g*), Wit (VIII *b* 6), Wyt (XV *d* 6), &c., *prep.* with, against, XIV *b* 36, XVII 138, &c.; (meet) with, II 510, VIII *b* 6, XV *g* 7; (together) with, among, I 54, 133 (see Wo), II 84, IV *a* 4 (*see* Beste), 5, XV *g* 30, &c.; *es noghte with*, does not associate with, IV *b* 2; at, XII *a* 142; *with þat*, thereupon, VIII *a* 239; with (*instr.*) II 106, IV *b* 62, XV *g* 8, 29, &c.; by (means, reason of), II 404, VII 142, XVI 160, 297, &c.; by (*agent*), V 348, 351, 358, VII 53, &c. *With al*, entirely, VIII *a* 76 (OE. *mid alle*); *with all this*, meanwhile, X 114; *wyth lyttel*, with little result, VI 215; *what with . . . and with*, what with . . . and, XVII 214. *Bowes . . . to schote with arwes* (to shoot arrows with) is normal ME. order, IX 258; *cf.* VIII *a* 259, 290, &c.

[OE. *wiþ* blended with *mid* (*miþ*).] *See* Þar(e), Þer(e).

Withal, Vithall, *adv.* withal, X 9; *forth withal*, straightway, XII *b* 82, 129. [OE. *mid alle*; *see* prec.]

Withdrawe, *v.* to withdraw; *intr.* retire, VIII *a* 324; *pp.* reft (from her), XII *a* 158. [OE. *wiþ* + *dragan*.] *See* Draw(e).

Wythhalde, *v.* to hold back, V 200; Withhelde, Withhylde, *pa. t.* V 100, 223, &c. [OE. *wiþ* + *háldan*.] *See* Holde(n).

Within(ne), Wiþynne, Vithin (X), &c., *adv.* inside, IX 141, X 13, 70, XIII *a* 16, XV *i* 2, &c.; in (his) heart, V 302; *prep.* within, in, VI 80, &c.; (freq. postponed) IV *a* 38, 40, XVI 282, &c.; (of *time*) XII *a* 29. [OE. *wiþ-innan*.]

Withoute(n), -outten, -owte(n), out, &c., *adv.* outside, X 68, XV *i* 2, XVII 127, &c.; *prep.* without, II 460, IV *a* 96, VI 30, XVI 300, XVII 149, &c.; *see* Ende, Lees, Nay, No, &c. [OE. *wiþ-ûtan*.]

Withtakand, *pres. p.* reprehending, IV *b* 9. [OE. *wiþ-* + ON. *taka.*] *See* Take(n).

Witnesse, *v.* to testify, VIII *b* 91. [From Wittenesse.]

Wit-sunday, *n.* Whitsunday (with pun on *Wit*), XI *a* 12. [OE. *se hwíta sunnan-dæg.*]

Witt(e), &c. *See* Wit, Wite(n).

Wittenesse, *n.* witness, testimony, XVI 279; *see* Drawe. [OE. *ge-wit(t)nes.*]

Wyues, Wiues. *See* Wif.

Wlaffyng, *n.* stammering, indistinct utterance, XIII *b* 14. [OE. *wlaffian.*]

Wlyteþ, *pres. pl.* pipe, warble, XV *b* 11. [Imit. of sound, or corrupt for ? *wrytleþ*; cf. OE. *writian*, warble, ME. *write-linge*, n.]

Wo, *n.* woe, grief, pain, sorrow, &c., I 168, II 5, XV *b* 8, XVII 40, &c.; Woo(e), XVI 18, 300,

&c.; **Wa(a)**, IV *a* 23, XVI 406, &c.; *wo was wyth* (*hym*), (he) was grieved, I 132; *me is wo*, woe is me, unhappy am I, II 331, 542 ; (with *nom. pron.*) *or ye be wo*, ere you are in trouble, XIV *d* 11 (*see* Ware, *adj.*) ; *with* (*mochel*) *wo*, (very) painfully, VII 169, XII *a* 105; *wepe and wo*, II 195, 234; *for wele ne wa*(*a*), on no account, IV *a* 2, *b* 74; *worþe hit wele oþer wo*, whatever happens, v 66 (*see* Worþe, *v.*). [OE. *wā*.]

Wod(e), *n.* wood(land), I 62, II 237, V 16, 84, &c. ; trees, XV *b* 14; wood, fuel, XII *b* 113, 123, &c.; *to wode*, into the woods, XII *b* 5. [OE. *wudu*.]

Wode, Woode (XVI), *adj.* mad, furious, II 394, V 221, XII *a* 138, XV *g* 17, XVI 344, XVII 426. [OE. *wōd*.] *See* Awede.

Wodehed, *n.* madness, recklessness, I 31. [OE. *wōd* + *-hēdu*.]

Wodenes, *n.* fury, VII 138. [OE. *wōd-nes*.]

Woderoue, *n.* woodruff, XV *b* 9. [OE. *wudu-rofe*.]

Wodewe, *n.* widow, III 23; **Wydwes**, *pl.* VIII *a* 13; **Wedows**, XVII 389. [OE. *wuduwe*, *wid*(*e*)*we*.]

Wogh, *n.* evil, misery, XVII 533. [OE. *wōh*.]

Woke, *n.* week, XIII *a* 28. [OE. *wucu*.] *See* Wyke.

Wol(e), Wold(e), Woll(e). *See* Wille, *v.*

Wolcome. *See* Welcom.

Wolle, *n.* wool, VIII *a* 13, IX 142, 238, 239. [OE. *wull*(*e*).]

Wolt(e). *See* Wille, *v.*

Woluer, *n. pl.* wolves, II 539; **Woluer-kynnes**, of wolf's kind, wolvish, VIII *a* 154. [OE. *wulf*; *wulfes* (gen. sg.) + *cynnes*.] *See* Kyn.

Wombe, *n.* belly, VIII *a* 168, *b* 54; *distrib. sg.* (*see* Herte) VIII *a* 209, 253; womb, XI *b* 30. [OE. *wámb*, *wómb*.]

Wom(m)**an**, &c. *See* Wyfman.

Won. *See* Wan(ne), Wynne(n).

Won(e), *v.* to dwell, abide, IV *a* 40, V 30, VI 44, XII *a* 191, XIII *b* 5, 7, &c.; **Wonne**, XVI 15, 235, 379, &c.; **Wonyd**, *pp.* dwelt, V 46; **Wont**, accustomed, VIII *a* 160, XII *a* 179. [OE. (*ge*)-*wunian*, dwell, be accustomed.] *See* Ywon(ed); **Wones**, *n. pl.*

Wonder, -ur; Wounder (XV *b*); **Wunder, -yr**; (i) *n.* wonder, amazement, (a) marvel, IV *a* 85, XIII *b* 42, XVII 265, &c.; miraculous deed, I 102 ; *mans wonder*, amazement of mankind, monster, XVII 408 ; *spake of hem wunder*, spoke wonderingly of them, I 225; **Wondres**, *pl.* marvels, XIII *a* 6; (ii) *adj.* (orig. loose compound), marvellous, XIII *a* 31, XVII 496 ; (iii) *adv.* (*cf.* OE. *wundrum*), marvellously, II 104, 356, V 132, XIII *a* 10, XV *b* 32, &c. [OE. *wundor*, *wúndor*.] *See* Wundred.

Wonderfol, Wondirful(l), *adj.* wonderful, IX 144, 266, XIII *a* 7. [OE. *wundor-ful*.]

Wonderli, Wonderlych, *adv.* marvellously, XII *a* 54, XIII *a* 14. [OE. *wundor-lice*.]

Wondringe, *n.* wonder, XII *b* 213. [OE. *wundrung*.]

Woned, I 189: ? read *wende*, went ; *see* note.

Wonen. *See* Wynne(n).

Wones, Woneʒ, *n. pl.* halls, II 365 ; (with *sg.* sense) dwelling, V 130, 332. [? ON. *ván*, expectation, occas. used as ' place where one may be expected to be' (cf. Norweg. *von*, expectation, haunts of game); but the word was infl. by assoc. with Wone, dwell (*q.v.*), with which it was often joined in allit. ME. rimes all require *wǫn* or *wān*.] *See* Wane, *n.*

Wonges, *n. pl.* cheeks, XV *c* 22 [OE. *wáng*, *wóng*.]

Wonne(n). *See* **Wynne(n)**, **Won(e)**.

Wonte, *v.* to be lacking; *yow* (dat.) *wonted*, you lacked, v 298; *ȝef me shal wonte*, if I do not have, xv *b* 34. [ON. *vanta*.]

Woo(e); **Woode**; **Woot.** *See* Wo; Wode, *adj.*; Wite(n), *v.*[1]

Worchinge, **-yng**, *n.* working, operation, IX 56; *wondur w.*, miraculous property, XIII *a* 32. [OE. *wyrcung.*] *See* Werche.

Word(e), **Woord**, **Wurde** (1), *n.* word, I 108, II 139, 222, V 305, XI *a* 10, XVII 380, &c.; plighted word, II 468; fame, in * þe word of him walkes ful wide*, his fame is spread abroad, XIV *b* 29; *worchip and wordes*, obsequious words, VII 174. [OE. *wórd.*]

Wore, *n.* ? troubled pool, XV *c* 30 (note). [OE. *wár* (in doubtful gloss), turbid, muddy water (see Napier, *O.E. Glosses*, p. 49 (note); but *cf.* OE. *wárig*, ME. *wóri*, muddy).]

Wore; **Workiis**; **Workeman.** *See* Was; Werche; Werkman.

World(e), *n.* world, earth, men, I 225, II 41, IX 72, &c.; **Warld**, II 403, XVII 70, 303; *warld so wide*, XVII 541; **Werld**, XIV *b* 16; *in world, of the w.*, on earth, XV *c* 25, IX 183; *werldes, worldes*, (gen.) of the world, worldly, in *worldes reches*, IV *b* 61; *worldes wele*, *see* Wele, *n.* [OE. *w(e)orold.*]

Worldly, *adj.* worldly, secular, temporal, XI *b* 2, 55, 96, 140, &c. [OE. *worold-lic.*]

Worm, *n.* snake, worm, II 252, IV *b* 27, XII *b* 195, XV *b* 31. [OE. *wyrm.*]

Worschipe, **Worschyp**, *n.* honour, VI 34, 119, IX 109, 333; **Worship**, VII 174; **Worshep**, VIII *b* 79; **Wurschyp**, I 91. [OE. *w(e)orþ-, wurþ-scipe.*]

Worschip(e), *v.* to honour, worship, VIII *a* 95, XI *b* 168; **Wur-schyppeþ**, *imp. pl.* I 84. [From prec.]

Wors(e), *adj. compar.* worse, XI *b*

75, XIII *a* 59, XVI 320, &c.; **Wers**(e), XVI 200; *neuer him nas wers*, never had he been more unhappy, II 98; **Wars**, *adv.* in *the wars*, so much the worse that, XVII 191 (*see þe, adv.*). **Werst**, *adj. superl.* worst, meanest, II 367; **Worst**, V 30. [OE. *wyrsa, wyrsta*; with *er-* forms *cf.* Werche, Scherte.] *See* Werre.

Worst. *See* Worþe, *v.*

Wortes, *n.* vegetables, VIII *a* 303. [OE. *wyrt.*]

Worþe, **Wrþo**, *adj.* worth, VI 91; worthy, in *þou were wrþe*, you would be worthy, you deserve, XV *g* 8 (*cf.* Worþy). [OE. *weorþe, wyrþe.*]

Worþe, *v.* to come to pass, become, be, and *auxil.* of *passive* (*esp.* with *fut.* sense); **Worst**, 2 *sg. pres.* wilt be, II 170, 174; **Worth**, 3 *sg.* will be, VIII *a* 48; will come to pass, VIII *a* 156; **Worþe**, **Worth**, **Wurth**, *subj. pres.* be, let there be, V 306, VI 2; *worþe hit wele oþer wo*, come weal or woe, V 66 (*see* Wo); *wel worth þe*, may it go well with thee, V 59; *wele wurth þe while*, good luck to the time, happy the occasion, XIV *a* 5, &c. (*see* Wel). **Warth**, *pa. t. sg.* in *hym warth*, accrued to him, VIII *b* 102; **Worþed**, *subj.* would fare, V 28; **Worþen**, *pp.* in *is w. to*, has turned to, is become (one of), VI 34. [OE. *weorþan, wurþan.*] *See* Yworth.

Worþy, **Worthi**, *adj.* merited, just, XVI 324; worthy, deserving (constr. *to* and *infin.*), IV *b* 10, IX 172, XVI 132; *w. to reherse*, worth repeating, XI *a* 4; *were w.* (*be*), deserve (to be), XVI 357, XVII 200 (*were* is *subj.*; *cf.* Worþe, *adj.*); worthy (of honour), worshipful, VI 134, IX 269, XI *a* 25, XII *a* 165, XVII 19; *worthiest* (*of*), most worshipful (in), XVII 489. **Worthier**, *compar.adv.* more honourably, VIII *a* 48; **Worþili**, *adv.* honourably, XIV c 67. [OE. *wyrþig*, merited.] *See* Vnworthi.

Wost, Wot(t)e. *See* Wite(n), *v.*[1]

Woth, Woþe. *See* Waþe, *n.*[1]

Wou, *adv.* how (is it that), why, -xv g 25. [OE. *hū*, ! infl. by *hwý*, &c.] *See* Hou.

Wouen. *See* Weue(n).

Wounde, *n. pl.* wounds, II 393; Woundis, x 51. [OE. *wúnd.*]

Wounder. *See* Wonder.

Woundit, *pp.* wounded, X 141, 154; Voundit, x 63. [OE. *wúndian.*]

Wowes, Woweþ, *pres. pl.* woo, make love, xv b 19, 31. [OE. *wōgian.*]

Wowyng, *n.* love-making, love-suit, v 293, 299, xv c 29. [From prec.]

Wrake, *n.* injury, XVII 138. [OE. *wracu.*]

Wrang(e), *adj.* and *adv.* wrong, unjust(ly), VI 128, xvi 264, 265, 305, XVII 188. [Late OE. *wráng*, from ON. *wrang-*, OIcel. *rang-r.*]

Wrappe, *v.* to wrap, xv f 10. [Obscure; ! cf. ME. *(w)lappen*, wrap.]

Wrastlynges, *n. pl.* wrestling-matches, 11. [OE. *wrǣstlung.*]

Wrath, *v.* to anger; *to wrath hym* (refl.), to become enraged, VIII a 146; Wrathed, *pp.* wronged, brought to grief, v 352. [From next.] *See* Wrethe.

Wraþþe, Wrathþe, *n.* anger, XI b 94; offence, VI 2. [OE. *wrǣþþo*, anger, injury.] *See* Wroþ, Wreth.

Wrechched, *adj.* afflicted, troubled, IX 317; Wrechidnes, *n.* misery, IV b 29. [From next.]

Wreche, *n.* unhappy one, II *333 (MS. wroche), 544; Wretche, XIV a 21, 23. [OE. *wrecca.*]

Wreke, *n.* vengeance, XVI 191. [OE. *wracu* or *wrǣc*, infl. by next.]

Wreke, *pp.* revenged, xv g 11; Wroken, Wrokin, (banished), removed, VI 15; revenged, XIV a

4, 5, XVI 199. [OE. *wrecan*, expel, punish.] *See* Awreke.

Wreth. *n.* anger, IV a 75. [OE. *wrǣþo*, *wrǣþþo.*] *See* Wraþþe.

Wrethe, *v.* to anger, offend, IV b 85. [Cf. OE. *ge-wrǣþan*, refl., to be enraged.] *See* Wrath.

Wryȝt, *n.* carpenter, I 176; Write, xvi 230. [OE. *wyrhta*, *wryhta.*]

Wrightry, *n.* carpentry, XVII 250. [Prec. + OFr. -*(e)rie.*]

Wryng(e), *v.* to wring; wring (the hands), IV a 65, XVII 211; Wronge, *pa. t. sg.* wrung, twisted and pinched, VIII a 168. [OE. *wringan.*]

Writ(e), Writt(e), Wryt, *n.* writing, III 36 (*dat. sg.*); Scripture, I 12, IV b 76, XI a 10, b 23, &c. [OE. *writ.*]

Write, Wryte, *v.* to write, VIII a 79, b 72, IX 122; Wrote. *pa. t. sg.* I 247; *pl.* VII 58; Writen, *pa. t. pl.* XI a 23; Write(n), Wryte(n), *pp.* I 37, 40, IV a 2, VII 31, IX 318 (*see* Putte), XII a 1, &c.; Ywryte, Ywrite, II 1, 13, III *introd.*, 33; Writyng(e), *n.* VII 23, XI b 305. [OE. *wrītan.*]

Write. *See* Wryȝt.

Wriþ, 3 *sg. pres.* covers, II 244. [OE. *wrēon*, 3 sg. *wrīþ.*]

Wryþe(n), *v.* to twist; bind, VI 151; turn aside (from the just course) VI 128. [OE. *wrīþan.*]

Wro, *n.* nook, corner, v 154. [ON. *wrá*, OIcel. *rá.*]

Wroȝt(e); Wroken; Wronge. *See* Werche; Wreke; Wryng(e).

Wrote, *v.* to root in the earth, II 255. [OE. *wrōtan.*]

Wroþ(e), Wroth, *adj.* angry, at variance, II 122, VI 19, xv f 7 XVII 36, &c.; *make hym* (refl.) *wroth*, become angry, I 10. [OE. *wrāþ.*] *See* Wraþþe.

Wroþely, *adj.* fiercely, V 221; Wroþeloker, *compar.* more severely, v 276. [OE. *wrāþ-līce*, -*lucor.*]

Wrouȝte(n), Wrouhte. *See* Werche.

Wrþe. *See* Worþe, *adj.*

Wruxled, *pp.* in *wr. in grene*, ! changed into, turned, green, v 123 ; but ' adorned ' is usually assumed here and for *wruxeled*, Purity 1381. [OE. *wrixl(i)an*, (ex)change. A sense ' adorned ' might be derived from an (un-recorded) earlier sense, ' turn, wind round ' (! rel. to *wrēon*, *wrigels*), or perh. from OE. *wrixlan (blēom)*, change colours, exhibit varied hues.]

Wulde. *See* Wille, *v.*

Wundred, *pa. t.* wondered, I 114. [OE. *wundrian.*] *See* Wonder.

Wunne, *n.* joy ; *gen. sg.* in *wunne wele* (*weole*), wealth of joy, xv *b* *11 (MS. wynter), 35. [OE. *wynn.*]

Wurde ; Wurschyp- ; Wurth. *See* Word(e) ; Worschip(e) ; Worþe, *v.*

Y- ; *see also* 3, I. For past participles in *y*- not entered below *see* the verbs concerned.

Yaf. *See* 3eue.

Y-arched, *pp.* in *y-arched of gold*, built of gold in the shape of an arch, II 362. [OFr. *archer*, *v.*]

Yarn. *See* Eorne.

Ybilt, *pp.* !lodged, II 483 (MS. ; *see* note) ; *see* Bilt. [See *N.E.D.* s.vv. *Build*, *Built.*]

Ybore, -born ; Ybounde. *See* Ber(e) ; Bynde.

Yclongen. *See* Clinge.

Yclosed, *pp.* enclosed, XIII *a* 24, 40. [ME. *closen*, from Clos, *q.v.*]

Ycore (orig. *pp.* of Chese, *q.v.*), chosen, excellent ; as mere intensive rime-tag, II 105, 148. [OE. *ge-coren.*]

Ydel, Ydill (IV), Hydel (VIII), *adj.* unemployed, idle, IV *b* 1, VI 154, 155, VIII *b* 27, &c. ; slothful, IV *b* 9, XI *b* 219. [OE. *īdel.*]

Ydelnesse, Ydyllnes (IV), *n.* lack of (useful) employment, idleness, IV *b* 7, XI *b* 64, 127, 197. [OE. *īdel-nes.*]

Ydronke. *See* Drynke(n).

Ye (=Ie). *See* Ei3e.

Yeaf, Yeaue. *See* 3eue.

Yei, *adv.* yes indeed, XVII 370, 458; oh yes (ironic), XVII 353. [! Reduction of a reiteration *3ē-3ē*, or assimilated to ME. *nei*, nay; see *N.E.D.* s.v. *Yea.*] *See* 3a, 3e.

Yelp, *n.* boast(ing), XVII 321. [OE. *gelp.*]

Yendles ; Yer(e). *See* Endles ; 3eer.

Yfere, *adv.* in *al yfere*, all together, II 223. [Orig. *yfere(n)*, OE. *ge-fēran*, pl., (as) companions.] *See* Fere, *n.²*

Yfet ; Yfou3te ; Yfounde ; Y3e ; Y3yrned. *See* Fecche ; Fight ; Fynde(n) ; Ei3e ; 3erne.

Ygraced, *pp.* thanked, VIII *a* 118. [OFr. *gracier.*]

Yhad ; Yhe(n). *See* Habbe(n) ; Ei3e.

Yhere, *v.* to hear, II 420 ; Yherd, *pa. t.* II 528 ; Yhyerde, III 49. [OE. *ge-hēran.*] *See* Here.

Yhy3t, *pp.* (adorned), arranged, XIII *a* 1. [ME. *hihten*, prob. from OE. *hyht*, pleasure (*hyhtlic* pleasant).]

Yhis, *adv.* yes, XVI 61 (MS.). [OE. *gise.*]

Yhonged ; Yiif. *See* Hange ; 3ef.

Ylefde, *pa. t.* believed, III 36. [OE. *ge-lēfan.*] *See* Beleue ; Leue, *v.³*

Yleft ; Ylent. *See* Leue, *v.¹* ; Lende.

Ylet, *n.* hindrance ; *3if þou makest ous ylet*, if you offer any resistance to us, II 169. [Not recorded elsewhere ; usual ME. form is Lette, *q. v.* Other MSS. read *ony let.*]

Ylokked, *pp.* locked up, IX 174. [ME. *lok(k)en*, from *lok*, OE. *loc*, n. ; cf. ON. *loka*, v.] *See* Loke, *pp.* ; Vnlokynne.

Ylond, *n.* island, XIII *a* 20, *b* 2, 44. [OE. *īg-lánd.*]

Ylore ; Ymad. *See* Lese, *v.¹* ; Maken.

Ymaymed, *pp.* maimed, VII *b* 35. [OFr. *m(ah)ainier*, &c.

cf. *meshaim, mayhem,* &c., n.]

Ymake, *adj.* becoming, comely, XV *c* 16. [OE. *ge-mæc.*]

Ymarked, *pp.* marked out, appointed, II 548. [OE. *mearcian.*]

Ympe, Impe, *n.* sapling, scion, XIV *c* 83, 89, 98. [OE. *impa,* shoot, graft.]

Ympe-tre, *n.* orchard-tree, II 70, 166, 186, 407, 456. [Prec. + *trēo.*]

Ynence, *prep.* towards, *IV *b* 22 (MS. ynesche). [OE. *onef(e)n, onemn* + adv. *-es.*]

Ynoȝ: Ynouh, *adj.* enough, XII *b* 123; **Ynowȝ,** XI *b* 190, 192; **Ynowþȝ,** XI *b* 149; **Inogh,** abundant, much, XV *a* 15; **Innoghe,** *pl.* many, in abundance, V 55; **Anouȝ,** *adv.* II 62, **Enogh,** XVII 532, **Inoghe,** VI 252; **Ynouh,** XII *b* 74; **Ynoȝ** (*of*), abundance (of), III 8; **Ynoh,** very, XV *c* 13. [OE. *ge-nōg, ge-nōh.*] *See* Ynow(e).

Ynome. *See* Nyme.

Ynow(e), *adj.* enough; as *sb.,* IX 160, 282, XIV *d* 13; **Ynowe, Enew,** *pl.* in abundance, great numbers, XI *b* 284, X 7; **Ynow,** *adv.* enough, XIII *b* 8; very, IX 4. [OE. *ge-nōg-,* oblique forms of *ge-nōh.*] *See* Ynoȝ.

Yond, *adj.*; as *pron.* that (over there), XVII 453. [OE. *geond,* thither; cf. Goth. *jaind.*]

Yone, *adj.* that (over there), XVI 340; **ȝon,** v 76. [OE. (once) *geon,* cf. Goth. *jain-s.* See *N.E.D.,* s.v. *Yon.*]

You(e), Yow. *See* ȝe, *pron.*

Ypocrisie, hypocrisy, XI *b* 12. [OFr. *ipocrisie.*]

Ypocritis, *u. pl.* hypocrites, XI *b* 7, 44, 56, 72, &c. [OFr. *ipocrite.*]

Yre, *n.*[1] iron, XIII *a* 44; **Yrne,** V 199; **Yrnes,** *pl.* irons (supporting injured leg), VIII *a* 130. [OE. *iren.*] *See* Irnebandis.

Yre, Ire, *n.*[2] anger, XVII 51; *in hor gret yre,* so as greatly to anger them, VII 181. [OFr. *ire.*]

Yrokked, *pp.* rocked, XIII *b* 22. [OE. (late) *roccian.*]

Y-se, *v.* to see, II 530; **Yzeȝ,** *pa. t. sg.* III 35, 41, 56; **Yseiȝe,** *pa t. pl.* II 328; for pp. *see* Se(n). [OE. *ge-sēon.*]

Yseye, Yseiȝe. *See* Se(n), and prec.

Ysene, *adj.* visible, II 354. [OE. *ge-sēne.*] *See* Se(n).

Ysode, *pp.* boiled, XIII *a* 30. [OE. *sēoþan,* pp. *ge-soden.*]

Yspent; Yspronge; Ytauȝt. *See* Spend(e); Springe; Teche(n).

Ythes, *n. pl.* waves, VII 106. [OE. *ȳþ.*]

Ytold. *See* Telle.

Ytuiȝt, *pp.* snatched, II 192. [Cf. OE. *twiccian.*]

Yuel(e), *adj.* evil, wicked, IX 237; difficult, VIII *a* 50; **Euyll,** evil, IX 83. [OE. *yfel,* adj.]

Yuel, *n.* evil, wrong, VIII *introd.,* *a* 220; **Euel(l),** IV *a* 76, IX 338, XV *g* 28. [OE. *yfel,* n.]

Yvsed. *See* Vse.

Yweddede, *pp.* (lawfully) married, VIII *b* 68. [OE. *weddian,* to betroth.] *See* Wedmen.

Ywent; Ywerd. *See* Wende; Were, *v.*[2]

Ywyte, *pres. subj. pl.* understand, III *introd.* [OE. *ge-* + *witan.*] *See* Wite(n).

Ywon, *adj.* accustomed, II 317. [OE. *ge-wuna.*]

Ywon, *pp.* *See* Wynne(n).

Ywoned, *pp.* accustomed, III 55, XIII *b* 37. [OE. *ge-wunian.*]

Yworth, Aworthe, *v.* to be, go on as before, in *late God yworth, late þow G. aworthe,* meddle not with God, it is God's affair, VIII *a* 76, 220. [OE. *ge-weorþan.*] *See* Worþe, *v.*

Y-yeue; Y-yolde. *See* ȝeue; ȝelde(n).

Yzede; Yzeȝ; Yzent. *See* Seie; Y-se; Sende.

Zayde, Zayþ, Zede, Zigge. *See* Sei(e).

Zelue, Zoluer, Zen, Zente, Zome, Zuo. *See* Self, Seluer, Syn(e), Sende, Som(e), Swa.

INDEX OF NAMES.

For the personifications in VIII, generic names (as *Bayarde*), and names of peoples (as *Brytouns*), see also the Glossary.